Shaking a Leg

JOURNALISM AND WRITINGS

BY ANGELA CARTER

Short Stories
Fireworks
The Bloody Chamber
Black Venus
American Ghosts and Old World Wonders
The Virago Book of Fairy Tales (editor)
The Second Virago Book of Fairy Tales (editor)
Wayward Girls and Wicked Women (editor)

Novels
Shadow Dance
The Magic Toyshop
Several Perceptions
Heroes and Villains
Love
The Infernal Desire Machine of Dr Hoffman
The Passion of New Eve
Nights at the Circus
Wise Children

Non-fiction
The Sadeian Woman: An Exercise in Cultural History
Nothing Sacred: Selected Writings
Expletives Deleted

Drama
Come Unto These Yellow Sands: Four Radio Plays

Collected Works
Burning Your Boats: Short Stories
The Curious Room: Dramatic Works

THE COLLECTED ANGELA CARTER

Shaking a Leg

JOURNALISM AND WRITINGS

ANGELA CARTER

With an Introduction by
Joan Smith

Edited by Jenny Uglow

Research Assistant Charlotte Crofts

Chatto & Windus
LONDON

Published in 1997

1 3 5 7 9 10 8 6 4 2

Introduction copyright © 1997 Joan Smith
Text copyright © The Estate of Angela Carter 1997

This copyright should be read in conjuction with the location of original
publications given in the chronology at the end of this volume.

First published in Great Britain in 1997 by
Chatto & Windus Limited
Random House, 20 Vauxhall Bridge Road,
London, SW1V 2SA

Random House Australia (Pty) Limited
20 Alfred Street, Milsons Point, Sydney,
New South Wales 2061, Australia

Random House New Zealand Limited
18 Poland Road, Glenfield
Auckland 10, New Zealand

Random House South Africa (Pty) Limited
PO Box 337, Berglvei, South Africa

Random House UK Limited Reg. No. 954009

Papers used by Random House UK Limited are natural, recyclable
products made from wood grown in sustainable forests. The
manufacturing processes conform to the environmental regulations of the
country of origin.

A CIP catalogue record for this book is available from the British Library

ISBN 0 7011 6336 4

Typeset by SX Composing DTP, Rayleigh, Essex
Printed and bound in Great Britain by
Mackays of Chatham PLC, Chatham, Kent

Contents

Editor's Note

This volume contains a substantial selection of Angela Carter's journalism from the 1960s until her death. It cannot be comprehensive, but I hope that the chronology at the end of the book, which lists introductions as well as articles and reviews, will guide readers further.

In arranging the contents, I have followed Angela's own lead in the earlier collections, *Nothing Sacred* (1982) and *Expletives Deleted* (1992), using categories to define and separate but also to tease and provoke. Inevitably, because her approach was so open and because she loved strange conjunctions and overlapping currents, many pieces could move happily between categories – she put reviews into sections on countries, for example, insisting that books were a guide to perception and should not always be fenced into literary divisions. I have adopted her line and have also followed her in dividing the final section into 'Stories and Tellers' and 'Writers and Readers', since her interest in genre, story-telling, magic and the way people make 'tales' out of ordinary lives, led her to see certain works in a different light to others. Within each section the pieces run in date order except where two reviews relate to the same author, when they appear together.

The chronology has been compiled after wide-ranging research, first by Mark Bell and then by Charlotte Crofts, but it is still provisional and we hope that this volume will provide yet more leads. Several people have helped in the quest and have dug deep into their own files. We are particularly grateful to Paul Barker, former editor of *New Society*, who was an enormous help in the early stages of collecting material, and to William Scammell, the editor of *Nonesuch Magazine* at Bristol University, where Angela Carter's work first appeared. We would also like to thank Carmen Callil, Susannah Clapp, John Ellis, Kim Evans, Malcolm Edwards, Michael Moorcock, Deborah Rogers, David Pringle and Brian Stableford. And we all owe a debt to the various publications from which these marvellous pieces come and to the many editors and literary editors who – as Angela herself said – often accepted the most surprising things, 'without batting an eyelid'.

Jenny Uglow, January 1997

Introduction

The first time I read a book by Angela Carter, it had such an impact on me that I rushed off to the local library in search of more. Knowing little about this author I had discovered – it was the late 1970s and novels like *Nights at the Circus* and *Wise Children* were a long way in the future – I devoured everything I could find, delighted to find that one woman had produced work as diverse as *The Bloody Chamber*, her sly re-casting of traditional fairy-tales, and a thrilling polemic like *The Sadeian Woman*. I had just returned to live in London after a long absence and Carter's hugely original engagement with the Marquis de Sade sustained me through a rather lonely Christmas in a borrowed flat near Kew Gardens; I remember wandering through the steamy palm house, mulling over her argument about the pornographic imagination beneath dripping green fronds, then the shock of stepping outside into the sharp winter cold. I wouldn't say reality intervened at that point, more that I'd been so caught up in a mental dialogue with this woman I'd never met that I'd forgotten what time of year it was. Carter's ideas were like that, staying in your head long after you'd put down the printed page, even when you weren't absolutely sure you agreed with her – a quality I don't want to describe as feminine, precisely, but which certainly struck me then (and again now, reading this collection of her journalism and shorter writings) as aeons away from the bombastic, know-it-all style of so much male discourse. One of the many things I like about *Shaking A Leg*, in fact, is the way in which the articles and reviews show Angela Carter's mind working, coming at a subject from different angles, changing its focus, trying out a thought and seeing where it goes. The result isn't tentative, far from it – few authors have been so passionately engaged – but it's a kind of writing which invites the reader to think, to argue back, to accost its creator with sentences beginning: 'yes, but what about . . .?'

From the very first pages of this book, which opens with Angela Carter's reflections on her family history, there is a sense of someone returning again and again to the same subject, seeing it from a different point of view. She has opinions but they are not set in stone; sometimes she pokes fun at her younger, more solemn self. You get the feeling that, by writing it down, she is trying to understand her background, a process which involves demolishing a few family fictions – and, perhaps, one or two of her own. Some of her relatives, her father and her maternal grandmother for instance, emerge vividly and immediately from her prose. Her mother, a shadowy figure compared to these domestic colossi, is revealed more slowly as a figure in her own right – and this gradual unveiling suggests, more powerfully than if it had been addressed directly, the uneasy relationship between the women of Angela Carter's generation and the one immediately before it. For she is in many senses a child of the 1960s, a decade which it has recently been fashionable to denigrate, and she lived through those extraordinary upheavals which amounted to a revolution in style, taste, politics – in everything from superficially trivial issues like fashion, about which she writes brilliantly and very funnily, to weighty matters like class. That decade changed people's lives, mostly for the better in my view, but it also created a generation gap more profound, I suspect, than anything that had gone before. This was especially true for women and when Carter writes about her mother, she does not hesitate to acknowledge limited aspirations and missed opportunities. There is also a muted note of self-interrogation, as though she is forever asking herself, as have many of us whose lives were shaped by the great wave of feminism which came out of the 60s, 'how do I come to be as I am?'

What she was, in Carter's case, is difficult to define. Novels, short stories, radio plays, fairy-tales, polemic, journalism: the scope of her writing, in an era when authors tend to be pigeon-holed as soon as their work begins to be published, is breathtaking. It is tempting, given this range, to characterise her as a Renaissance woman, were it not for that fact that it is writers like Carter herself who have taught us to be suspicious of such terms. It is easy to imagine her worrying at that phrase in one of her elegant essays, praising the humanism of the period yet taking satiric bites out of the rumps of the famous men – and they were all men – who created the great works of art for which the fourteenth and fifteenth centuries are famous. She seems to have been constantly aware that, for all the enduring problems women of our age have to contend with, this is the only century in which a woman like herself could flourish. In that sense, her feminism rings clear and true from these pages. She never whines, never indulges in self-pity, even when she is writing about a painful subject like her own anorexia; on the contrary, she displays an almost gleeful relish at the prospect of re-interpreting, from an intelligent feminist's point of view, cultural icons from Emily Brontë to Georges Bataille to D. H. Lawrence, and personal ones like her own female relatives. She is also, and this puts her in a separate category from many feminists, particularly the heavyweight Americans, acutely aware of the importance of class. It is one of the things, along with a sense of place – superbly evoked here in pieces about the north of England and about Japan – which make her such an acute observer of whatever scene happens to catch her attention.

But to adopt Angela's own kind of terminology for a moment, what emerges most powerfully from *Shaking A Leg* is her ability to detect bullshit at two hundred paces. Years before the term 'foodie' had been invented, she was mocking the pretensions of the cookery writer who insists on recherché ingredients not because of their qualities but their snob value. And it is a delight to find her, years before the porn star Linda Lovelace came out as a victim of the sex industry, deconstructing the actress's sexual *braggadocio* as a species of false consciousness – and discerning a profound rage behind Lovelace's notorious skill at *fellatio*. The permissive societies of which Lovelace is a product, Carter points out more than once, are actually deeply repressed: why else do people need permission to explore their sexuality? Only someone with an appreciation of the sweaty, earthy pleasures of sex could create this kind of critique, outspoken and completely unprudish; one of the delights of this book is the way in which the articles act as signposts, over a longish period stretching back to the 1970s, to to an emerging erotic sensibility which would one day create a bawdy, life-enhancing novel like *Wise Children*.

This is not to say that the pieces in this collection do not stand alone. They are connected to Angela Carter's other work but they also demonstrate the unique features of her journalism at its best: the writing is thoughtful yet immediate, concise but not shallow. Carter had a rare ability to use her own experience as a springboard for ideas. Where run-of-the-mill columnists turn a visit to their local shop into . . . well, a visit to their local shop . . . the reader could trust Carter to use it as, say, the starting-point for an exploration into the history and cultural significance of retailing. Everything interested her, nothing seems to have daunted her, and few journalists can claim to have such a sure grasp of both high and low culture. Clear-sighted and compassionate, she is the kind of radical thinker thrown up all too rarely in Britain; as I read these marvellously iconoclastic pieces, it strikes me how well they have stood the test of time. In a timid and conformist decade like the 1990s, when political debate is bogged down in platitudes, wry voices like Angela Carter's are sorely missed. Among the many pleasures of *Shaking A Leg* is the speculation it prompts about what she would have made, in her own highly original style, of the way we live now.

Joan Smith, March 1997

SELF

The Mother Lode

The first house in which I remember living gives a false impression of our circumstances. This house was part of the archaeology of my mother's mother's life and gran dug it up again and dived back within it when the times became precarious, that is, in 1940, and she took me with her, for safety's sake, with this result: that I always feel secure in south Yorkshire.

This first house of my memory was a living fossil, a two-up, two-down, red-brick, slate-tiled, terraced miners' cottage architecturally antique by the nineteenth-century standards of the rest of the village. There was a lavatory at the end of the garden beyond a scraggy clump of Michaelmas daisies that never looked well in themselves, always sere, never blooming, the perennial ghosts of themselves, as if ill-nourished by an exhausted soil. This garden was not attached to the cottage; the back door opened on to a paved yard, with a coal-hole beside the back gate that my grandmother topped up with a bit of judicious thieving for, unlike the other coal-holes along the terrace, ours was not entitled to the free hand-out from the pits for miners' families. Nor did we need one. We were perfectly well-off. But gran couldn't resist knocking off a lump or two. She called this activity: 'snawking', either a dialect or a self-invented word, I don't know which.

There was an access lane between the gate of the yard and the gate of the garden, so it was a very long trip out to the lavatory, especially in winter. We used chamber-pots a good deal - 'jerries' – cause of much hilarity due to the hostilities. My mother had a pastel-coloured, Victorian indelicacy which she loved to repeat: 'When did the queen reign over China?' This whimsical and harmless scatalogical pun was my first introduction to the wonderful world of verbal transformations, and also a first perception that a joke need not be funny to give pleasure.

Beyond the brick-built lavatory, to which we used to light our way after dark with a candle lantern, was a red-brick, time-stained, soot-dulled wall that bounded an unkempt field; this field was divided by a lugubrious canal, in which old mattresses and pieces of bicycle used to float. The canal was fringed with willows, cruelly lopped, and their branches were always hung with rags tied in knots. I don't know why. It was a witchy, unpremeditated sight. Among the tips where we kids used to play were strange pools of oleaginous, clay-streaked water. A neighbour's child drowned in one of them.

The elements of desolation in the landscape give no clue to the Mediterranean extraversion and loquacity of the inhabitants. Similarly, all this grass-roots, working-class stuff, the miners' cottage and the bog at the end of the garden and all, is true, but not strictly accurate. The processes of social mobility had got under way long before I had ever been thought of, although my mother always assured me I had never been thought of as such, had simply arrived and, as I will make plain, somewhat inconveniently, too.

We took this trip back, not to my mother's but to *her* mother's roots because of the war. My grandmother had not lived in her native village herself since she was a girl and now she was an old woman, squat, fierce and black-clad like the granny in the Giles cartoons in the *Sunday Express*, because she, an old woman, took me back to her childhood, I think I became the child she had been, in a sense, for the first five years of my life. She reared me as a tough, arrogant and pragmatic Yorkshire child and my mother was powerless to prevent it.

My mother learned she was carrying me at about the time the Second World War was declared; with the family talent for magic realism, she once told me she had been to the doctor's on the very day. It must have been a distressing and agitated pregnancy. Shortly after she began to assemble all the birthing bric-à-brac, the entire child population of our part of south London was removed to the South Coast, away from the bombs, or so it was thought. My brother, then eleven, was sent away with them but my mother followed him because my father quickly rented a flat in a prosperous, shingle-beached resort. Which is why I was born in Eastbourne, not a place I'd have chosen, although my mother said that if Debussy had composed *La Mer* whilst sitting on Beachy Head, I should not turn my nose up at the place.

So off they all went, my mother and my embryonic self, my brother, and my maternal grandmother went with them, to look after them all, while my father, in a reserved occupation, and who, besides, had served the whole term of the First World War, stayed behind in London to work but he came down whenever he could manage it and that was very often because he and my mother were very attached to each other.

My mother went into labour in Eastbourne but when she came out of it we were on the front line because Dunkirk fell while I was shouldering my way into the world; my grandmother said there was *one* place in the world the Germans would not dare to bomb so we all shifted ourselves to a cottage that my father now rented for us next door to the one in which my great-aunt, Sophia, my grandmother's sister, and her brother, my great-uncle, Sydney, lived. And though the Germans bombed hell out of the South Coast and also bombed the heart out of Sheffield, twenty odd miles away from where we had removed, not one bomb fell on us, just as she had predicted.

Uncle Syd worked down Manvers Main Colliery. He was a tall, gaunt man of a beautiful, shy dignity, who had, I understand, originally wanted to be a bookie but whose mother had not let him. I remember him all pigeon-coloured, soft greys touched with beige, the colour of the clothes he was wearing when I last saw him, when he came down south for my gran's funeral. And a pearl tie-pin. And a gold watch-chain, across his camel-coloured waistcoat.

Sophie was a teacher. She had no formal qualifications at all, I think, had simply never left school but stayed on to teach the babies the three Rs and did so until she retired in the 1950s, qualified eventually by experience, natural aptitude and, probably, strength of character. Besides, by then she had taught several generations of the village to read and write, probably taught most of the education committee to read and write. She, too, had a great deal of formal dignity; I remember how, unlike my grandmother, who had lived in London most of her life, Syd and Sophie both had very soft voices, country voices. Though we could hear Syd's cough through the wall, the dreadful, choking cough that all the men over forty in the village had.

The south Yorkshire coalfields are not half as ugly as they may seem at first glance. Rather like the potteries, they are somehow time-locked, still almost a half-rural society as it must have been in the early days of the Industrial Revolution. The wounded and despoiled countryside remains lush and green around the workings; sheep graze right up to the pit-heads, although the sheep I saw when I was a child were all black with soot, and Doncaster Market is far richer in local agricultural produce than the pretend-markets in Devon. There is a quite un-English pre-occupation with food; the pig is dealt with in a bewildering and delicious variety of ways but butter and cheese are good, too, and so is bread, the perfume of next morning's loaves nightly flavouring the air around the corner bakery.

The streets of the red-brick villages are laid out in grid-like parallels, cheapest of housing for working families, yet they manage to fold into the landscape with a certain, gritty reticence although it is one of gentle hills; there is none of the scenic drama of west Yorkshire, instead, a bizarre sense of mucky pastoral. The colliers were often famous poachers in their spare time. My granny taught me songs that celebrated the wily fox, the poacher's comrade, and his depredations of bourgeois farmyards:

> Old Mother Flipperty-flop jumped out of bed,
> Out of the window she stuck 'er 'ead –
> 'John, John, the grey goose is gone
> And the fox is off to his den, of!'

It is almost the landscape of D. H. Lawrence, almost that of the Chatterleys, Mellors was as tough on the poachers as only a true class-traitor could be. Lawrence ratted on it all, of course, Lawrence, the great, guilty chronicler of English social mobility, the classic, seedy Brit full of queasy, self-justificatory class shame and that is why they identify with him so much in British universities, I tell you. I know the *truth*. Him and his la-did-dah mother.

But I read *The Rainbow* a little while ago, searching for some of the flavour of the lives of my grandmother and her family eighty years ago, ninety years ago, in a village not unlike Eastwood, only a little more gritty, and there was Sophie, teaching school like Ursula Brangwen but making a much better job of it, I'm happy to say, perhaps since nobody sent her to Sheffield High School and taught her to give herself airs. At that, I hear my grandmother speaking in my head.

But Sophie *did* trek all the way to Leeds to go to art classes. Ruskin was a strong influence in these parts. To my knowledge, Sophie never drew or painted for pleasure when she was grown-up but she taught me the rudiments of perspective, and most of the alphabet, before I was five. Her father, my great-grandfather, had he owned a pub? At this point, they vanish into mist; there is a brewery in Sheffield with their family name, but it is a common enough name in south Yorkshire. Some connection was supposed to have been the cock-fighting king of the entire country but all this is irretrievable, now. I do not even know if they had seen better days, but I doubt it.

All the same, there was a beautiful parlour-organ in Sophie's pocket-handkerchief-sized front room and a grandfather clock so old it is now in the museum in Barnsley and a glass-fronted cabinet full of ancient blue-and-white china that must have been very fine because my mother always lusted after it but never managed to get her hands on it, in the end, because Sophie outlived her, to Sophie's grief. At night, the kitchen was lit by the dim, greenish, moth-like light of gas mantles; we took candles up the steep wooden stairs to bed. There was a coal range, that Sophie blacked; no hot water; a tin bath filled with kettles in which Syd washed off his pit dirt. There were no pit-head baths at Manvers Main until 1947, when the mines were nationalised.

Smelling of sweat and the sharp, mineral odour of coal dust, the miners came off the shift blacked up as for a minstrel show, their eyeballs and teeth gleaming, in their ragged jackets, braces, overalls, and I remember gangs of them exhaustedly swaggering home, so huge, so genial and so proudly filthy they seemed almost superhuman. I'm a sucker for the worker hero, you bet. I think most of them thought that nationalisation would mean workers' control and were justifiably pissed off when they found out it didn't, sold down the river by the Labour Party again, the old story.

Death was part of daily life, also; scarcely a family had not its fatality, its mutilated, its grey-faced old man coughing his lungs out in the chair by the range. And everybody was, of course, very poor. It wasn't until the 1960s that miners were earning anything like a reasonable living wage and by then Sophie had electricity, and a bathroom, and a gas-stove, benefits she accepted from the Coal Board without gratitude, for they were no more than her due.

Of course I romanticise it. Why the hell not. I cry with pure anger when I pass the pits beside the railway-line from Sheffield to Leeds; the workings, grand and heartless monuments to the anonymous dead.

We are not a close-knit but nevertheless an obsessive family, sustained, as must be obvious, by a subjectively rich if objectively commonplace folk-lore. And claustrophobic as a Jewish family, to which we have many similarities, even if we do not see one another often. I cannot escape them, nor do I wish to do so. They are the inhabitants of my heart, and the rhetoric and sentimentality of such a phrase is also built into me by the rich Highland sentimentality of my father's people that always made my mother embarrassed.

Since they were a matriarchal clan, my mother's side of the family bulked first and largest, if not finally most significantly.

My maternal grandmother seemed to my infant self a woman of such physical and spiritual heaviness she might have been born with a greater degree of gravity than most people. She came from a community where women rule the roost and she effortlessly imparted a sense of my sex's ascendancy in the scheme of things, every word and gesture of hers displayed a natural dominance, a native savagery, and I am very grateful for all that, now, although the core of steel was a bit inconvenient when I was looking for boyfriends in the south in the late fifties, when girls were supposed to be as soft and as pink as a nursuree.

Gran was ninety when she died ten years ago and wandering in her mind, so she'd talk about the miners' strikes of her girlhood, how they'd march in their pit dirt and rags with banners and music, they would play harmonicas, and she leaned out of the attics of the house where she worked as a chambermaid to watch. She would have made a bloody awful chambermaid, unnaturally servile until something inside her snapped.

My maternal grandfather, who died before I was born, originally hailed from East Anglia. There was no work on the farms so he joined the army and I think his regiment must have been sent to south Yorkshire to put down the strikes. Nobody ever told me this in so many words, but I can think of no other reason why he should have arrived there in time to meet my grandmother in the late 1880s or early 1890s. He met her; they were engaged; and he was sent to India.

When we were clearing out my grandmother's effects, we found a little stack of certificates for exams my grandfather had passed in the army. In Baluchistan, in the Punjab, in Simla, he had become astoundingly literate and numerate. He must also have learned to argue like hell. Furthermore, he became radicalised, unless the seeds had already been sewn in the seething radicalism of the coalfields. He wrote to my grandmother once a week for seven years. Characteristically unsentimental, she threw away their letters, with their extraordinary fund of information about an NCO coming to consciousness through the contradictions inherent in the Raj, but she kept the stamps. What stamp albums my uncles had.

Of all the dead in my family, this unknown grandfather is the one I would most like to have talked to. He had the widest experience and perhaps the greatest capacity for interpreting it. There are things about him that give me great pleasure; for example, as a hobby, later in life, he enjoyed, though only in a modest, yet a not entirely unsuccessful way, playing the Stock Exchange, as if to prove to himself the childish simplicity with which the capitalist system operated. My grandmother thwarted this flair, she never trusted banks, she kept his money in matresses, no really, in biscuit tins, on her person, in her big, black, leather bag.

When my mother's father came home, he married gran and joined the ILP and went to live in London, first Southwark, then Battersea, four children in a two-bedroom rabbit hutch. A yard, no garden. No bath. To the end of her life, my dotty aunt, who lived with gran, washed at the public slipper bath.

They were magnificently unbowed. There was a piano for the children, who played it; and did amateur dramatics; and went to see Shakespeare and Ibsen and Sybil Thorndyke in *Saint Joan* at the Old Vic. He was a clerk in the War Department; he used his literacy to be shot of manual labour, first rung up the ladder of social mobility, then worked in one of the first of the clerical trades unions. (Which may have been down a snake.) He got out of the slums, feet first, in his coffin; gran stuck it out until the street was demolished in 1956. Before the First World War, he chaired a meeting at which Lenin spoke. He shook Lenin by the hand and he led my eldest uncle, then a small boy, up to shake Lenin's hand, also. This uncle, however, grew up to adopt a political stance somewhat, as the Americans say, to the right of Attila the Hun.

My maternal grandfather died of cirrhosis. A life-long teetotaller, the years in India had wrecked his liver. My grandmother's house was full of relics of the Empire, an ebony elephant, spears, a carved coconut shell representing the Hindu cosmogeny, beautiful shells from tropical seas, some with pierced messages: A Present From The Andaman Islands. Also enormous quantities of souvenir china, mugs, teapots and sugar basins commemorating every coronation from that of Edward VII to that of Elizabeth II; there was even a brace of scarlet enamelled tin trays from Victoria's Diamond Jubilee. Contradictions of English socialism. And enormous quantities of books, of course, some very strange: Foxe's *Books of Martyrs*, not one but three copies; Macchiavelli; *Twenty Thousand Leagues Under the Sea.*

Their children were indefatigable self-educators, examination passers and prize-winners; those shelves were crammed with prizes for good conduct, for aptitude, for general excellence, for overall progress, though my gran fucked it all up for my mother. An intolerably bright girl, my mother won a scholarship to a ladies' grammar school, a big deal, in those days, from a Battersea elementary school. My gran attended prize-days to watch my mother score her loot with a huge Votes for Women badge pinned to her lapel and my mother, my poor mother, was ashamed because my gran was zapping the option her daughter had been given to be a lady just by standing up for her own rights not to be. (My mother used to sing 'The Internationale' to me but only because she liked the tune.)

Perhaps my mother was ashamed of gran, as well, because gran talked broad Yorkshire until the day she died, all 'sithee' and 'thyssen' and ''e were runnin' like buggery'. When she gracelessly shoved a plate of food in front of you, she'd growl: 'Get it down thee,' with a dreadful menace. She taught me how to whistle. She hated tears and whining to no purpose; 'Don't be soft,' she'd say. Though she was often wrong, she was never silly. When I or anyone else was silly, she would wither me: 'Tha bloody fool,' making a broken diphthong out of the long 'o'. How to transcribe it: half-way between 'foo-ill' and 'foyle'.

When I was eighteen, I went to visit her rigged out in all the atrocious sartorial splendour of the underground high-style of the late fifties, black-mesh stockings, spike-heeled shoes, bum-hugging skirt, jacket with a black fox collar. She laughed so much she wet herself. 'You wait a few years and you'll be old and ugly, just like me,' she cackled. She herself dressed in dark dresses of heavy rayon crêpe, with grey Lisle stockings bound under the knee with two loops of knotted elastic.

Her personality had an architectonic quality; I think of her when I see some of the great London railway termini, especially St Pancras, with its soot and turrets, and she overshadowed her own daughters, whom she did not understand – my mother, who liked things to be nice; my dotty aunt. But my mother had not the strength to put even much physical distance between them, let alone keep the old monster at an emotional arm's length. Although gran only actually lived with us in Yorkshire, and went back to her own house, five miles away, when we all went back to London at ceasefire, I remember her as always and ineradicably *there* until I was ten or eleven, by which time she was growing physically debilitated. I would have said, 'frail', but that is quite the wrong word.

But my grandmother's toughness was a limitation of its own. There was to be no struggle for my mother, who married herself young to an adoring husband who indulged her, who was subject to ill-health, who spoke standard south London English, who continued to wear fancy clothes long after she was both wife and mother. My grandmother could have known of no qualities in herself she could usefully transmit to this girl who must have seemed a stranger to her. So, instead, she nagged her daughter's apparent weaknesses.

With the insight of hindsight, I'd have liked to have been able to protect my mother from the domineering old harridan, with her rough tongue and primitive sense of justice, but I did not see it like that, then. I did not see there was a drama between mother and daughter.

At my wedding, my grandmother spread brown sugar on her smoked salmon and ate it with relish. She did not approve of the man whom I married because he wore a belt to keep his trousers up instead of braces. She wore her hair in a bun on the very top of her head and secured it with giant, tortoiseshell pins.

When I lived in Japan, I learned to admire their tolerant acceptance of the involuntary nature of family life. Love in the sense of passionate attachment has nothing to do with it; the Japanese even have a different verb to define the arbitrary affection that grows among these chance juxtapositions of intimate strangers. There is also the genetic and environmental snare, of course; they are they and you are you but, nevertheless, alike. I would have defended my mother with my grandmother's weapons.

I also admire the Russian use of patronymics, although matronymics would do just as well. Aeneas carried his aged father on his back from the ruins of Troy and so do we all, whether we like it or not, perhaps even if we have never known them. But my own father recently resigned the post to go and live with his own brother and father, moving smartly out of our family back into his own, reverting, in his seventh decade, to the youthful role of sib. At an age when most parents become their children's children, he redefined himself as the equal of his son and daughter. He can cope with the ruins of Troy very well under his own steam. He will carry *me* out of them, I dare say.

When my father attached a plastic parakeet he'd bought at Woolworths, his favourite shop, to a disused gas fitting on the ceiling of our kitchen in south London, my mother said to him in a voice of weary petulance: 'Age cannot wither nor accustom stale your infinite variety.' They had then been married for thirty-five years.

My father has lined the walls of his own new home with pictures of my mother when she was young and beautiful; and beautiful she certainly was, with a broad, Slavonic jaw and high cheekbones like Anna Karenina, she took a striking photograph and had the talent for histrionics her pictures imply. They used to row dreadfully and pelt one another with household utensils, whilst shrieking with rage. Then my mother would finally break down and cry, possibly tears of sheer frustration that he was bigger than she, and my father, in an ecstasy of remorse – we've always been very good at remorse and its manifestations in action, emotional blackmail and irrational guilt – my father would go out and buy her chocolates.

The gift wiped away all resentment, as it happened, because he often bought her chocolates when they had not rowed at all. He really loved to buy her things. She herself liked Harrods, especially the sale, and sometimes Harvey Nichols; he could never see the difference between these places and Woolworths except the restaurants but, since they very much enjoyed eating lunch out, he was happy to go with her, happy to carry the packages.

A morning's shopping was a major trip and they could indulge their taste for this diversion freely because my father worked from three o'clock in the afternoon until midnight most days. My mother was sometimes sorry for herself, to spend all her evenings alone, but he would come back in the middle of the night with the next day's newspapers and make her tea and bring her biscuits and they would chatter away for hours in the early morning. If I was awake, I could hear them through the wall.

Their life together was one of daytime treats and midnight feasts when I was usually at school or in bed. They spent more time alone with one another than do those parents who use children as an excuse for not talking to one another, and at times of the day when they were both rested and refreshed. No wonder they got on one another's nerves, sometimes. Then the storms were amazing. One could never rely on tranquillity, or not for long. But the rows were never conducted in hushed whispers – not of that 'pas devant les enfants' rubbish and were never about anything important, like money. Or me. At least, not yet. They were about nothing at all, a blocked-up lavatory, a blunt carving knife, my father's enthusiastic but not terribly scrupulous washing up. ('He'd like to wash up before we sat down to dinner.' 'He thinks we're going to want mustard all week.') Their rowing was the noisy music of compatibility.

It was a household in which midnight was early and breakfast merged imperceptibly into lunch. I can remember no rules, no punishments and I was expected to answer back. Once you were inside the door, a curious kind of dream-time operated; life passed at a languorous pace, everything was gently untidy, and none of the clocks ever told the right time, although they ticked away busily. We relied on the radio for the right time.

I went to look at this second house in which I lived last Christmas, the time for sentimental journeys. It was a good deal nicer than I had remembered it; a largish, even imposing Edwardian terrace house with a bay at the front and a little garden at the back, abutting on the Victoria-Brighton line. I had remembered it as smaller, poky, even. The entire street looked brighter and fresher than in the past; there were a few chocolate brown doors and the glimpse of a Japanese paper lantern in some front-rooms. Hardly any net curtains, now. The whole area is clearly on the up, again, but my father sold the house five years ago, sold it for peanuts, glad to be shot of it now she was gone, and went off.

My father and mother had settled down, as I've said, only a few miles away from her own family if 500 miles away from his, in Balham, then, in the mid-1920s, a solid, middle-class suburb, lace curtains, privet hedges and so on. They planted roses in the arid soil of the back garden and, unfairly enough, for my father only entered the garden to brutally prune them, they bloomed lavishly every June. They furnished the house with mahogany sideboard, leather settee, oak Welsh-dresser — handsome furniture; I wouldn't mind some of it, now, only my father abandoned most of it there. He has no affection for possessions, unless they have only sentimental value. He keeps my wedding dress. Perhaps in case I need it again. No, he'd want to buy me a new one. But my mother loved nice things and said, when I told her I was leaving my husband, to be sure to take with me some silver-plated teaspoons she had recently given me. I did not and have often regretted it.

Here, when we came back from Yorkshire at the end of the war to a street that had had the residue of respectability bombed out of it, we settled into a curious kind of deviant middle-class life, all little luxuries and no small comforts, no refrigerator, no washing-machine, no consumer durables at all, but cream with puddings and terribly expensive soap and everything went to the laundry. And we were too messy for genuine discomfort. But our household became increasingly anachronistic as the neighbourhood turned into a twilight zone. A social-realist family life for those first seminal five years, that I remember so well because the experience was finite; but the next ten years have a far more elusive flavour, it was as though we were stranded, somehow. A self-contained family unit with a curious, self-crafted life-style, almost but not quite an arty one, a very unself-conscious one, that flourished on its own terms but was increasingly at variance with the changes going on around it. My mother's passion for respectability in itself became a source of deviance; she actively encouraged me to wear black woollen stockings at a time when they were a positive sign of depravity. She forbade me lipstick in the days when only female beatniks did not wear lipstick. It was all very strange.

Since my father returned to his granite village beside its granite sea, returned not only to his native land – Scotland – but to the very house in which he grew up, triumphantly accomplishing the dearest dream of every migrant worker, I understand better how it was we were always somehow askew. I felt like a foreigner because my mother had married a foreigner, although neither she nor he himself ever realised it. Being a Scot, he never fully comprehended the English class system, nor did he realise he might have been socially upwardly mobile within it; he only thought he had not done badly, which is a different perspective upon it. He had seen what Dr Johnson, one of my mother's favourites, called the finest thing a Scotsman can see, the high road to England, and he took it; did well enough; married happily; ushered into the world two satisfactory children. And then he went home, a symmetric life. He was a journalist until he retired and, of course, journalists have a curious marginality on their own, a professional detachment. If he had pretensions, they would have been to style as such, I think. He remains something of a dandy. He has always enjoyed walking sticks, bow ties, selects a different form of headgear for different hours of the day.

So we did not quite fit in, thank goodness; alienated is the only way to be, after all. After the war, my mother was always trying to persuade him to move to a posher neighbourhood, as if she thought *that* was the problem, and a house big enough to have my gran live with us, as though the presence of my gran would not have cancelled the whole thing out. Mum fancied Streatham; she had her eye on one house after another and sometimes we were so near to moving that she would pack all the books up in cardboard boxes, but, when it came to the point, my father wouldn't budge.

He entered into the fantasy of the thing wholeheartedly, of course; estate agent after estate agent was led up the garden path by him, but, when the crunch came, he could not do it. I don't think it was the idea of living with gran that put him off; they recognised that, in their ways, they were a match for one another and treated one another with deference. But he was himself utterly oblivious of the way the neighbourhood was growing seedy, the way the house was falling down. 'Nothing wrong with the old shack,' he'd say, as the woodworm gnawed the rafters and the defective wiring ignited small conflagrations hither and thither. 'Nothing wrong with the old shack.' Not defensively – rather, with the air of a man startled that anyone might think otherwise.

No. He hated the idea of a big mortgage. He liked to have the odd bob in his pocket, for chocolates, for ice-cream, for lunches out, for nice things for my mother, for his own modest dandyism, for occasional taxis that turned into taxis everywhere after my mother grew ill. Also, he particularly enjoyed travelling first-class on the railways – oh, those exquisite night-trains to Scotland! We could not afford a nicer house and all those luxuries besides; he did elaborate sums on the backs of envelopes to regretfully prove it – and then would climb back happily to the little eyrie he'd made for himself in the attic, where he would lie on his bed listening to obscure continental stations on his radio, smoking his pipe. 'What are you *doing*?' she'd shout from the bottom of the stairs. 'Contemplating the futility of it all,' he'd say. 'Contemplating the futility of it all, you old trout.'

When she told him how much she hated being called an old trout, he'd riposte: 'The trout is the most beautiful of fish.'

Charm is our curse.

So they stayed put. After he retired from work, maybe the only move he really wanted to make was back to Scotland but she would not hear of that, so put herself at the tender mercies of his kin and of the deathly climate. After I left home, they turned increasingly in on themselves; a good deal of the joy evaporated from their lives with my mother's illness and there was her own mother's death, a great blow since the umbilical cord had been ill-severed. But that was later, when I was no longer a child.

My mother and father were well on in their marriage when I was born, so there is a great deal about them I do not know and I do not remember them when they were young. My father was older when I was born than I am now. But he loved to take snaps in those unknown-to-me days and there are dozens of albums of pictures of my mother. My mother in wonderfully snappy clothes with my brother in his photogenic babyhood; with a black and white dog they had; in an open tourer my father subsequently crashed; on beaches; in fields among cornstooks; at the piano; playing at typing on my father's typewriter, every inch the dimpled twenties' child-bride. My mother would often say what a lovely time she and my dad had before the war and there is the proof of it, trapped in the amber of the perpetual summer of the amateur photographer, redolent of a modest yet authentic period glamour.

I was not in any way part of that life, which had ended with the war; and the war ended with the onset of their middle-age. After the war, everything became drab and drabness, I think, instinctively repelled them both. Chaos, even mayhem, yes; but a drab, an austere time, no, even if my mother paid a lot of lip-service to respectability. Love and money only bought me lousy toys in the 1940s and I acceded to my brother's generation, I loved best his plush Mickey Mouse and his books, *Alice* and *Pooh*. Times grew less hard; then, at last, I acquired in full measure all the impedimenta of a bourgeois childhood, a dolls' house, toy sewing-machine, red patent-leather shoes with silver buckles, organdie dresses and so on, but these were all a little spooky in a twilight zone and the Cold War was a curious time during which to recreate a snug, privileged, 1930s childhood for their daughter. I went to primary school with apprentice used-car dealers and my best friend was a girl whose uncle trained greyhounds, whose mother was an office-cleaner. Not that my parents thought there was anything odd about that. And always, when I came home, the dreamtime engulfed me, a perpetual Sunday afternoon in which you could never trust the clocks, until, when I was fifteen, she was ill. And never fully recovered, was never really well again, always an invalid now. And the music of their rowing died to a soft *obligato*.

She once warned me: 'Children wreck marriages.' I had not realised how essentially satisfied they had been with one another until then; not that I think she meant my brother and I had wrecked *her* marriage. If anything, we were too much loved, I don't think she resented us. I do not think she was registering a specific complaint, but making a grand generalisation based on observation, insight yet also, perhaps, she felt a dissatisfaction that was also generalised, had nothing to do with any of us, did not even exist as an 'if only', but as if, perhaps unconsciously, she felt she might have mislaid something important, in the eccentric, noisy trance of that rambling, collapsing house.

But then, I do not think you ever know you are happily married until you have been unhappily married first.

She once gave me a rose tree.

It was for my tenth or eleventh birthday. I forget precisely which. It was a miniature rose tree, in a pot. I found it on my breakfast table, beside the other presents, of which there were a tremendous many, I was spoiled rotten. It was no more than a foot high and covered with pink blossom. I was a little disappointed with it, at first; I could not eat it, wear it or read it and I was a practical child and could not really see the use of it, though I could see it had been chosen with the greatest loving care.

I misunderstood my mother's subtleties. I did not realise this rose tree was not a present for my tenth birthday, but for my grown self, a present not for now, but to remember. Of all the presents of all the birthdays of a petted childhood, the rose tree is the one I remember best and it is mixed up, now, with my memory of her, that, in spite of our later discords, our acrimonious squabblings, once she gave me a perennial and never-fading rose tree, the outlines of which, crystallised in the transforming well of memory, glitter as if with properties she herself may not have been at all aware of, a present like part of herself she did not know about that she could still give away to me.

News Review, 1976

My Father's House

The dining room, never used except as an ancillary larder, a cool place in which to set jellies and store meat, eggs and fish for the cat, is unchanged in essentials since I first came here in 1945. This room has the air of formal disuse characteristic of the Scots company room of its period. It was assembled long before I was born and is now almost an informal museum of north-east Scots twenties style, heirlooms and memorabilia.

There is a Brussels carpet; a table of brightly varnished, heavily grained yellow pine built by a long-dead local joiner; wallpaper with cowed brown flowers; a mirrored sideboard piled with souvenir china, plastic bowls, flowers made of wood chips bought from whining tinkers, paper bags containing outmoded hats, a number of plastic dolls in blonde wigs and kilts brought back as giftlets for my now deceased aunt by cronies who tripped off to other parts of Scotland for wee holidays.

There is a glass-fronted cabinet where my great-grandmother's tea service is stored, stately shapes of white china teapot and slopbasin – clearly a better class of goods was available in the town in the 1850s than it is today. My father says she was a school-teacher and used to ride to work in Banff, across the Deveron, on a little pony. Banff, a small, granite, seventeenth-century town so obscure that letters directed to it are sometimes sent to Banff, Alberta, in error.

I tentatively identify this great-grandmother as the one whose antique sepia photograph on the wall shows her, good God, in a long cloak, wimple and modified steeple hat – and not as if it were fancy dress, either, but her normal apparel, a little touch of the Aberdeen witches. (In 1636, rope to bind witches at Banff cost eight shillings, a lot of money in those days.) But this lady has the stern face of a kirk-goer. There's the picture of a distant uncle who was killed while working on a railroad in Canada. Other family photographs, no longer identifiable, are curiously poignant. Who the hell were they? Why are they not remembered?

There are several pictures in heavy frames on the walls. Two are reproductions in oils of stags in depopulated Highland glens, school of 'The Stag at Bay'. There are charcoal sketches of similar scenes in all the bedrooms, the house is crammed with stags, there's even a little stag, made of lead, on top of the massive clock in the master bedroom. But there isn't a landscape that could harbour a stag within a hundred miles of this place. It's a purely emblematic Scottishness, this scenery of crags, spruce, glens, tumbling waterfalls, untenanted except for deer, post-clearance landscapes, in which man is most present in his resonating absences.

Clearly this family was once heavily into the mythology of Scotland. I keep trying to interest my father in the history of his people, now he's gone back to them at last. I sent him John Prebble's books about Culloden and the Highland clearances. But he's cast them aside after a preliminary, dutiful browse. He says they're too bloody depressing.

During the whole of his fifty years down south, he never showed any interest at all in his own foreignness. None of your St Andrew's Societies and Burns Nights, those folkmoots of the middle-class Scots expatriate. There's a joke he's still fond of, though. Jock goes down south for an interview and, on his return, is asked: Did you meet any Englishmen, Jock? 'Och, no; I only met heads of departments.' A self-defensive joke. Like the sort of Jewish joke told by Jews. And back he went, eventually. Back home.

It's a long day's drive to a stag-haunted glen from the north-east seaboard – soon, it's rumoured, to be oil-rich. The main evidence of the oil rigs off Peterhead, thirty miles away, is the way property values round here have shot up. Fish and farming remain the basics. The *Banffshire Journal* (sub-headed *and Northern Farmer*) carries stories about the price of fish, the shortage of pigs, the scarcity of fat cattle. Headline: STRAW DESTROYED IN BLAZE. Another: PORTESSIE MAN PRESUMED DROWNED, after he was thrown from the deck of an Aberdeen trawler when an oil rig supply vessel – ah! – ripped an eight-foot gash in her port side. That's the only mention of the oil in this issue.

There is ancient and graceful Banff; and there is the mouth of the beautiful Deveron, 'sweet Deveronside'; and then there is Macduff, where I come from. Correction. Where my father comes from: I am easily confused by my own roots. Where my father came from and went back to. Two towns separated by a river, and by invisible barriers of class. Brash Macduff was invented virtually as a new town by William Duff of Braco, afterwards first Earl of Fife, during the mid-eighteenth century. They were too busy putting in the harbour to even notice the Jacobite rebellion.

More to the point of this place than the crags and glens on the dining-room wall are the two fine colour prints of clipper ships in frames of birdseye maple. 'Whither, oh, splendid ship, thy white sails crowding, etcetera.' From these tight granite harbours, the clippers set sail for China, the immigrants departed for New Zealand.

I remember, about twenty years ago, a German training ship, some sort of triple-master schooner, put into Macduff harbour. It came floating like a tethered cloud past the little white toy-like lighthouse at the pierhead. It floated, it materialised, out of yet another vulgar, Technicolor, Cinerama sunset. The sun always goes down with amazing splendour over the Moray Firth.

I've never seen the town in such commotion before or since. Ancient fishers, with their flat caps, baggy trousers and characteristic rolling gait, thronged the foreshore, fêting the crew of the ship that shouldered aside the butch little fishing vessels with their touching names – the *Elspeth MacFee*, the *Rose in June*, the *Grace*, the *Fear Not*, the *Intrepid*. The ship came out of the past, carrying an invisible cargo of grandparents' memories. (Later, I think, it went down in the South Pacific.) That was something like an appropriate mythology.

I often wonder where the notion of the bustling industry of the Scots came from. Not from Macduff. They're competent, yes; but it's a sleepy town. Outside the church, there's a cross put up by the second Earl of Fife in 1783, whose pediment is inscribed thus: MAY IT FLOURISH AND LONG INCREASE IN NUMBERS AND OPULENCE WHILE ITS INHABITANTS GAIN THE BLESSINGS OF LIFE BY INDUSTRY, DILIGENCE AND TEMPERANCE. Wishful thinking on the part of the Anglo-Scots aristocracy, I'm inclined to think. 'Everybody takes things easy,' says the man who runs a taxi service, and does a lot of business ferrying drunks home at closing time. Poverty used to make them work hard; they had to. Temperance was always a more notional than an actual virtue round here.

All the same, a godly town. 'If the Lord will, the word of God will be preached on the Lord's Day at 5 pm. All welcome.' So says the sign on the door of the Tabernacle. The North Sea is a killer and those who work upon it pray a great deal, with good reason. 'Lost at sea', 'Lost at sea', 'Lost at sea', reiterate the gravestones in the churchyard, gravestones of Andersons, Pattersons, Shands, names reflecting the Scandinavian influence on this stretch of coast between Aberdeen and Inverness, a region less plastered with phony tartan than a lot of Scotland. I ought to remember that on those occasions when I'm tempted to don the tartan myself.

A couple of generations of my father's family are buried in Doune kirkyard. A theoretical distaste for nationalism, and the knowledge that the Anglo-Scot is the very worst kind, sets up disagreeable tensions within me in the gull-echoing, green place where, with fine self-regard, the dead have their academic qualifications inscribed after their names, BAs and MAs from Aberdeen mostly. Nevertheless, there they are – uncles and grandparents – all degreeless, alas. And another generation back is buried a few miles up the coast, in Portsoy; that's David, who fought at the battle of Waterloo and married a French wife. The stone was erected by his sons in memory of 'the most genial and indulgent of fathers', or so it says; extraordinary epitaph for a Victorian pater-familias in the Calvinist north-east. Either black irony; or else it was true.

He used to live in an earth-floored cottage that now lies in picturesque ruin on the foreshore. We have our little pilgrimages. My father likes to drive out to Davy's grave, Davy's cottage, and we stand and look at the relics, and I try to pretend I don't feel the cold hand of mortality on my heart, of mortality and also of something else. For the circumstances of life in that cottage are unimaginable to me. My family history remains, in some ways, inaccessibly foreign.

It isn't just the great-grandparents who seem impenetrable, either. My paternal grandmother would not light a fire on the Sabbath and piled all Sunday's washing up in a bucket, to be dealt with on Monday morning, because the Sabbath was a day of rest – a practice that made my paternal grandfather, the village atheist, as mad as fire. Nevertheless, he willed five quid to the minister, just to be on the safe side.

What fictional eccentricities are these? But all true, all perfectly well-documented. Everybody says I look just like my paternal grandmother, furthermore. I can't go out to buy morning rolls, those delicious regional specialities, without somebody who remembers the old lady grappling with me on the pavement and stressing the resemblance.

They're still a bit bewildered by my accent. My Aunt Katie used to explain, almost apologetically: 'Hugh marrit an English girl, ye ken.' And I'd stand there, smiling, feeling terribly, terribly foreign in that clean white town, under that clean, white unEnglish light which is nevertheless, in some dislocated way, home – which is where my ain folk are from.

The Japanese have a phrase, 'the landscapes of the heart', to describe the Romantic correlation between inside and outside that converts physical geography into part of the apparatus of the sensibility. Home is where the heart is and hence a movable feast. We used to come here for family holidays when I was a child, but there was bad feeling over my wedding and I hadn't set foot in the place for fifteen years, nor felt the lack of it, until my father decided to go home after an absence of half a century that his ain folk did not even seem to have noticed, so instantly did the town absorb him again. And I felt entirely at home here, the first time I got off the bus beside the harbour again. Nothing, nothing had changed.

Unacknowledged but dreadful pressure of roots? Or the last result of rootlessness and alienation, when you can say – and mean it – 'Anywhere I hang my hat is home'?

'Even the native, who has spent his life among these pleasing amenities, and has every detail imprinted on his mind's eye, is fain, of a Sunday evening, to betake himself to some rising ground, to the Gaveny Brae or the Hill of Doune, and feast his soul for the thousandth time on the well-beloved landscape.' So observed Allan Edward Mahood in his immemorial guide to *Banff and District*, a book my father assures me he kept at his bedside through all his years of London exile. Our rich sentimentality, obverse side to our rigorous cynicism. My ain folk – though they are simple, poor and plain folk. Se we proclaim with the characteristic disingenuousness of the colonialised.

Not that there's much nationalism of any kind in my family. When the Scots Nats seemed like so much Ealing comedy, long before they won the local seat, my late Uncle William was leaned on heavily for showing the Union Jack in his shop window at the coronation of Elizabeth the First of Scotland, and took it down for reasons only of pusillanimity. He didn't think his unimpeachable English connections were worth a broken window. England, half-English; Scotland, half-Scottish. Not much of a difference.

It's not even enough difference to make me a mongrel. I never really noticed the difference until I went back there, again, and found how different from home my home was. You don't choose your own landscapes. They choose you.

New Society, 1976

Sugar Daddy

I would say my father did not prepare me well for patriarchy; himself confronted, on his marriage with my mother, with a mother-in-law who was the living embodiment of peasant matriarchy, he had no choice but to capitulate, and did so. Further, I was the child of his mid-forties, when he was just the age to be knocked sideways by the arrival of a baby daughter. He was putty in my hands throughout my childhood and still claims to be so, although now I am middle-aged myself while he, not though you'd notice, is somewhat older than the present century.

I was born in 1940, the week that Dunkirk fell. I think neither of my parents was immune to the symbolism of this, of bringing a little girl-child

into the world at a time when the Nazi invasion of England seemed imminent, into the midst of death and approaching dark. Perhaps I seemed
particularly vulnerable and precious and that helps to explain the over-
protectiveness they felt about me, later on. Be that as it may, no child,
however inauspicious the circumstances, could have been made more
welcome. I did not get a birthday card from him a couple of years ago;
when I querulously rang him up about it, he said: 'I'd never forget the day
you came ashore.' (The card came in the second post.) His turn of phrase
went straight to my heart, an organ which has inherited much of his
Highland sentimentality.

He is a Highland man, the perhaps atypical product of an under-
developed, colonialised country in the last years of Queen Victoria, of oat-
cakes, tatties and the Church of Scotland, of four years' active service in
the First World War, of the hurly-burly of Fleet Street in the 1920s. His
siblings, who never left the native village, were weird beyond belief. To
that native village he competently removed himself ten years ago.

He has done, I realise, what every Sicilian in New York, what every
Cypriot in Camden Town wants to do, to complete the immigrant's journey, to accomplish the perfect symmetry, from A to B and back again. Just
his luck, when he returned, that all was as it had been before and he could,
in a manner of speaking, take up his life where it left off when he moved
south seventy years ago. He went south; and made a career; and married
an Englishwoman; and lived in London; and fathered children, in an enormous parenthesis of which he retains only sunny memories. He has 'gone
home', as immigrants do; he established, in his seventh decade, that
'home' has an existential significance for him which is not part of the story
of his children's independent lives. My father lives now in his granite
house filled with the souvenirs of a long and, I think, happy life. (Some
of them bizarre; that framed certificate from an American tramp, naming
my father a 'Knight of the Road', for example.)

He has a curious, quite unEnglish, ability to life life in, as it were, the
third person, to see his life objectively, as a not unfortunate one, and to live
up to that notion. Those granite townships on the edge of the steel-grey
North Sea forge a flinty sense of self. Don't think, from all this, he isn't a
volatile man. He laughs easily, cries easily, and to his example I attribute
my conviction that tears, in a man, are a sign of inner strength.

He is still capable of surprising me. He recently prepared an electric bed
for my boyfriend, which is the sort of thing a doting father in a Scots ballad might have done had the technology been available at the time. We
knew he'd put us in separate rooms – my father is a Victorian, by birth –
but not that he'd plug the metal base of Mark's bed into the electric-light
fitment. Mark noticed how the bed throbbed when he put his hand on it

and disconnected every plug in sight. We ate breakfast, next morning, as if nothing untoward had happened, and I should say, in the context of my father's house, it had not. He is an enthusiastic handyman, with a special fascination with electricity, whose work my mother once described as combining the theory of Heath Robinson with the practice of Mr Pooter.

All the same, the Freudian overtones are inescapable. However, unconsciously, as if *that* were an excuse, he'd prepared a potentially lethal bed for his daughter's lover. But let me not dot the i's and cross the t's. His final act of low, emotional cunning (another Highland characteristic) is to have lived so long that everything is forgiven, even his habit of referring to the present incumbent by my first husband's name, enough to give anybody a temporary feeling.

He is a man of immense, nay, imposing physical presence, yet I tend to remember him in undignified circumstances.

One of my first memories is how I bust his nose. (I was, perhaps, three years old. Maybe four.) It was on a set of swings in a public park. He'd climbed up Pooterishly to adjust the chains from which the swings hung. I thought he was taking too long and set the swing on which I sat in motion. He wasn't badly hurt but there was a lot of blood. I was not punished for my part in this accident. They were a bit put out because I wanted to stay and play when they went home to wash off the blood.

They. That is my father and my mother. Impossible for me to summon one up out of the past without the other.

Shortly after this, he nearly drowned me, or so my mother claimed. He took me for a walk one autumn afternoon and stopped by the pond on Wandsworth Common and I played a game of throwing leaves into the water until I forgot to let go of one. He was in after me in a flash, in spite of the peril to his gents' natty suiting (ever the dandy, my old man) and wheeled me dripping in my pushchair home to the terrible but short-lived recriminations of my mother. Short-lived because both guilt and remorse are emotions alien to my father. Therefore the just apportioning of blame is not one of his specialities, and though my mother tried it on from time to time, he always thought he could buy us off with treats and so he could and that is why my brother and I don't sulk, much. Whereas she –

She has been dead for more than a decade, now, and I've had ample time to appreciate my father's individual flavour, which is a fine and gamy one, but, as parents, they were far more than the sum of their individual parts. I'm not sure they understood their instinctive solidarity against us, because my mother often tried to make us take sides. Us. As their child, the product of their parenting, I cannot dissociate myself from my brother, although we did not share a childhood for he is twelve years older than I and was sent off, with his gas mask, his packed lunch and his name tag, as an evacuee, a little hostage to fortune, at about the time they must have realised another one was on the way.

I can only think of my parents as a peculiarly complex unit in which neither bulks larger than the other, although they were very different kinds of people and I often used to wonder how they got on, since they seemed to have so little in common, until I realised that was *why* they got on, that not having much in common means you've always got something interesting to talk about. And their children, far from being the *raison d'être* of their marriage, of their ongoing argument, of that endless, quietly murmuring conversation I used to hear, at night, softly, dreamily, the other side of the bedroom wall, were, in some sense, a sideshow. Source of pleasure, source of grief; not the glue that held them together. And neither of us more important than the other, either.

Not that I suspected this when I was growing up. My transition from little girl to ravaged anorexic took them by surprise and I thought they wanted my blood. I didn't know what they wanted of me, nor did I know what I wanted for myself. In those years of ludicrously overprotected adolescence, I often had the feeling of being 'pawns in their game' . . . in *their* game, note . . . and perhaps I indeed served an instrumental function, at that time, rather than being loved for myself.

All this is so much water under the bridge. Yet those were the only years I can remember when my mother would try to invoke my father's wrath against me, threaten me with his fury for coming home late and so on. Though, as far as the 'and so on' was concerned, chance would have been a fine thing. My adolescent rebellion was considerably hampered by the fact that I could find nobody to rebel with. I now recall this period with intense embarrassment, because my parents' concern to protect me from predatory boys was only equalled by the enthusiasm with which the boys I did indeed occasionally meet protected themselves against me.

It was a difficult time, terminated, inevitably, by my early marriage as soon as I finally bumped into somebody who would go to Godard movies with me and on CND marches and even have sexual intercourse with me, although he insisted we should be engaged first. Neither of my parents were exactly overjoyed when I got married, although they grudgingly did all the necessary. My father was particularly pissed off because he'd marked me out for a career on Fleet Street. It took me twenty years more of living, and an involvement with the women's movement, to appreciate he was unusual in wanting this for his baby girl. Although he was a journalist himself, I don't think he was projecting his own ambitions on me, either, even if to be a child is to be, to some degree, the projective fantasy of its parents. No. I suspect that, if he ever had any projective fantasies about me, I sufficiently fulfilled them by being born. All he'd wanted for me was a steady, enjoyable job that, perhaps, guaranteed me sufficient income to ensure I wouldn't too hastily marry some nitwit (a favourite word of his) who would displace him altogether from my affections. So, since from a child I'd been good with words, he apprenticed me to a suburban weekly news-paper when I was eighteen, intending me to make my traditional way up from there. From all this, given my natural perversity, it must be obvious why I was so hell-bent on getting married – not, and both my parents were utterly adamant about this, that getting married meant I'd give up my job.

In fact, it *did* mean that because soon my new husband moved away from London. 'I suppose you'll have to go with him,' said my mother doubtfully. Anxious to end my status as their child, there was no other option and so I changed direction although, as it turns out, I *am* a jour-nalist, at least some of the time.

As far as projective fantasies go, sometimes it seems the old man is only concerned that I don't end up in the workhouse. Apart from that, any-thing goes. My brother and I remain, I think, his most constant source of pleasure – always, perhaps, a more positive joy to our father than to our mother, who, a more introspective person, got less pure entertainment value from us, partly, like all mothers, for reasons within her own not untroubled soul. As for my father, few souls are less troubled. He can be simply pleased with us, pleased that we exist, and, from the vantage point of his wondrously serene and hale old age, he contemplates our lives almost as if they were books he can dip into whenever he wants.

As for the books I write myself, my 'dirty books', he said the other day: 'I was a wee bitty shocked, at first, but I soon got used to it.' He intro-duces me in the third person. 'This young woman . . .'. In his culture, it is, of course, a matter of principle to express pride in one's children. It occurs to me that this, too, is not a particularly English sentiment.

Himself, he is a rich source of anecdote. He has partitioned off a little room in the attic of his house, constructed the walls out of cardboard boxes, and there he lies, on a camp-bed, listening to the World Service on a portable radio with his cap on. When he lived in London, he used to wear a trilby to bed but, a formal man, he exchanged it for a cap as soon as he moved. There are two perfectly good bedrooms in his house, with electric blankets and everything, as I well know, but these bedrooms always used to belong to his siblings, now deceased. He moves downstairs into one of these when the temperature in the attic drops too low for even his iron constitution, but he always shifts back up again, to his own place, when the ice melts. He has a ferocious enthusiasm for his own private space. My mother attributed this to a youth spent in the trenches, where no privacy was to be had. His war was the war to end wars. He was too old for conscription in the one after that.

When he leaves this house for any length of time, he fixes up a whole lot of burglar traps, basins of water balanced on the tops of doors, tripwires, bags of flour suspended by strings, so that we worry in case he forgets where he's left what and ends up hoist with his own petard.

He has a special relationship with cats. He talks to them in a soft chirruping language they find irresistible. When we all lived in London and he worked on the night news desk of a press agency, he would come home on the last tube and walk, chirruping, down the street, accompanied by an ever-increasing procession of cats, to whom he would say good night at the front door. On those rare occasions, in my late teens, when I'd managed to persuade a man to walk me home, the arrival of my father and his cats always caused consternation, not least because my father was immensely tall and strong.

He is the stuff of which sitcoms are made.

His everyday discourse, which is conducted in the stately prose of a 1930s *Times* leader, is enlivened with a number of stock phrases of a slightly eccentric, period quality. For example. On a wild night: 'Pity the troops on a night like this.' On a cold day:

> Cold, bleak, gloomy and glum,
> Cold as the hairs on a polar bear's –

The last word of the couplet is supposed to be drowned by the cries of outrage. My mother always turned up trumps on this one, interposing: 'Father!' on an ascending scale.

At random: 'Thank God for the Navy, who guard our shores.' On entering a room: 'Enter the fairy, singing and dancing.' Sometimes, in a particularly cheerful mood, he'll add to this formula: 'Enter the fairy, singing and dancing and waving her wooden leg.'

Infinitely endearing, infinitely irritating, irascible, comic, tough, sentimental, ribald old man, with his face of a borderline eagle and his bearing of a Scots guard, who, in my imagination as when I was a child, drips chocolate from his pockets as, a cat dancing in front of him, he strides down the road bowed down with gifts, crying: 'Here comes the Marquess of Carrabus!' The very words, 'my father', always make me smile.

But why, when he was so devilish handsome – oh, that photograph in battledress! – did he never marry until his middle thirties? Until he saw my mother, playing tennis with a girlfriend on Clapham Common, and that was it. The die was cast. He gave her his card, proof of his honourable intentions. She took him home to meet her mother. Then he must have felt as though he were going over the top, again.

In 1967 or 1968, forty years on, my mother wrote to me: 'He really loves me (I think).' At that time, she was a semi-invalid and he tended her, with more dash than efficiency, and yet remorselessly, cooking, washing up, washing her smalls, hoovering, as if that is just what he'd retired from work to do, up to his elbows in soapsuds after a lifetime of telephones and anxiety. He'd bring her dinner on a tray with always a slightly soiled traycloth. She thought the dirty cloth spoiled the entire gesture. And yet, and yet . . . was she, after all those years, still keeping him on the hook? For herself, she always applauded his ability to spirit taxis up as from the air at crowded railway stations and also the dexterous way he'd kick his own backside, a feat he continued to perform until well into his eighties.

Now, very little of all this has to do with the stern, fearful face of the Father in patriarchy, although the Calvinist north is virtually synonymous with that ideology. Indeed, a short-tempered man, his rages were phenomenal; but they were over in the lightning flash they resembled, and then we all had ice-cream. And there was no fear. So that, now, for me, when fear steps in the door, then love and respect fly out of the window.

I do not think my father has ever asked awkward questions about life, or the world, or anything much, except when he was a boy reporter and asking awkward questions was part of the job. He would regard himself as a law-and-order man, a law-abiding man, a man with a due sense of respect for authority. So far, so in tune with his background and his sense of decorum. And yet somewhere behind all this lurks a strangely free, anarchic spirit. Doorknobs fall from doors the minute he puts his hand on them. Things fall apart. There is a sense that anything might happen. He is a law-and-order man helplessly tuned in to misrule.

And somewhere in all this must lie an ambivalent attitude to the authority to which he claims to defer. Now, my father is not, I repeat, an introspective man. Nor one prone to intellectual analysis; he's always got by on his wits so never felt the need of the latter. But he has his version of the famous story, about one of the Christmas truces during the First World War, which was *his* war, although, when he talks about it, I do not recognise Vera Brittain's war, or Siegfried Sassoon's war, or anything but a nightmarish adventure, for, as I say, he feels no fear. The soldiers, bored with fighting, remembering happier times, put up white flags, moved slowly forward, showed photographs, exchanged gifts – a packet of cigarettes for a little brown loaf . . . and then, he says, 'Some fool of a first lieutenant fired a shot.'

When he tells his story, he doesn't know what it *means*, he doesn't know what the story shows he really felt about the bloody officers, nor

why I'm proud of him for feeling that; nor why I'm proud of him for
giving the German private his cigarettes and remembering so warmly the
little loaf of bread, and proud of him for his still undiminished anger at the
nitwit of a boy whom they were all forced to obey just when the ranks
were in a mood to pack it in and go home.

Of course, the old man thinks that, if the rank and file *had* packed it in
and gone home in 1915, the Tsar would still rule Russia and the Kaiser
Germany, and the sun would never have set on the British Empire. He is
a man of grand simplicities. He still grieves over my mother's 'leftish'
views; indeed, he grieves over mine, though not enough to spoil his dinner. He seems, rather, to regard them as, in some way, genetically linked.
I have inherited her nose, after all; so why not my mother's voting patterns?

She never forgave him for believing Chamberlain. She'd often bring it
up, at moments of stress, as proof of his gullibility. 'And what's more, you
came home from the office and said: "There ain't gonna be a war."'

See how she has crept into the narrative, again. He wrote to me last year:
'Your mammy was not only very beautiful but also very clever.' (Always
in dialect, always 'mammy'.) Not that she did anything with it. Another
husband might have encouraged her to work, or study, although in the
1930s that would have been exceptional enough in this first-generation
middle-class family to have projected us into another dimension of existence altogether. As it was, he, born a Victorian and a sentimentalist, was
content to adore, and that, in itself, is sufficiently exceptional, dammit,
although it was not good for her moral fibre. She, similarly, trapped by historic circumstances, did not even know, I think, that her own vague discontent, manifested by sick headaches and complicated later on by
genuine ill-health, might have had something to do with being a 'wife', a
role for which she was in some respects ill suited, as my father's tribute
ought to indicate, since beauty and cleverness are usually more valued in
mistresses than they are in wives. For her sixtieth birthday, he gave her a
huge bottle of Chanel No. 5.

For what it's worth, I've never been in the least attracted to older men
– nor they to me, for that matter. Why *is* that? Possibly something in my
manner hints I will expect, nay, demand, behaviour I deem appropriate to
a father figure, that is, that he kicks his own backside from time to time,
and brings me tea in bed, and weeps at the inevitability of loss; and these
are usually young men's talents.

Don't think, from all this, it's been all roses. We've had our ups and
downs, the old man and I, for he was born a Victorian. Though it occurs
to me his unstated but self-evident idea that I should earn my own living,

have a career, in fact, may have originated in his experience of the first wave of feminism, that hit in his teens and twenties, with some of whose products he worked, by one of whose products we were doctored. (Our family doctor, Helen Gray, was eighty when she retired twenty years ago, and must have been one of the first women doctors.)

Nevertheless, his Victorianness, for want of a better word, means he feels duty bound to come the heavy father, from time to time, always with a histrionic overemphasis: 'You just watch out for yourself, that's all.' 'Watching out for yourself' has some obscure kind of sexual meaning, which he hesitates to spell out. If advice he gave me when I was a girl (I could paraphrase this advice as 'Kneecap them'), if this advice would be more or less what I'd arm my own daughters with now, it ill accorded with the mood of the sixties. Nor was it much help in those days when almost the entire male sex seemed in a conspiracy to deprive me of the opportunity to get within sufficient distance. The old man dowered me with too much self-esteem.

But how can a girl have *too much* self-esteem?

Nevertheless, not all roses. He is, you see, a foreigner; what is more, a Highland man, who struck further into the heartland of England than Charles Edward Stuart's army ever did, and then buggered off, leaving his children behind to carve niches in the alien soil. Oh, he'd hotly deny this version of his life; it is my own romantic interpretation of his life, obviously. He's all for the Act of Union. He sees no difference at all between the English and the Scots, except, once my mother was gone, he saw no reason to remain among the English. And his always unacknowledged foreignness, the extroversion of his manners, the stateliness of his demeanour, his fearlessness, guiltlessness, his inability to feel embarrassment, the formality of his discourse, above all, his utter ignorance of and complete estrangement from the English system of social class, make him a being I puzzle over and wonder at.

It is that last thing – for, in England, he seemed genuinely classless – that may have helped me always feel a stranger, here, myself. He is of perfectly good petty-bourgeois stock; my grandfather owned a shoe shop although, in those days, that meant being able to make the things as well as sell them, and repair them, too, so my grandfather was either a shopkeeper or a cobbler, depending on how you looked at it. The distinction between entrepreneur and skilled artisan may have appeared less fine, in those days, in that town beside the North Sea which still looks as if it could provide a good turnout for a witchburning.

There are all manner of stories about my paternal grandfather, whom I never met; he was the village atheist, who left a fiver in his will to every

minister in the place, just in case. I never met my Gaelic-speaking grandmother, either. (She died, as it happens of toothache, shortly before I was
born.) From all these stories I know they both possessed in full measure
that peculiar Highland ability, much perplexing to early tourists, which
means that the meanest, grubbing crofter can, if necessary, draw himself
up to his full height and welcome a visitor into his stinking hovel as if its
miserable tenant were a prince inviting a foreign potentate into a palace.
This is the courtly grace of the authentic savage. The women do it with
especially sly elegance. Lowering a steaming bowl on to a filthy tablecloth,
my father's sister used to say: 'Now, take some delicious kale soup.' And
it was the water in which the cabbage had been boiled.

It's possible to suspect they're having you on, and so they may be; yet
this formality always puts the visitor, no matter what his or her status, in
the role of supplicant. Your humiliation is what spares you. When a
Highlander grovels, then, oh, then is the time to keep your hand on your
wallet. One learns to fear an apology most.

These are the strategies of underdevelopment and they are worlds away
from those which my mother's family learned to use to contend with the
savage urban class struggle in Battersea, in the 1900s. Some of my mother's
family learned to manipulate cynically the English class system and helped
me and my brother out. All of them knew, how can I put it, that a good
table with clean linen meant self-respect and to love Shakespeare was a
kind of class revenge. (Perhaps that is why those soiled tray-cloths upset
my mother so; she had no quarrel with his taste in literature.) For my
father, the grand gesture was the thing. He entered Harrods like a Jacobite
army invading Manchester. He would arrive at my school 'to sort things
out' like the wrath of God.

This effortless sense of natural dignity, or his own unquestioned worth,
is of his essence; there are noble savages in his heredity and I look at him,
sometimes, to quote Mayakovsky, 'like an Eskimo looking at a train'.

For I know so little about him, although I know so much. Much of his
life was conducted in my absence, on terms of which I am necessarily
ignorant, for he was older than I am now when I was born, although his
life has shaped my life. This is the curious abyss that divides the closest kin,
that the tender curiosity appropriate to lovers is inappropriate, here, where
the bond is involuntary, so that the most important things stay undis-
covered. If I am short-tempered, volatile as he is, there is enough of my
mother's troubled soul in me to render his very transparency, his psychic
good health, endlessly mysterious. He is my father and I love him as
Cordelia did, 'according to my natural bond'. What the nature of that
'natural bond' might be, I do not know, and, besides, I have a theoretical
objection to the notion of a 'natural bond'.

But, at the end of *King Lear*, one has a very fair notion of the strength of that bond, whatever it is, whether it is the construct of culture rather than nature, even if we might all be better off without it. And I do think my father gives me far more joy than Cordelia ever got from Lear.

From *Fathers*, ed. Ursula Owen, 1983

Notes from a Maternity Ward

Towards the end of the thirty-eighth week, I grow bored with saying: 'Fine,' when asked at the ante-natal clinic how I'm doing. So I try a little joke. It backfires. God, how it backfires. 'How do you feel?' 'A bit apprehensive,' I say. 'Not so much about the birth itself as about the next twenty or thirty years.' The consultant, an unreconstructed Thatcher clone – that is, she looks like Thatcher minus the peroxide and the schlap – turns on me a face costive with high moral seriousness. 'You have done the right thing in not having an abortion,' she says. 'But there is still time. If you have any doubts at all, I urge you to seriously discuss adoption with your husband – I know he's only a common-law husband, of course.'

I'm overwhelmed by incredulity. Had I ever mentioned abortion in connection with this incipient cherub? Are my compañero and I not the Darby and Joan of our circle? Should I say we just got hitched? What business it is of hers, anyway? I lapse into outraged silence. Later, I will weep with fury, but, if I do so now, who can tell how she will misinterpret that. I seethe. Who does she think she is; or I am? And if she delivers this kind of unsolicited advice to the white middle-class – to a member of it who has given her occupation as 'journalist', to boot – then what manner of abuse does she feel free to dish out to the black proletariat? How come she's lived to long? And why don't I punch her in the nose?

I'll tell you why. Because she's chosen to insult me when I'm flat on my back, dress pulled up, knickers down, vulnerable, helpless, undignified.

I would publish her name to the four winds, and gladly. But the hell of it is, she turns out to be a good doctor, as far as the mechanics are concerned. Callous and insensitive perhaps; but quick to spot a malfunction. A gift not to be sneezed at. And, furthermore, a woman so straitjacketed by self-righteousness I doubt she'd ever understand why I want to crucify her. After all, her concern was only for what was best for the baby. And hadn't I virtually said I didn't want him? When she sees me, all pale and proud, on the ward after he's born – he chuckling in a glass box like a very expensive orchid – she's as nice as pie. Well done, she says.

'She'. Note how this consultant is female. I'm lying in at the embattled South London Hospital for Women, the last place I expected to be insulted. But there you go. Here, women treat women and she's the only one of them who treated me like a piece of shit.

I haven't been in hospital for thirty years, so I can't comment on the decline in the standards of the NHS; the floors aren't polished until they turn into lethal ice-rinks any more, which is no bad thing. The food has certainly improved, in comparison with the early fifties. The sheer wonder of the NHS remains; that they will do the best they can for us, that we are not at the mercy of a free market economy, that the lovely nurses smile as if they meant it and hug you when you are sad.

Inevitably, this particular hospital is scheduled for the axe. No amount of special pleading on behalf of women whose religion specifies they be treated by doctors of the same sex seems likely to save it; it is due to close down next April, its various wards – it's a general hospital – distributed around other local hospitals. The staff seems scarcely able to believe that some miracle won't save the place. If the Minister of Health turns into a woman tomorrow, there might be a chance, especially if (s)he then converted to Islam.

It is a rather elegant, red-brick building convenient for Clapham South tube station (the Northern line). It overlooks green and pleasant Clapham Common. It is, obviously, very well equipped; only needs a coat or two of paint and a few vases of plastic flowers to be fit for – who? The young woman in the bed next to me made a shrewd guess as to what would happen to the building once the NHS moved out. 'They'll sell it to bloody BUPA, won't they,' she opined.

The midwife shows me how to put the baby to the nipple. 'Look deep into his eyes,' she says. 'It helps with the bonding.' Good grief! Aren't we allowed any choice in the matter, he and I? Can't I learn to love him for himself, and vice versa, rather than trust to Mother Nature's psycho-physiological double bind? And what of his relationship with his father, who has no breasts? Besides, it's very difficult to look him in the eye. He fastens on the nipple with the furtive avidity of a secret tippler hitting the British sherry, glancing backwards to make sure nobody else gets there first. When he strikes oil, he instantly becomes comatose. Am I supposed to poke him into consciousness: 'Hey, baby, don't nod off, we're supposed to be bonding.' More like bondage. Constrained affection; what resentment it will breed, in time. It's all part of the mystification in which the whole process of childbirth is so richly shrouded. For he is doomed to love us, at least for a significant initial period, because we are his parents. The same goes for us. That is life. That's the hell of it.

Somebody gave us an American publication called *Giving Birth*. A collection of photographs of mothers and fathers sharing the experience. (Where's the lesbian couple? Discrimination!) The parents look ecstatic; radiant; touchingly, comically startled and so on. Lots of shots of little heads poking out of vulvas. Also quotes from participants: 'I felt I had to be very focused. It was almost like meditation,' says one mother. It is compiled by somebody called Mary Motley Kalergis, another name on my post-partural hit-list. (Isn't one allowed a year's justifiable homicide after the event?) The photographs are all in black and white, please note. And, indeed, colour film would have made souvenir snaps of the finale of my own *accouchement* look like stills from a Hammer horror film. While what was going on next door, an emergency Caesarian, well, *that* certainly wasn't like meditation, not half it wasn't! This truly nauseating book is designed to mystify. It is about as kitsch as a fluffy blue bunny, and as much to do with the realities of parturition as a fluffy blue bunny has to do with a real live baby.

OK, OK. So this notebook has submerged under a sea of babyshit. Mao Tse-tung called a pig 'a manure factory on four legs'. A baby is much the same, except it remains stationary. Some people suggest you chuck soiled disposables on the compost heap. There are a few other suggestions for utilising the formidable quantities of ordure produced by the average baby and heedlessly thrown away every day. To say nothing of the valuable amounts of methane they emit. At the end of *War and Peace*, Tolstoy has Natasha ankle-deep in baby shit; impossible not to read something vindictive into that, although he does make Pierre soil his hands, too. Anyway, there is nothing wrong with babyshit. The TV news gobs out fresh horrors into the living room every evening; insulted by the specific urgencies of the neonate, that appalling dichotomy – the one between our lives as we live them and the way that forces outside ourselves shape them for us - seems less desperate than usual. Under the circumstances, a mercy.

New Statesman, 1983

Fools Are My Theme

I'm very pleased and flattered to be here. More pleased and flattered than you might have thought when you invited me. I'd like to tell you how it came to pass that to be an honoured guest at a science fiction convention was a girlish dream of mine from a relatively early age. Since to most of you I suspect that I'm respectable but obscure, I thought that I'd indulge myself in a bit of autobiography. I'd run through my life as a science fiction fellow traveller, if you like.

When I was a child, about eleven or twelve, I suffered from insomnia and I very rarely slept. My father was a journalist and he worked at night. He'd bring in the next day's papers about midnight. This was very exciting. They'd smudge the sheets. He used to bring them to me where I lay on my sleepless bed and all the fresh print would smudge the sheets in a delicious way and get on to my fingers. I liked that very much. If I had a cut some of this printer's ink must have got into my blood. He'd bring *The Times* for my mother and the *Daily Sketch* for me. I wasn't very precocious and if any of you remember the *Sketch* it was about suited for a child of my age.

So it came to pass that in the small hours of those long ago sleepless nights I found myself reading a book called *The Day of the Triffids*, which was coming out in parts in the *Daily Sketch* at that time. Now, mock not; I'm aware that this is a book which is not taken terribly seriously these days by people like yourselves. I could be wrong, but I understand this is so. Maybe I was the right age for John Wyndham, who can say. But I enjoyed it very much, and to my enquiring mind, for indeed I had an enquiring mind, it wasn't the triffids that interested me at all. I don't like gardening much. I get very claustrophobic in the countryside because so much is going on. And I think I always thought that plants were like that really if you gave them a chance. It was the idea of a blind world that obsessed and indeed terrified me. A world which was irretrievably changed because of the loss of one single human faculty. And I think that book left a lasting impression on me because it taught me that writing didn't have to be true in order to have a meaning, and a catastrophe that was impossible, that was purely imaginary, could both move and disturb me.

So time passes, I continued to follow the career of John Wyndham, and I would read a little science fiction from time to time. But it didn't really take. Because it was the 'Golden Age', and I was already into prose style. I'd quarrel with people's grammar and I'd heckle the page and I'd generally throw copies of *Amazing* out of railway train windows.

What was important in this life I'm describing was when I eventually went to university, which I did at a mature age, I read English, and I was drawn to that section of our native literature which is actually mostly about monsters. Old English and medieval literature, in fact, which is how I came not to take J.R.R. Tolkien seriously. But it's also the part of our literature, our inheritance, in which literal truth isn't important at all. In *Beowulf*, for example, it's not a question of do monsters exist or can a monster have a mother? It's: how does a monster's mother feel?

And I also got used to an idea which I think is very important in science fiction, which is that the reader is doing a lot of the work, that reading a book is in a sense a recreation of it. That writing is not necessarily a personal activity, not a personal experience of my feelings or personality, but an articulation of a whole lot of feelings and ideas that happen to be around at the time. I won't bore you with a lot of stuff about medieval literature, which I still love very much, but I assure you that before the invention of printing reading was hard work. You really felt like you'd accomplished something when you'd read a manuscript in handwriting. Just as sometimes I feel that reading some of those books on very friable yellow paper that come apart in your hand, and come unglued from the spine, and the print's all over the page, and it seems to have been written for people who have magnifying lenses in their glasses, that's hard work too. Actually this remained true, about reading being hard work, right up to the eighteenth century with the regularisation of spelling. We were having a panel discussion about critics, and also about publishers and editors, just the other day; and I was thinking I do have a use for editors. It's because they can correct my spelling.

One of the things I love about science fiction readership, fans in fact, is that they really feel that they've made your book their own by reading it, which is a very respectably academic thing to do. That you've worked at it by reading it, that it's become yours. And people take a book personally. They tell you what it means to them. They tell you what should have happened in Chapter Seven. They take you to task over things that happened in Chapter Five. And if you didn't quite mean that yourself, well your interpretation is as valid as theirs, but you have to put up a very good case indeed to justify yourself.

Once the book is published it belongs to the fan, not the writer. And though this is a response which occasionally gets up my nose a lot, unfortunately I have a feeling that it's correct, that it is what happens to a book. Once it's written, once it's published, once it's read and somebody loves it, you cease to have any responsibility for it at all. It takes on a life of its own. It doesn't belong to me.

Anyway, into the booksian hermetic world which I've just described, at a time when I was doing research into the untold but not unchronicled early life of the magician Merlin – Robert Nye actually used a lot of that material, I was very annoyed he got there before I did – just as I was about to learn old Welsh and vanish entirely into a universe of dusty tomes, a magazine called *New Worlds* dropped into my consciousness. And it was exciting. It seemed to me, because I came to it freshly – I found a copy of it in a bookshop – that I didn't know any of the back-up to this. I didn't know what had happened. I didn't know why people suddenly began to write like that in the early sixties. I can't tell you how exciting it was. I was reading Ballard and Moorcock and Sladek as they came tumbling off the presses.

I was writing fiction myself at that time, and fiction that was nudging at the edges of possible experience, that was acutely dissatisfied with various formulas of what you'd call mainstream fiction. When I read those mid-sixties issues of *New Worlds* I realised it was possible to scrap almost every-thing I found oppressive about those apparatuses of fiction.

People talk about mainstream fiction and sf as though they were two quite different kinds of writing, and fantasy as well, as though it was quite different. But I think this is a false distinction, that it is a labelling that helps librarians, and people who know the kind of thing they like and don't want their prejudices to be disturbed.

I've just had a letter from a friend who's doing a little TV play about the relationship between a man and a woman, and she wants to set it in a cir-cus. The TV director she's working with says: 'No, you can't possibly have an affair between a high-wire walker and a trapeze artist. That's weird, that's unlikely. They've got to be ordinary people, like a solicitor and a social worker, that sort of person.' But Lorna says that if she gets them down to the ground and into a flat in Hampstead, that for her then it begins to get really weird, then it gets really strange. She doesn't know what's going to happen next. And that's how I've always felt. As my grandmother used to say: There's nowt so queer as folk.

I could relate instantly to the world of Ballard's *Crash*. It seemed to me that that was how the late sixties felt, that that was how it was like. That was how it felt to be living through the margin of the Vietnam War. And it was only, it seemed to me, the group of writers who were loosely connected with *New Worlds* that were actually dealing with the new circumstances in which we found ourselves, as British people in a society that had changed quite radically since we'd been grown up. And also as beings in the world, because we were the generation that grew up with the reality of nuclear weapons. I was five when the Bomb was dropped on Hiroshima, and I came of age roughly with the Cuban Missile Crisis, which I think was one of the great watersheds, certainly of my life. I think people who were born after the Cuban Missile Crisis, who don't remember it, are different because it was touch and go for a minute there. And I think you could say that nobody could ever be ordinary again – if anybody ever could be, which I don't think they actually could, except in terms of wish fulfil-ment. But we can't be ordinary now because there isn't the time.

The idea that first gripped me when I was a little kid and read *The Day of the Triffids* in the newspaper, that the literal truth might not be the whole truth, turned into a conviction that one way of asking questions – because

I think that one of the functions of fiction is to ask questions that can't be asked in any other way – is through constructing imaginary worlds in which ideas can be discussed. And speculations about the nature of our experience on this planet be conducted without crap about the imitation of life getting in the way, because whose life are you supposed to be imitating? Obviously a trapeze artist has got as much claim to be alive as a solicitor.

Autobiographically, what happened next, when I realised that there were no limitations to what one could do in fiction, was just what happened when people tried to get out of genre into mainstream – maybe what always happens when one tries to scramble one's labels – I stopped being able to make a living. Actually I didn't really stop being able to make a living because I've always found it easier to tailor my lifestyle to my income than the other way. So, shall we say, we took a significant nosedive in lifestyle, complicated by the fact that those who'd known me as a mainstream writer kept telling me I'd only gone into genre for commercial reasons, which certainly wasn't so. Novels of mine would resurrect themselves with naked women and tentacular monsters on the cover, but that didn't do the trick. I became the literary equivalent of a displaced person. I kept applying for my naturalisation papers in genre, as some of you probably know, but although some fans were ready and indeed eager to offer me resident alien status, basically someone else always seemed to smell a rat. You can't scramble labels as easily as that. So, with Channelcon, I do believe I have at last received my passport, resident permit and credit card. Thank you.

I'd just like to say a little more about the arbitrary divisions as I see them between straight fiction, sf and fantasy. It's not a question of making genre sf or fantasy respectable, because that would kill it. In mainstream terms my honoured co-quest, Mr Sladek, the Grand Demystifier, is quite outrageously experimental and it's his good luck, in a sense, that he's able to do what he does without disturbing the horses, because he's in a genre, instead of joining the great unread in the remoter regions of the John Cowler catalogue. Not being respectable often means that you are read by people with open minds who are not intimidated by the unorthodox, who love it in fact. It's interesting that one of the first English translations of a story by the great Argentinian writer Borges first appeared in *Ellery Queen's Mystery Magazine*. It was a story called 'The Garden of Forking Paths'. Borges, who only writes little philosophical investigations, has been adopted as a kind of household god by a lot of people who neither know or care that the publication of *Labyrinths*, which was his first collection, here in the seventies, rocked the entire mainstream to its foundations, opened up whole new possibilities for all kinds of writers. They showed, in fact, what lots of sf fans knew in their heart, that you don't actually need a plot, or characters, only an idea, and a monomaniacal obsession with getting it across.

It doesn't really matter why people read new things, strange things, unorthodox things, as long as they actually read them, as long as they get into the texts. And it was amazing for me to see in the Fancy Dress Parade last night all these people who've got into the texts to such an extent that for a few hours they actually live out these characters from novels. I think this is wonderful. You certainly don't get that at, for example, literary conventions. People turn up imitating themselves at dos like that.

The technological aspects of science fiction have always passed me by. For purely practical reasons. I can't so much as change a plug on an iron. This isn't because I'm a woman, I assure you, my brother can't either. It's kind of an inherited gene. Every time I look at a technological appliance it goes wrong. It's like King Midas in reverse. And theoretical physics has always seemed to be pure poetry, partly because I don't understand it. Fantasy is only what people think of when their minds are at play.

Just recently, in the last four or five years, there have been distinct signs of feedback from genre into the kind of fiction that gets respectfully reviewed in the Sunday papers, that wins the big respectable prizes. Which is difficult for me, because I'm a perverse person, and my response has been to start contemplating fiction about the international arms trade. I don't think it's impossible to do this in terms of the fantastic, far from it. But we live in very confused, confusing and dangerous times, and fiction, which is a kind of log of these times, changes its nature and expands and sucks in material from all manner of places and from all manner of styles and genres to be able to adequately describe ourselves to ourselves at all kinds of levels.

It's also supposed to give pleasure, too, and what's nice is that you're all here basically to have a good time, and you have fun reading books. As a visitor or a co-optee from another part of the literary forest, take it from me, that's odd. It's a real shot in the arm. Actually, it's very nice.

Notes from the Front Line

I've just scrapped my sixth attempt to write something for this book because my ideas get quite out of hand the minute I try to put them down on paper and I flush hares out of my brain which I then pursue, to the detriment of rational discourse. To try to say something simple – do I 'situate myself politically as a writer'? Well, yes; of course. I always hope it's obvious, although I try, when I write fiction, to think on my feet – to present a number of propositions in a variety of different ways, and to leave the reader to construct her own fiction for herself from the elements of my fictions. (Reading is just as creative an activity as writing and most intellectual development depends upon new readings of old texts. I am all for putting new wine in old bottles, especially if the pressure of the new wine makes the old bottles explode.)

The women's movement has been of immense importance to me personally and I would regard myself as a feminist writer, because I'm a feminist in everything else and one can't compartmentalise these things in one's life. My work *has* changed a good deal in the last ten or fifteen years; it would have been rather shocking if it hadn't, since, during that time, I've progressed from youth to middle age, and, for me, growing into feminism was part of the process of maturing. But when I look at the novels I wrote in my twenties, when I was a girl, I don't see a difference in the emotional content, or even in the basic themes; I recognise myself, asking questions, sometimes finding different answers than I would do now. I also see myself expressing myself in quite different ways now that I'm capable of subjecting to critical analysis problems that, when I was younger and perhaps bruised more easily, I perceived and interpreted in a much more intuitive and also much more self-defensive way. For example, I used the strategy of charm a good deal – I attempted to disarm with charm, in a way that makes me feel affectionately indulgent and maternal to the young person I was, who wanted so much to be loved.

I'm forty-two now; therefore I was a young woman during the 1960s. There is a tendency to underplay, even to completely devalue, the experience of the 1960s, especially for women, but towards the end of that decade there was a brief period of public philosophical awareness that occurs only very occasionally in human history; when, truly, it felt like Year One, that all that was holy was in the process of being profaned and we were attempting to grapple with the real relations between human beings. So writers like Marcuse and Adorno were as much part of my personal process of maturing into feminism as experiments with my sexual, and emotional life and with various intellectual adventures in anarcho-surrealism. Furthermore, at a very unpretentious level, we were truly asking ourselves questions about the nature of reality. Most of us may not have come up with very startling answers and some of us scared ourselves good and proper and retreated into culs-de-sac of infantile mysticism; false prophets, loonies and charlatans freely roamed the streets. But even so, I can date to that time and to some of those debates and to that sense of heightened awareness of the society around me in the summer of 1968, my own questioning of the nature of my reality as a *woman*. How that social fiction of my 'femininity' was created, by means outside my control, and palmed off on me as the real thing.

This investigation of the social fictions that regulate our lives – what Blake called the 'mind forg'd manacles' – is what I've concerned myself with consciously since that time. (I realise, now, I must always have sensed that something was badly wrong with the versions of reality I was offered that took certain aspects of my being *as* a woman for granted. I smelled the rat in D. H. Lawrence pretty damn quick.) This is also the product of an absolute and *committed materialism* – i.e., that *this* world is all that there is, and in order to question the nature of reality one must move from a strongly grounded base in what constitutes material reality. Therefore I become mildly irritated (I'm sorry!) when people, as they sometimes do, ask me about the 'mythic quality' of work I've written lately. Because I believe that all myths are products of the human mind and reflect only aspects of material human practice. I'm in the demythologising business.

I'm interested in myths – though I'm much more interested in folklore – just because they *are* extraordinary lies designed to make people unfree. (Whereas, in fact, folklore is a much more straightforward set of devices for making real life more exciting and is much easier to infiltrate with different kinds of consciousness.) I wrote one anti-mythic novel in 1977, *The Passion of New Eve* – I conceived it as a feminist tract about the social creation of femininity, amongst other things – and relaxed into folklore with a book of stories about fairy stories, *The Bloody Chamber*, in 1979. It turned out to be easier to deal with the shifting structures of reality and sexuality by using sets of shifting structures derived from orally transmitted traditional tales. Before that, I used bits and pieces from various mythologies quite casually, because they were to hand.

To return to that confused young person in her early twenties attempting to explicate the world to herself via her craft, the person in the process of becoming radically sceptical, that is, if not free, then more free than I had been. Apart from feeling a treacherous necessity to charm, especially when, however unconsciously, I was going straight for the testicles, I was, as a girl, suffering a degree of colonialisation of the mind. Especially in the journalism I was writing then, I'd – quite unconsciously – posit a male point of view as a general one. So there was an element of the male impersonator about this young person as she was finding herself. For example, in a piece about the suburb of Tokyo I lived in in 1969, I described the place thus: 'It has everything a reasonable man could want . . . massage parlours and, etc.' I used the phrase, 'a reasonable man', quite without irony, although, reading the piece in 1982, it is, ironically, most fitting –

the suburb *did* boast all the conveniences a 'reasonable man' might want, although a reasonable woman might have found them inessential, to say the least.

When the piece was republished in a collection of essays last year, I wondered whether to insert 'sic' in brackets after that 'reasonable man' but then I thought, no; that's cheating. Because my female consciousness *was* being forged out of the contradictions of my experience as a traveller, as, indeed, some other aspects of my political consciousness were being forged. (It was a painful and enlightening experience to be regarded as a coloured person, for example; to be defined as a Caucasian before I was defined as a woman, and learning the hard way that most people on this planet are *not* Caucasian and have no reason to either love or respect Caucasians.)

By the way, I make my living as a writer and have done so most of my adult life. This is no big deal and doesn't mean I always made much money. It has always been easier for me to cut my life-style to suit my income than the other way round so it's always been possible to manage. On the rare occasions when I've attempted to work within a hierarchical framework, when you have to get to an office on time and so on, and be nice to people you don't actually like, much, things have always gone badly. Because I've almost always been self-employed, I've had very little experience, as a woman, of the hurly-burly of mixed-sex working life. I get messages through from the front line that fills me with grief and fury for my sisters out there but this is different from personal experience. For some reason, I've almost always worked with women editors at my various publishing houses, and, even when one is dealing with a woman with zero feminist consciousness, there *is* a difference. Since it was, therefore, primarily through my sexual and emotional life that I was radicalised – that I first became truly aware of the difference between how I was and how I was supposed to be, or expected to be – I found myself, as I grew older, increasingly writing about sexuality and its manifestations in human practice. And I found most of my raw material in the lumber room of the Western European imagination.

Let me explain this. It seems obvious, to an impartial observer, that Western European civilisation as we know it has just about run its course and the emergence of the women's movement, and all that implies, is both symptom and product of the unravelling of the culture based on Judaeo-Christianity, a bit of Greek transcendentalism via the father of lies, Plato, and all the other bits and pieces. As a Japanese friend of mine once said, the spotlight of history is moving inexorably away from Europe towards Asia and Africa – societies that we (and white women can't get out of our historic complicity in colonialism, any more than the white working class can) comprehensively screwed, that owe us nothing and expect nothing whatsoever from us, which is just as well as the idea we might actually owe *them* something, like cash, doesn't go down too well, certainly in Britain. It is possible, assuming Western Europe is permitted to sidle out of the spotlight of history rather than going up with a bang, that, for the first time for a thousand years or so, its inhabitants may at last be free of their terrible history.

The sense of limitless freedom that I, as a woman, sometimes feel *is* that of a new kind of being. Because I simply could not have existed, as I am, in any other preceding time or place. I am the pure product of an advanced, industrialised, post-imperialist country in decline. But this has very little to do with my ability to work as I please, or even to earn a living from writing. At any time up to the early twentieth century, I could have told as many stories as I wanted, and made them as wonderful and subversive as I wished, had I survived the births of my children or the hazards of working-class or peasant life to a sufficient age to have amassed a repertoire of orally-transmitted fiction. If I'd been born an aristocrat, I could certainly have become very famous and honoured as an actual writer in medieval Japan, where there were many women writers of fiction and poetry, and where human ingenuity in sexual practice (unrestricted by the Judaeo-Christian ethic, which they knew nothing about) certainly seems to have made sexual intercourse less onerously fruitful than in the West. I could have been a professional writer at any period since the seventeenth century in Britain or in France. But I could *not* have combined this latter with a life as a sexually active woman until the introduction of contraception, unless I had been lucky enough to have been born sterile, as George Eliot must have been. Even if I had been rich enough to afford child care, wealth was no protection against puerperal fever, and being pregnant most of the time is tiring, enfeebling, and a drain on one's physical and emotional resources. In fact, most women were *ill* most of the time until the introduction of contraception and efficient post- and ante-natal care and you need to be quite strong and healthy to write big, fat books. (You do also need to have been around.)

And, just as I write this, I recall a bizarre contradiction. For the past three centuries in Europe, women have excelled – and been honoured for it – in the performing arts. Acting, singing, dancing, playing musical instruments. For some reason, the women's movement tends to overlook all that, perhaps because it seems less 'creative' to play somebody else's piano concerto beautifully than it is to write the thing. But it certainly takes a good deal more physical energy to perform a piano concerto than it does to write one, and weak, feeble women have been strumming away, sometimes in the last stages of pregnancy, ever since they were let up on the podium. It *is* odd. Like so many girls, I passionately wanted to be an actress when I was in my early teens and I turn this (balked, unachieved and now totally unregretted) ambition over in my mind from time to time. Why did it seem so pressing, the need to demonstrate in public a total control and transformation of roles other people had conceived? Rum, that.

However, A 'new kind of being', unburdened with a past. The voluntarily sterile yet sexually active being, existing in more than a few numbers, *is* a being without precedent and, by voluntarily sterile, I don't necessarily mean permanently childless; this category includes women who are sterile not all, just most of the time, after all. I/we are not the slaves of the history that enslaved our ancestors, to quote Franz Fanon (although he meant specifically chattel slavery).

So I feel free to loot and rummage in an official past, specifically a literary past, but I like painting and sculptures and the movies and folklore and heresies, too. This past, for me, has important decorative, ornamental functions; further, it is a vast repository of outmoded lies, where you can check out what lies used to be à la mode and find the old lies on which new lies have been based.

There are one or two lies in the lumber room about the artist, about how terrific it is to be an artist, how you've got to suffer and how artists are wise and good people and a whole lot of crap like that. I'd like to say something about that, because writing – to cite one art – is only applied linguistics and Shelley was wrong, we're *not* the unacknowledged legislators of mankind. Some women really do seem to think they will somehow feel better or be better if they get it down on paper. I don't know.

Writing – the only art form I know too much about, as practice – certainly doesn't make better people, nor do writers lead happier lives. How can I put it; although I might have liked to write poetry like Baudelaire's, I certainly would not, for one single minute, have wanted the kind of life that Baudelaire lived. His poetry is the product of terminal despair, and he was a shit, to boot. It is easy to forget that most of the great male geniuses of Western European culture have been either depraved egomaniacs or people who led the most distressing lives. (My two male literary heroes, Melville and Dostoevsky, were both rather fine human beings, as it turns out, but both of them lived so close to the edge of the existential abyss that they must often, and with good reason, have envied those who did not have enquiring minds.) I'm not saying it's great to be a cow, just keep on chewing the cud, although I have nothing against cows nor, for that matter, against enquiring minds. Only, that posthumous fame is no comfort at all and the actual satisfactions of artistic production are peculiarly lonely and solipsistic ones, while the work itself has the same compensations as those of any self-employed worker, no more.

To backtrack about the bit about 'applied linguistics'. Yet this, of course, is why it is so enormously important for women to write fiction *as* women – it is part of the slow process of decolonialising our language and our basic habits of thought. I really do believe this. It has nothing at all to do with being a 'legislator of mankind' or anything like that; it is to do with the creation of a means of expression for an infinitely greater variety of experience than has been possible heretofore, to say things for which no language previously existed.

One last thing. So there hasn't been a female Shakespeare. Three possible answers: (a) So what. (This is the simplest and best.) (b) There hasn't been a *male* Shakespeare since Shakespeare, dammit. (c) Somewhere, Franz Fanon opines that one cannot, in reason, ask a shoeless peasant in the Upper Volta to write songs like Schubert's; the opportunity to do so has never existed. The concept is meaningless.

The novel, which is my chosen form, has existed as such in Europe for only two or three hundred years. Its existence is directly related to the history of the technology of printing and to the growth of a leisure class with time to read. Much of that leisure class was female and the novel in Western Europe – unlike the forms it has taken when it has been exported to Latin America and Africa in this century – has tended to reflect the pre-occupations of the lives of leisured women. Perhaps that's why so many great European novels are about adultery, especially when written by men (*Madame Bovary, Anna Karenina*) who couldn't imagine what else women might get up to if they had a bit of free time. These are interesting historical facts, but they have nothing to do with me as a writer.

One important function of bourgeois fiction is to teach people how to behave in social circles to which they think they might be able to aspire. The novels of Jane Austen are basically fictionalised etiquette lessons and a lot of the fiction that has come directly from the women's movement performs, however unconsciously, the same functions. (Marilyn French's *The Women's Room* is really an instruction manual for the older woman post-graduate student.)

But all this bores me stiff, in fact, because it no longer seems particularly relevant to instruct people as to how to behave in a changing society, when one's very existence is instrumental in causing changes the results of which one can't begin to calculate. And I personally feel much more in common with certain Third World writers, both female and male, who are transforming actual fiction forms to both reflect and to precipitate changes in the way people feel about themselves – putting new wine in old bottles and, in some cases, old wine in new bottles. Using fictional forms inherited from the colonial period to create a critique of that period's consequences. Obviously, one is bound to mention Gabriel

García Márquez, although he must be getting pretty bored, by this time, to be the white liberal intellectual's pet fabulist, but there are lots of others and some very fine writing, often in a quite conventionally naturalist mode – I'm thinking of the Black South African writer, Bessie Head, who has utilised forms utterly alien to her own historical culture to produce complex illuminations of sexual and political struggle.

But, look, it *is* all applied linguistics. But language is power, life and the instrument of culture, the instrument of domination and liberation.

I don't know. Ten years ago, I'd have said that I, myself, wanted to write stories that could be read by guttering candlelight in the ruins of our cities and still give pleasure, still have meaning. Perhaps I still think that.

All this is very messy and self-contradictory and not very coherent or intelligently argued. It's been amazingly difficult, trying to sort out how I feel that feminism has affected my work, because that is really saying how it has affected my life and I don't really know that because I live my life, I don't examine it. I also feel I've showed off a lot, and given mini-lectures on this and that, in a pompous and middle-aged way. Oh, hell. What I *really* like doing is writing fiction and trying to work things out *that* way.

But I hope this will do.

From Michelene Wandor (ed.), *Gender and Writing*, 1983

Anger in a Black Landscape

I am no expert in anything, not history, not psychology, not medicine nor peace studies neither (least of all) strategic planning. I am, simply, a child of the nuclear age. I was five years old when they, or, rather, the Allies – that is, we – dropped an atomic bomb on Hiroshima, a small city of no strategic importance in southern Japan whose name, together with that of Auschwitz, has now entered our vocabulary, the most tragic legacies of the last war, names synonymous with horror that, hitherto, was unimaginable. Before Hiroshima, however, it might have been possible to predicate a future time in which people, savagely rendered sane by experience, would look back on the century of Auschwitz as the blackest period of human history; since Hiroshima, the possibility of that kind of hope for the future diminishes in direct ratio to the growth of the nuclear arsenal.

That act of warfare, the dropping of the A-bomb, perpetrated – obviously – without either my knowledge or consent, although they said it was for the sake of my future, changed irrevocably the circumstances in which that future life would be passed. Let me not be sorry for myself about this; it changed them less than if I'd been five in Hiroshima. But change them it did, and may well inexorably dictate the manner of my life's ending. For to plan for your old age, these days, seems an act of high optimism, of outrageous gallantry, even. I am, therefore, a child of irony and the absurd; of black humour, of guilt and of anger. These are my credentials for contributing to this book. I believe they are sufficient.

And, over the years, I've grown rather tired of rational, objective arguments against nuclear weapons. To approach rampant unreason with the tools of rational discourse is something of a waste of time. On the other hand, to pose the question: 'Do you really want you and your loved ones to be fried alive?' will always, even, presumably, from Thatcher, procure the answer: 'No.' Which isn't much help, either, even when it *is*, finally, as simple as that, since one way of forestalling this grisly fate might be to fry the Russkies first, mightn't it . . . well, then. Another way might be to build oneself a personalised bunker, in which to sweat out the thermonuclear blast. Terrific.

One of the most curious phenomena of the postwar period has been the growth of fictions about the blissfully anarchic, tribal lives the lucky fifteen million survivors are going to lead in a Britain miraculously free of corpses, in which the Man with the Biggest Shot-Gun holes up in some barbedwire enclave and picks off all comers. (Polygamous marital arrangements are often part of these fantasies.) The post-nuclear catastrophe novel has become a science fiction genre all of its own, sometimes as warning – more often as the saddest and most irresponsible kind of whistling in the dark.

Have you seen Goya's 'black' pictures in the Prado, in Madrid? You go through several rooms full of sunlit, happy paintings – children at play, beautiful young men and women dancing, picking grapes, a world of sensual delight – and, then, suddenly . . . paintings in black and ghastly grey and all the colours of mud, where swollen, deformed faces emerge from landscapes incoherent with devastation. The most awful one, that most expressive of a world of nothingness, shows a dog's head peering over the side of a mound of slurry. The sky, if you can call it a sky, is the colour of a bruise. And you know, from the infinite desolation of the scene, he is the last dog left, and, from the look of him, *he's* not going to last much longer.

Impossible, in that appalling room, to escape the notion, that Goya, in his famous despair, in *his* hatred of war and human folly, saw further than most people; there is something prophetic in these pictures, that have the look, not so much of paintings, but of photographs taken with some timewarped, heat-warped camera, of a Europe in a future that remains unimaginable . . . a wreckage of humanity, a landscape from which all life has been violently expelled . . . unimaginable; but not impossible.

We think people who sell heroin are very evil and, if we catch them at it, send them to prison for a very long time. The men who deal in instruments of infinitely greater destruction acquire great wealth and respect.

Yet the iconography of such catastrophe is, surely, familiar to us all, by now! Anyone who reads this book will have her or his own private nightmare of pain, loss, annihilation; my own private image is not a violent one. It is of a child crying in the dark, and there will be nobody to come, not ever. Which is the worst I can possibly imagine.

Yet somehow the hideous poetry of the *terminal* nature of nuclear warfare can exist almost in a dimension of its own, that deforms thought. As if we still saw war itself as a metaphysical scourge, one of the four horsemen of the Apocalypse, arriving from nowhere and dominating the world, our real masters. Not as war really is, the product of an interlocked tissue of political and economic causes, of human actions and decisions. But as if nuclear weapons themselves – symbolised by the Bomb – were the very transcendental essence of war, and, more than that, an externalisation of all our notions of the ultimate evil. The Bomb has become a very potent, perhaps *the* most potent, symbol of Original Sin.

Well, I've always thought the notion of original sin was pretty silly, anyway; and it certainly gets horribly in the way of any attempts to persuade human beings to behave better than they generally do. Because to deny that people are inherently evil isn't to say that the world isn't full of freaks, zombies and loonies, nor that such as they, with their limited imaginations and atrophied hearts, do not tend to rise to the top in the military or in those places where men and women (but mostly, I'm proud to say, men) sit down with a cup of coffee and systematically design bigger and better ways of causing pain. It is no good saying, 'Think of the children, crying alone in the dark!' to a person who hates children, and, given the opportunity, will beat and torture his own. Most people, on the whole, enjoy being alive but a significant number feel they have the right to deny this privilege to other people, for a whole complex of reasons. We live in a country where a good number of British citizens may not sleep easy in their beds due to the murderous activities of white racist thugs and it might even be possible to argue that such a country deserves the visitation of fire from heaven. (You see how easy it is to slip into biblical language, here.)

But such fire will fall upon both the just and the unjust, and upon the innocent, the helpless and the deluded, and some of the latter, alas, are just those with the kind of emotional limitations who can kill in cold blood, and who can certainly contemplate the use of nuclear weapons – on somebody else, that is.

However, demystifying the Bomb – that is, stopping thinking about it as the product of a Faustian bargain, infinite knowledge for infinite destruction, as if it were all somehow tragically fated, and also *trying* to stop thinking about it as a full stop in human history, certainly doesn't make the Bomb a friendly beast. Far from it, because, of course, it *is* just such a full stop. But not a necessary or inevitable full stop. The horrid poetry of it, that mankind was the species that Knew Too Much, doesn't help us understand how, for example, the idea of strategic bombing – that is, wiping out civilians – became so fashionable in the twentieth century. Nor does it help us try to do our best to prevent the circumstances in which nuclear weapons might be used. It certainly increases one's personal sense of impotence. And it doesn't help us to get *out* of this mess.

So. Let's start again, from another angle. How has it come to pass that this overcrowded, relatively poor, relatively insignificant little island of ours fairly bristles with nuclear installations? (I'm not being historic about this. I'm speaking out of blind prejudice.)

Surely you must have noticed what an exceedingly law-abiding race the British are? (Or, rather, we *like* to look law-abiding, whilst privately criminal. But, in practice, appearance is reality.) This was made very apparent in 1981, when a widescale attempt at civil disobedience was mooted after the Law Lords countermanded the fares cuts made by the Greater London Council on what is the most expensive, as well as the least efficient, public transport system of any capital city in the civilised world. One would have thought, considering how unpopular the fares increases were, that it would have been the simplest thing in the world to organise London transport users to revolt. All the revolt was supposed to entail, after all, was a simple refusal to pay. But did we? Did we, hell. And I include myself in this, because I didn't want to make any fuss – another British characteristic.

Admittedly, a speedy bit of legal sleight of hand meant all kinds of nasty and humiliating things could happen if you didn't pay up and play the game. But I don't think it was fear that made us put our hands in our pockets. No. We paid up out of simple, ingrained obedience. Desire to please the powers-that-be.

In Florence, when they put up the bus fares a few years ago, enraged Florentines torched the buses. And, more magnificently – for the British can torch things when they feel inclined, but usually only when there's no point to it, in a hobbyish way – far more magnificently, ordinary Japanese people contrived to halt the building of the new airport in Tokyo for *fifteen years* by systematic sabotage and vociferous civil disobedience. Peasants attacked the construction teams with rice flails. And this from a race the British are accustomed to regard as besottedly compliant with authority. At last, when all was lost and the runways built, overnight the protesters put up a large tower on the biggest runway, effectively halting proceedings for a few more weeks, as a final gesture. Admittedly, the fares in Florence went up – from a massive ten pence flat fare to a staggering twenty pence. And Narita Airport is now in operation, although the peasants on whose land it was built ended up with a fair bit of compensation.

OK. So you *can't* win. Although it is possible to negotiate the terms of defeat from a position of strength and so end up ahead of the game. Concerted and passionate protest against nuclear weapons in these islands may not achieve a global ban, and a universal end to war; but we might, just might, achieve a nuclear-free Europe, or, at least, a Britain cleansed of the diabolical things . . . Perhaps it is just that we aren't used to public protest doing any good, these days. We are most lugubriously accustomed to our own democratic absence from vital decision-making in this country. Why is that?

How *did* it happen that this island has become a moored aircraft carrier for instruments of destruction? The primary decisions about Britain's relationship with NATO were taken out of our hands long ago and all was accomplished with such a degree of secrecy that most people in these islands, if they think about it at all, think that British membership of NATO is a very good thing. Most of us also think that the British Army is a Good Thing and now, basking in the glory of our famous victory in the Falklands – at this time of writing – it is probably the worst possible time to suggest it is *not* a fine thing to kill or to die for one's country. That, instead, it is a profoundly monstrous and obscene thing.

There, almost certainly, isn't enough time left to us to set about those long processes of altering public consciousness in an island that has, hitherto, housed one of the most bellicose nations in the world. The British have an exceedingly long history of militarism and of compliance with authority and are reluctant to lose the residual conviction that to be British involves some kind of guarantee against destruction. ('Britons never shall be slaves.') After all, we haven't been invaded by a foreign army for a thousand years! No. Nowadays, we invite the buggers in and call it NATO.

But we don't know whether or not anything can be done about changing things unless we try. As women, perhaps we are more used than man to living with a real sense of personal powerlessness and that may give us, as a lobby, a kind of extra anger. Agitating for a bit less public secrecy – *as well* as against nuclear weapons – might be a start.

But let me, again, begin at *my* beginning – for a personal history of how this particular person, five years old in 1945, learned to live with the Bomb for all my adult life is relevant to us all, since our present impasse springs from a mass of personal accommodations to an intolerable situation.

Twenty years ago, yes, and more, I was in CND. And, truly, those long gone days of the marches from Aldermaston were some of the most moving and beautiful memories of my girlhood. It seemed, then, that in the face of those immense shows of serene public indignation – exhibitions of mass sanity, as they were – that, as had, after all, happened occasionally before, mass protest might change things.

I remember the Cuban missile crisis, as near the edge as we ever got. (As far as we know; much is concealed from us.) And, of course, it didn't happen. The weapons, so it seemed, *were* too terrible to be used. Just kept to frighten people with.

And, like most of us, after the emotional crisis of the Cuban missile crisis, I drifted away from CND. For, primarily, two reasons, neither of them anything to do with the comforting idea that, since the things hadn't been used, they'd *never* be used. No. One was:

Despair. It occurred to me that the reason why arms limitation talks and such were suddenly *on* was because those who enjoyed plotting ways of wiping us all out had decided to put nuclear weapons by for a while and concentrate on things that made less mess. Such as biological weapons, nerve gases and various other areas of research that were, from time to time, hinted at vaguely in *Scientific American*. It occurred to me that the superpowers were, far from learning to love one another, busily at work on instruments of warfare compared to which the thermonuclear flash might seem positively benign.

In other words, that the Bomb would indeed be banned – just as soon as they thought up something worse.

The second was:

Rationality. Applying my reason to the case in hand, I could see no qualitative difference between nuclear weapons and conventional weapons. (And the argument that we don't need nuclear weapons if we are armed to the teeth with the other kind still seems to me one of the most morally abhorrent, if one of the most commonsensical, in the anti-Bomb case.) Nuclear weapons were only the logical extension of the kind of warfare I'd been born into; the kind that unleashed its full fury against the civilian population. And, indeed, the next war will be the first in history in which those in the armed forces will stand a higher chance of survival than their loved ones at home. Maybe we should all sign on, now, as a mass gesture.

Although Tamburlaine the Great enjoyed reducing cities to rubble and slaughtering women and children, he usually did this after his band of paid killers had put down an opposing band of paid killers rather than before. The deaths of thousands, indeed, millions of non-combatants has never, hitherto, been a positive prerequisite for victory in armed conflict and it is this, rather than the nature of the weapons which inflict those deaths, that constitutes the moral difference between war in our time and old-fashioned kinds of wars. In *The Nuclear Barons*, Peter Pringle and James Spigelman suggest that strategic bombing was invented almost on the spur of the moment by Bomber Command, to save face when they found their target bombing was so lousy they'd deposited bombs on housing complexes instead of railheads and munitions factories. When I lived in Japan, people would tell me how the fire raids on Tokyo in 1944 had killed more people just as horribly as the Bomb on Hiroshima but nobody in the West seemed to have noticed, perhaps because John Hershey wasn't available to write it up. (Don't think the Japanese don't make jokes just because they don't smile, much.) Nuclear weapons are simply the most efficient way of 'bombing a country back into the Stone Age,' to quote an American president's plan for another Asian country some time later. (The New Stone Age seems the next plan on the agenda for us all.)

It came to me, then, that the only way to stop nations periodically going to war with one another in this new and morally indefensible way was a concerted impulse towards a federation constructed along humanitarian and egalitarian lines. Given my particular background and bias, this could only mean one thing – international socialism. (Note the absence of capital letters.)

Having reasoned myself into Utopianism, always the only rational stance, I asked myself: will it come in my lifetime?

After some thought, I reluctantly answered myself: no.

So, like most of my peers, I decided to put these heavy problems aside for a while and get on with living, for I was young, still, and it was the 1960s and, well, it was fun to be alive. Then – the Vietnam War, a focus for anger. And, increasingly engaged with the women's movement, there now seemed within that the possibility for actually creating a new heaven and a new earth, that this might even be within my own grasp, *as* a woman. For the private and public struggle of sexual politics was something that operated on terms I could more easily grasp than the one against the faceless enemy of militarism whose tentacles stretched everywhere. For *this* enemy had a face, a familiar and, indeed, often a beloved face, and I could understand the power system of sexual oppression because I had spent my whole life within it. Indeed, it was possible, in those heady days of the early 1970s, to lump all the oppressive, life-denying systems together under one label – Patriarchy – and ascribe all the blame to men. Capitalism is a patriarchal plot. *And* war. It was easy, then – it still is, dammit! – to make jokes about the presidents of the superpowers opening their raincoats and flashing their weaponry at one another ('Mine is bigger than yours,' 'It's not!' ' 'tis so!' and so on.)

Women have always had a tendency to despise men for their emotional impoverishment. Men feel superior to women for the same reason. Impasse.

I really don't know if it would be a better world if women ran it. My natural prejudice suggests it might, although Mrs Thatcher and Mrs Gandhi are *not* good advertisements for women in command. But this is no argument at all against women taking their fair share of policy- and decision-making, and, since it hasn't been tried, before, it might well make a difference, in the long term. If there *is* a long term.

It is certainly no argument against asking all women, all normal, every-day women who tend and nurture children, make them clean their teeth and eat up their greens so they'll grow up big and strong, to appreciate that such activity might well be futile. If.

That such activity probably *is* futile. Because.

But my forties began, as my twenties had done, in a fury of rage. Driving across East Anglia shortly after the Soviet invasion of Afghanistan, under a sky black with bombers 'exercising', listening on the radio to a selection of freaks, zombies and loonies from the Pentagon threatening the USSR with nuclear reprisals, it was easy to forget it was all a publicity stunt . . . as it, surely, has proved. Did the USA truly have the intention of teaching the Soviets a lesson by lobbing a warhead or two at the harmless population of the city of Kiev? Would that not have persuaded the belea-guered Afghans only of what they already thought, that the Infidel was as brutal, as foolish and as irrational as the imam had always said? It was all an exercise in frightening and I don't know what it did to the Kremlin, but, by God, it frightened me.

For I realised that, while my back had been turned, during those twenty odd years, the busy little bees in both the West *and* the East, the highly paid technocrats who live off the fat of the land and scribble away on their drawing-boards secure in the knowledge of those mink-lined bunkers to which they can retreat, if necessary . . . these criminal lunatics had been dreaming up, not only non-nuclear weapons of a kind to make the mind reel, but also infinitely more powerful nuclear weapons, more and more infinitely powerful nuclear weapons, as if, once they'd got the knack of it, they couldn't stop.

And something else became apparent, too. In all the threatening and frightening that went on over the invasion of Afghanistan (to no avail; the Soviets are still there), the idea of a 'weapon too terrible to be used' was still there. But this seemed to apply only to the very biggest and most devastating bangs. A whole new class of nuclear weapons that might be 'too terrible to use', but certainly weren't too terrible to contemplate using, had sprung into being. Maybe what has happened is this: since they keep on inventing bigger and better bangs, the one that is 'too terrible to use' is no more than the one they thought of most recently. So, in a sliding scale, *last* year's ultimate and unthinkable weapon becomes second in line *this* year, and, next year, will be perfectly all right.

I get dizzy, and lose count, and lose heart, but the formula, 'containing n warheads each one with n times the capacity of the bomb dropped on Hiroshima', now haunts my dreams. Notice, too, how this formula contrives to negate the reality of the Hiroshima devastation . . . as you might say, you ain't seen nothing yet.

We have, indeed, learned to live with the unthinkable and to think it. Last spring, I saw people, British people, not superficially psychotic-looking, wearing T-shirts with 'Nuke Buenos Aires' on the front. A new verb, 'to nuke'. So easily, in such an unacknowledged way, has the unthinkable slipped into our vocabulary. Note, too, how 'to nuke' is an active verb; it is easier to think of killing than of being killed, for obvious reasons. Can such atrocious garments be donned on Albion's shore without an enraged populace tearing them from the wearer's backs? They can.

The rational, objective arguments against Britain's participation in the scenario for blasting non-combatants off the earth in the name of military strategy and for subsequently rendering the planet uninhabitable have been deployed again and again, with increasing force, over the last three decades. And this is the result of it; the Argies had only to so much as tweak the lion's tail and, pow! How easily the final solution slips out! That the British do not have the capacity to unilaterally 'nuke' Buenos Aires is beside the point. The ease with which this neologism springs to the lips of the pro-nuclear lobby is unnerving in itself. There is a little man walks up and down the airport lobby in Boston, Massachusetts, carrying a hand-painted sign: 'Nuke Jane Fonda'. Useless to tell him you can nuke an individual only if she or he is standing alone in a very remote spot. I know. I've tried it. I didn't try snatching hold of his placard, throwing it to the ground and jumping up and down on it. Perhaps I should have.

As I said, I am no expert, although I possess a hereditary facility for vituperation. In the old days in my father's country, Scotland, the tribal chieftains deployed their poets in territorial disputes; they made them stand on ridges above the combatants, hurling abuse at the foe, until one or other was humiliated enough to leave the scene. Those were the days. Perhaps the time has come again to utilise these ancient skills – this time, against *both* sides.

It's sad but true that the 'irrational, subjective' arguments against nuclear weaponry, and, indeed, against militarism itself, are the moral and emotional ones – and morals and emotions might be more or less the same thing, at that. I've been engaged, here, in below-the-belt arguments, because these are, perhaps, the only ones left. We must plead, harangue, protest, demand – all kinds of things! A lot more democracy; a lot less secrecy; make (oh, horrors! oh, embarrassment!) a fuss, then a bigger fuss, then a bigger fuss again. The peace movement in the USA didn't rationally argue US troops out of Vietnam. It harangued. It shouted. It screamed. It took to the streets.

If the peace movement in Britain *cannot* persuade our (democratically elected) government, this one or the next, to review our position *vis-à-vis* NATO, the establishment of Cruise missiles in this country and our whole relationship with the obscene farce of modern warfare, then perhaps, morally, we do not deserve to survive and, almost assuredly, we will not.

One thing more. As women of this island, our traditional role in warfare has been to wave goodbye to our loved ones and then either to grieve, or else, at last, after an agony of anxiety, to welcome them home, when, perhaps, they have been physically mutilated, certainly psychologically damaged and when we had to hide from ourselves the dreadful knowledge that they had killed other women's lovers and sons. This role has been eroded in modern warfare, which offers a wide range of clerical and administrative roles to women and even, oh, thrilling! will let them into the combat zone if they are very, very good. It has, of course, never been true for, for example, the women of continental Europe, who, during wars, tend to trudge the roads as homeless refugees and be repeatedly raped by invading or victorious armies. It is always important to see our social roles not as universals but as relative to different situations, and a war with conventional weapons in the European theatre, of which we are a part, may well procure such a different situation.

Traditionally, we, as British women, are the loved ones for whom the boys fight, for whom they will return. But what – if we have been blown away? In the last war, those at home stood a good chance of violent death and, in a nuclear war, there will be scarcely any point in mobilising the troops except to keep down by force the sick and starving remnants of the civilian population. Non-combatants we might still be, but we will be on the front line and then, in a real sense, behind the lines, should we be unlucky enough to survive.

War is no longer the province of men and, as its most vulnerable potential victims, we *must* arm ourselves – not with weapons, but with rage, rage as if against the dying of the light.

From Dorothy Thompson (ed.),
Over Our Dead Bodies: Women Against the Bomb, 1983

BODY LANGUAGES

Fleshly Matters

Lovely Linda

Review of Linda Lovelace, *Inside Linda Lovelace*.

'Some people', our Lady of Hard-Core Porn reflectively begins her memoirs, 'are born to greatness, others have greatness thrust upon them.' Her own fame devolves partly upon her own sexual virtuosity but, more, upon the demands of a society that utilises limited libidinal gratification as a soporific in a time of potential social disruption. She, the archetypal swinger, is the product of the 'permissive' society she eulogises; but the notion of 'permissiveness' can only arise in a society in which authoritarianism is deeply implicit. Now I am permitted as much libidinal gratification as I want. Yippee! But who is it who permits me? Why, the self-same institutions that hitherto forbade me! So, I am still in the same boat, though it has been painted a different colour. I am still denied authentic sexual autonomy, perhaps even more cruelly than before, since now I have received permission to perform hitherto forbidden acts and so I have acquired an illusory sense of freedom that blinds me more than ever to the true nature of freedom itself.

With no surprise, one learns from the preface that Ms Lovelace is 'no adherent of Women's Lib'. She preaches sexual freedom divorced from social or spiritual emancipation: 'the only place she wants to be equal is in bed'. Nevertheless, she exemplifies what could be called 'porn pride' when she states: 'I have learned to do things with my mouth and vagina that few women anywhere can hope to achieve.' However, she gives credit for her training to Chuck, the 'sexual engineer', a libidinal Svengali who launched her in blue movies; she didn't even invent it for herself, or learn it from her mother (which, I suppose, would be the natural way in a less repressed society). In an interview published in the afterword, she claims always to achieve orgasm herself in the act of fellatio which is physiologically impossible. Therefore I suggest her relation to men and to her own sexuality is ambiguous, and, coloured by either a degree of self-deceit, or the desire to deceive.

Nevertheless, she can ingest an entire foot inside her vagina; we know not only because she tells us so (which wouldn't be the strongest evidence of veracity) but because she has been filmed doing it. Fame, however, came with *Deep Throat*, since when her name has become synonymous with a fellatory technique that looks, to the cold eye, uncommonly like a sublimation of a suppressed castratory urge of immense proportions. If my sexuality had been as systematically exploited by men as Ms Lovelace's has been, no doubt I, too, would want to swallow men's cocks whole; it is a happy irony she should have found fame and fortune by doing so.

Now, in spite of the respect she has for her achievements as a unique phoenix of fuckery, Ms Lovelace does only what any accomplished whore is expected to do in a society where the profession of prostitution demands specific sexual virtuosities. Any Bangkok prostitute can blow smoke rings through her labia minor and be certain of applause and thanks. Her own fellatory technique is derived from that of a Japanese geisha (via, of course, Chuck. You wouldn't find Ms Lovelace in a Japanese whore house, learning her trade the hard way.)

Not every girl can insert a foot inside her vagina and those with this talent are surely entitled to public recognition; but our society generally denies the prostitute both appreciation of and the opportunity to exercise particular sexual virtuosity and, besides, Ms Lovelace is no prostitute. Perish the thought. All is done for love. The pay in porno movies is 'lousy' until she hits the big time – that is, until the porno movies become respectable. Sometimes, in her movies, she plays the role of a whore, but she is not a whore herself. Her attitude to sex is not commercial. It is sacramental.

'My God is now sex. Without sex, I'd die. Sex is everything.'

In the service of the god, she has taken the repertoire of sexual display from the commerce and intimacy of the brothel and allowed her performance to be frozen upon celluloid, condemned to a sequence of endless repetitions. In doing so, she has removed any element of tactile immediacy from her exposition of the potentialities of the body and therefore completely defused the sexual menace implicit in her own person and her polymorphously perverse talents. And that menace is enormous. If she can engulf a foot, what else could she not engulf? The owner of the foot in his entirety? The world itself?

But, though the cinema has become an imaginary brothel, it is not one in which the flesh on display is for sale. Hence it can never be handled. On the screen, she is safe from real contact with the impulses she arouses. (She constantly reiterates her own sexual exclusivity; she does not fuck with *anybody*. They must be special. They must be 'swingers'.)

These defunct images of her sexual virtuosity do not involve nor implicitly challenge the potency of the spectator.

And, in the eternity of the celluloid, the cock exists as a thing in itself.

The exigencies of porno-movie making means that: 'Many of the cocks seen in the nitty-gritty close-ups don't belong to the guys that are seen leading up to the action.' Because those who can act can't fuck, and vice versa. Indeed, she reveals, many of the actors are homosexual; and the faces of the owners of the most active organs never appear on the screen. Dispossessed, then, of all human attributes but the anonymity of the genital organs, nothing is generated. Nothing will come of nothing.

Like a postulant, Ms Lovelace shaves herself before she engages in these primal yet abstract confrontations. She has removed all traces of the animal from her body, so that it has the cool sheen, not of flesh, but of a mineral substance. She is not an embodiment but a crystallisation, even a reification, of libido; her art or craft, the public exposition of sexual activity reduced to a geometric intersection of parts, her queasily kitsch prose style, her leer, her simper, her naïvety, her schoolgirl humour, effectively anti-septises all the danger from that most subversive and ambivalent aspect of our selves.

No more terror, no more magic. Sex utterly divorced from its reproductive function, its function as language and its function as warfare.

She is a shaven prisoner in a cage whose bars are composed of cocks. And she has been so thoroughly duped she seems quite happy there.

Each age gets the heroines it deserves and, by God, we deserve Linda Lovelace.

New Society, 1974

Fat Is Ugly

Review of Mara Selvini Palazzoli, *Self-Starvation*.

Mara Selvini Palazzoli is a psychotherapist who has researched anorexia nervosa for twenty years and has had dozens of demented female emaciates pass through her, I should imagine, on the whole, healing hands. My qualification for reviewing her book is that I am an ex-anorexic myself and so, in spite of her massive research, and deep and informed sympathy for women like me, still I know a trick or two that she does not (or so I fondly believe, doctor).

Anorexia nervosa is clearly going to be one of the fashionable ailments of the seventies, just as schizophrenia was the mode of the sixties. (I was a student when Laing's *The Divided Self* came out to form an instant focus for self-identification for young people away from home for the first time; they had to open a new ward in the local madhouse to deal with the resulting plague.) It will not, however, be quite as widespread as schizophrenia, since its ravages are primarily confined to young girls – or, rather, since there are more young girls than young boys, it will be just as widespread but rather more particularised. There is also the possibility that famine will convert the symptoms to a form of socially beneficial behaviour.

A historico-cultural diagnosis of the increasing study of anorexia nervosa ought to take the woman's movement into account, because the relation of the anorexic to her physical being implies extreme dissatisfaction with the physical being itself. I would not say that Women's Lib afforded me the final therapeutic strength to cope with my own residual anorexia, but it certainly helped.

Anorexia nervosa is a form of compulsive fasting which organises a number of personal and interpersonal dilemmas around the desire to lose weight. 'The true cause', says Palazzoli, 'is a deliberate wish to slim.'

There is, as we all know, considerable pressure on young girls to conform to the cultural standards of conventional aesthetics in Western society. Fat is emphatically *not* Beautiful, as it is in cultures where there is less to eat. Woman, regarded as an item of conspicuous consumption (though that is becoming somewhat less true), has traditionally the sole creative function of Dandy; she is tacitly encouraged to sacrifice much for the sake of appearances. Dandyism is the last resort of the impotent, and the protracted attempted suicide by narcissism (which is how my anorexic experience now appears to me), can be regarded as a kind of batty exhibition of heroics, which ironically underlines the impotence it was adopted to combat.

Palazzoli appears to take this view. She quotes another researcher in the field: 'All severe anorexics she has treated show a paralysing sense of helplessness.' Child, usually, of an overprotective mother, docile and well behaved in a family with as many kinks as Laing's families of schizophrenics, the anorexic uses food as a weapon to establish some kind of autonomy. Reading this book is like reading a guidebook to a country I know very well, but where I never bothered to identify the major towns, or industries.

Palazzoli defines two specific traits of anorexics. First, an unusual sensitivity to the ambiguous cultural role of modern women; second, a heightened sense of lack of personal autonomy, due to the nature of familiar relationships. To the potential anorexic, menarche – the first menstruation – arrives like a thunderbolt. I am prepared to accept that it happened that way, but it doesn't quite tally with my memories, menarche didn't even affect my body much, obese from infancy. It was the entry into the world that caused the trouble.

Inside every fat man there is a thin man screaming to get out. I had a firm conviction that fat was ugly, ludicrous, and disabling. And thin was wonderful. My mother's attempts to reconcile me to obesity – she would flourish Rubens and Renoir nudes before me and read aloud enticing descriptions of fat women from Victorian novels – I regarded with extreme suspicion. I thought she was attacking my thin-equals-attractive equation for malicious reasons of her own. Nevertheless, since enough is enough, she got me a proper diet sheet from a doctor and, with encouragement from my family, I embarked on a disastrous course.

Because obsession, compulsion, narcissism took over from reason when I reached about size 14. In the spring of 1958, I weighed fifteen stone; by Christmas of the same year, eight stone. At this point, I became an anorexic. The following month, I went down to between five and a half and six stone. Meanwhile, I was working ten or twelve hours a day and, when I returned home, writing a novel full of the most horrifying Freudian symbols. (Overactivity – this checks with Palazzoli.)

Amenorrhoea, suicidal depression, frigidity, moroseness – the cadaverous symptomology of this bizarre affliction set in. From Rubens to Grünewald in nine months flat. Further – and how I now despise it – I had set out on this crazy species of self-mortification out of pure sexual vanity. Consciously, at least. Clearly, more was going on in my psyche than that, but sexual vanity was my justification. I assumed that no man in his right mind could ever have been attracted to Fat Angie; therefore I reduced myself to a physical condition – that of Walking Corpse – that only a chronic necrophile could have fancied. (I had, of course, tended to regard marriage as the only possible release from a home environment bulging with all those Renoir nudes, although my father had always told me a good job was actually a better bet.)

My parents, at this stage, concluded I was batty and left me alone; but time does heal. I fell in with a group of picturesque eccentrics; I was working on a local newspaper which, at that time, functioned as a kind of benign day-clinic, where my patent insanity was taken in good part. I ceased to be docile at home and became obnoxious: first sign of autonomy. (Confessions of an ex-anorexic.) Tentatively, at first, I began to menstruate again.

I didn't eat bread for ten years, which was the time it took me to get used to being thin; I haven't touched white sugar, or filthy cake, or things like that, for coming up to seventeen years. I have wonderful teeth and blood pressure and everything, and anorexia nervosa is *not* the end of the world and can have some splendid side-effects, if you get through it.

But, far more traumatic than menarche for the adolescent girl, says Palazzoli, are the conditions attendant upon it: '– she experiences her feminine sexuality in a passive and receptive way; she is exposed to lewd looks, subjected to menstruation, about to be penetrated in sexual embraces, to be invaded by the foetus, to be suckled by a child'. She suggests it is this 'passive-receptive' aspect of feminine life which is revealed to the young girl at menarche, the 'concrete manifestation' of the passivity that has plagued her for so long.

The anorexic, in fact, is in desperate conflict with the woman's body she sees as a passive receptacle and the source of her own impotence; at the same time, she sees her own body – her sexuality? – as an all-powerful, invading force. Alienated, then, in totality from one's physical being. Yes, it felt like that. It did. But, thank God, nobody pumped me full of insulin or gave me electric shock therapy, as she says they do to other emaciates in her chapter on clinical treatment; that would have pandered much too much to the masochism inherent in the whole ghastly business. She herself believes only psychotherapy really helps. I should say so.

No, says Palazzoli, the anorexic does *not* reject femininity; she rejects only those aspects of adult femininity that 'conjure up the terrifying vista of turning into a succubus and a passive vessel'. Emaciation, therefore, equals emancipation; another false equation, but one way that presents itself to the baffled ego as a method of escaping a physical trap. Young men express the traumas of adolescence in other ways. I know it is not all jam for young men, far from it. But at least they cannot suffer unwanted pregnancy; and neither can a girl who does not menstruate.

And so we arrive where I suppose I must have started out, in the bosom of the 'anorexic family'. In 1967, Palazzoli founded the Milan Centre of Family Studies; in a chapter called 'The cybernetics of anorexia nervosa', she develops – I quote the flyleaf – 'an entirely new epistemology of the anorexic syndrome'. At this point, I pass. Get all the nutters responsible for provoking this particular manifestation of nuttery in one room and analyse the lot of them. Fine. I'm sure I'd have enjoyed it very much. But every family has two families behind it and so on *ad infinitum*. There were more nutters in my mother's family than mine, if only because it was a bigger family; and my father's too. Unlike Laing, Palazzoli acknowledges that you have to go on living with them after everybody knows the horrid truths they've spent so long concealing. But Aeneas fled Rome with his aged father on his back and so do we all.

I learned only by hindsight that I'd had anorexia nervosa. After the condition ameliorated, I attended the inquest on a fifteen-year-old girl who escaped from a mental hospital where she had been undergoing treatment for the affliction. She had laid down on the railway tracks at East Croydon station. (Anorexics *do*, I fear, commit suicide, though Palazzoli suggests they don't, or, at least, not often.) The evidence of her parents and her psychiatrists tallied with my own experience. Except, of course, that I hadn't been that bad; or else had somehow managed to conceal the extent of my folly from people who would have done something about it. But, you see, my parents, after verifying my amennorhea was not the result of pregnancy, concluded I was batty and left me alone. And perhaps I can attribute my survival in reasonable shape to that, as much as anything.

Palazzoli's book is, apart from anything else, a most valuable contribution to the field of woman's studies. The tone of this review may be attributed to that same gallows humour with which the seventeenth century approached the subject of syphilis; some existential ills are so savage, I believe one should approach them stoically. That is, lightly.

New Society, 1974

A Well-Hung Hang-Up

Cock modestly detumescent, Andrew Cooper III, *Playgirl*'s Man for June, leans against the bonnet of an extremely powerful car, both car and boy studies of potency *in potentia*. The winged symbol on the radiator suggests the erection the young man decently forbears to unfurl but it's plain to see he's superbly hung. The centre-fold shows him fresh from a sunset sea, white towelling robe falling away from his emblematic virility. He also displays himself for women's pleasure in tennis kit; in blue jeans and T-shirt; and in a sort of Chinese shroud.

Playgirl, the magazine for women, gives us Andrew Cooper III unclothed, as if his flesh were his function, like that of a beautiful woman, but his biography equates male sexuality with money and power in the traditional manner: 'he raked in his first million by the time he was twenty-one'. The biographical notes authenticate him; he has a history as well as a torso. We read of his endearing habits, he likes to climb mountains in the nude. Freedom, he says, is everything to him. He water-skis like a champ, plays tennis like a demon, handles a camera like a pro. Therefore, he exists. He has a soulful look, reminding us that his iconic derivation may be as much from the pin-ups of the rock stars in fan-mags of the sixties as it is from his lascivious sisters in the tit mags who part their legs and leer with far greater a culturally sanctioned abandon. He looks too butch to be true. He is hairy as an ape.

The pin-ups of male nudes in *Playgirl* and *Viva* serve at least one socially useful function; they gratify early adolescent curiosity as to the actual appearance of the male sex organ, which exercises pre-pubescent girls a

good deal until they are traumatised by their first flasher. But the magazines do not appear to aim at the pre-bra set, the tone of the contents is
resolutely sophisticated, so their purpose cannot be simply educational.

Playgirl, like *Playboy*, of which it is not the stable-mate, has a philosophy, which is one of responsible sexual freedom. The editor declares: 'I
do not trumpet behind the banners of women's liberation, yet I am not so
foolish as to deny that the success of individual liberation is the quintes-
sence of our survival. I believe vehemently in femininity and will do
everything in my power to promote it.'

The nature of this femininity is demonstrated by ads for vaginal deodor-
ants, vibrators, slenderising devices, bust developing creams, and exotic
underwear. The exotic underwear ad offers something called 'Bosom
Buddies', which seem to be artificial nipples, good heavens, out of style
since the *Directoire*. 'Soft rubber nipple pads help nature along. Natural
look and feel even under see-through tops.' There is a certain egalitarianism in that men are not spared these excesses, either; the *Playgirl* shopping
guide suggests, 'Give your man "Hot Pants" for Father's Day. Either
"Super Cock" or "Home of the Whopper" styles. 100% cotton stretch
waist band. Specify style and size (small, medium, large).' 'Small' and
'medium' is poignant. One letter on the doctor's page asks: 'Can they
really double penis size?'

Viva, stablemate of *Penthouse* and *Forum* so truly in the vanguard of the
sexual revolution, is less up-front, rather less brash than *Playgirl* with, perhaps, some pretensions to feminism as well as to femininity; nevertheless,
the *raison d'être* of both publications is the full frontal, male nude pin-
up, and, from the context, one can assume the purpose of these pin-ups is,
like all pin-ups, purely titillatory. And I assume, from the context, that the
person they want to titillate is a maturish professional woman not unlike,
perhaps, me.

Fat chance, I tell you, fat chance.

The poverty-stricken aesthetic behind these nudes cancels out all the
erotic promise of the flesh itself and all flesh, even that of Andrew Cooper
III, is potentially erotic. For one thing, in the ideology behind the aesthetic lurks the notion that, as a general rule, women are looking for love
and therefore the flesh, to please a woman, may not be presented specifically as flesh-in-itself. It is well known that women are not aroused by
hardcore porn so the titillation has a top-dressing of sentiment. A picture-
story in *Viva* actually depicts, in saccharine soft focus, a wedding night.
The sensitive, open-pored face of Jerry, *Viva*'s 'sexy yachtsman', spreads
across an entire page and he talks about love: 'First, of course, I'm attracted
to the body, but then the mind becomes important. The relationship is
really in the mind.' Ross, Case, Shep, Greg – such butch, emphatic,

deliciously brutal monosyllables! – make themselves and their limp pricks available for romantic fantasies rather than erotic ones.

The pseudo-biographies of the models in the tit-mags have, in contrast, a sprightly fakery; Marisa, Portland, Tracy know that nobody would recognise them with their clothes on, anyway, that they exist exclusively as ingenious articulated toys in a porno-Disneyland, and do not need to pretend to have hearts.

The aesthetic of the prick-and-bum mags is butch is beautiful. Jerry, 'young, light-hearted master of the waves', thrusts masterfully through the ocean, proudly naked steers his yacht. A pair of nude skiers have been snapped in mid-flight; naked sky-divers, even . . . the necessity to portray the male nude in action, demonstrating Hemingwayesque conspicuous virility, drops them straight into the absurd. It's not even kitsch, it's ridiculous. (*Playgirl* has a circulation of a million and a half, *Viva* something less.) Jacques Perrault runs eight miles a day to keep himself in trim, it says. Almost all the young men exhibit pale bikini marks on their deeply tanned, terribly hairy frames. They are joy through strength. The beaux of Muscle Beach engaged in as narcissistic a cult of the body as Hitler Youth.

Yet this must be an atavistic memory, in however vague and distorted a form, of the nude, discus-throwing youths, the Beautiful Athletes, the figures on vases, the pin-ups of the locker-rooms of Athens and Sparta so dear to the classical tradition, the principal models of the male body as an image of beauty and delight in our culture, hallowed by the public school tradition and the notion of a healthy mind in a healthy body.

And so, as images of delighted male sexuality, *Playgirl* and *Viva* toss we maturish professional women a few muscle-bound hustlers left over by a couple of millennia from the Symposium because the models we do have for lovely boys are too few to create a tradition and, perhaps, express far too explicitly the notion of the male body as an object of desire, as an instrument of pleasure – but not of woman's pleasure. Donatello's delicious David is, according to the colour supplements, a 'masterpiece of homosexual art'; hands off, girls! Similarly with Michelangelo's celebrations of vulnerable, narrow-chested striplings and Caravaggio's fat, sinister Bacchus with his fruit-hat *à la* Carmen Miranda; not a trace of such imagery as this to be found in *these* glossy pages. No room for complex sensuality, only for simple virility.

The picture of a naked man belongs to a different aesthetic convention than that of a naked woman. The female nude's nakedness is in itself a form of dress, since the lengthy tradition of European art clothes even the vulgarest pin-up with a heavy if invisible cloak of associations. She knows how to wear nothing; further, she is perfectly secure in that, so garbed, she can always expect approval. But what is sauce for the goose is not necessarily sauce for the gander.

The articles which will accessorise the nakedness of the pin-up, her erotic apparatus of beads, feathers, white stockings, black stockings, corsets, scarves, bodices, frilly knickers, hats, are sanctioned by a tradition that extends back as far as Cranach and beyond. Andrew Cooper III's towelling robe has no such cultural resonance; his blue jeans belong only to the modern tradition of porno-kitsch in which he himself is so firmly ensconced.

The dreamy narcissism of Dolores or Marsha, one hand straying towards her crotch, refers directly back to the slumberous Venuses of the Renaissance; Hélène, Natasha, Jane are continually peeking into little hand-mirrors with the intense self-satisfaction of a Titian goddess. Boucher's Madamoiselle O'Murphy is a Penthouse Pet already. It is a central contradiction in European art that its celebration of the human form should involve subsuming the particularities of its subjects in the depersonalising idea of the nude, rendering her – in the name of humanism – an object.

But women have the advantage of their disadvantages. Our relation to our own bodies is both more intimate and more abstract than that of most men to theirs. Naked, a woman can never be less than herself for her value in the world resides more in her skin than in her clothes. Though, naked, she loses her name and becomes a 'blue nude', 'the bather', 'woman dressing', 'Suzie', 'Gina', 'Europa', 'Eve', 'Venus', this personal anonymity is the price of a degree of mystification of her naked body that means she can accede to a symbolic power as soon as her clothes are off, whereas a man's symbolic power resides in his clothes, indicators of his status. The story of the Emperor's new clothes would have a different meaning were the hero an Empress; the spectators would have thought she had done it on purpose, that now she was displaying her real, female authority.

The tranquil and unconcerned pride with which nude women since the Renaissance display their usually generous breasts which are the rendezvous (remember) of love and hunger, means that, if not in the world, then, at least as art, the women have been certain of creating a positive response when they pretend to be a triumphant icon of nourishment and sexuality, of love, in fact. Madamoiselle O'Murphy and her look-alike, Marilyn Monroe might have been very confused about everything else but at least knew exactly who they were when they took their clothes off; their skin itself was the sign of their status, their nakedness their sole but irrefutable claim to existential veracity. The male models of *Playgirl* and *Viva* do not exhibit such self-confidence; and no wonder. There is a specific vocabulary of gestures and attitudes of sexual expression available for women in relation to men that does not exist for men in relation to women and so, erotically speaking, Andrew Cooper III and Gerry and Woody and all the chaps are posing in a void.

Further, they are playing deeply against the cultural grain. For there *is* a tradition of the male nude in European art and one so deeply part of our culture we don't even think of it as a male nude, which is what it is, though the genitals are not displayed. (They're not in any female nudes outside graffiti, either.) The icon of the naked woman as the source of nourishment and sexuality is balanced by the icon of the naked man in physical torment. 'It is no accident', says Kenneth Clark in *The Nude*, 'that the formalised body of the "perfect man" became the supreme symbol of European belief.' However, the formalised body of the 'perfect man' had to become a supreme icon of sado-masochism before that happened and the only heir to that tradition in our merciful age of unbelief is Francis Bacon. And it isn't simply two thousand years of crucifixions and pietàs working against the male body as an image of joy; it is two millennia of St Sebastian transfixed by arrows, St Lawrence with his gridiron, St Bartholomew being flayed, decapitated Holofernes, Prometheus with the birds gnawing his liver, martyrdoms, executions, dissections. Marat stabbed in his bath. Against this rage can beauty hold a plea? Not, certainly, in the timorous hands of the male pin-ups.

New Society, 1975

Health on the Brain

There's always been a human tendency to equate physical health with spiritual health. 'A healthy mind in a healthy body.' Disease is not seen as an accident of fate or directly related to bad working conditions, or mere bad luck. It is the physical manifestation of internal rottenness. How many adjectives for foulness relate to disease? Leprous; poxy; pestiferous; scrofulous. The notion of sickness is related to that indefinable 'something rotten in the state'. The porn and violence in the media, so the media constantly assure us, are evidence of a sick society. Sick with what, one may ask; but nobody ever says. Sick as such is bad enough.

As for the sick themselves, they must be wicked to deserve such pain. They've got themselves into their ghastly cancerous, bronchitic, syphilitic states entirely through their own self-indulgence, and they richly deserve their ulcers and coughs and dysentery and alcoholic psychoses.

The idea that sickness is, at some deep level, a moral failing is a comforting notion to promote when the National Health Service is reeling from the cuts. It is an even more comforting notion, when our choices are contracting as fast as the economy. We think we at least retain, or can gain control of our physical fates – that is, our bodies and their ailments.

The *Sunday Times*, ever quick off the mark to spot a trend, has just concluded a lengthy outline of do-it-yourself preventive medicine which might lead the unwary to imagine that the authentic *elixium vitae* resided in a jar of sunflower seed oil. For all I know, it may. Except I'm certain that I don't want to live until I'm a hundred. I'm not too sure I've got the energy to drag on until forty.

The *Sunday Times* has convinced me I ought to immediately start out on a new regime of positively conventual austerity in order to reduce the burden on a strained NHS by not forcing them to have to cope with my lung cancer or coronary. But the series hasn't altogether persuaded me that remaining alive is worth quite as much effort as all that.

Anyway, the zonking eight-part series that took butter off middle-class tables for at least a week was entitled 'The Art of Body Maintenance', presumably with a nod and a wink at the currently bestselling *Zen and the Art of Motorcycle Maintenance*. But zen acknowledges the effects of random chance. The concerned, committed *Sunday Times* team present an atrociously Calvinist model of the world. Sickness becomes the wages of an interesting kind of secularised sin. The pursuit of health is a moral imperative. Random chance – the universal spirit of black comedy that ensured an impotent Baudelaire would die of syphilis; that my grandfather, a lifelong total abstainer, should succumb to cirrhosis of the liver; that ten per cent of lung cancer deaths occur in non-smokers – is sternly eschewed.

Since the series dealt in a tone of high moral seriousness with matters of life and death and human suffering, I realise it's tasteless to approach it in a mood of bilious facetiousness. Nevertheless, the massive contribution the immorally unhealthy have made to our culture cannot be denied. The white spirochete coursed demonically through the nervous systems of Schubert, Nietzsche, Gauguin, Delius, Rochester, probably Shakespeare, certainly Maupassant, Freddie Keppard (the greatest New Orleans trumpeter of them all). It concentrated their minds something wonderful, before it wiped them out altogether. Alcoholics, depressives, cripples, Jarry, Kafka, Toulouse Lautrec.

Admittedly, most of them – except for Jarry, who didn't care, Kafka, who wouldn't have taken his tablets and Rochester, a recidivist – would have responded very favourably to modern treatments had their condition been diagnosed in time. But if you throw in people who probably weren't sick at all but took great pains to establish that they were, like Elizabeth

Barrett Browning and Florence Nightingale, it becomes apparent that there might be more to ill-health than meets the eye. Sickness offers all kinds of protection from the world, just as fatness and misanthropy do.

I submit that not one of the sufferers (mostly artists) listed above would have failed to repress a giggle at the very notion of looking after yourself as an *art*. No, one of them, Nietzsche, would have nodded appreciatively at the idea but we all know where that leads. Joy through strength and the thud of the jackboot.

The notion of 'body maintenance' suggests the body itself as a machine for living in. But though I scrutinised the series for some mention of the soul, I could find none, and therefore conclude there's no ghost in this machine. Man is fully automated, and must keep himself perfectly tuned. This machine for living in is a uni-cellular survival unit, a smoothly running tank which can take its occupant unharmed through all the risks attendant on living.

He stores it well with wholegrains, cottage cheese (made from skimmed milk) and non-animal-fat margarine. Thus he will avoid his coronary, that brutal spanner in the motor. No ashtrays inside, no cocktail cabinet, none of those harmful drugs that seduce whilst eroding the flesh, solacing one for the pains of living whilst reducing the ability to do so. None of that. This tank makes scrupulous detours around stress situations. The price of perpetual boredom is none too high. It takes care not to work in shipping, down the pits, or anywhere near asbestos. Let the ignorant and unwary do that. We know better.

There is a single bed. Celibacy is the best protection from the perils of generation and procreation, even if sexual intercourse is recommended to the old as good exercise for the heart and lungs. Had Rochester been told that fucking was splendid exercise, it is probably the only thing that would have put him off it and the world would have been the richer by a great poet.

However, if the well-maintained body decides, taking all things into account, that it should not deprive itself of sex because the physical advantages outweigh the disadvantages, it will maintain a strict monogamy. Not because of any romantic nonsense about love and all that. Didn't you realise fidelity was a health precaution? 'If you sleep with only one person, and you're both faithful, you should avoid gonorrhoea and syphilis.' That's some small compensation for marital boredom.

So the tank chugs on, negotiating a minefield of fat dinner parties, loose women and dark strangers, the Mephistophelean cigarette offerer, the wicked chocolate profferer ('Come on – just one won't do you any harm'), the fiends with bottles in their hands and perdition in their hearts. Finally it reaches the joys on an old age which the *Sunday Times* advertises with unretouched pictures of tangoing geriatrics and octagenarian joggers.

'Few people die of old age itself,' it says here. 'Most people who survive into their eighties die of the same diseases as the rest of us: heart disease, stroke and cancer.' Shame. Nevertheless, death itself as a fact, indeed the culmination of life, may still be balked by good diet, exercise, self-help, until presumably, the onset of irreversible senile decay. Great. That's a *perfect* way to go.

I specially liked part three, which had features on slimming, contraception, VD and suicide, all put together like a Rake's Progress, through no interconnections seemed intended. The section on slimming stresses the bane of obesity, though I doubt that, on a world-wide scale, obesity claims quite so many victims as malnutrition. Laugh and grow fat? Then cut out laughing. The life of the obese is nasty, brutish and short, as the insurance companies know.

They quote with approval the exemplary tale of Gail Ingham, who shed five and a half stone for love of the boy next door. Would it had been in a better cause, Gail; would it had been in the cause of your own narcissism, even, rather than somebody else's. 'It had been a long, hard struggle.' Conducted almost like a military campaign, or a primitive ordeal, necessary before marriage took place. I'd like a little more information about the motives of the participants, please, before I cheer. What kind of brainwashing is it that makes a presumably sane and normal girl say: 'I keep charts and calorie booklets and weigh everything. I have some marvellous scales. It's habit, now, I suppose, but every time I look at food, I just see a pile of calories.' That doesn't sound very healthy to me. It sounds like hallucination.

Bizarre ethnic groups and their habits always make a statutory appearance as little exemplary parables in every gospel of good health. These savage tribes usually subsist on a diet of cassava root whilst persistently, like Uncle William, standing on their heads or retaining every tooth in their heads until a ripe old age.

Now, do not think I am carping at the very notion of do-it-yourself health as such, though I find the idea of a life devoted solely to cheating death not a very exhilarating one. Obviously, any formulas that, in general, alleviate human suffering are to be applauded and the more widely they are disseminated, the better. But there's a gaping hole in 'The Art of Body Maintenance'. It says nowhere precisely what the purpose of it all is. It just takes it for granted that a healthy person is not only a more socially useful person than a sick person, but also a better one.

It seems to imply that good health, like any other form of virtue, is its own reward. But what is the well-maintained body going to do with its splendid strengths and resiliences and stream-lining, apart from saving the

NHS a few bob? Sit around in narcissistic self-admiration, flexing its new muscles in the intervals of its daily jobs and swims and the preparation of its wholefood meals? The body, in the context of this enormously well-intentioned series, exists solely as a thing in itself, not as an object of use or sensuality or delight.

There's a nice little moral coda, listing the things that baddies – it actually calls them 'baddies' – do, like giving sweets to children and not jogging, and using lifts, and pressing food and drink on reluctant guests. 'Goodies' do up seat-belts for other people, serve slimmers' menus, ask sex partners beforehand about VD and contraception (not, actually, the easiest thing in the world), offer their guests low-fat margarine and wholemeal bread.

I'm sure this is all very wise and sensible. But I can't, really, try as I may, see any implicit moral value, for good or bad, in a chocolate cream as such. Oliver Gillie, summing up the series, says: 'The great prospect for improving our health comes from making changes in the way we live.' But that's true for a lot of things besides health. To try to impose a heavy moral value on concerns which are a matter of knowledge and sense, seems rather silly and irrelevant. Not enough to make an art form out of, anyway.

New Society, 1976

Georges Bataille: Story of the Eye

There's a photograph – among the surrealist souvenirs – of the poet, Benjamin Peret, insulting a priest. One lesson of Georges Bataille's erotic novella, *Story of the Eye*, is that French intellectuals are made of sterner stuff than we are.

We think blasphemy is silly. They are exhilarated by it. Bataille's hero and heroine end up doing a lot more to a priest than just insulting him. The fine European tradition of anti-clericalism is central to the pre-occupations of this grand old surrealist fellow-traveller and sexual *philosophe*. It underpins Bataille's theory of active sexuality as the assertion of human freedom against the laws of church and state. There can be few texts that illustrate so precisely the cultural differences between the Roman Catholic and the Protestant sensibility.

Bataille puts pornography squarely in the service of blasphemy. Transgression, outrage, sacrilege, liberation of the senses through erotic frenzy, and the symbolic murder of God. This is a scenario alien to the secular heritage of Protestant humanism. It confirms the free-thinker's darkest fears about the nauseating madness inherent in Judaeo-Christianity itself. One can understand why Susan Sontag – whose worthy but dull essay, 'The Pornographic Imagination', is appended – refrains from commenting on the climax of *Story of the Eye*, where a priest is enticed into lapping up his own urine from a sacramental chalice. Sontag is concerned to define what kind of literature pornography might be; she doesn't notice that *Story of the Eye* is didactically lewd.

After the hapless cleric has drained the cup to its dregs of marinated Host, the polymorphously perverse heroine, Simone, orgiastically strangles him, gouges out his eye and pops it into her vagina, which she has already used as a repository for eggs, both raw and cooked, and the testicles of a bull. Roland Barthes, in *his* essay in the buxom appendix to the brief tale, points out the complex circularity of the dominant imagery of eye, egg, testicle. No content man, he; his whimsical formalism is too disingenuous by half. *Story of the Eye* was first published in France in 1928; two years later, French Fascists smashed up the cinema in which Buñuel and Dali's *L'Age d'Or* was celebrating erotic blasphemy. Bataille was dicing with death and *Story of the Eye* is about fucking as existential affirmation against death, who is also God. (Unless Bataille's own blind, paralysed father – syphilis, naturally – is God; he materialises horribly in an afterword.)

Now Simone, her lover, and an onanistic English milord set sail to America. They won't be able to raise Susan Sontag's eyebrows, whatever they get up to there; but since they crew their boat with black sailors, no doubt these guerrillas of the libido will think up a few stunts that will get up everybody else's noses.

That English milord, the non-participatory entrepreneur of obscene spectacles, is an unkind cut. The French have always thought we are sexually weirder than we have ever thought them, which is saying something. This has to do with the relativity of the notion of the sense of sin; and to do, too, with the way the metaphysics of *Story of the Eye* evaporate in the translation (by Joachim Neurgroschel), just as the crystalline rhetoric of Bataille's incomparable prose muddies in English. Nevertheless, this marvellous, scatological fairytale about the omnipotence of desire, as Barthes says, 'between the banal and the absurd' still enlightens.

New Society, 1979

Edward Shorter: A History of Women's Bodies

It is Edward Shorter's initial premise that the irreducible physical differ-ence between women and men – that is, the nature of the biological appa-ratus of femininity itself, essentially its reproductive system – has been, in the past, sufficient to account for most if not all the subjugation of women by men.

Put as badly as that, it is easy to see why Shorter adopts a combative stance. This is a tender spot *vis-à-vis* the women's movement and he states in his preface to this book, in the manner of one bristling for a fight: before 1900 or so, femininity was basically a negative concept for most women'.

The advances in medicine and surgery that had made childbirth virtu-ally risk-free and lengthened the lives of women cancer patients took place only within the last century. (Cancers of the womb and breast are, of course, specifically female and remain a scourge, if a less absolute death sentence than they once were.) Shorter argues – fiercely; he is a most iras-cible writer – that the ending of the physical victimisation of women, a victimisation not only social but also 'natural' in the form of those afflic-tions from which men do not suffer, 'was a *precondition* for feminism'. And, further, that men – that is, a medical profession that was then virtually an exclusive male preserve – were not only the allies of women in the struggle to survive but, in effect, created that very precondition. He assumes, puzzlingly, this is a controversial position.

This is an absorbing, most moving, informative, horrifying, exceedingly stimulating book. Yet, from the outset, the reader has a sense of happen-ing in upon a private fight, for Shorter is not only engaged upon a mas-sive survey of gender-related suffering but also in taking sideswipes at certain aspects of women's studies.

He burns with outrage at the millennia upon millennia of indescribable and largely unacknowledged pain which women have undergone solely on account of the physiology of sexual difference, at the uselessness of both academic and folk medicine in the face of the commonest gynaecological and obstetric mishaps in the past, and at the institutionalised ill-treatment of women by their menfolk.

Of this latter category, one example among many should suffice – of a 49-year-old French woman whose advanced uterine cancer was compli-cated by a similarly advanced pregnancy, forced upon her by the sexual importunity of her husband in the year of Our Lord, 1812, and I use the phrase 'Our Lord', advisedly. (Her doctor was aghast.)

Yet Shorter cannot refrain, again and again, from displays of sarcasm against those feminists who posit a 'woman's culture' at some mythical time in the past, in which female disorders were dealt with promptly and competently by the local white witch and the experience of childbirth – the appalling history of which is central to the book – was easy, spontaneous and celebratory, a 'fiesta of the oppressed', in fact. These gibes and asides impede the enormous drama of that triumph over nature which is essentially his subject, a drama which ends, as is rare enough, these days, on an upbeat note: for the tables of maternal mortality statistics alone are enough to reassure one as to the progressive nature of progress and, to my mind, make his case for him.

And femininity is certainly not a 'negative concept' now. And if women don't thank men sufficiently for permitting their emancipation, then nobody, except Margaret Thatcher, expects the entire industrial proletariat to turn round and thank the capitalist system for creating it, dammit.

Which is being terribly unfair to Shorter, whose ill temper I find wholly sympathetic. 'In recent times, we have heard so much about "wise women" of yore and their special kind of knowledge that represented centuries of practical experience etcetera. In fact, traditional lore existed for normal deliveries and was useless when anything went wrong.'

Well, yes, I know that. My mother told me that. My mother who died early from a heart condition aggravated by a protracted labour, a labour which, even a few years later, would have been speedily cut short by the kind of medical intervention some of Shorter's feminist sources despise. But his ongoing squabble with those silly sisters who, for ideological reasons, wish to deny the intractable nature of the past gets in the way.

He's tilting at windmills, at a particular kind of college-bred stupidity that flourishes on the north American continent, which regards the past as a Technicolor version of the present and twentieth-century medicine in its entirety as a system for producing ill-health. In a free market economy where medical care is a commodity like any other, the last attitude may be understandable but, if one of Shorter's projects, here, is to restore medical science itself to a positive role in the history of women's emancipation, then the abundant evidence he adduces is sufficient.

It is proverbial, hence automatically suspect, that joy in the newborn wipes out the memory of the pangs of childbirth. At a time when childbirth, at least in the advanced, industrial countries, may hold perils but rarely death, and pregnancy is no longer mandatory upon sexual intercourse, the memory of the common experience of childbirth in the very recent past has been almost obliterated, or rather has been consigned to the macabre folklore of the women's wards, where, ironically enough, it may be easily dismissed by some of the more enthusiastic ideologues of a triumphant 'woman's culture' as old wives' tales. Since the process of childbirth is 'natural', it is argued, then 'unnatural' medical intervention is what makes things go wrong.

'Woman is natural, therefore abominable,' said Baudelaire. Shorter is emphatically not of the Baudelairean tendency but much of his book is necessarily devoted to the ways in which the human female body can mal-function abominably during the 'natural' process of childbirth. The Lord assured Eve she would bring forth in sorrow and His blueprint for the female form ensured that, in perhaps the majority of cases, this would be so. Those societies that do not posit an Eve may order things somewhat differently, though the physiology is still the same.

Shorter does not explore such possibilities. He deals almost exclusively with the history of Judaeo-Christian bodies during what may loosely be called the 'European' period – that is, Europe and north America since the Romans. He cites only one or two pre-Christian Latvian folksongs as tenuous evidence that, sometime, somewhere, in that past he presents – I think accurately – as virtually unrelieved nightmare for women, some of us *did* experience an occasional modicum of *joie de vivre* before the mater-nal mortality statistics caught up with us; nothing about China or India.

Not, of course, that any system of belief, even one that was not based on the idea that women 'must be wicked to deserve such pain', could have been much use, before modern surgery, in the case of a baby who persis-tently refused to be born. Midwives used to carry hooks in their bags, so that, if tugging, pulling and poking around the birth canal (probably with unwashed hands) was of no avail, they could insert the hook in the baby's skull and bring it out that way.

This procedure was also followed in maternity wards. Shorter describes how recently the baby itself has received any consideration at all during the process of its own birth. Sometimes the hook proved redundant, if, for example, a birth attendant inadvertently pulled off the baby's head during the preliminaries. Sometimes the mothers recovered from these ordeals; sometimes not, surviving to encounter the hazards of puerperal fever, of chronic pelvic infections perhaps incurred after a husband insisted on copulation in the hours immediately after birth, of a prolapsed womb (for which no assistance was available until the introduction of vulcanised rub-ber in the nineteenth century). And so on; until, if she survived so long, the next pregnancy.

Caesarean section was a last resort and usually conducted upon a corpse, since the survival rate for the operation, until the late nineteenth century, was negligible. That is why Malcolm, in *Macbeth*, fulfilled the witches' prophecy by having been 'from his mother's womb untimely ripped'; he was not of woman born since by then she was dead. Today, in north America, Caesarean section is conducted very frequently. It is neat and tidy, the anaesthetised mother feels no pain at all and, furthermore, it offers the surgeon a big, fat fee. Towards the end of his book, Shorter starts to lose his temper with the medical profession itself, which, up till then, he has treated with an (occasionally sharply qualified) respect.

It is impossible to read *A History of Women's Bodies*, this black museum of female afflictions, without admitting that such a heritage of suffering has coloured the way men thought and, perhaps, still think about women, and the way women thought, and may still do, in secret fears and anxieties, about themselves. It is an essential book for women, in fact, a terrible enlightenment as to the real nature of the curse of Eve, its implementation over the centuries and its removal. Mercifully, Shorter's nice line in black humour astringently tempers the long-drawn-out agony of it all.

New Society, 1983

Eric Rhode: On Birth and Madness

This book begins like a novel: 'A woman attends a funeral. The coffin is lowered into the grave. A man approaches her and says: "He was not your father."' But the reader's expectation of continuous narrative is excited only to be disrupted; Eric Rhode prefers to work in discrete sections of speculation, each independently, often curiously titled – 'Father into Foetus'. 'Eyes Pregnant with a Mother's Babies'. This method of organisation is reminiscent of the collections of brief, aphoristic essays by Theodor Adorno, although Eric Rhode's intellectual method is rather less rigorous than Adorno's. Rhode's speculation centres on work as a psychiatrist in a puerperal breakdown unit – that is, a place where women are sent who have gone mad in connection with the process of childbirth. However, his scope extends far beyond the specificity of his book's title.

It is a favourite saying among women of my type that if men could have babies, then abortion would be as readily available as light ale. Nevertheless, it is in just this physical difference that the whole opposition of the sexes lies. If men could have babies, they would cease to be men as such. They would become the 'other'. They would become magical objects of strangeness, veneration, obloquy, awe, disregard, and oppression, recipients of all the effects of the syndrome of holy terror. I wonder if it has occurred to Eric Rhode that, but for a chance division of cells while he was an undirected foetus, he, too, might have had babies. Certainly he seems to imply that parturition is not a function of the psychiatric profession itself: 'Psychiatrists talk about a mental unhinging round about the seventh month: is this true? We need more evidence, especially from the pregnant delegates themselves.' So there aren't any women psychiatrists around who can supply the necessary?

Don't think I don't realise that Rhode doesn't mean this. It is only the sloppy way he has phrased it. Yet the question need not have remained rhetorical. Even if he does not know any psychiatrists who have been pregnant, if that is possible, then his list of acknowledgements includes known mothers who could have told him. Semantic sloppiness usually goes hand in hand with mental sloppiness. For example, is it just some psychiatrists or all psychiatrists who claim that women become 'unhinged' – whatever that means – in late pregnancy? If it is the opinion of the entire profession, as he implies, how was it arrived at – by a postal ballot or by a show of hands? Rhode is not fond of footnotes, on the whole. Nor, I suspect, of empiricism. On the other hand, he has far more female intuition than I do.

It occurs to me, thinking about this wayward, infuriating book with its shining flashes of metaphysics, its linguistic imprecision, its mass of references (Blake, Kierkegaard, Shakespeare, Giorgione, Walter Benjamin, and more, and more) how deeply psychoanalysis is concerned with culture. Not only broadly, with culture as opposed to nature, but also with culture in its narrowest sense – that is, high-bourgeois culture. Easel painting, symphonic music, literature. As if Freud had condemned the entire profession to the taste of a cultivated Viennese at the turn of the century.

Rhode is prepared to advance pure cultural product as the sacred book of the Freudian calling. By page three, he is already talking about 'a Greek play often read as psychoanalytic holy writ, Sophocles's *Oedipus the King*'. But he does not think of *Oedipus the King* as a cultural product, with the specific conditions of the time and place of its composition mediating its universality. Nor does he treat the play as if Sophocles had dreamed it. Rather, he seems to think of the Oedipus family as though they were real people with real problems, an approach similar to that of the literary criticism of A. C. Bradley. He talked about the Hamlets the same way; they might even be patients, although he does not pause to entertain the Bradleian-style gloss I've always put on the play myself: that it only makes sense if Hamlet is really the son of Claudius and not of 'Hamlet's Father' at all.

One could argue that *Oedipus the King* is really, deep down, about the overthrow of Mother Right, that the play contains, transforms, subverts, patricises the ideology of those antique, matrilinear communities around the Mediterranean celebrated somewhat circumspectly in *The Golden*

Bough, and increasingly cherished by women of my type as we reach a certain age, in which kingship was attained by marriage with the queen and terminated in ritual combat with the inevitable defeat by a more nubile successor when the hapless consort's hairline started to recede or his ardour flag. This is the version Robert Graves gives in his *Greek Myths*, and though Graves's anthropology is just as shaky as J. G. Frazer's, I love the poetic truth at the kernel of it. Certainly the question 'Who is your father?' only becomes pressing when property is inherited through the male line.

Children, since they are polymorphously perverse by nature and, furthermore, do not usually possess property, can be much nicer, wiser, and kinder than culture. In an early essay, Melanie Klein tells about a small boy who, informed how babies are made, is told that he can do it himself when he grows up. ' "But then I would like to do it to Mama." "That can't be, Mama can't be your wife [*sic*] for she is the wife of your papa, and then papa would have no wife." "But we could both do it to her!" ' The heart, or hearts, of many-breasted Cybele would warm to that. (I wonder if Melanie Klein believed women became unhinged in the seventh month of pregnancy.)

I understand perfectly well that Sophocles's play is about aspects of human relations that transcend the immediate circumstances of its composition. Oedipal conflict pre-dates Sophocles. On the other hand, the play isn't the pure product of Sophocles's unconscious either – art is not the dream of culture. But Sophocles and Rhode are both very much concerned with crude biologism *vis-à-vis* the Oedipal situation. Indeed, Rhode is so interested in paternity that he introduces a woman concerned about her own paternity in the first paragraph of a book that is supposed to be about maternity.

'He was not your father.' In the terms of the real world in which we live and where we try to cherish our dear ones, Oedipus *does* escape his fate. He does not murder the man who saved him from death, nurtured him, gave him a bicycle, had his teeth straightened, paid for driving lessons, etc. Nor does he impregnate the woman who wiped his bum, taught him to sneeze, and catered to all the indignities of childhood that effectively de-eroticise the relationship between mothers and sprogs. Oedipus's genuine filial feelings are not outraged. His biological parents are perfect strangers. To emphasise the biological aspect of parenthood is to deny culture in a way that makes us less human. That dreadful question – how do we know whose child we are? – has dogged patriarchy since its inception, yet it is a profoundly absurd question. Put it another way: an American friend discovered her son had financed his grand tour of Europe by selling shots of his sperm to an AID agency. 'My grandchildren!' she cried and then fell silent, suddenly aware of the absurdity, to even think of them like that.

There never has been a way to know. Not truly know. Until just now, in the late twentieth century, when genetics can help us. And that is somewhat late in the day for the human race, which has been forced to rely for so long on its mother's word when women are so notoriously duplicitous. But the question has been so pressing it has even resolved itself in metaphysics, in the invention of an omnipotent but happily non-material father to whom everyone can lay claim as a last resort.

'Father' is always metaphysics: a social artefact, a learned mode. Rhode is prepared to concede this, using his favourite device of the rhetorical question. 'Who is my father, my mother, my brother, my sister? In a sense, the answer is simple – in regard to our mother, at least.' (In regard to all the others, it may be unbearably complex.) 'There is documentation; and the documentation is unlikely to have been faked.'

Unlikely, but not improbable. Raising the unwanted child of a sister, or a daughter, as one's own is not uncommon among working-class families, often causing a good deal of existential anxiety. On the other hand, although a mother can fake the documentation of her condition, she cannot fake the physical event of birth.

The fact of maternity has become a good deal more problematic in the late twentieth century than it has been hitherto, however. For example, am I the mother of the fertilised egg I carry when it does not originate in my own ovary? I'd say: yes, of course. But where does the child who eventually comes out of this egg stand in relation to such a mother in terms of the incest taboo? What degree of kinship would the Sphinx ascribe? If Jocasta had donated a fertilised egg to Merope, what then?

These are academic, even scholastic points. But they underpin a good deal of the discussion about mechanical intervention in the processes of maternity, where the culture of high-tech surgery manifests itself at its most 'unnatural' by taking on, and succeeding at, a job that Mother Nature shirked. And if this train of thought is followed to the end, we must conclude that 'mother' is also primarily a conceptual category. Just like 'father'.

Yes, but. If these basic, physically determined relationships are not 'natural', then what is? And why do women, having given birth – the most natural thing in the world, as they constantly tell you at the antenatal clinic – so frequently go mad, as if the violent collision of culture and nature which is the event of childbirth shatters us?

Rhode does not really attempt to deal with this question. Instead, he manages to invest biological motherhood with an almost occult quality. Discussing Oedipus: 'That he fails to see the old man he meets at the crossroads (and murders) as his father is not improbable; that he fails to sense that the bereft queen (whom he marries) might be his mother strains credulity.'

Why? Some young men find older women quite attractive, and though Jocasta might be a touch long in the tooth, she is still capable of giving Oedipus four healthy children, so she can't be that old. Freud says the feeling of *déjà vu* is always inspired by the memory of the body of the mother – *déjà vue*. Perhaps Rhode feels that Oedipus, whilst having intercourse with Jocasta, was bound to have recognised his intra-uterine address. Or is he trying to warn young men off older women because if you screw them you will go blind? Because there is always the chance she might be his mother?

Surely it should be the other way around, anyway. Augustus John used to pat the heads of all the children whom he met when he walked down the King's Road because he wasn't sure who was or wasn't his and didn't like to leave anybody out. Similarly, we should all treat all old men with respect, just in case. Seed is a random thing. There isn't the same margin for error with mothers, for whom it is a case of one egg, one birth, as a rule.

Meanwhile, Rhode is constructing an edifice of radiant surmise around that extraordinary clash of culture and nature, childbirth. He is in love with the gnomic. He is so pleased with that sentence about our eyes being pregnant with our mother's babies that he repeats it twice, subtly varying it. He is rich in ideas that are marvellous, in the sense of the word that the surrealists used – magical, breathtaking, spurting from a sumptuous vein of his own unconscious. 'Adam's semen, the *semina aeternitatis*, contains all mankind,' he says. He has been discussing seventeenth-century philosophers; it has induced a seventeenth-century turn of phrase – or indeed, of mind. And the entire book is self-consciously in the form of a series of meditations of a doctor-philosopher, a sort of *Religio Medici* for our times. He condenses images into a dense, suggestive mass; he adores infinity.

And then one stumbles over a piece of nonsense. 'What does a father see when he looks at the beauty of his wife?' he demands rhetorically. But fathers do not necessarily have wives, nor, if they do, are these wives necessarily beautiful. I think I can see how this sentence has come about; Rhode is so concerned with the rhetoric of it he has not engaged in a little practical criticism. I suspect it ought to read: 'What does a father see when he looks at the beauty of his child's mother?'

The sentence remains a grid of patriarchal definitions: the mother is presented solely in terms of the gaze and vanity of the father, to whose credit it redounds to boast a 'beautiful' mate, and of her biological relations to both subjects. But at least it is no longer nonsense and the little bit of gratuitous romanticism about beauty suggests Rhode is really a nice man, even if carried away by his own rhetoric when he contemplates the fact of our arrival on this earth in its blood, its banality, its glory.

In fact, its romanticism is one of the most gripping things about the book, which could, perhaps, be subtitled 'A Psychiatrist in Search of the Soul'. Rhode is fairly sure he can locate that slippery concept even in the womb. 'Reluctantly I have come to the view that our heritage at infancy is some articulated yet unconscious Platonic idea, a necessary substrate to our capacity for having experiences.' Hm.

But then we come to the mad women themselves, in their bereft abandonment. He quotes from Etienne-Dominique Esquirol, who wrote down stark descriptions of women in breakdown in the 1830s. 'A woman feeding her child was startled by a clap of thunder. Her milk dried up. She lost her reason.' This makes Rhode think of a painting by Giorgione, *The Tempest*. It makes me think of Munch, *The Scream*. When he arrives at the voices of the women in the puerperal breakdown unit themselves, it is scarcely tolerable. This is suffering beyond metaphor:

> She just screamed and screamed when I tried to feed her. I thought, it's my own child and she doesn't want me. In the end, I didn't want to get up in the morning. I felt so guilty. I didn't feel capable of looking after her. My neighbour fed her and I sat there and cried.

'When I'm washing her clothes and squeezing them out, I think I'm wringing her neck.' A woman describes a recurring dream: 'I remember closing my eyes – and I could see a knife sticking into a baby. I could see someone swinging the baby in our hall at home, swinging the baby round and round in the hall.'

Language crumbles under the weight of this pain. Mystification of this pain is a lie. This is what it is to be a mother and be mad.

London Review of Books, 1988

Food Fetishes

The New Vegetarians

My neighbourhood wholefood shop – according to *Alternative England and Wales*, the best one outside London – is a genre masterpiece, a scrubbed pine and whitewashed gem of non-specific rusticity. There are baskets of splendid cabbages of many different kinds, of leeks, of kale, of ruddy-cheeked apples blotched and wenned as if on purpose so you can see at a glance no chemical spray has been near them. They're bakers as well: trays of solid, dark hand-thrown-looking loaves, a slice of which, with nut butter, is a nourishing meal in itself; and all manner of cookies and flapjacks and goodies made with honey and dates and raisins, all the natural sweetenings – never a trace of the killer white sugar.

They don't stock sugar at all, in fact – not even that earthy, treaclish, fudge-coloured sugar that comes in chunks, which I'd have thought would have been All Right. But they started a few years ago as a regular macrobiotic food shop, which cut sugar right out. The first sign they were, in other ways, declining from their original rigour was when they started selling tomatoes, which, macrobiotically speaking, are nowhere. Poison.

They collect old paper bags and egg-boxes and recycle them: there's a sign reminding one: 'It takes 17 trees to make one ton of paper – SAVE OUR TREES.' There's a back room, with bins, where you can weigh out your own beans and grains for a penny or two less than they cost if the staff has had to pack them themselves. There are moong beans; buckwheat; aduki beans; whole yellow millet; pot barley; lentils; black-eye beans; brown rice (Californian brown rice and Italian brown rice); red kidney beans; chickpeas; haricot beans; and much else besides. Also nuts and dried fruit. And a roomful of jars of herbs. I am very glad of all these peasant comestibles. It is a pleasure to shop in such a place.

It's a positive aesthetic of unrefinement transformed into refinement. They don't for example, wash their carrots. They may chip off a few of the bigger chunks of mud but those brick-coloured roots retain a substantial coating of the earth that bore them, a different order of foodstuff

altogether from the scrubbed, supermarket carrot in its condom-like plastic sheath. Sometimes they come from a place which is called Paradise
Farm. These are *real* carrots.

Wholefood makes you a whole person. The vendors themselves have a
gnarled, hand-woven, organic look about them, in their smocks and col-
larless jumble-sale shirts and woolly caps. They come and go on a free-
form democratic basis; it's a collective; it seems to work very well. Good
vibes. There's been a cat, a marmalade cat with white paws, though I
haven't seen him around lately. I asked them what they fed the cat on and
they said: canned cat food. But canned cat food may be made from ecologically endangered whales . . . They gentled me out of the shop, containing the possibility of aggro in a massive, vegetable calm.

The nice girl in the smock says she herself has nothing against people
who eat meat though she personally doesn't like the taste and, furthermore, she didn't like what our society did to its animals, locking them
up, pumping them full of hormones and so on. This is a favourite vegetarian ploy. I don't mind meat-eating in the least. If you want to poison
your body with noxious substances, go right ahead, you have free
choice; I don't want to preach to anybody. Diet has become a matter of
morality. There's something of the air of a Non-conformist chapel about
this shop.

I remember staying at a friend's where we'd reason to believe another
guest was a vegetarian and my hostess wanted to roast a large joint of pork
and so we asked, would that be all right? The perfidious vegetable eater
said yes, fine; she wasn't in the least dogmatic and she'd join us in a slice
or two of meat, probably, since it was planned as a special meal. When the
roast was actually on the table, though, she rejected it and piled her plate
with boiled potatoes. She said how good the potatoes were, really good.
They always say that. 'It's really good,' 'This is really nice,' as if to restore
'really' from its neutral qualifying status to its original, non-debased sense,
meaning 'authentically' of 'veritably'. Accept no substitutes. This is the
real stuff. *Really* real.

Then, while the rest of us tucked into the pork in an embarrassed
fashion, she remarked conversationally that she'd only become a vegetarian after a visit to an abattoir. She described the pools of blood, the gush-
ing entrails, the mild, dazed eyes of the harmless beasts while the leg of
pork lay there on its platter looking, every minute, more and more like
dead pig. (That's another thing vegetarians like doing – chanting: 'Dead
pig! Dead pig!' when they see a sausage.)

It wasn't the slaughterhouse reminiscences themselves that offended
me. It was that she felt she'd got the moral right to try to ruin the meal for
the rest of us, and, probably, she thought she was doing us a good turn. If

she shoved in sufficient emotive detail, this Sunday dinner would prove a Damascus Road. When she got to the bit where the little newly dead lamb's hooves twitched uncontrollably, we'd push away our plates crying: 'Never again!' and eat brown rice ever after. What a display of moral superiority! It was delicious pork. I enjoyed it.

It seemed to me, furthermore, that she dwelt on these gory scenes with a good deal of masochistic self-indulgence: mightn't there be some degree of repressed violence in all this? And, anyway, according to the best counter-culture sources, vegetables are sentient, too. What pain the grain must feel to be stone-ground! Pythagoras wouldn't eat beans because he thought they might contain the spirits of his forefathers. Why should re-incarnation abjure the kingdom of the plants? What is the ontological status of the carnivorous plant in the terms of the New Vegetarianism?

The New Vegetarianism – an alternative growth industry, a dietary sign system indicating spiritual awareness, expanded consciousness and ecological concern – has very little to do with the old vegetarianism, which was part of a lifestyle embracing socialism, pacifism and shorts, a simple asceti-cism expressing a healthy contempt for the pleasures of the flesh. Since Woodstock, you've got to *enjoy* your vegetarianism, dammit. 'Why live like vegetarians on food you give to parrots,' queried the man in the song, before expressing his own preferences for boiled beef and carrots. Because eating is a religious experience that's why. 'Pure men like pure food which gives true health, balanced mentality, sustaining strength, life long enough to search – pure food which has delicate taste, soothes, nourishes and brings them joy – pure food that promotes the knowledge of God.'

This epigraph from the Bhagavad Gita adorns *Super Natural Cookery*, a typically camp title, written in the queasily flirtatious style which seems to afflict all Aquarian cookery books. 'Salads of fruits are not acid oranges, desiccated (and dead) coconut and dyed cherries, or an overcooked peach on cardboard cottage cheese. Aren't you glad!' This is curiously flabby lan-guage in which to approach a sacramental food experience; a tone of sneering patronage, I call it. Some of the other manuals aspire to a hearty joyousness, often decorated with drawings of loopy-looking girls in smocks running through fields, which is really embarrassing. I mean, *really*.

The New Vegetarianism claims that you can chew your way back to a lost harmony with nature: the way to the Kingdom of God lies directly down the gullet. 'Food was the core, the centre of the experience – in Boston, I found a large, loose-knit community of people from every con-ceivable background – whose common link with one another was primarily the whole, naturally grown, unadulterated foods they chewed each day, food that was satisfying, delicious, healing. Food that was *alive*.'

This is a young man describing his first macrobiotic experience in a big,

fat American magazine called *East West Journal* they sell in my health-food
store, along with the *I Ching*, various books about massage, *The Well Body
Book*, and cook books.

Food that was *alive*. Curious choice of words. At least the Paschal lamb
stayed dead. Now this young man's making himself a farm, committing
himself to the 'mighty, healing land', embracing the mythology of a
benign nature as if he'd never heard of the Lisbon Earthquake which
shook Voltaire's belief in that benignity.

The ritual consumption of sufficient quantities of wholefood will
restore man's lost harmony with nature. That's the theory, then. When
did we lose that elusive harmony with nature, though?

It was, apparently, a shortage of the eggs, nestlings and fruit that formed
its diet that sent the original ape down from the trees to forage in the
undergrowth. He promptly almost exterminated a number of species of
lizards and porcupines and other small mammals and reptiles, before he
learned to kill larger animals by throwing rocks at them.

It's not surprising that the Aquarians and the New Age Seekers and the
Natural Lifers turn against this unedifying scenario. *Seed*, the Forum of
Natural Living, a home-grown publication, contains a brisk refutation of
Darwin – claiming, among other things, that, since Darwin himself looked
like an ape, he back-projected an analogy, rather than constructed a
theory.

'Grain, the foundation of civilisation', suggests the *East West Journal*.
Hunter becomes herdsman, plant-gatherer becomes farmer when ice fields
retreat about 11,000 BC. At this point, then, we can identify a natural
lifestyle superseding the unenlightened and unnatural past, about which
the less said the better. This is the Golden Age, when, as the Harmony
Foods ad on the back of *Seed* suggests, you could see the universe in a grain
of wheat 'and heaven in a wholewheat loaf'.

The New Vegetarianism posits man as a microcosm. He has poisoned
his own system with meat, white sugar, refined flour, chemical additives.
He has poisoned his ecological system, which is an image of himself. The
self-sufficient farming unit, beloved dream of most freaks – with its goat,
its bean row and its beehive – is a model of an environment over which
he will be able to exert maximum control. The macrobiotic diets are control systems in themselves. Dietary self-policing will keep the demons of
psychic disorder away. Regenerated, man microcosm/macrocosm retains
absolute control of himself, of life.

After its busy day working in the fields, the communion of the elect
gathers round the scrubbed pine table and consumes casseroles of chick
peas and wheat grains, or lentil and sesame paste pasties, or mixed bean
stews, ritually muttering: 'It's really good, it's really nice.' Gibbon thought

that primitive Christians, with similar ritual, were the straw that broke the camel's back.

New Society, 1976

Saucerer's Apprentice

It's probably due to Elizabeth David that I can tell the difference in colour and taste between olive oil from Greece and olive oil from Provence, and certainly due to her that I should find the difference at all significant. For the advent of Elizabeth David and her Gospel of Good Food marked the end of the era in which middle-class, educated Englishwomen took a positive pride in an inability even to boil an egg.

Before Her, or so the folklore goes, Englishwomen used to put a leg of lamb in the oven and leave it until it looked done, then float a scant spoonful of dried mint in a cup of malt vinegar and call it 'mint sauce'. We'd put a cabbage under the tap to rinse the slugs out, then simmer it odorously for half an hour. That, plus old, halved boiled potatoes doused with Bisto gravy, was Sunday lunch, the culinary peak of the English week.

Prior to the Elizabeth Davidisation of the English cuisine, food was so much fuel, a necessary but by no means necessarily pleasant adjunct to basic physical being. Batteries recharged by a crude injection of calories, one then got on with the stern, rigorous business of living, in which the sensuous appreciation of food and drink had no place.

God said, let Elizabeth David be! And all was light.

Now, twenty-five or twenty-six years on, foreigners say you get some of the best food in the world in English private houses. Though a Turkish acquaintance of mine, glutted on dinner-party fare of pork chops in cream and lemon sauce and *poulet à l'estragon* and terribly ethnic Italian things with veal, once asked me why all this delicious food in private houses was so very different, both in quality and type, from the vile stuff served up in caffs and cafeterias. In Turkey, he said, the rich and the poor would generally eat the same kind of thing, only the rich tended to eat rather more meat.

All this newly lovingly prepared food is a curious, hybrid cuisine, based on a vividly eclectic compilation of elements from other cultures and derived from the printed word rather than, as in countries with a vigorous traditional cuisine, one's mother's example.

It is, in fact, the cuisine of a particular class, of the new class of emergent intelligentsia that began to surge upwards in the 1950s, whose own mothers had to make whatever kind of meals they could out of the poor pickings of the depression, and the marge and spam and dried eggs of the 1940s. Elizabeth Davidisation owes a lot to the Education Act, 1944, as indeed I do myself.

When I began cackhandedly to put together my own first *coqs au vin* and *ratatouilles* from Elizabeth David recipes, I'd never tasted so much as a cup of *café noir* in its *pays d'origine*. Indeed I still know several women who cook marvellous food out of Elizabeth David and who've never set foot outside the British Isles, though they talk with consummate authority about the regional specialities of Bresse and the Ardennes and tell you exactly what it is that the natives of Parma feed their pigs with that gives the local ham such a very fine flavour.

For Elizabeth David's books are full of the essence of place. The Good Life is given a local habitation and a name. Of Provence, she says: 'Here in London, it is an effort of will to believe in the existence of such a place at all. But now and again the vision of golden tiles on a round, southern roof or of some warm, stony, herb-scented hillside will rise out of my kitchen pots with the smell of a piece of orange peel scenting a beef stew' (*French Provincial Cooking*).

This is cookery as pure witchcraft, invocatory cooking in which both the process of cooking and the comestible produced transcend the here and now. But it is not only verbal magic; she gives you the formulas to do it yourself. You, too, can prepare a similar *daube* which will contain in its vinous aroma all the magic of Provence. And this without any of the pain, inconvenience and inevitable disillusionment of actual travel.

It is certainly a far, far better thing for both the body and the spirit to eat nice things rather than nasty things, but all the same there's an element of exquisite alienation about a cuisine that depends to such an extent on the imaginative reconstruction of Abroad, and on a service industry which imports esoteric vinegars, obscure cheeses and specialised cooking utensils to back up the magic. However vigorously we cook, we still can't take decent food for granted.

Even the more recent revival of interest in whatever native British cookery there is has been largely confined to digging things out of antique cookery books that refer to a prelapsarian cookery that existed before, as Elizabeth David herself says, 'everything green . . . disappeared straight into the packet, the dehydrating machine and the deep freeze' (*Spices, Salt and Aromatics in the English Kitchen*).

Most people reckon the Industrial Revolution dealt a death blow to whatever native British peasant cookery might have existed. But there's more to it than that. I've got a book called *The North Midland School Cookery Book*; it's dated 1897. One of the general hints it gives to cookery teachers is: 'Bear in mind that economy of *time, labour* and *fuel* are of as great importance to working people as economy of material. Cottage cooking should be *simplified* as much as possible.' Not even the greatest peasant cuisine in the world could have survived the austerity of these institutionalised domestic science lessons, where the poor were sternly disciplined into cooking what was deemed good for them and giving no thought to what they might have enjoyed.

It's a tribute to the resilience of our native *charcuterie* that you can still buy black pudding, faggots and pork pies. Though the Industrial Revolution must have given cooked meat shops a terrific boost, since women could pick up a ready-prepared meal from them on their way home from the looms.

But the most drastic simplification of a cuisine is procured by extreme poverty. When Elizabeth David says that: '*Faites simples*' should be the good cook's motto, she means, away with fussy, pretentious, *haute cuisine* hotel restaurant food! rather than the reduction of a diet to its basic elements. My father tells me that Scots peasant eating in the late nineteenth century had been simplified until it consisted mainly of a dish called 'potatoes and point'; that is, the potatoes on the plate in front of you and the spectacle of your mother's finger directed upwards towards the hook in the rafter from which a side of bacon did not hang. Nothing destroys the palate like poverty; food as a sensuous experience is not the same thing as food which serves merely to alleviate hunger.

The Elizabeth Davidisation process began in the early 1950s, after we'd spent more than ten years eating a standardised, government-regulated, plain but adequate diet that gave a statistically significant proportion of the British public enough of the nutritionally correct things to eat for the first time, possibly, in the history of these islands, but left no margin whatsoever for the kind of meals of which dreams are made – though many opportunities for dreaming about food. Elizabeth David's first piece in print was called: 'Rice again'. She arrived at the end of the age of austerity, yet at a time when we were all sufficiently well fed to want a little more than bread alone.

The first edition of *French Country Cooking* was published with food rationing still in full force, in 1951 and contained hints for substitutions for cream, eggs, meat stock, bacon and so on; yet everything about the book heralds the rebirth of plenty. She is ready and waiting to tip over us a veritable cornucopia of good things – her books are books about the nature of food, as much as recipe books, books for a generation that had forgotten what food was like. And had also forgotten what Abroad was like.

Not only had we been eating the sort of food that would have gladdened the hearts of the devisers of *The North Midland School Cookery Book* for years; we'd been cut off from *la belle France* and the sweet south and all the mythological scenery of Europe, first, by the war, then by the currency restrictions. The early Penguin editions of *French Country Cooking* are decorated with lovely etchings by John Minton showing scenes of Gallic bucolic rusticity.

Fat, happy peasants cheerfully toast one another with brimming glasses; at their feet lies a gigantic ham and an equally gigantic artichoke. Everywhere about them, comestibles are heaped with the lavishness of the bacchanale. The cover is a picture of a kitchen straight out of one of Colette's rustic idylls; there's a dresser piled with jelly moulds, a table covered with *bain-maries*, casseroles and peppermills, a stick-backed chair, the glimpse of an old-fashioned range in the corner.

The current edition has a colour photograph on the cover, though Minton's decorations remain inside, giving the book a certain period charm. This cover shows a couple of huge bunches of garlic, some crates of rugged tomatoes and, slightly out of focus, a pair of butch, aggressive, gritty-looking French extras bustling about a marketplace. The difference between the two covers suggests, firstly, how greatly travel on the continent has increased in the last twenty years; nowadays, everybody knows that kitchens such as Minton drew may only be found in the Provençal *mas* and Dordogne farmhouses lovingly reconstructed by British expatriates. It also indicates the extent to which the first edition of the book was an object of contemplataion, of fantasy; and how the fantasy has become real.

Over the twenty-five or twenty-six years it's been in print *French Country Cooking* has accomplished the change from a dream guide to food as an aspect of the Good Life to a handbook of actual techniques for reconstructing the elements of the Good Life in your own kitchen. The fantasy of the age of austerity has become actualised on the scrubbed pine work surfaces of the age of affluence. And we are all cooks now.

Après Elizabeth David *le deluge*.

New Society, 1976

Jessica Kuper (ed.): The Anthropologist's Cookbook

First, catch your puffin. Anthony Jackson reports from the Faroes that puffins 'are captured in flight by a triangular net (*fleyg*) at the end of a ten-foot pole (*fleygastong*)'; after which feat it is rather a disappointment to find they are then roasted just like any old chicken. But a typically bizarre Faroese addition is the rhubarb jam with which they are served.

This is a delicious and erudite cookery book, culled from the culinary experiences of anthropologists in the more remote corners of the world. 'Food is not feed,' says Mary Douglas in her preface; and this is far more than a kitchen manual. It is a universal compendium of the methodology of the cuisine. Here, you may learn how to construct the earth ovens in which certain Pacific islanders roast dogs; that wombat meat is white when cooked; that human flesh is almost totally lacking in vitamin B and hence procures beri-beri amongst its addicts. And much else, besides; it is also a universal guide to the mores of the table.

For the people of Morocco, food is far more than mere sustenance; it is the expression of a complex ethico-religious system, incorporating sensual delight and the pleasures of social interaction in a series of sophisticated recipes and lavish meals. But Claude Lévi-Strauss does not care to dignify with the word 'recipe' any of the coarse cookery of the Amazonian tribes with which he worked.

And the Siriono of Bolivia do not regard eating as an aspect of socialisation at all. They are addicted to lonely midnight snacking, to avoid having to share whatever is going with anybody else. For them, eating is a solitary vice and, as one might expect, they have no table manners, just gracelessly shovel it all down as fast as they can, eyes well down, like bingo players. While the Trumai Indians of Brazil hedge the staples of their diet, such as fish-paste, with so many elaborate taboos it is a wonder any of them ever contrive to tuck into a square meal at all.

Rural Panamanians see elaborate sexual metaphors in food; and the analogy between food and sex, however unconscious, reaches a fine expression in the habits of the Joraie of Indonesia. They reluctantly interrupt a day filled with the voluptuous nibbling of enticing little bits and pieces for the hasty consumption of two square meals, necessary nourishment, 'taken, rather quickly – like the sexual act of a married couple', says Jacques Dournes. This chore over, they relax and start nibbling again, as if addicted to foreplay at the expense of intercourse.

The Thai and Indochinese recipes look even more voluptuous than the Moroccan and Jamaican ones; as for the cuisine of the Australian and South American aborigines, one could say of it what some Chinese said to me about English food: 'No doubt it suits the native sensibility very well.'

Jessica Kuper concludes her collection with a contribution from Lévi-Strauss at his most magisterial: 'It is not a little surprising, but extremely significant, to find certain genial philosophers of the mid-nineteenth century showing the same awareness of the contrast between knowledge and inspiration, serenity and violence, moderation and excess, symbolised in like fashion by the opposition between the boiled and the roast.'

She zips about in space and time from the medieval English kitchen to the mountains of Laos; and adds a list of shops where unusual ingredients may be bought. Any profits will go to the Royal Anthropological Institute. I can't think of a better present for greedy people with inquiring minds.

New Society, 1977

Barbara Tims (ed.): Food in Vogue

There's a smashing Erté on the cover of this luscious production, showing a woman dressed up as a carrot, though its point is by no means that Woman is only another edible, and an everyday, common or garden item of consumption, at that. Elsewhere, here, you can find her companions: an Erté onion woman, a celery woman, and a tomato woman, designs for George White's *Scandals* (New York, 1926). These costumes transform the most commonplace comestibles into something rich and strange via the medium of beautiful women.

To transform women themselves into food was evidently a favourite twenties' trick in stylish circles. There's an account of the Santa Claus Ball at the Kit-Kat:

The characters will present a typical Christmas dinner. Lady Grant will be Plum Pudding, Mrs Redmond McGrath Red Wine, Lady Dunn White Wine, Lady Ashley, Lady Jean Dalrymple, Dorothy Bethell, Lady Scarsdale are all parts of the menu; while Lady Patricia Douglas is Mince Pie and Mrs McCorquodale, who is organising the pageant, is to be Champagne.

So, although all the recipes in this something more than cookery book are perfectly viable and many are splendid, one can't escape the feeling that *Food in Vogue* is not purely food. Not food as fuel, pure and simple, but food as an aspect of style.

At the front of the book is a photograph of a girl with an oyster shell in one hand, a fork in the other, and, wedged – to her unsurprise – firmly between her teeth, a pearl, presumably out of the oyster. It's a striking image but not so much a concrete sign as a diffuse suggestion of a total environment of high living.

One of the interesting things about the sixty-year trek through *Vogue* back-number cookery columns is the point at which the women to whom those columns were addressed actually began to cook themselves, instead of employing other people to do it for them.

The early decades boast occasional references to bachelor girls frying themselves bacon sandwiches, but not half so many references as there are to cooks, cocktail bars, and dinners in restaurants, itself a helpless response to the post-First World War shortage of staff.

In the 1930s, when *Vogue* prose reached an apotheosis of tinkling breathlessness, cookery for the upper classes was introduced as a witty eccentricity:

> Some of the most unlikely people are cooking. The Hon. Mrs Reginald Fellowes has had a perfect little kitchen built next to her sitting-room and, if you think this is an idle gesture, consult some gourmet who has exclaimed his way through a dinner prepared by her own white hands.

But the contemporary tomato woman regards cooking as a stylish accomplishment and may look herself up in the index and find no less than ten ways to cook herself, including one recipe for tomato in horseradish-flavoured cream that is almost as stylish as a pheasant with gin and juniper from the 1930s, as elegant in its excess as Cole Porter. But tomatoes with horseradish, from the most recent pages of the magazine, is the sort of simple little thing that somebody who cooks every day might well do for best; pheasants with gin and juniper is the sort of one-off job that somebody who hardly ever cooks at all can spend a whole day of therapeutic endeavour on – especially when there is somebody to clear up the dirty dishes for her.

A recurring theme throughout the cookery columns is a curiously magical linking of recipes with famous names. As if something of the mana of ladies or gentlemen of wealth, birth, and distinction may be absorbed via the ingestion of dishes, or entire menus, synonymous with them. In the 1960s, Loelia, Duchess of Westminster, suggests *Homard frappé*, White Devil (which turns out to be just devilled chicken, no skull beneath the skin), and apples in rum for a 'magic' Sunday dinner. Back in the 1930s, Lady Portalington and Lady Juliet Duff and Mrs Syrie Maugham contributed recipes that, though perfectly sound, are so amazingly boring – Scotch collops, apple tart, pancakes with haddock – it doesn't seem surprising that English upper-class tables had such a bad reputation, nor that *Vogue* made sporadic forays into continental high life for fresh fare, sometimes with disappointing results. The Comtesse Mercati had a chocolate cake that no one could duplicate without the recipe – 'and she can't remember the recipe'. Tough.

With the arrival of Elizabeth David and Robert Carrier in the 1950s and 1960s, the cult of the personality tended to centre itself round the cook as magus, rather than the inspired amateur as cook. Miss David's magistral hauteur and Carrier's transatlantic exuberance and professionalism – 'During this new series of articles on food, drink and entertaining, I am going to dispel the maze of myths that surround *haute cuisine* – helped make cooking well a classy thing to do. And if the book ends with a flourish on Pamela Harlech's column titled, 'Seventies People and their Recipes' (Mrs Rupert Hambro's ginger soufflé, Anthony West's cucumber soup, Lady Elizabeth von Hofmannsthal's cabbage in cream) the upper classes clearly – by their fruits shall ye know them – spend a bit more time with the pots and pans than they did when top-flight cooks were ten a penny. This food has its own mana. It is magic because it is Good.

There is also, hereabouts, Arabella Boxer's recipe for wild green salad (sorrel, dandelion, watercress, and so on) which suggests that even after the collapse of absolutely everything, those of us dedicated to gracious living will still attack the weeds and roots and nuts and berries that may well form a staple diet with a bit of flair and verve. Cooking as dandyism.

Indeed, the most touching thing about these resurrected pages of early *Vogue*, their menus, their parties, their restaurants, their famous hostesses, and their table settings, is an absolute concentration on the frivolous that can, on occasion, aspire to the heroic. A wartime caption: 'On leave, he likes to dine against the sophisticated decor of Popote du Ritz. You in his favourite black, his favourite lace, feminine to the last flounce.' That'll show Hitler what we're made of.

And from the 1930s, the caption to a charming, minimal drawing by Cecil Beaton: 'Here you see a picnic in progress. The Marchioness of Queensberry and Miss Carley Robinson enjoy China tea out of a sprigged teapot and sit gossiping and watching the hovering butterflies.' Style as an end in itself; the exquisiteness, the rightness of that China tea, that a sprigged teapot – so much glamour would vanish had it been a brown earthenware one with a woolly teacosy. And some of the heartless innocence of style, as well, of a leisured class that took its leisure as a right and not as a privilege.

As an informal history of the changing diet and social mores of the English upper-middle and aspiring upper-middle classes, *Food in Vogue* does very well, and even better if read as the concretisation of a consensus wish-fulfilment fantasy about the nature of stylish living. 'How One Lives from Day to Day . . . Dinner hour at the Savoy; Surveying the kitchens at the Ivy; Supper at Rules; the Jardin des Gourmets has a delightful atmosphere of French rusticity; Entering the Spanish Grill at the Dorchester.' How one lived from day to day in the 1930s, until, in December 1939: 'In

Paris – Now – They shelter in the Ritz super-cellars in satin or wool pyjamas, hooded coats, warmly, gaily lined (Molyneux and Piguet) . . .' (Students of linguistics will be interested to note the usage, 'one', omnipresent in *Vogue* copy of the 1920s and 1930s and now confined, almost exclusively, to the Royal Family.) It is the stuff of modern-day fairytale.

This lavishly illustrated book is also an informal history of English illustration over the last sixty years, flowering in the 1940s, that heyday of English drawing; Keith Vaughan, John Minton, Edward Ardizzone, that beautiful agonised black and white with nostalgia already implicit in every line. Then the 1960s and the rise of the photographer, Penn, Lester, Bookbinder, of my, oh my. And with the 1970s, Tess Traeger's photographs that look exactly like oil paintings, Victorian oil paintings, at that; actual icons of nostalgia, images of a beautiful never-never land of fruit and beautiful children and flowers. This is the land where the tomato woman would like to live.

New Society, 1977

Elizabeth David: English Bread and Yeast Cookery

My corner shop sells wrapped, sliced white loaves that, at a pinch, could poultice a wound. It also, sometimes, stocks twisted, unsliced bread with sesame seeds on top emanating from a Cypriot concern on the other side of London which can fool the unwary into thinking it is somehow a more authentic product than the Mother's Pride stuff, though authentic in *what* way I can't say. The corner shop also sells plastic bags of pitta, which is fine, though it looks a bit odd filled with butter and marmalade at breakfast. (Kebabs à l'anglaise.)

Five minutes' walk away is one of those hot-bread outlets that sell poultices fresh from the oven. Seven minutes' walk away, virtually side by side, two shops stocking different varieties of those wholemeal breads that look hand-thrown, like studio pottery, and are fine if you have all your teeth. But, if not, then not. Perhaps the rise and rise of the poultice or factory-made loaf, which may easily be mumbled to a pap between gums, reflects the sorry state of the nation's dental health.

It is usually interpreted, however, as the result of a lack of moral fibre, as if moral fibre is somehow related to roughage in the diet. The British, the real bread lobby implies, are rapidly going, if they have not already gone, all soft, bland, and flabby, just like their staple food. The iron grip of the multinationals has squeezed all the goodness out of British bread, via the machinations of the giant miller-bakers, Allied Bakeries, Rank Hovis McDougall *et al.*, and the only way to fight back is to lob a homemade stone-ground wholemeal cob at them. (Which, in some cases, would indeed be a lethal missile.)

The real bread lobby has, of course, right, virtue, and healthy bowel movements on its side. On the whole, it is free from that paranoid nostalgia that afflicted Anthony Burgess, when he − I think it was he − laid squarely at the feet of the Welfare State the blame for the fact that Heinz baked beans no longer taste as tangy as they did when he was a boy.

The Welfare State it is, according to the formula of reactionary food fetishism, that has made us all soft and bland and flabby and that is why we dig into Mother's Pride and Wonderloaf and Sunblest with such enthusiasm. Behind this is an ill-concealed and ugly plot − not so much to swell the coffers of the hippy wholefood entrepreneurs who concoct those loaves that either go straight through you or else stay with you, heavily on the chest, for days, nay, weeks, as to get women back where they belong. Up to their elbows in bread dough, engaged in that most arduous and everlasting of domestic chores, giving the family good, hearty, home-baked bread.

Oddly enough, in all of Europe, the British housewife is, historically, the only one of all who found herself burdened with this back-breaking and infinitely boring task, for watching bread dough rise is the next best thing to watching paint dry, activity reminiscent of some of those recorded in early Warhol movies. The average black-clad Italian, French, or Greek mama, if asked to make bread, has always tossed her head with a haughty sneer. What else are bakers for? For herself, she's got better things to do − the meat sauce, the *coq au vin*, the dolmas, and so on. Of course, it's always been more difficult, given British cuisine, for our housewives to get away with that excuse. Since we've got to have something to shine at, it turned out to be baked goods, didn't it?

And, oh God, in my misspent youth as a housewife, I, too, used to bake bread, in those hectic and desolating days just prior to the women's movement, when middle-class women were supposed to be wonderful wives and mothers, gracious hostesses *à la* Miriam Stoppard, and do it all *beautifully*. I used to feel so womanly when I was baking my filthy bread. A positive ecstasy of false consciousness. I probably dealt the death blow to some local baker with a wood-fired brick-oven when I took away my custom, for in those days, there were old-fashioned bakers aplenty, no doubt then

closing down on all sides under the twin onslaughts of the newly fashionable anorexia nervosa and all that compulsive home breadmaking.

However, even here, twenty years later, in south London, there are a
couple of perfectly decent old-fashioned bakers within easy walking distance (both stocking that indescribable speciality, bread pudding). Even if
southern England *is* heavily saturated with chain bakeries, good bakers are
thick on the ground from Lincolnshire on to the north and Scottish bakers
are wonderful. Obviously, lots of people just pick up a Wonderloaf at the
corner shop or supermarket, perhaps even habitually: but I wonder
whether they don't make a distinction between bread for sandwiches and
bread for, as it were, eating. Certainly, sliced white comes into its own for
the former use – basically, a wrapping for a sweet or savoury filling, akin
to edible greaseproof paper.

Along with the notion that British factory-made bread is bad bread
comes the one that all artisan-made bread is *good* bread. Although the
recipe books of Tuscany are suspiciously full of handy hints for dealing
with large quantities of stale bread, it is still impossible to resist a sigh of
satisfaction when the waiter weighs down the paper tablecloth with the
basket of rough-hewn bread chunks in the somnolent, shadowless heat of
some Florentine lunch time . . . though, since the saltless, fatless bread of
the region will, by then, have been out of the oven for some hours, it is
now only good for carving into putti. Or dipping into the squat tumbler
you have just filled with red wine from a straw-wrapped (or possibly,
plastic-coated) bottle. And that's it! Pow! It hits you. The atavistic glamour of the continental holiday; the timeless, mythic resonance of the bread
and the wine . . . for what good is a continental holiday unless it is jam-
packed with resonances?

It always puzzles me that Christianity got off the ground, even to the
limited extent that it did, in those parts of the globe where its central
metaphor – the bread and the wine – were incomprehensible. A sacramental meal of shared rice and saké, the nearest Chinese equivalents to the
Mediterranean staples, suggests a very anaemic Christ indeed.

Wheat bread, in fact, is not only a specifically European staff of life, but
even a specifically Mediterranean one. Northern Europe tends towards
black, rye bread and wheat bread took a long time to penetrate to the
northernmost parts of even our own island, where all bakers still stock the
traditional crisp, flat, unleavened oat cake in large quantities. (When the
Scots first clapped eyes on grain, they knew immediately what to do with
it; they distilled it. No wonder the Scots proved averse to the doctrine of
transubstantiation. A deity with flesh of oat cakes and blood composed of
volatile spirit makes the mind reel.)

Nevertheless, part of the fuss we make when we think our bread – our

BREAD – has been tampered with must, surely, relate to the sacramental quality inherent in bread in our culture. Our bread, our daily bread, has been profaned with noxious additives. Although that bread is certainly no longer our 'daily bread' within the strict meaning of the prayer. In the sixteenth century, 'bread' meant 'food' just as 'rice' (*gohan*) in Japanese still means dinner. For most of us, in those days, food *was* bread – bread with, perhaps, a condiment of cheese, onion, or bacon grease to go with it, and maybe a chickweed salad on high days and holidays.

The menus of the Lambeth poor researched before the First World War by Maud Pember Reeves for her book, *Round About a Pound a Week*, feature bread heavily at all three daily meals. Two of those meals, breakfast and supper, are composed exclusively of bread plus a smear of margarine, jam, or sweetened condensed milk. The stunted, sickly, patently under-nourished, and often dying children described by Pember Reeves do not appear to have thrived particularly well on such a diet.

One should not, of course, ascribe to magic doses of Wonderloaf and Mother's Pride the almost intolerable health, strength, and vitality of the children of Lambeth at this present time. How these kids keep it up on salt 'n' vinegar flavoured crisps, orange crush, and fish fingers indeed perplexes me. One can only conclude that a varied diet of junk food is, in the final analysis, considerably more nutritious than a diet of not very much food at all and most of it starch.

In a culinary sense, though not, I suspect, in an emotional one, bread has been secularised in postwar Britain. It has become a food, like any other, no longer to be taken in large quantities. There are other things to eat, even other carbohydrate foods – rice, pasta. Yams. One of the things Pember Reeves's housewives liked about bread was its portability – a child did not have to sit down to eat a hunch of bread and marge and that was convenient if you did not have sufficient chairs, or even a table, on or at which to sit. Most families, nowadays, do manage occasional communal sit-down meals. Most homes, today, boast knives and forks. We no longer live by bread alone.

When one does not live by bread alone on a varied and interesting diet, bread changes its function while retaining its symbolism. Ceasing to be the staff of life but ever redolent with its odour of sanctity – an odour the hot bread-poultice shops have exploited commercially to the hilt – bread turns into a mere accessory, the decorative margin to a meal, or else into the material for a small but inessential meal, that very 'afternoon tea' beloved of the English upper classes, with which they used to stuff their faces in that desert of oral gratification between their vast lunches and their gargantuan dinners.

It is no surprise, therefore, to find that Elizabeth David's vast and highly lauded tome, *English Bread and Yeast Cookery*, is jammed full of tea-time recipes – buns, tea cakes, fruit breads and so on. For David, the high priestess of postwar English cookery, she who single-handed put an olive-wood chopping block into every aspiring home, to turn her attention to currant buns means that something is up.

English Bread and Yeast Cookery is a *vade mecum* to the art of home baking. And I use the word, 'art', rather than 'craft', advisedly, since her recipes are intended for the artist baker in her studio kitchen rather than the artisan in the common workshop.

David, ever apt with the up-market quotation, certainly knows how to add that final touch of arty glamour to the business! She whisks away the last surviving touch of dirndl skirt and Fabian Society from the concept of the home-baked loaf when she quotes a description of Virginia Woolf kneading away like nobody's business.

Virginia Woolf? Yes. Although otherwise an indifferent cook, Virginia could certainly knock you up a lovely cottage loaf. You bet. This strikes me as just the sort of pretentiously frivolous and dilettantish thing a Bloomsbury *would* be good at – knowing how to do one, just one, fatuously complicated kitchen thing and doing that one thing well enough to put the cook's nose out of joint. 'I will come into the kitchen, Louie,' she said to this young employee of hers, 'and show you how to do it.'

This attitude of the dedicated hobbyist reveals the essential marginality of the activity. David manages to turn the honourable craft of the baker into a nice accomplishment for refined ladies. Bread is put in its place; it is a special kind of art-object.

Here is, furthermore, the bitter-sweet bread of nostalgia, summoning up a bygone golden age of golden loaves, before Garfield Weston, of Allied Bakeries, the demon king in the real-bread scenario started buying up British bakeries in the 1950s and smirching with his filthy profane Canadian hands the grand old English loaf.

Although her book is full of quotations – Thomas Traherne, Keats, Chaucer – she does, however, let the heavy freight of symbolic significance borne by bread in our culture severely alone except, oddly enough, for a seventeenth-century French recipe for consecrated bread, This, she claims, sounds like brioche, which suggests it might have been used for a rather Firbankian mass. What *can* they have put in the chalice?

It is appropriate she leaves religion alone since *English Bread and Yeast Cookery* is already proving to be something like the holy book of the cult of the True Loaf, in which the metaphoric halo surrounding bread is turned back on itself, the loaf becomes not foodstuff nor symbol but fetish.

New Society, 1982

An Omelette and a Glass of Wine and Other Dishes

'Be modern – worship food,' exhorts the cover of *The Official Foodie Handbook*. One of the ironies resulting from the North/South dichotomy of our planet is the appearance of this odd little book, a *vade mecum* to a widespread and unashamed cult of conspicuous gluttony in the advanced industrialised countries, at just the time when Ethiopia is struck by a widely publicised famine, and the rest of Africa is suffering a less widely publicised one. Not Africa alone, of course, is chronically hungry all the time and acutely hungry some of the time: at a conservative estimate, 800 million people in the world live in constant fear of starvation. Under the circumstances, it might indeed make good twentieth-century sense to worship food, but punters of 'foodism' (as Ann Barr and Paul Levy jokily dub this phenomenon) are evidently not about to drop to their knees because they are starving.

'Foodies', according to Barr and Levy, are 'children of the consumer boom' who consider 'food to be an art, on a level with painting or drama'. It is the 'art' bit that takes their oral fetishism out of the moral scenario in which there is an implicit reprimand to greed in the constantly televised spectacle of the gaunt peasants who have trudged miles across drought-devastated terrain to score their scant half-crust. ('That bread alone was worth the journey,' they probably remark, just as Elizabeth David says of a trip to an out-of-the-way eatery in France.) Art has a morality of its own, and the aesthetics of cooking and eating aspire, in 'foodism', towards the heights of food-for-food's sake. Therefore the Third World can go suck its fist.

The Official Foodie Handbook is in the same format as, and it comes from the same firm that brought out, *The Official Sloane Ranger Handbook*. That is to say, it is 'a *Harpers & Queen* Publication', which means it springs from the loins of the magazine that most consistently monitors the lifestyle of new British affluence. These 'official handbooks' are interesting as a genre. The idea has been taken up with enthusiasm by *Harpers & Queen*, but the original appears to be *The Official Preppy Handbook*, published in the USA in the early days of the first Reagan presidency. This slim volume was a lighthearted checklist of the attributes of the North American upper middle class, so lighthearted it gave the impression it did not have a heart at all. The entire tone was most carefully judged: a mixture of contempt for and condescension towards the objects of its scrutiny, a tone which contrived to reassure the socially aspiring that emulation of their betters was a game that might legitimately be played hard just *because* it could not be taken seriously, so that snobbery involved no moral compromise.

The book was an ill-disguised celebration of the snobbery it affected to mock and, under its thinly ironic surface, was nothing more nor less than an etiquette manual for a class newly emergent under Reaganomics. It instructed the *nouveaux riches* in the habits and manners of the *vieux riches* so that they could pass undetected amongst them. It sold like hot cakes.

The British version duly appeared on the stands a year or so later, tailored to the only slightly different demands of a youth newly gilded by Thatcherism. *The Official Foodie Handbook* mentions two fresh additions to the genre in the USA: *The Yuppie Handbook* ('the state-of-the-art manual for Young Urban Professionals') and *The Official Young Aspiring Professionals Fast-Track Handbook*. There seems to be no precise equivalent for the Young Aspiring Professional in Thatcher's Britain: the Tory Trade Unionist (or TUTU) might fill the bill in some ways, but not in others. The Yuppie is, presumably, driven by an ambition he or she now has the confidence to reveal nakedly, an ambition to go *one better* than the *vieux riches*. In Britain, it is never possible to go one better than the *vieux riches*, who always own everything anyway. *Harpers & Queen*, the self-appointed arbiter of these matters this side of the herring-pond, identifies the strivers peremptorily as Noovos, or Noovs. There is something a touch Yellowplush Papers about all this, but there you go. It would seem that *The Official Foodie Handbook* is an attempt to exploit the nearest British equivalent to the Yuppie market, for, according to the arbiters, food is a cornerstone of this hysterical new snobbery.

Very special economic circumstances, reminiscent of those of the decline of the Roman Empire and also of the heyday of Edwardian England as described by Jack London in *People of the Abyss*, establish gluttony as the mark of a class on the rise. *The Official Foodie Handbook* notes: 'It takes several things to support a Foodie culture: high-class shops, fast transport bringing fresh produce from the land, enlightened well-paid eater-outers who will support the whole expensive edifice, lower-paid workers to make the food. Suddenly they are all present.'

Piggery triumphant has invaded even the pages of the *Guardian*, hitherto synonymous with non-comformist sobriety. Instead of its previous modest column of recipes and restaurant reviews, the paper now boasts an entire page devoted to food and wine once a week: more space than it gives to movies, as much as it customarily gives to books. Piggery has spawned a glossy bi-monthly, *A la Carte*, a gastronomic *Penthouse* devoted to glamour photography, the subject of which is not the female body imaged as if it were good enough to eat, but food photographed according to the conventions of the pin-up. (Barr and Levy, ever quick with a quip, dub this kind of thing 'gastro-porn'.) The colour plates are of awesome voluptuousness. Oh, that coconut kirsch roulade in the first issue! If, as Lévi-Strauss once opined, 'to eat is to fuck', then that coconut kirsch roulade is just asking for it. Even if the *true* foodie knows there is something not quite . . . about a coconut kirsch roulade as a concept. It is just a bit . . . just a bit *Streatham*. Its vowels are subtly wrong. It is probably related to a Black Forest gâteau.

A la Carte is an over-eager social climber and is bound to give the game away. 'Do you know the difference between a good Brie and a bad one? One made in a factory or on a farm? If *you* don't, your guests might.' Then you will be universally shunned and nobody will attend your dinner parties ever again. This mincing and finicking obsession with food opens up whole new areas of potential social shame. No wonder the British find it irresistible. Indeed, in Britain an enlightened interest in food has always been the mark of the kind of person who uses turns of phrase such as 'an enlightened interest in food'. If a certain kind of upper-class British cookery represents the staff's revenge upon its masters, an enthusiasm for the table, the grape, and the stove itself is a characteristic of the deviant subsection of the British bourgeoisie that has always gone in for the arts with the diligent enthusiasm of (as they would put it) 'the amateur in the true sense of the word'. This class is more than adequately represented by Mrs Elizabeth David.

In *An Omelette and a Glass of Wine*, a collection of her journalism dating back to the 1950s, there is an article describing the serendipitous nature of provisioning in London just after the war. Mrs David remembers how 'one of my sisters turned up from Vienna with a hare which she claimed had been caught by hand outside the state Opera House'. A whole world is contained within that sentence, which could be the first line of a certain kind of novel and sums up an entire way of life. It is no surprise to discover that Mrs David admires the novels of Sybille Bedford, nor that she was a friend of Norman Douglas. It *is* a little surprising that she has never turned her acclaimed prose style to fiction, but has always restricted herself to culinary matters, if in the widest sense, taking aboard aspects of history, geography, and literature. Her books, like her journalism, are larded with quotations, from recherché antique cookery books to Virginia Woolf, Montaigne, Walter Scott. Her approach is not in the least like the gastronomic dandyism of the 'food-for-food's sake' crowd; she is holistic about it. She is obviously a truly civilised person and, for her, knowing how to eat and to prepare good food is not an end in itself, but as much a part of civilisation as is the sensuous appreciation of poetry, art, or music. In the value system of the person who is 'civilised' in this way, the word carries the same connotation as 'moral' does in the value system of Dr F. R. Leavis.

Mrs David's journalism consists of discursive meditations upon food and foreign parts, but, in the course of *An Omelette and a Glass of Wine*, one learns a discreet but enticing amount about her private life, enough to appreciate that her deftness with the pans is not a sign of domesticity but of worldliness. She is obviously the kind of woman before whom waiters grovel when she arrives alone at a restaurant. One imagines her to be one of those tall, cool, elegant blondes who make foreigners come over all funny, and it is plain that she is the kind of Englishwoman who, like the heroines of Nancy Mitford, only fully come to life Abroad. Her recipes are meticulous, authentic, and reliable, and have formed the basic repertoire not only of a thousand British late twentieth-century dinner parties but also of a goodly number of restaurants up and down these islands. She has been the conduit whereby French provincial cooking and French country cooking, of a kind which in France is being replaced by pizzas and hamburgers, may be raptly savoured in rural England.

The eponymous 'Chez Panisse' of the *Chez Panisse Menu Cookbook* is directly inspired by Mrs David, who now spans the globe. The cook-proprietor of 'Chez Panisse', Alice Waters, says in her Introduction: 'I bought Elizabeth David's *French Country Cooking* and I cooked everything in it, from beginning to end. I admired her aesthetics of food and wanted a restaurant that had the same feeling as the pictures on the covers of her books.' It seems an unusual desire, to create a restaurant that looks like a book jacket, and most of the cooks from whom Mrs David originally acquired her recipes would think it even more unusual to learn to cook from a book instead of from Mum. But all this must spring naturally from the kind of second-order experience that lies behind the cult of food. Alice Waters is a girl from New Jersey who earned her culinary stripes by resolutely cooking her way through a compendium of French recipes assembled by an Englishwoman, using ingredients from northern California and serving them up to the me-generation in a restaurant named after an old movie. The result is a Franco-Californian cuisine of almost ludicrous refinement, in which the simplest item is turned into an object of mystification. A ripe melon, for example, is sought for as if it were a piece of the True Cross. Ms Waters applauds herself on serving one. 'Anyone could have chosen a perfect melon, but unfortunately most people don't take the time or make an effort to choose carefully and understand what that potentially sublime fruit should be.' She talks as if selecting a melon were an existential choice of a kind to leave Jean-Paul Sartre stumped.

Behind Ms Waters's wincingly exquisite cuisine lies some post-hippy Platonism to do with the real and the phoney. 'Depersonalised, assembly-line fast food may be "convenient" and "time-saving" but it deprives the senses and denies true nourishment,' she opines. Like anorexia nervosa, the neurotic condition in which young girls voluntarily starve themselves to death, the concept of 'true nourishment' can exist only in a society where hunger happens to other people. Ms Waters has clearly lost her marbles through too great a concern with grub, so much so that occasionally 'Alice Waters' sounds like a pseudonym for S. J. Perelman. 'I do think best while holding a tomato or a leg of lamb,' she confides. For a person of my generation, there is also the teasing question: could she be the Alice, and 'Chez Panisse' the *real* Alice's Restaurant, of the song by Arlo Guthrie? And if this is so, where did it all go wrong?

London Review of Books, 1984

Patience Gray: Honey from a Weed

I bought my first cookery book in 1960, as part of my trousseau. It was called *Plats du Jour, or Foreign Food* by Patience Gray and Primrose Boyd, a Penguin paperback with a seductive pink jacket depicting a large family at table – evidently not a British family, for its members, shirt-sleeved, aproned, some of them children, were uncorking bottles, slicing bread, eagerly tucking their napkins under their chins, faces aglow with the certain knowledge their dinners would not disappoint, which was, in those days, extremely rare in this country.

My copy of *Plats du Jour* now gives forth a mellow smell of old paper; the pages are crisp, brown, and dry as Melba toast. But it has outlasted the husband for whose pleasure I bought it by some eighteen years, proof positive of the old saw, 'Kissin' don't last, cookin' do.' And now it is a historic object, a prototype of the late twentieth-century British cookery book, a book to browse in as much as to cook from, its prose as elegant as its plentiful line-drawings. And, oh, that easy, graceful cosmopolitanism! 'For anyone who has eaten a well-prepared Gulyas in one of the little restaurants on the Buda side of the Danube, overlooking the lantern-threaded bridges and the electric glitter of Pesth on a warm summer night before the war . . .' The nascent genre infected an entire generation with wanderlust.

Patience Gray helped to instigate the concept of the cookery book as literary form – part recipes, part travel book, part self-revelation, part artobject. Now, some thirty years on, she has assembled what may be its culmination. *Honey from a Weed* is less a cookery book than a summing up of the genre of the late modern British cookery book. It is a book like very few others, although it has some of the style of the seventeenth-century commonplace book, replete with recondite erudition and assembled on the principle of free association, as when Mrs Gray lists uses for goose fat. In a cassoulet. In soups. On bread. On toast. 'On your chest, rubbed in in winter. On leather boots, if they squeak. On your hands if they are chapped.'

Above all, it is a book about a particular sensibility – a unique and pungent one – that manifests itself most characteristically in the kitchen. That is what the genre is all about. M. F. K. Fisher had pioneered the culinary autobiographical novel in the US years before the Penguin school of cookery writers found its greatest star in Elizabeth David in the late 1950s and early 1960s. For these writers, and for Patience Gray, cookery is what the open road was to Cobbett or the natural history of Selborne to Gilbert White. There is, however, a difference: these are women to whom food is not an end in itself but a way of opening up the world. And, indeed, they are all women: this is, at the highest level, a female form.

It is unique to Saxon culture, to my knowledge, that the ability to cook well is a sign of a woman of the world. Traditional plump home-bodies may deliver the goods in France and Spain and Italy, but in Britain and the US the classic cooks are awesomely sophisticated, aristocratically beautiful and often connected with the arts. Elizabeth David, friend of Norman Douglas, is eternalised in the lovely icon of John Ward's drawing, the epitome of chic in her companionable kitchen. M. F. K. Fisher is just as beautiful. Her most beloved husband was a painter, and her books are so instinct with upmarket bohemianism that it is no surprise to find her in a cameo role in the autobiography of the painter and photographer, Man Ray, in which a starring part is allotted to Lee Miller, the universal muse of the surrealists, who herself became a famous practitioner of gourmet cookery.

Patience Gray belongs to this nexus of cookery and the arts, although she has an earthy, hands-on approach to the real lives of the predominantly peasant communities in southern Europe where she has chosen to live, and to the arts: she works in silver and gold, making jewellery, and lives with a stone-carver whom she calls the Sculptor (she is refreshingly free from irony). Her book recounts their wanderings during a shared life dominated by the Sculptor's quest for suitable stone. Glamorous as this way of life may seem, it is no easy option. Patience Gray's kitchens have been exceedingly sparsely equipped. The hand-pump over the marble sink of one particular Etruscan kitchen did not work: 'I got the water in a bucket and lowering it into the outdoor cistern had a marvellous view of the glittering Monte Sagra and the Apulian Alps on one side and on the other a view to the Tyrrhenian.'

This combination of material asceticism and passionate enthusiasm for the sensuality of the everyday is at the core of the tradition from which Mrs Gray springs, with its obvious affinities to the style of Bloomsbury, where it was a moral imperative that the beautiful should always take precedence over the comfortable. Though 'beautiful' is not quite the right word – it is a kind of authenticity which is invoked here, as though water is more authentic, more real, wetter, drawn from an open-air cistern than from a city tap.

The metaphysics of authenticity are a dangerous area. When Mrs Gray opines, 'Poverty rather than wealth gives the good things of life their true significance', it is tempting to suggest it is other people's poverty, always a source of the picturesque, that does that. Even if Mrs Gray and her companion live in exactly the same circumstances as their neigh-bours in the Greek islands or southern Italy, and have just as little ready money, their relation to their circumstances is the result of the greatest of all luxuries, aesthetic choice. 'Poverty', here, is sloppy language – a rare example of it. Mrs Gray isn't talking about a pavement dweller in Calcutta, or a member of the long-term unemployed in an advanced, industrialised country; nor about poverty as such, but about a way of life which has a dignity imposed upon it by its stoicism in the face of a nature on which it is entirely dependent. The Japanese created an entire aesthetic, and a moral philosophy, out of this stoicism and this intimate relation with natural forces; as soon as they had a bob or two in their pockets, of course, they binged on consumerism, but the hard core is still there.

Then again, Mrs Gray and her companion are not too perturbed about the absence of piped water. Her companion, when pressed, expresses a preference for shitting beneath a fig tree, rather than in a flush toilet. When workers recruited from southern Italy moved into subsidised hous-ing in Turin, people used to say: 'No use giving them baths, they'll only grow basil in them.' Mrs Gray would think that was an eminently sensible thing to do with a bath. After a couple of days of toting buckets, my own appreciation of any view would have waned, somewhat. But arduous cir-cumstances never diminish Mrs Gray's rapt sense of wonder, and her book is dedicated to genuine austerity, an austerity reflected in many of the recipes she includes in her text. The section titled 'Fasting on Naxos' describes just that: 'The four weeks of the Advent fast and the six weeks of the Lenten one correspond with moments when on Naxos there was hardly anything to eat.'

She describes the harsh life of these Greek islanders without sentimen-tality, if with a degree of romantic awe, in a prose that will suddenly, effortlessly, fall into the very cadences of Sir Thomas Browne: 'In Homer's time, a King could go out to plough his land and build his bed of giant timbers.' Her prose is usually ravishing, sometimes breathtaking. The entire section titled 'Pasticceria and the Apulian Baroque' is composed according to the principles of the startling architectonics she describes:

> The city [Lecce] within the walls calls to mind the Bourbon Kings of Naples, who once a year ordered the construction of castle edifices made of stout edible materials – gigantic hams, cheeses, enormous mortadelle, and the fore and hindquarters of deer and Indian buffalo, in order then to gloat at the spectacle of the starving Neapolitans – admitted at the moment of completion – vociferously and violently vying with each other, to the accompaniment of martial music and gunpowder explosions, in their destruction.

The book moves among its venues at the whim of memory, according to no precise chronology. With Mrs Gray, we eat dried beans cooked a variety of ways in a variety of places. We eat potatoes and green beans boiled together, potatoes with alliums (the common name of the onion family) and olive oil, potatoes cooked in the oven with streaky bacon. Some of her recipes would certainly ease the plight of the long-term unemployed in advanced, industrialised countries because, even here, the ingredients cost so little. Then again, *Honey from a Weed* is a very expensive book. Such are the ironies of the politics of romantic austerity.

We make, with her, salads of hedgerow greens and boil up delicious weeds to eat hot with lemon juice – dandelions, comfrey, wood sorrel, field sorrel, wild fennel, fat hen, tassel hyacinth, purslane, field poppy. (When gathering your weeds, watch out for pesticides.) A meal may be made – *has* to be made – from whatever is to hand. M. F. K. Fisher's wolf ('How to Cook a Wolf', included in *The Art of Eating*) was metaphorical. Patience Gray 'met a number of people around Carrara not at all averse to cooking a fox', and tells you how to make fox *alla cacciatore* (with garlic, wine, and tomatoes). 'Exactly the same method can be applied to a badger . . .'

A connoisseur of free food, she waxes lyrical on snails, especially the *Helix operta*, oval in shape, golden brown in colour, 'with a beautiful logarithmic spiritual structure'. Surely, of all the creatures we eat, we are most brutal to snails. *Helix operta* is dug out of the earth where he has been peacefully enjoying his summer sleep, cracked like an egg, and eaten raw, presumably alive. Or boiled in oil. Or roasted in the hot ashes of a wood fire. In Catalonia, vineyard snails are laid out in rows on a bed of straw. 'The straw is set alight and the snails are retrieved from the ashes by jabbing them with sharply pointed sticks.' If God is a snail, Bosch's depictions of Hell are going to look like a vicarage tea-party.

Mrs Gray does not conceal the fact that the traditional communities she describes are now in the process of violent change. Her twenty years of wandering the limestone margins of the Mediterranean have coincided with the breakdown of ancient forms of village life:

> It sometimes seems as if I have been rescuing a few strands from a former and more diligent way of life, now being eroded by an entirely new set of values. As with students of music who record old songs which are no longer sung, soon some of the things I record will also have vanished.

This is partly what makes her book so valuable, and gives it an elegiac quality that sometimes recalls the recent work of a writer, John Berger, with whom she might seem to have little else in common except a respect for philosophical anarchism: Berger's majestic stories of peasant life, *Pig Earth* invoke the awesome severities and orgiastic celebrations of a past as recent as yesterday and already as remote as the Flood.

The point is, dammit, that they *did* have, as Iago griped about Othello, a daily beauty in their lives that makes ours ugly. In one of the stories in *Pig Earth*, a little old peasant lady goes out and gathers wild things in the mountains – wild cherries, lilies of the valley, mushrooms, mistletoe – and takes her booty into the city, where she sells it in the market for vast sums. She is selling not only delicious wild produce but glimpses of some lost greenness. She is the last remaining vendor of wild things, she is a kind of ghost. Mrs Gray describes Carrara twenty years ago:

> The feeling of the mountains was never far away: retired quarrymen sold bunches of herbs they had gathered there. In summer great baskets of bilberries and wild strawberries appeared. In autumn fresh cranberries, fungi and chestnuts were brought down from the Spanish chestnut woods. In this way a dialogue between town and country was maintained . . . In those days it was still possible to feel that the Carraresi were definitely in touch with the 'earthly paradise'.

If transplanted Calabrians do grow basil in their shiny new bathtubs, perhaps they know what's what.

Mrs Gray has taken the form of the late-modern English-language cookery book to its extreme in *Honey from a Weed*, producing a kind of baroque monument of which all the moving parts work (the recipes are very sound).

London Review of Books, 1987

Dressing Up and Down

Notes for a Theory of Sixties Style

Velvet is back, skin anti-skin, mimic nakedness. Like leather and suede, only more subtly, velvet simulates the flesh it conceals, a profoundly tactile fabric. Last winter's satin invited the stroke, a slithering touch, this winter's velvet invites a more sinuous caress. But the women who buy little brown velvet dresses will probably do so in a state of unknowing, unaware they're dressing up for parts in our daily theatre of fact; unaware, too, how mysterious that theatre is.

For the nature of apparel is very complex. Clothes are so many things at once. Our social shells; the system of signals with which we broadcast our intentions; often the projections of our fantasy selves (a fat old woman in a bikini); the formal uniform of our life roles (the businessman's suit, the teacher's tweed jacket with leather patches and ritual accessory of pipe in breast pocket); sometimes simple economic announcements of income or wealth (real jewellery – especially inherited real jewellery, which throws in a bonus of class as well – or mink). Clothes are our weapons, our challenges, our visible insults.

And more. For we think our dress expresses ourselves but in fact it expresses our environment and, like advertising, pop music, pulp fiction and second-feature films, it does so almost at a subliminal, emotionally charged, instinctual, non-intellectual level. The businessman, the fashion writers, the designers and models, the shopkeepers, the buyers, the window dressers live in the same cloud of unknowing as us all; they think they mould the public taste but really they're blind puppets of a capricious goddess, goddess of mirrors, weather-cocks and barometers, whom the Elizabethans called Mutability. She is inscrutable but logical.

The inscrutable but imperative logic of change has forced fashion in the sixties through the barriers of space and time. Clothes today sometimes seem arbitrary and bizarre; nevertheless, the startling dandyism of the newly emancipated young reveals a kind of logic of whizzing entropy. Mutability is having a field day.

Let us take the following example. A young girl, invited to a party, left to herself (no mother to guide her), might well select the following ensemble: a Mexican cotton wedding dress (though she's not a bride, probably no virgin, either – thus at one swoop turning a garment which in its original environment is an infinitely potent symbol into a piece of decoration); her grandmother's button boots (once designed to show off the small feet and moneyed leisure of an Edwardian middle class who didn't need to work and rarely had to walk); her mother's fox fur (bought to demonstrate her father's status); and her old school beret dug out of the loft because she saw Faye Dunaway in *Bonnie and Clyde* (and a typical role-definition garment changes gear).

All these eclectic fragments, robbed of their symbolic content, fall together to form a new whole, a dramatisation of the individual, a personal style. And fashion today (real fashion, what real people wear) is a question of style, no longer a question of items in harmony. 'What to wear with what' is no longer a burning question; in the 1960s, everything is worn all at once.

Style means the presentation of the self as a three-dimensional art object, to be wondered at and handled. And this involves a new attitude to the self which is thus adorned. The gaudy rags of the flower children, the element of fancy dress even in 'serious' clothes (the military look, the thirties revival), extravagant and stylised face-painting, wigs, hairpieces, amongst men the extraordinary recrudescence of the decorative moustache (and, indeed, the concept of the decorative man), fake tattooing – all these are in the nature of disguises.

Disguise entails duplicity. One passes oneself off as another, who may or may not exist – as Jean Harlow or Lucy in the Sky with Diamonds or Al Capone or Sergeant Pepper. Though the disguise is worn as play and not intended to deceive, it does nevertheless give a relaxation from one's own personality and the discovery of maybe unsuspected new selves. One feels free to behave more freely. This holiday from the persistent self is the perpetual lure of fancy dress. Rosalind in disguise in the Forest of Arden could pretend to be a boy pretending to be a seductress, satisfying innumerable atavistic desires in the audience of the play. And we are beginning to realise once again what everybody always used to know, that all human contact is profoundly ambiguous. And the style of the sixties expresses this knowledge.

The *Bonnie and Clyde* clothes and the guru robes certainly don't indicate a cult of violence or a massive swing to transcendental meditation (although *Rave* magazine did feature a 'Raver's Guide' to the latter subject in the November issue); rather, this rainbow proliferation of all kinds of fancy dress shows a new freedom many people fear, especially those with something to lose when the frozen, repressive, role-playing world properly starts to melt.

Consider a typical hippy, consider a typical Chinese Red Guard. One is a beautiful explosion of sexually ambiguous silks and beads, the other a sternly garbed piece of masculine aggression, proclaiming by his clothes the gift of his individual self to the puritan ethic of his group. The first sports the crazy patchwork uniform of a society where social and sexual groupings are willy-nilly disintegrating, the second is part of a dynamically happening society where all the individuals are clenched together like a fist. One is a fragment of a kaleidoscope, the other a body blow. One is opening out like a rose, the other forging straight ahead.

Of course, one does not have to go so far afield as China to see this dichotomy of aim. If you put the boy in the djellibah next to a middle-aged police constable, each will think of the other: 'The enemies are amongst us.' For the boy in the djellibah will be a very young boy, and the class battle in Britain (once sartorially symbolised by Keir Hardie's cloth cap) is redefining itself as the battle of the generations.

The Rolling Stones' drugs case was an elegant confrontation of sartorial symbolism in generation warfare: the judge, in ritually potent robes and wig, invoking the doom of his age and class upon the beautiful children in frills and sunset colours, who dared to question the infallibility he represents as icon of the law and father figure.

The Rolling Stones' audience appeal has always been anti-parent, anti-authority, and they have always used sartorial weapons – from relatively staid beginnings (long hair and grime) to the famous *Daily Mirror* centre-spread in superdrag. They are masters of the style of calculated affront. And it never fails to work. The clothing of pure affront, sported to bug the squares (as the Hell's Angels say), will always succeed in bugging the squares no matter how often they are warned, 'He only does it to annoy.'

The Hell's Angels and the other Californian motor-cycle gangs deck themselves with iron crosses, Nazi helmets, necklets and earrings, they grow their hair to their shoulders and dye their beards green, red and purple, they cultivate halitosis and body odour. Perfect dandies of beastliness, they incarnate the American nightmare. Better your sister marry a Negro than have the Oakland chapter of Hell's Angels drop in on her for coffee.

But this outlaw dress represents a real dissociation from society. It is a very serious joke and, in their Neanderthal way, the Hell's Angels are obeying Camus's law – that the dandy is always a rebel, that he challenges society because he challenges mortality. The motor-cycle gangs challenge mortality face to face, doing 100 mph on a California freeway in Levis and swastikas, no crash helmet but a wideawake hat, only a veneer of denim between the man and his death. 'The human being who is condemned to die is, at least, magnificent before he disappears and his magnificence is his justification.'

In the decade of Vietnam, in the century of Hiroshima and Buchen-
wald, we are as perpetually aware of mortality as any generation ever was.
It is small wonder that so many people are taking the dandy's way of asking unanswerable questions. The pursuit of magnificence starts as play and
ends as nihilism or metaphysics or a new examination of the nature of
goals.

In the pursuit of magnificence, nothing is sacred. Hitherto sacrosanct
imagery is desecrated. When Pete Townshend of The Who first put on
his jacket carved out of the Union Jack, he turned our national symbol
into an abstraction far more effectively than did Jasper Johns when he
copied the Old Glory out in paint and hung it on his wall. Whether or not
Pete Townshend fully realised the nature of his abstraction is not the
question; he was impelled to it by the pressures of the times.

Similarly, fabrics and objects hitherto possessing strong malignant
fetishistic qualities have either been cleansed of their deviational overtones
and used for their intrinsic textural charm, or else worn in the camp style
with a humorous acknowledgement of those overtones. Rubber, leather,
fur, objects such as fish-net stockings and tall boots are fetishes which the
purity of style has rendered innocent, as sex becomes more relaxed and the
norm more subtle.

Iconic clothing has been secularised, too. Witness the cult of the
military uniform. A guardsman in a dress uniform is ostensibly an icon of
aggression; his coat is red as the blood he hopes to shed. Seen on a coat-
hanger, with no man inside it, the uniform loses all its blustering significance and, to the innocent eye seduced by decorative colour and tactile
braid, it is as abstract in symbolic information as a parasol to an Eskimo. It
becomes simply magnificent. However, once on the back of the innocent,
it reverts to an aggressive role: to old soldiers (that is, most men in this
country over forty) the secularised military uniform gives far too much
information, all of it painful. He sees a rape of his ideals, is threatened by
a terrible weapon of affront.

A good deal of iconic clothing has become secularised simply through
disuse. It no longer has any symbolic content for the stylists and is not decorative enough to be used in play. Mutability has rendered it obsolescent.
The cabaret singer in her sequin sheath which shrieks, 'Look at me but
don't touch me, I'm armour-plated', survives as an image of passive female
sexuality, the *princesse lointaine* (or, rather, the *putain lointaine*) only in the
womblike unreality of the nightclub or on the fantasy projection of the
television screen. The tulle and taffeta bride in her crackling virginal carapace, clasping numinous lilies, the supreme icon of woman as a sexual
thing and nothing else whatever, survives as part of the potlatch culture at
either end of the social scale – where the pressures to make weddings of

their daughters displays of conspicuous consumption are fiercest.

On the whole, though, girls have been emancipated from the stiff forms of iconic sexuality. Thanks to social change, to contraception, to equal pay for equal work, there is no need for this iconography any more; both men and women's clothes today say, 'Look at me and touch me if I want you.' Velvet is back, skin anti-skin, mimic nakedness.

New Society, 1967

The Wound in the Face

I spent a hallucinatory weekend, staring at faces I'd cut out of women's magazines, either from the beauty page or from the ads – all this season's faces. I stuck twenty or thirty faces on the wall and tried to work out from the evidence before me (a) what women's faces are supposed to be looking like, now; and (b) why. It was something of an exercise in pure form, because the magazine models' faces aren't exactly the face in the street – not low-style, do-it-yourself assemblages, but more a platonic, ideal face. Further, they reflect, as well as the mood of the moment, what the manufacturers are trying to push this year. Nevertheless, the *zeitgeist* works through the manufacturers, too. They do not understand their own imagery, any more than the consumer who demonstrates it does. I am still working on the nature of the imagery of cosmetics. I think it scares me.

Constructing the imagery was an unnerving experience because all the models appeared to be staring straight at me with such a heavy, static quality of *being there* that it was difficult to escape the feeling they were accusing me of something. (How rarely women look one another in the eye.) Only two of the faces wear anything like smiles, and only one is showing a hint of her teeth. This season's is not an extrovert face. Because there is not much to smile about this season? Surely. It is a bland, hard, bright face; it is also curiously familiar, though I have never seen it before.

The face of the seventies matches the fashions in clothes that have dictated some of its features, and is directly related to the social environment which produces it. Like fashions in clothes, fashions in faces have been stuck in pastiche for the past four or five years. This bankruptcy is disguised by ever more ingenious pastiche – of the thirties, the forties, the fifties, the Middle East, Xanadu, Wessex (those smocks). Compared with the short skirts and flat shoes of ten years ago, style in women's clothes has regressed. Designers are trying to make us cripple our feet again with high-heeled shoes and make us trail long skirts in dogshit. The re-introduction of rouge is part of this regression; rouge, coyly re-introduced under the nineteenth-century euphemism of 'blusher'.

The rather older face – the *Vogue* face, as opposed to the *Honey* face – is strongly under the 1930s influence, the iconographic, androgynous face of Dietrich and Garbo, with heavily emphasised bone structures, hollow cheeks and hooded eyelids. Warhol's transvestite superstars, too, and his magazine, *Interview* – with its passion for the tacky, the kitschy, for fake glamour, for rhinestones, sequins, Joan Crawford, Ann-Margret – have exercised a profound influence. As a result, fashionable women now tend to look like women imitating men imitating women, an interesting reversal. The face currently perpetuated by the glossies aspires to the condition of that of Warhol's Candy Darling.

The main message is that the hard, bland face with which women brazened their way through the tough 1930s, the tough 1940s and the decreasingly tough 1950s (at the end of the 1950s, when things got less tough, they abandoned it), is back to sustain us through the tough 1970s. It recapitulates the glazed, self-contained look typical of times of austerity.

But what is one to make of the transvestite influence? Is it that the physical image of women took such a battering in the 1960s that when femininity did, for want of anything better, return, the only people we could go to find out what it had looked like were the dedicated male impersonators who had kept the concept alive in the sequinned gowns, their spike-heeled shoes and their peony lipsticks? Probably. 'The feminine character, and the idea of femininity on which it is modelled, are products of masculine society,' says Theodor Adorno. Clearly a female impersonator knows more about his idea of the character he is mimicking than I do, because it is his very own invention, and has nothing to do with me.

Yet what about the Rousseauesque naturalism of the dominant image of women in the mid-1960s? Adorno can account for that, sociologically, too. 'The image of undistorted nature arises only in distortion, as its opposite.' The sixties' face was described early in the decade by *Queen* (as it was then) as a 'look of luminous vacancy'.

The sixties' face had a bee-stung underlip, enormous eyes and a lot of disordered hair. It saw itself as a wild, sweet, gypsyish, vulnerable face. Its very lack of artifice suggested sexual licence in a period that had learned to equate cosmetics, not with profligacy as in the nineteenth century, but with conformity to the standard social and sexual female norm. Nice girls wore lipstick, in the fifties.

When the sixties' face used cosmetics at all, it explored imports such as kohl and henna from Indian shops. These had the twin advantages of being extremely exotic and very, very cheap. For purposes of pure decoration, for fun, it sometimes stuck sequins to itself, or those little gold and silver 'good conduct' stars. It bought sticks of stage make-up, and did extraordinary things around its eyes with them, at about the time of Flower Power. It was, basically, a low-style or do-it-yourself face. Ever in search of the new, the magazines eventually caught up with it, and high-style faces caught on to flowered cheeks and stars on the eyelids at about the time the manufacturers did. So women had to pay considerably more for their pleasures.

The sixties' look gloried in its open pores and, if your eye wasn't into the particular look, you probably thought it didn't wash itself much. But it was just that, after all those years of pancake make-up, people had forgotten what the real colour of female skin was. This face cost very little in upkeep. Indeed, it was basically a most economical and serviceable model and it was quite a shock to realise, as the years passed, that all the beauty experts were wrong and, unless exposed to the most violent weather, it did not erode if it was left ungreased. A face is not a bicycle. Nevertheless, since this face had adopted naturalism as an ingenious form of artifice, it was a mask, like the grease masks of cosmetics, though frequently refreshingly eccentric.

At the end of that decade, in a brief period of delirium, there was a startling vogue of black lipstick and red eyeshadow. For a little while we were painting ourselves up just as arbitrarily as Larionov did before the Revolution. Dada in the boudoir! What a witty parody of the whole theory of cosmetics!

The basic theory of cosmetics is that they make a woman beautiful. Or, as the advertisers say, more beautiful. You blot out your noxious wens and warts and blemishes, shade your nose to make it bigger or smaller, draw attention to your good features by bright colours, and distract it from your bad features by more reticent tones. But those manic and desperate styles – leapt on and exploited instantly by desperate manufacturers – seemed to be about to break the ground for a whole new aesthetic of appearance, which would have nothing to do with the conformist ideology of 'beauty' at all. Might – ah, might – it be possible to use cosmetics to free women from the burden of having to look beautiful altogether?

Because black lipstick and red eyeshadow never 'beautified' anybody. They were the cosmetic equivalent of Duchamp's moustache on the Mona Lisa. They were cosmetics used as satire on cosmetics, on the arbitrary convention that puts blue on eyelids and pink on lips. Why not the other way round? The best part of the joke was that the look itself was utterly monstrous. It instantly converted the most beautiful women into outrageous grotesques; every face a work of anti-art. I enjoyed it very, very much.

However, it takes a helluva lot of guts to maintain oneself in a perpetual state of visual offensiveness. Most women could not resist keeping
open a treacherous little corner on sex appeal. Besides, the joke went a
little too near the bone. To do up your eyes so that they look like self-
inflicted wounds is to wear on your face the evidence of the violence your
environment inflicts on you.

Black paint around the eyes is such a familiar convention it seems
natural; so does red paint on the mouth. We are so used to the bright red
mouth we no longer see it as the wound it mimics, except in the treacherous lucidity of paranoia. But the shock of the red-painted eye recalls,
directly, the blinding of Gloucester in Lear; or, worse and more aptly, the
symbolic blinding of Oedipus. Women are allowed – indeed, encouraged
– to exhibit the sign of their symbolic castration, but only in the socially
sanctioned place. To transpose it upwards is to allow its significance to
become apparent. We went too far, that time. Scrub it all off and start
again.

And once we started again, red lipstick came back. Elizabeth I seems to
have got a fine, bright carmine with which to touch up her far from
generous lips. The Victorian beauty's 'rosebud mouth' – the mouth so tiny
it was a wonder how it managed to contain her teeth – was a restrained
pink. Flappers' lips spread out and went red again, and the 'generous
mouth' became one of the great glamour conventions of the entire
twentieth century and has remained so, even if its colour is modified.

White-based lipsticks, colourless glosses, or no lipstick at all, were used
in the 1960s. Now the mouth is back as a bloody gash, a visible wound.
This mouth bleeds over everything, cups, ice-cream, table napkins,
towels. Mary Quant has a shade called (of course) 'Bloody Mary', to ram
the point home. We will leave our bloody spoor behind us, to show we
have been there.

In the 1930s, that spoor was the trademark of the sophisticate, the type
of Baudelairean female dandy Dietrich impersonated so well. Dietrich
always transcended self-pity and self-destruction, wore the wound like a
badge of triumph, and came out on top. But Iris Storm in Michael Arlen's
The Green Hat, the heroines of Maurice Dekobra, the wicked film star in
Chandler's *The Little Sister* who always dressed in black to offset her fire-
engine of a mouth – they all dripped blood over everything as they stalked
sophisticatedly to their dooms. In their wake, lipstick traces on a cigarette
stub; the perfect imprint, like half a heart, of a scarlet lower lip on a drained
Martini glass; the tell-tale scarlet letter, A for adultery, on a shirt collar . . .
the kitsch poetry of it all!

Elizabeth Taylor scrawls 'Not for sale' on her bedroom mirror in her
red, red lipstick in *Butterfield 8*. The generosity the mouth has given so

freely, will be spurned with brutal ingratitude. The open wound will never heal. Perhaps, sometimes, she will lament the loss of the tight rosebud; but it has gone for ever.

The revival of red lipstick indicates, above all, I suppose, that women's sense of security was transient.

New Society, 1975

Trouser Protest

When I started work in the late 1950s, it was as much as a girl's job was worth to arrive at the office in trousers, no matter how neatly or nattily cut they might be. Trousers for informal wear, in your own time – yes; in the company's time, no.

I remember, a couple of years later, a lengthy and increasingly batty debate in the extremist sect of the CND of which I was a member as to what women should wear for sit-ins. Because we were always being picked up and going limp and being carried into vans by policemen, trousers seemed the obviously seemly and practical garb. Besides, there always seemed to be some prurient photographer lurking about with a telephoto lens, to snap a flash of knickers or suspendered thigh if it were available, and then to gleefully splash it all over the national press – a form of punishment by humiliation to which women were peculiarly subject.

But, during this debate, one girl argued hotly that trousered female protesters would play up far too much to the public image of licentious beatnikery which already enriched the campaign. The sartorial style of the movement, she claimed, alienated potential support. Coats and skirts, she thought, and possibly even hats, a sort of Tory-lady look, would ram home far more effectively the point of civilised civil protest. Not just students and the disaffected, but thinking women in twin-sets and pearls could be seen to be involved. (We were all, I remember, rather on edge and these nutty scholastic disputations would break out from time to time; if they helped release tension for some, for others they racked it up inexorably to screaming point. I resigned, eventually and joined the Labour Party.)

At the time there was, in fact, a perfectly acceptable bourgeois female trouser in circulation – only none of us possessed a pair, of course. This was the knitted nylon taper trouser with a strap beneath the foot to keep the hem from rolling up. This garment, originally some form of skiing apparel, combined with a chunky Italian sweater and beehive hairdo, was standard lower-middle lounge bar gear. There were also a wide range of functional, middle-middle, and even upper-middle, country trousers available, best accessorised by Wellington boots, silk headscarves with pictures of horses on them and purple cheeks full of broken veins (a sign of being out and about in all weather). But, though some of us certainly had access to such 'invisible' garments (all functional garments are invisible), none of us had any intention of admitting it.

Because, of course, we *were* all disaffected and most of us were students and, for a variety of reasons, had adopted a style of dress which was a more or less conscious form of social affront or visual insult. Caught in a limbo of fashionable anti-style (that is, unofficial or 'underground' style) between the demise of the beatnik and the ascent of the hippy, we had adopted the only style there was around, the CND or generalised 'protesters' style, army-surplus sweaters and jeans usually manufactured by Levi-Strauss and Company. There was a lot of status about a pair of genuine Levis at this time.

We young chicks all wore Levis, of course, and we chose the men's styles because they offered a trimmer fit around the thigh. Though we did not know it, these trousers were a quite unambiguous sign saying, in effect, we could not, would not or did not need to work. That is, we were either workshy or else were students – the old excuse for not getting your hands mucky.

There was a horrid irony in our choice of men's working clothes to express our disaffection, because the number of jobs a woman who habitually wore jeans could have held down in 1961 were few and far between. They were usually connected, if they existed at all, with the arts – another area of activity which those engaged in productive labour often, with good reason, suspect has very little to do with work as such at all.

However when, last month, I noticed that the secretaries at my publishers all, every girl, seemed to be wearing jeans, yes jeans, I realised that one set of social conventions at least had changed completely during the maturation, or middle-ageing, of one generation. Blue denim has lost not only its last, lingering blue-collar connotations, but also its cultural references of teenage angst so dear to those of us who can still remember the day James Dean died, and what a personal tragedy it seemed. (Remember?)

Levis have become, quite simply, a style of trouser made in blue denim. (And they've branched out into other fabrics, too – oh, yes, I read the ads. But Levis are still blue denim to me.) And we are all wearing the pants now, we girls. Trousers have become respectable wear for respectable women – in other words, have become unnoticeable, except for particular elegances, individual expressivenesses.

Either trousers have become more formal or offices have become more informal. Something has changed, at any rate. I wonder what it means.

The word 'pants' derives from a name, Pantaleone, the clown in Commedia del Arte, and his characteristic garb, the loose-fitting pyjamas of the comic actor-acrobat. Informal, working wear. Yet trousers, of all garments, may claim to have revolutionary significance; the garb of the proletariat, adopted by the French revolutionists to replace the privileged breeches and stockings of the aristocracy. Even if the *enragées* who wished to extend the benefits of the revolution to their own sex were summarily laughed off the streets when they were foolish enough to venture out *sans culottes* but quite decently trousered, in carmagnole and cap of liberty. Ridicule has always been a potent weapon against women.

Not that to wear trousers is in itself a sign of an emancipated woman. Some of the most oppressed women in the world habitually wear trousers. Throughout Asia, from Turkey to Japan, peasant women perform back-breaking toil in traditional trousers whose origins clearly lie in pure functionalism. You can get more backbreaking toil out of a woman if she is not constantly tripping up over her skirts.

Mrs Amelia Bloomer, the American dress reformer, was more concerned with hygiene and propriety than with equal rights when she attempted to introduce a rather charming version of the Ottoman pantaloons and tunic into the Western world a hundred years ago, as a substitute for the bizarre crinoline. Nevertheless, those baggy trousers certainly looked like an attempt to usurp the contemporary male prerogative of legs; ridicule, again, killed the reform. Women wearing Mrs Bloomer's reformed dress were thrown out of churches, endured the mockery and abuse of the mob. Her name itself has entered the dictionary with a snigger of derision about it.

That women were working down the mines at the time wearing nothing but drawers (a male garment) and a shift was a matter that affected the sensibilities of very few in the same way; no woman, to my knowledge, was laughed out of a pit for wearing drawers. Indeed, during the twentieth century, the working and hence invisible trousers could be worn increasingly, from the First World War onwards, on the farm, in the factory, on the buses, in aeroplanes – though some form of hygienic boiler suit has never been introduced where it would seem most logical, in hospitals, as a uniform for nurses. But the wearing trouser bore no resemblance to the trouser-as-fashion; the trouser-as-fashion originates as delicious outrage.

A black satin smoking suit, with a waistcoat, worn with a monocle and a cigarette holder – the sort of thing Radclyffe Hall would have worn – intentional travesty, was a damn-your-eyes mockery of male dandyism, on sale at Debenham's in the 1920s. Its price, a whacking twelve and a half guineas, reflects the kind of woman it was manufactured for, who could spend so much on a whim. This garment, like the harem trousers of art deco fashion, suggests: 'She's only wearing it to draw attention to herself.' It is a world away from the munition worker's boiler suit, or the unisex tailoring of modern China. The glamour-pyjamas of the 1920s and 1930s were high-style and hence visible. If trousers became acceptable wear for women during the Second World War for reasons of practicality, and remained almost universal as informal wear, they didn't become really visible again until the high-style trouser suits of the mid-1960s. Then the female trouser once again acquired some martyrs; turned away from the Savoy Grill, or wherever it was. Even in your Courrèges pants-suit, with the white vinyl boots.

And yet, in the last decade, women in trousers have ceased to be either dramatically 'visible' ('Look at her!') or functionally invisible. (I can't remember if clippies wear trousers or skirts, these days; that's what I mean by invisible.) Trousers for women have become just another garment, in fact, more practical than most female garments; so prevalent that the stocking manufacturers feel forced to fight back with knocking copy. There's a poster in the tube stations at this very moment showing a pair of wonderful legs, accompanied by the legend – 'When was the last time a man said you had a pretty pair of jeans?' It's deplorably sexist, an invitation to narcissism. They must be really worried to stoop so low.

And these trousers are often quite indistinguishable from men's trousers. The taper-slacks of the 1950s were specifically female garments; they announced their sex by their side opening. The introduction of the frontal fly into women's trousers marked a change in the appraisal of a woman's body; it ignored a biological particularity in a truly egalitarian way.

This almost unqualified acceptance of trousers as regular, everyday wear for women suggests an emancipation more real than that offered by the mini-skirt, which was a form of systematic exposure that maximised sexual differentiation by sartorial means. Besides, the tights that went under the mini-skirt were the true successors of the tapered ski-trouser of the fifties, an ample and modest form of leg-covering that cancelled out the erotic promise of the shorn-off overdress. I observe that, after the loon-pants and bell-bottoms of the sixties and early seventies, straight jeans are coming in again. There is even a suggestion of a revival of the ski-pant, or tapered slack, without overdress or concealing smock.

The suggestion which is implicit in the advertisement – that universal female trouser-wearing will cancel out the erotic implications of the leg –

could be utterly misleading. We girls, in the fulfilment of one kind of sartorial emancipation, may yet have dug another pit of erotic narcissism for
ourselves. When will it end, O Lord? When will it end?

New Society, 1975

Year of the Punk

Bad Taste is the key to the emerging seventies' style. I think. In a changing world, amidst a bewildering welter of variables, at least you know
where you are when you can evoke offence. It's been a funny old decade,
the seventies, and, of course, it's not over yet. But, as its seventh segment
shambles towards Christmas like some not altogether rough – indeed, in
parts, vinyl sleek – yet certainly beastly beast, the mood of it all begins,
with hindsight, to shape up.

Since virtually every single event in the decade, from the property
boom to the Jubilee, has been in the worst possible taste, it seems only
right and proper that a mute sartorial response should surface as black shiny
plastic slit-sided dresses; camouflage combat trousers, as if either you did
not know there was a war on or else in ironic comment on the fact that
nobody seems to acknowledge there is a war on; chains everywhere, as if
you had not been born free; and blouses printed with excerpts from dirty
books. If you're terrible lucky, you might even get prosecuted for selling
obscene clothing, as did the King's Road boutique, Sex (now reborn as
Seditionaries, which name makes explicit its personal theory of sartorial
terrorism; its clothes are also very expensive).

Appearances, those magic representations of self, issue from an obscure
part of the unconscious that cannot be fooled, that never forgets anything
and recapitulates everything. Judging by appearances, there has clearly
been one of those massive changes in collective taste in clothes, in appearances themselves, that denote a change in the way people feel about themselves and the world about them, the kind of change that divides one
generation from another. This change has been shaping up since the soft-
focus, anarchic, eclectic fancy-dress ball of the late sixties. There is a hardening of outline; it is a hard-edge style and, this last year or so, it forced
itself on the attention in the form of an extreme.

This turned out to be an extreme of impropriety that cannot involve
nudity because there are tits all over the daily papers. So clothing itself
must become improper if Quentin (*On Human Finery*) Bell's fashion

function of Conspicuous Outrage is to operate, and conspicuous outrage – that is, sartorial terrorism – has remained, until now, a dominant teenage style. (I think this may soon phase itself out, but it's impossible to be sure, yet.)

The garments of soft-core pornography, the mesh stockings, the satin corsets, were easily incorporated into the regular grammar of fashion – oh, those frilly Edwardian chemises and petticoats of last summer! But it is easy to see there is no real impropriety in these garments, since soft-core porn embodies all the nostalgia men, fashion editors and lingerie manufacturers feel for the days when girls were girls. It is a form of eroticised sentimentality. And these are by no means sentimental times. At this point, Miss Stern totters into the sartorial arena on her six-inch spike heels and allows style to explore the rubber and leather garments of conspicuous deviance. These, furthermore, have the additional benefit of unisex and *really* get up your father's nose.

I'm perfectly prepared to believe, since the media tell me so, that the 'punk' style was originally, at any rate, long ago, a spontaneously generated phenomenon, a dandyism of the abyss put together out of odds and Army Surplus Store ends and mum's old clothes by the Savage Generation in its brief leisures between making Dole Queue Rock, vandalising telephone boxes and visits to the VD clinic and de-infestation centre. A visual representation of a conscious state of deprivation, in fact, the definition of a state of mind. (What state of mind? 'When I have inspired universal disgust, then I shall have conquered solitude,' as Baudelaire, himself often short of a bob or two, said at a not unsimilar time of conflicting ideologies).

As a style of conspicuous outrage, it abundantly succeeded, look at November's *19* magazine survey of patents on punks: 'They are the poisonous pus of a sick society.' 'Diabolical! Just a load of drop-outs!' Parents were saying the same things about the ethically impeccable flower children but a brief decade ago. (Sometimes, especially on trains, among people going to football matches, I get nostalgic for flower power, when they just sat there, covered in hair, and smiled). But each generation experiences generational conflict as if it were something new and, indeed, there are always new elements in it.

Yet the whole 'punk' thing was too self-aware, too conscious, too much like a put-on to be absolutely serious. Those babes in bondage, with coiffures and cosmetic effects as from an eighteenth-century madhouse, like a street theatre version of the *Marat/Sade*. And the French Revolution offers us an interesting example of self-conscious sartorial Bad Taste in another period of conflicting ideologies: the 'victim style' of the Directory, chalk-white face, convict hair-cut and the scarlet ribbon tied, or the red line painted, round the neck as a tribute to the guillotine. There is nothing new under the sun.

The victim-style of the seventies has a behavioural style to match. They never smile, these infants of the recession; they sneer. Defiant untouchables, tattooed at the extremities and accessoried with offensive weapons, lips and fingernails stained black and blue and the skin round their eyes painted up like rococo window-frames. This hard-edge, impersonal, constricted glamour, with its troubling elements of narcissism and fetishism, is almost too apt an illustration of a spirited reaction to impotence. There is too much irony in it, it is too knowing to be serious.

Irony is the self-defence of the down-and-out. The heavy irony of the punks blunts the style's offensive edge before it can even wound you. It makes you feel old, that is the cruellest thing, but it is basically a style of self-mockery. Arguing, perhaps, a low state of self-esteem in those who sport it. Warpaint was never put on to frighten the other side so much as to bolster the faint hearts of the wearers.

Punk is now busily diffusing itself and generalising itself and exercising a hard-edge influence over an enormous range of appearances. In a way, it is the visual recurrence of the persistent hard-edge element always present in working-class style. Remember the Skinheads, and the Rockers before them; and the Teds, who have turned into such genial folk heroes with the passage of time that nobody seems to remember just how nasty they were in their youth, with their razors and bicycle-chain knuckle-dusters.

All these styles, all predominantly masculine, were the specific uniform of an aggressive sub-culture with a taste for physical violence that remained universally offensive to everybody except the peer-group involved. Punk retains only the visual and linguistic aggression of these styles; it crosses with porno and self-mutilation; girls can do it and it has gone up-market, really up-market, with the most amazing speed, to fuse with the up-market vogue for tacky glitter that has been bubbling under since the early days of the magazine called *Andy Warhol's Interview*.

Styles of conspicuous outrage may start off as an expression of pride *in extremis*. But those who cannot work because there is none to be had and so make their play, their dancing, their clothes, into a kind of work, for reasons of self-respect, have a lot in common with those who either do not need to work or whose work is a kind of play, like pop musicians and fashion models. The only difference is, the rich have more money, Scott, and are prepared to pay through the nose for gold plastic wrap miniskirts, plastic raincoats, safety pins (sequinned specially for them) and bondage jackets made up, now, in specifically middle-class fabrics, like good tweed.

Therefore the style of the late seventies binds the underprivileged and the overprivileged in the same visual category, both bearing upon them the marks, as it were, the proudly born buboes, of what Reimut Reiche called, in another context in the late sixties, a 'pariah élite'. A self-conscious pariah élite, with an aesthetic of the tawdry, the parodic, a playbox decadence. And it is safe to say that punk or street styles on an up-market élite pariah do not denote low self-esteem at all, but a further degree of self-consciousness, the double irony of downward self-identification from an unassailable position of superiority.

Down-market self-conscious Bad Taste is naïve; a boy I know was wearing a swastika in one ear and a star of David in another last summer. He said it was to 'confuse people'. Which is a dangerous game. It is his innocence rather than his viciousness that gives me anguish, because he's not vicious at all. Up-market self-conscious Bad Taste, however, knows what it is doing; it consciously violates taboos.

As an example of this, fashion writers unblushingly dubbed last summer's dishevelled modes for women: 'après rape'; as a conscious trivialisation, a jokey piece of playbox anti-feminism — the taboo against mocking human misery, violated in the name, presumably, of irony. And yet it was almost too silly to be offensive, though the women's movement found it very offensive and quite right, too.

The pricey new glossy, *Deluxe*, has a set of fashion pictures in which the actors are garbed in jodhpurs, quilted nylon waistcoats, camouflage pants, mohair jumpers and drainpipes, and look very much as if they were mimicking sexual assault. This must represent some kind of glorious zenith or nadir of self-conscious Bad Taste and certainly cracks my own ironic impassivity right down the middle, though it's not really as offensive, as profoundly indecent, as the ads for the model agencies with the pictures of the girls plus their measurements. Like the visiting cards of a very expensive brothel. No doubt this resemblance is intentional. Isn't capitalism the brothel in which we all have our cribs? *That* must be what it means.

Deluxe, which itself might possibly be the zenith or nadir of the whole trend of Bad Taste, offers a wide variety of fetishistic apparel, a kind of summing-up of the up-market extreme. The use of rubber, with its comforting suggestions of the protective rubber sheet in the baby's cot; haircuts and cosmetic styles with the abstract stylisation of children's paintings of grown-ups; satin rompers and shorts of the kind Christopher Robin used to wear; the generally sexually exhibitionistic stance of the models; all these suggest a self-conscious pleasure in regression, a stirring of what Norman O. Brown calls 'the immortal child within us' in all its polymorphously perverse splendour.

But this pleasure in regression is of a very cerebral kind. The clothes, and the way in which they are photographed, seem to be expositions of ideas about relations of shapes and forms and textures to which the content and, indeed, the human body are almost incidental. At this theoretical level, you can see a new blueprint for the human body, and it is already working itself through in areas of clothes that have nothing to do with extremes, such as those in Marks and Spencer.

The underwear counters of Marks and Spencer are crammed with brassières such as I have not seen since the late 1950s, bras with underwired cups, padded cups, boned supports. And girdles, pantie-belts, even things that look very much like corsets. Breasts, so long left to their own devices, will be thrust up and out; the waist and belly bound in and flattened by garments that leave delicious bruises on the skin. The genuine article, back again, bondage undergarments for women, a reversion to the perpetual mild discomfort of constrictive clothing. Because the outline of women is changing, or reverting. Some of the magazines feature enormously bulky clothes for this winter, skirts, jackets and trousers that completely evade the lines of the female body, but this diffuse shape is the last gasp of the flow and spread of real flesh. There's a fad for second-hand men's suits, but I don't see it lasting; they fit too loose, are too comfortable.

The curious fad for the buttock-emphasising jodhpur suggests that bums will soon be back, to balance the new bosoms. Trousers and skirts are certainly tighter than they have been for years; tight trousers and long, tight skirts necessitate high, narrow heels – this is such an aesthetic invariable I think it must have something to do with golden sections.

Such clothes effectively hobble and restrict women as much as more explicitly fetishistic garments; they make it impossible for a woman to ignore her own physicality. You are aware of every breath you take; you have to walk carefully and totter when you run. Just as the use of cosmetics – and all the girls are doing it – makes it impossible to forget your own face. You must be always powdering and lipsticking in a one-to-one narcissistic relation with your self. I remember it all so well. I grew up with it – the taffeta petticoats that snag your stockings, the horror of it and, oh God, the little white gloves to protect your fingers from the gritty surfaces of real life.

Cropped hair, that elementary self-mutilation, is almost universal amongst young men and commonplace amongst young women. But it is the young men, with their clean-cut air, turned-up drainpipes, plaid shirts, who have the most uncanny air about them, like revenants from some pre-Vietnam campus where the matter of most moment was, whether you could borrow your father's car and who was bird-dogging whom. I could almost fool myself I was eighteen again, sometimes, back in that age of innocence when the young were poor and knew their place.

The polymorphously perverse infant of the Bad Taste extreme looks like he will grow up to be a good teen; he will know his place, this one. Girls, of course, are getting scared of the pill; and tight, bright clothes and hard bright faces are rarely, if ever, seen in cultures where sexual licence is the norm. We can stop being sexual subjects (that is, promiscuous) and revert to being sexual objects – 'après rape', in garments that will continually remind us of our socially induced masochism until they become, once again, like second nature.

Does recession always necessitate regression? Three steps forward, two steps back, the stop-stop-go of history, here it is, in the dressing-up box of appearances. What will happen next? Hard periods, like this one, always follow soft ones, like the sixties. The sixties were Rousseauesque, the seventies, as yet, Hobbesian. But, of course, they're not over yet – only this year is almost over, and I think it was a defining year. And I suppose I'm glad the year of the Jubilee was the year of the Punk, really. It was actually a very happy kind of irony, almost tasteful.

New Society, 1977

The Bridled Sweeties

Underwear exemplifies the existence – indeed, the chronic persistence – of the cultural taboo against nakedness that seems universal to all people at all times. In symbolic terms, a penis sheath or an ochre body rub is as good as a white tie and tails. We may see as stark naked many a man who perceives himself adequately, even impeccably, dressed. In the same way, a woman covered from neck to ankle in a woollen dressing-gown wouldn't dream of going down to the shops for a quarter of tea because she perceives herself as provocatively undressed.

Robert Graves prissily distinguishes between two kinds of unclothing. The naked (he poetically opines, I leadenly paraphrase) is sacred but the nude, rude. In other words, the pagan spectacle of the ritually and consciously unclad is the human in a glorious state of holy nature, which is why it is taboo. The nude, dressed up to the eyeballs in a lengthy art tradition, is clad in an invisible garment composed of generations of eyes.

Elsewhere – in *The White Goddess* – Graves describes how a numinous young Celtic person solved an enigmatic request to appear before her lover neither clothed nor unclothed by wrapping herself up in a fishing net. This non-garment performs none of the essential functions of clothing, neither protection from the elements nor chaste concealment of the parts, nor sign of status. Yet it fulfilled, while it subverted, the conditions of the taboo against absolute nakedness. Similarly, Baudelaire made his girlfriend take off all her garments but for her necklace. This made her look more naked by contrast, while offering a talismanic protection against what Graves might call the unleashed power of the goddess (though in that case she was a black one). From here, it is but one short step to the magical *déshabillée* of the Janet Reger catalogue.

Women's sexy underwear is a minor but significant growth industry of late twentieth-century Britain in the twilight of capitalism. In this peculiar climate, the luxury trades prosper. Perhaps a relationship with post-imperialism may be postulated; some folks call it 'decadence'. 'This collection has received enthusiastic acclaim wherever an appreciation for excellence as part of life's enrichment is sought,' declares the brief preface to Miss Reger's picture-book of her wares. The cover depicts a handsome pair of legs in gold kid mules, caressed in an auto-erotic fashion by a hand whose red fingernails are of a length that prohibits the performance of useful labour. The whole is sheathed in the unfolding drapes of a peach-coloured, lace-trimmed, full-length negligée; the eye automatically follows the line of the leg upwards, to a tasselled garter: the Rowena G. Garter. One size only. Colours: snow, champagne, palest green, soft apricot, ebony. The garter – than which there could not be a finer example of the luxury non-garment. The price list at the back of the mail-order catalogue offers it at £10.

Most of the colours of these fetishistic adornments are those of the archetypal luxury non-food, ice-cream – with the inevitable addition of black which, for some reason, remains synonymous with naughty underwear. The Reger catalogue hints subtly at the naughtiness: the girl posing legs akimbo in Corinna C. Negligée Ebony has scarcely perceptible bags under her eyes, and two black-clad models are pictured reclining on fur throws, perhaps to make some point about sophisticated carnality.

This luscious and expensive (£2) catalogue acts as a *vade mecum* via the post to the enrichment of your life through the non-garment. In itself, too, it is an *objet de luxe*, an invitation to voluptuous or narcissistic fantasy, depending on the sexual orientation of the browser. It also has enough of the air of the come-on brochure for an up-market knocking shop to risk causing creative confusion in those countries where brides as well as negligées are obtained through the post. This is part of the 'fantasy courtesan' syndrome of the sexy exec, a syndrome reflected admirably in the pages of *Cosmopolitan* magazine. Working women regain the femininity they have lost behind the office desk by parading about like a *grande horizontale* from early Colette in the privacy of their flats, even if there is nobody there to see.

The erotic point is inescapable. The models are dressed up in undress, in a kind of clothing that is more naked than nudity. Their flesh is partly concealed by exiguous garments in fabrics that mimic the texture of flesh itself – silk, satin-finish man-made fibres, fine lawn – plus a sublimated hint of the texture, though (heaven forbid!) never the actuality, of pubic hair.

The models are very heavily and ostentatiously made up, as if to demonstrate this civilised voluntary exile from the natural. They, too, are *objets de luxe*, as expensive to manufacture as the fragile ambiguities which adorn them. (The Leilah N. Nightdress, colours: rose, beige, black, in French lace, is really nothing more than a very sophisticated version of the Celtic young person's fishing net.) They are also elaborately coiffed, though occasionally in a style of reticent dishevellment, often with flowers in the hair, as if for some kind of bedroom *fête champêtre*. However informal, these garments are obviously public dress.

I remember reading somewhere how, in the 1950s, model girls were often reluctant to do lingerie jobs. Swimwear was fine; but respectable girls drew the line at modelling knickers, on the grounds that they should only be photographed in clothes in which they might be seen in public in normal circumstances. This quaint scruple seems to have vanished. The ostentatious glamour of the new lingerie (of which Janet Reger is only the most widely publicised purveyor), and certain changes in social relations, have created a climate in which this kind of non-garment is socially acceptable. It is breathtakingly expensive, and high cost is, in itself, a great moral antiseptic. The rich are different from us. The single-minded pursuit of excellence neutralises all kinds of waywardness.

Lingerie has become simply another kind of the non-garments characteristic of what you might call 'hyper-culture'. Others are some furs, evening dresses and ball gowns, real jewellery. All are, first and foremost, items of pure conspicuous consumption. Yet they also fulfil elaborate ritual functions. They are the garb for the Good Life in an opposite sense to that of the TV eco-serial – the pursuit of anti-nature. This includes the opera, eating in restaurants, parties, and, increasingly, sexual relations in which the gibbering old id, the Beast in Man, the manifestation of nature at its most intransigent, is scrupulously exiled. In hyper-culture, human relations are an art form.

The precious, costly fripperies on Harrods' underwear counter must do a roaring business among transvestites, whom I trust wear it in good health. For transvestites, the appearance of femininity is its essence. As I grow older, I do begin to believe this might be so. I'm just waiting, now, to aspire to the sexless grandeur of the ancients in Shaw's *Back to Methusalah*.

Of course, the whole notion of the 'natural' is an invention of culture, anyway. It tends to recur as an undertow in hyper-culture times as some sort of corrective to the excesses of those who see life as an art form without knowing what an art form is. But to say that nature as an idea is an invention does not explain the idea away. Clothing as anti-nature – as the distinction between beings under social restraint and beings that are not – can be seen in action in any circus. It is amazing what a number of non-garments – bridles, plumes, tassels – even the livery horses wear, to show to what degree they have suppressed their natural desire to run away. Relations between the non-garments of circus horses and those of professional strippers is obvious: they are seldom wholly naked, either.

Even the hippies were reluctant to strip off completely in their pursuit of the demystification of the human body. They could never resist the temptation to add a string of beads or two, or daub themselves here and there with greasepaint. Perhaps the promotion of the non-garment as decent wear shows a streak of culture within hyper-culture itself. This would come as no surprise to students of the whole messy business.

However, the real complexity of the taboo against nakedness may be seen most clearly in the catalogue of a firm like Frederick's of Hollywood – who, interestingly enough, use line-drawings rather than photographs. This is probably for reasons of cost, but it enables, all the same, a far greater degree of physical distortion. Mr Frederick is the man who offered you panti-girdles with padded or 'uplift' buttocks, and padded brassières that elevated the nipples while leaving them bare. Downmarket sexy underwear has a long, murky history.

In the early 1960s, even before permissiveness hit the West Coast, Mr Frederick – a world away from Serena French Knicker and Hattie Brief – was advertising the Pouf (sic) Panty, which had a puff of maribou at the front like a bunny girl's tail put on the wrong way round. His scanty bikini briefs were 'embroidered with lips at the nicest spot'. He urged his mail order clients how it pays to advertise: 'Wear our "Try it! You'll like it!" panty! Chances are . . . he will!' The acetate (no natural fibres here) non-garment bore this slogan stitched athwart the pelvic area. A vogue for sloganising knickers (and, indeed, underpants) has been a consistent feature of the downmarket, 'raunchy' lingerie market for years. Just, the slogans get ruder as time goes by.

Of all Mr Frederick's offerings the most striking is the 'all-nylon sheer lace brief pantie' that has 'daring derrière cutout edged in lace'. He calls this steatopygous gesture 'Back to Nature'. You couldn't put the whole ambiguous message of women's sexy underwear – upmarket, downmarket or in my lady's chamber – any fairer than that.

New Society, 1977

Ted Polhemus and Lynn Procter: Fashion and Anti-Fashion

There's a 'Compare and contrast' pair of photographs in this delicious book. One is of real Ozark hillbillies, mostly barefoot, in ragged, faded yet touchingly well laundered workclothes, the garb of decent, hard-working poverty. The other is of fake or cosmeticised or 'fashionalised' hillbillies, models demonstrating the 'Hillbilly Look' of circa 1975, crisp, print skirts and natty overalls, the fashion industry's tribute to the Simple Life, the garb of chic down-dressing. The former picture is a description of how people appear: the latter, a demonstration of what it is possible to look like.

And, unlike real hillbillies, those who choose the 'Hillbilly Look' today have the economic and social ability to don another look tomorrow – the Tart Look, perhaps, slit skirts, black stockings, stiletto heels. Though – see page 66 and discussion in the Introduction – *that* can cause a lot of confusion between those who espouse it for fashionable reasons, and real prostitutes, who wear it to show what they are. What they are – not who they are, which is another existential question entirely.

The 'Hillbilly Look' and the 'Tart Look' are fashion, and therefore part of the sartorial pageant of social mobility here today and into something else tomorrow. What hillbillies and prostitutes actually wear in the course of their working lives is anti-fashion, part of a sartorial code that maintains socio-cultural unity. This is the main thesis of the book; sartorial style and its relation to social function is what *Fashion and Anti-Fashion* is about.

The authors make a number of complex points with an amazing variety of pictures, some – like the lady swathed in cabbage leaves for a beauty treatment – sufficiently startling. They juxtapose happy families of pearly kings and Azanian tribesmen to represent stylistic continuity from one generation to another with a hippy son/straight father confrontation – 'Hiya, Dad!' 'Yarrggghhhh!!!!!') from a Furry Freak Brothers comic to show generalisational disjunction in stylistic terms. Pearlies (and primitives) look alike from father to son; where social mobility has queered the sartorial pitch, a pair of octagonal eye-glasses can be a red rag to a business-suited bull.

There is an exhilarating section on 'Anti-fashion as Utopia' – 'Utopian anti-fashions are the folk costumes of a mythical past, present or future' – featuring, amongst others, Frank-N-Furter *en travestie* from the *Rocky Horror Show* and the robot from Lang's *Metropolis*. At times, in fact, the pictures themselves threaten to run away with the argument, presenting as they do such a prodigious bouquet of sartorial bizarrerie. What does that picture of the fashion model in plastic mac and swimsuit, with a real gold-fish (poor thing) in a polythene bag of water slung round her neck – what does it mean? Has the world gone mad? Polhemus and Procter, however, probably *do* know what it means, at that.

It would be a pity if the pages of introductory text were skipped; they present a most cogent argument for the *seriousness* of the study of fashion, even if, after a brisk semiological run around, the authors finally settle for a definition of fashion as 'a grand illusion'. Which, after raising so many questions in the reader's mind, is a bit like saying: 'Well, you can wake up, now; it was all a dream, really.'

New Society, 1978

David Kunzle: Fashion and Fetishisms

David Kunzle starts off thinking about corsets from an angle which, I'm ashamed to say, had never occurred to me. It may be described most simply, thus: that women, as a whole, are *not* silly and, when they do things that, at first glance, may seem to be silly, like wearing extremely tight-fitting corsets, or tottering along in stiletto-heeled shoes, there is, at base, an impeccable, if unconscious, logic to it; that these voluntary self-mutilations are a paradoxical expression of sexual defiance and gender self-esteem.

Kunzle doesn't put it quite like that, but this is one message that may be drawn from his book, and it shocks me to think that, for so long, I went along with the standard feminist line on sexually specific clothing – that it showed women were the mere dupes of male fancy. How has it come about that feminists have picked up on the masculine notion that those women who aren't self-confessed feminists don't know what they're doing, half the time?

However, Kunzle's book is not an apologia for the corset but an argument conducted with awe-inspiring sobriety, about the role of certain practices involving the distortion of the female (and sometimes the male) form that become exaggerated at certain moments in history. His historical range extends from the wasp-waisted athletes of ancient Crete (both male and female, and they all wore padded codpieces, too), to Mrs Ethel Granger, of Peterborough, who has latterly entered the *Guinness Book of Records* as the possessor of the World's Smallest Waist (13 inches).

Nevertheless, the nineteenth century was the reign of Queen Corset, when everybody wore corsets, only some people wore them with more dedication than others. And this is the period in which Kunzle is able to elaborate most convincingly on his general predicate that tight-lacing was practised 'by women, always the disenfranchised *vis-à-vis* men, aspiring to social power by manipulating a sexuality which the patriarchy found threatening'.

He is interested primarily in excessive corseting, when, as he says in his Preface, ' "Fashion" (the culturally dominant mode of dress) and "fetishism" (the individual or group redirection of the sexual instinct on to an aspect of dress) collide and merge in the unique phenomenon of tight-lacing'. A practice that has never, precisely, been fashionable, since exhibitionism is always beyond fashion, though corsets were a European universal until this century.

He also provides a running historical commentary on the related sub-class of excessively high heels, which make a woman look either a quivering sex object always deliciously about to fall flat on her face, an erotic spectacle in itself with all the connotations of the 'fallen woman', or else the epitome of sexual aggression, ready to trample some prone man underfoot.

These forms of 'body sculpture' – of modifying, sometimes dramatically so, the natural human shape – obviously fly in the face of nature and therefore cock an all-too-visible snook at that god in whose form we were created. The Christian pulpit, always quick to pick up hints of burgeoning female sexuality, has fulminated consistently against 'unnatural' dress, from the horned headdresses of the Middle Ages to toreador pants, and directed considerable ire against the close-fitting corset, although Kunzle illustrates an iron corset of the sixteenth century that looks like a penitential garment and perhaps was.

Suffering for God and being ugly in a hairshirt was all right, apparently; suffering for the devil with a wasp waist and frilly petticoats was not. The corset it is that makes a woman's body an erotic hour glass, all tits and bum, yet armoured with whalebone and impossible to get at without permission.

Repression gives birth to austere, solitary pleasures and, in the nineteenth century, extravagantly sexual forms of women's fashions – the crinoline, the bustle, both emphasising a tiny, if not tiny-tiny, waist – blossomed in an atmosphere of general sexual repression, in which a particular veil was drawn over the reality of female desire. Kunzle quotes a shocked physician who discovered a young girl masturbating with the aid of her corset. However, there is rather more to sexual satisfaction than simple orgasm.

He provides extensive descriptions from practising twentieth-century tight-lacing fetishists as to the physiological satisfactions of the practice, the voluptuous palpitations, the 'disembodied', almost mystical feeling, the sense of mastery and achievement. These tally with letters to nineteenth-century women's magazines elaborating on the painful pleasure of a 15-inch waist, the sensation of being erotically in control, as in horse-back riding, the correspondence between self-control, self-discipline, and the magical ability to control the world. He suggests a relation between tight-lacing and the current female plague of anorexia nervosa, in which the irritating female flesh is curbed by dietary methods, often by young women who feel there is more to life than the conventional female role but may not know precisely what that something more might be.

He cites a Victorian phrenologist, thus: 'Compression produces inflamation, retains the blood in the bowels and neighbouring organs and thereby inflames all the organs of the abdomen, which thereby excites amative desires . . .' So that is the source of corset phobia! Especially since, once the corset has thoroughly awakened the sleeping demon in a woman's belly, the compressive organ itself will deal efficiently with the consequences. It was widely believed that tight-lacing procured abortion.

At this point, Kunzle's theory that tight-lacing was a means 'to protest the ever-breeding, child-centred mother' becomes hard to resist. And the foeticidal Victorian coquette, anxious to profit from her only capital, her body, by means of an upwardly socially mobile marriage or high-class prostitution, to do something, anything, to assert herself, becomes a sister under the skin.

Certainly, on the evidence Kunzle produces, fanatical nineteenth-century hatred of tight-lacing did not come from the female emancipation movement – which, after all, had far more important things to think of than what women did with their waistlines – but from those who saw women's primary function in terms of domestic labour and childbearing, both of which are activities contra-indicated by tight-lacing.

Renoir, celebrant of the 'natural' woman, spreading, naked, dumb, available for rape at any moment, hated and feared corsets. He told his six-year-old son that women who wore them must inevitably suffer from dropped wombs. In his memoirs, Pierre says, 'this idea of the womb tumbling down gave me nightmares'. You bet. Hogarth, however, adored 'stays', out of a metaphysical passion for a perfect, sinuous, rococo, artificial 'line of beauty' that is better than the natural, since it is a human creation. Baudelaire always preferred art over nature, and particularly enjoyed seeing men in corsets.

One of Kunzle's most curious and interesting byways is his discussion of the military corset, the tight waists of Russian and Prussian heroes. In an appendix, he includes an interview (made in 1969) with an English baronet, a Member of Parliament for fifty years, who habitually wore a corset and found he always delivered a House of Commons speech better when supported.

Though often witty, Kunzle is never facetious, although facetiousness has often been the way of making these fetishistic items socially acceptable, and also of reducing their implicit menace, somehow transferring the responsibility for their effect from women back to men again. Advertising copy from the wasp-waist revival of the 1950s demonstrates this admirably: 'Steel hand in the velvet glove' (but not your own hand); 'How can you look so naughty and feel so nice?'

Most histories of costume are lightweight gossipy journalism. *Fashion and Fetishisms* is, however, exactly how it describes itself: a piece of social history, instinct with intellectual curiosity and spiritual generosity towards the human race and its various contradictory ways of asserting its humanity.

From the photograph on the back-flap, it looks – though I could be wrong, and if so, I am sorry – as if David Kunzle may have donned, if not a waspy, at least a virile and inconspicuous corset of the 'military' type for the benefit of the camera.

New Society, 1982

The Recession Style

A poster advertising a certain women's magazine has been decorating the London underground for some time. It shows a girl wearing an assemblage of what are evidently supposed to be very high-style garments, so high-style as to represent an extreme of dandyism. The slogan rams this point home: 'Most girls wouldn't wear it.' This is the famous 'dare to wear' challenge – dare you blind 'em with your style, or are you (it is implied) content to remain a fuddy-duddy stick-in-the-mud.

But if you didn't know she was a fashion model, the girl in the poster would, in fact, look like nothing so much as a bag lady (or rather, person), in her asexually shapeless jacket, loose trousers and sagging socks, with a scarf of a dubiously soiled colour wrapped round her head, like a bandage beneath a hat jammed firmly down. Indeed, you can sometimes see, slumped on benches beneath this very poster, people in much the same get-up, utterly unconscious of their daring, or their involuntary dandyism, or anything at all.

In Green Park station, this poster has acquired the graffiti: 'Most girls couldn't afford it.' But to look like this need not necessarily cost much. You could put the look together for pennies. It has some of the qualities of late sixties thrift-shop chic, and many women of my generation have been going around looking like that for years, and looking like hell, in fact. Only the model's exquisitely painted face indicates that *her* get-up is intentional, and not some haphazard makeshift arrangement; that she has been paid to dress up like this, and hasn't been snapped at random at the Greenham Common peace camp. (As if to emphasise this resemblance, the poster has elsewhere been inscribed: 'Embrace the Base.')

She seems to be carrying a gas mask for a handbag, and is walking across a version of J. G. Ballard's 'terminal beach' – an arid stretch of pebbles devoid of the evidence of life beneath a sunless sky.

It is a very striking image, a gift for the spraycan commentators, and it captures the mood of the times almost to the point of parody, as if to say: we are all paper-bag persons, now, refugees in an empty world where, as well as all the other problems, you can no longer depend even on rouge to tell you what is male and what is female. Now that boys paint their faces, too, we only know she *is* a girl because the slogan tells us so.

The poster represents a public breakthrough for the aesthetic of poverty that has been operating strongly at street level since the punk styles of the mid-seventies, and may well prove (and is it any wonder?) to be the dominant mood of the eighties. It is a way of dressing that makes you look like the victim of a catastrophe.

Obviously, an aesthetic of poverty is quite different from looking poor because you *are* poor. The sisters with the spraycan interpreted the spirit of the poster correctly. The cash nexus enters into the whole thing as soon as you pay two hundred quid for your disintegrating leather flying-jacket, instead of digging it out of a garbage can.

Paying through the nose to look poor may well be a self-protective measure among those in work whilst the unemployment figures stack up. But it is ironic that rich girls (such as students) swan about in rancid long-johns with ribbons in their hair, when the greatest influence on working-class girls who *are* holding down jobs at ludicrously low wages, would appear to be Princess Di, herself always impeccably turned out and never short of a bob.

Princess Di look-a-likes work at the check-outs of every supermarket, often looking much prettier than her pictures, but, to quote *Honey* magazine: 'The way for clothes to look now is battered and crumpled, as though they've stood the test of time.' This is in itself an élitist concept, because only high-class, expensive fabrics *do* stand the test of time and, like the rich, look better as they get older.

Few can afford *real* old clothes of that kind. But cheap fabrics can simulate age if purposely crumpled, faded, torn and stained. (Leather, both real and artificial, is synthetically aged – the process known wittily as 'distressing'.) A poor fit is essential because garments must look twice-used, as if rescued from some nameless disaster. In its own unique way, the rag trade has acknowledged the recession.

According to the coverage, lavish as inscrutably ever, of last autumn's Paris fashion shows, the Japanese designers now in vogue seem to have been waiting in the wings until the time was ripe to off-load on to the backs of prosperous Occidentals a whole cornucopia of shapeless, arbitrary Zen styles, executed in impeccably Zen shades of earth, granite, foam and dung, and in fabrics which would appear to have been stored in cesspits since early Edo period. Now, clearly, they judge the time has come.

To force the filthy rich, in the name of high fashion, to dress up in garments derived from the Buddhist equivalent of Franciscan habits, the garb of conspicuous and unworldly poverty, may well seem richly humorous to the perpetrators of the jape and, perhaps, some small revenge for the Second Word War, or the entire history of European imperialism, depending on the personal bias of these designers. I suspect, too, a degree of class vengeance in some of the British designers (like Vivienne Westwood), who have arrived in international couture via anarcho-Dada.

All the same, imitation cast-offs, shrouds and coveralls are the coming thing. Up-market couture coincides with the sort of real cast-offs those people who are so down-market they scarcely figure fiscally within it have been making the best of since the economy first began to show stress.

This, as ever, leaves the middle class out in the cold, where they stay snug in their Marks and Spencer sweaters and Laura Ashley frocks. They usually remain in work, and are therefore at liberty to indulge in wishful thinking about eternal values and 100% pure natural fibres.

These days, the thing that really determines whether you look 'nice' (i.e., clean, neat and unprovocative) or 'nasty,' (i.e. messy, spiky, ominously black clad, riotously painted or tattooed) depends very much on whether you are in work or not. It behoves most of those in steady employment, especially white-collar work, to keep that white-collar scrubbed and trim because there are lots of people after it. Perhaps *that's* why most girls won't dare to wear the bag lady look until circumstances force them to it – though they might wrap a few token rags around their ankles.

Only top executives 'dare to wear' jeans to the office any more, or, indeed, jeans anywhere. Jeans have lost their outlaw chic since the class of '68 took them into the senior common room by a natural progression. They are now, more or less, a sign of grumpy middle age.

But, if you are *not* in work, you can wear what you bloody like. And they do. This emphasises more and more the basic distinction between those participating in the economic process and those exiled from it, a distinction which becomes daily more and more marked. The rich – which, nowadays, means almost everyone who has a steady job (except for those notable exceptions in the NHS and elsewhere) – may adopt the aesthetic of poverty for fun. Those who have no other option adopt it with ferocity and aggression. Once they know what they're doing, that is.

And often they do. Semiotic theory has clearly permeated the whole business. (I blame the art schools, especially their general studies departments; and the theory and practice of performance art has something to do with it.) Not only has the idea of the 'language of fashion' become a boring shibboleth, but much of the apparel you see about is clearly intended to be 'read', in no uncertain terms, as complex statements of affection and disaffection.

Literally, read. To hang around sheathed in leather covered with unimpeachable slogans like 'PEACE', 'BAN GOVERNMENT' and 'UTOPIA NOW', whilst writing 'CHAOS' on walls, gobbing a lot and lobbing crushed beer cans at passing cats, is to engage in a complicated piece of street theatre, which an illiterate person could be forgiven for getting entirely wrong.

The idea of appearance-as-visual-confrontation resurfaced with the punks in 1976 after its first Situationist outing in the heady days of 1968. Its roots go right back to Zurich 1917, and Petersburg just before the deluge. It is now common property, and it is used consciously by people who sometimes do not appear to be fully in control of what, precisely, they are expressing.

Pariah chic is more serious than outlaw chic. It produces ambiguities of which a girl with an anarcho-feminist lapel badge and a ring through her nose – the kind of ring with which animals are traditionally led to slaughter – is but the innocent victim.

Turning yourself into a slogan is, in the first place, a confrontational thing to do. Then comes the problem of the nature of the slogan, and who reads it.

The most extreme, and permanent way of turning yourself into a slogan is to tattoo that slogan on your skin, as if to say: My attitudes won't come off in the wash. But since tattooing is a form of self-mutilation, like pierced ears and noses, there is already an ambivalence about the tattooed provocateur. You must suffer in order to be provocative in this manner. And this kind of provocation can seem intended to prove suffering.

There was this skinhead, on the bus. He was adorned with two tattoos, both obviously self-inflicted. One went round his neck. It was a serrated line plus the instruction: SLIT HERE. The other, on his forehead was a swastika. He was twitching a lot, probably junked up to the eyeballs to give himself courage for the project he had evidently decided to embark on. He got off the bus at Vauxhall, and strode off in the direction of Brixton.

But to walk through Brixton with a swastika on the forehead, and an exhortation to slit the throat under one ear, is not so much provocative as suicidal – even if, along Electric Avenue, his appearance was certainly read as an advertisement of his own psychosis rather than a political statement. This kid had turned himself into a walking piece of racist graffiti. He filled me with rage, pity and terror.

The Dadaists used pity, rage and terror as the tools of the art that was supposed to end art, just as the First World War put an end (or so they thought) to civilisation. They sang, danced and screamed the scenarios of the end of the world in Zurich, among the cuckoo clocks. They caused a lot of fuss.

Something like fifty years ago, Yeats opined that things were falling apart, and many believed him and were distressed. Now the rough beast may well be amongst us, having chiselled the mark on his own forehead, and nobody makes much fuss. So accustomed have we become to the violent and desperate extravagance of the visual language which has accompanied economic catastrophe.

We must brace ourselves and wait while the Chinese curse works itself out: 'May you live in exciting times.'

New Society, 1983

Lou Taylor: Mourning Dress

People seem to be dying less often, these days. Though, statistically, that can't be true! The same number of people must continue to die as have been born, 'twas ever thus and ever will be, no way round it. Why then the demise of such *memento mori* jewellery as described by Lou Taylor, the rings with 'As I am so you must be' engraved next to a skull, the fob watches showing a young man sitting next to a tomb with the words: 'Welcome to bliss, how transient is human happiness'?

If we are less aware of death than our grandparents were, to say nothing of our medieval, Elizabethan and Jacobean forebears, it is no doubt because, these days, death most frequently occurs at those advanced ages to which it is appropriate. We are not less sensitive than our crape-draped ancestors, much of whose adult lives were spent, according to Lou Taylor, in weeds and weepers. Just that, on the whole, we have less to be sensitive about. Barring wars and road accidents, we can expect, with a degree of confidence, to encounter death when we are good and ready for it, when the engine has worn out and the bodywork eroded; death will probably not trip us up unexpectedly, nor our peers, nor our children, cross fingers, touch wood.

We may weep, we may regret, we may be reminded of our own mortality, but there is a logic to the death of an aged parent whose long, full life is done; there is none to the death of a child. And perhaps those bereaved women whose mourning extended even unto black ribbons threaded through their underwear were no more than expressing this bizarre illogic in a bizzarely illogical manner. But Lou Taylor associates the end of the high Victorian etiquette of mourning, the inexorability of black for, especially, widows, with the First World War. It was, she suggests, 'partly a question of morale, both for the troops on leave from the trenches and the public at large remaining at home. The sight of millions of women of all ages shrouded in crape would have been too much to bear.'

If she makes the wearing of mourning sound, very often, like neurotic rituals of compulsive obsession, then there is nothing like a good, strong dose of the reality principle to clean the air.

As death pertains more and more to those who are ripe to go, so the ceremonies and rituals of death lose their former, emblematic quality. The ghastly pomp and visual rhetoric of plumes, black horses, hearses are gone; the funeral ceases to be a tragic drama, becomes a small-scale, genre piece, at which the mourners wear clothes only slightly more formal than usual. Nowadays, not even a black tie but any old tie is a sign of respect.

Significant exceptions to this general rule are the funerals of combatants, victims of violence and innocent bystanders in Ulster, where sudden, violent, unexpected death out of season occasions funerals that are part military, loyalist or republican rhetoric, part displays of grief by an entire community. But Lou Taylor's brief doesn't carry as far as a discussion of the funeral as political statement, though her discussion of mourning dress involves her in a more general consideration of burial customs.

Those few funerals still celebrated as spectacle on mainland Britain are mostly those of royals or near royals. These are now nostalgically quaint, part of the tourist industry, even when the deceased has died in a politically controversial way. Lou Taylor reminds us of the state funeral of Lord Mountbatten, in 1979, after the IRA blew him up, where the procession was led by a riderless horse hung with its owner's riding boots reversed in the stirrups.

The origins of this custom lie in the mists of antiquity, at a time when a horse would be buried alongside its master to ensure he need not trudge on foot into the spirit world; it survives only as a detail of stage management, designed to bring a lump to the throat. It is a picturesque touch that would not survive translation into contemporary symbolism; a couple of garage mechanics pushing a driverless baby Fiat wouldn't move the crowd in the same way.

But on the whole, grief has been privatised and no longer needs special clothes to advertise its presence so that the entire world may see and participate in it. A funeral is no longer an invitation to share a common distress at the ubiquitousness of mortality. Lou Taylor cites an 'old-fashioned' funeral in Sussex, in 1971, when twenty black limousines followed a horse-drawn hearse; the deceased was a scrap merchant and the black-clad festival of his interment not so much of another time as from another culture, one in which life is theatre and needs an audience, not one in which life, like television, is best enjoyed in the privacy of one's own home amid a small circle of close kin.

However, grief is one thing; mourning is another, and though the one may express the other, mourning was (as funerals remain) big business. And if women, especially widows, bore the brunt of mourning in nineteenth-century Europe, wore black for the first two years, then black, white and the occasional touch of mauve for anything from six months to a lifetime after that, they were, argues Lou Taylor, publicly demonstrating the wealth and social status of their deceased mates whilst negating their own social identities.

And were egged on, perhaps, by a desire to emulate the Widow of Windsor, whose fetishistic attachment to both grief and mourning kept her in black crape for forty years after the Prince Consort's death in 1861. Queen Victoria made no concessions; she even wore a black bonnet and black dress for the Diamond Jubilee Procession in 1897, so determined was she to cast a blight on everything.

By then, the tiny lady's waist measured 48 inches round – Lou Taylor's book is crammed with fascinating facts like this – so the dress must have been virtually rectangular, almost a coffin shape in itself.

Queen Victoria's own death plunged the entire country into black. The wives of the bargees on the canals swapped their traditional white bonnets for black ones. The gold braid on the uniforms of the employees of the Glasgow underground railway was changed to black, an innovation which persisted for well nigh the next eighty years. The death of one's nearest and dearest might be one thing – evidently the Dockers' Union loaned out a black dress, shawl and bonnet to widows so they could wear decent mourning to their husband's funerals – but the death of princes is clearly something else.

Rituals of court mourning dominated the fabric industry. In the seventeenth and eighteenth centuries, when the French court was plunged into mourning by the sudden death of some second cousin twice removed of the king or the king's wife, the weavers of those brocades for which Lyon was famous were thrown out of work, and starved. Queen Victoria's years of mourning – and Lou Taylor quotes Lytton Strachey – 'exercised a highly deleterious effect upon the dressmaking, millinery and hosiery trades. The death of Edward VII in May 1910 left shops and manufacturers with vast, useless ranges of the new season's fashion fabrics.

Lou Taylor is particularly illuminating on this aspect of the history of fashion, one which historians of fashion generally skim over lightly or ignore altogether in order to get down to the serious business of the semiology of the skirt-length and things like that. There is a fascinating section on the fortunes of Samuel Courtauld's, which started out as one of the three firms in England who held the virtual monopoly of the production of mourning crape. (Dull-surfaced crape was an especially important mourning fabric because mourning demanded a lack of sheen – in extreme instances, cloth or wash-leather, rather than polished, shoes were recommended.)

Courtauld's boomed from 1850 to 1885, coinciding exactly with the peak of the Victorian passion for mourning etiquette. They scored a particular hit with a method of waterproofing crape, which hitherto had spotted dreadfully if rained on. The manufacture of crape was a steady trade, as steady as that of the coffin-maker, or so it must have seemed in those high days of the celebration of mortality; and if provident households would have preferred to lay by their black clothes once the first phase of mourning was over, store them away in mothballs ready for the next unexpected death, then a folkloric rumour was soon established that it was unlucky to keep crape in the house.

Interestingly, Courtauld's sales of crape dropped during the First World War, in spite of the widowing that went on but, happily for the shareholders, the firm had already diversified into coloured silks and were about to diversify yet further into rayon. In June 1940, crape production in England ceased altogether and was not resumed again after the war, the history of this fabric encompasses an immense change in looking at the world, described in this erudite, intelligent book.

If, as Lou Taylor says, widows' weeds had an especial function, that of stressing the way a woman's identity and sexuality were subsumed to her mate's and so 'died' with him, a death symbolised by the veils and drab, *unlively* clothes she might then wear for the rest of her life, not only changes in the social position of women but the randomised deaths of a war in which the civilian population of Britain took their due share of the violence for the first time, helped make the widow herself a somewhat anachronistic figure.

By the way, the black dress, bonnet and shawl loaned out by the Dockers' Union was in use from 1880 to 1914 – the same outfit, that is. Clearly trade unionists, though as keen as anyone on showing respect to the dead, were not superstitious about laying away crape.

New Society, 1983

Elizabeth Wilson: Adorned in Dreams

'The serious study of fashion has repeatedly had to justify itself,' observes Elizabeth Wilson in the introduction to *Adorned in Dreams*, a study of fashion which, in itself, may help to render such justifications redundant; her book is the best I have read on the subject, bar none. Fashion is part of social practice: it is an industry whose demands have helped to shape modern history, and choosing our clothes is the nearest most of us will ever get to practical aesthetics. Yet analysis of this hybrid phenomenon has largely been left to the copywriter and the pop psychologist, so that the subject may appear trivial because it has been endlessly trivialised.

It is tempting to hypothesise that this is because fashion, the province of the woman's page, is deemed, like childcare but unlike cricket, to be of interest to only one gender and therefore a marginal taste. A contempt for fashion as a particularly pernicious form of manipulative consumerism is also to be found among those who believe it to be a plot devised by men in order to turn women into sex objects, a view held with as much passion as was once used to promulgate an earlier theory: that fashionable clothes were devised by male homosexuals in order to render women terminally unappetising to heterosexual men. Elizabeth Wilson, however, approaches fashion as if with the commendable motto: 'Nothing female is alien to me.' Because women *do* love to dress up, and also to dress down: we dress to cheer ourselves up, to reward ourselves, to transform ourselves, to amuse ourselves, to incur the admiration and/or envy of other women, to pass unnoticed in the crowd, to pass messages about ourselves, to pass the time. 'Women do not always dress for men,' as Elizabeth Wilson observes tartly. 'The belief that they do has confirmed many fashion writers in their view of women as essentially silly.'

Nobody who feels superior to fashion can write well about it. In her haunting fragment of autobiography, *Mirror Writing*, Elizabeth Wilson presented herself as always strikingly *clothed*. The garments that she wore on well-remembered occasions form an integral part of the memory of those

events, as if her relation to her clothes, in their changing glamour and personality, is somehow more reassuring and constant than her relation to her
own remembered self.

Mirror Writing discussed dandyism and style informally, as one of the
ways in which identity is constructed. *Adorned in Dreams* continues and
considerably extends this discussion in much more concrete terms. The
book is, as she says, an attempt 'to view fashion through several different
pairs of spectacles simultaneously – of aesthetics, of social theory, of
politics'. She succeeds so well in this project that one only becomes aware
of its ambitiousness as she starts pulling together the threads of her main
argument. This is adequately summed up by the quotation printed on the
jacket: 'Fashion is essential to the world of modernity, the world of spectacle and mass-communication. It is a kind of connective tissue of our
organisations.' She is setting out, in fact, to restore its *clothedness* to the
modern world, especially to the modern city, of which fashion itself is the
offspring: she is giving the Emperor back his clothes, you might say, and
in the process finding out why he needs so badly to wear them. Since he
is 'adorned in dreams', we may very well learn more about reality from the
secrets revealed by his disguises than we do from the naked truth, whatever that is.

'Dress is the frontier between the self and the not-self,' she says in the
introduction, indicating some of the genuine strangeness of her subject,
with its anthropological links with magical ritual and its almost metaphysical connection with the notion of the individual. Most commentators on
fashion are themselves so powerfully seduced by the dreams that they
never realise – or can't bear to remember, or can't be bothered to do the
research, or simply forget – that the dreams, in the concrete form of
clothes in shops, are the product of hard and ill-paid labour. Sweat-shops
and factories turn out the raw commodity; they exploit a primarily female
work-force today, just as they did in the nineteenth century, when much
feminist disapproval of fashion sprang from an awareness of the conditions
in which it was made. (Around 1915, women blousemakers were being
paid nine shillings a dozen for fancy garments in fine fabrics, fourpence
each for ones in cheap silk.) The sweat-shop and the factory are central to
the history of fashion, for fashion is the child of the machine. There were
certainly fine clothes before 1851, when Singer patented the sewing-
machine, and styles could change with just as giddy a speed as they do
now, but fashion as a hobby for everyone, and especially as an activity
associated with looking at and choosing from the exultant displays of
goods on sale in the great cities of the Industrial Revolution – this is the
result of mass production, and of capitalism. Indeed, as Wilson says,
fashion 'expresses the ambiguities of an economic system which

manufactures dreams and hope as well as squalor, devastation and death'.

Some of these ambiguities are explored in the chapter titled 'Fashion and City Life'. The new cities of the nineteenth century, typified by London and Paris, and New York – which was to become the characteristic city of the twentieth century – created new classes of people, strangers living in anonymous propinquity, for whom appearances, trusting appearances, not going by appearances and keeping up appearances, were of immense importance. These cities of strangers developed a whole culture based upon looking and innovation and consumption, the culture of shopping. There is a certain romantic grandeur about her account of the inevitable rise of the department store, concurrently with that of manufactured goods, and its speedy triumph as a free museum of the latest thing. Often the architectural style of the stores themselves was the latest thing. Victorian department stores share something of the style of those other unprecedented palaces of the period, the great rail termini.

These stores made a very great deal of difference to women's lives. They provided new forms of employment for large numbers of women, mostly of the lower middle class; and, for their customers, they came to function as almost the equivalent of men's clubs, places where bourgeois women could venture without chaperone or escort, meet friends, enjoy a snack, and live for a while in surroundings of a plush and marbly splendour that matched the aspirations the stores had helped to create. Zola's marvellous novel *Au Bonheur des Dames* evokes the wild joy of a sale in one of these emporia during the heroic age of consumerism: 'women were reigning supreme. They had taken the shop by storm, they were camping in it as in conquered territory, like an invading horde which had settled among the wreckage of goods.'

Zola saw his store, the Au Bonheur des Dames of the title, as a vast juggernaut crushing traditional tradespeople and small shopkeepers beneath its wheels in its headlong progress and, above all, transforming business methods. These department stores, abandoned hulks, may now be seen, empty of stock and bereft of custom, in the deserted downtowns of those American cities that have already committed themselves to the twenty-first-century vision of the total shopping environment embodied in the shopping mall. And when Elizabeth Wilson reaches the period when classical Modernism disintegrates in a mass of self-contradicting signs, she also loses confidence, somewhat, and her writing loses some of its beautiful clarity, although on the nature of Post-Modernism itself she is wonderfully cogent: 'Post-modernism, with its eclectic approach to style, might seem especially compatible with fashion: for fashion, with its constant change and pursuit of glamour, enacts symbolically the most hallucinatory aspects of our culture, the confusions between the real and the not-real, the aesthetic obsessions, the vein of morbidity without tragedy, of irony without merriment, and the nihilistic critical stance towards authority, empty rebellion almost without political content.'

Here she sums up the present condition of aesthetics with positively majestic severity. Yet it is precisely when she discusses fashion in the present day and the recent past that bits and bobs of fashion journalists' argot creep into and disfigure her prose. 'Fashion anarchy', she says, speaking of the demise of 'the single, Paris-dictated line' which evidently once existed and now does not; she talks about 'the ethnic look', and this look, and the other look, with neither irony nor apology, but almost a kind of exhaustion, as if all that is solid really is melting into air, this time, but 'wolf' has been cried once too often. She fails to appreciate adequately the incorporation of fashion into the leisure industry; she, mysteriously, seems to admire Mary Quant.

Elizabeth Wilson blames the sixties for a good deal, especially for the promotion of decadent images of Woman as Waif, and as 'the art nouveau nymph, stoned and tubercular'. It is as if the capacity for dialectics deserted her when faced with something of which she did not approve, and evidently she does not approve of that ramshackle yet glorious decade. As a result, she tends to misread icons. For example, the whole point of Twiggy, whom she fingers as waif incarnate, was the contradiction between the extraordinary refinement of her features and the raucous cheerfulness of her personality. She looked, and, indeed, still does, like a creature from another planet where people are more beautiful than we are: and she sounded, as her then boyfriend remarked, like 'a demented parrot'. She was promoted as an authentic working-class heroine. Twenty years later, she is not dead or mad, but a huge star on Broadway. She had very little effect on the way girls looked because, of course, it was impossible to look like her without that distinctive bone structure – but also, I suspect, because she led an utterly blameless life. Mums and dads were the ones who really thought she was lovely. Marianne Faithfull, now . . . Interestingly enough, Twiggy sponsored a range of clothes marketed under her own name in the late sixties and it was a failure. Yet it is always difficult to achieve an objective stance towards the day before yesterday. I cannot in reason castigate Elizabeth Wilson for failing to stand sufficiently far back from something when there isn't sufficient existential room to do so.

London Review of Books, 1985

Roland Barthes: The Fashion System

The Fashion System isn't about fashion, as such. Instead, it concerns itself with 'the written garment'. That is, with 'King Coat the First', and 'the famous little suit that looks like a suit', and 'the sailor top open over a knit dickey' and the rest of the verbal representations made not by the dressmaker but by the fashion copywriter. Barthes states his purpose at the outset, in the foreword: 'The object of this inquiry is the structural analysis of women's clothing as currently described in the Fashion magazines.' He usually gives fashion a capital 'F', as if it were a proper name. I haven't worked out why.

Barthes combed *Elle*, *Le Jardin des Modes*, Vogue and *L'Echo de la Mode*, scrupulously noting the way in which some of these publications were more down-market than others. He found almost too rich a trove of samples from the luxuriant hedge of verbiage the fashion industry interposes between the object and its user; here is a feast of overripe prose. 'Banal poetry', he calls it at one stage. 'Petticoats, creamy and dreamy. 'Gauze, organza, voile and cotton muslin, summer is here.' 'Prints win at the races.'

Barthes exhibits an awed, horrified fascination for the raw material of his project, yet be would seem to revel in that for which he feels distaste. He just can't leave that phrase, 'prints win at the races', alone. He worries away at exegesis for pages, like a puppy disembowelling a slipper. There is an air of sublimated camp about much of this.

Although the fashion rhetoric he cites might well have come out of this month's *Vogue* and *Elle*, it turns out that Barthes was scrutinising these magazines all of twenty-five years ago and more, proving one of his points about the timelessness of the written garment – 'imagine a woman dressed in an endless garment, one that is woven of everything the magazine of Fashion says – as opposed to the constantly changing nature of the *real* fashion garment.

Begun in 1957 and completed in 1963, *The Fashion System* was published in France four years later and now belatedly arrives in Britain following well in the rear of many of the ideas it contains.

But even by the time Barthes wrote his foreword, presumably in 1967, he seemed already somewhat embarrassed by this comparatively early exercise in what he calls 'the new intellectual art' of semiology. He virtually apologised for himself: 'This book forms a slightly naïve window through which may be discerned . . . the beliefs, the temptations and the trials of an apprenticeship.'

All the same, *The Fashion System* is tougher going than later Barthes because it is crammed with complicated diagrams, quasi-algebraic symbols and series upon series of inventories, sets of classifications and lists of categories, each subdivided into further subsections with the scrupulous obsessiveness of a medieval schoolman, until you start wondering how many semioticians could dance on the head of a pin.

Barthes consumes page after page with sets of minutely differentiated definitions, such as: 'Certain species can "head" other species; a *knot*, for instance, is the species of the genus "Fastener", but it can form subspecies of its own; *hatter's knot, cabbage-knot, butterfly-knot*; this means that a hatter's knot is set in signifying opposition to all other knots before being more generally opposed to all other fasteners.' And, at random from the chapter titled, 'Inventory of Genera', the entry: PLEATS Drapes, gathers, godets, darts, pleats (fan-), fold ruffle. For the lay person, all this has the compulsive mystification of a Borges short story. If it weren't all so finicking and anal, it would be taxonomy run riot.

But though *The Fashion System* may have started out as a description of a method, replete with specifications for the tiniest nuts and bolts, the lapidary epigrammist of the later texts cannot resist peeking seductively through the elaborate semiological apparatus, nodding, winking, beckoning and making strange.

He cannot resist astonishing the reader: ' . . . think for a moment of the magazine as a machine that makes Fashion'. This is such a dazzling image it stops you in your tracks, quite taking your mind off what he might be getting at in the first place. And then, far from giving you time to get your breath back, he will embark on an intellectual aria executed with the liveliest and most elegant grace.

For example, how, in Fashion, a place that is somewhat adjacent to Utopia, there is, appropriately enough, neither pain nor harm nor suffering. Fashion is 'the language of a mother who preserves her daughter from all contact with evil'. This insulation from the facts of life procures that systematic euphoria peculiar to fashion: '(it formerly belonged to all literature for young girls)'. If it is the sign of an anal-retentive character to tidy up and store away and assign a place to everything and put everything in its place, then there is a paradoxically prodigal looseness of the bowel about a man who can throw away an idea like that as he does in a parenthesis.

But that is something Barthes is fond of doing. '(We could say that the stereotype functions like a poorly recalled memory.)' He enjoys consigning fascinating, if dubious, facts to obscure footnotes that you might miss if you were in a hurry: 'In the Renaissance, as soon as one got a new costume, one had a new portrait done.' And it is strangely moving to come across this seminal thought, 'Fashion presents the woman as a representation,' and realise how far, when projected in a straight line, it was going to go. (There are certain pleasures of hindsight to be got from reading *The Fashion System* out of context with the rest of Barthes.)

The Fashion System is nevertheless an unsatisfactory book for somebody whose mind doesn't function like clockwork on odd days and fireworks on even days, which is surely how Barthes's mind must have operated. The book is rather like a complicated and elaborate ladder, which Barthes has constructed in order to be able to climb to an unexpected place, and then climbed – and now balances on the top rung on one leg, poised to kick the ladder away and see what happens next. But almost incidentally, *The Fashion System* does tell you a great deal about how the imaginative structures of mass culture, of which fashion is part, operate.

New Society, 1985

Arthur Marwick: Beauty in History

Back in the sixties, a decade which evidently I enjoyed rather more than did your contributor, Janet Watts (*London Review of Books*, 8 December 1988), Kenneth Clark published a contribution to art history called *The Nude*. A disgruntled friend of mine opined that if the author had any integrity, he'd have started off his opus: 'Wankers, ahoy!' (Oh, the jaunty irreverence of those days of intellectual ferment, and its reassertion of the best characteristics of British humour – funny, vulgar, true.)

Arthur Marwick's book almost deserves the same put-down. Almost, but not quite, because he's somewhat less po-faced, if a good deal more prurient, than Kenneth Clark, and perfectly vulgar himself, though not particularly funny, alas.

True? Is beauty truth, or was it ever? Not necessarily, says Professor Marwick. But he certainly knows what he likes and a fitting subtitle for *Beauty in History* might be: 'Women I have fancied throughout the ages with additional notes on some of the men I think I might have fancied if I were a woman'. He does not permit himself any more complicated permutations of sexual preference than this.

Beauty in History is a big thick, amply illustrated tome devoted to proving to Professor Marwick's own satisfaction that physical beauty in human beings is not a socially determined characteristic but an essential harmony of feature and proportion that does not change from age to age, or rather, does not change much, and is subject to only the mildest fluctuations of fashion. There are echoes here of the revisionist Ruskinian aesthetic of Peter Fuller, although Marwick adds an erotic sub-plot to ginger things up, quoting Freud: 'There is to my mind no doubt that the concept of "beautiful" has its roots in sexual excitation and its original meaning was sexually stimulating".'

This adds a peculiar force to his statement of intent: 'In evaluating beauty we should not, as all previous writers have done, look simply at what painters *painted* or fashion writers *decreed*, nor even at one or two individual beauties and what was *said* about them: we must look at what people actually *did*.' (Italicised, this statement is printed on the book's jacket, so everybody can see exactly what the book is about.)

It is a relief to find that Marwick does not do anything quite so crude as to evaluate good looks, as depicted in painting and photography of the past, on a scale of ten. He also believes there was a 'traditional' view of beauty in Western Europe derived from Platonism and early Christianity, which saw beauty as a moral, even a spiritual quality, more to do with the soul than the body, and this meant that good looks weren't so highly valued then as they are now, when personal appearance is, as Marwick claims, more important for worldly success than it has ever been before. (And, presumably, people have more sex, therefore.)

He is also happy to take on those feminists who argue that ideas of beauty are essentially political, part of the male plan to subjugate women. 'All the complicated talk of politics and power struggles and male conspiracy and oppression seems to miss the simple heart of the matter: the sheer uncomplicated joy of going to bed with a beautiful woman.' He is more than happy to concede, as a sop to feminists, that women probably feel the same way about going to bed with handsome men, although a dishy premature ejaculator may find that women shun him.

He certainly has a low opinion of the feminist sexual imagination. He applauds the way women abandoned brassières in the late 1960s, and believes that for some of the women who did so it was 'part of the realisation that (something feminists ignored) there were few more enticing sights than the outline of breasts unconstrained by a brassière.' There is something almost – but, again, not quite – touching about the boyish enthusiasm Professor Marwick evinces towards his subject. There are whole pages off which one can feel the acne rise. Then he adds, piously: 'My earnest hope . . . is that this book should not be sexist.'

In fact, it is beyond sexism. A man who, with a perfectly straight face, can describe the photographer hero of Antonioni's movie *Blow Up*, as having 'a corps of lovely cavorting dolly birds at his disposal' clearly has some difficulty in defining what constitutes sexism and the language in which it habitually expresses itself.

To castigate a man, on the one hand, for his use of sexist language and then to turn on him for lack of chivalry may seem quixotic; besides, Professor Marwick covers himself by invoking another Professor Marwick covers himself by invoking another Professor, Sir John Plumb, but these two gentlemen between them certainly have no respect for the feelings of the dead. 'George III's wife, Charlotte of Mecklenburg-Strelitz, was so manifestly ugly that the King's bouts of madness, Professor Sir John Plumb has suggested, may have been due to the strain of having sexual relations with her.' Could not George III have closed his eyes and thought of England, as women were frequently told to do in the circumstances? Or put a pillow-case over her head? And obviously neither George III, nor Professor Sir John Plumb, or possibly even Freud, had ever heard the ancient piece of folk wisdom: 'You don't look at the mantelpiece while you're stoking the fire.' (Also current with the cruder variant, 'poking'.)

This saying is either extremely sexist. Or, not. Depending on how one looks at it. After all, women traditionally copulate with their eyes shut, whether or not they think of England, and sometimes have a nice time, even so, which suggests that the mantelpiece, though mute, might have its own opinions on what makes a good stoke.

Then again, if having sex with an ugly woman sent George III mad, the neurasthenia to which married women of the eighteenth and nineteenth centuries were so notoriously prone might well have sprung from having to go to bed with the monstrously ugly old men their fathers picked out for them for pecuniary reasons. This reintroduces the problems of politics, and of conspiracy and oppression (male), into the scenario again by a convenient side-door, but Professor Marwick himself is perfectly prepared to do so under certain circumstances, provided the boot is on the foot of the opposite gender.

'Angie Dickinson, successful, influential, wealthy, middle-aged Hollywood actress, famous for her affairs with men much younger than herself, put a practical perspective on the matter when she revealed that she was well aware her young men did not find her particularly sexually desirable but hoped that she would help them in furthering their film careers.' In other words, one woman's 'uncomplicated' joy in going to bed with a handsome man is a toy boy's cynical power politics. Or perhaps Ms Dickinson is simply more prepared to acknowledge the complications than, say, Henry Kissinger, or any other of the ill-favoured middle-aged men of wealth, status and power who enjoy the company of attractive younger women. But Ms Dickinson, come off it! is *far* prettier than Henry Kissinger, even if she won't see fifty again, and I doubt her boyfriends urge her to put a bag over her head unless that is what they always like to do.

However, horizontal mobility has been characteristic of the careers of great beauties of both or all sexes for millennia, and the potted histories with which Marwick illustrates his thesis that good looks assist social advancement are full of it. Indeed, the better-looking you are, the more you are, or seem, forced to do it: Marilyn Monroe slept with some repulsive studio bosses on her way to fame, alcohol and barbiturate abuse, psychiatric illness, emotional shipwreck and premature demise. (Marwick is decent enough to note briefly that being beautiful does not necessarily make a person happy.)

But Marwick is prepared to down-pedal the lure of status and the imperiousness of power when it belongs to a man the cut of whose jib he admires: 'I would surmise that, without the magic of royalty, Charles II would still have been pretty successful with women.' Except that, like what song the siren sang, or whether or not Rubens really liked fat women (something Marwick makes much of), this is beyond conjecture.

Now what is particularly irritating about this presentation of the past as a giant Miss Universe pageant, with a lady-pleasing subsection for dishy gents, is that tucked away within it, and relatively unexplored, are some interesting propositions. One of them Professor Marwick puts with, I trust, calculated banality: 'if it was a woman's duty to be beautiful, could a beautiful woman exploit her looks without having to utilise her sexuality? If she did grant sexual favours, could she remain respectable?' He says these questions became pressing issues in the nineteenth century, although, if literature is any evidence, they have been of intimate concern to women since the time of Homer. (And the answer to the second question is obvious, anyway: yes, of course, provided nobody found out.)

But the way in which appearance functions as a kind of visible sexuality for women only ceases to matter in periods of sexually relaxed behaviour. Marwick's book is a study in an eroticism of the eye that does not take into account the fact that the eye is not a sexual organ, as such: the eye envies, the eye desires on its own account. He remarks that the model girls who became famous in the 1960s – Jean Shrimpton, Twiggy et al – were beauties who, unlike the fabulous courtesans of the Belle Epoque, led wholly respectable private lives, according to the manners of the time. (In fact, their private lives in those days, involving cohabitation without marriage, would have been sufficiently scandalous at the turn of the century.) Their romances belonged to a different order of fantasy than the liaisons of women like Polaire and La Belle Otéro, Cora Pearl, 'Skittles' and so on. Twiggy and Justin de Villeneuve, Jean Shrimpton and Terence Stamp – these affairs were not the stuff of male erotic reverie but of female fantasy.

And their appeal was primarily to women. However much men may have admired them, it was women who made Twiggy and Jean Shrimpton stars and they modelled for women's magazines and the women's pages of newspapers, not for *Men Only*. They were offering themselves to be looked at by women; even if the photographers who mediated the images were men, the editorial staff who promoted the various 'faces of the year' were largely women and the consumers of the imagery almost wholly so. There is a complexity to this that Professor Marwick, with his implicit criterion of beddability, does not explore, even if he is keen to explore the vexed question of Twiggy's bosom in the days of her early fame and confirms that, yes indeed, she was adequately endowed. 'Twiggy, with her 31-inch bust, had beautiful, small but perfectly proportioned breasts, as can be seen from the photograph of her in a bikini reproduced III,116.'

It is surely the kindest thing to regard this bizarre trip around yesteryear's pin-ups as a one-off aberration from a perfectly reputable historian who has stretched out a simple, if debatable proposition – that, through Western European history, all human beings have always fancied the sort of people he fancies – to accommodate a degree of, to me, incoherent theorising which is not without its unintentionally comic side.

London Review of Books, 1989

HOME AND AWAY

What the Hell – It's Home!

Bradford: Industry as Artwork

At times, Bradford hardly seems an English city at all, since it is inhabited, in the main, by (to all appearances) extras from the Gorki trilogy, huddled in shapeless coats – the men in caps and mufflers, the women in boots and headscarves. It comes as no surprise to hear so much Polish spoken or to see so much vodka in the windows of the off-licences, next to the British sherry, brown ale and dandelion and burdock. Though, again, it might be a city in a time-machine. Those low, steep terraces – where, at nights, gas lamps secrete a mean, lemon-coloured light which seems to intensify rather than diminish the surrounding darkness – and the skyline, intermittently punctuated by mill chimneys, create so consistent an image of a typical Victorian industrial town everything teeters on the brink of self-parody and the public statuary goes right over the edge.

Like monstrous *genii loci*, petrifications of stern industrialists pose in squares and on road islands, clasping technological devices or depicted in the act of raising the weeping orphan. There is something inherently risible in a monumental statue showing a man in full mid-Victorian rig, watch chain and all, shoving one hand in his waistcoat *à la* Napoleon and, with the other, exhorting the masses to, presumably, greater and yet greater productiveness.

The same impulse to ennoble commerce must have dictated the choice of the Gothic-revival architectural style, that of the instant sublime, for which the city is famous. The Wool Exchange pretends to be a far more impressive cathedral than the cathedral itself, and most of the public buildings strive in their appearance to transcend their origins, becoming in the process authentic chapels to Mammon. Mysteriously enough, the city museum is housed in a mansion imitating another kind of grandeur; it and the formal gardens surrounding it are just like the hotel and grounds in *Last Year at Marienbad*, a curiously wistful palace of culture set in a rather romantic public park. The building is guarded by a statue of Diana the Huntress. All this is irrelevantly gracious and unnervingly out of context, reflecting, presumably, the place of the arts in the context of the culture which produced it. The mills, however – reflecting, perhaps, a more honest respect for the muck which signifies brass – are built on heroic proportions.

Their chimneys are monumental in size and design, like giant triumphal columns or pediments for Brobdingnagian equestrian statues. On some days of Nordic winter sunshine, the polluted atmosphere blurs and transfigures the light, so that the hitherto sufficiently dark, satanic mills take on a post-apocalyptic, Blakean dazzle, as if the New Jerusalem had come at last, and the sky above is the colour and texture of ripe apricots. A russet mist shrouds the surrounding moorland, which is visible from almost every street, however mean. On such mornings, it is impossible to deny that the scene is beautiful.

Snow, however, brings out the essential colours of the city. Everything is delicately veiled in soot which fortuitously unifies the eclectic urban scene to such a degree that those public buildings which have been scrubbed back down to their native stone look ill at ease, as though they no longer belonged here, like millhands' sons who have gone to Oxford. But the soot, although it paints in monochrome, does not create a monotonous scene, for here one may appreciate and enjoy an infinitely rich collection of blacks, from the deepest and most opaque to the palest and most exquisitely subtle, through an entire spectrum – brownish-black, greenish-black, yellowish-black and a cosy, warm, reddish-black. The air, which often has the metallic chill of freezing metal, is full of the sweetish smell of coal smoke. Snot is black.

The weather is brutish. The cold has moulded the stoicism of the inhabitants and, perhaps, helped to determine their diet, rich as it is in heat-supplying fats and carbohydrates – so rich in fat, indeed, that persistent local folklore relates how Bradford Royal Infirmary is forced to discard pints of donated blood due to the high fat content it contains.

Fish and chips; pie and a spoonful of reconstituted dried peas the colour of mistletoe, swimming in grey juice; the odorous range of Yorkshire charcuterie, haslet, sausage, tomato sausage, black pudding, roast pork, pigs' trotters, pigs' cheek, jars of pork dripping, every variety of cooked pig the mind could imagine or the heart desire, for the succulent pig appeals to the native thriftiness of its eaters since every part of him may be consumed.

All this powerful cityscape of strangeness and unusual harmonies seduces the eye of the romantic southern visitor so much he finds it easy to forget that, thirty years ago, Lewis Mumford defined such places as Bradford as 'insensate industrial towns'. J. B. Priestley's Bradford was a good place to have come from, bearing in mind one would be able to remember it in tranquillity far, far away; and John Braine's postwar

Bradford expressed only an appreciation of those affluent parts of the place
that might be anywhere else in Britain. But now it is easy to find it charming here.

It is partly charming because it is so strange; the presence of so many
Pakistanis creates not so much the atmosphere of the melting-pot for, at
present, the disparate ethnic elements are held in an uneasy suspension, but
an added dimension of the remarkable. Signs everywhere in Urdu; young
girls with anoraks over their satin trousers; embroidered waistcoats; unfamiliar cooking utensils in hardware shops; and cinemas with even their
names up in Urdu. On Sunday afternoons, the man next door spends
perhaps three or four hours practising upon some inexpressibly exotic
musical instrument which sounds as though it has only a single string. He
chants constantly to his own accompaniment and, to this Asiatic threnody,
the wuthering of the Brontë winds from the moors lends a passionate
counterpoint.

But thirty years ago would I have found all this charming? Or would I
have flinched that human beings should be forced to live and work in
these conditions which might well have reminded me of the workers'
dwellings in Lang's *Metropolis*; and if, unwillingly, I had found a quaint
attraction in the scene, I would probably have identified it as the same
attraction/repulsion the late eighteenth-century intellectual experienced
at the spectacle of the Horrid. Just as the uneasy aesthetic of the Horrid
modulated into a positive pleasure-reaction to the same spectacle redefined as the Picturesque and thence into that expansion of the sensibility
involved in the discovery of the idea of the Sublime, so the Horrid – i.e.,
the working-class environment, Victorian Gothic architecture, the detritus we now refer to as examples of industrial archaeology – began its modification towards the picturesque twenty years ago, if not before. It is now
well on the way to becoming a new type of the Beautiful, although we
have not yet found it a fitting name, a type of the beautiful first consciously
rendered visually in those British films of the late 1950s which featured
endless arty shots of gasworks reflected in canals and pit wheels outlined
against storm clouds.

A hundred years ago, Daumier found such spectacles perfectly hideous;
forty years ago, George Orwell found only a poignant desolation in these
industrial cityscapes, marked with the grisly stigmata of poverty. They are
probably still seductive principally to the bourgeois romantic intellectual
who sees them with the fresh eye of one not born and bred in a back-to-
back house or to those afflicted with a sad case of Hoggart nostalgia. (I
have a peculiarly rich reaction to Bradford due to a confusion of both
kinds of response, plus some piquant memories of an early childhood in a
more southerly Yorkshire environment which really looked more like

Tolkien's Mordor than anywhere else.) On the other hand, the history of taste may well be that of the obscure and probably warped predilections of the bourgeois romantic intellectual gradually filtering down through the mass media until everybody knows for certain what they ought to like. After all, only a handful of eccentrics enjoyed mountains until a mountain got up and followed Wordsworth across a lake.

I often feel that Manningham Mills are rolling inexorably after me on ponderous wheels down Oak Lane.

Yet Bradford has the virtues of a total environment where work and life goes on side by side, and the hilly streets, following as they do the (indeed) majestic contours of the surrounding hills, retain some kind of organic relation with the countryside in which a chance combination of natural elements, wool and water, produced the city in the first place. It is not a handsome city as Leeds, nearby, is handsome; it does not wear its muck with such conscious, assertive pride. It is more domestic, earthier. The contrast between the splendid front and the squalid asshole are not nearly as great. It is far older than Leeds. At times, it even feels almost medieval, with its windy, winding streets. It is a city with such a markedly individual flavour that even though it will take an aesthetic *volte-face* of seismic proportions before even the most entrenched preservationists hail it as the Florence of the north, that day might some day come; Bradford will indeed be seen by all to be beautiful if it escapes the fate of the rest of Britain, which is plainly that everywhere will be done over to look like a universal continuous North Cheam. Then we will wake to a shocked consciousness of the visual pleasures we have lost.

New Society, 1970

Fin de Siècle

It looks like the *fin* has come a little early this *siècle*.

So old she ought to be superannuated, an infinitely accommodating whore, painted thickly over the stratified residue of yesterday's cosmetics and the day before yesterday's cosmetics and, under all the layers, deep in the pores, the antique, ineradicable grime. London: over-ripe, voluptuous, oppressive, corrupt, self-regarding, inward-turning who costs twice as much to love as any *grande horizontale* in the entire history of the world.

Things have changed while I've been away. Or, perhaps, they have just intensified.

Age, alas, cannot wither nor accustom stale her; I only wish it could –
beautiful, baleful London, melting sweetly in her own decay as the property speculators burrow away at her innards with the vile diligence of
gonococci, a monstrous harlot heaving away in the birthpangs of an ill-
favoured offspring, all concrete, glass, steel, chrome and dead.

The cure for homesickness is worse than the disease; all you have to do
is to come back.

There is, of course, a war on – although this is a fact most people, with
a considerable degree of success, contrive to ignore. The telephones very
often do not work; when they do, one frequently encounters the familiar
surprise of the obscene telephone call. Unknown callers announce themselves by urinating through the letter box. Go away to Portugal for a fort-
night and your semi in Coulsdon will have appreciated by £50,000 in
value when you return. If you belong to the incipient hereditary caste of
rent-controlled tenants, gorillas in dark glasses will burst in and smash up
your lavatory. There is a state of emergency.

I see the Conservatives really do keep their promises.

A feverish, hysterical glamour plays like summer lightning about certain
of the arteries of sixties' consciousness, although the King's Road has long
gone the way of Carnaby Street towards an ultimate apotheosis in candy
floss and Kiss Me Kwik hats, while the petals drop remorselessly from the
full-blown Gate. London, never a city formed around a central core but
always a constellation, a galaxy, of separate planets each with its own peculiar forms of life, linked together as tenuously as unravelling knitting by the
creaking subways that shudder to a halt at midnight and roads so choked
they often seize up altogether. Sometimes buses come; sometimes they do
not. Everything costs the earth.

'Mustn't grumble,' said the old lady at the bus stop who could no longer
afford to visit her daughter in Luton since it cost 50p each way. 'Still,
mustn't grumble.'

If the British weren't so bloody nice, there'd be a bloody revolution.

To my now stranger's eye, London wears the self-conscious quaintness
of parochialism like a singularly unbecoming national dress. In the sixties,
London, for the first time, became aware of itself as – in the jargon of those
dear, dead days – a centre of consciousness, a city with a certain characteristic style expressive of a radically changing mode of life. For a brief
season, it seemed the old barriers of class and privilege were, if not actually
down, at least crumbling.

Nobody had ever accused the British of sophistication before and, in
our innocence, the very idea we had, however accidentally, created a
mode went to our heads. Perhaps we mistook permissiveness for liberty.
But a permissive society is still a profoundly authoritarian society – who is

it, do you think, who is *permitting* you to do all those exotic things . . .

However, having gone away, and returning now from two years in the trim dementia of Japan, where structured permissiveness has always been the preferred structure for the exercise of enlightened fascism, I can see innumerable signs of change here – but no signs of growth. As though the London style, in spite of a small number of variations, is imitating itself helplessly over and over again, with an increasing degree of hysteria.

It has become a very noisy city. Even the walls shout at you. The city is scribbled all over, a perpetual gabble of graffiti. Some walls are a positive palimpsest, on which one can chart the ideological blossoming, waxing and waning of the consciousness of a decade, of the sixties. Over the underwriting (CND symbols, BAN THE BOMB), are beautiful thoughts for the pure in heart, fading now, influence of Paris '68: 'Authority is the mask of violence', 'Crime is the highest form of sensuality', 'Psychiatry kills', 'Love only ME' (that's a funny one). Then brute reminders of the brutalism at the fag end of the decade: BOOT BOYS, SKINS UNITE. BOOT TOWN. BOOTS FOR EVER. BOOTS RULE.

And so, into the seventies – bearing, not peace, but a sword: 'Support the Stoke Newington Eight', 'Armed love', 'To hell with the Stoke Newington Eight', 'Support the dockers', 'Smash the dockers', 'Support the IRA', 'Smash the IRA', 'Workers' control – not controlled workers' (don't you know there's a class war on?). 'Gay is angry' (don't you know there's a sex war on, either?). It says on the walls of Holloway Prison: 'We are women – we are angry'.

Nevertheless, I am astonished to see that a good half of the female population of London is in the grip of a common false pregnancy this summer – a curiously disturbing phenomenon. Over their maternity smocks, they tie elaborate pinafores such as those formerly worn by Victorian nursemaids. Fabrics often retreat to the nursery – pastel cottons printed with designs featuring the three pigs, or Wynken, Blynken and Nod. This summer's footwear has reached a peak of fetishistic strangeness unknown since the spike heels of the late fifties – a public insanity expressed by the feet.

Two shapes dominate. One is a monolithic clog that has acquired such a thickness of sole it affects the entire balance of the female body. As an alternative to these brutalised versions of traditionally peasant apparel, there are authentically deviant shoes – ferocious, ankle-strapped monsters, lugubrious parodies of the styles of the forties, with stilt heels five or six inches high and platform soles several inches thick, executed in a series of fantastic leathers, polka dot patents, tartan suedes and so on; shoes that resemble nothing so much as the kubkabs or bridal pedestals, more furniture than apparel, on which Syrian brides totter to the altar in a demonstration of chronic helplessness. Women are once again precariously elevated in a display of masochism.

Conceivably, these diabolical contraptions, and the outfits that go with them, are a mute, derisive response to the Women's Liberation movement. Certainly the girls who stump along in their enormous shoes, with their bellies thrust out and their eyes painted red so they look as if they have been weeping, have the iconography of sexual oppression scrawled all over them. Yet these styles, which parody femininity, may be one response to the state of emergency we ignore in every other way but the unconscious signs of taste. Hems always drop when hard times are coming, as if women feel the need to retreat into the defensive pseudo-vulnerability of womanliness. This resurgence of role-defined clothing, of garments that, however drab or lurid, indicate emphatically there is a special being, a woman, inside them, seem a symptom of the detectable hardening of the social arteries.

The flavour of this summer is the sickly-sweet flavour of nostalgia. As though a defensive retreat into the recent past is the only defence against an ominous tomorrow. The hamburger heavens and the ice-cream parlours purvey nursery food to thronging crowds, in surroundings as bright, cheerful and uncomplicated as a kindergarten. Extra-thick milk-shakes; chips with ketchup; hamburger sandwiches – the food we of the deprived, postwar years used to lick our lips over in the glossy advertisements of American magazines that came in Bundles for Britain. To this generation, the food and the surroundings come without any such overtones; it is pure dream food. A nostalgia for the eternal verities is expressed in health foods, brown rice, tisanes and corn fritters. We have re-entered an age of unsophistication.

There is a revival of the music and the styles of, God help us, the early fifties, a move to embrace the innocence of the style of the Rockers, which was one of urban pastoral – the Rocker as a kind of noble savage: indeed, there is a resurgence of interest in the appeal of the totemic virility of the Ted. No hint of the pansexual revolution there.

The frenetic simplicity of the music is that of the age of innocence before Vietnam, before LSD, before the public embracement of the illusion of permissiveness. The style of the early seventies is that of a sensibility at the point of exhaustion. Perhaps the collective consciousness can expand only so much, and then the shift back to the known, the familiar and the safe begins. They are selling drainpipe jeans in jet black and ice blue in the King's Road. Bill Haley and his Comets are on tour.

Nostalgia is itself a sickness of the sensibility. Nostalgia, accompanied by the impotent rage that shrieks and gibbers from the hoardings, adds up to a manic-depressive sickness.

Returning to London. It is like coming to a new city, where all the signs have changed and people speak another language. The infrequently visiting, wistfully tarnished north Atlantic sunlight of this inclement summer plays upon a soon-to-be-altogether-unrecognisable skyline of unpopulated towers that must have been designed to look at its best in ruins. On the hoarding at Hyde Park Corner, a prophetic hand has daubed: GOOD-BYE LONDON.

It is the more than Asiatic patience of the crowds that appals me most.

New Society, 1972

The Oss Has His Day

You pass the Ambrosia creamed rice factory; then, after a while, the Mother's Pride bread factory on the Devon/Cornwall border. These two monuments to British traditional cuisine behind, you're into Britain's little Sicily, grim stone townships, grim, sullen moors . . . But we are bound beyond bleak Bodmin to the little town of Padstow, with its seafood restaurant, its steakhouse, its tropical bird garden. And it is May Eve.

Everywhere is hung with flags, and boughs of sycamore decorate all the doorways. Padstow is *en fête*. The Harbour Inn – stable of the Blue Ribbon Oss – is packed out, but a bit of dancing goes on. One agile man has stripped off his shirt, pissed out of his head, terpsichorally too extravagant to be a visitor.

The crowded bar sings the May Song, Padstow's own. It says: let us all unite, for summer is acome in today. But it will, in fact, come tonight, at 12 p.m. precisely. We shall sing in the summer in front of the Golden Lion, up the street.

The Lion has an elaborate sign on its front executed in Merrie England style. This announces that it is the stables of the Old Oss, or Red Ribbon Oss, one of the two hobby horses who will parade tomorrow's streets. The narrow access fills up as soon as the pubs close. Young kids sing and raucously dance the May dance and May Song while there's room to dance; before they pass out, anyway. Their dancing has been affected by discos. They only seem to know the one verse: 'Unite and unite', 'Rejoice and rejoice'. And the strange cry, 'Oss! Oss!' with its response, 'Wee Oss!'

In a lighted upper room of the pub, a man in purple underwear persists in sticking his bum out of the window. At first, in my innocence, I thought that this, too, was a folk tradition. But the growing hubbub of discontent in the crowd soon disabused me of that. After a while, people began to heckle him. But he didn't take any notice and eventually put a tape recorder on his windowsill. It was playing the May Song. He must have recorded it earlier. A little flicker of alienation.

A cultured voice demanded total silence, so we could hear the bells. We hadn't heard the bells for years, it complained. And wasn't that the tradition? – that everyone waited quietly outside the Golden Lion until they heard the church bells ring, and then we got on with the night singing, as soon as it was actually May Day. Half the crowd muttered and grumbled, and the other half shushed them. Then somebody began to heckle the publican and his wife, who'd appeared at a first-floor window. The bloke upstairs displayed his purple backside again, and turned his tape recorder up very loudly.

So we missed the chimes at midnight; but a stern woman, who commanded immediate attention, announced when they had taken place. I liked her immediately because she seemed genuinely hostile to visitors like me, trippers, though she assured us coolly that Padstow was glad to welcome its May guests, provided they didn't get in the way. Her welcome had the formal chill of an Aeroflot stewardess. Then she introduced the night song. It's slower, it's got special words. 'No hollerin', mind.' Now I'll give you the key.

Early to rise tomorrow. All but the most dedicated and the most curious are off to bed, though now the carollers will tour the town. There are special verses for rich men. (You have a shilling in your pants. And I wish it were mine.') for married women, and young girls. Those who are visited like very much to be visited, have kept awake specially, come down to their doors to listen, provide the leaders with beer. And it must be a fine thing to be sung to in this antique fashion. It must refresh one's sense of home and continuance, even though lewd visitors are taking advantage of the promiscuous dark, the unexpectedness of everything, to neck in the churchyard.

Cool, dark air; a moonless night but fine stars; swishing trees, all very Hardy. The singers invoke the 'merry morning of May' again and again, and it is magic. Really. Even though a man in the crowd mutters to me that there's nothing to keep young people here; everyone stuck in their parlours in front of their tellies all winter; is serving Cornish cream teas to trippers a fit life for a man, I ask you?

We start at the Golden Lion; by 2 a.m. we have circumnavigated the town. When one of the visited plays back his aubade on a tape recorder, somebody sourly mutters that next year only one bloke armed with a tape recorder need make the tour. At the harbour, the hot-dog stand reluctantly puts up its shutters. In the ladies' public lavatory, already pungent and awash, a young girl grimly cleans her teeth. Good night.

Refreshed by a brief sleep, the town wakes about seven-thirtyish. Old men are out, decorating the base of the maypole with fresh flowers – furze, bluebells, cowslips so dewy they must have been picked this morning. The maypole is impressive enough to recall its totemic origins, tall as a telegraph pole and stuck all over with paper flowers and ribbons.

Children in maying gear, white shirts and white trousers, run about self-importantly already, wearing the colours of the respective hobby horses, red sashes and neckerchiefs, blue sashes and neckerchiefs. (You can buy them in the gents' outfitters, together with authentic Padstow sailor caps; and many have.) Cafés open, queues form. In the newsagent's a woman snarls: 'Drink and profit, that's all Padstow May Day is. An example of man's inhumanity to man.'

Another resident joins in. She hadn't been able to buy a loaf of bread, and she'd lived in Padstow all her life. Both agreed, while the newsagent sycophantically smirked and nodded, that May Day now was nothing to what it had been. Each lady, essential shopping completed, would presumably return home and sweat out the entire bright, beautiful May Day in a state of siege.

But we, we're waiting for the hobby horse. Drums herald it. Ten o'clock. Here comes the Blue Ribbon Oss, the first out. It starts from the Institute under a bower of green boughs. The road is so crowded, now, so many cameras going, that it can hardly dance properly, its partner, the Teazer, can hardly swing his club.

Nevertheless, it is appalling, magnificent.

Controversy rages amongst folklorists as to which is the most authentic survival – the Blue Ribbon Oss, started up again by a group of soldiers home from the First World War, or the Red Ribbon Oss, which has the support of the establishment of folklore preservationists. They both look alike anyway, but for the colours of the teams, the factional in-fighting, a few blue stripes on the Blue Oss and his beard of wool. Both are of vast antiquity.

The Padstow hobby horses, or Osses, are shining black monsters, grotesque, alarming, snapping, leaping, magic, beastly anachronisms. The Osses are, or were, a fertility symbol, a rain charm, a mark of death and resurrection, the summer-bringer, and now the glad harbinger of the tourist season to a region that would relapse altogether into more than Sicilian poverty without the extra revenue from the sale of cream teas, full-cream fudge, and Cornish-clotted-cream-sent-to-any-address-in-Britain-by-first-class-post.

Oss is built on an elm hoop, 5 feet 9 inches in diameter and 18 round. Over this foundation is stretched a gown of sailcloth, suspended from webbing braces on the shoulders of the dancer. On his head, the dancer

wears a conical cap topped with a tuft of horsehair. Over his face is a mask
of such striking design its origin is said to be African. In the nineteenth
century, ships from Padstow went all over the world, the days when the
maypole was a mast from the shipyard. If nobody did bring the mask back
from West Africa, or Borneo, or Java, then God knows where it comes
from. A ferocious red, black and white witch doctor's mask, with red eyes.

The elm hoop boasts a vestigial horse's head and tail at either end. The
entire apparatus weighs about 100 lb. The dancer makes several tours of
the town, each tour lasting two and a half to three hours. It is tough work.

His partner, the Teazer, dances backwards before his spirited adversary.
The marching band of melodeons, drums, accordions, plays the May
Song. The teams march before and behind, arms linked, singing. Teazer,
an elegant high-stepper, baits Oss with his patently phallic club; Oss makes
ferocious darts and sallies at him, at the crowd. Once young married
women pursued him, and young unmarried women fled him. If you were
pulled under his skirts and danced with him, that was good luck. Which
meant, you got pregnant. Great.

Sometimes Oss will die. He sinks down, a hush falls. Teazer strikes Oss's
frame with his club. We change to the second tune, a bizarre dirge about
the whereabouts of King George. Who is 'out in his long boat. All on the
salt sea'o!' time has tampered with whatever it once meant, to make luminous nonsense of it.

> Up flies the kite
> Down falls the lark-o,
> Aunt Ursula Birdwood she had an old ewe
> And it died in her own park-o.

The festival walks a delicate tightrope between authentic bucolic rum-
bustiousness and squalid riot, and some bugger is always trying to film it,
which the Blue Team, especially, can hardly bear, such are the tensions
between local pride and local exclusivity and the desire not to be relegated
into an exhibit in a living museum.

Mid-afternoon on May Day; a certain exhaustion, intimations of
tomorrow's hangovers. Numerous coppers, hovering. More and more
trippers. You can easily tell the trippers from the natives; the natives are
wearing their best clothes. An embarrassing clown person in red nose,
fright wig, check pants, silver boots, performs an inscrutable mime in front
of the fish bar on the quay; hopeless! He's been upstaged by too much real
street theatre. His private fantasy that he is enriching events (though
nobody stops to watch him) adds a little estrangement to the scene; and
now the teeny-drunks are reeling about. In an upper window of a house

with a fine view of the sea, an old lady established herself early this morning and has jabbered at the crowds all day in a comminatory fashion. A pair
of large dogs, succumbed to the festive spirit, fuck boisterously directly in
the path of the Red Team; here they come again.

Shall we stay for the evening dance around the maypole? Somebody
warns me there was a bit of fighting, last year. A crash of glass decides it;
probably the newsagent's window. A head emerges from upstairs, gesticulating furiously, and two of the lurking coppers close in on a youth and
lead him away. We pick our way over the puke and empty beer bottles to
the car. Five miles outside Padstow it starts to pour with rain.

New Society, 1975

Bath, Heritage City

Getting a buzz off the stones of Bath, occupying a conspicuous site not
fifty yards from the mysterious, chthonic aperture from which the hot
springs bubble out of the inner earth, there is usually a local alcoholic or
two on the wooden benches outside the Abbey. On warm summer afternoons they come out in great numbers, as if to inform the tourists this city
is a trove of other national treasures besides architectural ones. Some of
them are quite young, one or two very young, maybe not booze but acid
burned their brain cells away, you can't tell the difference, now. Jock will
dance while his mate attempts to play the concertina. I remember a
demented youth banging a cider bottle against the bench and singing a
tuneless song with the refrain, 'I am an angel', which clean French and
Scandinavians – we only get upper market tourism – ignored.

I once saw a man puking exhaustively inside the Abbey, surrounded by
memorial plaques of soldiers and sailors who seem to have come to die
here in large numbers. Bath is dotted with blue plaques, Wordsworth was
here, Southey was here, Jane Austen was here, almost everybody came for
a weekend but Malthus was actually buried here. My favourite plaque is
in Brock Street. 'Here dwelt John Christopher Smith (1712-1745),
Handel's friend and secretary.' Such English self-effacing modesty! Why
not come out with it; 'I was a sycophantic arsehole-licker.'

On the Abbey façade, angels climb up the ladder towards God, sort of
nutty Disney. The Palladians who turned Bath into what it is today pulled
down almost everything else, they must have left the Abbey façade standing because it was so charming. Charm, the English disease; charm, mask

of dementia? The fine-boned, blue-eyed, characteristically English madness; foreigners, who see both charm and madness at the same time, tend to diagnose the combination as hypocrisy. I had a Japanese friend who said: 'When I see a pair of blue eyes, I think of the Opium War.'

There's a lot of fine-boned, blue-eyed English madness in Bath, part of its charm, a population with rather more than a fair share of occultists, neo-Platonists, yogis, theosophists, little old ladies who have spirit conversations with Red Indian squaws, religious maniacs, senile dements, natural lifers, macrobiotics, people who make perfumed candles, kite-flyers, do you believe in fairies?

Down the Lansdown Road stride a blue-eyed, Aryan, straight tall couple garbed in colourful rags and chinking with crucifixes; the young man carries an open Bible, from which he declaims in a stentorian voice the more lugubrious assertions of Ecclesiastes. Past Hedgemead Park, favoured venue of the local flashers, bearing the word of the Lord. Past Steve the Tattoo Artist's shop. Steve can inscribe a nice Pietà on your back if you want, and he's got a pamphlet stuck in his window called, 'The Fall of Babylon', Radical Traditionalist Pamphlet No. 2, 'A message of comfort to the latter-day citizens of that great city'. The peripatetic evangiles skirt the West Indian grocer as he loads yams into his mobile shop, he's a member of the New Testament Church of God, himself; crying, 'Hallelujah!' they disappear into the heart of heritage Bath. Nobody turns to look. Too much fine-boned, blue-eyed English dementia around here already to raise an eyebrow.

Constructed in a navel-like depression of hills, Bath's omphaloid location induces introspection, meditation, inwardness, massive sloth. Some of us disappear right down our own navels and never come up again, in fact; famous madmen lived here – William Beckford, the irascible Captain Thickness, enshrined in that monument to the English disease, Edith Sitwell's *English Eccentrics*. But the Anglo-Saxons wouldn't live here, they thought it was haunted. Too cack-handed and primitive themselves to build in stone, they thought that only giants or devils could have done so and left the Roman ruins well alone. There is an Old English poem describing their superstitious dread of the place.

Some of the anti-conservationists, even some of the City Fathers, seem to feel the same terror, as though this masterpiece of planning had been built with the aid of unholy powers and so presents a dreadful menace to we punier beings. Best let the old place quietly fall down. Such things are not for us. Of course Bath is a masterpiece of town planning. As the alternatives murmur to one another over their halves of cider, anywhere you live, you're only ten minutes' walk from the Social Security; apart from the sheer convenience of everything, the Georgian city has the theatrical splendour, the ethereal two-dimensionality of a town of dream.

It has crazy skies, like those beneath which the blue-eyed dements of the novels of John Cowper Powys, also occultists and neo-Platonists, disport themselves. And certain luminous skies of early evening irradiate with gold the haze through which the church towers in the valley are always peeking, so that, then, the terraces thrown with such artful asymmetry across the hillsides have a deserted look. The beautiful trees in this city are so huge they look as if they had been here before the houses and will outlast them. Marvellous, hallucinatory Bath has almost the quality of concretised memory; its beauty has a curiously second-order quality, most beautiful when remembered, the wistfulness of all professional beauties, such as that of the unfortunate Marilyn Monroe whom nobody wanted for herself but everybody wanted to have slept with.

In front of Lansdown Crescent, that stunning bone-white terrace which contrives the perfect solution to the middle-class English desire to live in a town house in the heart of the country, a horse grazes on the downward dipping hillside. It is so peaceful you can hear him crunch. All those magisterial chestnuts in the hollows! From this elevation, the entire city is laid out before us, like a splendid toy for the very rich who still live here in large numbers, people of rank and fashion, taste and means. Bath is enjoying a revival. Such a civilised place to live. In a green dishevelment of waste-land and disused allotments a little way along, sprightly young foxes tumble and cuff one another. Soft, mauve shadows cast by the golden light.

That golden light, the light of pure nostalgia, gives the young boys in their bright jerseys playing football after tea in front of Royal Crescent the look of Rousseau's football players, caught in the amber of the perpetual Sunday afternoon of the painter. The sound of the voices of the children contains its own silencing already within it: 'Remembered for years, remembered with tears.' Nostalgia is part of the aesthetic, time's sweet and inevitable revenge.

The haunting silences of Bath are those with which the English compose intimacies.

The uselessness of the city contributes both to its charm and to its poignancy, which is part of its charm. It was not built to assert the pre-eminence of a particular family or the power of a certain region. It had no major industry in the eighteenth century, except tourism. The gentleman whose tastes this city was built (speculatively) to satisfy had no interest in labour as such, only in his profits from a labour he hoped would take place as far away from his pleasures as possible; Bath was built to be happy in, which accounts for its innocence and its ineradicable melancholy.

The younger and elder Woods did not even build the Circus and Royal

Crescent, those monumental pieces of domestic design, the Olympian apotheosis of the terraced house, to glorify themselves, as a Renaissance architect might have done. They, and Baldwin, and Palmer, and Finch, and Eveleigh, and Goodrich, and so on designed to demonstrate and also help to create the taste of a certain class, a taste the dominance of that class would help to institutionalise as 'good taste'. The demonstration and embodiment of that taste was also the demonstration of greatly enlarged economic power of a greatly enlarged upper-middle class, but in one sense, this was incidental to the main plot. Only rich madmen like Beckford went in for conspicuous consumption and vulgar display.

Order, space, harmony, what Mumford calls the Olympian qualities. A residential town for a gentleman, which could also house the service industries that catered to his elegant and civilised pleasures. His main indulgences were not the gross pleasures of boozing and fornication, but the subtler debaucheries of dandyism, that is, systematised narcissism and gambling, an activity that performs at least one radical function, that of robbing money of its exchange value and making it, at least temporarily, a plaything. He liked to dance primly under the stern eye of Beau Nash, surely one of the most boring men who ever lived, boring and totalitarian, a veritable Stalin of good taste.

The narrow, cluttered alleys of the medieval city did not suit such a gentleman's needs, although he liked to keep one or two of them around because they were so charmingly picturesque. No. Best of all, he liked to bowl along in a curricle or a gig, in control of his own direction, high above the mob that plodded through the mud his wheels had agitated, so he enjoyed wide boulevards. Pulteney Street, the perfect neo-Classical street. On foot, the walk to the two-dimensional focal point of what is now the Holbourne and Menstrie Museum, an amazing bit of architectural *trompe l'œil*, soon palls. The wide road, flat as a pancake, the front doors passing by with the grim regularity of telegraph poles. You are not meant to linger here. On the other hand, a car goes much too fast. You whizz past the splendid façades in a moment; they hardly impinge upon the eye at all. But, in a horse-drawn carriage, the twin terraces flow past on either side like exquisite back projections, to be viewed as part of a city of views, to be decorously enjoyed at a distance and to be soon – but not *too* soon – over.

The lucid and serene architecture of this city confronts me with an Englishness I attempt to deny by claiming Scottish extraction. I always give Jock a shilling when he pan-handles me.

Bath, in its romantic, dishevelled loveliness, is no longer the city the Woods built; two hundred years of the history of taste have modified the crisp outlines of its rational harmony, and this has changed its appearance far more than time itself has done. Our perceptions of the city are modified by those of everybody else who has ever been here and thought that it was beautiful. It is more than the sum of its parts.

The softly crumbling stone; those tumultuous skies across which, now and then, the wild swans fly; that light, with the elegiac quality that brings a lump in the throat; that sense of pervasive pastoral, the feeling for the countryside typified in wild gardens, it isn't really anything to do with the countryside at all but a liking for parks, for landscaped meadows, for contained nature, for garden cities . . . the water-colour aesthetic as of English art, whose favourite seasons are the moist ones, early spring, early autumn, and all of whose landscapes are gently haunted. Bath, a city so English that it feels like being abroad, has been so distorted by what Pevsner called the Englishness of English art that the city itself has become almost an icon of sensibility. This particular Englishness, this particular sensibility, had a last major high art revival in the late forties, in the pictures of John Piper and Michael Ayrton and the Nashes. Mervyn Peake showed its demonic aspect. In fiction, the novels and anthologies of Walter de la Mare; in music, Britten's setting of 'The splendour falls on castle walls'.

It devolves on an aesthetic of mood and feeling, not of form or idea; the sensibility is common to all the examples above, regardless of the medium in which they were executed. It is an art that does not bear the marks of having been jostled in the market-place, and such a jostling would have brushed away a good deal of its melancholy bloom. It is not so much bourgeois art – that would be vulgar – as a truly middle-class art, and, since the English middle class is unique, then perhaps this class origin is what gives the sensibility itself its characteristically English charm. It is reflective, the production of reverie and introspection. It is typical of Bath's quality as a product of the English artistic sensibility that one of its ghosts should be a lyrical creature who manifests its presence by an odour of jasmine.

On the hill beyond the river, they illuminate at night, a folly called 'Sham Castle'.

New Society, 1975

What the Hell – It's Home

It's a shame the name Habitat incorporates the suffix 'tat', a rich source of cheap jokes, even if the people who go on most about 'habitattiness' are often to be found shamefacedly slipping stoneware crocks into their wire baskets in the china departments of that very store because they can't find them anywhere else any more. Neighbourhood hardware stores are rapidly ceasing to stock certain traditional items of Staffordshire pottery, such as brown earthenware teapots and hot-pot jars.

No publicity is bad publicity, and Terence Conran must laugh all the way to the bank; a cheap joke is a sure sign of public acceptance. And when a trade name turns into an adjective – 'habitatty' – then you know you're on your way to becoming a national institution. The Habitat catalogue is already almost the equivalent of the old Sears Roebuck catalogue, a sort of secular consumers' bible. No good home is without one. It is browsed in more than it is ordered from, but still it exercises its benign influence on taste. Because the catalogue gets about so much, and because of the mail-order bit, Habitat goods turn up in the most unexpected places, like the Outer Hebrides and the south of France, spreading Good Design wherever they go. The Habitat vision of home has contrived, in ten years or so, to become the dominant domestic style of a generation.

Not that the Habitat catalogue contains precisely the stuff that dreams are made on. The furniture and home accessories it advertises are not of offensive lavishness. No Italian black leather beds with mirror headboards. No malachite-topped coffee tables to provoke a pure, acquisitive lust and flights of outrageous fantasy. Far from it. There's not much inducement to conspicuous consumption or wishful thinking in those glossy, well laid-out, beautifully photographed pages. Everything is practical, sensible, reasonably priced and available on HP. It is all blissfully within reach; or may be next year.

The Habitat catalogue room-sets show a planned environment into which the browser can, in his imagination, insert himself with no trouble at all. It all looks lived in. Beds are personalised with gollies and teddies; cats and dogs dash through the rooms; and the mess of pets and children won't disturb the whole scenario, all surfaces can be wiped down with a damp cloth.

Even the models lolling about on Habitat floor cushions are only the tiniest bit more glamorous than real young professionals. They look, in fact, very much as we hope we do: television actors rather than movie queens, only very slightly idealised. There are always lots of beautiful children in the Habitat catalogue; some of the models are even black, or yellow. Some of them – oh, courageous realism! – are even old.

Look at the page showing the duvet covers. Under one design, a bed-jacketed, bespectacled lady of uncertain age eats breakfast; under another, a young man apparently naked, investigates Mailer's book about Marilyn Monroe (a racy touch, that). A child puts together a Habitat jigsaw. (Children are encouraged to acquire the Habitat habit young, via colourful and imaginative toys that have the air of home accessories themselves. So they can be left lying around the living room and still look part of the total interior design.) This isn't an advertisement for bed-linen but for living. An ad for a lifestyle with no class tag. Only the very determination not to be typed by class and age imposes a certain uniformity.

The furnishings themselves are subtly anthropomorphised. Items have been given names like those of a family in Highgate Village: William, Emma, Eleanor, Bella . . . These armchairs and sofas will be part of the family. Habitat purchasers are not over-awed by their own dining-room suites. They will live *with* their furniture, not alongside it – as my mother did. My mother always thought her mahogany table was too good to use *as* a table. It inhabited the rarely used dinging-room like a rich lodger.

The Habitat style ingratiates itself. It speaks aloud to sense and yet whispers gently to sensibility at the same time. Good design, it says, can be functional *and* fun. And Good Taste can be as much fun as Bad Taste – a fairly radical perception in the early days of Habitat. I remember how, in the late 1950s, interior design seemed split three ways. There was heavy trad, with deep-buttoned leather chesterfields and alabaster table-lamps. There was Scandinavian teak. And there was freakish neo-Dada, featuring phrenologists' heads and stuffed elk – an uncompromisingly vulgar statement about just how boring the Good Taste of the other two styles was. With a certain sprightly élan, the Habitat style manages to combine all three elements in one catalogue. It suggests one ought to buy one's household goods with a clear eye for value and yet a light heart.

But if I can easily imagine myself sitting on a piece of the William range ('Craftsman-built furniture which has a solid frame of beechwood'), reading the *Sunday Times* colour supplement, waiting for my Elizabeth David lunch to be ready, I can't imagine, say, a Rembrandt on the wall opposite, even if it were an unframed repro pinned up as casually as all hell. A Rembrandt would look hideously out of place in this room-set. You could have a flight of plaster ducks there, that would be fun; or a pair of romping plaster Alsatians on the coffee table; or even a Cherry Girl or a Whistling Boy. All these would be fine; they would be unpretentious chic. But art, real art, which does not come into any category of good or bad taste – no. A Habitat interior does not aspire towards the insurrection of art, which cannot find a place in it.

Habitat is currently doing a delicious range of seventeenth-century fruit and flower prints. (They used to offer a set of contemporary graphics but I can't find any trace of it in the current catalogue; sold out, probably.) This season's prints are the perfect decorations for Habitat room-sets. They are almost too pretty to be pure fun, yet they are entirely lacking in that troubling quality that distinguishes fine art from applied art. They're not going to hang there and demand to be looked at or construed. They are there only to please and they are obviously pleasing: a visitor doesn't have to puzzle his head over what on earth you've got those things up for. (Come to that, he wouldn't with a Hockney print, either.)

Alice, in *Room at the Top*, told upwardly socially mobile Joe to buy old maps in antique frames for his room because old maps pertained to a consensus of Good Taste: they wouldn't give anything away. There is certainly something of this about all the Habitat merchandise. It is obviously Good Design and Good Value. The purchaser knows that, if the shop stocks it, he's on safe ground. Those fruit prints are a more sophisticated version of Joe's century maps.

It's interesting to see that Habitat went over the top a bit with their Art Deco repro 'Zozo' sofa – a charming old-fashioned sofa that has been lovingly made in an old-fashioned way', the catalogue calls it. It has round shoulders and round arms. The designers let fashion run away with them. It is pastiche a little too close to home. You can still pick up that sort of thing in auction sales for about £5. Mum may even be just on the verge of slinging it out, in the wake of Cherry Girl and Whistling Boy. Many an upwardly socially mobile Habitat browser may have felt they were trying to sell him or her a pup.

I love the shops. Twenty-two of them now, including a warehouse in Oxfordshire with a playground. The shops are the antithesis of the department store, with its hushed decorum and imposing, beadle-like, senior counter-jumpers, where merchandise is mediated between the firm and you by supercilious assistants who fetch items from locked glass cases, items known only to themselves, and spread them out on counters which mark the division between buyer and seller with absolute precision. There is no sense of a ritual exchange in a Habitat shop.

The staff, usually young, wearing name tags, negotiate with the informally clad customers on friendly, easy terms. Merchandising is democratised. There is music, a pleasant sense of subdued bustle. Everything for sale may be felt, handled, touched; no locked showcases. The goods are displayed with such reckless prodigality it is easy to forget they have to be paid for. The Aladdin's-cave-like glass and china and linen departments, especially, with their supermarket layout and those choice carousels of mugs and so forth, are a positive invitation to impulse buying.

In this free-and-easy atmosphere, buying furniture seems the most commonplace activity in the world. It's nothing like the once-in-a-lifetime grand slam it was for my parents, who bought the major contents of their house when they were married, and that was that. Indeed, marriage itself was a once-in-a-lifetime grand slam for my parents, and their furniture was part of the visible apparatus of their weddedness. The rise of serial monogamy must have done wonders for the home furnishing industry. If Wife No. 1 gets Conran's Country House suite at the first division of property, you can experiment again next time around. Acquiring one Habitat room-set in the course of matrimony doesn't cancel out the opportunity of living with any of the other room-sets. The interiors are renewable every seven years, about the time of the seven-year itch. Habitat's stock is geared to upward social mobility and the collapsible marriages that tend to accompany it.

In seven years' time, we may have graduated from Habitat's 'Basic' range. ('The "Basic" range was conceived as a solution for anybody setting up home on a low budget who considers it economic folly to buy furnishings that are likely to fall apart in a couple of years' time'.) By then, we may even aspire to the Conran Shop. 'Conran Shop' is part of the Habitat Group, but quite different. Not all the things we see, and which we really like, can be sold in Habitat: chocolate suede-covered Italian sofas, handmade glass light fittings, Baccarat goblets so fine you can squeeze them gently between your finger and thumb and they give a little . . .

The typical Habitat home is something of a caravanserai and might be on the move tomorrow. It is at the same time a very good imitation of the Last Homely House (lovely welcoming kitchens filled with traditional cooking pots), yet infinitely modifiable. It can be broken up and reassembled in a dozen different forms. A wide variety of personal taste can be accommodated within a general standard of acknowledged good taste, without straying outside the catalogue. There's nothing wrong with any of it!

And *that's* what seems wrong about it, really. The complete Habitat home is a mobile home, a refuge yet maybe a launching pad. The catalogue reflects a narcissistic preoccupation with lifestyle, as if a lifestyle were an adequate replacement for real life.

New Society, 1976

The Donnie Ferrets

You get to Doncaster market from the station by going through one of those monumental, multi-tiered shopping precincts with branches of every chain-store you can think of in it, a total merchandising environment with artificially modulated lighting and controlled temperatures. It must have seemed like a good idea at the time. There are lots of them, as

monolithic in design as the buildings of the Thousand Year Reich, constructed in the expectation of universal, everlasting affluence at the end of
the 1960s. Now they already have some of the quaint appeal of the ruins
of those giant churches built in Paraguay by the Jesuits in the fallacious
hope of the conversion of the Amerindians.

This one has a piazza with a concrete pool in it, dry now. The citizens
of Doncaster have made an informal agora of this area and sit around it on
the seats thoughtfully provided for them, reading the sports pages. When
they're finished with their newspapers, they throw them into the dried-up
pool. It's busy enough, now, on a Saturday afternoon. But at night, when
the shoppers have all gone home, this gleaming temple of Mammon will
become the echoing domain of alienation, fit only for vandalisation. It's
the spitting image of the shopping precinct in Stephen Poliakoff's *Hitting
Town*, where the waitress used to come in the evenings to have herself a
good scream.

However, a modest stream of customers now commute between British
Homes Stores and the branch of Brown, Muff's. Under a black leather
poster of Alvin Stardust, menswear in the butchissimo style favoured in
south Yorkshire vanishes from the racks with a speed surprising in a recession. The supermarkets are packed, though God knows why. A hundred
yards away, belly is king and the stalls are groaning with the sort of food
south Yorkshire likes to eat.

Out, then, into the mild drizzle, across the main road; and, like a little
touch of Ballets Russes, you see before you the peaked hoods of the market stalls in the distance, beyond O & A's. It's a different world, a different shopping experience, like stepping into a space-time warp. A little
town of stalls dominated by the austere classical lines of the Corn
Exchange Market and, by the serene and lavishly embroidered towers of
Doncaster parish church across the main road.

It's confusing, at first. There's so much of it, and such an extraordinary
variety of things for sale, from once-used co-respondent's shoes to plastic
tiger lilies. And the market looks like it's been there a long time, which
it has. The stallholders are not fly-by-night, here-today-and-gone-
tomorrow rip-off artistes, like so many of the stallholders of London's
remaining street markets, but solid burghers with a reputation to maintain.

And, furthermore, it's also *meant* to be confusing. These markets are not
so much for shopping as for browsing, for a randomly structured prom-
enade that takes you in a leisurely fashion from stall to stall, comparing
prices and qualities, jostled by one's fellow men, exhorted by persuasive
barkers, stopping off for peas and chips at Irene's Corner and so forth. A
time-and-motion study man would go mad rationalising the movements
of a typical weekend shopper in Doncaster market.

Meat, dairy products, bread and cakes are all under cover. The market traders advertise themselves with the up-front self-confidence of the time before advertising became an art-form. 'The egg-people', says one sign; 'pies of perfection', announces another, emphasising the message with a very nice naïve painting of a straight-walled pork pie with a token tomato slice or two at its base. If you look up from the counters long enough, you'll see lots of fine primitives aloft. The stall with the game licence is decorated with medallions of hare, pheasant and guinea fowl. Best beef may be bought under a cameo portrait of a heavy bull with a ring in its nose, all complete, as if to suggest some of the bull's virility will be imparted to those who eat its meat. This is the carnivorous north.

Most of the cheese comes in plasticised cartwheels but some, if you're lucky, may be found in authentic mired bandages and that is often fine. There's a sweetish, musty odour from row upon row of open biscuit tins. I'd forgotten how you used to be able to buy biscuits loose. And lots of cut-price confectionery. 'These are *not* misshapes', says a hand-written sign on a notice on a spilling sack of Mint Imperials. But greedy children who don't pay much heed to symmetry can stock up on warped liquorice allsorts and at very competitive prices.

Cakes. Curd tarts. Slab cakes in various flavours, fruit, seed, coconut, cherry, plain, at 20 pence a small loaf. 'The luxury crumpet.' Balm-cakes. Everything displayed just within reach, as it is on your own tea-table.

There is a lack of reticence about the displays, a lack of guile and arti-fice in the presentation of the wares, that suggests the food is not designed to appeal to the jaded palate via the eye but directly to the active digestive processes. It grabs you at a visceral level. Meat lies on the slab in moist, bleeding chunks – everything, tongue, liver, kidneys, terribly recognisable as such. They don't hide the eggs away in boxes but heap them up like pebbles on a beach. The baker's stall, called 'The Crusty Cob', tumbles its bread on to the counter prodigally, all dusty with flour and straight from the delivery tray.

There's butter too ('Yorkshire farmhouse butter, 50p a pound') in lavish blocks. These are the very archetypes of basic foodstuffs, not the stereo-types you find jostling promiscuously in the troughs at the supermarket, anonymous sections of meat that might be cunningly synthesised from the look of them, and never even seen a slaughterhouse, and those geometric sections of cheese all sheathed in cellophane so that a hundred hands can shuffle them without the hygiene regulations being broken.

In this market, only the butcher is privileged to handle the meat until you've paid for it. Money is transformed into food before your very eyes, elementary magic of the market-place. The girl at the cheese stall brusquely offers you a sliver of Cheddar on the end of a murderous knife.

All is grimly personalised. The rituals of buying and selling involve a direct, face to face confrontation.

This confrontation is especially direct in Doncaster, where they engage in the service industries with a positively Soviet egalitarianism. The cheese lady does not attempt to charm with a smile. She has a black-dyed, piled-up hairdo like a country music star; her eyelids are painted a vivid green. If you don't like her style, so much the worse for you.

The fish and poultry market is even more direct. Under the vaulted architraves, the white marble slabs all aslither with hunks and fillets remind you why they used to call it 'wet fish'. One stall calls itself the 'modern fishmonger' and has a sign showing a very dapper fish in a topper and monocle, smoking a cigarette; modern is a relative term. Eviscerated rabbits lie in mauve mounds, only their kidneys left in the cavities where their bellies were; above them swing racks of rabbits still in their pelts. These are counters where you can buy saucers of whelks and mussels and shrimps and eat them on the spot, from tiny saucers; kids rummage through discarded boxes of whelk shells. It's cold and wet underfoot, here. It's getting on in the afternoon and they're slapping the fish about something dreadful. The rituals surrounding real food can ravage one's sensibilities, rather.

Fruit and veg outside, mostly; and the occasional flower stall. And clothes; and hats; and used paperbacks; a sheet music stall, a porn stall, a brassware stall – dozens of brassware stalls, some of which have branched out into knick-knacks such as miniature pottery lavatories with money-box slits in them and, written on them, 'Put a penny in the little pot'.

Heavy market-traders in sawn-off Wellington boots against the rising damp, many wearing those characteristic fingerless mittens and the bag of change strapped round their aproned waists, make lavish promises. One offers a ballpoint pen guaranteed to write 40,000 words; but, then, part of the trip is the side-shows, the complete dinner services for a fiver to you, and so on.

And it goes on, stall after stall; and a little roundabout to amuse the kiddies. There's a fire engine on the roundabout, with Doncaster Fire Brigade written on the side. This rambling encampment of goods for sale, where buying is as much of an art as selling and it can all come down to a battle of wits between the stall-holder and you.

Maybe Yorkshire never really left the Third World. These enormous markets of the great northern cities and towns are like the peasant markets of Europe, or even like oriental bazaars, solid, institutionalised – one of the Sheffield markets is housed in multi-storeyed, concrete erections scarcely distinguishable, from the outside, from any Arndale Centre in the world.

But you can't buy live pigeons in any Arndale Centre that I know of.

And there they are, in Donnie, a cage full of beautiful, plump pigeons, their heads sunk into their necks, pigeons all the smoke and slate colours of Doncaster on an autumn morning. A little old man came, and brushed his hand over the outside of the cage, cooing at the pigeons so that they all stirred from their trance and cooed back at him. 'Just you eff off,' said the pigeon vendor, in his flat aggressive cap. 'I've had enough of you.'

But he had more than pigeons to sell. He had canaries, and budgies, and a white dove, and a solid lump of black puppy that separated itself out at random into five puppies, and a tea-chest full of guinea pigs. Also lop-eared rabbits and huge, robust white rabbits with black blotches on them, like Dalmatian dogs, good, I should think, eaters.

And ferrets. I'd never seen a ferret before. Arching its wickedly articu-lated back, the small, vicious creature, creamy-white, like ermine, snarled delicately at the fascinated children pressed around the cage. Ferrets. Of course, they'd sell ferrets. We're in Yorkshire, aren't we? The regional hunting beast, the questing beast; teeth too sharp to make a nice pet, really.

But this little boy wanted a football from the toy stall and even the sight of the ferret wouldn't distract him. He was whinging away about the foot-ball until his granny lost patience with him entirely. 'Bugger t' football,' she said, with the air of somebody utterly exhausted by the traditional total south Yorkshire shopping experience, 'Bugger t' football.'

Outside, among the fruit and vegetable stalls, it had started to rain in earnest and the cabbage stalks and shed lettuce leaves were turning to soup in the puddles. It's very tiring, not being alienated from your environ-ment.

New Society, 1976

The Paris of the North

Since I propose to describe a literary festival, let's adopt a suitable tone.

Sometimes the rain crashed and pounded on the already empurpled moors; sometimes it hung like a hint of immanence in the air, teasingly seeming to be always on the point of falling, so you did not know if it was safe to go out without your raincoat or not (and got the point of the old song about Ilkley Moor and hats immediately). But sometimes the rain fell more gently, and caressed the bluebells and dandelion clocks and tousled hawthorn bushes almost with love. And once or twice it stopped alto-gether, albeit reluctantly, to make way for that fine, pale, Nordic sunshine which is the summer blessing of these high uplands. But, on the whole, the weather at Ilkley was inclement. Wettish.

The mill-owners' grey stone houses gleamed like moist pebbles, and limply dangled the Jubilee flags in the high street. The street theatre company, medieval in their colourful rags and white-painted faces, would cluster to play their musical instruments under a canopy of dripping trees.

The Transylvanian backdrop of west Yorkshire hangs oddly behind the small, clean, pleasant town of Ilkley, with its boutiques, its cafés, its discreetly reticent proximity to the darkly handsome, polyglot, multiracial cities of Leeds and Bradford.

Ilkley itself has less in common with the industrial cities of which I suspect it to be rapidly becoming a commuter suburb, than with certain small towns in France or Germany – towns like I thought you didn't get in England any more, where an affluent middle class is heavily into what we used to call 'straight' culture. A visitor from the south, or even from defiantly philistine south Yorkshire (home of punk rock's answer to *Rolling Stone*, they call it *Gun-Rubber*), feels, at first, confused. Because, you see, they care.

I thought at first, well, if it was France, at least there'd be a decent restaurant. But, hell, there is a decent restaurant in Ilkley. It's supposed to be one of the best in England, but I couldn't afford to go there (to complete the French comparison). Nevertheless, it's the sort of restaurant featured on gastronomic tours. Good grub is evidently part of the cultural trip in these parts.

Ilkley *en fête*. The black and gold logo of the literary festival on every tree. The notion of a literary festival is in itself an odd one. Books are inner-directed things. There is a direct, one-to-one, silent, private relationship between writer and reader. Reading aloud is something else. Yevtushenko wanted to book the Haringey Arena for a reading. But I understand that writers have always been dowered with a certain messianic resonance in Russia, or else, maybe, they share some of the respect that Russians traditionally reserve for Holy Fools. Nevertheless, I can imagine a festival with Yevtushenko at the helm actually being fun.

Festival, in the context of literature, or poetry, or art, or movies, or music, seems now to mean a moderately eclectic gathering of people with vested interests of some kind or other in the medium concerned. These vested interests need not necessarily be strictly financial; they may be strictly PR. Festivals keep the organisers busy and happy. They bring extra benefits of tourism. They enable the participants to meet old friends without having to pay their own fares; they may even make new ones. Who am I to jib? I went to Ilkley. Met old friends, made new ones. Bought a nice picture of some sheep.

But how to organise a literary festival that is not hopelessly academic? I remember once arriving by chance in Sligo when the Yeats festival was in process, and the whole town full of Yeats look-alikes sheathed in plastic macs (if Ilkley is inclement, Sligo never knew the meaning of the word 'clement'). They all turned out to be associate professors from mid-Western universities come to talk for three hours each on the imagery of 'Sailing to Byzantium'. The residents of Sligo had all been pushed into the deepest recesses of the back bars, where they muttered mutinously in between trying to take the visitors for a fiver.

Ilkley does not fall into this trap of erudition. It wants to involve the locals. Therefore it feels forced to go multi-media. Nobody there is fool enough to sit on their backsides for three hours while some dement drones on about seminal influences.

So the festival commissioned Graham Collier to blend a spoken text from Lowry's *Under the Volcano* with jazz. Lord David Cecil came to talk about Jane Austen. There was a live, staged version of a well-known television book discussion programme. A theatre group named Phantom Captain, with an interesting line in bourgeois apologetics, started off poorly supported, but gathered its own momentum by a judicious bit of street theatre, and ended up a bit of a rave in the Youth Centre. Marguerite Duras came and talked about her movies, in French. Adrian Henri, fresh from another festival (of performance arts, in Brighton), and Roger McGough and Brian Patten, together performed their always well-received Liverpool poets number, as a grand finale.

An eclectic bill. And there were lots of other things besides: events for kids, exhibitions, you name it. But, in spite of the Box Tree Restaurant and Madame Duras, no, we are not actually in France. Besides, is not the pay-train from Leeds disgorging a clutch of poets every lunchtime, to read authentic texts aloud?

After the first few days, I began to hope against hope the next pay-train would disgorge, say, Verlaine, announcing to the festival at large: *Je suis Verlaine, poète et pédéraste.* No, were he to arrive at the ICA like that, they'd probably make him director on the spot, and slip him five quid on the side to get plastered with. Such a performance alone would authenticate his artistic worth. Down south, it would be a breach of taste to be shocked. Up north, though, I suspect he'd still be able to raise a few eyebrows before he'd even read a stanza. Why not. What else is outrage for?

Not Verlaine but Jeff Nuttall, the Wild Man of Leeds, blew into the festival club on the Monday night, insulted everybody roundly, and vanished as darkly as he had come. And I saw it all; it was like a revelation. *Of course*, the British avant-garde is alive and well in the provinces. Down south, nobody knows or cares enough about art any more to know what's mainstream and what isn't. The establishment is supple enough to evade all attacks. Attacking it is like hitting a jellyfish with a stick. Thwack! it slithers away. Thwack! again, it slithers off in another direction. Thwack! thwack! thwack! You score a direct hit. It opens and engulfs you.

To use the French analogy, again: fights broke out in the audience when Cornelius Cardew's *Triumph of Time* was premièred in Paris. In London, it was greeted with lugubrious respect. Hardly anybody in the audience knew enough about what was going on to have any firm opinion on it at all. In Ilkley, they have firm opinions. It is probably the Paris of the UK.

Anyway, to get back to Ilkley. What was I doing in Ilkley? I and the Welsh poet, Allan Perry, with his laconic Swansea humour, and Mrs Perry, Jean, come along for a holiday, were the Writers in Residence there. Kind of guardian angels to the concourse.

It had been a whimsical lodging. It wasn't just the lack of a bar that got to us, after a while. It was the display behind the reception desk, unconnected I may say, with the festival. 'Books to buy or borrow', said a sign. Such as: *I found God in the Soviet Union; The Jesus Generation;* the complete works of Billy Graham. And mine host was apt to slip you a tract. 'Are you the poetry lady? Here's a little book of poems. They're godly but super':

> I have drunk the wine of failure,
> Been drunken thru and thru,
> Have worn old clothes that did not fit,
> When every flower was blue.

We looked at it but could not believe it. Verlaine should have been there.

From this eyrie, every day, we descended to the festival – to greet the relays of lunchtime poets; to engage with those who wanted to engage with us; to be gently patronised by the street theatre because we hadn't the nerve to go up and relate to people by shaking rattles under their noses; to spend hours organising spontaneous readings; to get things going; to keep things going; and sometimes it rained and sometimes it did not.

A very nice man who edits a magazine called *Rabies* came and did a modest Verlaine. He performed a poem containing a variety of farmyard impressions. We all liked it very much but afterwards a crisp, grey-haired lady put us down terribly by saying: 'I suppose he thinks we don't know what Dada is in Ilkley.' She turned out to be a marvellous primitive painter.

She was mad as fire about the way people like me sneered at people like her – 'little old ladies', she said. 'They go on and on about little old ladies not knowing nothing about anything.' She had a painting of a waterfall, done in silver paint. She said it had been especially difficult to do, since she was trying to get the sound.

On the other hand, a lady, admittedly rather older than she, had said, the night before – at the discussion group we were supposed to hold at the end of each day's events – that it was a pity Rupert Brooke had died so young since she was sure he would have done marvellous things. But then, she did not come from Ilkley. And, God knows, it is a reasonable enough thing to say if you actually care about poetry, even if it is God-awful poetry you care about.

Besides, the north is a different country. Actually, the north is two different countries. I live in Sheffield; and I've lived in Bradford, just off Lumb Lane, by Manningham Mills. Nothing in either of these places prepared me for Ilkley. It was the secondhand clothes shops, rather than anything in the festival itself, that demonstrated to me the absolute otherness of this town.

Jean and I soon discovered the Oxfam shop and the Shelter shop and combed them, exclaiming. Nothing but good tweed, sturdy jersey; name brands. I had spent the money I'd earmarked for a winter coat on Barbara Whalley's paintings but, lo and behold, I managed to purchase a square-cut early sixties coat in a fabric we used to call poodle cloth for the price of a kebab and chips in The Smoke.

The lady volunteer at the tea bar in the festival club admired it, but she said she herself never dared buy anything from the Shelter shop – though often tempted – for fear she might meet its donor in the street when she was wearing it.

That is what I call real life. You could write like Balzac if you lived in a town like that. Indeed, it would require the intransigence of a Brontë *not* to write like Balzac in a town like that.

There was a black coat with a fur collar I asked them to put aside for Verlaine.

New Society, 1977

D'You Mean South?

Like Budapest and Istanbul, London is a city divided in two by water. George Melly's version of transpontine south London (enshrined in an early Flook story) was innumerable quarters of undifferentiated seediness, populated by men in flash ties and flat caps, doing shady deals with one another about used cars or three-legged greyhounds in gravy-coloured pubs whilst drinking brown ale.

A typical south London headline from the local press was: BABY IN PRAM BITTEN BY RAT. The local cuisine was jellied eels and mashed potatoes, consumed in white-tile eel-and-pie shops. Kids all wore plimsolls but never socks, and had grey candle-drips of snot depending from their nostrils. Nights were made hideous by the rhythmic jangle of the swung bicycle chains of Teddy Boys who often stabbed one another on late buses and were then subject to gross miscarriages of justice.

Useless to complain it was not precisely so, that a *lot* of London was poor in the 1950s and much of it poorer than the south-west postal districts. But all this poverty was less visible than poverty is now because posh people did not, as they do now, buy houses in poor areas. So they thought that all of London must be safe, secure and clean.

It was not so much poverty and squalor and petty criminality that I remember best of south London in the 1950s but the seedy respectability of soiled net curtains and well-attended dancing classes, classical and tap, held in bay-windowed front rooms.

The girls, I remember, always had wild aspirations to style. Around their fifteenth summer, they spread out all their petals – like flowers with only one season in which to cram all their blossoming. I recall a giggling flock of girls, some white, some black, at the tube station entrance in 1959. They must have assembled there in order to go 'up west' (i.e., to the West End). They were as weird and wonderful as humanoid flora from outer space, their hair backcombed into towering beehives, skirts so tight you could see the clefts between their buttocks, and shoes with pointed tips that stuck out so far in front they had to stand sideways on the escalators. There was a shoemaker in Brixton who custom-built these shoes to the girls' requirements.

It was a style they had invented all by themselves. They were shackled by those skirts, crippled by those shoes, as if the clothes they had selected symbolised the cramped expectations of their lives in the cruel confinements of sex and class. Their dandyism triumphed over the limitations of their circumstances, and made them objects of bizarre and self-created beauty, a triumph of mind over matter. My mother would never have let me go out looking like that. Hadn't I gone to a direct grant school?

After an absence, I now live in south London again. And the girls, I see, still do have a style all of their own. Last autumn, it was ankle-length, knife-edged pleated tartan skirts, with ankle socks and plastic sandals. This summer it seems to be a decorous punk – tapered jeans, rouge, and a lot of chains everywhere – as if to indicate that, however much things might seem to have changed, everything remains fundamentally the same.

In 1960, I went for a job on a glossy magazine and said, with typical south London sullen defiance: 'Balham', when the editor asked me where I lived. She drummed her enamelled fingertips on her leather desk for a long time, then inquired, almost solicitous: 'Do you find that perfectly convenient?' It was terribly convenient for the Northern Line, but she did not mean that. Where I live now is only two stops nearer the West End on the Northern Line; but these days she would be more likely to say: 'Clapham? Why, some friends of mine have just moved there.'

When the bourgeoisie got priced out of, first, Hampstead and Highgate – how long ago it seems! – and then from Camden Town and Islington, and the alternatives got priced (who'd have thought it?) out of Ladbroke Grove, there was nowhere else for *all*, repeat all, the poor sods to go, was there? That's typical south London usage. Every statement is converted to a rhetorical question. Similarly, every question is thrown right back into the lap of the questioner. 'What's the time?' 'Do you mean, what's the time, guv?' Do not trust them when they call you guv, though 'squire' is more openly contemptuous.

We are always on the defensive. We rarely look you straight in the eye. Shiftiness is the prevalent mode of demeanour. And we are always complaining, in a characteristic querulous whine. For us born-and-bred south Londoners, sun is always the herald of rain. Things are always less good than they were; or, we prophesy with relish, not as bad as they're going to be. We exhibit many of the more unattractive personality traits of the colonialised. We lugubriously enjoy the area's reputation for violence.

The lady in the newsagent's on the Wandsworth Road told me that every week, regular as clockwork, five of her customers – five little old ladies – get mugged. Always the same five? How little? How old? And was it mugging or dipping? Because to have your pockets non-violently picked is not the same thing at all as being hit over the head with a bottle. Well, she said, maybe dipping. Still, it's a rotten thing to do to a little old lady, isn't it? She had me there. I could only concur.

But the Teds used to enjoy waylaying little old ladies, and they used razors, too. I don't think it's got much worse. It's probably stayed the same. But more people notice. Fewer people regard it as simply one of the hazards of inner-city life. We had certain techniques of urban hygiene drummed into us from an early age: never cross the Common at night, unless accompanied by a responsible adult who has not offered you sweets. May marks the beginning of the open season for flashers on the Common. Lock all doors and windows. Lock all car doors, even if you are only gone for a moment. Do not leave your washing unattended in the machine at the launderette. Even so, they'll probably get you.

They got us the first week we moved in. Property Redistribution

Anonymous called, and did not leave a card to thank me for my involuntary co-operation. Since I had no valuables to steal, they were reduced to taking odds and ends they thought the wife might fancy: a pretty teapot, all the forks and spoons but, oddly, no knives except the carving knife. (Ooooer, as my mother used to say, a typical south London expression of fear and anxiety). Also a pair of black velvet trousers and a straw boater: probably somebody will turn up in them eventually at the talent night at the pub down the road to do a soft-shoe shuffle. Burglars and embourgeoisification go together like a horse and carriage.

At the crossroads, the Queenstown Road is dominated by the magnificent pile of Battersea power station, a monolithic backdrop like a still from a Soviet propaganda film of the 1930s. On the corner, on a wooden bench, at the foot of a hoarding, occasionally lie red-eyed men with bottles in paper bags. Nearby, an Italian ice-cream parlour does a roaring trade. A couple of Indian grocers, two bistros and a brace of antique shops – as if everything round here goes in pairs, like coppers traditionally do.

Things are clearly looking up. But something is wrong. The inherent charmlessness of the architecture down here? The ceaseless roar of the traffic? It is a curiously unsettling intersection, on which the bistros and antique shops sit as uneasily as a top hat on a Bradford millionaire.

Round Clapham Common, of course, it has always been more or less posh and always pleasant, though never possessing that raffish chic the newcomers hanker for, or the seediness the alternatives relish. Here you may find Victorian and Edwardian residential Clapham with its interesting quality of unflashy, solid, unshakeable money. And, somehow, also, of worth. The founder of the *Church Times*, G. J. Palmer, lived round here. Lots of evangelists and do-gooders. William Wilberforce, even. Marianne Thornton, who organised ragged schools, boys' schools, girls' schools, Sunday schools, infants' schools, and one particularly offensive one – a school for the daughters of tradesmen, 'my Middlings', she called them.

You get the picture? Piety and good works: plain living and high thinking. It must have been round here, in one of these substantial but discreet red-brick villas, that the man in the Clapham Omnibus lived, the solid, sensible, rational chap with his natural sense of justice and decency.

These houses are solid, decent, English, middle-class values, rendered in bricks and mortar. They are constantly leafleted by the Socialist Party of Great Britain, the International Marxist Group, the Workers' Revolutionary Party and the Socialist Workers' Party, some of whom even live there. But I kind of hear Elgar playing when I look at these houses. I suspect it is from here the Afghan hounds come who are walked on the Common on summer Sunday afternoons, beneath the kites flown by clean children and laughing alternatives.

These houses were only briefly, if ever, down. They're now almost fully recovered from the indignity of multi-occupancy. You can't walk home from the tube, these days, without seeing somebody moving their Swiss-cheese plants into a white-painted room, probably with a chrome and glass coffee table and maybe spotlight fittings. The newcomers who've just moved into Clapham must all be the same kind of young professional couples. A health food shop has opened to sell them black beans. The book-shop has display cases of Picador Books, the publications of Pluto Press, *Spare Rib*, and God knows what else besides. The entire Rive Gauchy bit, in fact, from seedy bohemia to radical chic, to kids called Gareth and Emma playing with their Galt toys on the floor of the bank while – *at the same time* – down the road, an old lady in the pub removes her teeth in order to sing 'Some of these days' with passion and vibrancy, to tumultuous applause. Even the Rastas in the front bar applaud her.

It is all very confusing indeed and, hypocrite that I am, I've made it sound absolutely delicious, haven't I? Anyway, if you just stand still, social mobility will catch up with you anywhere, these days.

If, at any point in history, the one thing you can always be sure of is that the middle class is always on the rise – then it seems to me that there's a whole new middle class on the rise now. They're bred of the proliferation of the media and further education expansion maybe. They all want somewhere cheap and cheerful to live and if they can't find it, have to settle for somewhere cheap and lugubrious. So here they come, and I come back, don't I? And try to pretend I've never been away.

New Society, 1977

Poets in a Landscape

Ghosts of dead poets don't walk the Lake District, no – they hike. Fell-walking ghosts as mad as hatters, high as kites . . . you feel you might surprise them at the rim of Rydal Water, or spot their phantom reflections in the magic mirrors, Grasmere, Windermere – I bet the glassy tarns looked terrific on opium! Although the story goes the Wordsworth sibs, ace pedestrians and compulsive water-viewers, only took laudanum for medicinal purposes, your honour. In Lakeland, among daffodils shuddering in April snow, how easy to imagine the Wordsworths, freaked out as all hell, trudge, trudge, trudging the miles from Dove Cottage to Windermere to check if their connection (probably Humphry Davy) had delivered.

For surely they *must* have been smashed out of their skulls all the time, Wordsworth and his sportive sister with her crazy eyes ('wild and startling eyes', opined de Quincey, noting, no doubt, and who more knowledge-ably, her expanded pupils). Why else should they have gone striding off in all weathers, whirling blizzard, serrating frost, braving the peculiarly wet Cumbrian rain, to take in yet another peak or mere in a different light? How else could they have stood it, had they not been smashed? They took bits of cold pork or mutton in their pockets, to snack on. Wordsworth, absent-minded as only a genius or an incompetent, kept forgetting his gloves or his cardigan and having to go back for them.

Behind every great man is a silly woman who thinks the sun shines out of her darling's arse-hole and believes his over-sensitive fingers will rot off if he does the washing up. Conversely, behind every great woman is some irascible fellow who says, for example: 'Of course you can't tie a clove hitch, don't be silly; give me the rope.' And she gives it to him, all right, the Reverend Patrick Brontë is a perfect example of this latter type; his daughters were bound to be geniuses, in order to spite him. But, alas, poor Dorothy Wordsworth, how could she protest her own genius in the face of a man who freely acknowledged it, yet couldn't have tied a clove hitch to save his life? There is no role so thankless as that of the muse of a per-son who needs looking after.

All the same, the addiction to hiking. Of course, the Wordsworths were fleeing a stress situation at home. In the confined space of Dove Cottage, they must have been bumping into one another all the time and then jumping apart as if they'd both simultaneously touched a live wire, mum-bling 'Sorry' and looking out of the window to see if it had stopped rain-ing. What a finely wrought atmosphere of sexual tension! Where else to go – even if it hadn't *quite* stopped raining, yet – but out into God's good fresh air, among the insolent grandeur of the snow-clad mountains, let the boisterous winds blow it out of their systems. Look, William; daffodils.

And we know that William looked.

Sometimes, on their walks, Dorothy was so overcome with *everything* that she had to stick her head into a babbling mountain stream to cool off. Then, when they'd got home, she'd take to bed.

There is no denying that the home life of William Wordsworth at this time was rather odd. The Dove Cottage years; William and Dorothy, he just a year older, turning thirty, at his creative peak. *Lyrical Ballads* in the bag, *The Prelude* on the boil. She, his amanuensis, his willing victim, his sycophant, glorying in it. They were acquainted with plenty of solid members of the Lakeland bourgeoisie and even one or two peasants but it is their junky friends, Coleridge (a frequent visitor) and de Quincey (although he arrives a little later) who finally complete the group.

English artists are supposed never to congregate together and form groups in the way that French artists do. Indeed, it is the proud boast of modern masters like Kingsley Amis and Margaret Drabble that the whole point of the thing is the bourgeois individualism with which it is done. Nevertheless, form groups they always have, in fact, ever since Shakespeare and Jonson at the Mermaid Tavern; the Pre-Raphaelite Brotherhood, the Camden Town Group, the Bloomsbury Group. The Lake Poets are not unique in their peer bonding.

The congregations operate with that hypocrisy of which foreigners so often accuse us, for not only do they exist when they should not, and while their very existence is denied, but they also embrace deviant behaviour with considerable enthusiasm, the while overlaying it with such a thick coat of plain living and high thoughts that the man in the street thinks all artists are great bores until the biographies appear after they are dead and the laws of libel no longer apply.

Sexual aberration and dope (in which I include ethyl alcohol) are the prime specialities of these groups, sometimes simultaneously, occasionally favouring one rather than the other. Offhand, I cannot recall any Bloomsbury junkies but their deviance rating was high enough to recall the zero-population growth slogan coined years ago by Anthony Burgess: 'It's sapiens to be homo.' The Lake Poets, on the other hand, tended to concentrate on laudanum and whatever it was Humphry Davy concocted in his test tubes.

Wordsworth and his sister were, however, very close. All agree on this. Impossible not to start to see such entries in Dorothy's journal of the first two years in Grasmere, when they lived in picturesque isolation together: 'I petted him on the carpet.' But Wordsworth wasn't Byron, of course. He was quite clear on that point. They must have lived together as in a perpetual latency period where puberty was postponed; and these rare nursery caresses were permitted only on these rare, sweet evenings beside the parlour fire, when William had not taken himself to bed early with a bad head. Since all art springs from repression, it is no wonder that parlour nourished great poetry. Since Dorothy had less access to sublimation, one may assume most of the tension came from her. But what did *she* get out of it? Reflected glory?

We all know what William got out of it. Oh, that delicacy of observation of hers! Ah, the exquisite language of her journals, the filigree precision with which she logs the lovely scenes around her! And was she not his unique reference book where flowers and trees and the quality of weather were concerned? Which was just as well since, as Robert Graves crustily observed: 'Wordsworth had a very cursory knowledge of wild life; he did not get up early enough in the morning.' Certainly the journals never note a breakfast earlier than nine o'clock, which was past lunchtime by the standards of the peasant farmers around them. Sometimes they have breakfast about the time I have my tea.

They were playing at the simple life, of course. William would stake out a row of peas in the vegetable garden and then retire, clapped out with manual toil, to his bed – he spent a lot of time in bed – leaving the rest of the plot to Dorothy. She did the washing; cooking; endless baking – bread, bread, bread, and giblet pies, which seems to have been her speciality. (Nowadays, this type of person is into health foods). She coped with the servants for, although the Wordsworths were not rich, they were quite far from poor. She dealt with the beggars, the two or three a day who asked for a crust and ha'pence, she interviewed those one-legged soldiers, idiot boys, orphaned children, itinerant leech-gatherers, gypsy ladies, whose dossiers her brother later versified so diligently. She copied out the interminable results of his labours, she edited, she criticised, she polished, not ever the muse herself, but the hand-maiden of the supplicant to the muse. Funny role. Rum.

Now and then, William's one wild oat would raise its ugly head, Annette Vallon, seduced and abandoned in France years before. 'Letter from Annette', Dorothy notes impassively from time to time. These entries are usually followed by the announcement of a headache, for Dorothy, too, was prone to headaches. They are both of them always reeling under terrible headaches. Toothache; colic; piles; insomnia. 'I lay down unwell.' 'William still poorly.' Gastric troubles. Colds – a five-mile tramp soaked to the skin always leads to a week in bed, but any fool, I should have thought, could have foretold that!

So that sometimes it looks almost as though they went in for all that healthy outdoor activity simply in order to procure the temporary refuge of sickness. But both of them were sick as dogs half the time yet rarely with anything catching; I submit that the evidence in Dorothy's journals of the chronic, low-level, ill-health in the household and the exultant submission to sickness when it came is proof-positive of acute, long-term nervous strain.

Yet not, I think, the strain of repressed sexuality so much as the strain induced upon them both by Dorothy's importunate, obsessive, self-abnegating devotion to the brother who is her more-than-self. 'The fire flutters and the watch ticks. I hear nothing else save the Breathing of my Beloved and he now and then pushes his book forward and turns over a leaf.'

This is not the language of love; love is more abrasive. It is the language of the fourth form. She must have had a crush on him. Poor Dorothy; poor William, trying to read his book uneasily conscious of her crazy eyes.

Eyes mad not with passion but her own ambition for, if he is *not* a genius, then she might as well be dead.

Later on, when he was married and famous and she was paralysed and demented, she could still recite her brother's poetry perfectly. Perhaps by then, resurrecting her stillborn self-esteem in the privileged licence of madness, she thought she had written it all herself.

New Society, 1978

So There'll Always Be an England

When I was a little girl just after the last war, we used annually to celebrate something called Empire Day at my primary school in south London. The neighbourhood was, as it still is in spite of superficial changes, an upper working, lower middle class one, of an arduously arrived-at respectability. But an attempt to revive Empire Day there, today, would provoke either wild mirth or riots. Even in Attlee's England, it was already an anachronism. Attempts were made to re-christen it Commonwealth Day, but the old name stuck.

I should stress that this was a state school, where one or two of the teachers were, I think, closet members of the Communist Party. Not, however, the headmistress, Miss Cox, who always wore tubular pastel satin dresses trimmed with diamanté in the style of the late (though then flourishing) Queen Mary. She had staged this pageant since the 1920s.

Assembled in a playground strung with Union Jack bunting, those children who had been assigned no special roles sang patriotic songs: 'Land of hope and glory' and 'There'll always be an England'. There was a procession of flags and emblems: England, Scotland, Wales, Ulster. The emblems, of cardboard carried on poles, were a Tudor rose, a thistle, a daffodil and a shamrock. Those who carried the Scottish, Welsh and Ulster flags wore national costume – kilt, steeple hat, Kathleen Mavourneen headscarf; but the little girl who bore up the cross of St George wore just a regular gymslip. The lesser breeds, evidently, were picturesque; the English, not. No. As it turned out, they were romantic.

For then the Rose Queen arrived. She was always the blondest and bluest-eyed of the 11-plus entrants. Her girl attendants scattered in her path tissue-paper rose-petals out of the silver baskets they carried. She was helped up to a throne, which consisted of a chair placed on a table and draped with cloth. She was crowned with artificial roses. Some of the boys carried in a maypole. Then came the dancing.

The commonwealth and the empire, in all their manifestations, were sufficiently represented by symbols of England's first colonies and acquisitions. They were all subsumed, in this emblematic pageant, to England. For the Rose Queen must have, in some sense, stood for England. Perhaps there was a vague memory, here, of Isaiah – how a little child shall lead them. Otherwise, all was just as we had learned in our history lessons: that certain different elements, the crosses of St George, of St Andrew and St David, had come together to form a sum far greater than the individual parts: the Union Jack.

Ireland, the one that got away, was written out of the script, although Miss Cox kept firm control of the Six Counties.

Nevertheless, this display represented the fact that the *idea* of Britain was an English invention, like the spinning jenny and the steam engine. Why else did we celebrate the British empire by singing: 'There'll always be an England'? Great Britain = Greater England. The greedy flag swallowed up its constituent parts and became a sign, not of a nation but of a state of mind.

Yet, at the core of the ritual, the essential nub of Empire Day was – of all things – a cut-down version of an operetta, *Merrie England* for juveniles, in which south Londoners, several generations removed from the soil, skipped round in circles whilst plaiting and unplaiting the ribbons – could they have been red, white and blue ribbons? – on a purpose-built maypole which was far removed from the phallic splendour of the ethnic originals.

The Rose Queen on her wobbling throne looked straight ahead for fear of falling. (England, as legend has it, always does better under a queen . . . a legend that surely cannot survive the reign of the second Elizabeth.) In our childish trebles, we piped a song: 'Rose of England, breathing England's air, Flower of majesty [or was it 'liberty'?] beyond compare.'

The rose-in-the-fist logo of the European socialist parties; the flowers of the mill girls who led the strike in Lawrence, Massachusetts, and wanted 'Bread and roses, too' – not from such flowers as these had fallen Miss Cox's paper petals, whirling in the gritty breeze created by our plimsolled feet. If you turned up in plimsolls without socks, Miss Cox slapped your hand with a ruler and sent you home.

For sentimental, chauvinist reasons, I always wanted to be allowed to carry, if not the Scottish flag, then at least the thistle. But this was denied me for, I think, the simple reason that my father was patently and unashamedly a Scot. This has a bearing on the intentional unreality of the charade.

Miss Cox retired in 1951, coincidentally the year of the Festival of Britain, which was the same kind of thing on a bigger scale, and perpetrated by a Labour government, too. Some of the props from Empire Day arrived in the playground, as toys, Miss Cox must have realised that her successor would not wish to keep up the event. I remember somebody skimming the cardboard shamrock through the air as if it were a prototype frisbee.

This living fossil of a pageant of Empire Day taught me one thing: that patriotism is theatre. As Albert Speer said of the Nuremberg rally: 'those fabulous, fabulous visual effects'. Since it is theatre, it is designed both to create the suspension of disbelief and also to *mean* something. But the meaning is 24-carat kitsch.

Kitsch – which is to sensibility what pornography is to sex – informed the notional 'Englishness' at the climax of Empire Day. But the nature of this Englishness was oddly acknowledged. It was initially evoked via . . . normalcy.

It first arrived disguised as a child in a school uniform, carrying a flag. One must qualify the conditions of that normalcy: think it out. It was, God help us all, a *child in uniform*. A *Mädchen*. Then came the antithesis to this blood-chilling thesis: a celebration, or rather a definition, of Englishness as a soft, pink mood, with the fake Tudor rusticated trim of a maypole.

These two images – the child in uniform and the child as rustic rose – sum up the double thrust of Englishness: the hard edge, and the soft focus. There is the rigid authoritarianism that presumes a passive submission; and then there is the marshmallow sentimentality with which the English have chosen to smother their bloody, bellicose and unexemplary history in order to make it digestible.

The English are an unhistoric nation. Think of the costume of the Yeoman of the Guard which the leader of the English National Party dons to enliven by-elections. Intended, presumably, to invoke England's glorious past, it is reminiscent only of Gilbert and Sullivan (operetta, again). The reality of it is as if, in 400 years' time, some patriot, touting for votes on a nostalgia ticket, chose to don the garb of our present-day SAS.

But should this entire planet survive so long, by then all may be changed. We will have our personal Utopias, our own versions of William Morris's *News from Nowhere*. Looking on the bright side, there is just a chance, however faint, that this England of the remote future will resemble a kind of permanent Notting Hill carnival.

Real familiarity with history cannot coexist with the sense of a special destiny. It must be a fine thing, should such a country exist, to live in a place that does not now, nor ever has had, the consciousness that it has been singled out for a special fate. Or in a place that has lost it to such an extent that one could answer Blake: 'And was the holy lamb of God on England's pleasant pastures seen?' with a resounding No. (Or, in the words of the old joke, to reply: 'I've got news for you. She's black.')

What a curious legend, that the boy Jesus visited Glastonbury. (How? On a freighter taking saffron from Phoenicia to Cornwall? And how did he get through immigration?) As strange an idea as the lie perpetrated by Geoffrey of Monmouth, who also invented King Arthur, that the British (sic) are the descendants of refugees from the Trojan war. Evidently, if England is a melting pot now, it must have been so for a very long time.

The Glastonbury and the Arthurian legends are evidence of a deep-rooted, long-term desire to get in on the mythological action, whatever it might be. Once they decided they were a people with a special destiny, the English couldn't create myths fast enough. Any myth, however trivial. In the 1960s, we even contrived to fool ourselves that the Beatles invented rock and roll – when what really happened was that British working-class youth took like ducks to water to the music created by the most oppressed and deprived section of the advanced industrial world, the urban poor of the southern states of the United States.

'There'll always be an England.' But this is an England enshrined in foreign stereotypes of the comic toff, milord, district commissioner or sahib; rarely is it enshrined in those English whose historical struggle is described in E. P. Thompson's *The Making of the English Working Class*. Americans always assume that, because you are British, you have met the Queen, or at least, a duke or two. By 'British', here, they mean, 'English'. Foreigners always do.

The same confusion permeates English life. The English person, lucky enough to have a job, who earns his bread by the sweat of his brow is increasingly referred to as 'the British worker', as if the English had finally washed their hands of him. And it would seem that the toffs, in fact, have done just that. (The British worker is, of course, always 'he', which bias is part of the entire scenario.) Indeed, isn't the very idea of 'the British worker' a joke, in itself? More like the British *non-worker*, ho, ho, ho! An English joke which joyously survives the reality of the dole queues.

As a national symbol – if adopted by democratic consent – this Schweik-like, fiddling shirker, who treasures the right to strike above rubies, would make a most appealing one. Much more sympathetic than the Queen, although there is some justice in the patriotic enthusiasm for the biggest social security claimant of them all.

But this 'British worker' is no more than a figment of the fevered imaginations of *Daily Express* leaders. So he and his fictive comrade, the ganja-crazed Rastafarian mugger, are examples only of just how much Englishmen hate, fear and despise other Englishmen.

There is something here that relates to the soft, pink absence at the heart of the Empire Days of my childhood. Most of the poor but honest parents watching the display in that dingy suburb supported the Conservative

Party. I know so because a teacher (probably a red) asked us. Out of forty-five children, some sitting on their feet to conceal their socklessness, only a handful went against the trend. Imperialism indeed begins at home. To wave a Union Jack whilst singing 'There'll always be an England', is to do something very nasty indeed. OK, so there'll always be an England; but what are the English doing to stop it?

On Albion's shore, in 1982, a statistically significant proportion of the population may not sleep easy in their beds lest white racist thugs chuck petrol through their letter boxes and follow up with a lighted match. The destitute beg alms in every street. Insane old men address the elements in public places with the passion of a Lear. Crazy old women expire in door-ways.

We have just enjoyed the birth of a potential hereditary monarch, less than a year (as if family planning clinics never existed) after a royal wedding celebrated in a manner of which both Miss Cox and Albert Speer would have approved. We have just rejoiced at victory in a small colonial war.

I know lots of perfectly ordinary, ethnically English people who think all this is *terrible*. But they don't get any media coverage, dammit, and that's a fact. The legendary English virtues – of tolerance, decency and fair play – are rarely manifested by the media, to such an extent one could easily think the new commonwealth had inherited them all. For these qualities are far more amply demonstrated by people of Asian and West Indian origins, in the face of most intolerable abuse, violence and prejudice.

If it's only a minority of the English who've been infected by the greed, envy and contempt of the English ruling class, then nobody is brave enough to scrub off the graffiti. And, alas, that includes me.

Every day, when I pass the foul slogans scrawled in illiterate hands on the walls at the council block at the end of the road, I thankfully marvel at the generosity of spirit, the true English phlegm, of those whom it is meant to insult, and who 'just feel sorry for them', as a black girl said to me. And she is no more English than I am. Like me she was only born here.

New Society, 1982

Masochism for the Masses

Of all the elements combined in the complex of signs labelled Margaret Thatcher, it is her voice that sums up the ambiguity of the entire construct. She coos like a dove, hisses like a serpent, bays like a hound; a protean performance that, on occasion, rises to a clarion call or rallying cry. When she clarions, one imagines she can hear herself crackling over the radio waves to outposts of the empire: 'Britain calling.'

It is, in a real sense, a voice from the past. Apart from anything else, it has adopted a form of 'toff-speak' now reminiscent not of *real* toffs, but of Wodehouse-aunts. A voice as artificial, both in its well-modulated, would-be mellifluous timbre and its over-precise diction, as that of a duchess in a farce or a pantomime dame. In itself, a voice with connotations so richly comic it's a wonder her perorations aren't drowned by peals of mirth each time she opens her mouth, and unpleasantly significant that they are not. Because just what makes her sound so ludicrous are the barbarous echoes of past glories that shape her vowels and sharpen her consonants; yet it is also these echoes that make some of us, as a reflex action, snap to attention and touch the forelock.

But how come the voice's perpetrator is not sometimes helplessly overcome by its funny side? Rallying the Scottish Tories at the election campaign kick-off: 'Let us go forth from Perth . . .' How did she manage to spit out that phrase from the elocution class with a straight face? Gods knows, there've been sufficient pompous windbags at the helm of this nation before, but never one who's combined a script straight out of *The Boys' Own Paper* circa 1909 with the articulation of Benny Hill *en travestie*. And got away with it. That's the grievous thing.

But, when Thatcher modulates from the dulcet if bellicose contralto with which she cajoles her own side to the shriek, as of ripped linen, with which she subjugates the Commons – and which, interestingly enough, she also uses to address open-air meetings, so it may be involuntary – then, it chills the blood. For, then, hers becomes the very voice of the implacable, arbitrary, irrational authority known and feared in childhood. Voice like a slap on the wrist. Voice that broke in on your game with the little boy next door. 'What *are* you doing? Put your knickers back on, this instant!'

Small wonder, then, she is widely known as 'the nanny' and, on television during the campaign, has given the impression that if you don't vote for her, she'll tan your bottie. (She'll tan your bottie even if you do, unless you're very rich, but as is well known this is *le vice anglais* and the rich have always got it in the private sector; certainly Thatcher has democratically extended the joys of masochism to the entire population.)

The nanny. Although Anthony Barnett scrupulously refined the image – rather the governess who feels a cut above the rest of the staff whilst despising her bosses, and has now kicked out the squire since she knows far better than her employers what's good for him.

But, of course, we're *not* the rest of the staff and though the squires in the Tory Party might have been foolish enough to first promote her within their enclosed little world, they are no longer her employers. *We* are. Her contract is up for negotiation again, now, and it is, perhaps, characteristic of the overweening upper servant that she appears to believe there is no chance it will not be renewed.

But most of us have little direct experience of hiring staff and have seen nannies and governesses only on television, the medium, of course, by which she has infiltrated every home. A rather less cosy association, and one which gives the client less choice in her appointment, is with the lady magistrate who sends the menopausal housewife – as it might be one's mum; or, oneself – down for two years for shoplifting. ('Society must be protected from women like you.' Thatcher is fond of protecting society from people, as if people did not constitute societies.)

Certainly she rams home the point of the atavistic middle-class authority figure with her lady magistrate's two-piece costumes and her lady doctor 'sensible' shoes. Never one to miss out on the exploitation of her gender by fair means or foul, she, unlike Shirley Williams, has always known what garb intimidates. Yet, even when you cannot see her, even on the radio when she's occupying the Jimmy Young Show like an army with banners – and what other politician than this Housewife Superstar would have spotted the potential of the Jimmy Young Show – her scourging voice identifies her instantly as Class Enemy Number One.

Well, it does to me. It does to the bloke next door, who doesn't believe in hanging because it's too good for her. It does to all those who are not dissipating their energies during this election campaign by engaging in the voluptuous but non-productive luxury of Thatcher-hatred – I'm told the Bingo callers in Sheffield say: 'Number ten, Thatcher out' – as though she were somehow greater than the sum of her party and, if she saw the light and joined the Poor Clares tomorrow, the Tories would be perfectly all right. As they used to be, under decent, magnanimous, welfare socialists like Heath. (Remember Heath, who gave us the three-day week?) One of the wickedest things Thatcher has done is to make her Tories seem tolerable.

Yet she and her media advisers, and how odd it is one should discuss a British prime minister in terms of those who tell her how to powder her nose, have worked damn' hard to blot out the Class Enemy bit, to turn the Tory Party's greatest liability, both in terms of gender and fanaticism, into a comicbook superheroine. ('Superwoman', as Jean Rook of the *Daily Express* calls her.) They've done this, not by toning down her patent absurdity but by playing it up. If her colonial war helped, then it did so only with the aid of the most cynical manipulation of blood lust and

militaristic nostalgia of a kind we can ill afford. By turning the absurd into
something ineffable, something glorious.

All the qualities that make her like the 'bad guy' in wrestling, the 'Man
you Love to Hate,' like Mick MacManus, have gone into the resultant
Thatcher package. She is loathsome for precisely those reasons for which
she is most admired. For conviction, read monomania. For strength of
purpose, read pig-headedness. For cleverness, read low animal cunning.

If the media were as besotted with Michael Foot as they are with
Thatcher, he could be transformed overnight from the shambling loony as
which they now present him into a lovable eccentric, vastly wise, figure
of almost saintly heroism, whose sheer greatness of heart – there's Jean
Rook's headline! 'Mr Great-Heart' – shines through the somewhat outmoded rhetoric originally designed to address a packed Welsh mountainside rather than to suit a *tête-à-tête* with a television camera. (In fact, that's
all that's wrong with Foot on TV. He persists in addressing it as if it were
a public meeting, while Thatcher knows very well she is partaking in a
soap opera, with a role somewhat like, say, Alexis Carrington in *Dynasty*.

Indeed, if Foot were Tory leader and not Labour leader, think what the
notorious Jak, the *Standard*'s cartoonist, would do with him. Every time
he tripped over his terrier's lead, it would be proof his mind was on higher
things, such as saving the working class from the rapacity of the trade
unions or voluntarily repatriating Siamese cats to Bangkok. All this is to
do with the *artificiality* of the presentation of Thatcher, which is stressed by
the constant emphasis on her personal appearance, in which she appears
enthusiastically to condone the sexism of the media, gladly giving information about her tinted hair and the hours spent in the dentist's chair
(what courage!) having her teeth capped.

We are told exactly how she does it and then invited to applaud her
appearance of youth: 'Four years on and looking ten years younger,' by
Jackie Modlinger, fashion editor of the *Daily Express*. Even if one might
be forgiven for assuming that, like a latter-day Elizabeth Ba'thory, the
Countess Dracula of Hungarian legend, she retained the appearance of
youth by bathing each day in the blood of unemployed school leavers.

The ends to which this youthful radiance are put are balefully iconic.
That face of Thatcher is more stylised than even her voice, and nothing
about it is comic, especially its striking Aryan quality. The blonde, immaculate hair; the steel blue eyes glittering like bayonets, and always with a
glazed expression as if fixed on the vision of some high Tory apotheosis
such as the crucifixion of Arthur Scargill. The up-thrust chin, as if crest-
ing the waves, like the figurehead as which Steve Bell has so often depicted
her. Possibly, hideous thought, to her secret satisfaction, since, for
Thatcher, the image is more important by far than the meaning behind it

and a figurehead remains a figurehead, whatever its satirical intent.

It is the face, and the pose, too, of a Person of Destiny – and there seems no denying she has personally associated herself with that 'fulfilment of our nation's destiny' of which she spoke to the Scottish Tories, no doubt in serene confidence there was not one devolutionist amongst them who might have queried the appropriateness of the possessive pronoun.

However, the nature of that 'destiny' is as imprecise as the location of the 'Shining city on a hill' invoked as the destiny of the USA by Ronald Reagan during his pre-election debate with Jimmy Carter on American TV. Possibly her destiny and his destination are, in fact, the same city, luminous with radioactive dust and no longer identifiable.

Latterly, she's been sporting a silver and enamel Union Jack on her lapel, as emblematic a jewel as the accessories in the portraits of Elizabeth I as Gloriana. She's also developed a tendency to look vaguely red, white and blue, all over, unless the strain of all this is beginning to tell on me, as it is on Steve Bell's *Guardian* penguin. Union Jack jewel, patriotic colours – all convey the same story; that hers is a transcendent Britishness rising above mere sectarian strife such as the class struggle. Her cult of the personality, establishing her as an emotionally unassailable figure divorced from the sordid business of party politics, peaks on the cover of *The Economist* for 14-20 May. This shows her (up-thrust chin, commanding eyes, as ever, but with a new, positively Mussolini-esque meditatively brooding expression she must have practised in front of the mirror for ages) beneath a rampant Union Jack. The flag, for once, is out of focus, either an oddly tasteful touch or an indication that Thatcher is even more patriotic than it. The legend on the cover of this self-styled centrist publication: 'The issue is Thatcher.'

For the point of *The Economist* cover, constantly emphasised by Thatcher's appeal to the metaphysics of Britishness, is that a vote for Thatcher is a vote, not for the Tories, but for Britain. If you believe in Britain, clap your hands, and Britain, like Tinkerbell in *Peter Pan* will rise from her deathbed. And. And then, do what? But what Britain will do after this, to change the metaphor, Lazarus-like resurrection is also left vague, except, like any revenant, she will be less corporeally substantial and, presumably, no longer need nourishment, health care, education or employment.

The scarcely credible words of the Thatcher campaign song – and it is a *Thatcher* campaign song, not a Tory campaign song – concentrate on those undoubted qualities of leadership she shares with charismatic lemmings. The song also leaves unstated the place to which she proposes to transport us. 'Who do we want, who do we need, It is the leader who is bound to succeed – Maggie Thatcher, Just Maggie for me.'

Yet the issue in this election is most emphatically *not* Thatcher, who is no more than the representative of certain vested interests, and it is only her vaunting personal ambition and readiness to use the dirtiest resources of right-wing populism that give the illusion she is 'Mrs Big', as Jean Rook calls her. Me, I'm only a writer of fiction and a coarse semiologist by profession and must use the words of a far greater person than I, Theodor Adorno, to sum up adequately what Thatcher represents and a vote for her means.

Whatever was once good and decent in bourgeois values, independence, perseverance, forethought, circumspection, has been corrupted utterly . . . In losing their innocence, the bourgeois have become impenitently malign . . . The bourgeois live on like spectres threatening doom.

He saw it all, years ago, and said it in *Minima Moralia*.

And here she is, spectre not at the feast but at the famine, symbol – though only a symbol – of our bane and, possibly, an eventual enlightenment, like the plague in Camus's novel, except we may more easily be rid of her than Oran could purge itself of *pastorella pestis*. She can be exorcised with a mere cross on a voting slip. However, what then?

Years ago, during the February 1974 election campaign, the cover of the French news magazine, *L'Exprès*, carried the question: 'La Grande Bretagne: Chile ou Suède?' Curiously enough, this is the very choice Thatcher herself has offered us in this campaign, between 'a society coerced and a society free under the rule of law', although she might not agree the former phrase is an apt description of Chile under Pinochet while for me the latter sums up Sweden, with all its petty regulations and amazing virtues, well enough. In those days, the electorate pondered, wavered and finally plumped for the Swedish option. And the Labour government they put into power blew it. Blew it so badly that, as a result, this time round, a real choice might no longer exist.

Perhaps it was inevitable that in our post imperial anomie, the hangover after the two-hundred-year spree, Britain should throw up the apparatus to create a twopenny halfpenny demagogue of the kind known and feared throughout the Third World. Should release the madwoman who'd always been gibbering in the Tory attic, with its lugubrious lumber of Union Jack draped gallows, the personification of the Tory lady who'd grounded successive Tory Party conventions in a morass of meanness and cruelty. And should give this symbolic entity the keys to the whole asylum.

But nothing is inevitable; history seems inevitable only by virtue of hindsight. There is a conspiracy to create the impression that Thatcher is the kind of leader who goes down in the history books. I rather suspect that, should these islands survive so long, the ethnically complex, polyglot, joyously egalitarian inhabitants of these islands in 2083 will think of Thatcher only as a footnote to the history of graphics. 'Gave inspiration to Steve Bell, Ralph, Steadman, Gerald Scarfe, q.v. See, also, under Mère Ubu.'

New Statesman, 1983

Michael Moorcock: Mother London

This epic portion from the kitchen of Michael Moorcock's imagination is a vast, uncorseted, sentimental, comic, elegiac salmagundy of a novel, so deeply within a certain tradition of English writing, indeed, of English popular culture, that it feels foreign, just as Diana Dors, say, scarcely seems to come from the same country as Deborah Kerr.

Mother London contains obvious input from the music hall – Josef Kiss, the central character, himself started out working the halls as a mind-reader. And Moorcock tends to create his characters with a few, swift, sure strokes, brilliant and two-dimensional, just as the characters in music-hall sketches, or, indeed, the personas of the performers themselves are created.

He also does not deny the influence of pulp fiction – a whole generation of English youth nourished its dreams on Western novels – nor of *The Magnet, The Gem*, nor certain kinds of teddibly, teddibly Bridish popular history. (He quotes copiously from Arthur Mee.) But across the *ad hoc* structure and the unapologetically visionary quality of it all necessarily falls the incandescent shadow of William Blake, for whom there was no distinction between the real and the imaginary and whose phantom rises again every time we see a way out of that particular trap.

It isn't really a question of 'magic realism', that much-abused term. For Moorcock's Londoners, nothing could be more magical than the real fabric of the city they love and the stories with which it echoes.

A city is a repository of the past. Therefore *Mother London* is organised as an anthology of memories – recollections from the pasts of a group of men and women who meet regularly at an NHS clinic (under threat) to collect their tablets and enjoy group therapy.

Not that any of them are deranged, exactly. But they are all sensitives, some of them perhaps too sensitive to the stories of the city and its myriad voices. The grandly eccentric old man, Josef Kiss, can hear what people think. Sometimes it drives him mad.

We can hear the voices, too. The narrative is seamed with them, voices in a multitude of tongues, speaking platitudes, mouthing sexual paranoia, prejudice, gossip, wild talk, abuse . . . the city talking to herself. She is not a loving mother. But we must take her as we find her; she is the only one we have.

During the Blitz, Josef Kiss put his talents as a mind-reader to work, seeking survivors in the burning ruins. He did not find the beautiful Mary Gasalee among the ruins, however. She walked out of the flames by herself, carrying her new-born baby in her arms.

In spite of this authentic miracle, Mary's daughter grows up to be a best-selling historical novelist, not the new Messiah. Though the novel ends with the joyously consummatory marriage of Josef and Mary, there is no suggestion this event might cue in the arrival of yet another saviour, even though the city that survived the fire from heaven might now be in need of divine intervention to save it from the effects of late capitalism – the property boom, the demise of history, the exile of the working class from the city they built.

For the London Moorcock celebrates is working-class London, whose history has always survived by word of mouth, in stories and anecdotes. He takes you on a grand tour of the forgotten, neglected parts of London, as far as Mitcham in the south, but always coming back to W11, where, twenty years ago, you could see the Proverbs of Hell chalked up on the walls.

And if Josef and Mary turn out to be indestructible, as they do, perhaps there is hope in the infinite resilience of narrative itself.

Not for Moorcock the painful, infrequent excretion of dry little novels like so many rabbit pellets; his is the grand, messy flux itself, in all its heroic vulgarity, its unquenchable optimism, its enthusiasm for the inexhaustible variousness of things. Posterity will certainly give him that due place in the English literature of the late twentieth century which his more anaemic contemporaries grudge; indeed, he is so prolific it will probably look as though he has written most of it, anyway.

Guardian, 1988

Iain Sinclair: Downriver

Iain Sinclair, in the profane spirit of surrealism, has chosen to decorate the endchapters of his new work of fiction with a dozen unutterably strange picture-postcards. They show scenes such as that of six men, heavily veiled, veils held down by brimmed hats, posed with long-barrelled rifles. And two men in grass skirts, with feathers in their hair, intent on a game of billiards. They are Africans. And here are twenty-odd white men, in straw boaters, surrounding a prone crocodile. Joblard, Sinclair's friend, arranges the cards so that they tell a story. At once they become scrutable: they are images of imperialism. Joblard titles this picture story, what else, 'Heart of Darkness'.

But the twelve interconnected stories in *Downriver* don't match up with the numbered postcards, unless in such an arcane fashion it must necessarily remain mysterious to me. *Downriver* is really a sort of peripatetic biography: Iain Sinclair's adventures at the end of time, at the end of his tether, in a city of the near future with a hallucinatory resemblance to London. The decisive influence on this grisly dystopia is surely the grand master of all dystopias, William Burroughs. Jack Kerouac, asked for a quote for the jacket of *The Naked Lunch*, said it was an endless novel that would drive everybody mad. High praise. *Downriver* is like that, too.

It is mostly about the East End. This reviewer is a south Londoner, herself. When I cross the river, the sword that divides me from pleasure and money, I go north. That is, I take the Northern Line 'up west', as we say: that is, to the West End. My London consists of all the stations on the Northern Line, but don't think I scare easily: I have known the free-and-easy slap-and-tickle of Soho since toddlerhood, and shouldered aside throngs of harlots in order to buy my trousseau casseroles from Mme Cadec's long-defunct emporium, undeterred by rumoured crucifixions in nearby garages. Nothing between Morden and Camden Town holds terror for me.

But I never went to Whitechapel until I was thirty, when I needed to go to the Freedom Bookshop (it was closed). The moment I came up out of the tube at Aldgate East, everything was different from what I was accustomed to. Sharp, hard-nosed, far more urban. I felt quite the country bumpkin, slow-moving, slow-witted, come in from the pastoral world of Clapham Common, Brockwell Park, Tooting Bec. People spoke differently, an accent with clatter and spikes to it. They focused their sharp, bright eyes directly on you: none of that colonialised, transpontine, slithering regard. The streets were different – wide, handsome boulevards, juxtaposed against bleak, mean, treacherous lanes and alleys. Cobblestones. It was an older London, by far, than mine. I smelled danger. I bristled like one of Iain Sinclair's inimitable dogs. Born in Wandsworth, raised in Lambeth – Lambeth, 'the Bride, the Lamb's Wife', according to William Blake – nevertheless, I was scared shitless the first time I went to the East End.

Patrick White says somewhere that there is an intangible difference in the air of places where there has been intense suffering, that you can never get rid of the memory that pain imprints on the atmosphere. London's river runs through *Downriver* like a great, wet wound. Almost all the stories are affected in some way by the swell and surge occasioned when the pleasure boat, *Princess Alice*, sank after it collided with the *Byewell Castle*, a collier – a high-Victorian tragedy recalling the loss of the *Marchioness*, although Sinclair does nothing with the analogy, lets it lie there in the water. An estimated 640 people went down with the *Princess Alice*, including the husband and two children of Elizabeth Stride. Her family gone, she took to drink, went on the streets. She became one of the victims of Jack the Ripper – the kind of ominous coincidence that fiction needs to avoid if it is to be plausible. Life itself can afford to be more extrovert.

So can Sinclair, who has no truck with plausibility but allows or persuades his densely textured narrative to follow a logic based on the principle of allusion, engaging in a sort of continuous free collective bargaining with his own imagination. For example: there is sardonic, virtuoso description of the *Princess Alice* disaster:

> The victims chose an unlucky hour to enter the water. They were discharging the sewage from both the north and south banks into Barking Creek. Outflow. Mouths open, screaming, locked in a rictus. Rage of the reading classes. Public demand for the immediate provision of swimming-pools for the deserving poor. Let them learn breast-stroke.

Then the narrative moves like this:

> Something happens with the draw of time. With names. The *Alice*. Fleeing from the extreme interest of Lewis Carroll (weaving a labyrinth of mirrors for his English nymphet) into the tide-flow of Thames. Can you row, the sheep asked, handing her a pair of knitting-needles. Dodgsons. Dodgeson. Out on the river with another man's daughters: Lorina, Alice, Edith.

And thence to the enigmatic Canadian performance artist, Edith Cadiz, whose story we already know. By day, she worked as a nurse, nightly subsidising herself – for that income would never keep her – as a prostitute of the least exalted type. Edith Cadiz haunts the text, with her disinterested love for the mad children in her care, her unnerving stripper's act involving a dog and a set of street maps. One day, after copulating with a dog at the request of a Member of Parliament – this text is rich in dogs, some of them memorably unnerving – she disappears.

She is no less haunting a character because Sinclair makes plain she is not his own invention but the invention of another of the characters he has also invented. But many of the other characters, including Sinclair himself in a memorable walk-on ('a flannelled Lord Longford: on sulphate'), are drawn, kicking and screaming, one assumes, from real life. Some of them I recognise. One or two of them I know. That is Sinclair's autobiographical bit. Think of *Donwriver* as if Alice had wept a river of tears, rather than a pool; this river, like memory, full of people, places, ideas, things, all with ambiguous reality status.

King Kole, the Aboriginal cricketer, standing at the rail of the *Paramatta*, watching a pilot-boat butt its way across Gravesend Reach, knew he had arrived at the Land of Death. Gravesend did for Pocahontas, the Indian princess, too: she died there, on her way back to Virginia. Sacrificial victims of imperialism. But less fatal presences include a writer, Fredrik Hanbury, a name transparently concealing one familiar to readers of the *London Review of Books*. There are painters, vagrants, Jack the Ripper, Sir William Gull, ritual murder, cricket, Homerton, Silvertown, 'The Isle of Doges' (VAT City plc).

Alice herself features at considerable length, in an extended meditation on Tenniel's illustration to *Through the Looking-Glass*, the one that shows Alice in the train. Alice 'allies herself with the order of birds; a feather grows from her severe black torque'. That feather might be a clue to the solution of the murders. What murders? Why, didn't you know? Spring-heeled Jack has returned. 'VAMPIRE AND BRIDE-TO-BE IN DOCKLANDS HORROR'. Edith Cadiz might have been a victim of this man.

But that is to suggest too much interconnectedness, to imply that a plot might be about the happen. *Downriver* is jam-packed with teasing little hints at possible plots, but these coy insinuations of resolution, climax, dénouement are marsh-lights designed to delude the unaware reader into imagining that some regular kind of story might be in the offing. Fat chance. These stories, flowing all together, form a river without banks in which you sink or swim, like the victims of the *Princess Alice*, clutching at associations, quotations, references to other writers, if you can pick them up.

I picked up one or two. The American horror writer H. P. Lovecraft, is economically invoked with the single phrase, 'a gibbous moon'. T. S. Eliot is constantly quoted by Edith Cadiz both before and after her disappearance; she passes round a hat that once belonged to him after she does her strip. The scarlet-haired opium addict, Mary Butts, makes a brief guest appearance and Sinclair borrows a minatory quotation from her autobiography: 'I heard the first wraths of the guns at the Thames's mouth below Tilbury.'

With this mass of literary references, the sex magic, the degradations, the torture, the rich patina of black humour, this is a book that triumphantly rejects any possibility of the Booker short-list in advance. It wears its contempt for all that on its sleeve. It is, besides, a work of conspicuous and glorious ill-humour. Sinclair doesn't seem driven, like Burroughs, by an all-consuming misanthropy: he's too romantic for that. But whenever Sinclair writes about the media, he goes pink and sputters. There is a section titled 'Living in Restaurants', about trying to make a television movie about Spitalfields. 'The *consiglieri* like the sound of it, the authentic whiff of heritage, drifting like cordite from the razed ghetto.' The media lunches, four months of heroic eating. He hates them all. He constructs stiff, epigrammatic insults, more insult than epigram. The TV producer 'has that combatant attitude so prevalent among people who spend their lives bluffing genuine enthusiasts into believing they know nothing about their own subject.'

There is an *unhandiness* about Sinclair's prose, here. It creaks. His satire is splenetic but also heavy-handed. 'The Widow was a praise-fed avatar of the robot-Maria from *Metropolis*; she looked like herself, but too much so.' No prizes for guessing who *that* is. However, *Downriver* is set just a significant little bit further forward in the future, after the privatisation of the railways. And the Widow is *still* in charge. Who could have guessed, when *Downriver* went to press, that Margaret Thatcher would have resigned by publication date? Not Sinclair. When he appears in the third person of the final story, he babbles 'some bravado subtext about considering his book a failure if the Widow clung on to power one year after its publication'. Unless he wants to claim a pre-emptive strike, he'll have to concede that, like Blake, to whose prophetic books his own bears some relation, he had, as prophet, zero success rate.

At one point, the Fredrik Hanbury character opines: 'Obsession matures into spiritual paralysis.' *Downriver* is far more than the sum of its obsessions, compelling as these are. Who can ever forget that dog of dogs, the one with *no eyes*, not a dog whose eyes have been put out but one who *never had any*, grey fur there, instead. This is an image so horrifying I don't want to understand it. What is the opposite of dog? This question begins and ends the book, this manic travelogue of a city about to burn, and I can't even begin to answer: I will have to read *Downriver* again, to find out.

Yet, in spite of, or perhaps in order to spite that central, dominating motif of the river, none of these twelve stories flow easily. There are swirls, eddies, and undercurrents but precious few stretches of clear water. When these occur, as they do, for example, two separate times in the section called 'Prima Donna' (the Cleansing of Angels), the limpid narrative achieves genuine supernatural horror; the bristling begins. One is the anecdote about Cec Whitenettle, driver of the hell-train bearing nuclear

waste through Hackney. The other is the story of the Ripper's only per-
sonable victim, the 'Prima Donna' herself, that begins impeccably, better
than Lovecraft, almost as good as Poe: 'I had not, I think, been dead
beyond two or three months when I dreamed of the perfect murder.'

But Sinclair obviously isn't interested in plain sailing. His everyday
prose is dense, static, each sentence weighed down with a vicious charge
of imagery. Fighting the current, this reader was forced to ponder the ultimate function of fiction. This was very good for me. Is it to pass the time
pleasantly, I asked myself? If so, they put some quite good things on television these days. But something is happening in this text that makes it
necessary to go on reading it, something to do with time itself, even if, in
order to go on, you must – to mix metaphors – crack open each sentence
carefully, to inspect the meat inside.

All writers of fiction are doing something strange with time – are *working* in time. Not their own time, but the time of the reader. One of
Sinclair's milder obsessions is with ritual: the project of ritual is to make
time stand still, as it has apparently stood still in David Rodinsky's room
in the Princelet St Synagogue since the day, twenty-odd years ago, when
he disappeared. (See Tale No. Five, 'The Solemn Mystery of the
Disappearing Room'.) If time could be persuaded to stand still for even
one minute, then the thin skin that divides Victorian London,
Pocahontas's London, Blake's accursed London, Gog and Magog's
London, The City of Dreadful Night, Jack London's London (*The People
of the Abyss*), *Downriver*'s London of the near future, might dissolve altogether. The partitions of time dissolve in the memory, after all. They dissolve in the unconscious.

At one point, Joblard and Sinclair watch Pocahontas being carried
ashore to die, but that is altogether different, a purely literary trick with
time. It is an easier one because the reader watches it being done on the
page rather than experiencing it in the act of reading. The thing is, you
can't skip bits of *Downriver*. You have to move with currents as violent and
mysterious as those of the Thames.

Its vision of London is pure hell. Madmen, derelicts, visionaries, 'wet-
brains' live in the towers of abandoned mental hospitals. Academics voluptuously drown themselves in chains. Bohemians live with a dedicated
ferocity. Oh! that Imar O'Hagan, with his trained snails and his 'fridge full
of blocks of frozen vampire bats like an airline breakfast of compressed
gloves'.

It describes a city in the grip of a psychotic crisis. One image makes this
concrete – a room in Well Street ('Grade 2 listed husk'), former home of
a mad, addicted girl, now a suicide. The walls are covered with shrieking
graffiti, protests, denunciations, phone-numbers, pyramids, quotations,

lingams, crucified sparrows, horned gods, walking fish. 'The floor was
clogged with mounds of damp sawdust – as if the furniture had been eaten,
and, conically, excreted. Bas-relief torcs of blood were plashed over the
skirting-boards. "Dogfights," Davy explained.' This, even more than the
voodoo ritual later to be enacted on the Isle of Doges (sic), is the true heart
of darkness within the city.

On the whole, the English, except for Dr Johnson, never have liked
London. Cockney Blake saw, within a crystal cabinet, a refreshed, regen-
erate, a garden city:

> Another England there I saw,
> Another London with its tower,
> Another Thames and other hills.

Sinclair and two companions precipitate themselves out of that nightmare
voodoo ceremony by an act of will and find themselves transported to just
such an earthly paradise, freshly designed for the 'Nineties by a snappy
Post-Modernist', a 'morning-fresh Medieval city', a 'transported Siena.
Beneath us, along the riverside, a parade of windmills.' Windmills, the
green sign of harmless energy. Benign, harmless windmills, the herbivores
of the energy world. But when they look closer, they see the windmills
are not windmills after all, but the sites of crucifixions.

Downriver is an unapologetically apocalyptic book that has, alas, found
its moment, even if the Widow is now reduced to soundbites. Mother
London, says Sinclair, is splitting into segments: a queasy glamour extin-
guishes the mad, bad past in Whitechapel, the rest of the places go hang
. . . and yet these stories show how impossible it is to pull down an
imaginary city. As Sinclair walks round London, he reinvents it, and
remembered pain will always dance like heat in the air above the spot in
Whitechapel where the Ripper struck down poor Lizzie Stride. The
singing that turned to screaming continues to impress itself on the water
where the *Princess Alice* went down. Listen, you can hear it on the slapping
tide.

London Review of Books, 1991

Travelling

My Maugham Award

What did I do with my Maugham award? Well, in the end I found I had gone round the world, which surprised me a little; I became a connoisseur of cities, of American, Asiatic and even European cities and encountered, amongst others, the most beautiful transvestite in the whole of Greenwich Village; a Russian wrestler who had a wallet of photographs showing himself wrestling with a bear; a frayed Japanese with nicotine-stained teeth who told me Dostoevesky was his spiritual father; a six-foot-tall girl from Reading striding about Tokyo in a Victorian velvet mantle who modelled for sake ads on Japanese television; hippies, GIs fresh from Vietnam, an ex-para who had jumped into Algeria – and innumerable others.

In America, I saw a great many hallucinatory midnight bus stations and lived in a log cabin in a redwood forest for a while. I heard the windbells of San Francisco and the picturesque cries of the street traders of the Haight-Ashbury quarter . . 'hash . . . lids . . . grass . . .' I made a sentimental journey to the jazz museum in New Orleans and looked at a glass case containing Bix Beiderbecke's collar studs and handkerchief through a mist of tears. Around the Berkeley campus of UCLA, saffron-robed figures sang and danced 'Hare Krishna', to my exquisite embarrassment, and everywhere they advertised burgers – hamburgers, bullburgers, broiler-burgers, every kind of burger including Murphy's Irish Shamrockburger. Then I left America and went to Japan, where people smile and smile but never show their teeth.

Tokyo blazes at night like a neon version of the collected works of Marshall McLuhan and the taxi-drivers wear white gloves. The autumn umbrellas and the willow trees in the streets give this ugliest and most enchanting of cities the atmosphere of a painting by Renoir. At night, beside the vast departmental stores, the fortune-tellers sit at their little stands, each advertised by a neon hand marked with the lines of power, and do a roaring trade. Japan is utterly different from anywhere else in the world. I thought, at first, 'Well, maybe this is just Asia,' but then I went to other Asiatic places and, no, nowhere is the same as Tokyo. And this country, which voluntarily exiled itself from the world for 250 years, is like no other country. I can't say whether I liked it or not, really; not that I was never, even for one moment, bored there.

The Japanese language itself poses – or, rather, annihilates – many problems for the European. For example, there is no Japanese word which roughly corresponds to the great contemporary European supernotion, 'identity'; and there is hardly an adequate equivalent for the verb 'to be'. Further, in a language without plurals, the time-honoured European intellectual division between the one and the many cannot exist except in a kind of intuitive meta-language, the existence of which I very much doubt. Now that I am trying to learn Japanese, I find myself having to turn my head inside out – always good therapy. Japan is like going through the looking-glass and finding out what kind of milk it is that looking-glass cats drink; the same, but totally other. In the campus at Waseda University, beautiful young men with the faces of those who will die on the barricades were lobbing hand grenades at policemen. However, I also went to several other countries.

I travelled, therefore, a great deal, especially for someone who had, previously, never been further than Dublin, Eire, and I saw a great many things: a devil dancer who was, I think, bewitching a luxury hotel in Bangkok, which is an unholy blend of Edmund Dulac's illustrations to the *Arabian Nights* and Crawley New Town; sunset over Hong Kong harbour, the waters of which are impossibly green; and finally felt a hunger for the familiar and went to Paris for, though I had never visited there before, I had read about it in Balzac and seen it often in my favourite movie (which is Marcel Carné's *Les Enfants du Paradis*). And it was better than I would have believed possible, and so was the Midi, although the mistral was snarling. In a café in Arles, I saw a madman remove the battered top hat he wore on his head, take from this receptacle the raw chicken which it contained, and eat it.

After that, I came home and tried to sort out, a little, the effects of the enormous barrage of imagery to which I had been subjected and found the task, as these somewhat disconnected paragraphs will indicate, exceedingly difficult. However, I am working on it.

The Author, 1970

The Back of Beyond

Time runs at different speeds in different parts of the world. In southern Anatolia, the clocks don't register global village time, they register Third World time. Which is the time of yesterday and tomorrow. But not today. Not yet.

If this part of Turkey had a colour, it would be purple; its texture is that of slightly soiled velvet. One can be more precise and less allusive about the smells. There is the rich, lively stench of horse urine; a subtle, furry scent rising from sun-warmed heaps of fat peaches, so ripe they are about to rot; the sharp, sweet scent of the eau de cologne with which the inhabitants continually douse themselves. Blended with these Levantine and primordial odours is that heady mixture of unwashed flesh, goat and woodsmoke redolent all together of nothing so much as socks that have not been washed for a very long time. This is the authentic smell of the Third World.

A number of specific indicators tell us just where we are. You don't even have to look at the economic index. The telephones rarely, if ever, work. Any encounter with bureaucracy is fraught with screaming hysteria. The service trades – cafés, restaurants, hotels – all appear to be run, with sufficient efficiency, by nine-year-old boys. But then, it is the school holidays.

The male inhabitants are all officer class, every one, with their straight backs, direct and piercing regards, martial dignity of bearing. Middle-aged middle-class Turks at seaside resorts advance upon the sea as if subduing it. They all carry a good deal of weight before them and favour long, decent boxer shorts to swim in. They are, inevitably, heavily moustached. A moustache means a man is always dressed, even when he is naked. Occasionally they will smoke a cigarette as they stride slowly forward into the water, to minimise the significance of the occasion. Portly and majestic, they advance upon the sea until the water covers the lower slope of the belly and touches the pendulous nipples. Then, without any undue haste, they launch themselves splendidly forward.

It is also a fine sight to see a group of Turks, all of them moustachioed like comic opera brigands, eating chocolate pudding from cut-glass dishes, with tiny spoons, in the ubiquitous pudding shops. Cultures that do not use much alcohol tend towards a sweet tooth. The pudding shops sell crème caramel, ice-cream, desserts made from creamed rice, rosewater, cornflower, all manner of quivering, opalescent, nut and cream-topped puddings. You never see women in the teahouses but occasionally, you see them in the pudding shops. Not half as often as you see men, though.

In this country, hair and apricots are the colour of dark amber. The people look more British than the British, sometimes, with their red-gold hair and their fierce blue-grey eyes; the Arabs have no monopoly of Islam. Isn't half southern Russia Moslem? (Or is that because the Ottomans went there?) Some parts of the Turkish landscape, those vast fields of sunflowers taller than a man, the quivering enfilades of poplars and the neo-classical railway stations with rail-side tea-gardens, can imperceptibly modulate into that of southern Russia – if you ignore the Coca-Cola signs and keep out of the cities.

During the Ottoman empire, the Mediterranean was the Turkish lake and maybe a residual sense of imperial destiny accounts for that clean-limbed straightly tall demeanour. They look you straight in the eye even when they are cheating you blind. Nevertheless, the Turks themselves, no less than their vassals, were liberated from the bonds of empire by Ataturk. Ataturk's Turkey, nationalist, secular and republican, was the very antithesis of its Ottoman predecessor. Perhaps they walk like republicans. Every town has a Republic Square and an Ataturk Boulevard. Even the meanest teahouse has its portrait of Mustapha Kemal Ataturk over the gas jet on which they make the Turkish coffee, although he has been dead for more than thirty years. Perhaps the British should study Turkey; God knows, we need models for de-imperialisation.

Ataturk's argument for the emancipation of women, remarkable for an Islamic country in the 1920s, and one that time has not rendered unsophisticated, was that Turkey was losing half its human resources through locking them away. But, inevitably, a peasant culture is a device for locking up human resources in the soil. It is just impossible to escape role-defined labour in a peasant culture, even if the women seem always to have done most of the work, while their menfolk sat in teahouses smoking waterpipes and conversing with Russian loquacity but no trace of Slavonic gloom.

Ataturk, when asked what quality he most admired in a woman, replied: 'availability'. He abolished purdah; nevertheless, veiled of their own free will, the women of the countryside retain a magnificent archaic style. They dip their fingertips and anoint their palms in henna; they arranged henna-dyed hair in innumerable braids under their cheesecloth headdresses; they persist in carrying water from the well in amphoras, with that stately grace typical of non-industrial countries.

The clothes of the women differ from district to district. The characteristic baggy trousers, or *shavlar*, more of a voluminous divided skirt, seem to predominate in the south, in that more women seem to wear them than anything else. It is both a picturesque and unbecoming garb; the bulky drawers appear to organise the physiques of those who wear them so that they develop swag bellies and quickly become steatopygous. They look just like those dolls with spherical bases that cannot fall over no matter how hard you push them. Even when the *shavlar* are made from glossy, brilliant velvets or paisley prints, they are, since they are always worn with a blanket stiffly folded across the head and over the lower part of the face, quite plainly garments designed to distinguish women as women but to keep them as anonymous as possible as human beings.

The paradox of a peasant culture is that, though it has some of the formal elements of the collective in terms of thought patterns and lifestyle and offers no scope for the cultivation of psychological individuation, the men and women are quite ferociously individualised.

But women in *shavlar*, from a distance, can bear a fleeting resemblance to ambulant mosques. And one of the paradoxes of Islam is the iconography of the mosque; the lascivious, curvilinear domes, architectural versions of the statue of the many-breasted Diana of Ephesus, guarded on all sides by the bristling, phallic spires of the minarets. As if to demonstrate how firmly the male principle keeps the female principle in check. As we feminists say to one another, never trust a spire. On the other hand, Turkish men are, on the whole, very nice to women, which is more than can be said, on the whole, for the British.

Ataturk hauled Anatolian menswear into the late nineteenth century. Men wear big, peaked caps – though the old and devout still don skull-caps of pin-tucked linen. Their waistcoats are garlanded with watchchains. The young men in their wide-shouldered suits, with the cloth caps that reveal the childlike bulge of the back of the head, have a curiously touching air; they look like Robert Tressell's ragged-trousered philanthropists, or early immigrants in America. An entire class, or caste, or section of humanity is defined by its dress. Sartorial inegality. Yet the style is in perfect harmony with the surroundings and is not *experienced* as inegality; and it is a decorous, beautiful style.

These are prosperous Third World peasants, with lots of delicious things to eat and pure air to breathe and a rich texture to their lives that we in Britain lost about the time of the Industrial Revolution. Life is harsh and savage in the east, in bandit country, where the Kurds are; nevertheless, it is not impossible to suspect that the world of the prosperous Third World peasants may be, if not the best of all possible worlds, at least one of the more tolerable versions of the world presently available. There is a Luddite lurking in the hearts of most of us. The back of beyond is not necessarily the asshole of the universe.

In a mountain village, a young boy took me to his home in order to try to sell me a carpet. So I was able to take one of the more romantic of these 'snapshots' of Third World life.

Two cows, one black and one brown, their backs grey all over with dust from the road, stood quietly by the gate, which was propped permanently open with a stone. The house itself was a square, white, single-storeyed structure with small windows and, before it, a vine-covered porch. Granny had such an enormous belly it raised up the waist-band of her black skirt until it met the safety pin that fastened her brown cotton shawl in front. There was a selection of small children, donkeys and cats milling about. None of them took the slightest notice of me at all.

The house was arranged around a square, white-washed kitchen which contained a large refrigerator and a calor gas, two-burner stove arranged on a box in the corner. The concrete floor was carefully swept. Lined up against the wall were a number of tall sacks made of a white, homespun material; these contained dry foodstuffs such as beans, rice and millet. There were two other rooms. In one stood a loom of such primitive design one could have deduced from its structure how weaving was invented in the first place. The housewife was engaged in making rugs and bags in bright, simple, geometric patterns. The room was tiled with carpets and there were banks of cushions for seating, arranged around two walls. All was clean, decent, cheerful and proper.

I looked at the carpets but did not buy one and the young boy, as if congratulating me on my decision, shook me forcefully by the hand.

New Society, 1972

Triple Flavour

The bus moves off to Larnaca, a town built, it is said, on the site of a city founded by a grandson of Noah. Like Ireland, Cyprus is an island unusually rich in legendary history. Like Ireland, it has only the appearance of tranquillity.

In this town, as in all the towns of Cyprus, the streets pretend they are elsewhere than Cyprus, since they are named after Greek or Turkish places and heroes: Athens, Socrates, Ankara, Ataturk, Byron and so on. And Windsor, even. 'He who holds Cyprus holds the key to the eastern Mediterranean.' Her factual history has been imposed on her from outside. Everybody trampled on her: Arabs, crusaders, Venetians, Turks and British. ENOSIS (Union with Greece), says the flaking white graffiti. You would have to pull the island up by its moorings and tow it round the

Aegean to get it. But it *is* a Greek island. Except where it is not. It is a Greek island nestling snugly in the armpit of Turkey.

And in the Turkish quarter, in any Turkish quarter, beyond the United Nation's lookout post and the tangle of barbed wire, you can see, for example, a young girl with the perfect oval face of an Ingres odalisque. Her black hair is parted in the centre, a striped silk handkerchief is tied round the low chignon. She is all complete, sitting at an open window like an invention of the romantic imagination, or a sign that says: 'The Levant'.

The island, predominantly Greek, presents the triple flavours of Greece, Turkey and a little bit of Blighty. All three of these, in their separate ways, have contrived to make themselves so much at home that the very land-scape alters according to whoever lives there, even if, all the time, its tranquillity is only apparent.

The triple flavours do not blend at all. The Greeks maintain about them a vibrant and electric atmosphere. They seem always on guard, for they have been long enough on the island to have grown insular; and some-times the place feels as though it had been provincial for ever. So they have the implicit wariness of provincials. Their swarthy women go about in chattering covens, revealing gold teeth in subtly ambiguous smiles that flash like knives. They bind up their abundant hair in coarse snoods and wear black, shapeless dresses that stop abruptly somewhere between knee and ankle. They kiss the hands of chignoned priests when they meet them in the street and kiss the tin-plated icons in the sombre churches. They kiss vociferously and often and they screech.

At the seaside, the beach boys flex; the young Greeks perform exhibitionist callisthenics, displaying harmoniously proportioned torsos that match their classically straight noses. But where the excessively green sea laps against the Turkish beaches, the men are old and fat and sit in the shade of an immense tree on uncomfortable wooden chairs, sunk in the heavy, waking lapse of consciousness that is quite alien to Europe. Yet it is not quite Asian; more slavonic. And the Turks drink spiced tea made in samovars, when they can afford it. If the Greeks are vibrant, the Turks are slumberous. They are equally proud and murderous, only in absolutely different ways.

Nicosia, the capital of the island, is a Greek name. The Turkish name for the same city is Lefkosa and, in fact, they are two different cities divided by barbed wire and improvised barricades of broken furniture and dented oil cans. Soldiers of various denominations – Greeks, Turks, and those who go under the blue United Nations flag – patrol these ramshackle borders of a tumbledown world. The people in the Turkish quarter, on the whole, are poor and live in cavernous tunnels hollowed out of cliffs of crumbling, plastered stone. The quarter is pocked with

craters that look like bomb sites and probably are. It is another world from
the suave, provincial boulevards where island intellectuals in short-sleeved
shirts and ties sip café frappé in front of the photographs of Makarios in his
canonicals; and there is a Wimpy bar and you can buy the *News of the
World*.

These rutted alleyways are haunted by sleek, elegant cats. They are
pampered and beloved, for the Turks love cats. In Lefkosa, the cafés have
floors of dusty tiles and inadequate washing-up facilities and use only
sweetened, condensed milk. Men sit here all day, sometimes with a thim-
bleful of coffee before them, more often without and gaze into space –
gripped in a silence so heavy you could touch it with your hand. The
infrequently appearing women, wimpled and enormous, move like swans
and never show their teeth when they smile – which, anyway, they do
rarely. It throbs with dry heat and the *cicadas* go chug-chug-chug. A man
calls the muezzin; it sounds like Jewish liturgical singing. Amplified on a
crackling speaker, his voice performs such a rich trajectory of emotive
sound, it cuts directly through the noises of the city and pierces the heart
– though not, that is, the hearts of the Greeks, to whom it must be a perpetual irritant.

And then we step delicately back over the barbed wire into another
country. The soot-stained chimneys of the open air grills already belch
smoke odorous with searing lamb; it is suppertime and the Greeks will eat
kebab and hot bread and crudities splashed with oil and vinegar.

The curdled stucco ziggurats of modern Mediterranean architecture
overshadow the Hotel Victoria, which has tiled floors; high echoing
rooms; tall windows with slatted shutters; corridors open to the weather;
and all the paraphernalia of nineteenth-century romanticism. It's a run-
down place where travellers stay and breakfast is over by 6.30 a.m. It is
something of a find among the tourist hotels that deep fry eggs in olive oil,
and contemptuously roast the bacon. English is spoken all over the island,
although the Turks do not speak it as well as the Greeks; and this hotel,
named, of all people, after Queen Victoria, dares refuse to prepare an
English breakfast at the hour of nine because, for the vendors in the streets
and the householders behind their curlicued double doors, the morning is
then half over.

Like Ireland, Cyprus is unusually rich in tragic irony. They managed to
get rid of the English, but, no sooner had they done so, we crept in at the
back door again, disguised as tourists and expatriates, and emptied our tea-
leaves all over them. Not that they seem to care. Murderous in their
separate ways, divided by centuries, refusing even to unite against us, the
Greeks and the Turks eye one another across the barricades, indifferent to
the pink brick housing estates, with their roads named after towns in the

Home Counties, where the British still stake their claim to an interest in the eastern Med. The inhabitants of this harsh and beautiful island exhibit only the appearance of tranquillity, and sometimes not even that.

New Society, 1973

Wet Dream City

The *Morning Star* carries an ad for a seven-day package trip to see the work of the communist city councils in Bologna and Venice. That puts the Queen of the Sea in fresh perspective; '*Venise la rouge*', as Alfred de Musset said.

Forget about the top dressing of international glamour, knocking back cocktails of champagne and peach juice in Harry's Bar. Harry fixed martinis for Hemingway and isn't called Harry at all. He has named these upper market beverages 'Bellinis', probably easier for foreigners to pronounce than Giorgiones. They cost the earth. They are as irrelevant to Red Venice as the Doge's Palace, with its vast, echoing, pointless rooms, and its oil paintings clearly commissioned by the square yard.

The city is a perfectly ordinary one, of tenements, groceries, back alleys, and graffiti, of which the currently most inscrutable is '*Armenia Libere*' and the most enterprising 'Bakunin lives'. A run-of-the-mill kind of city, whose inhabitants are subtly discommoded by the fact that the streets are filled with water.

What can they have been thinking of when they built it? On 25 March 413, at midday, refugees from Padua laid the first stone at the Rialto, putting up the first homesteads out on an island in the sea safe from the barbarians at the moment ravaging the remains of the Roman empire. No doubt it seemed a good idea, in those troubled times. They must have felt like *The Survivors*. But the long-term impracticality of it, the inconvenience of the construction work . . . All that effort to put up the largest pedestrian precinct in the world. And now it is falling down.

> Oh Venice! Venice! When thy marble halls
> Are level with the waters, there shall be
> A cry of nations o'er thy sunken halls,

prophesied Byron. True enough; there will be a Venetian ball, with madrigals, at the Royal Naval College, Greenwich, in aid of the Venice in

Peril Fund in July, tickets (including wine and dinner) £15.

Venice in Peril, jet-set ecology; charity balls and benefit concerts to fund the conservation of the place; shoring up the fiction of our cultural heritage, as if this most extravagantly and improbably beautiful city (as, of course, it is) has become almost an image of European culture itself. The waves remorselessly erode the stones that Ruskin lovingly logged. The rats industriously gnaw our own cellars. The tide recedes a little less far each time it goes out, comes in a little further. It stakes, on every turn, a larger claim to the old sandbank, hunkered up with art treasures, slum property and garbage, on which we eke out an ever more precarious existence. Venice is sinking at last. How apt.

Venice is at once a real and an imaginary city, a place and an idea. 'The greenest island of my imagination,' Byron called it, like many other northerners before and after him, for whom Italy itself was the land of perpetual summer – where the lemon trees grow, domain of love and passion, of personal liberation. Italy was for the nineteenth century what Nepal was for the 1960s.

Venice, the water navel of Italy. The golden lion with wings and agate eyes, on its pole by St Mark's, sufficiently symbolises Venice – a fabulous beast. A sacred cow would also suit. However, a mammal with avian accessories suggests ambiguity; the ambiguity of a water-borne, even water-logged city, neither land nor water, not fish nor fowl and only intermittently good red herring.

Prostituted so often, she has acquired a raddled dignity. There is an introspective silence at nights, as of a brothel when the lights go out. It is a secret place. The natives, on the whole, are dour.

Those nights are very spooky, disturbed only by the voices of late-wandering visitors and the occasional anachronistic splash of the oar of a gondola on a midnight boat trip. The silence is introspective and also sinister. You remember what dangerous places Renaissance cities were: robbers, assassins behind every bridge, in every doorway; and nowhere in this city to run away to but the canals, into which a plunge is probably a fate worse than death.

Intrepid Byron, of course, used to swim home from dinner parties, down the Grand Canal. Sometimes he would carry a lighted torch in one hand to warn boatmen of his approach, so that they would not inadvertently batter his head with their oars. He must have risen up on the steps of the Palazzo Mocenigo like a clubfoot triton wreathed in turds. In those days the Grand Canal was both the main highway and the main sewer of Venice. I trust to the city council it is not so now.

But I cannot imagine it is a healthy city. Its atmosphere seems especially fatal to exotics from northern climates. Browning died here; Wagner died here; Diaghilev died here, as if it was all too much, suddenly. Byron, to whom too much was never enough, survived it. But death in Venice seems imminent on any cold day in spring.

I think Thomas Mann used Venice as an image of destructive sensuality in the same way Europeans use Asia ('The beds in the East are soft' and so on.) Mann's von Aschenbach, the rigid personification of the Protestant ethic – super-ego, made man – surrendered at last to his repressions at the sight of a beautiful boy on the beach at the Lido. He became, in his love-enfeebled state, a fit prey for the virus of the European disease, the sickness of decay, brewing in the city that always used to function as the place where east met west. The incoming tide of mortality rotted his will to live. I was not particularly well in Venice, either. I saw the city through a feverish influenza haze. So it looked more like a hallucination than ever.

In this unusual state, it was the water everywhere that made Venice all so strange. The enormous, pale, amniotic lagoon that surrounds Venice, and of which you are never unaware, glitters in all the colours of green from jade to oil. The water invades the city itself, and veins it with those bottle-green canals the water of which never moves. Venice seems an interuterine city, place of birth and hence (by all the laws of equivalences) of death. The silence of the night is the claustrophobic hush of the womb. This is probably why the city has such a regressive effect on its *aficionados*, especially those from the masculine and Protestant north. They go to the dogs here.

In Venice, the bad Lord Byron acquired 'the first gonorrhoea I have not paid for'. He cohabited, with easy egalitarianism, first with a draper's wife, then with a baker's wife, who attacked him with a breadknife. He got so fat you could no longer see the knuckles of his hands. And he never cut his hair.

But Byron, 'a broken dandy lately on my travels', he called himself, had gone to the dogs already. After Venice, there was nowhere to go but up. Greece, the fight for freedom, a hero's fate.

Incorruptible since already done for, even his work improved in Venice. The city nourished his profound frivolity. He penned the sprightly *Beppo*, started *Don Juan* while balked inamoratas hurled themselves into canals. No lolling about on beaches, leering voyeuristically at children, for him. Venice did him good. It seems to do so for those with least to lose.

Poor von Aschenbach. He should have met Baron Corvo. It was a wonder he did not. Corvo was always sculling about the Lido. He would then have surrendered to his repressions in a less morbid, if a more reprehensible way. Corvo knew all the addresses.

But von Aschenbach is a fictional character and Baron Corvo has some claims to a real existence. All they have in common is the interrelated fiction of a place and its baleful atmospherics.

Corvo's hold on reality had been tenuous enough, at best. At his first glimpse of Venice, this snapped for good. Easy to see how it happened. Venice allowed Corvo to abandon himself utterly to the fictions of a life that had been all his own invention in the first place. An imaginary person stepped into an imaginary place. The irony was that both of them were perfectly real.

Corvo went to Venice, as Isherwood did to Berlin, for boys. He found them – boys with wicked knees and shorts open to the navel; boys like simpering tigers; boys, radiant with adolescent *machismo* in the white light of dawn, poised on the poops of gondolas. Some boys he could only imagine. 'Real medieval *gondolieri* in long fantastically striped hosen of silk, proud in the pomp of brocade, poised on lofty poops in the luminous shade of some small canal,' he fantasised in a letter home, in his ineffably jewelled style, sumptuous and vulgar as the screen in San Marco's. How he would have admired von Aschenbach's half-grown and athletic Tadzio, with his hyacinthine curls, his face of a Greek god, and his striped sailor suit with red breast-knot.

Improbable cities attract improbable lovers. Who more improbable than Frederick Rolfe, who claimed his baronetcy had been given him by a lady called the Duchess of Sforza-Cesarini. Catholic convert and failed priest, he rewarded himself for his expulsion from the seminary by writing a novel *Hadrian VII*, in which he became Pope. After that, only an authentically fabulous city would do. He came to Venice on a holiday paid for by somebody else, with a change of clothes packed in a laundry basket, a ring that had a spike in it for blinding Jesuits, and a fountain pen filled with a quarter of a pint of red ink. Venice swallowed him at a gulp.

It is all far odder than a novel, even than his novel, *The Desire and Pursuit of the Whole*, a romance of modern Venice in which a lucid dementia reigns. Corvo wandered homeless on the Lido in the piercing cold. He fired off begging letters and plaintive cries by every post ('every day I live here, something hurts me'); took boys off across the lagoon by steamer to the island of Burano for beefsteak, red wine, solace. He sent snapshots home. 'I think the ones of Carlo are very sweet. Pity he has but one ball.'

On a thousand pounds sponged unscrupulously from a visiting clergyman, he splurged on a gondola of his very own, with sails painted by his own hand, and rowed by four boys 'Young Venetians poised on lofty poops out in the wide lagoon' – a dream come true.

He hung his bedroom with antique robes of cardinals and, shades of von Aschenbach, dyed his hair bright red. Penniless again, in 1913, he is reduced to sleeping in his boat, with the rats biting his toes. A month later, another death in Venice, one far stranger than Thomas Mann's fiction if less resonant. Dropped down dead in that city which seems a perpetual bizarre carnival. As Byron had noted with relish, *carnival* means: 'farewell to flesh'.

Think I'll take that trip they advertise in the *Morning Star*, next time. It seems safer, that way.

New Society, 1977

A Petrified Harvest

The soil around Caldas da Rainha, a small town about forty miles north of Lisbon, is a vivid, foxy, reddish brown; mix it with water, bake it and you will have earthenware. For several centuries, this town has been a famous centre of the ceramics industry, with a unique style of its own. Although, on Mondays, an itinerant vendor sets up his stall in the market square to sell bowls, dishes, jugs and casseroles of the most elementary shapes and glazes, these are peasant artefacts whose function is rapidly being superseded by the enamel saucepans and plastic bowls in the supermarkets.

And is it any wonder; the earthenware is so friable it crumbles in your hand. Use it, break it, replace it, was the old way but these wares no longer cost a penny or two. A large dish costs about a pound and you can buy something in the hardware store that will last a lifetime of several of them for that much money. So the peasants eschew these primitive and beautiful things, which will find a more welcome home in the stripped pine kitchens of developed countries. Besides, any artisan potter from here to Kabul could make them; they are not the pots for which Caldas has been and is famous.

Contemporary Caldas ware is piled on stalls that remain in place all week and its prime function is that of souvenir. Since the tourist industry in Portugal is not yet fully recovered from the down-turn it took with the revolution, the proprietors of these stalls have a wistful air, these days, as do the vendors of straw hats, though they live in hopes that all will soon be as it once was.

At first sight, a stall of Caldas ware looks like a petrified harvest festival. Since the market is filled with local produce, apples, peaches, peppers, tomatoes, strawberries, cardboard boxes containing twitching rabbits, chickens and ducks on their way, all alive oh! to the pot, it seems as if there has been a direct transposition into ceramics of fruit, fur, feather and veg. In this ceramic feast, however, the red apples are far too beautiful to eat; so they have been mounted on wall plaques. These wall plaques are what you notice first, like icons of plenty to be hung on the kitchen wall in times of famine. If you could eat with your eyes, you wouldn't need agrarian reform.

The wall plaques do not feature apples alone. The scarlet pigment with which they have been painted is suited, also, to peppers, tomatoes and strawberries, mounted on leaves of brilliant green – all those bulbous fruits of testicular shape seem to delight the ceramicists of Caldas most. Some of the higher priced platters are decorated with bas-reliefs of seafood, lobster and fish.

There are many other items on the stalls, too; noble cabbages have been turned into soup tureens, sometimes with a spoon in the shape of a cabbage leaf emerging from a hole in the lid. There are also dishes shaped like chickens sitting on baskets and others, indeed, in the shape of bunnies and ducks. All the fare of the market faithfully reproduced, even ceramic rings of sausages.

Here and there, a nod and a wink to the idea of functionalism. A brace of walnuts have been serrated, to turn them into salt-shakers. Another salt-shaker is in the shape of a corn cob, with a mouse clinging to it. Another favourite line is the money-box in the shape of a bread-roll, with a pot mouse perched on that one, too. The local style in ceramics is one of intense realism. Stalin would have loved it.

However, the market offers other, more special souvenirs of Caldas. Here is a row of little figures, a monk, a policeman, a footballer clasping before him the pennant of his club. Though the figures are made of painted clay, their clothes are of real fabrics and the monk's robe, the policeman's greatcoat and the footballer's pennant may all be lifted to reveal, beneath, his dangling prick.

They say there was an ancient cult of the phallus in this part of Portugal. Certainly, phallic-shaped cult stones may be seen dotted here and there about the countryside; but I think the ceramic pricks of the market place bear only the most obscure relation to them. Besides the figurines, the stalls have little baskets full of teeny tiny pricks for sale, made into lapel badges to wear, presumably, *under* the lapel and flash in moments of high hilarity. These objects are adorned, at one end, with a dab of dark brown paint, representing pubic hair, at the other with a dab of startling red. Others of these pricks are presented as if a miniature coat of arms, on a shield-shaped base equipped with fins of a fish. There are also matchboxes containing pricks; and lipstick holders, with the legend 'A Souvenir of Caldas', on the side, with the things inside them.

Almost every stall sells joke mugs with pricks inside; these are rather larger than the tie-pin pricks. The shaft is a bright peach colour, there is, again, the fiery dollop of red at the tip and the brown base. With fiendish exactitude, there is a hole at the tip of the prick. These mugs are also sold in some, though not all, of the shops in Caldas that also specialise in the local ceramics, of a rather higher technical standard than those sold in the market place.

But I should say that these objects seem neither less nor more prurient or obscene than the bulging ceramic apples and peppers, though, in fact, somewhat more crudely made. But they seem to be the same sort of thing, really – a ceramic joke, in the worst possible taste, about the nature of reality, its fragility and its glazed intransigence.

The most interesting and curious wares in the market are objects about the size of mouse-traps. These show an actual copulation, a man equipped with one of the red-tipped pricks of Caldas crouching over a woman who lies on her back. Both parties are naked except for his moustache. A string hangs from the base of the mouse-trap; when you pull it, yes! he jerks forward; and, yes, his prick fits into the red-daubed orifice of the woman. These items come in two styles; woman on her back, woman on her front, hinting at a surprising sophistication of sexual mores for such a respectable Catholic town. But nothing else about this crudely articulated encounter suggests Iberian puritanism does not hold Caldas da Rainha securely in its grip; they describe sexual intercourse as a brief, mechanical operation accompanied by an audible click of unaccustomed musculature. Only one stall sells these things: it is the one that also sells wall plaques of the Virgin and child. In the market place of Caldas da Rainha, I began to understand Buñuel better.

The stuff in the market seems pressed rather than moulded, produced by the cheapest possible methods of mass production. The shops offer a higher class of product, though the themes are the same. The cabbage soup tureens, often accompanied by matching bowls, are larger, glossier, perhaps more subtly coloured; there are cauliflower soup tureens; *hors d'oeuvres* dishes in the shape of corn cobs; lidded bowls in the shapes of giant strawberries, artichokes and pineapples, with cups to match, a gigantesque horticulture as if to mock the puny efforts of the local farmers. There is some evidence here of charm, wit and a kind of ceramic sleight of hand.

A large ceramic lizard crawls across the façade of one shop, accompanied by a monstrous crab. Inside, are heads of bull and moose somewhat larger than life. These are evidence of an older style of ware, as are the occasional ceramic portrait studies of quaint peasant folk, grotesque grannies and gnarled fishermen. Yet the final degeneration of the style is hinted at in certain shops by a cabbage soup tureen that is pink instead of green. And cheek by jowl with bodily executed faience cockerels are kitishily elongated cats and jars in the shape of weeping onions that speak in a universal language of bad taste rather than in the specific vulgarity of the region which is, after all, sanctioned by time and exonerated by tourism. Because you can always it on tourist taste.

But they've been potting these abortions in Caldas for years, for centuries. The local museum was unpacking a retrospective exhibition of the ceramic art of the place; 200 years of the god-awful, they could have called it. A lot of the taste is very nineteenth century, said the curator. Suspended from the museum wall, a cabbage leaf, one single cabbage leaf, five feet long. There is a vase shaped like an arum lily, the size of a well-grown dwarf, on four vegetable feet; the stopper of the jar is the pistil of the lily. The curator stretched out her arms to indicate the size of a ceramic crab still in its crate; eight feet across. Here is a group of giant mushrooms, the size of bar stools; there, a top hat with a pair of kid gloves potted on to the brim.

She showed me a prize piece, a platter full of sardines under a net. The taste is ghastly but the technique is superb, she said. Each sardine individually moulded, every scale, the glint in every fishy eye, and laid in place, then the net woven subtly, breathtakingly out of clay and superimposed thereon. How to fire such things in, presumably, wood or charcoal burning kilns? Great, plain sixteenth-century urns from some remote period of artistic purity hulked in the background; the museum staff unpacked yet another purple vase the handles of which were formed of crabs writhing as if to the very life.

The curator hints at items they have decided not to display; the fucking machines of the village square, just like the cabbage tureens, presumably boast their high-class ancestors here. The souvenir pottery of Caldas da Rainha can hardly be said to represent the degeneration of a tradition, except from the point of view of pure technique. Nothing could be more degenerate than the beautifully executed caricature figures of old peasants, granny crouched over a fine seam, granddad in an apron cobbling a shoe, their wrinkled faces twisted in the sickly grin of the Uncle Tom.

Not so much an erosion of sensibility as a lapse of sense – who *needs* a pot crab eight feet across? And doing it ('the technique is superb') more important than the thing done. The curator kept saying that the contemporary ceramics were awful; but everything in her exhibition was really exactly the same as everything outside, the only difference being the subtle and academic one between high vulgarity and low vulgarity, in an aesthetic where nothing is real but everything looks real. The local potters, like the copulating couple that, in the context of the rest of their wares, begins to seem a masterpiece of the naïve style, perform their circumscribed actions, forward and backwards, forward and backwards, when the string is pulled. It's not that they want to; it's that they can't do anything else. Only illiterate old men turn the red earth into flowerpots and saucepans, after all.

I would draw only one very hesitant and general conclusion from the tourist wares of this town: it is, that there has been something funny about the relation of man to labour in Portugal for a very long time. And it doesn't seem to have changed much.

New Society, 1977

Bread on Still Waters

When my dear friends, Shirley Cameron and Roland Miller, performance artists, suggested I go with them to a festival of contemporary art in Portugal at which they had a pressing invitation to appear, I said yes. Fine. I'd never been to Portugal. And here was something gripping, twelve days of exhibitions, debates, films, performances and God knows what else besides.

Besides, I like their work a lot. They've done performances involving Christmas trees, chairs, mirrors, enormous cakes made of paper, in rough pubs and public places where, if you tried to read a poem aloud or, heaven help you, essayed a string quartet you'd be eaten alive. And emerged unscathed, even applauded. When people know nothing about art and care less, they tend to be willing to show interest in anything that interests them, and cheerfully make imaginative connections they might not be bothered about in the normal course of things. So I was curious and excited about the things that might happen in a country where the virus of modern art has been isolated in quarantine wards in Lisbon and Oporto, or sent off to Paris with a grant.

Cut, therefore, to Caldas da Rainha. A small town not too untypical of southern Portugal except the weather tends to be lousy. It is neither a charming nor yet an unattractive town; it looks like everything should wear antimacassars, but it boasts two bustling markets, one for fruits and veg and one for fish, where denim jeans and T-shirts are also sold by gypsies, hucksters of extravagantly villainous appearance. These illiterates, the oppressed (to coin a phrase) of the oppressed, are – ironically enough – marks for the right wing, who love and cherish ignorance and, put it to work for them. It was the gypsies who gleefully mucked in with the fighting on the last day of the festival.

There is also a fine museum, filled for this occasion alone with abstracts and Dada-ish things and pop things and slogans, consorting uneasily with gilt-framed canvases of children playing in sunlit meadows and picturesque village scenes, that hung on the walls all the time.

So far, so good. This prim, stuffy place, this prim, stuffy museum, invaded for twelve days by the European avant-garde, all in festive mood. It was a delicious spectacle. Not quite like an Ealing comedy, though we Brits did our best; in England (Cheltenham, say), we'd have known the script by heart before we set out, but here were subtle differences that began to make us a little uneasy.

All the same, surely only a very slightly different kind of light comedy? A French domestic-market comedy, with the habitually outraged major and the perpetually expostulating museum curator; exclamations over the girl who took off her clothes and rolled in liquid chocolate; the fuss over the rude candle lantern. The artists behaving exactly like artists, the small-town bureaucrats behaving like stereotypical small-town bureaucrats, and a whale of a time being had by all.

We used to go to one particular café because it stayed open until late, and there we met a deaf-and-dumb lottery salesman, who was a great mime; after all, he had to be. He turned two paper napkins into a pair of birds that flapped their wings for the Cameron/Miller babies, and then he showed us a photograph of a friend of his who had been shot under Salazar in the square right outside the café, just in front of the building that is now the Maoist headquarters.

Graffiti everywhere, some of it two and a half years old. LONG LIVE STALIN in very big letters, here and there. I congratulated a teacher on the charming mural of flowers and rabbits on the wall of a school, and he told me how the headmaster had the kids paint flowers and bunnies over the slogans with which the wall had been covered.

Art is scandal, art is outrage, said some of the grosser bits and pieces of French avant-garde kitsch who had arrived in great numbers, were rumoured to want to stage a *séance d'amour* in the park (oh! the shock and horror of the mayor), and often sported lapel badges with slogans like REMEMBER THE FUTURE. Then there was the woman who used her body as a canvas because art, she claimed, was prostitution. This thesis went down OK with the cognoscenti in the discussions in the museum, but it went down like cold sick on the general public. Art from a different order of experience, again.

How did she, Orlan, use her body as her canvas? Well, she had lots of pictures of herself taken in classic poses, Watteau's Miss O'Malley, the Rokeby Venus, Ingres's Odalisque. What was most touching about her was that she always took off her glasses to pose for the nude photographs.

She'd had the Odalisque picture blown up to lifesize and often stood in front of it, will all the vulnerability of the myopic. She also used to go out wearing a dress with a nude painted on it, tits on the front, arse on the back. She wore a ring featuring a design of a triple copulation; that upset the waiters a lot.

On the last day, she'd plastered the town with come-on posters. Orlan will sell herself in the fish market. She had a handcart piled with photographs of various parts of her anatomy and a price list, so many escudos for a hand, for a breast, for a pubic triangle and so on. Isn't the artist doing just this when s/HE exposes bits of his or her being for sale in a gallery? Whore, opined the fishwives, who'd never been inside an art gallery in their lives and are, perhaps, even less likely to venture into one now. Art is scandal, art is outrage. The fishwives pulled her hair; they were big, strong women in rubber skirts and boots; and the gypsies joyously egged them on.

Things were getting ugly when a group of men the Lisbon newspaper later described as 'right-wing thugs' created a diversion and smashed up a sculpture somebody else had been making in another part of the fish market. It seems they had arrived from a nearby town by tram expressly to have a bit of a go.

Remember the future, indeed, since it looks as though it might prove to be much the same as the past. However, if art is indeed scandal and outrage, why did everybody cry 'philistinism' when scandal and outrage were, in fact, provoked? Unless it was not art at all that caused the fuss, but the old scandals, sex and politics. However, if it *was* the sex that was so shocking, why not demonstrate at the porno-movie theatre? But they don't, you know.

Maybe not even the organisers of the festival had quite got the measure of the town, with its Maoists and Stalinists and communists and anarchists, its unusually high number of refugees from Angola, its respectable poverty, its sordid poverty and its Chekhovian middle class, who have the air of always listening to make quite sure that the sound of the hatchets on the trunks of the cherry trees has, in fact, as they are now beginning to suspect, more or less ceased.

They put us up at Edouardo's house, a detached residence on the hill above the town, with a Moorish-style garden, a fountain, a goldfish pool, orange trees, and the biggest dog I've ever seen, to keep off marauders. Edouardo said that, since the revolution, all the peasants wanted a car, a cabbage patch, a deep freeze and a colour television set. He was a very nice man. He said that when he found out the house-keeper had never had a holiday in her life, he sent her to the seaside for a week.

I started making up aphorisms, to try to explain things to myself. For example: Those with enough know they have not got too much, but those

with nothing cannot make such fine distinctions. And, again: If the rich
have good hearts, they would like the poor to have more money, but only
if it meant that they themselves did not have less. And yet another: In a
country where bread is scarce, one should feed the birds with discretion.

The more I think about this one, the more it seems to sum up the
twelve days of art activity in Caldas da Rainha and how it went wrong.
Because desire, imagination and dream – the domains of art – these, too
should be distributed with care in a country where the very possibility of
such things might seem to mock the reality of the inhabitants. To say
nothing of hope. But I actually invented it to sum up the inauguration of
the Caldas da Rainha Society for the Prevention of Cruelty to Animals.

I think Maria Marcellina was behind this. She was married to one of the
festival organisers, her favourite adjective was 'wonderful', she was a kind
of avant-garde raver, and maybe she wanted to ingratiate the festival with
the local ladies who tended, themselves, to eat cake rather than bread (such
cake shops!) and worry a lot about the donkeys. So Maria or some of her
friends, but I think it was mainly Maria, organised an event to get the
Society for the Prevention of Cruelty to Animals off to a good start.

It was a very sweet and pretty event. She put lots of pieces of broken
bread, left over from our communal evening meal, into envelopes; and
wrote the name of each participant in the festival on every envelope. Then
she strung up these envelopes from the branches of the chestnut tree that
shaded our communal open-air lunch table, so we found them all dangling
there when we came to eat our soup. Inside them, as well as the bread,
was a behest, in French and Portuguese, the two languages of the festival
(you'd never believe the cultural imperialism) to feed the crusts to the
pretty birdies.

Lots of the locals, who kept wandering in and out of the park as if they
owned the place, dammit, got very pissed off to see a lot of hippies chucking good bread all over the place. What about a society for the prevention
of cruelty to the proletariat, eh?

The local Communist Party came and sedately leafleted the artists on
the last day. The whole festival had been a lot of bourgeois crap, they'd
decided and invited the artists to go up to the CP headquarters and apologise. We would have gone, at that, to discuss the proposition. But, by
then, the square was a seething mass and it seemed best to keep a low profile. It seemed a shame. It seemed a terrible shame.

A light comedy about modern art – which is, according to the ideology
of such comedies, of course, inherently comic in itself – taking place on
the surface of a bitterly tragic country. The Portuguese government has,
of course, stopped the grants for the theatre groups, artists and musicians
that they first funded, in the flush of revolutionary zeal, to go out and visit

remote villages. A sculptor acquaintance of Roland's has now chosen to work on a housing project, helping with the water supply.

As for me, I don't know what to make of it all. They did a performance in a wood, which involved a picnic in which they ate not bread but stones. A group of housewives, the unemployed, children, gathered around enthusiastically, as if, somehow, the imagery reflected their experience, clarified it. Posthumously, as it were, I see the relevance of that.

New Society, 1977

Munch And Antibiotics

At seven, a comfortable evening calm has settled down already on Oslo and the rain stopped at last. In the largely pedestrianised streets that comprise the city centre, the veritable hub of Oslo, there are kiosks selling pancakes. And the kids are coming out, to cluster like starlings, dressed in denims and anoraks – casual, low-profile styles, nothing elaborate – with the plan, maybe, of raising as much hell, later on, as they can afford to, before the last sky-blue tram departs for the suburbs.

Can this tranquil, rather anonymous city be the expressionist and hallucinatory Christiania, which the hero of Knut Hamsun's *Hunger* roamed, starved and crazy? These are the streets Edvard Munch populated with pallid, spectral beings in the grip of terminal angst. The great-great-grandchildren of Munch's demented burghers are beautiful as only those cared for from the cradle by a remorseless welfare state can be. Straight teeth, straight limbs. No squints, no badly sewn harelips, no forceps marks on those smooth foreheads. Sound, whole and, probably, sane.

Somebody told me there's a growing problem with drugs, because Norway is so boring. But there's a growing problem with drugs in Italy, I said, and nobody accuses *Italy* of being boring. This idea, that a welfare state equals the death of the soul, is implicit in a lot of discussion about Scandinavia. It is very nice for the British, because it means that we are doing ourselves a deal of spiritual good by dismantling such remains of our welfare state as are left. But you can still lose your soul, besides a good many more tangible and more important things, just as well *without* a welfare state, dammit.

The great delicacies of the national cuisine – smoked salmon, marinated raw salmon, game – are raw and rotten foods, as Lévi-Strauss would say. They denote past hardships heroically borne. In a fairy story, a peasant

family is making Christmas dinner for some trolls, so it had better be good.
The menu is porridge and sausages. Norwegians deserve their present
affluence and the 'nannying' of which even my guidebook complains (the
negative side of the "welfare state"') has transformed Hamsun's and
Munch's city of dreadful night into – into what?

It's hard to say, because Oslo is a diffuse and airy kind of place, hard to
pin down.

Descending from the air into Oslo, it is possible for the traveller to
imagine he or she is indeed flying, like a gull, skimming over the ragged
sleeve of coast – over an inlet where a sailboat rocks on dimpled water,
over forest that, from this altitude, appears so close to the roads, to telegraph poles, that it does not look in the least as it, in fact, is, trackless . . .
blue flash of a lake . . . woods, again, in which nestle a handful of wooden
homesteads with vast gardens; then the land abruptly vanishes, beneath us
only the enormous sea and now we are almost down, into an airport clean,
bright and leisurely as a child's idea of an airport. On a day of white sunlight at the end of summer, descending into Oslo by air is enough to justify the invention of the aeroplane on aesthetic grounds, alone.

A long arm of the sea runs beside the freeway into the city, as crowded
with boats as the freeway is with cars. And the only vulgar thing to be seen
on the ride downtown is the simulated banana on top of the Chiquita
banana warehouse.

This rather awesome lack of vulgarity does not appear to be the
product, as it is in beautiful, beautiful Stockholm, of a rigorously austere
taste. Is seems, instead, almost accidental, the result of a genuine lack of
pretension.

There is a throwaway unpretentiousness about the entire city. Few, if
any, pompous civic buildings – except, maybe, the vast, brick-built
National Theatre, with the statue of Ibsen outside – proof that it is perfectly possible to be ethically impeccable while hardly ever boring. Even
the cathedral (brick built, again) has a sober, unassuming air, the house of
the Lutheran god who was born into the artisan class. Perhaps it is as much
a state of mind as a city – in the suburbs, you might meet an elk. (Difficult
for a Brit to appreciate that elk, like reindeer, are not fabulous beasts.) Oslo
covers, according to the guidebook, 175 square miles, with a population
of just under half a million.

A little Norwegian girl named Sonja Henie went to Hollywood and, as
they say, skated her way into the hearts of millions, married a shipping
magnate and, with him, built a pastoral version of the Museum of Modern
Art in a wood beside the fjord in Greater Oslo. Besides their collection of
pictures, and the special exhibitions (this month, Joseph Beuys – heavy
European mainstream stuff), there is a roomful of Sonja Henie's skating

trophies, dozens of them, all silver, on glass shelves. (Who polishes them?) The combination of elements – the skating star, the millionaire, the Hollywood bit, the lovely building itself, the blithe setting, the abstracts, the silver cups and skates and pickle forks, are unexpected and satisfying, a True Romance with something for everybody.

There is a terrace, where you pay the earth for excellent coffee and watch the sailboats on the ruffling water. Yesterday's sunshine has gone, replaced by soft, grey light, and the outlines of the wooded hills are smudged as if with a charcoaled thumb. Exquisite.

Like a chocolate box. No. *That's* not right. Chocolate boxes look like this. This is the original of the photograph on the calendar. This is the actual scene the photographer snapped for the travel brochure. I've never been here, before, yet the view moves me like a memory and yes, of course, I *have* seen – not this precise view, but this *sort* of view before, this view with the same sense of nostalgia built into it. It is a typical landscape of the old country, the home country, 'remembered for years, remembered with tears'; one of those places that somebody has looked at and thought, quite consciously, 'I'll always remember this,' framing it already in the mind's eye. A landscape already misting over with the tears of departure, selected not so much for its specialness as for its typicality. (Did Sonja Henie chose this site herself?)

As cruelly depopulated by emigration in the nineteenth century as by the Black Death in the fourteenth, this country lost almost a million inhabitants to terrain almost as inhospitable as itself. The poor peasants went to farm land never ploughed before, to Minnesota, to the Dakotas, to Nebraska . . . hence the crazy liquor laws of the stern, Scandinavian midwest, which they made blossom.

The emigrants would take with them, to remind them in the wilderness of the people they once were, the place where they had been born, almost the same souvenirs as a tourist might take home from a holiday visit – a painted chest, or some easily portable item of furniture, an embroidered waistcoat. And the landscape of the old country, enhanced by absence, sticks in the mind in the heightened and unnatural colours of picture postcards in an album.

These old country scenes, somehow or other, enter the common domain, perhaps by their sheer force of the emotion with which they are charged – think of the way our perceptions of the landscape of Ireland have been formed by expatriates' nostalgia. 'Home thoughts from abroad.' But Browning could afford to come home and go away again as he pleased. Once you got to Nebraska, you were stuck.

The National Gallery of Oslo is full of landscapes, many of them – by artists shamefully unknown to me – very fine. But these are landscapes

selected for qualities of the sublime, rather than the familiar. And perhaps
the landscape itself, the mountains, waterfalls, the grandeur of it, renders
the painter redundant; he or she must take a back seat, not to his or her
creation but the actual subject of the painting.

I refer to the painter as 'he or she' advisedly, by the way; it is a typically
sneakily self-righteous Scandinavian trick that two of the very best nineteenth century Norwegian painters are women, Kitty Keilland and Harriet
Backer, landscapes and interiors respectively.

Landscapes and interiors – many landscapes and also innumerable genre
paintings in the National Gallery. Scenes of rustic life, many of them oddly
uninhabited. (Did the owners of the small, poor houses refuse to pose?)
Unpeopled interiors of sparsely furnished wooden rooms, the bed set in
the wall as in nineteenth-century Scotland, a painted chest, a bare table, a
row of summer dresses on a hook. Interiors showing peasant congregations at church. But, yes, peopled interiors, too, and portraits of the
anonymous poor.

Whatever the intention of these painters, whether or not it was to document the lives of the poor or seek out true Norwegian roots among the
peasants, the models themselves helplessly participate in the reconstruction
of their lives in the terms of the picturesque. They can't help it; the
painters can't help it. They're all caught up in some irony of the artistic
process. And yet. And yet.

There's one portrait head, dated 1886, of a young farmer in traditional
dress, by Olaf Isaachsen – a ruddy, golden-haired young farmer with the
terrible beauty of innocence and vulnerable dignity of those who are
utterly at the mercy of circumstances, so that you look at him as if he were
just glimpsed before being swept away by some storm . . . and then the
content of the pictures on the walls breaks through the spurious consolation of a vast amount of highly accomplished, glossy brushwork and, dear
god – it isn't an art gallery at all; this is a terminal ward.

So many pictures of death-beds, sick children . . . and one old woman
gives the game away altogether; she is titled: *Tuberculosis*. Then you know
the sick children are all incurable. On the faces of those still undiagnosed,
a hectic, lively pallor that bodes no good. All Edvard Munch did was to
apply a lively expressionist technique to the common iconography of his
place and time – the death bed, the fatal diagnosis, the child who will not
live and therefore, must be idealised, sentimentalised, or the death will be
quite intolerable. Already, even as he paints her, she exists only in
memory, so that children, too, become souvenirs of the past, not our connection with the future.

Ours is the first century in human history in which parents have been
confidently able to anticipate their children will outlive them; when one

may expect to see adulthood in the company of all one's siblings; when women don't expect to die of the effects of giving birth. The particular Protestant tradition of this country acknowledges human responsibility for human suffering to an uncommon degree; that is why the woman, mother or sister, in Munch's *The Sick Child*, daren't look her red-haired child in the eye, because she knows quite well someone is to blame but she doesn't know who or why her little girl has to suffer so.

Munch's vision is incompatible with antibiotics, and strict regimes of preventive medicine and community health clinics. He himself would undoubtedly have felt the benefit of a course of lithium and the attentions of a sympathetic psychiatric social worker, though if fewer of his sibs had died in infancy he might have been less obsessed by death, to begin with. Today, of course, that red-haired child in his painting would have, barring wars and road accidents, a life expectancy of 78.73 years. And they say there's no such thing as progress.

New Society, 1982

Constructing an Australia

Australian writers seem to spend all their time travelling from festival to festival. Writers' festivals proliferate throughout the continent, they are like folkmoots or union meetings except for the time it takes to get there. Five and a quarter hours by jet from Perth in Western Australia to Brisbane in Queensland. Festivals certainly help to assuage that sense of isolation in a country where all writers, in a sense, are regional.

From Melbourne to Brisbane is only as far as from London to Rome and no sooner had the writers' festival in Melbourne ended than the major part of the participants emplaned for the north, to take part in another round of panels and readings, to be again cosseted and feted, to have egos gently massaged by the general public even if one's peers can be somewhat more abrasive.

If finding out what other people are up to is part of the fun of the thing for the writers, the general public fully avails itself of the opportunity to acquire, as it were, 'hands on' experience of those whom they admire. Australians are not indifferent to the word. It makes you realise how unlike the British they are. It is awesome.

'I'd like to kiss the hem of her dress,' confided an admirer of Antonia Byatt's. Another girl knelt briefly at my feet. This in allegedly staid

Melbourne. If this is how they respond to foreign writers, what do they do to their own? Later on on this trip, at a reading in a pub in Sydney, the fiction writer Elizabeth Jolley was virtually mobbed by kids young enough to be her grandchildren. She is the poet of alienation, death and black humour. She is published in Britain but not sufficiently appreciated here. Maybe we don't think she's Australian enough. Not butch enough. And she quotes Rilke a lot. Hmm.

It is exhilarating, to say the least, to be in a country where fiction matters. And, ho! the passions involved! In Melbourne, the playwright and novelist Louis Nouwra swung a punch at a critic who gave him a bad review. They story arrived in Brisbane well before Louis did, already embellished somewhat – now they said Louis had lurked in the pub until the hapless reviewer was taking his overcoat off and hence in a vulnerable position, a foul lie. The whole event was turning into a tall tale before one's very eyes, becoming part of the mythological literary history of Australia.

But where have all the new writers come from? Well, you can write as much as you like but nobody will read it unless it gets published and, in the last ten years, an indigenous Australian publishing industry has brought into national prominence an entire generation of writers addressing themselves specifically to questions of which the sub-text is post-colonialism. Even if the writers are conscious of it or not, the anguished urban romances of Helen Garner, Frank Moorhouse's urban paranoia, Peter Carey's precise outrages are taking place in the context of a society in which the points of reference are no longer British, are still in the process of defining themselves.

There is also an elaborate and enlightened structure of state patronage in Australia and even if books are vastly expensive – imports subjected to crippling mark-ups of anything from 25 per cent to 50 per cent or more, home products highly priced because of small print runs – still books shift off the shelves in amazing numbers. It is evidence of a society inexhaustibly curious about itself, about the way it works, how it feels to *be* Australian.

Which, nowadays, means to live in a vast urban conurbation, to have maybe Italian, Yugoslav, Laotian kin, to slip as easily as a dolphin through a sea of mingling cultures and, presumably, to sometimes feel as lost as the girl who came to see me in Sydney did, who broke down in tears because she'd found the neighbourhood where I was staying, where she'd lived herself as a student, utterly changed, the gingerbread cottages gone, the crumbling colonial mansions gone, replaced by battalions of high-rise apartments. She felt a stranger in her own city, she said, and she was only twenty-five.

(To a foreigner, Sydney still looks pretty good.)

Alienation, of course, is a necessary prerequisite of good art in the late twentieth century. Maybe the construction industry will have an important role in the history of the novel in Australia.

The whole Bicentennial business, from close up, looks suspiciously like the invention of the construction industry, in cahoots with the newly booming tourist industry. Tower blocks rise everywhere, in Melbourne, in Sydney – especially in Brisbane, that pungently unique, sub-tropical city from which so many Australian writers, Tom Shapcott, Rodney Hall, Peter Porter and more, have fled.

You can still see traces of a devilish exoticism. A few ornate colonial faces have been restored; a current fashion in Australia is to retain the façade of a building while ripping out its insides and installing a steel and glass tower therein. The streets are still lined with flowering trees. In the suburbs, the unique Queensland architecture, houses built on stilts to catch the breeze with latticed verandas to filter it, lingers on here and there. A massive police corruption scandal has just broken, to give a *film noir* edge to the jasmine-scented nights.

But although Sir John Bjelke-Petersen, the Queensland premier, may be, in John Pilger's words, a 'dinosaur', you can't trust ultra-conservatives to sequester themselves in the past these days. Far from it. Sir John's Brisbane is dynamic as Victorian London. The sound of the jack-hammer reverberates in the jacarandas. Sir John plans to build the tallest building in the world, here, on the banks of the sluggishly undulating Brisbane River, a tower to cap all the rest of the towers that have suddenly transformed the city's skyline into a rough facsimile of Chicago.

No. Not Chicago. We are in another hemisphere; possibly in the historic long view, in another sphere of influence. Sir John's models, presumably, are Singapore, Tokyo, and Hong Kong, the dynamic cities of the Pacific basin, whose wealthier inhabitants are increasingly investing in deliriously covetable waterfront properties in Australia's great cities, besides chunks of real estate as such. And it is from Asia that the tourists come.

A pink stretch limo collects a Japanese honeymoon couple from the gate of the wild-life reserve in the Brisbane suburb. The bride cuddles a toy koala – a fake fur koala, I trust, not one of those made of kangaroo fur, both ecologically unsound and invalid on humanitarian grounds. The chauffeur bows in the Japanese manner as he closes the door on them. Ironies of history.

The koala, Australia's favourite mascot, is probably about to die out. It has been stricken by a sexually transmitted disease, an affliction that severely damages its reputation as the marsupial most suitable for children.

The plight of the koala is itself like one of those savage Australian jokes. To lose your koalas to syphilis in the year of the Bicentennial would be proof of what I take to be an abiding Australian suspicion about life, underneath the surface optimism – that, at the end of the rainbow, lies not a pot of gold but a crock of shit. (One of the reasons why I love Australia is because I, too, think this is the only sane existential position to hold.)

The opening panel of the Writers' Festival in Melbourne, part of the glorious Spoleto festival of the arts, was titled: 'Shadow-boxing with Colonial Ghosts'. Graeme Gibson (Canada), Catherine Lim (Singapore), Archie Weller (the other Australia – Aboriginal Australia), Manning Clarke. The chairman, a historian named Stuart Macintyre, used the phrase 'the British diaspora', which set me brooding about the sheer strangeness of the British empire, that cast its net so wide and carelessly, paid no heed to the future, played fast and loose with a world that has now abandoned it. Australians don't care that Britain is in an even greater state of post-colonial anguish than they are; why should they? They can more easily face the future without us than we can without them.

Guardian, 1987

Japan

Tokyo Pastoral

This is clearly one of those districts where it always seems to be Sunday afternoon. Somebody in a house by the corner shop is effortlessly practising Chopin on the piano. A dusty cat rolls in the ruts of the unpaved streetlet, yawning in the sunshine. Somebody's aged granny trots off to the supermarket for a litre or two of honourable saki. Her iron-grey hair is scraped into so tight a knot in the nape no single hair could ever stray untidily out, and her decent, drab kimono is enveloped in the whitest of enormous aprons, trimmed with a sober frill of cotton lace, the kind of apron one associates with Victorian nursemaids.

She is bent to a full hoop because of all the babies she has carried on her back and she bows formally before she shows a socially acceptable quantity of her gold-rimmed teeth in a dignified smile. Frail, omnipotent granny who wields a rod of iron behind the paper walls.

This is a district peculiarly rich in grannies, cats and small children. We are a 60 yen train ride from the Marunouchi district, the great business section; and a 60 yen train ride in the other direction from Shinjuku, where there is the world's largest congregation of strip-shows, clip-joints and Turkish baths. We are a petty bourgeois enclave of perpetual Sunday wedged between two mega-highways.

The sounds are: the brisk swish of broom on tatami matting, the raucous cawing of hooded crows in a nearby willow grove; clickety-clackety of chattering housewives, a sound like briskly plied knitting needles, for Japanese is a language full of Ts and Ks; and, in the mornings, the crowing of the cock. The nights have a rustic tranquillity. We owe our tranquillity entirely to faulty town planning; these streets are far too narrow to admit cars. The smells are: cooking; sewage; fresh washing.

It is difficult to find a boring part of Tokyo but, by God, I have done it. It is a very respectable neighbourhood and has the prim charm and the inescapable accompanying ennui of respectability.

I can touch the walls of the houses on either side by reaching out my arms and the wall of the house at the back by stretching out my hand, but the fragile structures somehow contrive to be detached, even if there is only a clearance of inches between them, as though they were stating emphatically that privacy, even if it does not actually exist, is, at least, a potential. Most homes draw drab, grey skirts of breeze-block walls around themselves with the touch-me-not decorum of old maids, but even the tiniest of gardens boasts an exceedingly green tree or two and the windowsills bristle with potted plants.

Our neighbourhood is too respectable to be picturesque but, nevertheless, has considerable cosy charm, a higgledy-piggledy huddle of brown-grey shingled roofs and shining spring foliage. In the mornings, gaudy quilts, brilliantly patterned mattresses and cages of singing birds are hung out to air on the balconies. If the Japanese aesthetic ideal is a subfusc, harmonious austerity, the cultural norm is a homey, cheerful clutter. One must cultivate cosiness; cosiness makes overcrowding tolerable. Symmetrical lines of very clean washing blow in the wind. You could eat your dinner off the children. It is an area of white-collar workers; it is a good area.

The absolute domestic calm is disturbed by little more than the occasional bicycle or a boy on a motorbike delivering a trayful of lacquer noodle bowls from the café on the corner for somebody's lunch or supper. In the morning, the men go off to work in business uniform (dark suits, white nylon shirts); in the afternoon, schoolchildren loll about eating ice-cream. High school girls wear navy-blue pleated skirts and sailor tops, very Edith Nesbitt, and high school boys wear high-collared black jackets and peaked caps, inexpressibly Maxim Gorki.

At night, a very respectable drunk or two staggers, giggling, down the hill. A pragmatic race, the Japanese appear to have decided long ago that the only reason for drinking alcohol is to become intoxicated and therefore drink only when they wish to be drunk. They all are completely unabashed about it.

Although this is such a quiet district, the streets around the station contain everything a reasonable man might require. There is a blue movie theatre; a cinema that specialises in Italian and Japanese Westerns of hideous violence; a cinema that specialises in domestic consumption Japanese weepies; and yet another one currently showing *My Fair Lady*. There is a tintinnabulation of chinking *pachinko* (pinball) parlours, several bakeries which sell improbably luxurious European pâtisserie, a gymnasium and an aphrodisiac shop or two.

If it lacks the excitement of most of the towns that, added up, amount to a massive and ill-plumbed concept called Greater Tokyo, that is because it is primarily a residential area, although one may easily find the cluster of hotels which offer hospitality by the hour. They are sited sedately up a side street by the station, off a turning by a festering rubbish tip outside a

Chinese restaurant, and no neighbourhood, however respectable, is complete without them – for, in Japan, even the brothels are altogether respectable.

They are always scrupulously clean and cosy and the more expensive ones are very beautiful, with their windbells, stone lanterns and little rock gardens with streams, pools and water lilies. So elegantly homelike are they indeed, that the occasional erotic accessory – a red light bulb in the bedside light, a machine that emits five minutes of enthusiastic moans, grunts and pants at the insertion of a 100 yen coin – seems like a bad joke in a foreign language. Repression operates in every sphere but the sexual, even if privacy may only be purchased at extortionate rates.

There are few pleasant walks around here; the tree-shaded avenue beside the river offers delight only to coprophiles. But it is a joy to go out shopping. Since this is Japan, warped tomatoes and knobbly apples cost half the price of perfect fruit. It is the strawberry season; the man in the open fruit shop packs martial rows of berries the size of thumbs, each berry red as a guardsman, into a polythene box and wraps each box before he sells it in paper printed with the legend, 'Strawberry for health and beauty'.

Non-indigenous foods often taste as if they had been assembled from a blueprint by a man who had never seen the real thing. For example, cheese, butter and milk have such a degree of hygienic lack of tang they are wholly alienated from the natural cow. They taste absolutely, though not unpleasantly, synthetic and somehow indefinably obscene. Powdered cream (trade-named 'Creap') is less obtrusive in one's coffee. Most people, in fact, tend to use evaporated milk.

Tokyo ought not to be a happy city – no pavements; noise; few public places to sit down; occasional malodorous belches from sewage vents even in the best areas; and yesterday I saw a rat in the supermarket. It dashed out from under the seaweed counter and went to earth in the butchery. 'Asoka', said the assistant, which means: 'Well, well, I never did,' in so far as the phrase could be said to mean anything. But, final triumph of ingenuity, Megapolis One somehow contrives to be an exceedingly pleasant place in which to live. It is as though Fellini had decided to remake *Alphaville*.

Up the road, there is a poodle-clipping parlour; a Pepsi-Cola bottling plant heavily patrolled by the fuzz; a noodle shop which boasts a colour TV; a mattress shop which also sells wicker neck-pillows of antique design; innumerable bookshops, each with a shelf or two of European books, souvenirs of those who have passed this way before – a tattered paperback of *The Rosy Crucifixion*, a treatise on budgerigar keeping, Marx and Engels on England; a dispenser from which one may purchase condoms attractively packed in purple and gold paper, trademarked 'Young Jelly'; and a swimming pool.

I am the first coloured family in this street. I moved in on the Emperor's birthday, so the children were all home from school. They were playing 'catch' around the back of the house and a little boy came to hide in the embrasure of the window. He glanced round and caught sight of me. He did not register shock but he vanished immediately. Then there was a silence and, shortly afterwards, a soft thunder of tiny footsteps. They groped round the windows, invisible, peering, and a rustle rose up, like the dry murmur of dead leaves in the wind, the rustle of innumerable small voices murmuring the word: '*Gaijin, gaijin, gaijin*' (foreigner), in pure, repressed surprise. We spy strangers. *Asoka*.

New Society, 1970

People as Pictures

Japanese tattooing, *irezumi*, bears the same relation to the floral heart on the forearm of a merchant seaman as does the Sistine Chapel to the graffiti on a lavatory wall. *Irezumi* is tattooing *in toto*. It transforms its victim into a genre masterpiece. He suffers the rigorous and ineradicable cosmetology of the awl and gouge (for the masters of the art do not use the needle) until, unique and glorious in his mutilation, he becomes a work of art as preposterous as it is magnificent.

He is a work of art with an authenticity peculiarly Japanese. He is visually superb; he exudes the weird glamour of masochism; and he carries upon his flesh an immutable indication of caste. Bizarre beauties blossom in the programmed interstices of repression. The puppets of the Bunraku theatre are the most passionate in the world; *ikebana* is the art of torturing flowers. *Irezumi* paints with pain upon a canvas of flesh.

During Japan's first encounter with the West in the 1880s, *irezumi* was banned, but the practice continued to flourish and the laws were later rescinded. Though the art is now in its decline – due, perhaps, to the bourgeoisification of the Japanese working class – the ultimate pictorial man may still be seen in his rococo but incontestable glory on summer beaches around Tokyo; on construction sites; in the public baths of certain quarters; anywhere, in fact, where members of the urban proletariat take off their clothes in public.

Those who traditionally wore tattoos – carpenters, scaffolding workers, labourers, gamblers, gangsters – wear them still, almost as an occupational badge. Among gangsters and the underworld, the practice still has elements of an initiation rite since it is both extraordinarily painful, extremely lengthy and also exceedingly costly. It is often carried out at puberty.

There is an active appreciation of the art, which extends to other styles of tattooing. An Australian prisoner of war among the Japanese happened to have been extensively tattooed in the occidental style. He was often called out from among his comrades to exhibit himself to high-ranking visiting military and received many small gifts of candy, biscuits and cigarettes from the fascinated and admiring guards. This tattoo fancy extends to the collection of skins. In Tokyo there is a private museum, devoted to the display of particularly fine specimens. It is said that, in the heyday of *irezumi*, some enthusiasts would buy the pictures off a man's very back, making an initial down-payment and waiting for the demise of the bearer of the masterpiece to collect it. So, for the poor workmen, tattooing may have been a form of investment or even of life insurance.

The origins of the practice are lost, like the origins of the Japanese themselves, in the mists of antiquity. Tattooing is endemic to Oceania. One recalls Melville's 'living counterpane', Queequeg; and the English word, 'tattoo', is derived from the Tahitian. In the third century AD the custom was ascribed to the Wo, the aboriginal inhabitants of Kyushu, the southernmost of Japan's islands, by the Chinese chronicle, *The Records of Wei*: 'Men, great and small, all tattoo their faces and decorate their bodies with designs . . . They are fond of diving in the water to get fish and shells and originally decorated their bodies in order to keep away large fish and waterfowl. Later, however, these designs became merely ornamental.'

Irezumi has recently been primarily the pursuit of the lower classes but the Edo era (1603-1867) was the classical age. Even the great artist, Utamaro, forsook his woodblock prints in order to design a great number of tattoos. Tattoo contests were held, where firemen, artisans, palanquin-bearers, and dandies of both the merchant and the samurai class, vied in the display of their colours. The geishas of the pleasure quarters were often tattooed with remarkable finesse, especially on the back. In one of his short stories, the modern novelist, Junichiro Tanizaki, with characteristic acumen, ascribes a socially acceptable, but extremely active, sadism to a tattoo artist of the period: 'His pleasure lay in the agony men felt . . . The louder they screamed, the keener was Seikichi's strange delight.'

Today's favourite designs are still based on those popular in the eighteenth and nineteenth centuries. They include the Dragon, giver of strength and sagacity; the Carp (perseverance); folk heroes like the infant prodigy, Kintaro, who stands for success; Chinese sages and Japanese deities. If there are relics of superstitions behind these choices, they are as tenuous as those behind the names of Japanese baseball teams – the Hiroshima Tokyo Carp, the Chunichi Dragons, the Osaka Tigers. Many designs have no such significance but are chosen only for their intrinsic beauty. Flowers. The sea. Lightning. Famous lovers. Young ladies astonished by snakes.

Traditionally, the Japanese have always felt a lack of interest, verging on repugnance, at the naked human body. Lady Murasaki, the eleventh-century novelist, wrote with a shudder of distaste: 'Unforgettably horrible is the sight of the naked body. It really does not have the slightest charm.' Even the erotic actors in the pictorial sex-instruction manuals of the Edo era rarely doff their kimono. The genitalia, bared, are rendered explicitly enough, but the remainder of the human form is heavily draped, either because it was considered irrelevant to the picture's purpose or because nobody ever told the Japanese the human form was supposed to be divine.

Modern Japanese men have come to terms with the female nude, to a certain extent, in that there is now an active appreciation of its erotic quality – as though they said, with Donne: 'Oh, my America! My new found land!' but the indifference of 2,000 years, whatever created this indifference, lends a peculiarly borrowed quality to the reaction to, for example, a strip-show.

Now, a man who has been comprehensively tattooed – and the *irezumi* artist is nothing if not comprehensive – can hardly be said to be naked, for he may never remove this most intimate and gaily coloured of garments. Stark he may be, but always decent, and therefore never ashamed. He will never look helplessly, defencelessly, indelicately nude. This factor may or may not be important in the psychological bases of *irezumi* – which provides the potentially perhaps menacing human form with an absolute disguise. In Japan, the essence is often the appearance.

A tattooed Japanese has, in effect, been appliquéd with a garment somewhat resembling a snugly fitting Victorian bathing costume. The finished ensemble covers the back, the buttocks, both arms to the elbow and the upper thigh. The middle of the chest, the stomach and the abdomen are usually left in the natural state. This enhances, rather than detracts from the 'dressed' look, because the bare skin, incorporated into the overall design acquires an appearance of artificiality.

This is the method of *irezumi*. First, the design is selected, possibly from a chapbook of great antiquity. Then the design is drawn on the skin with black Chinese ink, or *sumi*, which gives its name to the technique. *Irezumi* is derived from *sumi* and *ireru*, which means 'put'. The dye is then applied, following these outlines. A series of triangular-shaped gouges or chisels are used. The full-dye brush is kept steady by the little finger of the left hand, while the gouge is held in the right, rubbed against the brush, then pushed under the skin. This is repeated, until a thick, clear line is achieved. To keep the working surface clean, the master must wipe away blood all the time. Finally, using the full, traditional palette, he works the design into the epidermis.

The traditional palette remains that of the Edo era. The primary tint is, again, *sumi*, which turns an ineffable blue under Japanese skin. Green is also used, together with a light blue and a very subtle red of such extraordinary excruciating properties that the client can tolerate only a few new square inches of it a week. The brush, and the human form on which it works, together indicate a curvilinear technique. The design flows around the body with the amorous voluptuousness of Art Nouveau. There can be no straight lines in *irezumi*. The effect is that of coarse lace. It is an over-all, total and entire transformation.

It is this absolute sense of design that is unique to *irezumi*. Not the eclectic variety of the tattoo produced by the needle – a dragon here, a tombstone marked 'Mother' there, and, on the biceps, the name 'Mavis' surrounded by rosebuds. The masterpieces of the European tattooists are essentially imitative of painting. If they utilise the nature of the body on which they are depicted, it is by way of a happy accident – as when a tattooed hunt follows, in full cry down a man's back the fox which is about to disappear into his anus. There is nothing whimsical about *irezumi*. No slogans. No skulls or daggers.

It may take as long as a year of weekly visits to a tattooist before the *oeuvre* is complete. These visits will last as long as the customer can endure them, perhaps several hours. The process of covering large areas of skin with a single pigment can be extremely painful. Soreness and itching are concomitant with the growth of the garden on one's skin. *Il faut souffrir pour être belle.*

The tattoo-masters themselves tend to inherit the art from their fathers. The apprenticeship is long and arduous, and requires a high degree of artistic skill. They are conscious of the archaic dignity of their profession and may be found in the old-fashioned quarters of Tokyo, where they still cultivate the hobbies of ancient Edo (Tokyo's name before the Meiji restoration), such as keeping crickets in cages and breeding songbirds.

Irezumi is a favourite motif in popular art. Japan produces, for her domestic market, a number of leisurely sagas about the native gangster, the *yakusa*. The word, 'gangster', with its overtones of Capone, does not do full justice to these racketeers, who wear kimonos and often fight with swords. Even today they possess a strange kind of outmoded respectability. The *yakusa* films are usually set in the 1930s, though the only indications of period may be the occasional Western-style suit, pick-up truck or revolver. The heroes will display handsome, though greasepaint, *irezumi* as a simple indication of *yakusa* status.

The motif of the tattooed bride, the girl from the gangster class or the brothel, who has successfully 'passed' and tearfully reveals the evidence of her past on her wedding night, is not infrequent. Involuntary tattooing, for both men and women, is also a recurring motif. They may be tattooed as punishment for the infringement of group rules, or from revenge. Women are also stripped and lengthily tattooed in certain kinds of blue movie. The tattoo-master, with madly glittering eye, and awl poised above the luscious flesh of his defenceless prey, appears in many stills in the series of publications called *Adult Cinema – Japan*, among pictures of young ladies hanging upside down from ceilings during operations for amputation of the breast.

Masochism and sadism are different sides of the same coin, and perhaps a repressive culture can only be maintained by a strong masochistic element among the repressed. In Japan it is rare to hear a voice raised in anger, and rarer still to see a fight in public. It is considered subtly offensive to show the teeth when smiling, for a public display of teeth may be mistaken for a menacing snarl. If I am angry with my friend, not only do I never tell him so, I probably never speak to him again. More Japanese die of apoplexy than from anything else, as though they have bottled up their passions and bottled them up and bottled them up . . . until one day they just explode.

Perhaps one must cultivate masochism in depth if one is to endure a society based on constant expressions of the appearance of public goodwill, let alone try to maintain it. And, though it is difficult to ascertain the significance of *irezumi*, it is almost certainly one of the most exquisitely refined and skilful forms of sado-masochism the mind of man ever divined. It survives strangely but tenaciously in modern Japan.

New Society, 1970

Mishima's Toy Sword

The Japanese may not have any specific philosophy of life but they decidedly have one of death, which may sometimes appear that of recklessness.'
– *Daisetz T. Suzuki, Zen and Japanese Culture.*

That evening in November, the television screen filled with the face of the novelist, Yukio Mishima, quite unexpectedly; but this soon dissolved in a sea of lights, to reveal an orchestra playing the *Romeo and Juliet* fantasy overture. A reverent voice began to speak over the music and the camera panned to a popular musician, a kind of Eric Robinson figure, who was intoning a requiem. I was given a translation. He was thanking Mishima for showing, by his suicide after 'invading' army headquarters, that the spirit outlives death, and for revealing again what it meant to be Japanese. He lowered his lids and whispered: 'Sayonara.' The swelling finale was accompanied by that face, again. It was quite orgiastically sentimental.

Then came the commercials for Johnny Walker whisky; and for a hotel which offers, in addition to its other services, topless can-can dancers. We were all safe again amid the iconography of the economic miracle. Next, a beautiful girl sang *White Christmas* in subtly peccable English and the news carried an account of the dismissal of an official from an influential post in southern Japan after he had claimed, incorrectly, that several colleagues were engaged in a right-wing conspiracy. Asked for his opinion of Mishima's action, he had replied that it expressed the essence of the Japanese spirit. Then came the sports news. We turned to another channel and found a samurai movie stylistically locked in a complex dialectic with the Italian Western. A typically eclectic evening's viewing. During a sword fight, several died horribly but stoically.

Either immune to, or transcending, Freudian symbolism, Mishima – whose real name was the less euphonious and easy-to-remember Hiraoka – 'displayed his sword' to the commander of Japan's Eastern Self-Defence Force (euphemism for 'army'), at its headquarters in Ichigaya, Tokyo, and then killed himself. The Self-Defence Force is small but well equipped and very well trained because like the samurai of the seventeenth and eighteenth centuries, it is never called upon to fight. It was the enforced tranquillity of eighteenth-century Japan that saw, ironically enough, the compilation of the *Hagakure*, a complete exposition of the samurai code and of *bushido* (the way of the warrior). The book was banned under the American occupation and Mishima wrote an introduction to a recent edition. *Bushido*, says the *Hagakure*, is 'to find the place to die'. It would seem this quest took Mishima, leading a group of members of his Society of Shields, to the balcony at Ichigaya, where he proclaimed both insurrection and allegiance to the Emperor.

Mishima was well known at the headquarters because his Society of Shields had trained there. The Society of Shields was a civilian defence organisation, or private army, which Mishima had formed. (The Self-Defence Agency had been pursuing a policy of allowing members of the public to use Self-Defence Force space and equipment.) The platform of the Society of Shields was virulent anti-communism, approval of violence and enthusiasm for the Emperor system. Mishima was once asked if it was legal to carry his sword in the street (which it isn't). He said that it was, because the sword was a registered art object.

All the aspects of the Mishima débâcle carry several levels of irony. For example, the government is already taking a much firmer line with right-wing organisations. But had Mishima not written in his *Guide to Actionism*: 'Once an action is launched, it cannot stop before it comes to its logical end . . . Once a Japanese sword is drawn from the scabbard, it cannot return until it completes its mission of cutting.'

Under duress from the Society of Shields, a thousand or so Self-Defence Force troops assembled at Ichigaya to hear Mishima urge them to cast off the shackles of Japan's war-renouncing constitution and pledge themselves afresh to the service of a divine Emperor. Mishima wore the Ruritanian uniform he himself designed for this men. The real soldiers, looking less dashing, laughed and jeered. The director-general of the Self-Defence Agency, Yasuhiro Nakasone – in effect, the Minister of Defence – was asked his opinion of the Society of Shields some time ago. He replied: 'They remind me of the Takarazuka Girls.' These perform sprightly operettas, where all the boys are girls *en travestie*. However, when Mishima stepped back inside the building, away from his cavalry, he removed his dress jacket in order to disembowel himself.

He made a 13-centimetre gash – deep enough to let the intestines out. This impressed a postmortem official, who said, it showed 'a superb strength of will power'. As used to be the tradition, his boy-lieutenant decapitated him in order to cut short the death agony. 'Every samurai should be able to cut off a man's head,' says Lord Redesdale, English observer of nineteenth-century hara-kiri.

The boy (Mishima's soldiers were mostly students) also disembowelled himself, but he did so less efficiently. He only managed an incision of ten centimetres; so shallow he lost hardly any blood. But a comrade decapi-tated him, anyway. In his time, Mishima had staged nightclub acts. He was a superlative showman and, if his career ended at the age of forty-five in an *acte gratuit*, he had, after all, been compared to André Gide. The bizarre routine stopped after two deaths. Who, anyway, if it had gone on, would have cut off the head of the last of the squad from the Society of Shields? Not one of the Self-Defence Force, certainly – even though local right-ists, on their way to work, do stop them to shake their hands. After the death of Mishima and his lieutenant, the police came. Photographs show only the two heads, neatly put side by side, looking queerly dehumanised and faintly comic. 'What can be achieved by such an action as that taken by Mishima? He may have believed he was logical but the impression of a clown cannot be denied,' asked Shigeru Hayashi, Professor of Modern Political History, at Tokyo University. He had a point.

Yukio Mishima, novelist, playwright, film director, body builder, karate expert, military man, died in such a positive gesture of contempt for the lack of militarism in modern Japan that this was widely interpreted as a sign of revived militarism in itself. Mishima's death received all the more publicity abroad because he had achieved – through novels like *The Sailor Who Fell Out of Love with the Sea* – an international fame that the vagaries of fortune have denied many perhaps more distinguished Japanese artists.

Mishima's act was an orchestration of certain elements: sado-masochism; the homo-eroticism inevitable in a culture which has, for the past 800 or 900 years, systematically degraded women; a peculiarly nutty brand of fidelity; narcissism; and authoritarianism. As these elements unhappily do not fall into those areas of the human psyche that the Japanese repress, they tend to seem, sometimes, characteristics that are especially Japanese. Certainly the general conclusion the world seemed to have reached, as reflected in the international press, was more or less this: just when the Japanese had revealed their blessedly commonplace and comprehensible materialism, they go and do something weird and inscrutable *again*.

Nineteen seventy was the year of Expo, but also the year a group of radical students known as the Red Army hi-jacked a plane and held all who flew on it to ransom, and, as finis, the year of the attempted *coup d'état* by the Society of Shields. If both these last events are the poles of the first two and, ideologically, the poles of one another, both utilised the tactics of terrorism. Perhaps the dreariest lesson to be learned from the Mishima incident was that left-wing terrorism feeds right-wing terrorism. These events are also, though for entirely different reasons, protests against the first – against what the left, with a great deal of justification, called a crazy carnival of capitalism, and what the right, with self-indulgent romanticism, called the degeneration of the Japanese spirit.

'But,' said my friend, S, 'a European could never understand a thing like Mishima did, because Europeans haven't any passion.'

Passion apart, the Mishima incident seems perfectly scrutable in terms of the man's own personality as revealed in his books, pronouncements and activities. He had made, and starred in, a film in which an army officer committed hara-kiri (or, to use the more refined term, *seppuka*) after the 1936 insurrection. The connection of hara-kiri with a metaphysical notion of Japaneseness depends on what weight one gives such intangible nostra. Mishima's notion of Japaneseness seems as much a bookish stereotype as Enoch Powell's notion of Britishness. However, by the use of rhetorical gesture – which is particularly suited to a culture where appearance often assumes an abstract importance – Mishima may have presented the Japanese with an idea that some remember seemed authentic, once.

Many do feel that prolonged contact with the West has deculturalised Japan, and not only those who, as proof, point to the fact that the young read Marx and often believe him. But it is easy for the comfortably off (and for the European) to mourn the passing of the folk-ways of a peasantry who contrived to put the most respectable face in the world on their misery, or to regret the social stability of the Edo area, the scarcely rippled domestic and foreign peace between 1603 and 1867. In that era anyway, the Tokugawa shogunate ensured stability by making Japan an aesthetically harmonious man-trap.

Japan is no longer by any means a man-trap. The price of deculturisation may prove to be, for the majority, three square meals a day, a flush toilet and a ferro-concrete home which, if unpicturesque, at least does not let the wind through. There is, besides, the intellectual freedom of a country which has transcended its own cultural boundaries. It seems a fair bargain.

Nevertheless, there remain these complaints of a confusion of identity – the loss of a sense of self, rooted in a glorious past that everybody accepts as glorious. Japan's past is, on the whole, as inglorious as that of any other nation. There is just one exceptional period, the Heian Era of the ninth and tenth centuries, which produced a shining pinnacle of civilisation, when Japan must have been the only place in the world, at that date, where there was no such thing as capital punishment. But those who look backward rarely, regrettably, look back as far as the Heian. And, if a 111 million characters are indeed looking for an author, then one can only hope they would have too much collective sense to light on someone like Mishima.

Among his massive oeuvre are plays about Hitler and de Sade and a monograph on St Sebastian whose punctured body features as a masturbatory object in his first major novel, *Confessions of a Mask* (an account of a boy's progressive awareness, and subsequent stern repression, of his sadistic homosexuality). Mishima grew to believe that there was nothing left to salvage from traditional Japanese culture. If his early work was influenced by Dostoevsky and he was compared to Genet (as well as Gide), he became so steeped in the Japanese feudal myth that, when the members of the death squad met in the luxurious Palace Hotel the day before the visit to Ichigaya, all of them composed the traditional poem of parting with the world. Mishima once again used the imagery of the sword: 'A man of valour has waited in vain for so long a time, nourishing a sword in his grip; this year too has so far advanced that already the frost is here at hand.' They had already posed for their memorial photograph.

An exhibition of photographs of Mishima closed, on pre-planned schedule, in Tokyo at the date of his death. He was seen posed in loincloth, with sword, on *tatami*; without loincloth, among discreet foliage; and in black leather, on a motorcycle. A poorly developed notion of the ludicrous lends his writing an over-heated quality. Interestingly enough, he dealt at length with the Herostratus syndrome in *The Temple of the Golden Pavilion*, which was based on an actual case of incendiarism, involving a monk and a historical monument shortly after the Second World War. Like most of his novels which have been translated into English, it exudes a monstrous and compulsive weirdness, and seems to take place in a kind of purgatory for the depraved.

Though these fairly early novels contain a good deal of the conventional bric-à-brac of japonaiserie – the bamboo flutes, the sliding screens and so forth – there is little evidence of political aspiration or of the latterday blooming of Mishima's right-wing evangelism. They come later, in a body of writing of which *Sun and Steel*, published this month, is an example. Together with his increasing use of hard-to-read characters (which predate the postwar simplification of Japanese script), his resonating anti-communism, his student soldiery and his cult of body-building, these made of him in Japan a personality who, though widely admired, was also something of an ageing *enfant terrible*. His suicide, if it did nothing else, at least authenticated his genius, for nothing enhances a talent like violent death.

'Mishima's death is the final volume in his collected works,' one Japanese assured me. And that is the conclusion to which most intellectuals came – it was the climax of a life spent on the dangerous borderland between life and art. The highly literate Japanese allow writers as much regard as do the French and they give them certain privileges of public recognition, denied the English or American writer. The official line, however, is reflected in an *Asahi Evening News* editorial, which sharply observed: 'Democracy is not a playhouse in which to stage a theatrical performance by writers and artists.'

Yet many Japanese express admiration for the public exhibition of such stoical courage even if it is sometimes wry. (He had guts and he sure showed them.') And some are abandoned enough to wish to tease a foreigner. 'I'd like nothing better than to kill someone and then kill myself,' a laughing man with pig eyes confided to me in a coffee shop. And, for days afterwards, nobody could talk about anything else.

Yet Japan *is* a functioning democracy, where the needs and sharply increasing demands of a great many people occupying a small land-mass create a sufficiently concrete proliferation of actual problems – roads; sewage; a politically debilitated left and a militantly actionist far left; a right vociferously feeling the pinch of the war-renouncing constitution; the lack of social services. There is also the presence of that massive irony of history, the People's Republic of China, which shows increasing irritation at her prosperous neighbour's relationship with the West. It is the existence of China which may well force a perfectly genuine crisis of identity on the Japanese in the near future – not one of swords and samurai, but of actual survival or disaster.

China has again become a megalith in Asia and it owes only certain philosophical aspects of its self-consistent internal logic to that West of whose manners and technology Japan has been such a diligent student for the past century. Japan's as yet hesitant attitude towards China will require the perhaps painful consciousness of a wider, Asiatic identity that she has, since her experiments in colonialisation, preferred to ignore. A philosophy of death – as perceived by Dr Suzuki – may have spring from economic factors which made life, for many, scarcely worth living, even within the carapace of a stoical indifference. But in the context of the rice and circuses of modern Japan, Mishima's action seemed wishfully laughable. In the context of her potentially tragic predicament, it seems profoundly trivial.

New Society, 1971

Once More into the Mangle

They contain practical and explicit advice on sexual problems, and glossy, full-page nudes to cut out and pin up. The nudes are equipped with a variety of phallic props (French loaves or those round-headed Japanese dolls), and they all wear faintly anxious smiles, as if to say: 'Am I being erotic enough?' with that prim lack of inhibition peculiar to the Japanese. Full-page ads feature chubby, immensely trustworthy-looking men holding aloft bottles of magic elixir while demanding: 'Come too quickly? Having trouble with *your* erection?' One can see at a glance these Japanese comics are not for children.

Indeed, from their contents, they would appear to be directed either at the crazed sex maniac or the dedicated surrealist. The picture strips are a *vade mecum* to the latent content of life – pictorial lexicons of the most ferocious imagery of desire, violence and terror, erupting amid gouts of gore, red-hot from the unconscious. However, it is respectably suited Mr Average who buys them to flick through on his way home to peaceful tea, evening television and continuous, undisrupted, absolute propriety.

The incidence of death, mutilation and sexual intercourse remains roughly constant in Japanese comic books, whatever the narrative. Each book is an anthology of several stories, plus pin-ups, a doctor's column and humorous cartoons. Though there are no specific war comics in Japan, there are often war stories in these comics (and when they deal with the

Pacific War, they are often extremely anti-Japanese): no specific horror comics, but the heritage of the *kwaidan* (the ghostly tale and its hideous goblins) cannot be concealed. On the whole, the adult comics deal either with sex and violence against a background of perspectives of skyscrapers, iconographic representations of present-day Tokyo; or they deal with sex and violence among the pine forests, castles and geisha houses of the glorious but imaginary past. They are printed in black and white, with an occasional use of red, on the usual absorbent paper.

The comics of modern life often contain stories based on incidents which actually happened: the exploits of blackmailing bar-hostesses, of bank robbers, of gangsters, of embezzlers and of the abductors of school girls. School girls are a perennial bloom in Japanese erotology, because of their distinctive uniforms, middy blouses, pleated skirts and black stockings, clearly designed by Colette's first husband.

The narratives are stylistically banal and, in the international habit of low art, often take time off to moralise – though the tenor of this moralising can bring the outsider up with a start. Two young girls, in floppy hats, long skirts, high boots, bleached hair and false eyelids, abandon themselves to dissipation. They attend pot parties (where the strip suddenly goes into negative, as in an old-fashioned avant-garde movie); fornicate with pop singers; find only ennui; and conclude their careers by jumping, hand in hand, off a bridge. The last picture where in mid-air, they endearingly clutch their hats, has this caption: 'For life is as fleeting as the dew in the morning and the world is only the dream of a dream.'

The technique of all the comics seems to derive rather from the cinema than from American comic-book art, just as the themes relate more to the B feature film than to the self-conscious whimsy of the super-hero comics. Since the strip, as a form, is essentially a series of stills, unfolding only in the personal time of the reader, the effect is one of continuous static convulsion. This is a condition sufficiently approximating to that of modern Japanese society.

Typically, the strip begins with a pre-credit sequence, sometimes spread over two pages. In the period stories, this may show a detailed, picturesque and action-packed panorama of a battle or an execution. In a modern story, it may show the climax of a horse race or a boxing match, or the hero or heroines, or both, in a striking pose (the heroine lying on her back perhaps, with a racing car roaring out between her legs). This is an overture or appetiser.

The narrative itself is composed in a series of long-shots, close-ups and angle-shots, with an elaborate use of montage. A typical montage sequence in a samurai comic might show: a bird on a bare branch against the moon; the dragon-tailed eaves of a castle roof; an eye; a mouth; a hand holding a sword. Some use is also made of techniques equivalent to panning or tracking shots: for example, a series of different sized and shaped shots of a night sky with moon and clouds.

It would be possible to use any of the stories as an unusually detailed shooting script. Latterly, there has been a vogue in Japan for what looks very much like comic-book versions of Italian Westerns, another form that has a heightened emotional intensity and stylised violence.

Some artists, however, use elements of traditional Japanese graphic art. Until the twentieth century, there was a flourishing trade in pictorial chapbooks, detailing heroic adventure and tales of life in the brothel quarters. The Japanese script itself is more of a visual medium than the Roman one and tends to sharpen the visual sensibility. The comic books, however transmuted, do not in themselves represent a complete break with tradition or reveal the beginnings of a post-literate period. But it is some indication of the mental relaxation they offer that particularly obscure Chinese characters, when they occur in headlines (though not, for some reason, in the text), often have their phonetic transcription in the syllabic *hirogama* printed in little letters beside them.

The period stories especially often borrow their graphic line from the past. This makes them more beautiful than the modern stories. They also sometimes use calligraphic insertions in especially breathtaking scenes, rather than putting the words in balloons coming from the actors' heads.

What is actually going on in the pictures often looks rather odd to me because I cannot read Japanese. When a translation is provided, it usually turns out to be worse than I could have imagined. Why isn't this girl fighting back during a gang rape? Because they forethoughtfully dislocated all her limbs, first. Why is this weeping old lady in bed with this wild-eyed boy? She is his mother; she has given herself to him as rough-and-ready therapy for his persistent voyeurism. Can this really, truly, be a close-up of a female orifice? Yes, it can.

One also finds the marvellous.

The ceiling of a castle hall is pierced with swords, each grasped in a severed hand that drips blood on to the floor below.

A man the size of a flea plants a kiss on the nipple of a giantess as though it were a flag upon a virgin peak. Waking, she cracks him between her two fingers.

A feudal lord, afflicted with ulcers, sees the head of the son he has murdered rising up out of each pustule. In a fatal exorcism attempt, he vigorously scoops the damned spots out with his sword until he falls, gashed in his entirety.

The samurai comics offer the most stunning harvest of sadism, masochism, nervous agitation, disquiet and dread, perhaps because the inbuilt mythic quality of the pseudo-historic time with which they deal excites creative energy. The hieratic imagery occasionally stuns. The virtue of a low-art form is that it can transcend itself. An artist named Hachiro Tanaka stands out from the visual anonymity of his genre by a style of such blatant eroticism and perverse sophistication that, in the West, he would become a cult and illustrate limited editions of *A Hundred and Thirty Days of Sodom*.

Tanaka perpetrates lyrically bizarre holocausts, in décors simplified to the point of abstraction. His emphasis on decorative elements – the pattern on a screen; on a kimono; that of the complication of combs in a girl's hair – and his marked distortion of human form, create an effect something between Gustav Klimt and Walt Disney. His baby-face heroines typify Woman as a masochistic object, her usual function in the strips.

Formed only to suffer, she is subjected to every indignity. Forced to take part in group sex where it is hard to tell whose breast belongs to whom, her lush body unwillingly hired out to reptilian and obese old men, the eyes of a Tanaka woman leak tears, and her swollen lips perpetually shape a round 'o' of woe, until the inevitable dénouement, where she is emphatically stuck through with a sword, or her decapitated but still weeping head occupies one of his favourite freeze-frames. But, whichever way the women go, they all go through the mangle – unless they are very wicked indeed; when they obey the Sadeian law and live happily ever after.

If the ravaged dove is the norm, Woman in the strips is nevertheless a subtly ambiguous figure. One series specialises in erotic futurology. Again, the artwork is at a high level. The latent content presumably reflects the fears that haunt the doctor's columns. ('How can I enlarge my penis?') A race of superwomen has bypassed the male in its search for sexual gratification, and, in designs of a peculiar purity, uses devices, masterpieces of Japanese technology, such as chairs with breast-massaging hands, and electronic lickers. These last are elongated, quivering tongues on legs that produce spasms of extraordinary delight, though (significantly) they often fuse.

In another context, a fat harpy lolls on a cushion of little, crushed men in blue business suits; into her ravenous mouth she crams TV sets, washing-machines and all the other booty of the modern industrialised society. Again, an old woman crouches over a sleeping boy, painting a young face on top of her own withered one with juice extracted from her victim. A culture that prefers to keep its women at home is extremely hard on the men.

But human relations either have the stark anonymity of rape or else are essentially tragic. Even at the level of the lowest art, the Japanese, it would seem, cannot bring themselves to borrow that simplistic, European formula: 'then they lived happily ever after'.

The girl dies from her rape in the arms of the knight who saves her; he walks off alone, Hemingwayesque, into a lonely landscape under a waning moon. The girl and the knight murder the lord who sold her to the brothel; they immolate themselves. The deserted bar-girl consumes sleeping pills. Love is a tragic, fated passion; yet, still, heroically, they love. Japan's is a very romantic culture, even if the Japanese jab enormous daggers in the bellies of the comic-strip girls, and flay them alive, and crucify them, and even jump on them six or seven at a time.

The narratives are interspersed with humorous cartoons. A man raises his bowler hat to reveal a bald head topped with a nipple. A determined lover sharpens his penis with a knife, while a girl watches with justifiable appreciation. An extraordinary cartoon, revealing God knows what stresses in the inflexible family structure, shows a baby at the breast sucking its mother literally dry – until she is nothing but a deflated bag of skin. Unabashed scatological humour proliferates. A man rises above the door of a cubicle propelled by a rising mountain of his own excrement; unperturbed, he continues to read his newspaper. A man strains and strains and eventually excretes his entire bowel. (The indigenous floor-level, seatless lavatory invites a close and painful relationship with one's own shit.)

Essentially, the comic books are plainly devoted to the uncensored, raw subject-matter of dream. They are obtainable at any bookstall for about 10p. They are not meat for intellectuals; when Yukio Mishima disembowelled himself in public, he can hardly have been influenced by the delirious representations of *seppuka* in the comic books. They are read at idle moments by the people whose daily life is one of perfect gentleness, reticence and kindliness, who speak a language without oaths, and where blasphemy is impossible since the Emperor abdicated his godhead. Few societies lay such stress on public decency and private decorum. Few offer such structured escape valves.

In imported editions of *Playboy* and in the home-produced nude and adult cinema magazines, pubic hair, if ever it appears by chance, is scrupulously blacked out with ink; the male genitalia, unless in a comic context (a man bowling a row of penises with a ball shaped like a pair of testicles), might not exist. A knight disgarbs to reveal loins as marmoreal as those in Blake's 'Bright day'. Another paradox.

New Society, 1971

Poor Butterfly

A friend of mine, who is an English teacher of English, asked one of his Japanese students: 'What is the quality that you would require in a wife?' The student, a young lawyer who had graduated from one of Japan's best universities, replied in all seriousness: 'Slavery. I can get everything else I need from bar-hostesses.'

I recently visited a hot springs resort in the mountains near Tokyo; a spot where companies hire hotels to accommodate employees' annual outings. The town was full of souvenir shops, strip-shows and shooting galleries. Most of the latter were deserted, but one was crowded with laughing, shouting men. On examination, the targets at which they aimed their air-guns proved to be small, china statuettes of naked and beautiful women. If you shattered a nude Venus with your pellet, you received, as a prize, a large, cuddly fluffy toy. This seemed to me a fitting parable of the battle of the sexes in Japan. True femininity is denied an expression and women, in general, have the choice of becoming either slaves or toys. Not long after this epiphanic revelation, I found myself in the front line of the battle.

The *mama-san* explained that, as a special attraction during the festive season, she had originally intended to dress her fifteen resident hostesses in colourful national costumes from all over the world. Owing, however, to the printer's error, the postcards she commissioned to advertise her special attraction read: 'During the days before Xmas, your drinks will be served by charming and attractive hostesses . . . from all over the world.' Therefore she had to go out and search for a clutch of foreigners and she was prepared to pay well over the odds for them, since the notice was so short – 30,000 yen, about £35 sterling, for five nights' work in shifts of two and a half hours.

'This must be the only country in the world where it's cheaper to buy women than to do two bunches of advertising,' said Suzy, a friend who came from Long Island and who once worked as a hostess in a club where an amorous customer, whilst giving her a good-night kiss, bit her lip so savagely the blood spouted across the room. She also worked, another time, in a club that had a special games room full of pin-ball machines where one directed one's balls towards the pictured orifices of women, and so on.

Our bar was called 'Butterfly', and it was in the most expensive and allegedly exclusive area of Tokyo night life, the Ginza. It was about the size of a largish studio apartment in Hampstead and somewhat tastefully panelled in beige pseudo-wood, with two chandeliers in a tiered,

wedding-cake style. A whole lot of tinsel, a white Christmas tree fabri-
cated ingeniously from synthetics, and the presence of Suzy and myself
announced that the holiday was at hand. Some of the fifteen hostesses who
worked there all the time were indeed decked out in subtly Japanified
saris, cheong-sams and other exotic clothing – including one extraordinary costume consisting of a turquoise satin, crotch-length shift,
which had a multiplicity of abdominal slits. 'Harem-style', said the wearer.

However, the hostesses were lumpy girls, on the whole, and, as they say
about race-horses, aged. The *mama-san*, a kimono'd pouter pigeon, had
the slightly harassed, professional joviality of a woman who has not yet put
enough by for her old age – though her place, handsomely subsidised as it
was by the Japanese government via the expense account system, was very
plainly coining it.

In most bars, the regular visitor purchases his own bottle and drinks
from that. But as the drinks are all poured out by a hostess, (there may be
as many as five hostesses at a single table at any one time) and also because
all the girls quite freely order extras – peanuts, dried fish, chocolate, and
so on – the customer has no means of estimating the size of his bill. This
will include, of course, a generous charge for the hostesses. In Japan, it is
notoriously bad form to question a bill, anyway. Besides, the company
usually pays. However, the bill for an evening at 'Butterfly' might cost,
perhaps, £30 or £40 – an evening of innocent fun, watered whisky and
the company of complaisant young women trained in the art of decorously
lewd conversation: the last vestige of the traditional arts of the multi-
talented geisha.

Clearly, though, the hostesses do not really need to speak and no doubt
soon will cease to do so. They are not selling their charms; they do not
usually sell their flesh. If they do, it is strictly a private arrangement; and
since, at all costs, the pretence must be maintained that they are not *de facto*
prostitutes, they rarely get honest cash paid down for the transaction, but
only something useless, like a kimono.

It would be easy to construct a blueprint for an ideal hostess. Indeed, if
the Japanese economy ever needs a boost, Sony might contemplate
putting them into mass production. The blueprint would provide for: a
large pair of breasts, with which to comfort and delight the clients; one
dexterous, well-manicured hand for pouring their drinks, lighting their
cigarettes and popping forkfuls of food into their mouths; a concealed
tape-recording of cheerful laughter, to sustain the illusion that the girls
themselves are having a good time; and a single, enormous, very sensitive
ear for the clients to talk at.

Japan must surely be the only country in the world where a man will
gladly pay out large sums of good money to get a woman to listen to him.

Possibly slaves do not make good listeners. However, the hostess – the computerised playmate – may conceivably be an illustration of the fact that Japan is just the same as everywhere else, only more so; perhaps she is indeed the universal male notion of the perfect woman.

'Butterfly' is a bar typical of two or three thousand others in the Ginza alone. It is a sufficiently respectable place, patronised by solid businessmen. These include a number of, if not captains of industry, at least first mates and pursers. Of the twenty or thirty men who will visit it during the course of an evening, not one will arrive alone and not one will bring a woman with him. Why, the company man might well ask, bother to bring coals to Newcastle?

Yet a throbbing sensuality is by no means the dominant quality of such places. The atmosphere is curiously similar to that of an English domestic charabanc outing, or even the kind of family New Year's Eve party at which drunken uncles pat the buttocks of their nieces. The plump company men would probably eagerly don paper hats with 'Kiss me Kwik' and 'I am a Virgin (Islander)' on them if some enterprising entrepreneur were to tour the bars selling them. 'I am a naughty boy!' they surreptitiously confide. And 'he is a naughty boy!' they whisper, giggling, about their friends, while, under the table, a continuous groping goes on.

In the warmth and privacy of the bar (as, indeed, of the rush-hour subway), the Japanese abandon their aversion to public heterosexual touching. The hostesses touch and are touched freely, though their status as interchangeable non-persons negates, to a considerable degree, the sensual – or, indeed, purely tactile – connotations of such touching. This depersonalisation process also applies to the customers. Both customers and hostesses are interchangeable commodities. The hostesses move from table to table as fresh customers enter, leaving the drinks, conversations and seduction attempts half-finished. The dirty glasses are instantly removed and the other attentions at once transferred to whichever hostess remains. When a customer leaves, he abruptly terminates interaction as though he suddenly remembers he is paying for it all. Without any warning, he gets to his feet and rarely bothers to bid his hostesses a civil goodnight, even when the girls move to the door with him in a chattering convoy, carrying him to a waiting taxi if he has become helplessly drunk.

But the price the customer pays, over and above the bill, for such boosts to his male self-esteem is a palpable loss of identity in the warm bath of spurious affection and indulgence supplied by the hostesses. It is hard to say which sex is most exploited by the system; yet both customers and hostesses, as if in diabolical complicity, remain blissfully unaware of the dubious existential status of the interaction. In the course of the evening, the customers, petted, fawned on and indulged, regress to behaviour of a masculine crassness sufficient to make a Germaine Greer out of a Barbara Cartland.

For example, the girls even go so far as to feed their large infants food. 'Open up!' they pipe, and in goes a heaped forkful of raw shellfish or smoked meat. Unaware how grossly he has been babified, the customer masticates with satisfaction. Meanwhile the *mama-san* herself takes ice from the crystal ice-bucket with a pair of silver tongs and pops it into her customers' drinks with gestures of (in the circumstances) ludicrous refinement. And a hostess can hardly call her breasts her own for the duration of the hostilities.

Double entendre, bawdy allusion and a constant reference to sexual performance and phallic dimension stoke the continuous conflagration of mirth, which will occasionally modulate into the authentic, empty hysterical sound of the laughter of the damned.

Such bars will employ Caucasian girls as exotic extras, like a kind of cabaret. A black girl would be far more exotic and could probably command any price she liked for such work. A curious double standard prevails among the clients; a man whose cigarette has just been lit by a Japanese girl will often produce his lighter to light the cigarette of a foreign hostess. Foreign girls also get more pay and exercise far greater job mobility, having different notions of the nature of employment. These things make the Japanese girls overtly hostile to the alien competition, especially when the foreign girls stage strikes for more money, and walk-outs over obscenity. A girl whose livelihood depends on the hostess bars simply cannot afford to have the self-respect to strike.

The Japanese hostess is locked in a remorseless dialectic. Save for the very few who regard hostessing as a profession which – plus, perhaps, a little prostitution on the side – will lead, one fine day, to their very own bars with their very own flock of hostesses, most of these girls are working in bars at night to supplement the monthly income from a daytime job that does not provide them with a living wage. The hostess, poor butterfly, is selling her youth and time and energy at a very cheap rate to people who could not afford to pay for them out of their own salaries. They usually charge her up to a firm which would refuse to give her enough money on which to live if she were officially on its pay sheet. Such are the ambiguities of acute capitalism.

The actual position of a foreign hostess is, however, sufficiently ambiguous as a social phenomenon. We are asked to exercise the customers' English in a kind of dexterous, cross-cultural, tightrope dance. I transcribe the following conversation verbatim:

Customer: I will provide you with accommodation during your stay in Japan.

Hostess: Will you buy me a house?

Customer: Only if you do it three times a night.

(Roars of delighted applause from the rest of the table, at which are seated three company men and four hostesses.)

Hostess: Will there be room for my children?

(Whoops of appreciation at such wit.)

Customer: I will have my pipes cut (*sic*).

(They all cried the Japanese for: '*Touché!*')

Hostess: I mean, the children I have already.

(Cries of: 'Huzzah! Huzzah! *Bis! Bis!*')

Customer: How many children?

Hostess: Eleven. There will also be my mother; my father; my two sisters; my brother; my aunt; and my husband, a *sumo* wrestler of incredible proportions and invincible strength . . .

At this point, the customer said to his friends: 'Let's move on to the next bar.' They did so, somewhat precipitously. The *mama-san* was a mite peeved and suggested we foreign girls behave in a more lady-like manner, that is – to laugh more and talk back less. She herself laughed almost all the time, even when nothing funny happened.

One customer's English was limited to the single word, 'masturbation', which he pronounced very frequently and with a singular relish. Another raptly muttered the phrase, 'sexual intercourse', over and over again. Suzy claimed to observe a man stifling the signs of an orgasm, while another grasped my thighs quite unexpectedly and then announced: 'I want you tonight.' It is no good turning wrathfully on the poor things and crying: 'What do you think I am? A prostitute?' They *know* you aren't a prostitute. 'No charge, of course,' he added categorically.

After we finished work the first night, Suzy and I walked round to look at the shop on the next block that advertised 'adult toys' and keeps open until all hours. On the way, we passed a mournful transvestite in a kimono, who was warming his hands on a baked sweet potato, hot from the charcoal glowing on a peripatetic vendor's cart. We passed a tea-room that advertised the presence of 'exciting New World bunnies'. It was nighttime in the world's most exciting city.

The adult toyshop carried a splendid selection of whips; some tooledleather chastity belts; all manner of electronically operated dildos; a variety of books and records, including one entitled *Fornicating Female Freaks*, which offered the authentic sounds of some 'bold butch lesbians having AC/DC sex', imported from America, and many other things. The salesman offered for our inspection a fat fish made of foam-rubber. When he pressed a switch, a red light on top of the fish's head glowed and the whole diabolical contraption started to shudder convulsively. With an enviable, deadpan expression, the salesman explained: 'a masturbatory device for gentlemen.'

Which is, presumably, the same function Suzy and I had performed for the last two and a half hours.

New Society, 1972

Death in Japan

One young man was executed because he slipped four nappies for his baby into his wife's rucksack, thus displaying dangerous petty bourgeois tendencies. A girl was executed for shamelessly wearing earrings; a boy and a girl for making love when they should have been making the revolution (the boy's two brothers helped to kill him). Another girl died because she climbed into her sleeping bag a few minutes later than the others and that showed that she was lacking in discipline.

Meanwhile, the radicals argued vehemently as to whether the revolution should be waged with guns and bombs or with guns alone. Those who, by word or deed, revealed they were not ideologically in line with the leaders were stabbed to death with knives, or left outside in the snow without any food. At the latest estimate, 17 members from a complement of 29, had been purged – as the newly formed group that called themselves the United Red Army moved by night from hideout to makeshift hideout in the frozen mountains of the harsh Japanese winter. It is not the scenario for a Godard film; unfortunately, it all happens to be true.

Always hungry for a nine days' wonder, the Japanese public has almost gagged on a surfeit of sensation. As the captured leaders of the Red Army spilled out confession after confession, it was easy to forget the spectacular conclusion of the extraordinary tragedy – the siege of Karuizawa. Some of the fleeing radicals, the police on their trail, took the wrong road and accidentally ended up in Karuizawa – a most respectable mountain resort, deserted for the winter. Cornered in a villa with a hostage, they held a 1,000-strong battalion of police at bay until the police destroyed the villa and charged, receiving several casualties and fatalities.

In all their dealings with militant radicals, the Japanese police have shown enormous efficiency, restraint and courage. However, one sometimes feels that the militants are merely engaged in elaborate psychodramas rather than in any serious attempt to overthrow the actual state.

The national television network had cameras on the site for the duration of the whole of the last day of the siege. Work came to a temporary halt throughout Japan as men and women glued themselves to their sets to watch a drama that moved with ponderous slowness to its inexorable conclusion. Then the father of one of the youngsters who was involved committed suicide, from shame.

As the police arrested other members of the group, parents began publicly to apologise for the misdeeds of their children and vociferously attempt to take the entire blame on themselves. Members of the Diet, the Japanese parliament, have demanded the resignation of the principals of some of the universities the Red Army members attended. The weekly magazines speculate on the sexual problems of the two leaders of the group, Tsuneo Mori and Miss Hiroko Nagata, both aged twenty-seven. Meanwhile, the police continued to exhume corpses, as Mori and Nagata indicated the location of more and more graves.

The radicals first went to the mountains in December to form an 'entirely new party' from the extremists in the complicated, eternally dissident Japanese militant student group. They included the violence-professing Keihin Ampo Kyoto and a faction of the Sekigunba – the group that first gained notoriety in 1969 when it hijacked a Japanese airliner to North Korea. (The men who were involved are apparently still there, undergoing, it is said, 're-education'.)

Since then, members of this new party have been jailed for bank raids and armed robbery, and are thought to be responsible for a number of random bombings. From behind bars, these terrorists now denounce their comrades. The Red Army débâcle is distressing in every detail, even to the astonishing facility with which the leaders have confessed and the amazing lack of any solidarity within the various factionalised groups themselves. It is almost possible to feel as if Mori and Nagata and the rest, like guilty children, want to be punished by the stern father against whom they rebelled; as if they rebelled solely in order to be punished.

The nature of the revolutionary group they created is rather startling. The 'entirely new party' had, first of all, to purify itself of all bourgeois elements, and it fell to carrying out this task with savage glee. Yet, in Japan, even terrorism – like gangsterism – is hierarchical.

The members of the central committee signified their status by carrying knives. The leaders had bread and coffee with their meals; the others made do with barley. The central committee had the right to start a criticism session, or trial, whenever it pleased and usually chose the middle of the night – until the rank and file grew too frightened to go to sleep and some of them ran away. But, since the executions were conducted by the entire group, those who ran away could not go to the police without incriminating themselves of murder and could scarcely go to other radicals for help for fear of reprisals. There is a history of internecine murder among the radical groups, but this would seem to be the first instance of the internalisation of murder within a group.

One of the runaways described the organisation as 'feudal', Nagata's revolutionary fervour appears to have been accompanied by a degree of emotional disturbance; she is said to have 'detested affairs between men and women to an abnormal degree'. Since the organisation of the new party involved an attempt at communal living and there were a number of women in the group, hysteria was very likely, since the Japanese function well as groups only in familiar and clearcut situations, sanctified by social ritual, and are prone, at the best of times, to sexual tension.

The group members were the products of middle-class families with, interestingly – or, perhaps, inevitably – no tradition of left-wing involvement within the home. Both Mori and Nagata, with most of their comrades, experienced Pauline conversions to the cause of violent revolution whilst they were attending what the Japanese call 'prestigious universities'.

It is debatable that the extremist students absorbed more than slogans from Mao; in its rigid structure, its savage authoritarianism and its sadistic excess, the new party could, ironically enough, well be denounced by Peking as evidence of the revival of Japanese militarism. As it is, the débâcle is a body-blow to the authentic Japanese left, just as it has making significant inroads in the industrial cities, and a positive godsend to the right. Those who died in the mountains might well prove to have been martyrs for the right wing, in a drive to stamp out dangerous progressive tendencies once and for all.

Though the Japanese press has luxuriated in an orgy of emotionalism, the comment sometimes makes the point that the habit of submission to authority, and the sado-masochistic sensibility it has produced, is so very engrained in Japan that, it can, if unchecked, override ideology. It is, of course, easier to blame the students' excesses on over-liberal schooling and lack of home discipline, than to examine the role that traditional Japanese values have played in the action.

It would probably take more than a mass hara-kiri on the part of the entire Diet to make the vast majority of the Japanese face up, in fear and trembling, to the psychological heritage of 2,000 years of acute authoritarianism.

It is less than two years since Yukio Mishima killed himself out of rage and regret at the apparent decay of the authoritarian ideal which is exemplified in the Emperor. Mishima once said that there was a curse on Japan.

The nature of the curse was, perhaps, defined by one Japanese intellectual's comment on Sergeant Yokio, the member of the imperial army who hid away in the jungle of a Pacific island for twenty-eight years because he was ashamed to come out alive after promising that he would die rather than surrender himself. 'Yokio-san is living proof of how terrible things may happen to individuals in a society that denies individualism.'

Mishima and the corpses in Gumma Prefecture are defunct proof. The prospects for change in Japan are not particularly good. Maybe revolutionary change could never arrive spontaneously in Japan, due to the inertia of submission created over centuries. Perhaps, to paraphrase Lenin, the revolution will have to be brought to Japan on the points of (alien) bayonets – for it is difficult to escape the haunting sense that some of the Japanese inhabit a quite different reality than the rest of us.

New Society, 1972

A Fertility Festival

Somebody stole the blueprint of hell and, with it, they built Nagoya. The super-express whizzes you to Nagoya from Tokyo in two hours through a landscape of imminent despoliation. Tangerines hang on the trees, tea-bushes cover green slopes, but these pastoral landscape accessories already have a timorous air. Festering industrial blight spreads remorselessly around the artery of the New Tokkaido Line. Soon, one endless city will stretch from Tokyo to Osaka. It won't be a very nice city.

But, thank God, we are only passing through Nagoya, we will not stop there. We are going to attend a fertility festival in the countryside, half an hour or so outside the city. This festival celebrates the marriage of the god called Takeinazumi-nomikoto to the goddess, Arata-hime-no-mikoto. It is a beautiful day in spring, just the season, just the weather, for a fertility festival. Yet all the gods in the Shinto pantheon, working together in one great concerted sacred copulation, could not revivify the concrete desolation of Nagoya.

There is a long queue at the bus station. But they do not look like devotees; most of the potential celebrants carry several cameras and have a prim yet salacious air. They might be about to visit a strip-club. There are more foreigners in the crowd than I expected; we all look a little sheepish. Has anthropological curiosity or mere prurience brought us here? For the focus of this famous fertility festival is a wooden phallus of immense size, borne in triumphant procession through cheering crowds. Surely none of these natty city dwellers has come out of a desire to increase his or her own fertility in this over-populated country that has alienated itself from the sense of the signs that we are about to witness, to the tune of a million abortions a year.

They are running relays of buses to the two temples, one of which enshrines the female principal, the other the male. Since the sexes are polarised in Japan, the two temples are about a quarter of a mile apart. We go to the female shrine first. As soon as I get off the bus, I smell something unfamiliar. Organic pollution. Horseshit, by God! What a surprise! I've never smelled horseshit in Japan before! Are we about to enter the unrepressed past?

But a drove of cameramen are here already, bustling about floats set on trucks, about to drive off to the female temple. The floats are decorated with tigers; with Disney deer; a rainbow; the fat-faced, laughing god of joy. And lots and lots of plastic flowers. On each float sits a girl, carrying a plastic rose. I do not know if these girls have any traditional ritual function, or are a modern tribute to the spirit of carnival. They are all dressed in fancy kimonos and their faces made up like geisha, white and impassive as if carved from plaster-of-Paris. They sit quite still.

One float contains an enormous wood and plaster mushroom, plainly phallic in inspiration. At the end of the float, large, humorous, vulgar, plaster feet stick out on either side. Beneath the phallic mushroom sits – 'Wake me early, mother, for I'm to be Queen of the May' – the plainest of all the chosen girls, wearing a shimmering kimono of gold brocade that must have cost a bomb. She alone has an air of faint embarrassment.

The floats move off slowly down the road towards the female temple. At this shrine is a rock shaped like the female orifice and, in a portable shrine in an auxiliary temple a little way away, there is a large clam. Shops along the path are selling live clams, indisputably vulvic in appearance.

The floats reach a junction in the paddies and halt; the rest of the procession approaches to join them. This part of the procession is altogether more hieratic in character. It is led by a Shinto priest with a bobbing, black, horsehair chignon, in a white robe, mounted on a white horse from whom the horseshit must emanate. The priest is followed by a detachment of middle-aged women in pink and red garments, with red scarves wrapped round their heads and shoulders, carrying staffs decorated with bands of little, jingling bells, trimmed with red ribbons. These women are heavily into the ritual of their roles. All the same, they seem to be daring the spectators to titter. How should a pious lady behave in a situation where piety necessitates obscenity? Aggressively.

Now comes a lorry full of drummers: young men with sweatbands round their heads, many of them in spectacles, all wearing cotton jackets open to the waist. They beat their drums in archaic rhythms, laugh and shout. And here is a troupe of men carrying bunches of wire sticks stuck with favours of red and purple paper that have white marks at the centre. Possibly stylisations of the female orifice. The crowd, shouting, tussles for these favours the bearers toss to right and left. But it is not a very large crowd, and mostly comprises cameramen.

And now, what we've all been waiting for! The cameras click again and again. Another priest, on horseback – and his retinue bears a waving banner with, painted upon it, a perfectly explicit female orifice which could serve as an illustration in a gynaecological textbook. Hair and clit and everything. Click! Click! Click! And this black and gold portable shrine approaching now must contain the sacred clam. It is being carried along by bare-legged young men, some of them with spectacles, some without.

The shrine bucks back and forth, and it now threatens to topple into the thin crowds standing in the stubbled fields at either side of the path. Good fortune is supposed to spill from the shrine when it does this. Click.

We adjourn to the male temple. Inside the temple itself, men in green, butterfly-sleeved garments flutter about mysteriously behind the paper screens; but outside, in the compound, is all the fun of the fair and lots of people enjoying it in a decorous way. There are stalls selling waffles filled with chopped octopus; goldfish made of barley sugar; hot chestnuts; hoop-la stalls; bowls of real goldfish, that you fish for with a little net and take home in a polythene bag. Toffee-apples. Pop-corn. Hot grilled cuttlefish. Candy floss. Trinkets. Lucky pot cats. Lucky pot badgers. And the round-based, eyeless, gold and red things they buy for luck and paint the eyes in as the luck comes. Or not, as the case may be.

Somebody has asked me to buy them some little clay models, or icons, they thought were sold at this shrine. I've seen samples, bought here years ago. Icons basic as graffiti, two-in-one symbols that combine phallus and vulva in one little pierced knob of white clay. And, really, very beautiful to look at. I look and look for these tokens but they are nowhere to be found. They must have gone out of production. Not kitsch enough for nowadays, perhaps. They illustrate exactly Henry Miller's distinction between obscenity and pornography; it is possible to buy pornography.

One stall sells cocks made of bright pink sugar at 75p a time. In the course of the afternoon, they sell 300 of the things – their entire stock. One other stall, and one other stall only, sells cookies in all manner of phallic and vulvic shapes, as well as lollipops on sticks with a coy little striped candy cock nestling in a bed of pink sugar. But the temple virgins at the amulet booth sell only the tie-pins and charms in brocade bags you can buy at *any* Shinto shrine.

Dozens of kids run about, splashing themselves with water at the holy well as they drink from the bamboo dipper. It is just another fair, to them.

A few old men, in cloth caps, with grave faces; they are not here for a cheap thrill. And lots of grannies, pushing empty wicker prams up and down, up and down. Is this not a fertility festival? Their faces are grim, as if to say, Isn't this a serious business? Fierce grannies in drab kimonos, with shocks of grey hair and seamed, wizened faces. The old ladies are out in force, today, attempting to re-establish, by sheer force of their iron wills, the time – still fresh in their memory – when this festival of the male and female principle indeed revivified the soil, quickened the womb, and so forth.

But who else has come here for a blessing? Some of the family parties, perhaps, who look like gangsters on an outing from Osaka. (Japanese gangsters are repositories of tradition.) But not me, certainly. Nor the parties of holidaying company men, giggling to hide their embarrassment. Nor the cameramen, from the picture magazines. Nor the television crews. There is a gnarled European who says he is from *Paris Match*. My friend Harold hopes to sell his pictures to *Stern*. But all of us, with various emotions, are waiting for the procession that will bring the fabled Mighty Cock back to its home.

Meanwhile, a snake-charmer entertains. A plump, sweating man in shirtsleeves and dark glasses, he talks of the many advantages of owning a snake. How it makes a snug muffler – he wraps it round his neck: you can tie children up with it – eek! the children squeal. And, during the recent toilet paper shortage . . . at that, he draws the snake back and forth between his legs.

There is a strip-show beside the main temple building. A female barker with a loud-hailer stands outside the entrance; beside her, a window in the tent reveals the head and shoulders, and only the head and shoulders, of the girl inside, who is shortly going to take off her clothes for your pleasure. It is the stately, artificial head of a geisha, matt white, bewigged, hung with shiny ornaments. These sideshows give the scene a medieval quality.

Over the tannoy system, the police, continuously solicitous, urge the crowd not to fall over and injure itself. Not to dart out into the main road in the path of oncoming traffic. Not to trample one another underfoot in their eagerness to witness the procession as it approaches.

Behind the shuttered temple is a shrine containing hundreds and hundreds of phalluses of all sizes. A large crowd is gathered here, taking photographs. In front of this shrine is a large stone phallus, set on a low pediment.

An uneasy, smutty relish pervades the reactions of most of the visitors. They are as much strangers here as we Europeans are; as great a distance separates them from the enthusiasm of the grannies. Perhaps an even greater distance, since they have only just learned the titillation of prudery, while we have struggled all our lives to overcome it.

At last, in the distance, the sound of weird music of bamboo pipes and drums. A breath of strangeness hushes us all. Here it comes – out of the animistic, pagan past, a relic of the days before the Japanese lost their *joie de vivre*. The crowds surge. Click! Click! Click! Someone has climbed into a tree to get a better view. The police order him down. First, a group of Shinto priests, on foot, in white robes and sugarloaf hats of horsehair, bringing a banner which shows a medical illustration of the male organ in a state of advanced tumescence. Then about twenty of those astonishing, prim women who look like members of the local Women's Institute; and each woman cradles in her arms a succinct wooden phallus, about the size of a cricket stump.

Now. Ah! Cheers and lewd cries. The crowd jumps up and down and climbs over itself to fire off its cameras in the direction of the Mighty Cock, as, serene, radiant, triumphant, an explicit glory of varnished wood, golden brown in colour, it sails over their heads. Good heavens, it is eight feet long. Nine feet long. Ten feet long? Immensely long! In a palanquin borne by jovial obscene ancients, laughing and showing their teeth. The round tip and the immense superstructure of the Mighty Cock emerges from the white curtain of the palanquin. And the ancients shift it this way and that way, so that it seems to move about according to a life of its own.

The photographer from *Paris Match* has broken through the barriers and dances backwards in front of it, clicking away. Harold has joined the procession itself to click at it from close quarters and the ancients are too jovial or too drunk to shoo him away.

The palanquin is attended by acolytes and musicians in white regalia, playing a haunting, archaic melody of drones and beating drums. There are men carrying poles with mops of coloured rags on top of them, all laughing, all singing. And, in spite of the cameras, in spite of our common alienation from the meaning of this ritual, the festival takes hold of us all for a little while – just a few seconds. A magic strangeness, a celebration; the paddies are quickening, it is spring. The god has married the goddess and now returns home. The grannies thrust forward their empty prams and scream shrilly. The old men wave their female favours ecstatically. Here comes a jolly old dancing man bearing yet another phallus in his arms and, after him, a line of dancing men carrying a pole with, hanging from it, a six-foot phallus of unvarnished wood. Phalluses, phalluses everywhere.

All singing, all dancing, they process in authentically orgiastic fashion into the temple. The old folks are having a whale of a time. The priests have an air of suspended disbelief. The children are enjoying themselves, in their pre-pubescent innocence. But the persistent click of the cameras indicates the festival has become one of mechanical reproduction. The day will be fertile only in spool after spool of images of itself processed on film. Perhaps, next year, it will be sponsored by Fujicolor.

It isn't quite over, yet. Amidst screaming and laughter, the priests throw a hail of rice cakes from the balcony of a temple building. The crowd screams and jostles for them; but Harold's girlfriend tells him not to go and take pictures of the scene because the rice cakes are hard and might break his lens.

The vendors already begin to pack up their stalls. Dusk draws on. The snake-charmer is gone. The temple virgins have closed the shutters of the talisman booths. Anti-climax. Post-coital depression, perhaps. Over the tannoy, the police now urge the crowd to take care not to get run over in the car park and to drive carefully on the road back to Nagoya. It is getting cold and we must all go back to Nagoya. The restaurant beside the bus stop has upped its prices by 10p per dish in honour of the festival.

New Society, 1974

Murasaki Shikibu: The Tale of Genji

translated by Edward G. Seidensticker

The Tale of Genji is a masterpiece of narrative fiction and was written a thousand years ago by a woman whose real name we do not know (she's always been known by the name of her own main heroine, Murasaki). Its most immediately affecting quality is that of an exquisite and anguishing nostalgia. Not a whisper of the morning of the world, here; all regret at the fall of the leaf and remembrance of things past.

It is also endlessly long, constructed with great skill and composed in a Japanese so archaically elusive that many modern Japanese will use Seidensticker's definitive English translation as a handy crib. Murasaki Shikibu had the capacity for dealing with emotional complexity of a Stendhal and a sensibility rather more subtle than that of Proust.

Kyoto, the imperial capital of Japan of the Heian period, which is her setting, was a dazzling place, where fine handwriting, a nice judgement in silks and the ability to toss off an evocative 60-syllable tanka at the drop of a cherry blossom were activities that achieved the status of profound moral imperatives for the upper classes.

The major work of English literature extant at roughly the same period is butch, barbaric, blood-boltered *Beowulf*, a fact that makes the Japanese giggle like anything. Though Murasaki does not by any means capture all the world in her silken net; cultured as all hell her courtiers may be but they are the élite of an élite and when her hero, Genji, in exile, catches a glimpse of the life of the common fishermen, he finds it difficult to believe other people are altogether human. Murasaki's imperial court is a claustrophobic place.

And it is a curious fact that a novel so variously beautiful, so shot through with rainbow-hued poetry, so sophisticated, so instinct with that heart-wrenching sense of the impermanence of the world the Japanese call 'mono-no-aware' (the sadness inherent in things) should procure in this reviewer at least the sense of having gorged herself on a huge box of violet-centred chocolates.

At least Arthur Waley's Bloomsburyish and truncated version (which Seidensticker's monumental achievement is bound to supersede) gave the inescapable lady-novelist quality of *The Tale of Genji* its due. Seidensticker's chaste, occasionally transatlantic, idiom errs only on the side of a lack of self-indulgence.

The polygamous and promiscuous Heian court – 'court life is only interesting when all sorts of ladies are in elegant competition,' opines Genji – produced a bumper crop of lady writers; in the endless boredom of rarely visited harems, in the well-screened apartments of retired empresses, there were dozens of bright, clever, highly educated, twitching, neurotic women, scribbling away – poems, novels, diaries, commonplace books, anything to pass the time.

Life revolved around the suns, the shining ones, the emperor, and chief ministers. The character of Genji himself, the sentimental rake who never forgets a one-night stand and always commemorates it in a wee personalised poemlet on the loveliest notepaper, the first great romantic fictional hero in the world, is indeed supremely fictional. It is not a characterisation but an idealisation, a model for polygamous husbands.

But the life of the imperial sprig, Genji, is not the whole meat of the novel. It is essentially a family saga, the family the enormous clan of the imperial family, with the extraordinary network of relationships that multiple wives, child marriage, and institutionalised illegitimacy makes possible. It flows on and on, with no apparent reason for stopping, and then halts abruptly in midstream – possibly because Murasaki died, or became a nun.

After Genji dies, about three-quarters of the way through, Murasaki concentrates her attention on the tormented love affairs of the frivolous Niou, and of Kiaru, with his repressed sexuality and general oddness. There is a definite change of emphasis, now, a sharpening of focus, an increase in psychological realism. It is as though the lives of Genji and his lovely consort, Murasaki, had been an account of a golden age, now past;

the world is running downhill, no more descriptions of snow-viewing or incense-making competitions. The glamour of all those beautiful people is definitely tarnished.

Beautiful people Niou and Kiaru certainly are, but as deeply unpleasant as most beautiful people. As one ex-concubine remarks of the father of her child: 'The Prince at Uji was a fine, sensitive gentleman but he treated me as if I were less than human,' and the unfortunate product of this liaison is hounded to the point of suicide by the conflicting attentions of our predatory heroes.

One suspects that, by page 1,000, it is beginning to occur to our narrator herself that the Heian court, from the point of view of one of those ladies in elegant competition, is really a meat-market with a particularly pretty decor. That ineffable Buddhist gloom, which makes Calvinism look positively sprightly, begins to suffuse the text.

Nevertheless, the décor is absolutely ravishing. Murasaki depicts an exquisite, pictorial life. The first chapters unfold themselves like a succession of painted screens, in which the beauties of nature and the seasons and the weather have the function of pure decoration. There are the rituals of bird and butterfly dances; the shuttered, sequestered women with their black-painted teeth and six-foot swatches of hair, in robes of white silk lined with red, yellow lined with russet, arrange and rearrange those iridescent sleeves that are all custom allows of them to be seen beneath their curtains, sleeves often wet with tears due to the demands of their highly cultivated hearts.

Flowers, everywhere; women named for flowers. Gardens. Ruined houses where neglected ladies sit like Mariana in the moated grange ('he cometh not,' she said). And, dominating everything, an absolute tyranny of good taste, a Stalinist regime of refinement. Choose a singlet of the wrong shade of red and your life is as good as over.

Yet the ominous thunder of the river in which poor Ukifune tries to drown herself reverberates through the last chapters like the very voice of stern Buddhist morality itself. It's all the dream of a dream, you see. All of it. It is curious that this wonderful and ancient novel that Seidensticker's translation makes so voluptuously deliciously readable should have so little hope in it.

Guardian, 1977

Ian Buruma: A Japanese Mirror

Shinto deities abhor immaculate conception; their geneses are maculate as all get out. They spring up from the vomit, faeces and urine of other deities. They crawl out of their eyes and nostrils. The god of fire badly burnt his mother's privates on the way out. The entire pantheon often shakes with ribald laughter, sometimes sparked off by the sight of the exposed genitals of a female deity improvising a striptease. One god, Sarutahiko, 'blessed with a long red nose', is himself a walking penis.

Ian Buruma believes the modern Japanese remain spiritually close to these originals gods they created before the black ships brought Japan's self-imposed seclusion from the world to an end in the last century. Indeed, these gods were in existence long before the importation from China of Buddhism and Confucianism, with their ethics and sobriety, which can sometimes seem as much of an irrelevant top-dressing as Westernisation.

The violent, sexy and grotesque mythologies of Shinto, with their notable absence of sin and guilt and their unabashed enthusiasm for the sexual organs and the bodily functions, certainly underpin a different sensibility than that underwritten by the one about the virgin mother and the father who went to endless trouble to secure the crucifixion of his only son. This sensibility, expressed in terms of popular culture, is remarkably upfront about its obsessions.

In the stately and beautiful city of Kyoto, there may be seen a striptease show which concludes with the performers handing round magnifying glasses and hand-torches so that the audience can inspect the parts on exhibition as closely and carefully as they please. Buruma remarks: 'All this is a long way from the austere, exquisitely restrained, melancholy beauty most people in the west have come to associate with Japan.' It is hard to tell from his tone, which is a mixture of awed fascination and mild distaste, just how great his personal disappointment originally was when he discovered what he terms the 'raunchy' side of Japanese culture.

The 'nopan kissa', for example. These are coffeeshops with nude waitresses. The name is derived from an abbreviation of 'no panties' plus a short form for 'kissaten' (coffeeshop). Here, the décor will feature inflated condoms 'hung up like balloons at a children's party'. Then there is the Takarazuka Young Girls Opera Company, where all the parts in romantic reviews – *Gone with the Wind, Romeo and Juliet* – are played by women, to an audience almost exclusively female, who tend to dress in pink in order to match the colour scheme of the theatre. The girls of the

Takarazuka troupe play male roles more beautifully than men ever could, it is said, just as the female impersonators in the Kabuki theatre are more feminine than women could ever be. H'm.

Sado-masochistic pornography is everywhere. As Buruma says, it probably isn't as hard as that to be found in Amsterdam or New York, but it is exhibited shamelessly on every street-corner news-stand. He seems to think that makes it worse, somehow. He describes the career of the recently retired porno movie star, Tani Naomi, who 'spent almost her entire career being tied up, beaten with whips and shoe-horned by impotent brutes'.

Buruma relates the violence inflicted on women in this kind of pornography to a national mother fixation. Tani Naomi 'even looked like a Japanese mother . . . she was the Mother Goddess in bondage, the passive cross-bearer of masculine inadequacy'.

He broods a good deal on the significance of the mother-child relationship in Japan, a country in which a shady businessman cleans up his image with a campaign of television commercials showing pictures of himself when young gallantly carrying his mother on his back.

There is a special genre in the Japanese cinema (and latterly TV soap opera) dedicated to maternal sacrifice and suffering. Japanese mothers – and Buruma finds this especially sinister – carry their babies in slings on their backs, 'not pushed ahead in a pram to face the world alone'. Deprived from birth of the lonely existential anguish of the European baby due to the absence of a perambulator, he asks if it is any wonder the Japanese – Japanese men in particular – never grow up but decorate their naked cafés with inflated condoms and alternately suck and berate the breast. From this it may be seen that Buruma is on safer ground when he sticks to straightforward descriptions of Japanese popular culture than when he ventures into social psychology.

He has clearly watched a tremendous amount of Japanese television, gobbles up 'B' feature movies, roams the streets with an ever-open eye for the latest innovations in sleaze – he is an irresistible and occasionally very funny guide to the demotic manifestations of a sensibility that is an extraordinary blend of the tight-lipped and loose-jointed. But much of his material is oddly familiar.

The popular culture he describes is curiously like an electronic version of Boccaccio or Chaucer, who would both have relished a theology not so different in practice from their own, however different in theory. A Renaissance businessman might not have won approval by publicly exhibiting himself carrying his mother, but he might very well have commissioned Titian to paint him as Aeneas bearing his father on his back away from the ruins of Troy. Buruma says that Japan is in many ways 'closer to the European Middle Ages, before Christianity obliterated the last vestiges of paganism', than to present-day Britain.

On the other hand, it would be interesting to see a book on British or American popular culture by a Japanese semiotician as culturally omnivorous as Ian Buruma. What would they make of blood sports, football vandalism and the public fertility of Princess Diana?

New Society, 1984

Junichiro Tanizaki: Naomi

It is Tokyo in the early 1920s, a city in effect the bed in which Japan is consummating its ecstatic honeymoon with the twentieth century after 250 years of isolation. There is a heady, fizzy feeling in the city, a sharp appetite for the new – which is to say, for things and ideas from the West. For cafés; for beefsteak; for cocktails, high-heeled shoes, three-piece suits; for mixed dancing. Everyday life and the relations between the sexes are in a state of flux. In a very real sense, people don't *know* themselves, can't recognise themselves any more.

The heroine of Tanizaki Junichiro's novel (the family name comes first in Japan) is in some sense the embodiment of this city, in which, as Tanizaki said in another context: 'Old Japan had been left behind and new Japan had not yet come.' If it was a honeymoon time, that implies plentiful, painful tensions; it was also an adolescent time, neither one thing nor the other, and the eponymous Naomi, the perfect child of this temporal lacuna, is a teenager before the concept has even been thought of, lithe, heedless, sexy, venal, gauche, a new kind of new woman.

Whereas, in the West, the New Woman was an unprecedented phenomenon which could be blamed on nothing but ourselves and our own moral decline, in Japan she was an import, not their fault but squarely *our* fault. Europe and the United States shipped her there between the covers of foreign novels. Most contagiously of all, she leapt into vivid life upon the cinema screen out of the spools of American movies.

Tanizaki Junichiro is one of the greatest of twentieth-century novelists, of the rank of Thomas Mann. *Naomi* was written shortly after the earthquake of 1 September 1923 devastated the Tokyo of the Taisho Emperor and its feverish liveliness. Tanizaki, then thirty-seven, moved from the capital to live near the old merchant city of Osaka. There, almost against his will, this thoroughly Europeanised writer, profoundly influenced by

Baudelaire and Wilde, rediscovered his own Japaneseness and embarked on a series of novels, of which *Naomi* is the first, that describe the profound sense of loss and alienation caused by the shock of the collision of a traditional culture with modern history.

It is one of the ironies of this collision that Tanizaki used the form of the European nineteenth-century novel of bourgeois realism to depict it. Of this series of novels, *The Makioka Sisters*, published after the Second World War, is an analysis of the last, precarious days of an old Osaka family as that war becomes inevitable, and is one of the masterpieces of realist fiction. Tanizaki died, approaching eighty, in 1965.

If, while he was writing *Naomi*, Tanizaki was in the process of rediscovering, with profound pleasure, the Kabuki theatre and the Bunraku puppet theatre, he continued, like Naomi and her husband, to love the movies and kept big scrapbooks of his favourite stars. *Naomi* must be one of the first novels to describe sensibilities formed by Hollywood and, perhaps, the first to depict the precise nature of the cultural imperialism disseminated by Hollywood. For the images on the screen have made his characters thoroughly dissatisfied with their own physicality.

Kawai Joji, the narrator, falls in love with Naomi because he thinks she looks like Mary Pickford. When she wears a bathing costume, he remembers Mack Sennett's bathing beauties. She could, he thinks wistfully, even pass for a Eurasian . . . and, best of all, her name is Naomi.

For Kawai, Naomi stands for all the allure of the exotic – but she only *stands for it*, she does not embody it. She is, in reality, just as Japanese as he is. His own sense of self is never at risk with her, as it would be with a real foreigner, as it is with the White Russian countess who teaches them ballroom dancing, whipping their feet if they take a wrong step. (Such vigorous detail abounds in Tanizaki.)

When Kawai-san dances with the countess, his face jammed against her prominent chest, he feels as though he is doing something 'absolutely forbidden'. The power and strangeness of the West has been eroticised; to possess the foreign woman would be to eat of the very fruit of the tree of knowledge. But Kawai-san is essentially a comic character. His relation to the countess serves to reveal how ridiculous he is.

In *Some Prefer Nettles*, the novel Tanizaki wrote shortly after *Naomi*, the hero puts himself existentially at risk through a liaison with an 'exotic' Eurasian prostitute, though here the threat the woman represents may be contained precisely because she *is* a woman who may be hired. *Some Prefer Nettles* deals with precisely the same themes of alienation and sexual estrangement as *Naomi* in an incomparably more subtle way. And it must be said that Edward G. Seidensticker is a rather more elegant and persuasive translator than Anthony H. Chambers.

But the most interesting thing about *Naomi* is that it is very, very funny, with all the sprightly, heartless vivacity of a two-reel silent comedy. With expectations bred of the lugubrious Mishima, we do not expect Japanese literature to be funny. But Tanizaki, in this book, is.

Naomi is drawn entirely from the outside, the very type of the faithless female lover that haunts the universal male imagination, tacky, meretricious and irresistible. But *Naomi* may be read as the story of a fine man destroyed by an unreciprocated passion for a worthless woman only with the greatest difficulty. The novel's Japanese title is *Chijin no Ai*, usually translated as *A Fool's Love*. Whether Kawai is ridiculous because of his affectations or would always have been foolish is impossible to say. Certainly he was born to be a comic cuckold and it was only a matter of time before his fate sought him out.

Then again, Naomi was only fifteen, perhaps less, when Kawai plucked her from the bar where she worked and installed her ostensibly as his maid. They invest in a Western-style bathtub so that he can sponge her down every night. He starts to keep a diary in which he notes down every detail of her changing body as it grows 'strikingly more feminine every day'. He gives this diary a title: 'Naomi grows up.'

Such goings-on would be rum in any culture and are no less so in Japan. But Kawai is blessed with such a strange kind of askew innocence they seem utterly banal. Part of the joke of the novel is its narrator's lack of self-awareness. In the bleak, dark, short novels of the end of Tanizaki's career, *The Key* and *Diary of a Mad Old Man*, the principal characters are drawn against their reason into a downward spiral of fetishistic sexual obsession. But Kawai would hotly deny there was anything wrong with him. Except love, of course. He has the matter-of-factness about his pleasures of the true pervert. His masochism is not a hobby but a way of life and Naomi, as she matures into a tramp, does him the service of gratifying it.

Day by day, she looks more and more Eurasian. Day by day, Kawai grows more enslaved until, inevitably, the worm turns; forced to acknowledge her copious infidelities with the pimply youths with whom she engages in beach parties and other teenage goings-on, he throws her out. And, of course, she soon comes bouncing back, having transformed herself meanwhile into a complete occidental.

Naomi sets out to make the final bid for Kawai's heart and bank account clad in, not a kimono, but a smart French crêpe frock; on her feet – like Luis Buñuel, Tanizaki relished a pretty foot – not Japanese sandals but 'highheeled patent leather shoes decorated with fake diamonds'. (He enjoyed attractive footwear, too.) Kawai has a sudden, intense vision of her beauty and her evil, one of the places where the novel sounds an odd note from the Japanese past, that of the profound misogyny that Buddhism shares with all monotheist religions.

The novel's ending finds the odd couple installed in a Western-style house in Yokohama, where the smart foreigners with whom Naomi likes to socialise live. The focal point of this house is its mistress's grand ceremonial bed, which her husband does not share. Naomi dances all night with men called McConnel, or Dugan, or Eustace. Sometimes she calls her husband not Joji but 'George'. 'The more I think of her as fickle and selfish, the more adorable she becomes.'

She is still only twenty-three, he thirty-six. They have a lifetime before them, a chilling thought. Japan has ahead a headlong career of fascism, militarism, victory, defeat and economic triumph, more history in a lifetime than many nations manage in a millennium. Naomi must have been born in 1904, from internal evidence in the text; she would be in her eighties, alive and kicking, today.

New Society, 1986

Amerika

Tom Wolfe

When he was younger and more supple, Tom Wolfe introduced The Kandy Kolored Tangerine Flake Streamline Baby in the diction of Holden Caulfield: 'I don't mean for this to sound like "I had a vision or anything" but.' . . . This established at once – by the well-known technique of affirmation by denial – that Wolfe had indeed been granted some kind of vision (unless it was, rather, the gift of tongues) in the early 1960s. But by the time he's putting together an anthology of the new journalism, and titling it portentously The New Journalism, the flatulence of middle age is apparent and Wolfe ponderously comes the heavy father over his offspring non-fiction genre. 'The most important literature being written in America today is in non-fiction, in the form that has been tagged, however ungracefully, the New Journalism.'

Perhaps, though, the most important literature being written anywhere, ever, has always been non-fiction; Rousseau's Confessions was more important (whatever 'important' means) than Laclos's Les Liaisons Dangéreuses; The Wealth of Nations than Tom Jones, and so on. But I don't think the whilom Pleonastic Kid means quite that. Now, ten years on, he's doffed, more or less, spurious reticence and now announces a signal victory. He's wiped out the novel as 'literature's main event', no less. That's what he's done, with a little help, that is, from Truman Capote, Gay Talese, Terry Southern, and all the other aces featured in the anthology.

He says so himself. It's all here in black and white in this piece called The New Journalism, which occupies some sixty pages of the eponymous anthology (published in America in 1972 and in Britain, this summer, by Quartet). I was terribly surprised and impressed. Also a bit nonplussed; it never occurred to me that the novel had the kind of status Wolfe takes such glee in demolishing. All I know is, from my own experience, writing novels is a precarious way of making a living. Clearly they must order things differently in the United States. All the same, what a shock! Here's Wolfe briskly castigating John Barth and Borges and James Purdy and Gabriel García Márquez (some of whom are not even American), whose mortal sin is a tendency towards non-naturalistic fiction. Neo-Fabulists, Wolfe labels them, who've sold off their birthright as social chroniclers – the birthright of the novelist – to the New Journalism. For not even, it would seem, a mess of pottage. The only novelist Wolfe seems to have even half a good word for is the incredibly boring Philip Roth; probably for reasons of pure masochism.

I suppose, vaguely, I must have thought Wolfe was dead, like Bryan Jones, Janis Joplin, Jimi Hendrix, Carnaby Street, Candy Darling and all the other culture heroes. So it's nice to find he's alive and kicking. I wonder if he's aged. I remember being very struck by the oddly gentle, curiously old-fashioned fellow pictured on the flyleaf of *KKTFSB*, with his quizzical smile, the lock of hair falling over his brow like a Georgian poet, the carnation in his buttonhole as if he'd been snapped on the way to a wedding, the spotted handkerchief in the breast pocket and, off all things, a suit with a *waistcoat*. He looked rich, as though he probably did not need the money, and so was spurred on by pure ambition; therefore, perhaps, a dangerous man.

Soft-featured, anachronistically dandified, his appearance was at variance with the content of his reportage. Not with his style. Though his content was raucous – Vegas, Park Avenue potlatches, Kesey's bus blasting out *Carmina Burana* across California – his style was paper-tigerish and could not roar for long.

His up-front bravura often lapses into odd little camp mannerisms . . . like 'so – so Beyond Pop Art, if you can comprehend', in the piece about Jane Holzer and, in the same piece, 'The press watches Jane Holzer as if she were an exquisite piece of . . . radar.' (Not now, it doesn't. Who wants yesterday's papers? But in the deep freeze of Wolfe's prose, she's stored away in her youthful beauty; hard-cover, a longer shelf-life, the eternity promised by the poet.)

Ten years on, in a quite different context, wee Tom's still putting in these arbitrary breathing spaces that seem to mimic real speech. 'If you tried to put one of those lumpy mildew mothball lumberjack shirts on them – those aces . . . they'd *vomit*.' And that comes from an introduction Wolfe did for a book about the sociology of fashion by a perfectly respectable German professor, René König's *The Restless Image*. That dash, those three little dots: the pause for thought made visible, then the flop of the limp wrist as, exhausted with the effort of celebration, Wolfe falls back on the word he'd thought of first. And so achieves an effect of surprise by means of a piece of typographical sleight of hand.

None of the flash is necessary. As a theoretician of fashion, Wolfe has the percipience of the born semiologist, but it is semiology in a vacuum. Some innate dandyism in him insists on the appearance of a negligent brilliance. He wants no intellectual structure (which is to say, a moral structure) to obtrude upon the recreation of effortlessness.

Wolfe's artfully spontaneous, tessellated style, is not so much impressionist as imagist. It is a mosaic of brilliant bubbles. You could describe it with a title of Boris Vivan's *Froth on the Daydream*. In the Jane Holzer piece, there's one particular felicitous image and, if you lay it out nicely, you get:

> and two eyes opened
> - swock! -
> like umbrellas

See? Prévert. Such a jamboree, filigree way of writing — so oddly at variance with this passionate, indeed, polemical stand for social realism. What *can* he be up to?

'My argument is that the genius of any writer — again, in fiction or non-fiction — will be severely handicapped if he cannot master, or if he abandons, the techniques of realism,' pontificates Wolfe. Yet in this lengthy advertisement for the New Journalism as an art form and for the novel of realism or documentary novel, the novel based on legwork and research, Wolfe still utilises his very own particular style of shellacked, self-defensive facetiousness. This is designed not so much to disarm criticism as to render it ridiculous before it can even be formulated. Before he got so heavy, Wolfe used to remind me rather of the poets in Donald Davie's poem, 'Remember the Thirties':

> They played the fool, not to appear as fools
> In time's long glass. A deprecating air
> Disarmed, they thought, the jeers of later schools.

But now Wolfe seems to want to manipulate his image in time's mirror in order to gain the cheers and thanks of posterity. Still, always the ironist. (Irony is debonnaire, Davie's poem goes on.) Wolfe concludes his essay on the theory of aesthetics of the New Journalism with a larky description of his demise at the hands of a (presumably) Mongol horde. The horde bears down on Tom Wolfe. 'Friends! Citizens! Magazine readers! What a *scene* this is going to make! So help me, this is the way people live now! This is the — (gork))))))' So the reverberating parentheses of death closes in upon him, still observing, still sparking off, still reporting for all he's worth.

Perhaps it is a failure of his technique that I cannot summon up a tear for this hypothetical death of Wolfe. But since his work has always had a sprightly surface heartlessness, concealing, probably, the iron stoic pessimism of the true dandy (and that is why I like him really), he deserves neither tears. Nor jeers, indeed.

But I can't think why he's started pontificating about social realism in this fashion. Though his work is obviously about real things that actually happen, somebody like Jane Holzer or even Leonard Bernstein (though I'd heard of him before) are just as fictional to me as Old Goriot or Charlie Chan. And Wolfe's notion of social realism is narrowly connected with the idea of literature as a market commodity. Not a whisper of social realism and proletarian humanism. Never a suggestion of the ambivalence of realism as an artistic genre, now an instrument of oppression for keeping people in their place, now a methodology of liberation, revealing the world as it is, yet capable of change. Nothing of that.

'The novel no longer has the supreme status it enjoyed for 90 years (1875-1965),' says Wolfe, after he's stated categorically that prevailing styles amongst novelists are washed up. Which is what we've all been saying for years, although no new style – he's right – which has achieved a total acceptance as the way a piece of narrative should be has emerged.

Sometimes, as in the case of Charlie Manson, a straightforward documentary realism acquires all the obscene titillation of Grand Guignol. Then, perhaps more than ever, we need the mediation of fiction to show us what it is like to be human. (If, that is, we wish to remember.) I don't think journalism can ever do this. It deals in only the particular event, the unique personality.

Wolfe says he and the other new journalists found they had the whole 'hulking carnival' of New York in the 1960s to themselves, and the psychedelic fiesta of California, too – the big novels on these subjects the publishers were expecting never materialised. And where's the great Vietnam novel? Where, indeed? Perhaps a Vietnamese is writing it. No Frenchman wrote a great novel about Napoleon's retreat from Moscow: but a Russian did. Anyway, it seems an odd way of regarding a novel – almost a version of, 'you've seen the movie; now read the book'. You've witnessed the event; now write the novel. But the gestation of any novel that's a bit more than a good read is a lengthy and curious process: it is a process of synthesis.

Wolfe laid down an invaluable amount of documentation about the 1960s. His legendary demonic inaccuracy as regards fact is of no importance to the researching novelist, who will regard his style as part of his content. *The New Journalism* is a useful pocket guide to some more bizarre aspects of the same period. The New Journalists have done so much of the legwork! The rest of the statistics are in the libraries.

Rarely can a period have been so well or so lovingly documented, nor with such a deadpan lack of obvious moralising. Under the gratuitous nastiness of Ed Saunders's book about the Manson Family glimmer the sulphurous bones of a novel waiting for a Dostoevsky or a Melville to flesh out with horror and pity. 'Thanks a lot, Ed. Wouldn't have liked to have done *that* kind of research, myself.'

It won't be a documentary novel, either. The novel, fictional narrative, will be with us as long as the bourgeoisie is with us. They've got some kind of complementary relationship.

New Society, 1975

That Arizona Home

I remember riding the Greyhound bus through Arizona, one burning August afternoon, a most desolate region of rock and scrub and tundra. The road passed through a township or kind of collapsed and sprawling system of habitations miles from anywhere. Abandon hope all ye who enter here. Everything as tumbledown and derelict as, in America, you usually only see in inner cities – single-storey wooden buildings with sagging verandas and iron bedsteads out in the open air; presumably so that the sleepers could catch a little of the cool of the night.

The odd, lean dog nosing in the garbage, of course. Otherwise, scarcely a sign of life but for an Indian child chucking stones at a wrecked Chevvy with a certain indifferent, apathetic hostility.

That bored Indian child was the only glimpse I caught in all my travels in America of the vanishing American himself. But these Indians certainly did not *look* as though they were vanishing. There was quite sufficient evidence of their presence, all right – beached as they were on a singularly inhospitable piece of terrain, making the best they could of a bad job.

Apocalyptic religions had let them down. The shirts of the Ghost Dance cult were *not* alas, proof against bullets. But the booze must help. And if you're smashed out of your skull all the time on peyote, then even the bizarre patronage of Marlon Brando must seem tolerable. Peyote might, however, be a bit too exotic for those unsuccessful used-car dealers.

The bus driver said they were some kind of Comanche, though he wasn't terribly specific about it. Then again, they might be Apache, he suggested without interest. In the bad old days, when the Spanish bought a slave girl from the Comanche, the Comanche made a point of raping her before handing her over: 'Here she is,' they used to say. 'She's spoiled now.' Losers have their own method of self-defence, of which spite is one. It may be better to be raped by the devil you know rather than the devil you don't, though that's a moot point. Nevertheless, even a woman can sympathise with this horrid yet defiant custom.

That was an Indian village as I saw it. But what of the legendary arrow-swallowing, snake-handling Navaho, with their sand paintings, their basketry, their turquoises? They haven't done too badly, considering. They got into the handicraft and pageantry business. And the Iroquois, with their dominating rituals of torture and religion, their long houses, their twisted and grotesque ritual masks, their slow deaths by torture, their cannibalism? Gone into the construction business up north. I don't know about the Choctaw, with their feather mantles and their bodies painted with swirling suns and serpents and their interesting family life, in which a father had no authority over his children. Most of the picturesque mores of yesteryear have gone down the great, thirsty drain of history; and that's that.

'By and large, Indians are poor. They range from poor to horribly poor. They are, when they wish to be, extremely picturesque and they are objects of great interest to tourists' – Oliver La Farge, *A Pictorial History of the American Indian*. Yes, indeed. It is a hard thing to be imprisoned in one's past because one has nothing left to sell. It's a fate of which the English had better be beware, especially in this jubilee year.

I wish that some examples of twentieth-century South Western Scrap Metal (Comanche?) could have found its way into the exhibition just ended at the Hayward gallery in London. But I wonder what religio-sociological function the imaginative catalogue would have ascribed to them. The *Sacred Circles* show was heavily into myth, especially the current myth of the Red Man as mystic.

As if the American Indian hadn't been sufficiently dogged by mystification. He's had the myth of the Noble Red Man thrust upon him. This is a myth on which, like many Europeans, I was raised. So I was always rooting for the painted savages to fall upon the cowboys with infinite violence. I always saw him as a Noble Red Man, even when he was presented to me in terms of the alternative myth – that of Murderous Brute. Ariel and Caliban at the same time.

When the hippies discovered that the Indian had natural rhythm and was, besides, in tune with the infinite, he received a new and more meretricious incarnation as an ecological Prospero.

This new myth invites the red man as magician-scholar to return from exile and preside, along with Don Juan, the Yaqui sorcerer, and J. R. R. Tolkein, the Middle English scholar, over every aspect of inner reality. This attribution of spiritual authority contrives to assuage the Great American guilt over the decimation of the red man – once eloquently expressed by Edmund Wilson in the words of his book-title, *Apologies to the Iroquois* – by allotting him a comfortingly false ascendancy. If you can accompany this with a lot of ritual self-abuse and breast-beating (such as the Americans indulged in over the My-Lai massacre), as if Wounded Knee happened yesterday, then so much the better.

It gives me great, chauvinistic pleasure – and God knows, that's rare enough, these days – to know that most of the Indian tribes sided with the British during the American War of Independence. It probably proves nothing but that they were born to lose. Given the chance, they had tended to ally with the French, for preference.

I also relish the doubt about the nature of the purchase of Manhattan. Did the Dutch, indeed, buy the island for $20 worth of geegaw and knick-knacks from the Indians who lived there? Or was the transaction made with a band of Indians from a totally different tribe, who merely happened to be passing through? I like to think of the red men murmuring, 'Property is theft' (the natives of New York state were famed for their philosophical bent), ripping off the Dutch and disappearing into the thickets, indulging for once in their infrequent laughter.

The red man has suffered the curious fate of many ethnic minorities. He is a screen for projective fantasies, rather than a phenomenon of reality. If *Sacred Circles* was anything to go by, this process hasn't stopped. It seemed to be in full flood, too, in Robert Altman's film, *Buffalo Bill and the Indians*, where the demystification of the Wild West seemed to necessitate a mystification treatment of Sitting Bull, whether Altman wanted it to or no. The Indian in *One Flew Over the Cuckoo's Nest* is heap big myth, too. What I'd like to see is a movie featuring the Navaho marines in the Second World War who found their native language was a code no foreigner on earth could crack, and so become lynchpin communications teams. Something straightforward, like that.

Some of the fantasies have been benign, and some have not. Some of them have even come near the truth. Engel's particularly eulogistic approach in *The Origin of the Family*, even though perhaps not precisely an accurate description of the Iroquois, is a far better view of Indian life as the Good Society than those fantasies of tribes under the sway of bloody ritual, superstition and hallucinatory drugs that the San Franciscans of the 1960s found so enticing. 'And a wonderful constitution it is,' applauded Engels.

'No soldiers, no gendarmes or police, no nobles, kings, regents, prefects, or judges, no prisons, or lawsuits – and everything takes its orderly course. There cannot be any poor or needy – the communal household and the gens know their responsibilities towards the old, the sick and those disabled in war. All are equal and free – the women included.'

The red man must often have been surprised to find himself used as a moral example, a kind of super-ego, for Whitey. Alternatively, he was perceived as the id in person. There's a picture in La Farge's book of Billy Two Legs, a Seminole chief on the warpath, all shaggy mane and warpaint. Voracious, bloodthirsty, sparing – you can tell by one glance at him – neither woman nor child, the bogeyman come straight out of nightmare to get you.

During the Enlightenment, the red man was enlightenment itself. John Locke opined: 'In the beginning, all the World was America.' The Indian was Adam rediscovered, an Adam who had not eaten the forbidden fruit, and so retained not the naïvety of a child of nature, but innocence in the form of an intuitive sense of truth and justice, innocence as a lack of corruption. The red man's sane and democratic social institutions were, for Locke, a positive disproof of Hobbes. Adam; but not yet the old Adam. That comes later, with Billy Two Legs.

It's a little known literary fact that Polly Peacham, bigamous wife of Captain Macheath, finally pledged herself to an American Indian after she had followed Macheath to Virginia, whence he had been transported. All this is in *Polly*, Gay's sequel to *The Beggar's Opera*. Gay's Indians are positive paragons of good sense and morality, never losing a chance to score off Whitey.

There's a mezzotint of an Indian chief who came to London to visit Queen Anne. He wears a good cloth suit, like a country squire. He's pictured in a forest glade, displaying a length of fine beadwork. He looks a proud and decent man whose conversation would be edifying, and who would not abuse his own authority. For a moment, the Emperor of the Six Nations is not just a fantasy projection, but real.

There's a desperate picture by George Catlin, primitive painter and Indian lover, that shows how, 150 years later, both Noble Red Man and Murderous Savage could be replaced only by another fantasy, the self-tormenting European one of the red man corrupted by the white man. You could subtitle Catlin's picture: *the degrading effects of civilisation*.

It's a double portrait, of the same person: 'Wi-jun-jon, Pigeon's Egg Head, going to and returning from Washington'. On his way out, he's a respectable kind of savage, in beaded, fringed buckskins, with a crest of feathers and sensible shoes. On his way back, what a change! Now he is Pigeon Egg's Head, such a comic name in English, for good and all. In the white man's garb, he's a grotesque figure, a painted fan in one hand, a furled brolly in the other, white gloves (of all things), and a silly red feather stuck in the front of his stovepipe hat. His poor feet are crippled in high-heeled boots. There's a fag stuck in his mouth. Worse, bottles stick out of both back pockets of his dandified black coat with the gold epaulettes.

Indian as drunken clown. Indian as stooge of history. Indian gone to hell, aping white man's ways as he tries to get himself out of the cage of Indianness.

That somnolent Arizona township is at least home, and not a fantasy.

New Society, 1977

Snow-Belt America

The *Providence Sunday Journal* weighs as much as a six months child. Aspiring folks take the *New York Times* on Sundays, too, in a touching Chekhovian fiction of 'keeping up' – New York City is only a couple of hundred miles away, four hours by rail as Amtrak winds its leisurely course south-easterly along the coastal creeks, inlets and nuclear submarine bases. Together, these papers add up to a lot of dead trees.

Few take the Boston paper, although Boston is only one Amtrak hour in the other direction. There's a historic rivalry between Providence and Boston, admittedly felt less keenly, if at all, by Boston. There is a bit of 'the world forgetting, by the world forgot', about Providence. Perhaps that's why the Mob, or so they say, chose it to run the whole of New England up to New York State from.

Inward-looking as the city is, the *Pro-Jo*, as it is affectionately known, does not confine itself to local news. That account of the Ku Klux Klan fish fry and barbecue in Santa Fe . . . Nor, in its lavish international coverage, culled from the syndicates and agencies, does the paper operate with an inflated sense that the eye of the world is on Providence, Rhode Island, capital of the smallest state in the union and one, indeed, that grows smaller day by day.

The census theoreticians concur that people are quitting Rhode Island, and the whole of the declining north-eastern Snow-belt, in droves, heading for the Sun-belt. Florida. California. Texas. I think this is incorrect. I think they're just dying off. Don't think they could afford the fare. And I've got friends who *came* here from Texas, dammit. OK, they're black. Couldn't keep up with the social life, down there. All those fish fries and barbecues.

But the standards of its journalism are not the reason why we few remaining paupers left in Providence, RI, make a weekly dive for the *Pro-Jo*. Tucked between the leaves, like the apfel in a strüdel, are the advertising supplements. Why pay more?

It's dollar dynamite. Every week, some firm in Providence or its surrounding urban sprawl, is slashing prices. 20 to 25 per cent off all cribs,
chests, dressers. A ready-to-assemble multi-purpose wall unit in rich rustic
Malibu finish at 23 per cent savings! Sheets; hi-fis; TVs; video-recorders;
cameras; washing machines; refrigerators. Clothes for men, women, children and a category called 'juniors', presumably covering those who are
none of these things. *Why* pay more, after all?

On Sunday mornings, therefore, with the aid of the sheaf of advertising
supplements, you plot your forthcoming seven days' consumer strategy.

Even 10 cents here and 50 cents there add up. I've seen people in the
supermarket pay for a cart-load of groceries with a combination of federal
food stamps and discount coupons from the *Pro-Jo*. This is the other side
of consumerism. Shop exclusively from loss leaders, and you are ahead of
the game.

Of course, all this takes time and energy and the discipline of a quarter-
master sergeant, and you can never buy anything just because you fancy it,
and none of all this is possible without a car in the first place, because the
big discount stores and supermarkets are way out on the edge of town.
And some of the stuff is on sale because it is rubbish. The local drugstore
currently has superabsorbent tampons on sale. Well, only one brand, now
banned, has been specifically associated with toxic shock syndrome.

So just laying in the week's necessities turns into an IQ test, an
endurance test, another of those obstacle races for the poor in which you
know, if you can't keep up, it's your own fault.

Not that everybody in New England, or even Providence, is a pauper.
No, indeed! Far from it! Lots of rich doctors and old money! The stark
deprivation of the north-eastern seaboard is a myth put about to explain
why Rhode Island stayed Democrat in the recent débâcle. Nevertheless,
there are a fair number of people in the city who seem to be just getting
by.

If the state stayed Democrat, the specifically local politics of Rhode
Island defy brief summary. Suffice it to say that, traditionally, it has been
for years the arena in which the Irish and the Italians have slugged it out.
The governor of the state is called Garrahy. His challenger in the recent
gubernatorial elections – why, Providence's own mayor, Vincent 'Buddy'
Cianci! By whom hangs many a tale. Oh, those hotly denied rape allega-
tions! The peculiar business of the concrete pine-nut in Little Italy! The
way he likes, riding on a white horse, to review the mounted police patrol!

Does it sound like comic opera? Very well. It is like comic opera.
Providence itself has that quality, which is given visual affirmation by the
white marble dome of the state Capitol, which may be seen from most
parts of the city. It is a vulgar, pretentious, Edwardian, inappropriate and

therefore endearing wedding cake of a building, like the palace of the ruler of an archduchy whose economy subsists entirely upon the sale of postage stamps.

When the Capitol was built, at the turn of the century, they wanted to put up a statue of the founding father, Roger Williams, on top. But nobody could find out what he'd looked like. So they put just any old statue up there and said it was 'independent man'.

Roger Williams was expelled from the Commonwealth of Massachusetts in 1636 for saying he didn't think the king had any right to cede land that belonged to the Indians. He had a good civil rights record all round, and let in Jews and Quakers once he had a place of his own. That place he called Providence, because it demonstrated 'God's merciful providence unto me'. The first Indian that he met, here, he is supposed to have greeted with a breezy 'What cheer?' Wot'cher. Wot'cher, me old cock.

Providence is old New England, and proud of it. In the harsh, white light of the new world, that unyielding, dense light that hits you like a blow from the eye of a watchful God, the saints settled down inch by inch, and, at first, Providence appears to present an apt and homogeneous face. That bony, uncomfortable, New England face, with the blue, fanatic's gaze.

Here was born, and died, the most characteristically demented of all New Englanders, the horror-story writer, H. P. Lovecraft, who believed he was about to be engulfed by alien forces. On his gravestone is the ominous legend: I AM PROVIDENCE.

On closer examination, this New England face, in appropriately Lovecraftian fashion, disintegrates.

The black lady in the washeteria addresses me in such beautifully formal Boston Brahmin American it sounds like she's taking the piss; the place is full of mumbling preppies from the local Ivy League university, after all. When her son comes in, she and he revert to the Portuguese Creole of the Cape Verde Islands.

A few weeks ago, the Cap Verdeians celebrated Amilcar Cabral Day in a community hall in Fox Point, a section of the city which has a stripe in the colours of the Portuguese flag painted down the middle of the road. Similarly, Little Italy, the Italian section, has a red, white and green stripe. The Black-Hispanic ghetto in South Providence, on the other side of the interstate highway that cuts the city in two, has not yet decided on the colours of its stripe, apparently, for, as yet, it has none.

The Lusitanian Americans come from, predominantly, the Cap Verde Islands, off the coast of what is now Guinea-Bissau, and from the Azores. The origins of the community are romantic. The whalers out of New England ports picked up and brought back fresh hands from those remote places. Others came after under their own steam.

What is impressive about the community is, it doesn't aspire. Young men hang out outside bars. Old folk train vines over poles in their back-yards and sit outside in the shade in summer, sipping beer from cans and watching the passing scene. Fox Point looks like what it is: a prosperous part of the Third World transported *in toto* to an inner suburb of an indus-trial city. If they realised they were American, they would know they were poor. As it is, poverty is its own reward. Fox Point is a very nice place indeed.

But Providence as a whole has richly reaped the reward of poverty. The city has been down so long it is now looking like up. Downtown is com-posed of pretty, turn-of-the-century stores and warehouses which are being turned into tourist attractions. The residential areas are all exquisite nineteenth-century gingerbread houses. There was no profit in pulling down all this in the thirties, the forties, the fifties. Now there is plenty, plenty profit in restoring it.

This, obviously, involves getting the people already living in them out and selling the houses to people like me.

I was walking home this evening after buying some tough, peppery sausage called *linguica* on which no discount was offered. A local child, no more than twelve, addressed me. She was sitting on a fence in dungarees and dayglo sox, swinging her legs.

'Excuse me, but do you rob kids?' she demanded Brechtianly. I said, 'Of course not,' and walked firmly on. I heard her behind me, muttering: 'Of course not,' trying out a British accent. Ethnic music poured out of Manny Almeida's Sporting Bar and Grill. Next year it will be a soyburger joint run by a brace of geriatric hippies into macramé and role reversal.

The trouble is, I understand none of all this. Providence is a nice place, a pretty, sleepy, seedy place, a relaxed and, on the whole, not-ungenerous place. But the city falls apart in my hands, the way the Sunday paper does; it slips open in five, six, seven sections, and none of them fit back together again. I can't get a grip on it.

You cannot say the centre does not hold, because I don't think it has a real centre; it is a plurality of worlds. If I take the rigorous way of life posited by the advertising supplements as the core of the whole, shifting mass, it is because the fringe-of-town bargain stores are, in some sense, the new cathedrals of the community, the only places where the multitude of people and conditions in this one tiny city ever actually gather together, holding those supplements as if they were prayer books.

The city opens out like the rooms in an immense flat. You go from one room to another and the door slams behind you; you go into another room. Bang. Rich suburb. Bang. Little Italy. Bang. Mount Pleasant, where the French Canadians live. Bang. This is Camp Street, for socially mobile blacks. Bang. This is South Providence, which looks like the end of the world. I can't put all these separate conditions together and make sense of them and nobody seems to try, anyway.

Walk the half mile from Fox Point to the East Side, which varies from posh to seedy intelligentsia. The streets empty. The houses retreat behind prim hems of grass. No more shops. No bars. A woman calls her cats: 'Plato! Samantha! Midnight!' No laughter of children. No more graffiti in Portuguese, no hearts or names of footballers.

Only a swastika in red paint on the wall of the playing field across the street.

New Society, 1981

The Rise of the Preppies

So I am teaching this course in fiction-writing for the year at what I shall call, as H. P. Lovecraft did before me, the University of Miskatonic, and one of my students, D, asks me anxiously if his spelling is up to par. He confides in a conspiratorial whisper: 'You see, I went to public high school.'

I don't immediately see. I am a foreigner. There is a public (i.e. funded from taxes) high school in our New England town called the Classical High. It seems to exist in order to feed very bright students to classy colleges such as Miskatonic. But D doesn't want me to run away with false impressions.

'You see, I'm from California,' he said, as if that explained it all.

It certainly explains his anxiety here in the north-east. He means that I must make allowances for him because he was processed through a vast, multi-ethnic, mixed-ability, unstreamed learning centre.

If the American north-eastern mythology about multi-ethnic, mixed-ability, unstreamed (and free) high schools, let alone about California, had much reality, D ought to be a semi-literate, coke-sniffing sociopath. As it is, he's got a lovely prose style; his spelling is no worse than most and better than some; and there he was, chatting in Spanish to Hispanic ladies, on the 'US out of El Salvador' demo. Which is more than I can say for those disaffected preppies with Trotsky badges on their lapels who are taking the 'Marxism and Literature' course. Not that these latter are characteristic preppies.

Preppies. Yes, preppies. The noun (also used as an adjective, as in 'those trousers are a bit preppy') is derived from the word, 'preparatory school', and signifies both preparatory (or prep) school alumnae and their style. 'Preppy' is what the Italian-American public high school alumna derisively calls the WASP prep school alumnus in Erich Segal's *Love Story*, thus initiating the usage. There are quite a lot of preppies at Miskatonic, though it is not true you can tell them by their Fair Isle cardigans. The intellectual preppies are the hardest to handle, as they believe they have been trained to think for themselves.

Of course, I *had* heard of a couple of American private boarding schools before I came here. Two names, in particular, stick in the mind, because they sound like unpleasant but not fatal diseases of small children: 'I'm afraid the little fellow's come down with a nasty touch of Choate,' 'Nothing wrong about a tricky case of Groton that four years' re-education in the canefields won't put right!'

That being preppy might have hardened into a style a goodly number of non-preppies might either aspire to, or feel obscurely threatened by, was a notion beyond my ken.

Yet so potent is the myth of the democratic function of the American high school that, when I read *The Catcher in the Rye* in the 1950s, I never even registered the implications of Holden Caulfield's boarding school. Now I can diagnose his condition with authority: he was suffering from mild Choate. And therefore, in spite of all appearances and his highly idiosyncratic grammar, he was a member of a tiny, highly privileged élite. How did be become a culture hero?

Might not Holden Caulfield's emotional problems, let alone his prose style, have been alleviated by the healthily abrasive environment and vibrant social mix of a public high school?

It might have been permissible for liberals to ask this question ten years ago, and perhaps in California it still is. Radical southerners are solidly behind public education. But the question does not present itself much in the north-east, these days. The north-east is very big on the private sector. If you can't go private sector, make damn sure your kids have what it takes to go highly selective.

It may seem no privilege to pay through the nose for the acquisition of basic literacy, but putting your child into private school – any kind of private school – is only the tip of an iceberg. At its apex remains, as ever, the antique, private, venerable Ivy League universities, most of them strung out along the railway line through the north-eastern corridor that runs from Boston through New York City to Washington.

Not that preparatory school automatically leads to an Ivy League. There are other places preppies like to go; these days you never know whom you might find yourself rooming in with at an Ivy. Nevertheless, it is a Miskatonic alumna who has just perpetrated an odd little book called *The Official Preppy Handbook*, of which over half a million copies are in print. It has topped one of the *New York Times* bestseller lists ever since it came out, last year, at about the same time that Reagan was elected.

The handbook is edited by Lisa 'Bunny' Birnbach with help from friends. It describes itself as: 'The first guide to *The* Tradition. Mannerisms. Etiquette. Dress Codes. The Family. How to be Really Top Drawer'. It is a tightly schematic compilation of lists, diagrams and photographs, describing a selection of upper-class educational institutions, residential areas and social types.

This belongs to a literary tradition at least as old as the journalism of Addison and Steele in the eighteenth century. This tradition discusses emblematic figures (the 'preppy' is such a one). The mode of this genre is usually, but not necessarily, ironic. The writer professes an encyclopaedic knowledge of the world, which he describes down to the last detail. ('Twenty verbal expressions for vomiting'. OPH, page 129). In this tradition, the inner life of a social class is deduced from the outer appearances of imaginary representative types.

In the 1960s and early 1970s, Tom Wolfe offered confirmatory accounts of types and lifestyle with an oscillating focus, as though he could not decide whether Old Money, New Money or Hippies were more glamorous. His role models reflect the confusion of the times.

As the seventies firmed up, our very own Peter York characterised the 'Sloane Ranger', transatlantic cousin of the female preppy, in a more precisely schematic, focused way. Probably a far-sighted person could have predicted the election of the Thatcher government from York's parting shot: 'There is nothing wrong with being a Sloane Ranger.' The discreet charms of the bourgeoisie are being celebrated again.

The widely syndicated strip cartoon called *Doonesbury* has a nostalgically 'Class of '68' quality of social comment. (The *Guardian* has now started to run it in Britain.) Just after the OPH hit the bookshelves last autumn, *Doonesbury* ran a strip which featured an interview between a concerned, hairy, radical radio chatshow person and 'Muffy Harkness, lead singer for the hot new preppy band, Muffy and the Topsiders'. (Muffy is evidently a traditional prep nickname.)

The hairy one asks Muffy: 'Isn't the prep movement limiting its appeal by suggesting that élitism and privilege have become hip?' 'Maybe,' she answers, 'but the political climate is just so right for that, don't you think?'

These galleries of types, and comprehensive guidebooks to the customs of invented stereotypes, are not to be confused with simple etiquette manuals. Etiquette manuals tell you how to behave in circumstances of hardened ritual in which you have not previously found yourself. When etiquette manuals appear on the bestseller lists, it is a sign that a good deal of social mobility is going on. Just as a plethora of sex manuals is a sign that people unaccustomed to doing so are now having sex.

But Addison in the eighteenth century, and Wolfe, York and, in her frivolous way, Birnbach in the late twentieth, are in the business of helping consolidate the idea of a certain social class as an object worthy of emulation. They tell you how to spot style leaders, and, if you wish, to ape them. They are not telling you how to entertain them in your own home, nor how to meet them on equal terms.

However. La Birnbach has gone on record as saying that anyone can be a preppy 'with a proper frame of mind'. She has even taught a course on 'how to be a preppy' in an exclusive New York bar, according to a press hand-out. (Note that 'exclusive'.) And, of course, the appurtenances of significant style have never before been so easily available. It would be easy to mistake the OPH for an extended advertising supplement, not only for the preparatory schools and colleges which it lists, but also for lists and even addresses of all manner of suppliers of high-class goods and merchandise.

So far, so much good clean fun. But to *look* like a preppy, to *feel* like a preppy, does not mean one *becomes* a preppy, since the essence of being a preppy is being second-generation middle class. A decision about the kind of education you are to receive which is taken in early adolescence, is a decision that is taken *for* you. So the OPH might serve as a handy guide to enable the upper class to define its own secret code of distinctions between the real and the fake. For, of course, it is simply not true that anyone can be a preppy.

Unlike Addison, who took it for granted his readers would know, La Birnbach and Co. do, in fact, let on that you need almost unlimited amounts of old money to be 'really top drawer': 'The thing about money is that it's nice you have it. You're not excited by it. You don't talk about it. It's like the golden retriever by the chair – when you reach out for it, it's there' (OPH, page 32).

How you get your hands on it in the first place is left a tactful blank. The *real* preppy is born, not made.

There are signs that OPH started as a joke that got out of hand. Another is the handy hint about not mentioning *The Communist Manifesto* in the section about what to say at your prep school interview. And there is a kind of giggling fascination with the minutiae of the lives of the rich and privileged in the book that is wearily familiar to a Brit. These are the very accents of the public school (old-world style) rebel, biting the hand that fed it and, lo and behold, gorging on it all the way to the bank.

But a college in-joke that gets out of hand to the tune of half a million or more copies – the book circulates widely at the Classical High, what's more – is funny peculiar, rather than funny ha ha. Snobbery is never good clean fun. Books like the OPH feed on anxiety. The laughter it provokes outside the magic circle of reference it both records, and helps to create, is anxious and self-defensive.

The kids in the Boston public school system would, of course, find the whole thing completely inscrutable, and not funny at all. Just this minute, the radio newscast announces that Boston will sack 23,000 of its teachers next week to ease its financial load, and that's no laughing matter, either.

All this makes me feel like Mr Jones in the old song. Something is happening, but I don't know what it is.

New Society, 1981

Anne Campbell: The Girls in the Gang

The lives of the three women members of New York street gangs, the subject of Anne Campbell's piece of investigative sociology, are curiously anachronistic, as though there were a time warp in New York City and a sizeable segment of its population were living, not in Reaganite affluence, but the terrible, brief lives of the poor of medieval Paris or Victorian London. Sun-Africa, one of the women whose lives Ms Campbell has partially shared and whose tape-recorded voices she transcribes for us, seems, says Campbell, to 'perceive life as a kind of jungle in which another gang, the police or a bullet are all likely to stop her in her path'. This is Hobbesian talk, but Sun-Africa's perception appears to tally quite well with the recorded facts.

This is a book about one aspect of the schizophrenic geography of the United States, in which the First World co-exists cheek by jowl with the Third and the inhabitants of both worlds watch the same soap operas on television. The girls in the gangs, or, rather, the female auxiliaries of the boys' gangs – named with such baroque invention, the Dragon Debs, the Turban Queens, the Emperor Ladies – all adore soap opera. The soaps take place in surroundings of extraordinary luxury; the Sandman Ladies, the Elegant Queens, the Devil's Rebels (Ladies), live in roach-ridden apartments on burned-out blocks. But the soaps are saying, see! the rich have problems, too. Problems can't be solved by money. It is not the life-style but the melodramatics of *Dallas* and *Dynasty* and *All My Children* with

which Campbell's informants identify, for their own lives are conducted
with similar passions more like those of grand opera than of soap opera.
Passion is free and the girls are poor: criminality in these boroughs does
not procure rich dividends. The steadiest source of income remains the
welfare cheque – the price, as Gore Vidal once said, that the United States
pays for keeping ethnic minorities out of the mainstream of economic life.
Of Campbell's three women, two are Puerto Rican and one is Black but
not Black American – Sun-Africa's family are emigrants from Panama.

Gangs have been a feature of New York life since the earliest days of
the city; the territorial groupings, the sense of family ties imparted by gang
membership, all these created, and still create, a sense of community in the
featureless space of the new city, the new and unknown society. Gangs
seem to be growing more and more psychologically important as most of
New York that is not Manhattan grows daily to look more and more like
the suburbs of Hell.

Violent death is the constant companion of Sun-Africa, Weeza and
Connie. Sun-Africa has suffered the deaths of not one but two lovers (both
shot while committing burglaries). Weeza loses her common-law husband, probably killed by a rival gang, during the course of Campbell's field
work. Connie is forced to move house because of death threats to her
family. They all fight in gang wars; sometimes beg and steal; discipline
errant girls; give succour and advice, but the women's movement has had
no appreciable effect on their contingent status. They join the gangs for
love of a man, or because their brothers are members, or for fun, or for all
three. The girl 'dressed outlaw', with the flick-knife at her belt, is a mother
and a lover, first and foremost. The gangs present no radical alternative
lifestyle for women. Nor for men.

'The gang is not a counter-culture but a microcosm of American
society,' concludes Campbell. She quotes Bob Dylan, ironically: 'To live
outside the law you must be honest,' and the gangs readily subscribe to the
myth of the romantic outlaw, but they are hypocrites. For all those whom
Campbell talks to, crime is something other people do; when we do it, we
have no other choice and are absolved of responsibility. The gangs like to
think of themselves as vigilantes, keeping their neighbourhoods safe; in
fact, they commit most of their depredations right there on the block. The
characteristic crimes of the alarmingly named Sexy Boys and Girls (of
which Weeza is a member) are to rob Saturday-night drunks and hit old
ladies on the head before snatching their handbags. The Sandman, into
which Connie has married, confine themselves to dealing in dope, which,
in the circumstances, is behaving like boy scouts.

The Five Per Cent Nation, though, is something else, even if the New
York Police Department define it as a gang. Five Per Centers are the

enlightened ones, 'the Muslims and the Muslims' sons'. Sun-Africa, who took that name when she joined them, is a refugee both from the lower middle class and also from a promising career as a juvenile delinquent. Before she became Sun-Africa, she distinguished herself in an autonomous, exclusively female gang. Style and shop-lifting were their thing and they were known as the Puma Crew, after the brand of sneakers they liked to wear. Subsequently Sun-Africa donned the long robe of an 'earth', as the men, or 'gods', of the Five Per Cent Nation call their women, and now lives in a kind of harem – the 'gods' are polygamous, as befits good Muslims. Her family wanted her to go to college and they are startled and upset by her present way of life. But it is almost as if Sun-Africa, terrified by her experience of the freedom of the criminal, deliberately sought out for herself a life bound by the most stringent limitations.

Although the Five Per Cent Nation is notorious for the murders and robberies connected with it, and has recruited existing gangs into it, it has, unlike the Angels of the Night and the Shadows of Death, an ideology that makes sense of its members' experience. When Sun-Africa says that if it were not for the Nation she would probably be dead, it is impossible not to believe her. In an anomic world, any value system may seem better than none. Sun-Africa is sixteen.

Times Literary Supplement, 1984

Edmund White: The Beautiful Room Is Empty

This account of an American sentimental education starts off according to the conventions of such things: 'I met Maria during my next-to-last year in prep school.' In the US, prep school prepares you for college; the narrator is on the threshold of adulthood but, although an intense friendship with Maria, painter, socialist, Lesbian, nascent feminist, will be central to his life, she is far from being the romantic heroine who will administer his lessons of the heart.

Yet, in a sense, she saves his life, or, at least, his sense of self by introducing him into the hard-working, easy-going Bohemia of the 1950s, where our existentially dishevelled hero can feel, if still not quite at home, at least less abandoned in the world.

Love as such will come much later, almost at the novel's end. As for passion – well, perhaps the preconditions for passion won't arise until after the novel is over, because you need high self-esteem to engage in a passionate attachment, you need to believe yourself worthy of one, and the narrator of this lucid book spends the greater part of it coping, with considerable fortitude, with the conviction he is depraved, or mad, or worthless.

After he has finally found, and lost, his first great love, he tries to exorcise the pain by writing about it: 'Yet how could I like myself, or ask the reader to take seriously a love between two men?' The novel itself is an answer to that question.

The Beautiful Room Is Empty is a sequel to Edmund White's *A Boy's Own Story*, and takes the anonymous hero of the earlier book from late adolescence, to the further shores of youth, his late twenties. It also takes him from the stern repression of the mid-West to New York City; from the 'frumpy cuteness' of fifties Middle America to the ravishing diversity of the late sixties; from the solid, merciless, deranged, white middle class to the rootless urban intelligentsia with its mix of race and class and desire.

But, essentially, the narrator's sentimental education concerns neither men nor women but the nature of his own desires. It begins in a painful contradiction: 'As half-consciously I inched towards my desires for men, I clung to my official goal of stifling these desires.' Driven by a curiosity he believes to be as perverse as its promptings are irresistible, his encounters are bleak with irony, characterised by a deliberate absence of pleasure, as if to enjoy them would make them even more wicked. The narrator's secret life, indeed, most of his sexual life, consists of meeting anonymous flesh in the public toilets he obsessively cruises, the 'long sentence' served on his knees from which Edmund White extracts an astonished poetry.

In a coffee shop, on a night out with a reckless gaggle of queens – 'Grab your tiaras, girls' – he notes straight couples stare with open disgust. 'I was no longer a visitor to the zoo, but one of the animals.' Meanwhile, the narrator's father grudgingly coughs up for the analysis that is supposed to 'cure' his son. But the ministrations of Dr O'Reilly, speed freak and alcoholic, teetering on the verge of his own breakdown, collapse, only induce more anxiety: 'If I started from the premise I was sick (and what could be sicker than my compulsive cruising?) then I had to question everything I thought and did. My opinions didn't count, since my judgement was obviously skewed.'

Damaged ghosts, victims of America, drift past. Annie Schroeder, real-life Warhol superstar *avant le jour*, yearns to be a top New York model. A bulimic, she blocks up the drains when she regurgitates the whole ham and entire turkey from which she has made a midnight snack during a Christmas visit home with the narrator; her gesture of disgust and rejec-

tion is so comprehensive, if involuntary, that it is a wonder the narrator
never thought of bulimia himself.

In to this world of guilt, lust, and occasional fierce excitement erupts
Lou, the 'handsome, ugly man', scarred, alcoholic, heroin-addicted, irresistible, who loves Ezra Pound, and 'everything deformed by the will
towards beauty', and who loves, too, the 'beautiful poetry of gay life'. The
narrator clearly hadn't thought of it like that before.

Lou's own huge potential for tragedy has been arrested by his equal
potential for the dramatic glamour of the life of homosexual crime celebrated by Burroughs and Genet, the lure of, the necessity for transgression.
In terms of the period, you might say that Lou *enjoys* being a pervert.

It speaks volumes for the narrator's good sense and emotional stability,
in spite of all, that he eschews the 'demon lover' aspect of his new friend
and cultivates, instead, a loving friendship. His scandalised mother, for
whom the enigmatic Lou is the last straw, suggests an implant of female
sex hormones will solve her son's problems: '- oestrogens neutralise your
sex drive altogether; they neuter you and soon you're free to lead a normal life'.

And yet she loves her son. She truly believes she has his welfare at heart.

Lou suggests the narrator leave Chicago for New York with him, the
archetypal journey for the American writer, the mid-West to the Big
Apple. Here, normalcy is a more flexible condition; the sixties are just
beginning; the streets are full of what Lou calls 'Cha-cha queens, hair-
burners and glandular cases', and the narrator begins, for the first time, to
see homosexuality not as deviancy but as a way of being.

And the beautiful stranger arrives at last. The blond Sean. Perhaps love
is not so inaccessible, after all. Yet Sean soon cracks up, breaks down,
because loving another man is too much evidence that he is homosexual
– a recurrent theme of the book, the wish to gratify desire whilst evading
stigma, whilst avoiding self-identification whilst evading membership of a
stigmatised group. That's putting it in bare, sociological terms. It was a
system of repression that killed. Sean goes to live with a cowboy; nobody,
he writes, would ever guess this cowboy was gay . . .

The narrator despairs. 'If as a child I'd known my whole long life was
going to be so painful, I'd never have consented to go on leading it.'

But the novel is not over. It is quietly moving towards a remarkable and
joyous conclusion that takes place, unfashionably enough, on the barricades, probably the first barricades in the history of street warfare manned
by people who saw the funny side of a revolution.

On the day of the death of Judy Garland, the narrator and Lou find
themselves in a gay bar, one summer's night; the police raid. There is a
riot. The bar was the Stonewall; at this point, the novel enters real history.

'Lily Law shouldn't have messed with us the night Judy died,' says Lou. Somebody shouts out: 'Gay is good.' Gay Liberation is about to be born. The Stonewall riot was, the narrator says, 'The turning point of our lives.' The rioters were not protesting their right to depravity, neuroses, or psychic derangement, but a simple right to be human.

This exemplary novel is written in prose as shining and transparent as glass; it lets you see life through it. It describes how the survivor of a psychological terror campaign retains his humanity.

It I were a teacher, I would recommend this book to every student who asked me why it was necessary to fight the amendment to the Local Government Bill presumably designed to prevent me doing just that. Nobody who has seen the inside of the closet would wish to condemn anyone to return to it.

Guardian, 1988

LOOKING

Animalia

At the Zoo

Last week, summer holidays, ice-cream weather, the apes at the zoo were drawing the usual huge crowds with their comic antics and their wistful air of being almost human. Part of the fascination of the monkey-house is the arbitrariness of it. The primates are behind bars and we, apparently quite fortuitously, have escaped this fate; visiting a mad-house in the eighteenth century much have been rather like this. There is pleasure in the relief with which we leave the monkey-house – 'There but for the grace of God'.

At London Zoo, of course, there are only invisible bars in the monkey-house; the apes live in a nice, low-rise brick-built complex and their apartments have huge picture windows in which visitors can see their own reflections almost as if moving about inside the apes' lovely homes, with their Design Centre exercise bars, their Habitat stylishness.

Only a whimsical quirk of evolution has separated Guy the gorilla, in his massive, obsidian repose, from an executive desk in an international corporation. As it is, he is trapped behind his glass panel as if on a TV screen, the daily functions of his life performed before an impersonally curious audience, the helpless star of a long-running soap opera of ape life – you could call it, 'My Brother's Keeper'. The most intimate details of his domestic life are on display; when Lomie, Guy's mate, struck a blow for the Women's Movement by showing herself a careless and unnatural mother, it caused as much stir as the death of Grace Archer years ago. Since Lomie had been forcibly impregnated by another ape, the whole episode smacked more of *Peyton Place* than *The Archers*, but we were spared the dreadful scenes that must have taken place in the relative privacy of their sleeping quarters as her time drew near.

After the birth there followed a most touching spectacle, that of the infant gorilla, repellently named 'Salome' (why?), cradled in her green-uniformed keeper's arms as he sat in her enclosure, the cynosure of all eyes. The gorilla couple achieved a certain revenge on their script-writers; they managed to get one of them written into the serial.

The terminology of the animals' attendants brings home the analogy with the mad-house. 'They are 'keepers', as in an old-fashioned lunatic asylum, not 'guardians', as in a poor-house, even if the apes do not engage in productive labour. Yet the keepers, although men, perform functions that are not altogether human, such as teaching baby giraffes how to walk and suckling orphaned baboons from bottles. They are ambiguous link-men between the world of men and the world of beasts and the animals may well regard the keepers as entirely in complicity with them, though their discreet presence ensures we never forget the fact that a zoo is a world of beasts, for beasts, built entirely by men for their own purposes.

The Zoo's Royal Charter of 1829 gives the objects and aims of the Zoological Society of London, which owns both London and Whipsnade Zoos, as: 'The advancement of zoology and animal physiology, and the introduction of new and curious subjects of the animal kingdom'. In the zoological gardens, the beasts are themselves like sentient plants, laid out as in flower-beds, objects of study, contemplation, surmise and fantasy. Like lilies of the field, they are not bred for food or service. They have another function, they are there just to *be*, in the best conceived of all pos-sible paternalist utopias.

The mandrills at London Zoo have a spacious garden to play in, with climbable rocks and exercise bars; a hedge of roses divides it from the visitors, such a hedge that, if untended, would grow into as huge and thorny a barrier as protected the lapse of consciousness of the Sleeping Beauty. In their lives as mobile vegetation themselves – in their great wastes of perpetual leisure, what can the apes be thinking of?

The patriarch of the mandrill family (*Mandrillus sphinx*, West Africa) has a face indeed like a tropic flower. A luscious snout of the tenderest red; white, bulbous, blue-veined cheeks like the calyx of a pitcher plant; and delicate, pointed, leprechaun ears almost hidden in a foliage of speckled fur. He is the most magnificent, the least human-looking, therefore superbly dignified. Like all the enclosed patriarchs, he ceaselessly patrols the perimeter of his enclosure. He has a sunset-coloured rump.

Last week, however, most of the rumps of most of the primates appeared to be in full bloom; must be the season. The sexual organs of the Sooty Mangaby (*Cercocebus atys*, West Africa) are undeniable as mouths, like the transposed orifice in Magritte's *The Rape*, sore, inflamed, a visible reminder of the persistent irritation of the flesh. Carnal. A wound. It is almost as if they were doing it on purpose.

The chimp patriarch patrols the chimpanzee enclosure, round and round and round, on all fours, his flaming rump jutting well out and his tongue, also, stuck out at full length; on his tongue, he balances a great lump of the bright yellow shit produced by a fructarian diet. 'What's he doing that for, mummy?' Possibly a too scrutable sign. What *can* they be thinking of, in their chronic unemployment, their ideal housing, their life as objects of instruction and amusement.

There are nice monkey-houses and nasty monkey-houses. The nastier the monkey-house, the more exemplary the quality of ape life, the more they seem to be staging some sort of primates agitprop.

The baboon enclosure in Turin Zoo is like a penal colony. Twenty or thirty of the animals are housed in a perfectly round, shadeless, concrete arena with some branches of a dead tree in the middle in which one or two immobile baboons usually perch. These yellow baboons have curious, leonine muzzles with virtually concave noses, enraged eyes and well-barbered, bristling manes. Like crew cuts. Like convict cuts.

It was midday and very hot. In spite of, or because of, the heat, the baboons were engaged in almost ceaseless activity, some copulating, some masturbating, others stalking about the concrete floors. Many were engaged, with some tenderness, in delousing others and gobbled up the lice as they picked them off the pelts with mechanical relish. Often, the louse-pickers would form a busy chain of three or four baboons. Directly below us, for a terrace offers a God's eye view of this microcosm, we would see how white their flesh was as one baboon parted another's scanty fur, and how pitted with the bites of insects.

Their buttocks were so extravagantly in bloom they seemed to experience some difficulty in walking. The thin skin over the purple cushions of flesh was stretched so tight it shone like cheap satin and looked as if it would spout pus if it were lanced. This grotesque appendage appeared to cause some difficulties with hygiene, one way and another, there was a lot of shit around the baboon pit. All the despair emanating from this pit had a specifically anal quality. Genet.

Too much like Genet. Konrad Gesner observed baboons in the six-teenth century and noted: 'When he is signed to, he presents his arse.' A sexual offer, but also a general token of humility. Male baboons of low rank display female mating behaviour towards those of high rank. 'The smaller and younger male can obtain a good many advantages by submit-ting to a more powerful male. The superior male will protect his favourite against the attacks of other apes. When the stronger partner is about to take food away from the weaker, the young male will frequently offer himself sexually and in return will be allowed to keep the food.' (*Sex Life of the Animals*: Herbert Wendt).

Suddenly one baboon stopped delousing another and raised his head, as if all at once on the alert. Then he barked sharply. One after another, they all started it, after that – each stopped whatever he was doing until every baboon in the pit was barking in unison in the still heat of lunchtime, when the other animals in the zoo were fast asleep.

They went on barking for a long time, almost a minute. Then stopped. Three of them began to drearily work the treadmill for a while; the delousing parties began again; and one or two of them started to pick over the piles of straw-coloured shit on the floor of the arena, extract from it undigested husks, and eat them.

They order their monkey-houses more existentially than we do in Turin; grief, despair, degradation, defiance, hopelessness. A pecking order. A lice-picking order. Easy to see what *these* chaps are thinking of – such a pitch of rage they'd never be fobbed off with a Habitat lounge suite; I had thought that one baboon was buggering another but, when I looked more closely, I saw the one had climbed upon the other's back only in order to reach, to claw as high as he could up the perpendicular surface of the perfectly smooth concrete wall that surrounded them.

There was a lovely zoo in Verona, though, that seemed to have been designed by people who saw the beasts' side of things almost completely. At the entrance was a notice: 'Attention – this is the only chance most animals have to observe the behaviour of human beings. Make sure they receive a good impression.' The yaks had a hillside to run in, the vultures obscured themselves in the branches of real trees. Next to a somnolent tiger, another notice announced didactically: 'When a man kills a tiger, we call it sport; when a tiger kills a man, we call it ferocity.'

A small colony of monkeys inhabited a roomy cage full of greenery; all was not oppressively chic, but green and decent. As in a very good sanatorium, all was order and decency. A pair of baboons sat together on a bough like Darby and Joan. In an adjoining cage, a very nice black gibbon with a white beard did a few press-ups.

He swung to the front of his cage when he saw us and thrust both his long arms through the bars, opening and closing his black, wrinkled, distressingly humanoid hands but not quite as if he were begging for food, more as if beseeching us for something. And he must have known we would not give him food for there were notices everywhere: 'It is vehemently forbidden to feed the animals.' (When I was working at the zoo in Bristol, once, I saw a man feed a little rhesus monkey with a ball-point pen.) No. It seemed as if he wanted to hold hands.

When nothing was forthcoming from us, no reciprocal gesture, he reached right out to the grass that grew outside his cage, pulled up a few stalks, all that he could reach, and munched them. So it *was* goodies he was after! But his bowl was full of lots of delicious-looking fruit; did the grass outside his cage have a different flavour? Or perhaps, since we had not responded to him, he was saving face, was now showing us that of course he had not been reaching out to us at all, at all.

But, as we turned away from the cage, he thrust his hands out towards us again; and followed us, padding after us as far as his commodious cage would let him, and then he pursued us further and further with his dreadful speaking eyes as we went off.

The nicer the zoo, the more terrible.

When darkness falls and the crowds are gone and the beasts inherit Regent's Park, I should think the mandrills sometimes say to one another: 'Well, taking all things into consideration, how much better off we are here than in the wild! Nice food, regular meals, no predators, no snakes, free medical care, roofs over our heads . . . and, after all this time, we couldn't really cope with the wild, again, could we?'

So they console themselves, perhaps. And, perhaps, weep.

New Society, 1976

Animals in the Nursery

W.C. Fields wouldn't have thought there was anything odd about the natural affinity children seem to feel for animals. Both categories, infant and beast, are irrational, irresponsible, a prey to the most violent impulses of untamed instinct and, worst of all, damn them, cute. But sometimes it's almost as if children feel an unspoken alliance between themselves and animals against us adults: small children and pet animals, especially – both helpless passengers in a world where they're mercilessly subjected to a total caring process, fed, clothed, housed, loved, while denied all access to the apparatus of decision-making. They're allowed to exist, in the main, only as decorative appendages to other people's lives. Tough on kids. Tough on Puss. Tough on Rover.

Merchandisers for the child market realised early on that the formal division between beast and child is acquired, not inborn. It is learned late and is apt to be unlearned under stress. There are those dramatic cases in Freud: that small boy who thought he was a chicken, exhibited solidarity with chickens by only singing songs about them, crowing a lot and – bless the wee innocent and his totemic ambivalence – taking special pleasure in watching chickens being slaughtered for the pot.

Most writers for children latch on to and vulgarise that Garden of Eden world of wise, talking beasts, sentient flowers, sermonising stones, that children appear to inhabit effortlessly. Sexual unawakedness is a feature of this primitive world, where extraordinary miscegenations take place. An owl can marry a pussy cat, for example. A mouse, a bird and a sausage set up a *ménage à trois*.

Adults regress to this privileged place at peril. You can glimpse it, as in a broken mirror, in poor Christopher Smart's *Jubilate Agno*: 'Let Elimelech rejoice with the Horn-Owl who is of gravity and amongst my friends in the tower.' Or in the magnificent and pathetic confusion of schizophrenia. Like Louis Wain, the feline dement, who progressed inexorably from drawing picture books filled with cats in hats having tea and playing croquet to a total absorption in hallucinated abstractions of cats, all psychedelic around the edges, cats that looked like colour negatives of Persian rugs, cats that became the visible magic carpet of his own madness, bearing him off in perpetuity to a sinister kingdom of omnipotent cats.

Which, maybe, goes to show that the prelapsarian world of wise talking beasts is really but a hop, skip and a jump away from paranoia.

Yet children seem to relish the notion of their pets and toys sitting around after lights out, discussing their owners – all grist to the enormous mill of infant vanity. Pets are a little less convenient as objects of fantasy than toys. They have more autonomy. But books, and especially books for young children, tend to confuse animals and toys. They mix up the animate and the inanimate. This convention helps to introduce otherwise unfriendly animals into the nursery. Rupert Bear, Winnie the Pooh and D.C. Thompson's own, inimitable Biffo are obviously not bears as such, even if they constantly refer to themselves as bears and exhibit well-known bear tastes, such as a predilection for honey.

The toy both is, and is, not the animal it represents. Similarly, the animal in the various imaginative worlds created for children both is, and is not, the animal it purports to be. Its presence may be supported by a wealth of detail from the naturalist's notebook. But it is a modest and ingenuous article that knows its place. Like a good child itself, in fact.

The animals in Kipling's *Jungle Books*, who are allowed uncommon amounts of magnificence, ferocity, maturity, law, justice and sensibility, nevertheless conspire to bolster the esteem of the human child. Not one of them, not even the wisest, dare look Mowgli between the eyes. As Bagheera the panther says 'thou art wise – because thou hast pulled out thorns from their feet – because thou art a man.'

Mowgli has his cake and eats it. His Man credentials give him uncommon amounts of status in the jungle, and his impeccable Beast connections lend him all kinds of mythic resonances when he returns to his human kith and kin after his long exile in Eden. Kipling's jungle is in India, a country in which man was not necessarily created in God's image. Animals, therefore, may be credited with rather more autonomy than in England, even if they all lick Mowgli's arse like mad. His adopted human mother can stammer, when he returns home: 'My son! But it is no longer my son. It is a Godling of the Woods. Ahai!'

He is indeed a fine sight. 'As he stood in the red light of the oil lamp, strong, tall and beautiful, his long black hair sweeping over his shoulders, the knife swinging at his neck, and his head crowned with a wreath of wild jasmine, he might easily have been mistaken for some wild god of a jungle legend.' He got hold of the knife quite early on, so he could skin game with it. No doubt a chimpanzee gave him lessons in the elementary use of tools, though Kipling is anti-monkey, on the whole. Kipling seems to regard monkeys as a cruel parody on the human race, which was probably perpetuated by some particularly sardonic minor deity in the Hindu pantheon.

Mowgli's apprenticeship among the wise beasts turns him into a perfect Noble Savage. Kipling gives him an exemplary fate very different from the sad and terrible ones of the real wolf children, like Kasper Hauser, described by Lucien Malson. 'Children deprived too early of all social contact – those known as feral or "wolf" children – become so stunted in their solitude that their behaviour comes to resemble that of the lower animals.' Those wolf children the Reverend Singh painfully repatriated into human society were mute and brutish for a long time. The acquisition of a reasonable competence as a wolf is all a human being brought up as a wolf can reasonably hope to achieve. Kipling's animal impersonators are all the more spurious because their furry clothing is so lifelike. Real wolves and panthers do not venerate us at all. All fictional animals are imaginary animals. Adult writers take an unfair advantage of child/beast solidarity to perpetuate animal fables that are really systems of moral instruction.

Various conventions dominate the language of fictional talking beasts. Mowgli shows off: 'The Jungle has many tongues, *I* know them all.' But his conversations with bear, snake, panther, wolf and monkey suggest, not separate languages for each species – nor even for each genus – but only different dialects. The beasts use 'thee' and 'thou', and speak in ornate, rhetorical periods. Theirs is a stately kind of speech, considerably distanced from that of Stalky and Co. It is exactly the same as the speech of Kipling's villagers. It all reads like translations from Urdu.

Inventing different speech patterns for different animals is too arduous a task for most writers, in fact. It would mean taking the animals too seriously, and having to try to explain a great many complicated zoological things. There's a hypothesis of a basic animal lingo, fish, flesh and fowl Esperanto. The whole of animal creation converse together in a linguistic freemasonry that suggests the beast Tower of Babel is yet unbuilt. The whole heterogeneous global zoo is lumped together as 'animals' on one side of the fence, with 'human beings' on the other side. Nice, sympathetic children and the occasional favourite uncle – an eccentric savant such as Dr John Dolittle – are allowed as go-betweens.

This convention simplifies the bewildering variety of the world in a very consoling way; and consolation derived from imposing human forms on apparently mysterious creatures is probably part of the role played by these make-believe animals. Yet the arbitrary division between man and beast obliterates the fact that man himself is only another animal with particularly complex social institutions. And very often make-believe animals conspire to make the human world disappear altogether, the final revenge of the child/pet axis on their masters, especially when they are entirely creatures of the imagination, with no roots in biological actuality. Six-year-old Sybil Corbet defined Animal Land as the place 'where there are No People'. (For people, read grown-ups.) But her Animal Land is, at second look, rather a spooky place.

'Animal Land where there are No People is quite near, only you can't see it. It is a kind of Garden Cage, with the North Pole and the sea always roughling and wavy. In the summer they like to be hotter and hotter, and in the winter colder and colder. They live by the North Pole and in the leafy places near. It is always light there, always day, they climb the poles and always play.'

Sybil was a Late Victorian child, from, I should think, a rather sheltered background that she probably resented. In 1897 she published a little book of drawings of animals she'd invented herself. Autonomous, parentless, grotesque, these beasts inhabit a sort of landscaped maximum security prison where the keepers, like Kasper Hauser's keeper, deposit the food invisibly by night, and stay well out of the way the rest of the time. The animals chatter away like mad, of course, which is more than poor Kasper could do when they let him out. It is just the kind of place which W.C. Fields would approve of for keeping savage children and tame animals in.

New Society, 1976

In the Bear Garden

I see that Paddington Bear has now progressed from the storybook to that pitch of fame where he may be impersonated by ingenious actresses at the birthday parties of rich children while Paddington food, such as marmalade sandwiches, and appropriate games such as Hunt the Paddington Parcel, are played. Toyshops bulge with actual Paddington Bears differentiated from other toy bears by the requisite shaggy hat and duffle coat, with that tag around the neck bearing the message 'Please take care of this bear', that no child ought to resist.

Like several other storybook heroes, such as Pooh or the inexpressible Wombles, Paddington himself derives originally from a stuffed toy, but his passage through the printed page has worked a change on him. He has acquired a depth of character which has transformed him. This always seems to happen. The very first Womble of all, to whom I was once introduced, was nothing like the current Womble toys. He was a very small, snouted proto-animal whom only a child could have loved, and that for the sake of familiarity alone.

The Paddington Bear books, Michael Bond's seemingly endless saga of the adventures of this engaging beast, have endowed him with a very particular kind of personality. It is this fictional personality which is now re-created in the marketplace, at the earnest behest (presumably) of children everywhere, to the accompaniment of a resonant carillon of cash registers. As a market, children are sitting ducks.

Paddington is a toy who became real through the medium of fantasy. Now, a fantasy reconstituted, he is up for sale as plain toy again. At the moment, he's peaking. Top of the heap of the toy superstars. Will his success continue? Might the generic name for a toy bear cease, with the years, to be 'teddy' and become 'paddy' (leading to a whole toyland sub-mythology about Irish bears)?

The teddy bear has a singular genealogy. He appears to derive from a genuine bear cub, if the myth of his genesis has any truth. During a bear hunt in Mississippi in 1902, it's claimed, President 'Teddy' (get it?) Roosevelt refused to shoot a cub that crossed his line of fire. Photographs of the president, with the bear at his feet, led to the mass production of the nursery hero, who proved instantly beloved as soon as he arrived. The prototypes broke all records at the Leipzig fair in 1903.

I've seen a photograph of a teddy bear dating from about 1907. He is only about seven inches high, and has not yet acquired the portly shape of the post-Pooh teddy. E. H. Shepard modelled Pooh on his son's and Christopher Milne's own toys. But the pictured Pooh asserted his own identity, and this modified the appearance of later teddies. Paddington is hairier than most toy bears, and has dark ears. But I suspect this will not be enough to alter the whole idea of the toy bear.

Bereft of the signs of his identity as Paddington – and any child worth his salt will make short shrift of that hat, that duffle coat, that label – he will be, naked and unashamed, virtually indistinguishable from any other teddy bear again. It was the genius of A. A. Milne and E. H. Shepard to put Pooh into the world with nothing on. So any teddy bear could become Pooh at the whim of its owner, rather than degenerate into not-Pooh by losing the visible apparatus of Poohness.

But time passes and fashions change, even the conservative fashions of the toy-shop. And the differences between Paddington and Pooh are very striking.

For one thing, Paddington is a foreigner. A Peruvian bear. Pooh is as much a symbol of Englishness as Winston Churchill, with whom he shares the affectionate diminutive that caused me so much confusion as a child. Paddington is sharp as a tack; Pooh sweet, addle-pated, dozy, a poetaster, an idler.

Paddington is resolutely urban, living in the vicinity of the Portobello Road. He has a bank account, a tailor, rides in cars, engages in a middle-management lifestyle (though never, perish the thought, in productive labour; mustn't give kids the idea that life is hard). Pooh is a creature of pastoral, rarely straying from the confines of the Hundred Acre Wood and, for all his iconographic function for the middle class, he himself transcends class, just as Colin Clout, Hobbinol, Strephon and Phyllida do. Creatures generated by literary convention alone, the class struggle passes them by. They live the intuitive life of natural man (or bear – though Pooh, of course, is a most unnatural bear by any zoological reckoning).

Most significant of all, Paddington's familiars are neither children, nor toys, nor other domesticated animals. His friends aren't even young; they are middle-aged: the housekeeper, Mrs Bird, the antique dealer, Mr Gruber. He is a wise child in a bearskin, mixing with adults on equal terms, just as precocious children believe they do. But Pooh's familiars are the hallucinatory dream-child, Christopher Robin, a Wordsworthian creation, and the other denizens of the nursery (a specifically little boy's nursery – not a doll in sight), stuffed animals of all shapes, sizes and types. One of Milne's triumphs was to project the middle-class nursery of the 1920s as a locale for idyll, where the toys live on easy, egalitarian terms with their owner and engage in adventures which do not reflect, but parallel, real life.

Paddington's world is the real world, more or less. The bear moves in a position of privilege. His youth makes him naïve; but he is not innocent. Pooh's world is a privileged domain of perpetual childhood, an arcadia of boy and bear eternally in a wood together, a sunlit, late Georgian glade in which the toy stands for innocence and by simply existing, suggests its own demise.

When the toy's owner himself loses his innocence, then he will see the toy as just a rag, a bone and a hank of hair – no longer Arcadian companion and wise friend. He will always mourn the loss of that pristine vision.

I think that Paddington may *not*, in the long run, make it as one of the

tutelary spirits of the fiction of childhood. Charm Paddington may have
in spades, but mythic resonance – no. He is no more than the hot-shot
contemporary manifestation of the toy bear.

But Pooh, for a time at least, became the earthly reflection of the Great
Platonic Teddy Bear in the sky, whose shadow John Betjeman glimpsed
upon the brow of Archibald, his 'safe old bear':

> I used to wait for hours to see him move.
> Convinced that he could breathe.

Unlike Pooh, who had Christopher Robin, or Archibald, who had
Betjeman, Paddington has no child as mediator, who can display, by
mutual devotion, the touching innocence of childhood, or to show, by
growing up and discarding him, how brief and fleeting that innocence is,
and what a terrible ache of nostalgia will always torment us for the lost
dream. Paddington (rather honourably, in fact) is content to live his life as
a bear among men. But that means Paddington can never become a *real*
teddy bear. Teddy bears insist on remaining teddy bears as such; to maintain this mode of being, they demand that the man becomes a child.

Cara, mistress of the noxious father of the noxious Sebastian Flyte in
Brideshead Revisited, put her finger on it: 'Sebastian is in love with his own
childhood. That will make him very unhappy. His teddy bear, his nanny
. . . and he is 19 years old.' Flyte, thank God, is presumably long dead in
his Carthaginian cloister, disembowelled, I trust, by a boy, but the
Sebastian Flyte syndrome lingers on. Media personalities retain balding
teddy bears into middle age without a blush. It's as if they were convinced
that this fetish demonstrates their own purity of heart, or that the very possession of a teddy bear were some kind of magic wrinkle-remover.

Poor Pooh took the brunt of it. Pooh clubs at our oldest universities.
The ponderous, senior common room fun of a Latin translation of Pooh.
Gatherings of Pooh aficionados where grown men gather to solemnly play
such holy games as Poohsticks and sing in unison: 'The Hums of Pooh'.

But Pooh is not the only totemic teddy bear to preside over these half-
serious, half-playful, wholly nauseous re-creations of an illusory childhood. There is also the pastel-toned, nattily-trousered Rupert Bear. I have
seen men of over forty wearing Rupert Bear T-shirts! And there's that
anonymous tribal horde of picnicking teddy bears, featured in the ursine
national anthem – even if the song gave the game away in the last line:

> At six o'clock their mummies and daddies
>   will take them home to bed,
> 'Cos they're tired little teddy bears.

So the child *was* the bear *all the time*. Blessed prepubescent delusions.

Business acumen is certainly not one of Pooh's original characteristics. He must owe his recent access of it to his adoption by Walt Disney and subsequent emigration to the States, where he had a facelift. In doing so, he acquired too much worldly wisdom for his image, while the books themselves look more and more 'period', not the sort of thing you could dish out to infant Rastafarians in an inner-city primary.

Paddington's success in business is entirely predictable. He is clearly a bear with an eye to a quick buck. He may even be the first crack in the façade of the moral rectitude of the toy bear. Is the way now open for pro-letarian bears, rock-star bears, junkie bears equipped with tiny toy syringes. Godfather bears from Sicily who'll feel about spaghetti the way Pooh felt about honey . . . punk bears?

A suitable prototype for a punk bear might be the hero of *Grizzly,* the follow-up to *Jaws,* eighteen feet or thereabouts of muscle and ferocity, decimator of camp-sites. He has a face not unlike the mean features of those Russian wooden dancing bears, gorebellied, portentously clawed, whose limbs convulsively jerk when a string is pulled. Bears as malign as only bears from a country where bears come from could be.

Only a real child – not a grown-up in love with childhood – could empathise with a bear like that.

New Society, 1977

Little Lamb Get Lost

I'm sure Blake was wrong about the tigers of wrath being wiser than the horses of instruction. Apart from the question of the long-term efficacy of wrath as a tactic, hadn't Blake ever seen an angry horse? 'Imagine twenty thousand of them breaking into the midst of a European army, confound-ing the ranks, overturning the carriages, battering the warrior faces into mummy, by terrible jerks from their hinder hoofs.' The judicious, right-eous, fearless, unanimous anger of the Houyhnhnms; wrath after reflec-tion, anger in solidarity.

Also, I wonder if Blake had ever actually seen a live tiger. The fubsy beast that illustrates 'Tyger, Tyger' in the *Songs of Experience* looks as if he should have a zipper down his back and a pair of pyjamas inside him. I always rather hoped this was Blake's own ironic comment on the singu-larly unpleasant familiar of Nobodaddy whom he describes in the text,

'What immortal hand or eye, Dare frame thy fearful symmetry', from the picture, Walt Disney, it would seem.

But, of course, he is not talking about tigers at all. He is talking about something blind, furious, instinctual, intuitive, savage and *right*. If Blake's placid and didactic horses are delegates from the Fabian Society of the superego, his tiger is the representative of the unrepressed subconscious, even the id, possibly the mob storming the Bastille.

Of course, all this is patently unfair to real tigers (and, indeed, to the mob, whom I see more as Houyhnhnms). Tigers are no more savagely in tune with chaos than the rest of us. In their natural habitat, they are just part of the ecological juggling act, the 'prey-predator' triangle that so upsets sensitive children when they first come across it in biology text-books.

Tigers keep themselves to themselves unless provoked. Blake's libels upon them only shows how shit-scared mankind has always been of car-nivores. Its fear of its own subconscious is another matter.

We're scared of carnivores because, presumably, they would eat us, if they got half a chance. Which must be why we pusillanimously prefer to eat herbivores rather than the carnivores. Herbivores lie still on the plate. (The Chinese, admittedly, have an enviable sangfroid about dogs.) And why we retain a curious ambivalence towards the pig.

Even when it is not proscribed for socio-religious reasons, we all know how easily pork taints, and how speedily it can poison us. Probably because the pig eats anything he can get: tea leaves, ordure, cabbage stalks, its young, wellington boots and, if the farmer has been foolish enough to leave his feet inside them, feet plus socks.

The omnivorous pig has no equal at its promiscuous table but ourselves. Human flesh is supposed to taste like pork, at that. Maybe the taboo on pork, like the more universal one against eating daddy, is based on the notion that like should not eat like. Carnivores, flesh eaters, predators, are dumb beasts, and beastly. Herbivores are just dumb.

If we're scared of carnivores, then we patronise herbivores, especially when they come in small editions. 'Little lamb, who made thee?' It is a sufficiently fatuous question to ask a lamb. But would Blake, who (how-ever intermittently) possessed a sense of the ridiculous, have dared submit this poser to a grown sheep?

But I do not wish to appear hard on Blake, who in spite of these irra-tional projections, in general had a sound if sentimental line on animals. (If a robin red-breast in a cage put all heaven in a rage, one hopes heaven would be similarly aflutter at the caging of less attractive birds such as those vultures with the appearance and the habits of hanging judges.) Nevertheless, it is one of the more insinuatingly baleful effects of Judeao-

Christianity that we can't treat the beasts as, in any sense, equals, but persist in projecting on them either our own beastliness or our fantasies of innocence. In other cultures, beasts may have to bear a heavy burden of myth. But they are not forced to be exemplary.

I know someone who once hitched a ride in a bullock cart in the Hindu Kush. As night drew on, they were still far from home, and the driver began to belabour his bullock unmercifully around the head and shoulders, in a futile attempt to get it to speed up. 'Oh, don't do that,' said our traveller, an English animal lover. 'Can't you see the poor bullock is tired?' 'Of course he's tired,' snapped the driver. 'He's only human, like the rest of us.'

It used to give me a deep sense of inner peace, in the Far East, to know I was among people who had never built into their cultural apparatus some notion of anthropocentricity, because they thought they'd been made in the image of a god. Not that this makes them any nicer to animals, of course. That isn't the point.

People treat the animals they have in their power according to their expectations of their treatment by people who have power over them. (As, indeed, men do their wives.) But it does put our co-tenancy of the world with the teeming multitudes of furred, clawed and feathered things on a different existential basis. It means you can't ponce about like the lord of creation. There, swinging from a tree or perched on a branch, but for a genetic quirk, goes one. Or, if an adherent of one of the more logical forms of reincarnation, one goes.

Our relation to snakes has been irretrievably distorted by the Book of Genesis, though snakes seem to cause an almost universal psychic ripple. It's due, no doubt, to the venomous quality of some of them, and the gratuitously phallic aspect of all of them, especially when poised to strike. They suggest, as do certain fungi, that somebody in that design centre in the sky has a very dirty mind and a concomitant Puritan streak. Our attitude to snakes combines a rational apprehension and a strong element of psycho-sexual pathology.

It is from this precarious fusion that the whole concept of the beastliness of beasts springs. There is a basis of rational fear (based, properly, on respect), of which, since it is real, you need not be afraid because you can take steps to deal with it. And there is internalised orchestration of that fear, helped along by centuries of bad relations with the beasts, which is far more difficult to tackle, since it is nothing to do with animals at all.

We return, in fact, to the notion of the carnivorous animal as id. Look no further than the connotations of the word, 'wolf'. In the wild, wolves have impeccable domestic institutions. Not only are they fine mothers but, as Mowgli, Romulus and Remus will attest, also excel at fostering.

They are certainly less sexually voracious than the rabbit, but if Red Riding Hood had found a bunny in granny's bed, all it would have meant was that it was Easter. Yet the wolf is virtually synonymous with 'id', and with a particularly bestial type of ravening lust.

All wolves do, to acquire this reputation, is simply be prone (if they get half a chance) to bite us. If they are not quickly stopped, they will then, as will any dog whose teeth aren't rotten, gobble you up.

Nobody likes to be reduced to the status of comestible. But there is more to it than the indignity of turning into a factor in the prey–predator triangle when we thought we were half-way between ape and angel, and so out of the running as regards dogs' dinners. Dogs are more like wolves than cats are like lions. Some dogs – and I recall certain uneasy encounters with police dogs – are very like wolves indeed. Our relations with dogs are even more ambivalent than our relations with pigs, because less honest. At least we simply *eat* pigs. We don't practise emotional imperialism on them.

Rabies may be transmitted by any warm-blooded mammal, including bats. But though it was a boy badly bitten by a rabid wolf on whom Pasteur carried out the first successful treatment, it is a disease synonymous with mad dogs.

Rabies is both the beastliest of maladies and the malady of beasts. It is the *ne plus ultra* of the sickness unto death; not only, if untreated, always fatal, but also it transforms you into the object of the darkest fears of beastliness – a nightmare come true. And it is transmitted to you by the furry innocent in your home and heart.

Worst, most atavistic of all, it is spread by oral contact, reawakening all manner of primal terrors of the fatal kiss, the vampire's love bite, the sharp teeth of beasts inimical to man. One or two recent thrillers, and a striking movie, have exploited the considerable amount of pathological eroticism that may be mined out of rabies. It suggests that the 'beast in man' thesis of innate human nastiness is, alas, making a strong comeback. All the stuff about the inimical beast is projection. Animals are perfectly indifferent to us, unless under certain circumstances of enforced or voluntary intimacy. Even then, they are usually benign, though I can't think why. They never behave in a beastly fashion, unless abused. Or rabid.

What do you do with a mad dog, after all? You shoot it. The madness of dogs is of a different order of ideas from the wrath of tigers. We know we're right to shoot mad dogs. In our hearts, we always knew Rover wanted to get his own back; now he comes slavering in for the kill. The rabies novels all make great play of the putsch of pets, the breaking of the bond between man and domestic animal in an orgy of slaughter, as if the only way to rid ourselves of beastliness was to rid ourselves of beasts.

I only trust that this wave of Gothic dread may be usefully harnessed to halt the advance of the virus. But that is an enterprise in the domain of reason. Rabies, like bubonic plague and leprosy, is a sickness that bears an obfuscating freight of myth with it.

But should one logically extend the theory of equal rights of all creation to the virus? The virus does not know what harm he does. Or is the virus our common enemy? That lays the way wide open for a kind of secular Manicheism of which the microbiologists are the prophets. That way lies madness, and not the madness of the unfortunate dogs, either.

As it happens, the only person I can think of who genuinely saw no rational division between man and everything else was as mad as a hatter, and a religious maniac, to boot. It was as if the church had played a dirty trick on Christopher Smart in Bedlam:

> For I have a providential acquaintance with men who bear the name of animals.
>   'For I bless God to Mr Lion Mr Cock Mr Cat Mr Talbot [turbot?] Mr Hart Mrs Fysh Mr Grub and Miss Lamb.
> Everything – animal, vegetable, mineral, fish, fowl and good red herring – rejoices in the lamb, and no questions asked; like who made thee, or whence came we, or whither goeth we.
>   Let Ross, house of Ross, rejoice with Great Flabber Dabber Flat Clapping Fish with hands.

New Society, 1978

All Creatures Great and Small

There used to be a terrific schools' broadcasting programme when I was a kid; it was called, *How Things Began*, and purported to be actuality transmissions from our roving reporter in the prehistoric past. On one ocassion, transmission terminated abruptly when, dropping his microphone with a shrill cry, he fled, pursued by dinosaur. David Attenborough would never lose his cool like that.

Life on Earth is the apotheosis of the lantern-slide lecture, a *How Things Began* with moving pictures. It is in fact, a sort of natural history version of movies like *Gone with the Wind* or *Intolerance*, a smasheroo life-science epic that takes as its scenario the entire story of life upon this planet. There are still a few hundred million years to go, too.

Call it the rebirth of awe. Impossible not to gasp with delighted amaze-
ment as, every Tuesday, regular as clockwork, Attenborough effortlessly
produces fresh astounding rabbits from the evolutionary hat, accompanied
by a refulgently Korngoldesque score, in the wonder of living colour. I am
sure impressionable children think he is God.

There is certainly a strong sense of an omniscient and omnipresent
Attenborough, whose eye is on both cat-fish and sparrow, who was there in
the beginning, analysing the primordial slime, who is with us now, lovingly
watching the baby croclets peer between the fangs of the mother crocodile.
I am sure his own apotheosis as the guardian angel of terrestrial creation has
been effected unintentionally; but it was bound to happen because of the
organisation of the series of terms of evolutionary chronology.

His presence as link-man is not reflected in the actual contents of the
programmes. They are not intended as accounts of Attenboroughs adventures in the wonderful world of wild-life. But, because Attenborough, as
the inquiring representative of homo sapiens, is trying so hard to take a
back seat to the beasts, he comes across even more strongly as the guiding
principle himself. The beasts can't speak for themselves so he has to do it
for them and he knows more about them than they do themselves. The
exigencies of the shooting schedule give him a lack of actual physical
continuity; he never wears the same shirt twice. So he pops up, now up
to his knees in a hot spring, next moment in polar waste, with a magical
ubiquity.

But the series requires just this kind of link-man, a specialist who can
pass for a enthusiast, an amateur 'in the true sense', as they say. A lover. A
hero. It would have had quite a different effect if they had got a bird man
to do the birds, a snake man to do the snakes. *Life on Earth* is a romance
about evolution, not an Open University course in elementary zoology.
Therefore dissections are out, though some of the wee beasties on the
screen must have anybody with O-level biology itching for the knife.

And Attenborough's transcontinental odysseys, the time and effort in
the making of the series, the knowledge that it is a massive technical
achievement – all these are part of the romance, too. So is all the back-up
slow-slow-slow motion camera work, technological marvels in the service
of natural marvels. All this highly mechanised awe in the face of nature is
a mite disingenuous; the programme demonstrates just how much we
have mastered nature by the fact it has been made.

There is also a curious 'now it can be told' atmosphere about it all.
Attenborough is much too sophisticated to say things like: 'At last nature
unlocks her secrets.' But the idea is there, all the same. It is all disconcertingly like a summing-up or a conclusion; almost an end-of-term report.
Messiaen's *Quartet for the End of Time* might have been good theme music.

The feeling, to this layperson at least, that one is being introduced to a finite body of knowledge, that this is the revealed and final truth, is only slightly tempered by Attenborough's humble acknowledgement to the birds, that they are still the only ones who know the logic governing migration and they're not letting on.

Life on Earth bears an intriguing relation to last year's wonderful recreation of Darwin's voyage on *The Beagle*, something like the relation of *The Godfather* to the second part in which Brando does not appear. Darwin, unseen but acknowledged, hovers over *Life on Earth*; it's the outline format which he is very largely responsible for. Both series apply the full decorative resources of Hollywood, swooning strings and all, to the wonders which surround us; but the Darwin series was rich in interpersonal relations, in intellectual conflict, in tall ships battling with head winds, and was distanced from us by its period setting. It was a popular drama about the birth of a scientific theory.

In *Life on Earth*, that theory – evolution – is itself the drama, the birds, beasts, little fishes, the micro-organisms co-star with Man the Inquirer. Curiously, in a context of scientific objectivity, the scaly and feathered actors, the very blobs themselves, are thrust into dynamic roles; the episodes have titles like: 'The conquest of the waters', 'The lords of the air'.

In the eponymous book of the film, Attenborough says how one mustn't think that species ever decided to evolve. Yet we live in functionalist times, so a frog will 'give itself a varnish' from wax-producing cells on its body, and Attenborough talks about 'that major insect invention: flight'. Scientific objectivity offers no real refuge from the ideology of the age; in the *Life on Earth* book, it is a shock to come across this kind of mercantile anthropomorphism: 'The appearance of flowers transformed the face of the world. The green forest now flared with colour as the plants advertised the delights and rewards they had on offer.' One senses evolution as the project of the life force.

Attenborough, being a man of the twentieth century, scrupulously avoids the kind of anthropomorphism that finds sermons in stonefish. The anonymous author of *Half Hours in the Tiny World,* Victorian entomology for tots, animadverts on the subject of flies: 'Help every helpless, be it a drowning fly or a brother floundering through the difficulties of life's first tasks.' This sort of thing hasn't been on for years. Attenborough will show you how the fly *works;* slot it in its place in what, as the weeks pass, is looking more and more like a revamped twentieth-century version of the Great Chain of Being; and move smartly on to the next item.

When he tells us that the hag-fish has no backbone, he is casting no aspersions on the moral fibre of the hag-fish. No use asking: 'But what is it *for,* Daddy?' There isn't any answer because there isn't any question. But that doesn't stop those nervous whimpers in the dark – does it – nor, if not the search for an answer, then at least the attempt to pose the right questions. It is not the brief of any romantic epic to ask questions, however – unless they will be posed in episode 13, when Man makes his appearance.

Yet, as a result of this loving cool that asks nothing of other life-forms than us except that they be, the metaphorical implications of the lifestyle of individual species stand out in unstressed relief for those whose cultural training forces them to see them. (This is either the blessing or the bane of those on the arts side.) Evolutionary culs-de-sac such as the dinosaur, with us only in his relics, or the ostrich must surely strike a sympathetic chord in any human heart. But from all the early episodes of *Life on Earth* the unnerving message comes loud and strong – that the mission of all creatures great and small is to propagate their kind. Engender and die. And species longevity goes to those who propagate most efficiently. It is a disturbing thought for any fan of Malthus.

Once the butterfly has mated, its wings drop off. 'Bye, bye, butterfly. 'Its purpose done, it dies,' says Attenborough in a voice of brooding tenderness. In the book of the film, he is even more explicit; certain female spiders post-coitally snack on their mates – 'But in terms of the success of the species as a whole, that individual disaster is of limited consequence: he lost his life after, not before, he had completed his purpose.'

Nietzsche got off on Darwin, didn't he? Attenborough waxes positively Wagnerian about the salmon, who circumnavigate the globe and then return, swimming strongly and witlessly upstream, to the gravel beds where they were spawned, in order to rip one another apart, mate and die. Our intermediary with the life force surveys a river full of dead and rotting fish with the air of one surveying a battlefield of fallen heroes.

But it is the ants that make my blood run cold. Busy, busy, busy; and what for? To keep the whole ant-universe going; to ensure that the timeless eternity of the ants, of which the whole is the summation, no more nor less, of its parts, can carry on in the same way that it did at the time when our roving reporter was frightened by the dinosaur. Ants are too much like us. It was horrible. Attenborough on the ant hill suddenly turned into Virgil in Hell.

And yet the tenor of the whole thing is: that evolution is not the same as progress, that all living things have equal rights. The whole movement of *Life on Earth* is towards exorcising terror and mystery from our relations with our furry, finny, scaly and mucus second cousins twice removed.

The programme about fish was a particularly striking example of this kind of exorcism; or perhaps it is censorship. In the Middle Ages, they hypothesised that the ocean was the mirror image of dry land, in which everything found its own strangely barnacled re-definition. And, indeed, the Bosch-like inhabitants of the deep swam on to the small screen like vile emblems of our lusts, our depravities, our endeavours. Oh God, the gulper, no more than a swimming, voracious mouth; the aptly named ghoul, with its Gothic, poisoned spikes; the shark whose nose has turned into a saw; the spherical, bewhiskered ostrocod. (That's what it sounded like, at least.)

To these satirical monsters, Attenborough extended the same loving kindness as he had done to the Disneyesque, harmless frogs. Quite right, too, of course. It is not for any life scientist to acknowledge these strange beings straight away as the nameless things that glide through the mind before sleep. How did they get out of the ocean bed into the nightmare – that's one inadmissible question.

Life on Earth is dedicated to pure wonder and the dissemination of fact. It suffers, obviously, the limitations of the grandiose simplifications that are necessary to all forms of popular science. 'The wonderful beauty of all the works of creation . . . may help to give us some idea of the yet more wonderful power of the Creator, from whom all beauty proceeds.' – *Silver Wings and Golden Scales*, anonymous, undated, circa 1870. It is curious to see how the realisation there is no Grand Designer after all has not affected the notion of the Grand Design; the Sunday evening repeat of *Life on Earth* acquires the air of a sermon for our time.

New Society, 1979

Song and Show

Now is the Time for Singing

Says Nell to the farmer it's a fine summer's day,
While the rest of the farmers are off making hay,
Come to the barn where we won't be seen,
And the two of us start working our threshing machine.

O Nell she stepped forward and into the house,
The boss got the harness and strapped her right on,
Nell took the handle and turned on the steam
And the two of them start working the threshing machine.

O six months being over and nine coming on
Nell's skirt wouldn't meet nor her drawers wouldn't go on;
It's under her oxter like a young fairy queen,
I will have you transported for your threshing machine.

These verses from the traditional song 'The Threshing Machine', still very
widely sung by country singers all over the British Isles, can be dated by
reference to the fourteenth edition of the Encyclopaedia Britannica:

> A workable threshing machine was invented late in the eighteenth
> century, and was gradually coming into use early in the nineteenth; it
> was driven by water or wind power, sometimes by horse labour, and
> later by steam. But it was not until the 30s of the nineteenth century
> that steam began to be applied at all extensively to agriculture.

The study of the traditional song of these islands is something of a liberal
education in itself; this song may well contain what is one of the earliest
instances of the use of imagery derived from modern technological
appliances.

One is perhaps reminded of the pylon poetry between the great wars;
or perhaps of the 'keen, unpassion'd' beauty of Rupert Brooke's great

machine. Or again, perhaps not.

And of course you also learn very quickly if you listen to any traditional songs at all, that the English have been telling big lies about themselves for years.

During the latter part of the nineteenth century and the earlier part of the twentieth, the English middle classes foisted two enormous myths on the whole wide world. Myth A – that of the cold unemotional Englishman who would rather have a good dinner, or a good game of cricket than . . . h'm, clears throat, blushes, stutters, 'you know what'. And no wonder, when one contemplates Myth B – the cold, unemotional Englishwoman, behind whose twinset and double strand of pearls beats a heart bound up inextricably with the welfare of her Scotch terrier.

However, while John was out empire-building and occasionally penning tongue-tied letters home to his girlfriend in which he referred to her as 'old girl', no doubt, the anti-middle-class figure of Jack, unencumbered by the white man's burden and the benefits of a public school education, was engaged in totally other pastimes, with the willing aid of his own girl.

> My father and mother
> In yonder room do lie,
> Enjoying of one another,
> Then why not you and I?
> Enjoying of one another
> Without a fear or doubt;
> Then roll me in your arms, love,
> And blow the candle out.

In the English tradition, this song goes to an enormously virile tune that strides up and down the scale like a man in big boots. It is one of the great love songs in the English language and it expresses no yearning, no phony idealisation, no sentimentality, but a great warmth, a kind and easy loving that accepts men and women as they are with no fogging notions of sin or shame. And there is no room for regret when the young man goes away:

> It was six months ago and after,
> Six months ago today,
> He wrote to me a letter
> Saying he was going away;
> He wrote to me a letter
> Without a fear or doubt,
> Saying he would never return again
> To blow the candle out.

And that's that, and there's no point in grieving. On the printed page,
this looks like a piece of doggerel; sung, it becomes a celebration of sexual enjoyment, a piece of complete emotional honesty. For the texts are
nothing without the tunes, which give them a further dimension of meaning. The whole – the song – does not exist except in performance. Yet,
from the words of the song, which is meaningful for us today when electricity has replaced candle power in all but the most primitive or hyper-
sensitive of surroundings, one can see the frankness and directness and the
human warmth so much English song expresses.

Just as the frankness and directness of 'Three Maidens A-milking Did
Go' is meaningful for us today, though young girls no longer go to the
greenwood with any but the most symbolic of milking pails.

> Three maidens a-milking did go,
> Three maidens a-milking did go,
> And the wind it did come forth and the wind it blew about,
> And it blew their milking pails to and fro.
>
> They met with some young man they knew,
> They met with some young man they knew,
> And they asked him if he had any skill
> In catching a small bird or two.
>
> O yes, I've a very good skill;
> O yes, I've a very good skill;
> So it's come along with me to yonder flowery tree
> And I'll catch you a small bird or two.
>
> So away to the greenwood went they,
> And away to the greenwood went they,
> And he tapped on the bush and the bird it did fly in,
> Just a little above her lily-white knee.
>
> Here's a health to the bird in the bush,
> Here's a health to the bird in the bush,
> And we'll drink down the sun and we'll drink down the moon
> Let the people say little or much.

Forget the contemporary idiom: the 'bird in the bush' has nothing to
do with girls up trees. This song has a tune of incomparable, melting
beauty; it deals with Lawrence's sort of sexual tenderness.

Sam Larner, the octogenarian Norfolk singer, speaks like a song, it is his idiom of speech: 'Lovely! I wished . . . that's all gone from me now and that's the reason I don't care if I live or die now, cause that was the . . . one of the main things I lives for, cause I loved it.'

Here's a health to the bird in the bush . . .

Larner spent most of his working life on the sea – it very nearly killed him; yet it gives a false picture of him as a singer to call him a 'singing fisherman'. In the country, worthwhile singers are treated with respect and admiration; they and their repertoires were – and in some places still are – the major sources of entertainment in places away from large towns, and so they were cherished and their whims were pandered to and some of them were quite prima donna-ish.

Larner was at one time a star performer at fishermen's concerts up and down the eastern seaboard and like all country singers, he is a splendid conscious performer, with spectacular timing and control. Your country singer is by no means just some one who gets up to give a song, all casual-like, as he sups his beer.

Songs that came from his father, from crews of ships he worked, from friends and acquaintances – Sam Larner sings them in a plain, straightforward 'let me tell you a tale' way. He has a repertoire of about sixty-five songs, which seems large enough by any standards but those of the major traditional singer.

Another, and a finer, East Anglian singer, Harry Cox – surely the best of all living singers in the English tradition – has so many songs that people have lost count. His father was visited by some of the early collectors, the pioneers who went out to record and note down words and music from country singers so the songs could be preserved for our entertainment and enlightenment. One day Cox senior told a collector he wasn't going to sing any more, he was going to retire; however, he had taught all his songs to his boy Harry, who would henceforth take over his position in the community. Whether or not this story is apocryphal, it shows the pride and sense of artistic responsibility of the country singer.

To hear the present Harry Cox is to be immediately aware that one is listening to an artist, and a conscious artist. He does not sing with his heart on his sleeve, as a grotesque parody of folksong like Joan Baez does, he sings from the heart. And a savage song about the brutal ill-treatment of a young boy by a ship's captain:

> With my marline spike I cruelly gagged him,
> Because I could not bear to hear his cries

is grim and sardonic and frightening. Or he sings about an encounter between a sailor and an Aboriginal Australian girl:

> Her hair hung in ringles, her colour was black,
> She said, kind sir, watch me float on me back
> On the streams of my native Australia.

and the inevitable happens and she's left with something very concrete
indeed to think about on the shores of her native Australia:

> When six months was over and nine being done,
> This beautiful babe she brought forth a fine son;
> But where was the father? he couldn't be found,
> And she cursed the day she lay on the ground
> On the shore of her native Australia.

And the intervening verses are warm and loving and illustrate precisely
Miller's distinction between obscenity and pornography. Or he sings
about something as far away from us in time as the hardships of the con-
victs on the cruel shores of Tasmania, 'Van Diemen's Land', and history
lives because the people have remembered it with such vividness.

His style is a compound of subtle and beautiful rhythms; there is a marvellous pulse to his singing and he modulates the tune of a song from verse
to verse and decorates, with great taste and economy, the basic melodic
line so that it grows with organic logic, with the rightness and inevitability
of a natural growth. His musical personality – and it is his musical personality only which he imposes on a song, he never allows his own emotional
responses to a song to come through but lets it speak for himself – is part
of the expression of his songs.

And this style of the performer is one of the things that makes folk song
a unique and vital form. The performer is something more than the interpreter of his material; he is helping to formulate it basically. One learns
more about the importance of style from hearing Cox, or traditional
singers from other parts of the British Isles like Davy Stewart, the wild and
passionate Scots tinker singer, or Joe Heaney, the virtuoso singer, than one
ever will learn from looking at books.

That Cox, though, who does represent the best of the present English
country tradition, can only be heard in unsatisfactory gobbets here and
there on anthology records is a crying shame. He should have an LP to
himself – or preferably, a whole series of LPs. God knows, enough
material has been recorded from him. But real folk song has been somewhat ignored in the late hootenanny boom; and hootenanny music, as
commercial folk music was recently christened (or foke, which is what
you hear at fokenites) is about as closely related to authentic traditional
music as trad, that happily defunct phenomenon, was to the jazz of King
Oliver. Or even less so.

You can hear Joe Heaney on record, which is a great thing. He is from Galway, and represents a tradition which is something other than the English. It is far more complex in structure, with decoration (i.e. grace notes, vocal twiddles that enrich a song's musical meaning) that is almost baroque in its elaboration; yet never seems imposed from the outside, but is structurally essential to the final impact. And he demonstrates the almost magical ability of a great traditional singer to create a new whole out of elements of text and tune.

He sings a song called 'The Bonny Bunch of Roses', which is typical of many pieces of pro-Napoleon propaganda, which circulated among the pagentry of the British Isles at the time of and shortly after the Napoleonic wars. (We all felt pretty sorry for Napoleon at the time and some of us felt especially sorry, as he seemed to them a better bet as ruler of England than those we had then ensconced on the throne.)

The text of 'The Bonny Bunch of Roses' is the typical product of a hack broadside writer, and the words have obviously not been much altered by the people, as was their usual custom with the texts of broadsides. Broadsides were collections of verses, usually pretty bad doggerel, but sometimes initially based on popular country songs much as record companies might now 'cover' a hit; these collections were sold up and down the country for a few pennies, by peripatetic ballad sellers, and were one of the means by which songs circulated throughout the country and new songs arrived for the people to do as they pleased with.

In Heaney's text, there are an astonishing number of high-flown infelicities and some of it verges almost on Macgonagallese:

> By the margins of the ocean one pleasant evening in the
>   month of June
> When those feathered, warbling songsters their liquid
>   notes did sweetly tune,
> There I overheard a female, and on her features signs of
>   woe,
> Conversing with young Bonapart concerning the bonny
>   bunch of roses, oh.

'The bonny bunch of roses' probably refers to the red coats of the victorious British army; or it might refer to the United Kingdom, England, Ireland, Scotland.

Heaney sings totally without sentiment. His tune is sharply angular, almost spiky; he stylises it through superb control and this very free, very beautiful decoration; and the song takes wing from its origins, because a powerful lament on the vanity of human wishes.

> O mother dear, I bid adieu, I now lie on my dying bed,
> If I'd lived I'd been more clever but now I droop my
>   youthful head,
> And while my bones lie mouldering and the weeping
>   willows o'er me grow,
> The name of young Napoleon will enshrine the bonny
>   bunch of roses oh . . .

From the song, which is a conversation between young Napoleon and his mother detailing Bonaparte's ambitions and their defeat, and his son's tragically early death before he could avenge his father, one learns all one need to know about the historical context of the song for it is not really about Napoleon and the Napoleonic Wars at all, not when Heaney sings it, say, in a folk-song club in 1964; his song is about how all brave men must finally meet their Moscows, and how all worldly ambition is finally brought to nothing.

And a singer not born in the tradition as Heaney was, but who has devoted time and love and skill to the study of traditional style can finally give this ultimate dimension of meaning to a song. A. L. Lloyd, the doyen of non-traditional folk singers, does it with every song he sings. And a young man from County Durham, Louis Killen, whose style embraces the elaboration of the Irish technique and the rhythmic directness of the English one, sings 'The Bonny Bunch of Roses' (and a deal else) with power and authority, and wakes the same echoes.

A. L. Lloyd was one of the major figures in the recent revival of interest in folk song, which is now a *fait accompli*; and what the best of the revival singers are doing is making a tradition that was once the perquisite of a certain section of the community available for us all to enjoy and be moved by and learn to express ourselves in.

Yet much of what is loosely termed revival singing is curiously irrelevant to the real why and wherefore of authentic folk song. The form of folk song is unique, as I've said; it is unique in the seminal importance of the performer, and his attitude to his material in its lack of sentimentality as a means of expression, and its directness and human warmth.

Until the last few years, the tradition was the basic means of creativity available to most of the people in these islands, for mass social mobility is only a recent thing, and really, folk song represents the great body of non-intellectual achievement of England, Ireland, Scotland.

It is beautiful and expressive by conscious design, not by accident. A song is not an *objet trouvé*, no matter where you find it. Its simplicity is deceptive. It is very difficult to sing initially with the proper impact, even with texts and tunes learned from recordings of singers – without love and knowledge of the forms which produced these songs, it is all too easy to produce a hideous, rootless hybrid with bits of an imperfectly apprehended American tradition (which, again, is quite a different kettle of fish) obscuring all.

And it is well-nigh impossible to write convincingly in the style of a folk song, just as it is well-nigh impossible to write convincingly in poetry of any kind if you haven't got the specific sort of talent. And however great your initial poetic talent, you've got to write in a very well-defined mode if you want to produce something that sounds, smells and feels like a folk song. Most of the 'composed' folk song one hears so much about these days are species of political rant that are more bastard descendants of Brecht and Weill (whose hypothetical parents, screaming in horror, would disown them) than anything to do with folk song. Even a great poet like John Clare, who was a countryman, too, came a cropper when he tried to imitate folk song lyrics, probably because he had not treated the form with sufficient seriousness.

And again, many of the most pleasing verbal effects in a song are not the result of one person's creative talent, but the cumulative talents of years, even centuries, working over a song. And not only did they have a certain sort of verbal creativity, but it was closely linked with a musical creativity, and a working technical knowledge of how some phrases are poetry but unsingable and others become poetry when sung.

Even so, it is possible to find great beauty — by any standards — in the texts alone, even apart from their beauty, as a skeleton has beauty of its own. The most usual form of expression is that through pictorial images of great clarity:

> I leant my back against an oak
> Thinking it was a trusty tree
> But first it bent and then it broke
> And so did my false love to me.

and:

> The week before Easter, the dawn bright and clear,
> The sun it shone brightly and keen blowed the air,
> I went down to the forest to gather wild flowers
> But the forest would yield me no roses.

and:

> The trees they grow so high and the leaves they grow so green
> The day is past and gone, love, that you and I have seen;

It's a cold winter's night, and I must bide alone
For my bonny lad is young but a-growing.

and:

Her hair it was three-quarters long,
The colour of it was yellow;
She's wrapped it round his middle so small
And carried him home to Yarrow.

The extraordinary image of this last – the girl letting down her long, yellow hair and wrapping her dead lover up in it, to protect him or to keep him warm – we know to be one created by the working over of a text.

The song it comes from, the classic Scots ballad 'The Dowie Dens of Yarrow', is of some considerable antiquity; and these verses seem to have been transposed into it at an early date from another song from the times when young men themselves had long, yellow hair, for the song concerned a girl who pulled her drowned lover out of the river by his long, yellow hair. It was obviously something that cried out to be worked over.

It is also quite clearly not a naturalistic image. It is meant to work on an allusive and symbolic level; as is the sympathetic magic of the oak that bends and breaks. The young man in 'The Week Before Easter' also quite obviously did not go down to the forest to pick any wild flowers at all; the erotic symbolism of folk poetry makes great play with flowers of all kinds, especially roses.

Down the green meadows where the young girls go,
Gathering flowers just as they grow,
She gathered her flowers and away she came
But she left the sweetest rose behind.

And so she's going to have a baby, and she's so unhappy she wants to die. And even with the moving sparseness of the language of this text, one must realise that it is the tune which is an elegiac, lamenting one, and the gentle unsentimental singing of the English gypsy, Tom Willet, that gives it true poetic life.

Yet the richness and allusiveness of imagery in folk poetry, which reaches on through singing almost on a subliminal level, means one's appreciation of the mode grows with one's knowledge. And so, naturally, does one's imagination, one's ability to think in images oneself, one's sensibility and one's perceptions, because folk song is an art, and these are the things all the arts do.

And because folk song is easy to understand, you don't have to jump through any intellectual hoops to receive the dubious lump of sugar of a meaning at the end, which you have to do when 'Old Possum hits you with a teaball' (in Kenneth Rexroth's pregnant phrase.)

The importance of the folk song revival is really the recreation and, through it, the emergence of a meaningful art form which can be appreciated by and can immeasurably enrich anyone with ears and a heart. The revival is in such an infant stage that it has only yet produced a handful of singers who have worked hard enough at the form to learn the authentic magic that transmutes old songs from books into songs freshly new-minted through themselves, and has so far produced only the most minor new songs that have anything like the elements of honesty and imaginative beauty of the old ones.

But – regardless of what *Melody Maker* called the folk boom – folk song has now been emancipated from its function of pressure valve of the creative urge of the anonymous masses, as jazz music was in its time so emancipated; and we can all appreciate it for what it is and what it can be and what it can mean to us.

Nonesuch Magazine, 1964

Bob Dylan on Tour

Performing, he's nothing but a shadow to look at, thin and black-clad and linear, a Beardsley hobgoblin. The little pointy face, so white it is almost blue in the spotlight, is shadowed by a baroque mound of curls. His gestures are harsh, angular and sketchy – insolent, asexual, frequently reminiscent of those of the Scarlet Hex Witch of the comic books. He seems at times to be sending up the overtly sexual writhings of the English pop stars of the new wave (i.e. Jagger, etc.)

Bang, bang, drums, organ, amplified guitar. He does a black and white devil dance clutching a black and white amplified guitar and you can hardly hear a word he's singing. Maybe this is part of the plot. But it's alright, ma, he's only howling.

Thus Bob Dylan, erstwhile Wonder Kid of Protest, demonstrated to packed and baffled theatres up and down the British Isles that he is approaching an artistic maturity of a most unexpected kind.

Once, he was embraced by innocent liberals as a folk-singer whose songs ('The Times They Are A-Changing', 'Masters of War', 'The

Lonesome Death of Hattie Carroll') pointed committed youth's way to an understanding of the twentieth-century predicament. And this predicament might be solved just by singing them. It was a comfort. People like comforts. But maybe comfort doesn't finally help all that much.

Dylan is no longer comfortable. The fat-cheeked, Huck Finn-capped youth of the early records who dealt in idealism and excruciating do-it-yourself romantic imagery (white doves, mountains, seas, rainbows – and, for God's sake, clowns) – has grown up into the first ever all-electronic, all existential rock and roll singer. He's singing for Kafka, Kierkegaard, Dostoevsky and all the boys down home on Desolation Row.

His singing is exceedingly stylised. He never hits a note true. He chews vowels like ju-jubes. He cries like a wolf (or like Howlin' Wolf). But what matters most is the songs.

Which now have a tough urgency, a strained sense of critical involvement with twentieth-century America and a kind of moral satire which is akin to Dean Swift and William Burroughs. Certainly, he's still got a long way to go on a peculiarly harsh and unrewarding path; but his beginnings are spectacular. The best of the songs on his latest all-electric LP, *Highway 61 Revisited*, songs such as 'Like a Rolling Stone' and 'Ballad of a Thin Man', have a mature savagery and a scary kind of wit which is new and extraordinary in music of mass appeal.

He has become a prophet of chaos and those who once accepted him as a blue-denim Messiah of a Brotherhood future once the times had changed may sense a personal betrayal. If not, then not.

He attempted to pacify the old fans by doing the first half of his concerts in this country with acoustic guitar and mouth organ. As a matter of fact, 'Desolation Row' sounds pretty silly without a beat backing and he seemed curiously apathetic and a bit lonely, all by himself on stage.

At Cardiff, the audience greeted the opening lines of 'Mr Tambourine Man' with relieved recognition and a round of applause; he did not even give a thin smile in return but threw the song away as if he wished he could throw his harmonica after it. No introductions, no nothing. He scrambled through the troubadour of song bit.

To jerk into life when the group came on in the second half and the noise bit began. This Dylan is clanging and vulgar, neon and plastic and, at the same time, blackly, bleakly romantic. And exhilarating, akin to reading *The Dunciad* or a strip cartoon version of *Wuthering Heights* while riding a roller coaster.

Dylan is a phenomenon. He never used to be. The smug outrage of the 'I hate *Time* magazine' attitudes of his early songs was easy and shallow, but there are no easy answers, no easy imagery. He's on his own (like a rolling stone or like a Rolling Stone) and what happens now should be best of all.

London Magazine, 1966

A Busker (Retired)

Charlie is a walking piece of social history but few stop to listen to him for he is a storyteller in the style of the Ancient Mariner, a chronic lapel-grabber, and, once started, nothing can halt his flow. He talks so rapidly, in such a toothless, bronchial rumble, that not many people can follow him when they first hear him. As he talks, he watches you anxiously from his round, rheumy eyes to see if you are getting bored; at the first signs of boredom, he nudges you into fresh attention, talking with more and more desperate intensity.

He has the face of a withered urchin and the body, too; he is no more than five feet tall and slightly built. The front of his long overcoat is crusted with snuff, which he will offer freely around secure that nobody will accept it. He walks in a slow shuffle, with the aid of a stick; this stick defines his centre of gravity outside his body and, together with the characteristic cap – worn with the buttoned peak pulled well down on his forehead – helps to determine his silhouette.

He takes this checked cap from his head very rarely and, when he does, it is a shock to see his iron grey fall of hair, still boyishly glossy and thick. He is seventy-six years old. When he feels poorly, either with his heart or with bronchitis, his face becomes as grey as the sea. He was a busker, playing fiddle and banjo and singing comic songs; this is how he earned his living until he retired.

At home, he has a seven-string banjo which he made himself, but no fiddle of his own now. When we first used to talk to him in the pub, he would tell us of his musical prowess and illustrate it by putting his stick under his chin and pretending to play that. We thought all was fantasy and he was a silly old man about his fiddle until we met him one night in the street and I happened to be carrying a fiddle.

Standing in the street under a lamp, he instantly tuned up the fiddle and began to play. He reeled off a bunch of music-hall tunes, using much double and treble stopping and a very flamboyant bow technique; he grunted alarmingly as he played. He said he had to give up being a busker since he had a bad heart, a poor old heart. He had not played the fiddle for fifteen

years. He sang a song to the tune of the hymn, 'Far, Far Away': he said he
had made the new words up himself. He plucked the tune on the strings:

> Where is my mother-in-law?
> Far, far away!
> Where is her nagging jaw?
> Far, far away!

There is a verse about how he went to the races and put his money on
a horse named Kidney Pie (due to the exigencies of the rhyme). Kidney
Pie headed the field but when he went to collect his winnings he found
the bookmakers had already packed and gone 'far, far away'.

He also has a parody of the song 'My Grandfather's Clock'. This begins
promisingly:

> My grandfather's socks were too big for his shoes
> And his shoes were too big for his feet.

One of the verses asserts that his grandfather's teeth were too big for his
mouth so they stood ninety years on the shelf. He says, 'Clever, isn't it?
Eh? Eh?' Nudging away with his elbow. Songs such as these kept the
money rolling in when he was in the profession. He says he was earning
as much as £5 a night during the 1930s, playing pubs all over our city and
in neighbouring towns, as well. And this was during the Depression. Even
allowing for Charlie's tendency to exaggerate, he must have done well.

The first job he ever had was that of newspaper seller with a pitch fifty
yards from the pub where he now spends his evenings. That was during
the Boer War. But he soon turned to busking and after that never looked
back.

He says he made his first fiddle out of a corned beef tin, whittling the
neck from the leg of a chair. That was a corned beef fiddle, haven't you
never heard of a corned beef fiddle? He could play anything on it. He
bought his second fiddle at a newsagent's. It cost 4s 9d. It had a back like
glass but there was a big scratch on it. He played it for years and, when he
finally sold it, he doubled his outlay on it. Part of his act is a lengthy piece
of innuendo about learning the fiddle. 'Playing the fiddle is just like court-
ing a lady, you got to treat her gentle, treat her nice. You got to love a
fiddle. Stroke her belly, gentle. Just like when you're new married, you
might have a bit of trouble with your bow, it ain't stiff enough. You got
to practise. Practice makes perfect. Then, after you've finished, you got to
wipe your bow off with a rag.'

He will sing 'Swanee' and 'Waiting for the Robert E. Lee' in his cracked old voice that has forgotten the way the notes should go, and he will sing 'Moonlight Bay', one of his favourites, while plucking out the notes banjo style on the fiddle. He has a large repertoire of tunes, songs and jokes; his favourite tune is a waltz called 'Sweet Dreamland Faces'. He wrote to the old tyme dance programme on the wireless with a request for them to play this but they never did.

He elaborates everything into comic fantasy, describing how the mice in the basement where he lives sit in front of his shaving mirror preening their whiskers or how he once saved the life of a pet cat injured by a car. 'It was run over and all its brains burst out and I scooped them up and put them back and it lived for years. Lived for years.'

When he speaks of his father, all is Munchausen-like excursions into a higher imaginative reality. His father was a man of many trades but he never went busking. Charlie says it was because he hadn't got the guts. But his father had the guts for almost every other venture since, according to his son, he was a pub pianist, a puppeteer and an unqualified (though practising) doctor and dentist. At first Charlie said his father was a surgeon in the American civil war but subsequently revised this, saying instead he had worked as a doctor in the last Indian wars in America. He still has his father's needles and surgical instruments in their cases. He said he had a clock set with human teeth which his father had pulled. Sixpence a time, a whiff of ether, out came the tooth.

'My old dad used to hypnotise my mother, he used to raise her right off the ground. She had lovely long hair right down to her boots. My mother were a frail little woman, ailing. She had beri-beri, she slept a lot. One night she came home from the pub and she fell down and cut her nose, cut it so bad it was hanging off, and my old dad stitched it back on again with fifteen stitches. I held the candle and my old dad put in fifteen stitches and it was good as new in the morning. She fell down because she was drunk.'

At one time, his father ran a puppet theatre. Charlie has given away the last of the puppets, which were almost life size and included such things as a policemen, a skeleton and a comically bewhiskered Irishman with bog-trotter hat and corncob pipe, but he still has a photograph showing his father standing in front of a stage where all the dolls are taking a bow. His bearded father sports a top hat and flowing cape; in the picture, his eyes are unusually grave and mysterious and it is not hard to imagine them producing a mesmeric effect.

This is one of a selection of well-thumbed photographs Charlie keeps among the litter in his pocket. One picture is that of the fattest woman in the world, a music-hall personality he new socially. When she died, she had to have two bullock carts to tow her body away. He has handled her picture so often in showing it to people in pubs that her face has worn away, giving her the disturbingly blurred features of a figure in a Francis Bacon painting.

When he plays, sings or tells a story and there is laughter, the years drop away from him and he congratulates himself with delight, saying: 'See, I can still make people laugh. Eh? Eh?' He is anxious not so much for company as for a chance to entertain.

In his room, there is a photograph of himself as a young man, very smart and spruce; and a number of dusty cases of musical instruments: and his father's clock, decorated with human teeth. Also his father's magic box, of which he often talks. This is a peepshow, in a cardboard box, giving you a tiny glimpse of fairyland.

New Society, 1967

The Good Old Songs

In a small pub on a main road in an area of Bristol due shortly for demolition, a very small man playing an ornate silver and ivory piano accordion, which seemed almost too large for him, sat perched on a bench by the bar, his feet did not touch the floor. He had a fat, pale mole on his jaw, his hair was white, he wore a grey pullover, he seemed grey and silver all over. Everyone was joining in singing, though they continued to drink and chat at the same time. A girl, the only young girl present, was kissing a whippet, covering its milk chocolate-coloured muzzle with lipstick in doing so.

When everyone started singing 'If You Were the Only Girl in the World' a man with a bristling moustache said:

'That's a melody that's lasted fifty years and will last for fifty more, not like this wretched jungle beat of today that will hardly last till tomorrow. This song is full of nostalgia for me. It brings back to me all that bloody awful blood bath of the First World War and Waterloo station and the soldiers clasping their women, knowing they would never see them again. I was in the army for twenty-nine years. In the army, they used to say: "Never stand up when you can sit down, never sit down when you can lie down."'

With that, he sat down. The piano accordionist began to play 'When I Grow Too Old to Dream' and everybody began to sing that except the moustached man, who said in an aggrieved voice: 'I don't know the words of this one.'

He and his moustache were out of their class in this pub, where empty
Woodbine packets spilled from the ashes of an unused grate. He was there
on purpose to buy a birthday drink for an employee, an old man in his seventies with a tattooed snake round his left wrist. This old man is a virtuoso banjo player in the British style; he plays solos such as 'La Marguérite',
'Bless This House', 'Mr Jollyboy', 'Land of Dreaming Darkies' and
'Niggertown' (these last two presumably relics of the days of coon shows
and blackface minstrels). The publican is also a banjo player; they plan, one
night, to play duets together in the bar. That should be worth waiting for.

Sometimes one hears a banjo in a pub, but usually it is either a piano or
a piano accordion, with perhaps a rhythm section of spoons or drums.
Small electronic organs and organ attachments on pianos, however, are
becoming more and more popular. One will occasionally find rock
groups, fossils from the late 1950s; these are essentially noise machines and
only to be found in the rowdiest pubs. These electric musicians have
ornate, swept-back hairdos, are smartly dressed in navy suits and shoestring
ties and perform with such a manic abandon that they all run with sweat
by the evening's end.

They are usually in their late thirties, if not older. They play early Little
Richard, Presley, Jerry Lee Lewis and Gene Vincent hits such as 'Bee-
bop-a-lula' and 'Great Balls of Fire'. Sometimes one is even lucky enough
to hear 'Rock Around the Clock'.

In the main, the atmosphere of the public bar is predominantly middle-
aged. The musician's task is rather to promote general singing in the bar
than to provide background music. There is music of some kind in perhaps two-thirds of the pubs of any size that have not gone over to muzak,
elaborately arranged plastic bouquets, petty bourgeois interior decoration
and the lager and vodka-and-lime trade.

Even in pubs without music, singing – usually unison but sometimes
solo – will break out spontaneously at the saturnalian season of Christmas
through to the New Year.

Then the solo singing will be in the nature of a party piece; every New
Year's Eve, for example, there is a ritual of persuading the regulars to do
pieces such as the patter song 'Sylvest' ('My brother, Sylvest, got a row of
forty medals on his chest. He beat a thousand niggers in the west . . . My
Brother Sylvest'). But, in the main, singing in our city is a communal
thing. It has only been permitted in pubs for five years. Bristol is deeply
puritan. No music, no singing; the only thing you used to be able to do in
a public house was to get drunk.

On a Saturday night, every sing-song pub in the city must be echoing
with the same repertoire. There are the songs that never die; whose broad,
catchy melodies and lyrics expressing either honest sentiment or sometimes

surreal humour insinuate themselves into the mind and are absorbed though never consciously learnt. The repertory ranges widely over time, from music hall favourites such as 'Down at the Old Bull and Bush' and 'My Old Man Said Follow the Van' through pops of the intervening decades up till contemporary songs in the traditional idiom.

These are the songs the mums and dads put into the hit parade, the songs of Ken Dodd, Val Doonican; the Australian group, The Seekers, ('The Carnival is Over', 'Morningtown Ride'); and the American country and western singer, Jim Reeves. A chart-topping country number, 'The Green, Green Grass of Home', won a golden disc for the super-dramatic singing of Tom Jones. It was primarily the shillings of the public bar that must have kept him at the top for six long weeks. This song sells nostalgia and love of home; there is a savagely dramatic sting in the last verse. The singer has described in glowing terms the beauty of home; then –

> I awake and look around me,
> See the four grey walls that surround me,
> And I realise that I'm only dreaming;
> For there's a guard and there's a grey old padre,
> On and On we'll walk at daybreak
> And they'll lay me 'neath the green, green grass of home.

It is such a hot favourite that, at the football match, the entire throng sings aloud with it when it is played over the loudspeakers.

The sweet predictability of tune and the directness with which they view the human predicament must account for the popularity of American country songs. 'Distant Drums' by Jim Reeves went straight from the mass media into the pubs, 'Mary, marry me, let's not wait, For the distant drums may change our wedding date.' Reeve's 'Release Me' has similarly caught the imagination – 'Please release me, let me go, For I don't love you any more.' You can't get a much more bald statement of the death of love than that. Everybody seems to know the words of the song.

Inspirational songs are heavily featured, such as 'I Believe' and 'Climb Every Mountain'. The popularity of 'Climb Every Mountain' is an indication of the popularity of the film, The Sound of Music ; every town where it is shown has had a story in its local paper about someone who has become hooked on The Sound of Music and seen it about 100 times. Most people have seen it more than once. But songs that have an arty flavour about them or are more specifically hymnal in type are left to the solo singer.

These are such songs as 'Bless This House' and 'Ave Maria'. Also, 'Oh, My Beloved Father', which has somehow developed religious connotations.

When a person gets up to sing solo, he or she will feature a slightly different range of material, for example, 'The Song of the Clyde', 'It's a Grand Night for Singing' or 'The Spaniard Who Blighted My Life'. They are all so different in that they sing both chorus and verse of songs, inciting the rest of the pub to join in on the chorus with ritual gestures of the hands. When everybody is singing together, verses are usually jettisoned since the choruses are what everybody knows. Who ever heard, for example, the verse of 'Daisy Bell'?

Teen music in general passes the pub by. Neither its rhythms nor its sentiments suit the Saturday-night-out singers. The only Beatles song to make the pub scene here (though it might be different in Liverpool) is 'Yellow Submarine', as being bouncy, humorous, panto-type song not too different in mood from 'The Woody Woodpecker's Song' ('Ha-ha-ha-ha-ha, Ha-ha-ha-ha-ha, That's the woody woodpecker's song': opportunities for bird and animal imitations are always welcomed, it is a fine thing to hear thirty or forty people all barking together in 'How Much Is That Doggy in the Window?')

The melodic patterns of modern pop, which often ultimately derive from American Negro blues, and the harmonic complexity of the music of the Beatles or the Beach Boys are from and of a different world, the all-at-once world of the twentieth century, the postwar world. The public bar is stuck in a time before them. The linear melodies favoured in the sing-song pubs, hopelessly and forever square, belong to an older world and retain, however remotely, some connections with the linear tunes of our own folk song.

Similarly, the massive sophistication of the lyrics of Donovan, Bob Dylan and Lennon and McCartney pass most people by; the singers round the piano don't dig abstruse imagery and hippie allusion. They see the world with a grand simplicity just as in the old songs. Maybe this simplicity is often blurred by sentiment but that is nothing new and the basic concerns of affection and fidelity remain the same. There is also a cosy familiarity in singing the songs you have always known; many of these songs are loved just because they are known, are remembered because they are always sung.

The genius of the public bar remains Vera Lynn, whose voice, says Richard Hoggart, sounds the way a mill girl sings inside her head. Vera Lynn still represents a style of straight-out, open-throated singing from the heart which is distant, very distant, but all the same, not too unimaginably removed, from English traditional singing style. And English traditional singers will sing most of the pub favourites mixed up with far older ballads with perfect equanimity, anyway.

Margaret says she does not like music like the Rolling Stones and, besides, it would be too difficult for her to play even if she did.

Margaret is the resident pianist at a pub down by the river; the walls of this pub are decorated with sailors' hatbands, arranged in squares. She is accompanied by a drummer. She is plump and smiling, with carefully coiffed grey curls; she always wears a nice dress for her public appearances and appears brisk yet sedate. She dominates the bar. She can play anything and will pick up a tune the bar starts singing spontaneously and accompany them in any key they choose. Her experience is more or less typical.

She says: 'The favourites are songs like "A Shanty in Old Shanty Town", "You Made Me Love You", "Underneath the Arches", "Heart of My Heart" and all the Al Jolson songs. Everybody seems to know them, young or old, and they all join in. I never go into a pub except when I come here to play.

'I started entertaining at the piano at the age of fifteen, doing amateur concert party work. My husband is a drummer. We played together at clubs until we got married; then I dropped it. It's not my husband who plays here with me; he plays somewhere else on Saturday nights. Well, five years ago, when the ban on music was lifted, I came in here and sat down at the piano and the landlady gave me a permanent engagement. I've been playing three nights a week here for the five years since. I also play one night a week for keep-fit classes.

'I get 30s a night from the management. They collect money in a beer mug for the drummer. Most pub pianists get 30s a night. I get a lot of pleasure from playing but I do it for the money, really. I need it, with two young children.'

Noël Coward made someone in *Private Lives* say: 'Strange how potent cheap music is.' Even flattened out by the rolling bass and smash-bang-wallop attack of the pub pianist's typical style, a style emulated by the accordionists, the potency remains. Nothing brings back the past like a tune, especially a good old tune, just as the man with the moustache says. The sense of togetherness in a sing-song pub is marvellous. The unmusical voices blend, somehow, and there are smiles for strangers. It is a very good scéne.

New Society, 1968

Giants' Playtime

The ring is a concrete parenthesis. It is an area of privileged space inside which the rules of the game exert an absolute dominance, and are the only things that – for the duration of the game – are true. Into this ring, plummet harsh parallels of very white light. This light has the peculiar, theatrical quality of making bare flesh, however increasingly bedabbled with real sweat, or even blood, look like a costume. This light clothes the wrestlers.

Sometimes professional wrestling is like chess, and sometimes like ballet, and sometimes like a crude morality play: the good guy who plays according to the rules, versus the bad guy who 'bends' them, mocks them and sometimes flouts them altogether. Sometimes it's like folk drama masquerading as sport; occasionally vaudeville – 'There's a Black Maria outside!' announces the referee, and, quick as a flash, Johnny Kwango retorts: 'It must be my sister.' ('No Colour Bar in Wrestling,' states *The Mick McManus Wrestling Book.*)

Or else it is physical display decked out with certain elements of antique theatre, masks, hieratic posturing, menace, dread, violence, pain – all the apparatus of the Theatre of Cruelty except its metaphysics. This is Theatre of Cruelty played for laughs, in which injury is a regrettable accident. (I remember once being at the Colston Hall in Bristol when Judo Al Hayes, I think it was, tripped over his bootlace and sprained his knee. A dreadful hush fell over the audience; how solemn the referee as he led the hero limping away!) A game with all the appearance of merciless combat, and all the trimmings of diverting make-believe.

There's always a very intimate atmosphere at a wrestling show. A subdued babble of conversation all the time. Nothing like the oppressive silence to which the audience at a real theatre is condemned. And we sit, not in the alienation of absolute darkness but in only a cosy dimming of the light. You can read your newspaper for a while, if you should start to feel bored. There is a good deal of audience participation as well. Old ladies do indeed rush screaming down the aisles and beat their fists against the ropes.

The first impression of a gathering at a wrestling match isn't one of frenzy and blood-lust at all. The atmosphere is relaxed, homely, comfortable. There are lots of family parties, a lot of kids. There is the odd baleful woman on her own who will shriek: 'Get 'em off! Get 'em off!' during the mimic de-balling that seems to have become a new routine. There is usually a sprinkling of old ladies in the best seats, waiting for the offchance a heavyweight, lobbed out of the ring, might drop like an over-ripe fruit into their laps. It's lovely to see the old dears enjoy themselves. They know what they like. The innocence of their pleasure absolves them from understanding its nature, whatever that is.

The Exorcist was supposed to top this particular bill, but he's been out of action for some months now, following a neck injury. I was disappointed to miss him. He enters the ring in a black robe with a candle in

one hand and a bible in the other. He's one of the subgenre of masked
mystery wrestlers, of whom the doyen is Kendo Nagasaki, the 'man from
nowhere'. Kendo sports a heterogeneous collection of pseudo-Japanese
apparel, including a sword and a mask of the kind Japanese fencers wear.
He never takes his mask off, not even in the dressing-room shower. His
anonymity is his identity.

Now, it is fair to assume that Steve Veidor or Judo Al Hayes, facing
Nagasaki for the fifth or sixth or umpteenth time, is no longer intimidated
by this bizarre apparition, although its obvious intention is intimidation.
The audience, to whom he's just as familiar, will greet him with a mixture
of hooting derision and camped-up dread. The mystery of his mystery is
a piece of showbiz. His weirdness is sufficient to itself. Its meaning is that
it doesn't have any meaning. As soon as he sheds his cloak and strips down
to his leotards, he then engages on his real business – which is that of the
regular bump-and-grind of a working wrestler, a man who is working at
playing.

The sound of a wrestling bout is pure *musique concrète* – the thwack of
flesh upon canvas; the deep grunts of stress; 'one-two-three' in the inexorable voice of the referee; the brisk clanging of the bell. Then up spring
the wrestlers, miraculously revivified from the prone. The stricken, the
almost done-for, go to their corners, rinse out their mouths, are ready and
roaring for another go.

In this improvisation, there's a certain physical rhythm which is specially
apparent on nights when there isn't that electric tension in the air that
sparks the most brilliant invention. Nights, in fact, in small provincial halls
at the end of a tour like this night. The rhythm is that of a mutual system
of sudden reversals of fortune. It goes something like this.

First, there's a preliminary circling, heads down, clenched fists up. Then
one or the other makes the first grab, catches his opponent in a painful
hold, head trapped between his thighs, say. ('Grab his fruitbowl!' a patriarchal and white-bearded figure may suggest at this.) Grunt, moan, pain,
tension – a long-drawn out tension, broken by a sudden burst of action.
The aggressor now receives a foot in his face, and back he goes! Legs
up in the air, bouncing as if he were made of rubber. 'One . . . two . . .
three . . .'

This is almost a moral rhythm. The aggressor, the over-reacher, is foiled
by his victim, who in turn becomes the torturer. The serial play of violence denies pain by the sprightly vivacity with which the participants
demonstrate it and the speed with which they recover from it. John Elijah
came into the ring in a fur hat and a fur jacket *à la russe*. This probably
means he will one day graduate into a bad guy; they tend to run to furs.
Now, stripped, he goes crash! against the post, which shudders. Elijah v.

Kirkwood. Bob Kirkwood twists the other's arm in an appalling fashion for an endless moment; then up he goes, high over Elijah's head, squeaking with affront, kicking his heels in their quaint, archaic wrestling boots which look like a Roman gladiator's. But as soon as he's back on his feet, he knocks down Elijah flat. That'll teach him to be a bully.

Bad guys subvert the rules, good guys play clean. Bad guys, however, bend the rules in such a way that they can be seen to be bending the rules. How else could they show they were bad guys? And since their crimes against the game are a secret shared with the audience, they validate the rules by their infractions of them. It is not only excessive violence and blatant bad sportsmanship that make the bad guy. Moral defects, such as boasting, displays of cowardice, arguing with the referee, and refusing to shake hands with the winner after losing a match, all help towards giving him a bad reputation.

The mayhem routines of Adrian Street, Esq., who believes he is a reincarnation of an Ancient Greek, 'often have the crowds howling with hate', says *The Mick McManus Wrestling Book*. I remember seeing Adrian Street back in the 1960s, when he'd just started out in the rather specialised role of the 'pretty boy' wrestler. He'd mince into the ring under a barrage of the foulest slander, wearing red robes trimmed with fur. 'Hit him with your handbag!' they'd urge him and positively scream with fury when he won.

The bad guy often does win. The morality play element, never very far away in the physical drama of wrestling, does not mean that right inevitably triumphs. Far from it. It's too much like real life for that. Rather, when the bad guy wins the championship, the audience has the positive assurance of its prejudice that he has only done so by low cunning and sleight of hand, although the 'mask' or persona of the wrestler bears no connection at all with his actual prowess.

The Mick McManus Wrestling Book is a storehouse of information about what it calls the stars of biff. For five years Masambula wore a grass skirt, and a mask with fangs and horns. After a spectator at Darlington, Co Durham, put a match to it, he subsequently always entered the ring in a full-length leopard skin, a sign of negritude as emblematic as the kilts habitually sported by Scots wrestlers and the green trunks of Irish wrestlers.

Ricki Starr always wears ballet shoes in the ring and once danced with the Ballet Russe de Monte Carlo. He'll give a pirouette or two before getting down to business. Big John Cox, the seventeen-stone ex-York ambulance driver, has memorised thirty-six of Winston Churchill's speeches. Dory Dixon former world light heavyweight champion, plays the harp. Josef Zaranoff is 'masculine, muscular, mighty; but the love of his life is his cat, Pom Pom'. 'Big Bruno six foot five inches of flame-red hair and ogre's beard, hates women, adores poodles.' Joe d'Orazio, 'Bard of the biff business', paints in oils and writes poetry. He is quoted as believing that 'the world would be a better place if we could all talk poetry to each other'.

Wrestling Review, the magazine-cum-programme that Dale Martin Promotions sells at its presentations, is full of the same kind of chatter, as if to reassure the spectators the men in the ring are in no way mythic beings. 'Sid Cooper is taking things easy for a couple of weeks as far as wrestling is concerned. He has to get back to Yorkshire to supervise the disposal of his pigs for the Festive Season.'

These details have an extraordinary irrelevance to the one-dimensional grandeur of the participants in these contests, which fulfil every definition of Roger Caillois's definition of play – 'an occasion of pure waste, waste of time, energy, ingenuity, skill'. The prodigality with which these giants play is its own justification.

New Society, 1976

Wagner and the Mistral

The mistral got into Birgit Nilsson's robes and tossed them hither and thither, all her moth and mulberry draperies in a wonderfully Gothic confusion. From the topmost-but-one tier of the amphitheatre, she looked like a Brünnhilde in Lilliput, tiny and perfect in her silver jerkin and wing-like draperies. She'd first appeared with some form of silver antennae on her red hair, resembling, from this distance, more a miniature, exquisite insect, out of some less stirring epic, Drayton's *Polyolbion* or *Nymphidia*, perhaps. But the headdress had been discarded by the second act; maybe the mistral had threatened to whip it away.

But if, in one sense, the mistral was definitely on Wagner's side, turning her and her sister valkyries into the brides of a wind that seemed imminently about to bear them off with it, in another sense, it was not, since it very often snatched the voices out of their mouths and blew them clean away.

And the wind began to exhibit positive Wagnerophobia when it grossly amplified the technological clamour of trains arriving and departing from the station at Orange, especially during the quiet bits, when the subtlety of the orchestration is so important; and what's more, blasted we 14,000 odd culture lovers on our stone benches with great gusts that got chillier and chillier as the night progressed, helping to give the performance something of the therapeutic quality of an ordeal. But perhaps this aspect of the wind was indeed in complicity with Wagner; after all, God knows, he had not intended we should come to the theatre in order to merely enjoy ourselves.

On the cliffs surrounding the amphitheatre, hard-eyed cops in kepis kept guard, outlined dramatically against the sunset, policing the culture-ordeal going on below in the tiny, lighted eye of the stage where the cosmic argument – which had become primarily one between superstars and the wind – was doubly distanced from us by the necessarily well-lit orchestra pit, and the orchestra sawing away in their monkey suits.

Wagner may have been inspired by the theatre of Ancient Greece to embark on revolutionising the concept of the music drama; all the same, I can think of no more unsuitable a place for a performance of *Die Valkyrie* than a Roman amphitheatre in sun-drenched, neo-classical Provence, except, perhaps, an actual Greek amphitheatre on say, the coast of Anatolia.

But, if one is committed to presenting a 'grand spectacle' in a Roman amphitheatre with exceptionally poor acoustics, so that the music must be loud, what other composer is there who will do? *Aida*, with or without elephants, is a cliché. *The Trojans* might not have quite that crowd-pulling attraction that will fill up 14,000 exceedingly uncomfortable places. Now, Wagner especially with Birgit Nilsson, with an all-star cast, with Rudolf Kempe conducting – that'll bring them down from Paris in their special trains! That's the stuff of which 'grand spectacles' are made.

Poor Wagner, so concerned about the acoustics at Bayreuth – his spirit must have been beside itself, half overjoyed at a theatre built to celebrate the gods themselves, half immensely put out to find the troublesome wind, probably blowing directly from Israel, wreaks havoc with the score – and, worse, that the gods to whom the theatre had been dedicated were the *wrong* ones. Serene in his niche in the brick wall thirty or forty feet above the participants in the excessive goings-on below, the marble statue of Apollo presiding over the stage had the air of one listening, himself, to Monteverdi.

As a first tribute to chaos, we started something like three-quarters of an hour late and the audience energetically booed a party of VIPs who had the temerity to enter the auditorium after the conductor. (Later, the audience would roundly boo the orchestra.) House-lights dimmed; a rather vulgar bit of *son et lumière* – the sheer cliff of brick bathed lugubriously in red light, suggesting a waterfall of blood. Hundings house somewhat inadequately suggested by three piles of bricks of which the largest is to double as Brünnhilde's catafalque, when Wotan finally puts her to sleep. This open-plan staging does nothing to suggest the appalling claustrophobia of the atmosphere of the Ring cycle, a claustrophobia of which the incestuous coupling of Siegmund and Seiglinde is a metaphor.

Without any visual glamour in the settings at all except the fabulous but inappropriate glamour of the amphitheatre itself with the great scoop of sky above it, the vivid, subtle and sensational music must carry all the drama; and, of course, in the privacy of the study, hi-fi turned up, lights turned down, it can. But Wagner's inwardness mitigates against the whole notion of a 'grand spectacle', anyway. Let's quote the master himself: 'The only picture of human life that may be called poetic is the one where all motivations that have meaning only for the abstract intelligence give way to purely human motives rooted in the heart.' The perfect theatre for Wagner, then, might be the private opera house of the individual sensibility, where the music itself, with the curious, opiate quality that Baudelaire recognised, can create visions just as exotic as Xanadu. Not if the rude, Mediterranean mistral is blowing most of the music away.

And the scale of the amphitheatre would daunt even Wagner's own stage directions, those props that could only exist in the gigantic greenroom of his imagination. Ram-drawn chariots, fiery steeds, ash trees, forests, castles would look like objects from a toy shop, under the cool eye of the chaste yet sensuous marble god perched up there half-way to the stars (though not as far towards them as we in the topmost-but-one tier are).

Unless the gods were propped up on stilts, equipped with enormous, padded capes, given huge, painted masks, equipped with bull-roarers – unless treated explicitly in the Graeco-Roman fashion, which Wagner, who loathed historical accuracy, abjured, unless exhibited on the stage with that degree of artificiality necessary to all realistic representations of godhead, they will look distressingly unreal. Wagner, of course, hoped to assert humanity by denying historicity. 'I abandoned once and for all the domain of history, and established myself in legend . . . Whatever the epoch or nation it belongs to, legend has the advantage of incorporating exclusively what is purely human in the given epoch or nation . . .'

But history, in the all-too-concrete shape of a Roman amphitheatre, contrives to exert such a massive pressure on Wagner's legendary beings, they diminish to the scale of the botched abortions of a Tolkien, that whimsical don on a perpetual sabbatical. The smug marble god up top scores a signal victory. The Teutons were too primitive to have theatres, anyway.

Back-projections of monstrous horses with fire darting from their hooves and nostrils, of storms, of crags, might do the trick, matching the

excess of the whole conception. Perhaps the singers shouldn't even appear
on the stage but send mimes on stilts to do the acting for them and manifest themselves musically only via an excellent amplification system.
Offhand, Antonin Artaud is the only director I can think of who could
have done true justice to Wagner, poor Artaud, another nutter, another
bedsit megalomaniac creating huge cosmogonies between rarely changed
sheets that permanently reeked of last week's bacon fat. A universal genius
who never got the breaks.

But Wagner did get the breaks, of course, and was not a nutter at all –
indeed, sometimes seems the only dangerously sane man in his whole
exotic entourage. Look at them – Ludwig II with his mad eyes in his
Lohengrin outfit, the very king a republican might choose for patron if he
wanted to bring the whole concept of monarchy into disrepute and bankrupt the exchequer into the bargain. The various complaisant cuckolds
who felt their virility enhanced by sympathetic magic when Wagner vigorously screwed their wives. In his book on Wagner, Bryan Magee says he
modelled the character of Siegfried on 'his friend (good heavens!) Michael
Bakunin' – and so another unlikely ingredient goes into old Klingsor's
cauldron. And, of course, there was always Nietzsche.

One jump ahead of the debt collectors, megalomania rigorously kept
within the bounds of self-interest, Wagner never quite let it blossom into
dementia. Not so much a case study in the pathology of genius but one of
the great con men of all time, who saw around him an incontinent yearning for a universal genius and hurry-scurried to fit the bill.

Ardent, despotic, expressing 'all that is excessive, immense, ambitious in
both spiritual and natural man', said Baudelaire; poetic, musician, philosopher, magician, the whole bourgeois notion of the artist rolled up into
one eczematous fornicator who took it into his head to institutionalise
myth as a form of psychic history and upon whom history took its ghastly
and inevitable revenge in the form of his apotheosis by Hitler. Better be
an Artaud, perhaps, and languish in a madhouse for most of one's life than
provide the musical accompaniment for the Götterdämmerung of the
Fuhrer.

Because it's not the music of Wagner that offends me, I love it, even if
that gut-rotting pessimism of he who sympathises too passionately with
the love-suicide warps the, yes, nobility of the whole conception. (They
say he never got over Louis Napoleon's *coup d'état* of 2 December 1851.
'When the success of the *coup d'état* was confirmed and it appeared that
what no one had thought possible had actually happened and had all the
appearance of enduring, I turned my back on this incomprehensible
world as a riddle not worth the attempt to solve.' Oh, that bourgeois
despair! Even young Siegfried's dauntless optimism isn't going to save

him from the noose the Norns have prepared for him.) No. It is the idea
of drama as a religious occasion, the elevation of the artist to the role of
priest or philosopher that's Wagner's real crime. This is the con-trick of
all con-tricks and though, like all confidence tricks, it contains a great element of vengeance, it has also taken in artists themselves, which is a great
pity.

Because old Klingsor does his tricks with the aid of the same maths Bach
used, and all the magic of art – finally – boils down to a few coloured lights
and tricks of sleight of hand. Magic, like a Humean miracle, is the one
thing which is categorically impossible; anything else, however unlikely,
since it is less impossible than magic, explains the phenomenon.

Meanwhile, watching the false universals of myth unfold their admittedly mesmeric, even plausible unrealities on the stage far, far beneath me,
I thought how splendid it was that Milton abandoned his project for
writing an Arthuriad, embalming all that nonsense in the phoney amber
of an institutionalised Matter of Britain. The pile of bricks upon which
Birgit Nilsson lay lit up with a muted, magi-coal effect; Wotan, in his
silver rabbits-ears helmet, kisses her sleeping eyes and creeps slowly,
silently away, to keep an appointment with the atrocious destiny reserved
for people who confuse art and life.

New Society, 1975

Fun Fairs

The idea of 'fun' is an odd one. Fun is quite different from pleasure, which
has obscure overtones of the erotic. Barbarella's machine killed you with
too much pleasure; a machine that killed you with too much fun suggests
a far less swooning death. Death by tickling, perhaps. (*The World's Fair*
advertises tickling sticks, 'ideal for Glasgow Fair'.) Fun is also quite different from delight, which is a more cerebral and elevated concept. You
might get pleasure, or delight, from a good performance of *The Marriage
of Figaro*; if you found it fun, or worse, 'great fun', it would only go to
show what a camp little number you were.

According to the *OED*, 'fun' originally meant a cheat, a hoax, a practical joke; widened to involve ridicule ('to poke fun') and, heartlessness,
always an aspect of the comic, only finally settled to a significance of guilt-
less enjoyment at around the turn of this century. Perhaps some folk
memory of its earlier meaning is what lends a certain ambivalence to fun

fairs. (Which are not the same as fairs.)

Since fun is pleasure without guilt, as in the euphemistic 'fun-loving', we are bound to feel it must be inherently trivial; in a Judaeo-Christian culture, half the fun of the thing is the guilt, anyway. Adultery is never fun; look at Anna Karenina. Swapping *is* fun, or so the writers to *Forum* claim. Promiscuity isn't fun and will land you in approved school but 'having a bit of fun' with a consenting adult suggests that nobody minds a slice off a cut loaf. Fun is pleasure that does not involve the conscience or, furthermore, the intellect. (Hegel is never fun.) Fun, in fact, might be the pleasure of the working class, as defined from outside that class.

Nevertheless, it's a shibboleth that socialism can never be fun; it won't be much *fun* after the Revolution, people say. (Yes; but it's not all that much fun, now.) But perhaps this means that a degree of alienation is necessary before the full 'fun' effect takes place; unalienated fun might be something unimaginably else.

You cannot be overwhelmed by fun, as you can be by pleasure. This kind of estranged fun is in the nature of a holiday; doing something 'for fun' is to act gratuitously. Yet fun is *per se* harmless; it is often good and clean, while pleasure can be unnatural. Even de Sade couldn't think up unnatural *fun*. Fun costs something – what doesn't? – but, like thrills, may often be obtained remarkably cheaply.

Fred Loades's vast model fairground, working models exactly to scale of roundabouts, coconut shies, big wheels, swingboats, rock stalls, all the fun of the fair, constructed between 1929 and 1977, a life-work, features midget pantechnicons bearing such legends as: 'Loades of Fun, Fun On Tour', etc. You press the time-switch; the lights go on; everything clicks into motion. Then stops. Until you press the switch again. Discontinuous as the peripatetic fair itself.

There was a man in Hammersmith market, he sold shirts, he used to shout: 'We're not here today and gone tomorrow, we're here today and gone today!' Fun is peripheral to one; here today and gone today, unless you have it in your heart. To the provider of fun, of course, it is so much hard work, dismantling the ride at two in the morning, driving a hundred miles, getting your ride built up again when you get there and so on. The technology of fun is a hard task-master; its reward is a consciousness you do no harm to anyone. And an unusually cohesive lifestyle. The In Memoriam columns of *The World's Fair* are even more affecting than those of the *Morning Star*; the wedding announcements suggest grand alliances between friendly clans, reports of parties staggering folkmoots.

In 1934, Mitcham fair covered 17 acres. There were 35 riding devices, 168 hooplas or similar, ten circuses, 50 darts stalls, 14 coconut shies, 59 refreshment stalls, palmists, ices, the fattest lady, the biggest rat, boxing booths, performing fleas and Wild West shows. Those were still heroic days. By the time I started going to the fairs on the south London commons, it was postwar, lean times, menace of Teds and flick-knives, no more fat ladies or sharp-shooters to gawp at. Candy floss had come in – women with turquoise eyelids and stacked hair twisting the bouffant pink stuff on to sticks out of the whirling drum; and lots of peppermint rock and toffee-apples, because none of these things were covered by sweet coupons, were, in fact, 'off ration', somehow legally illicit, oddly similar to the fair itself. But, no hot dogs; absent, that pervasive aroma of dehydrated onion simmering in a vat of hot water that hits you between the eyes at fair-grounds nowadays.

Yet there are still gallopers on the road, gallopers staked through the back with the barley-sugar stick supports to which you clung, gallopers with scarlet nostrils and gilded manes, after which real horses seem such a bitter disappointment. In my childhood, only the very youngest children rode them, everybody else preferred the dive-bombers, caterpillars, dodgems, speedy, flashy things that whirled you round and sometimes turned you upside down. Yet round and round the gilded horses still went, to the music of an organ that emitted a bronchitic wheeze of pure nostalgia, and so they do still, those marvellous horses whose feet never touch the ground, although, one by one, Victorian roundabouts retire to museums. Just as fun art, with the passing of time, turns into fine art, so the frivolous technology of the roundabout turns into industrial archaeology.

The fun of the fair, like the magic of the music-hall, has a capacity for procuring instant nostalgia in the hearts of people whose parents never let them go to fairs at all in case they picked up germs, and who can't even remember music-halls. The bourgeoisie always prefer to experience popular art at second-hand, in museums, art galleries and the pages of coffee-table books; that way, you run no risk of actually having any fun, or being forced to submit to the indignity of the Demon Whirl or the Lightning Jets. Since the fun of the fair is entirely sensational – that is, a direct, visceral assault on the senses – and may be experienced cheaply and without guilt; it has no connotations, not of the erotic, which is all in the mind, but of the straightforwardly sexual, which is all in the flesh and blood. Best to keep it in the quarantine of other people's experience, then. At the fair, you play games with vertigo, the quaking attraction of gravity which makes us want to plunge when we see an abyss – falling, spinning, the systematic derangement of all the senses and no harm done. All in fun. Oh, the titillation of the infernal apparatuses for whirling, bouncing, whizzing, swooping down! People scream when the dive-bombers swing out on their chains; all the fun of the centrifuge. Pleasures of incipient nausea; of feeling danger when one is absolutely safe. Of concealment and revelation;

do you remember the Caterpillar, that sped round its circumscribed track under a retractable awning of green canvas? Young couples loved it, the awning creaks up, creaks down at mechanical random.

Exhilaration of speed; and of not being in control, sombody else is in control, the gnarled, muscular showman for whom all this secular magic is only so much real life. 'It's thrilling.' 'It's terrifying'. 'It's exciting.' 'It's fun for all,' opine the signs in their ineffable agitated lettering. All around, the shrieks and crazed hysterical laughter of those in the grip of orgiastic physical excitation. And the inescapable music, remorseless as the juke-boxes of hell.

In the exhibition of fairground art at the Whitechapel Gallery in 1977, there was an electric-shock machine, built around 1900, the first ever to utilise electricity for amusement. This comes as no surprise. All the fun of electro-convulsion. No doubt the ancient Chinese, had they got around to inventing electricity, would have thought it best to keep it exclusively for fairground sideshows, just as they couldn't think of any other use for gunpowder but fireworks.

A fairground is a fun cathedral for the poor. It is visually a hard-edged world, in which most of the decorative detail is two-dimensional, executed in that kind of *trompe-l'œil* which deceives nobody and is intended to deceive nobody, not so much rococo as almost a conscious parody of rococo. Compare the work of the fairground artist, Fred Fowle or you could even buy the set of Twist cars decorated by him advertised in the fairground and circus trade paper, *The World's Fair*, if you had the nerve – anyway, compare a scenic panel by Fred Fowle with the effects inside a 1930s super-cinema, the Tooting Bec Granada, say. Fowle's work is up-front, straightforward, it hits you in the eye; it was he who introduced primary colours into the fairground, in the 1930s. It is decoration which is part of machines whose function is not to procure dreams but to excite the senses. Not the delineation of an invented reality but an exaggeration of concrete images to do with real sensation. On the other hand, Tooting Bec Granada, with its cyclorama of moving cloud and gallery of mirrors, is an interior constructed wholly of fantasy, of illusion. That is why the marble there is real.

Fred Fowle uses marbling techniques, but knows that it must not even *look* real, for his purposes. 'The thing about marble is that you exaggerate it more than it is. If you go in the Natural History museum you see marble there, but if you were to copy them. . . . it wouldn't have the same effect, of course' (interviewed by Ian Starsmore in *The Fairground*).

Super-cinema architecture, with its velvet drapes, crystal chandeliers, marble interiors, post-Symbolist murals and ritualistic screenings of movies showing, in the main, very rich people behaving extremely oddly, was designed for consolation during the Depression; you paid your money and you entered a better world. Fairground design was dedicated to the proposition that even if you didn't have a penny to bless yourself with, you could still have a bit of fun. Admission to the site was free; you could just walk around, look at the bright lights, enjoy the paintings, listen to the music and the ululations of those actually undergoing the ordeals by speed and mild terror. Fun, in fact, not unlike that which the Catholic church offers in its rococo pleasure domes in southern Mediterranean countries.

Certain crafts turn into art when people stop doing them, so you see that the craftsman was an artist all the time because the things they made stay beautiful after they have ceased to be functional. The beautiful beasts from old fairgrounds that Lady Bangor has collected together will probably convince the Chinese archaeologists that a particularly jolly kind of totemism flourished in Europe in the nineteenth century; the preternaturally alert gallopers, a furred, saddled seal, a cow with a golden horn, a fluorescent ostrich, a cat with a fish in its mouth, a llama, a cockerel. To ride round and round on one of them a hundred years ago must have made you feel you were the Lord of motion; it is around these items from the archetypal fairground of the pseudo-memory of nostalgia that the lustre of an actual art-object begins to gather. They are ceasing to be fun; now, on their stands, where you can walk all round them and see how perfect the finish is, they give quite a pure kind of delight. The fairground, of course, with its project of sensual immediacy, has rendered them obsolete; even the kiddies' rides in open-air markets have more fire-engines and motor-bikes aboard than gilded goats, nowadays.

I once read an interview with Fred Fowle in the *Evening Standard*. He said: 'Balham was a Disneyland to me when I was a kid and every place outside was as foreign as the moon . . . I used to ride on the swings at old Bedford Hill Fair and wonder if there really was anything outside of south London.'

I suppose there isn't, really, if you have an eye like that. On his own terms, he is a great social-realist painter. The fairs he works for are themselves stylisations of, exaggerations, heightenings of real life, as, ideally, holidays should be – not time off or out, but time, as it is, enhanced. The time of your life.

New Society, 1977

Carlos Moore: Fela Fela

Fela Anikulapo-Kuti, the Nigerian musician, is widely tipped by the British musical press as the Third World superstar most likely to succeed the late Bob Marley in seizing the First World by the ears and the pockets. If Fela indeed makes it in the UK, chart-wise, then it seems we can look forward to the appearance on *Top of the Pops*, for the first time, to my knowledge, of the child of a recipient of the Lenin peace prize.

That Fela's mother, Funmilayo Ransome-Kuti, was awarded the Lenin peace prize in the early 1960s ('I think they gave it to her in Lagos') is but one of the surprises in this messy but fascinating book, which would almost be the raw material for a novel by V. S. Naipaul. Except that Naipaul would get it all wrong, since Naipaul does not relish iconoclasm.

Fela's records – some of them, anyway: he makes as many as eight albums in any one year – have been randomly available in Britain for years, among the handful of imports marked 'African jazz'. But Fela isn't a jazz musician pure and simple. And he clearly doesn't want to be. If, at one time, he really wanted to be president of Nigeria, or of a united Africa, then Carlos Moore, whose interviews with him and his associates comprise a good deal of this book, doesn't draw him out on those aspirations.

The book concentrates more on Fela's discords with the Nigerian authorities and his allegedly irresistible charisma than on what he actually plays. Which is a pity, because when you hear it, you understand immediately why he's such a scandal at home, such a pain in the neck to successive Nigerian governments, such a sulphurous legend and why, if his troupe, once called Africa 70, now Egypt 80, *does* tour here, it is going to be a furious festival. We don't combine anger with *joie de vivre*. Fela does.

His music is big band agitprop, a neurotically exciting mix of jazz, funk, African hi-life with the man himself on saxophone, sometimes keyboards, and providing vocals which take the form of hypnotically repetitive, furious sermons. For which, as a general text, may be taken one of the sayings of Fela printed on the sleeve of the *Black President* album: 'According to the estimation of Africa's riches every Blackman should be a millionaire. Why are we so poor? It's time to investigate.'

One big hit was titled: 'ITT: International Thief Thief'. You can't say fairer than that. He is the scourge of internal corruption in Nigeria, of 'colonial mentality', of the multinationals; and the celebrant of Africanness. His music also reeks of a shamelessly up-front sexuality, which has, it seems, led many young girls to throw in their lot with his flamboyant career.

Fela Fela: This Bitch of a Life regrettably, for the foreigner, skimps on the general background of West African politics during its hero's forty-odd years of life, but usefully incorporates a brief history of his Yoruba people. A number of collages of newspaper headlines give a broad historical context ('6 January 1959: Troops Halt Congo Riot: Belgian Cabinet Called', '1 June 1967: Lagos Orders Blockade of Seceded East'). This device, by itself, politicises the text.

Two sections disconcertingly purport to be spirit communications from Fela's late mother. But these, it turns out, are the 'poetically and spiritually inspired' contributions of Shawna Moore, wife of the Cuban journalist who toted the tape recorder. She is also credited with translating the book from French (*Fela Fela: cette putain de vie*). This is odd, because the interviews themselves certainly sound unmediated by translation, an English flavoured with Pidgin, that linguistic *cordon sanitaire* with which both oppressors and oppressed protected themselves against verbal contamination from alien cultures.

Fela emerges from the taped interviews as awesomely foulmouthed and contentious. Yet that battling mother – first Nigerian woman to drive a car, to visit China, fighter for woman's suffrage, friend of Nkrumah – was married to the Right Reverend Israel Oludotun Ransome-Kuti, grammar school principal, first President of the Nigerian Union of Teachers. Fela's siblings are paediatricians, surgeons and such. In his early twenties, he himself spent four years in London studying music in a perfectly legit fashion. Few pop superstars have credentials so impeccably radical *and* middle class.

Fela jettisoned the 'Ransome' – the name a gift to the family from a missionary, way back – and adopted Anikulapo ('he who carries death in his quiver'). He paints his face with white 'spiritual dust', lives in a compound with a plurality of women, is rarely out of trouble with the law and makes a spectacle of himself for a living. In European terms, his life could be seen as a long-term, and magnificently successful, fight against respectability. In Nigeria, it probably seems like that too.

All this adds up to a mass of contradictions, of which the star himself seems richly aware and has resolved in that startling synthesis of politics and show-business which thrives in Africa, Latin America, the Caribbean, Greece – and sometimes tries to raise its head over here.

His albums consistently log confrontation. A 1975 brush with the police over marijuana produces an album, *Expensive Shit*. *Shuffering and Shmiling* was composed after the sacking and burning of his home by soldiers of the Nigerian army. The cover of his 1981 album, *Coffin for Head of State*, reproduced by Moore, features a photograph of his mother's coffin being utilised in a demonstration against the then head of state.

Fela Anikulapo-Kuti clearly possesses a positive genius for the dramatic presentation of self, an ability to orchestrate – literally and metaphorically – the events of his own life as a continuous exposition of outrage. It is a sort of populist situationalism and it happily accommodates any amount of hype and charlatanry. The basic position, never quite spelled out here, seems to be permanent rebellion in the name of Africanness as life force.

This, presumably, provides the ideological basis for Fela's polygamy. In a generous gesture which puts to shame all other pop stars, Fela went through a form of marriage with twenty-seven of his groupies in Lagos in 1978. By the time of the writing of *Fela Fela: This Bitch of a Life,* only a hard core of fifteen remained, plus the original Mrs Anikulapo-Kuti, who has stuck with him since London, 1961, and cultivates, according to the book an 'Olympian detachment' in her own residence. It's not fair to call the girls groupies, though; they all work in the act. Their photographs are all smashing.

None of those interviewed by Carlos Moore expressed dissatisfaction with her lot, although their husband seems to slap them around somewhat. He made his position on women quite plain with a hit called 'Mattress'; that is how he sees a woman's role – prone. Punishment for insubordination in the Anikulapo-Kuti home is exile from the marriage bed. He calls them his 'queens'. According to one queen, 'Jealousy is not an African word', which is just as well.

Social custom is relative and the rhetoric of the woman's movement may be out of place in West Africa, though havoc might well be wrought in the Anikulapo-Kuti household by the introduction of a few of the novels of Buchi Emecheta. Nevertheless, the image of superstud, extravagantly promoted by this book, ill becomes a radical iconoclast now well into his forties. Proud as she doubtless was of her son, his mother sounds the better man.

New Society, 1982

Phyllis Rose: Jazz Cleopatra

'She just wiggled her fanny and all the French fell in love with her,' said Maria Jolas to Josephine Baker's biographer, Phyllis Rose. Maria Jolas, evidently still bewildered after all these years by the insouciant ease with which the washerwoman's daughter from St Louis, Missouri, conquered Paris in 1925.

But by all accounts that wiggle was an unprecedented event even in the uninhibited world of Parisian spectacle. Her posterior agitated as if it had a life of its own. Phyllis Rose theorises about it: 'With Baker's triumph, the erotic gaze of a nation moved downward: she had uncovered a new region for desire.' Surely Ms Rose is being a little unfair; the French reputation for sexual sophistication may be exaggerated but the *habitués* of Montmartre cabaret *must* have seen a bare bum before.

And, of course, it wasn't as simple as that. Baker herself put her finger on the source of her attraction: 'The white imagination sure is something when it comes to blacks,' she said. When Baker sailed the Atlantic in 1925 with a group of African-American artists, including Sidney Bechet, to take a little taste of show-stopping Harlem nightlife to Europe, she left behind nascent Broadway stardom as a comic dancer, an elastic-limbed, rubber-faced clown, grimacing, grinning, crossing her eyes, to find herself freshly incarnated as a sex-goddess without, it would seem, changing her act very much at all.

She even, although glammed up to the nines, continued crossing her eyes at odd moments: she must have felt it necessary to make her own ironic comment on herself to her audiences, so rapt and breathless was the Parisian reaction to the *Revue nègre*. 'Their lips must have the taste of pickled watermelon, coconut, poisonous flowers, jungles and turquoise waters,' enthused one scribe.

Yes, of course there is an implicit racism behind that purple prose, but it is a better thing to be adored for one's difference than shunned for it and Phyllis Rose describes eloquently the extraordinary sense of liberation these black artists felt when they arrived in Europe. Life acquired a grand simplicity; any bar would serve them, and waiters said: 'sir' and 'madame'. They could check into any hotel they wanted. To use a public convenience did not provoke a race riot. Later on, in the US in the 1950s, Baker would battle valiantly in the Civil Rights Movement; in Paris in the 1920s, she allowed herself to enjoy being a girl. She was Cinderella, the papers said; all she need do now was try on the slipper and marry the prince.

As toothy, exuberant, not-precisely-pretty Josephine Baker grew into her new role of jungle queen, savage seductress and round Baudelairean Black Venus, she left off making faces. At night, she hit the town in Poiret frocks. She never married a prince but Georges Simenon always said he would have married her had he not been married already; then, staggering thought, she would have been, in a sense, Madame Maigret. She had plenty of other offers, too; Phyllis Rose does not drop many names, although she gives a teasing vignette of the architect Le Corbusier, whom Baker met on an ocean liner. 'He and Josephine became great pals and he went to the ship's costume ball dressed as Josephine Baker, with darkened skin and a waistband of feathers.'

She acquired a pet, a leopard named Chiquita, 'a male despite his name', who sported a diamond collar. (She had a Bardot-like passion for animals.) Chiquita went everywhere with her, her exquisite objective correlative; the French wanted her to be herself a jewelled panther and good humouredly she gave them what they wanted. Baring her breasts, she danced in the Folies Bergères wearing a girdle of bananas and sealed her fame. From henceforth, this garment, which is, I think, unknown in any form of dress in any part of the world, which is purely the invention of a mildly prurient exoticism, would be associated with her.

In 1928, she danced in Berlin. Louise Brooks, there to film *Pandora's Box* for Pabst, and something of an expert in the methodology of exploited sexuality, saw her. When Josephine Baker appeared, naked except for a girdle of bananas, it was precisely as Lulu's stage entrance was described by Wedekind: 'They rage there as in a menagerie when the meat appears at the cage.' Phyllis Rose doesn't record Brooks's observation, suggesting as it does that there was, perhaps, rather more raw eroticism about Baker's early performances than Rose lets on.

La Baker came back to the Casino de Paris and sang: 'J'ai deux amours. Mon pays et Paris.' That became *her* song. In return for her youth, her sex, her exoticism, the French gave her love, cash, and respect. She briefly returned to Broadway in 1935 and arrived at a party for Gershwin in full drop-'em-dead French glamour-queen glad rags: 'Who dat?' said Bea Lillie. In France once again, now and then she'd change the words of her song: 'Mon pays, c'est Paris.' After a war in which she proved her loyalty to her adopted country, smuggling secret information in invisible ink on her sheet music, would you believe, the French gave her the Légion d'Honneur.

She died in her seventieth year, in 1975, in the white heat and ostrich plumes of her umpteenth come-back, an institution, a heroine, mourned by the dozen children – her multi-ethnic 'Rainbow Tribe' – she adopted in her forties, something glorious if faintly touched by the ludicrous, at last, a geriatric sex queen cherished in old age by the French loyalty to the familiar as she had been fêted when young by the French passion for the new.

Tatler, 1990.

Screen and Dream

Femmes Fatales

Review of G.W. Pabst, *Pandora's Box*, and Josef von Sternberg, *The Blue Angel*.

PRINCE ESCERNY: Can you imagine a greater happiness for a woman than to have a man wholly in her power?
LULU: (jingling her spurs): Oh, yes!

This illuminating exchange comes from Frank Wedekind's *Earth Spirit*, the first of the two 'Lulu' plays that Wedekind thought were about abnormal psychology but turned out to be really about everyday life, as these things so often do. What is interesting about this repartee in the dancer Lulu's dressing-room (hence the spurs – part of her costume), is that Escerny does not pay the slightest attention to her reply.

With a little probing at this point, Lulu might have been willing to give him the answer to that version of the riddle of the sphinx – 'What do women want?' – that was exercising the mind of a certain Viennese *savant* at this very time. But Escerny is not concerned with that. In a roundabout way, he is telling Lulu what *he* wants, which is for her to destroy him. Since she is a good-natured girl, she would probably be prepared to gratify this desire were it not for the exigencies of the plot, that must now whirl her away to lesbianism, murder, incest and a final epiphanic *crise* at the hands of Jack the Ripper. Which is what, presumably, Wedekind thought an attractive girl like Lulu would actually prefer to having a nice time.

But Wedekind himself could not consult Lulu as to the nature of her own real wishes since she does not exist except as the furious shadow of his imaginings. But at least he gives her credit for some kind of life beyond his imaginative grasp; it was left to one exceptional actress and one exceptional film-maker to flesh out that life and show that it is in absolute contradiction to the text.

Pabst's screen version of the Lulu plays, *Pandora's Box*, remains one of the great expositions of the cultural myth of the *femme fatale*. It is a peculiarly pernicious, if flattering, myth which Pabst and his star, Louise Brooks, conspired to both demonstrate irresistibly in action while, at the same time, offering evidence of its manifest absurdity.

They've just shown this particular piece of emotional dialectic at the National Film Theatre as part of the Surrealist season. Brooks is the greatest of all the Surrealist love-goddesses, pitched higher in the pantheon, even, than Dietrich and Barbara Steele because she typifies the subversive violence inherent in beauty and a light heart. She is the not at all obscure but positively radiant and explicit object of desire – living proof, preserved in the fragile eternity of the film stock, that the most mysterious of all is, as Octavio Paz said, the absolutely transparent. And, indeed, Lulu is transparent as sunshine; which is why her presence shows up all the spiritual muck in the corners. So she gets blamed for the muck, poor girl.

Time and permissiveness have dimmed neither the medium nor the message one whit. Brooks's face and presence remain unique; God knows, one would think she was quite enough woman as she is, but nobody, of course, can leave her alone for one moment. Desire does not so much transcend its object as ignore it completely in favour of a fantastic recreation of it. Which is the process by which the *femme* gets credited with fatality. Because she is perceived not as herself but as the projection of those libidinous cravings which, since they are forbidden, must always prove fatal. So Lulu gets off with the countess and obligingly sets up an Oedipal situation for her stepson when she shoots his father.

The conviction that women ought to live for love remains implicit in the idea of the *femme fatale*, despite the continual evidence of the behaviour of the *femme fatale* herself that this is not so. But the main contradiction inherent in the *femme fatale* is that, though she seems to live for love and often lives by it, she is, in fact, quite incapable of it. Or, so they say.

Lulu keeps repeating cheerfully that she has never been in love. This is the main thing that is wrong with her, according to Wedekind. No heart, see. A lovely flower that, alas, lacks perfume. Her loyalty to her old friends; her fidelity to her first seducer, the repulsive Schön; her willingness to support her adoptive father and effete stepson by the prostitution she loathes – Wedekind records all this but cannot see it as any evidence of human feeling at all. She is the passive instrument of vice, he says. That's all.

Pabst concentrated on the physical integrity of his leading lady and so the plot turns into something else. Lulu's negative virtue, her lack of hypocrisy, illuminates the spiritual degradation of every single other character in the movie, with the possible exception of the honest Egyptian brothel keeper. This slight imbalance is created, in part, because Pabst had to tone down the part of the lesbian countess who exploits Lulu less viciously than anybody else does. The hypocrisy of censorship has, therefore, only served to strengthen the point that the movie is actually making about hypocrisy.

There are, of course, not one but two classic German expressionist cinematic *femmes fatales* and if Louise Brooks is the more magical, then Marlene Dietrich is the most succinct. At every point, these two women present mirror images of one another, just as their names – Lulu, Lola-Lola – teasingly echo one another. Dietrich was Pabst's second choice for Lulu if Paramount had not released Louise Brooks. *Pandora's Box* is a silent film; Brooks speaks with her body. The image of Dietrich in *The Blue Angel* is inseparable from her plangent, sardonic voice.

The Blue Angel, made by Josef von Sternberg, né Joe Sternburg of Brooklyn, made of Dietrich not a cult legend but a major icon of the cultural imagination of the twentieth century, serene, heartless, androgynous, a lovely cobra poised to strike, and so on. This is a curious transformation wrought on the actual character in the movie by, again, those strange projections of desire that have turned Lola-Lola into a drag-queen.

At the core of the didactic Pabst's abstract melodrama of bourgeois hypocrisy is the American Brooks's exhibition of lyrical naturalism. That is part of the artistic tension of the movie. The central jewel in the formal rococo of von Sternberg's parody of provincial life is, in fact, a virtuoso piece of harsh realism – Dietrich's attractive, unimaginative cabaret singer, who marries a boring old fart in a fit of weakness, lives to regret it but is too soft-hearted to actually throw him out until his sulks, tantrums and idleness become intolerable. If that is the story of a *femme fatale*, then some of my best friends are *femmes fatales* and anybody who feels ill-used by them has only himself to blame.

Lola-Lola can't love, either. She's much too sensible. She sings 'Falling in Love Again' with the ironic self-indulgence of one about to embark on a sentimental interlude that might give her a little fun but not much lasting profit. She has the look of somebody planning a brief holiday. So much the worse for the unfortunate professor, who is vain enough to think she is offering him her all. But as for him, is he so capable of human feeling himself?

He doesn't actually propose to Lola-Lola ('Men don't marry women like that,' as Schön, her seducer, says of Lulu) until he gets the sack for making a fool of himself over her. Maybe he thinks she owes him that much. Why? His marriage to Lola-Lola looks less like the surrender to a fatal passion than a grab at the chance of a lifelong meal ticket. How anybody has ever been able to see this film as the tragedy of an upright citizen of Toytown ruined by the baleful influences of a floozy is quite beyond me. The professor is a monster at the beginning and a monster at the end; he has toughened Lola-Lola up a bit and, perhaps, that is *her* tragedy, but clearly she will not brood. Neither will the toughening process kill her, as it does Lulu.

Dietrich's Lola-Lola is, of course, another wonder of the cinema and quite sufficient, in its sheer self-confidence, to serve as the projection of a fatal woman. And she is far more of an affront to male self-esteem than Lulu could ever be, because Lulu, being a child of nature and not a professional woman, has very little self-esteem herself. So *Pandora's Box* is never as criminally misread as *The Blue Angel* is. I have only ever seen one interpretation of *The Blue Angel* that seemed to tally with the movie I've seen and that is by the Surrealist, Ado Kyrou.

Kyrou, however, is so *bouleversé* by Lola-Lola that he goes right over the top. He simply can't believe Emil Jannings's luck. The famous scene, often regarded as the apogee of the ex-professor turned clown's humiliation, where he helps Marlene Dietrich on with her stockings: Kyrou shakes and stammers at the very thought. Is there a man living, who would not regard a lifetime spent helping Marlene Dietrich on with her *stockings* as the very highest fate to which he might aspire? Kyrou can hardly bear it; he wants to jump right into the screen, knock Jannings out of the frame and take his place tenderly at her feet. The professor's real tragedy, opines Kyrou, is that he is offered, if not love then a reasonable simulacrum of it, by a woman who is patently well worth a bit of hard work, and he is too great an idiot to see it.

'A woman blossoms for us precisely at the right moment to plunge a man into everlasting ruin; such is her natural destiny,' states the spineless sponger, Alwa Schön, in Wedekind's play. The horrid professor might have said the same. But what about her own life, if she can retain it, after the ruin has been accomplished? That is a gap in the scenario which, if she manages to get out of the mess, she must fill in herself. The pragmatic Dietrich packs her bags and exits with a sympathetic vaudeville performer, who will not ask of her more than she is willing to give. The more metaphysical Lulu can only hope, now, to accede to death as if it were some kind of grace.

So Lulu, the reluctant prostitute who never wished to sell the body she regarded as an inalienable possession, will be murdered by a sexual maniac, a man whom repression has turned into a monstrous scourge of whores, and on Christmas Eve, too, poor girl. She pays the price of expressing an unrepressed sexuality in a society which distorts sexuality. This is the true source of the fatality of the *femme fatale*; that she lives her life in such a way her freedom reveals to others their lack of liberty. So her sexuality is indeed destructive, not in itself but in its effects.

Repressive desublimation – i.e. permissiveness – is giving the whole idea of the *femme fatale* a rather period air. But this is only because the expression of autonomous female sexuality is no longer taboo. To clarify the point, a remake of *Pandora's Box*, or even *The Blue Angel,* ought, perhaps, to star a beautiful boy in the *femme fatale* role. Fassbinder could direct it. The significance of the *femme fatale* lies not in her gender but in her freedom.

New Society, 1978

Japanese Erotica

Review of Nagisa Oshima, *Ai No Corrida*

The blowfish (*fugu*) is the Japanese culinary speciality *par excellence*, the greatest treat of all, but one to be approached with caution. It is exceptionally delicious, it is a delight to the eye, it is inordinately expensive and, if you aren't careful, it will – the final thrill – kill you! Certain of its internal organs are fatally toxic. The Japanese feel about blowfish like they feel about the love of women.

Maybe *The Blowfish Feast* might have been a better title for Nagisa Oshima's sumptuous period piece – you can't call it a costume drama, because the principal actors usually appear unclad (contrary to the lengthy tradition of Japanese eroticism). *The Bullring of Love* is a rough translation of *Ai No Corrida* though the image of the bullring does express the erotic antagonism between men and women that the film so amply illustrates: sex as an exhibition of athletic skill and physical stamina, in which the man is the blundering, witless, phallic bull, the instrument of female pleasure, the passive, adoring victim, perpetually desired, easily exhausted. And the woman, the toreador, derives her ultimate orgasm from the *coup de grâce* with which she then dispatches him.

But it is not as simple as that.

Kichi knew what was coming to him, all right, just as somebody who wilfully consumes the blowfish out of season knows he stands a running chance of taking his after-dinner nap in the morgue. And, in Japan, nowhere but the morgue is the right, true end of passion. Innkeepers near famous waterfalls, precipices, volcanoes (love suicides like beauty spots), cautiously refuse to let rooms to young couples who arrive late, indecorously hand-in-hand, suspiciously without baggage.

In a country happily free from the notion of original sin, ethics is part of the process of socialisation. A society in which, traditionally, the common goal is the good of all and marriage a liaison of reason, it is erotic passion that turns the communard into the bourgeois individualist. It turns Oshima's Kichi from complacent stud to clapped-out murderee, Sada from submissive maid-servant to demented castratrix.

Libidinal gratification may be pursued with wholehearted enthusiasm and nobody pay it any attention. It is the unique assertion of the self in erotic passion that is the secular sin which necessitates a self-inflicted punishment. At some point in all this, just to fall in love becomes an act of rebellion against society, as the Surrealists always said it was. But the lovers of *Ai No Corrida* have no consciousness of the nature of the society from which they retreat into emotional seclusion. You could call them rebels without a cause.

Yet the events *Ai No Corrida* describes took place in 1936, when Japan, in the thick of imperialist expansion, was purging the left wing through a series of assassinations and preparing for war. A time of rage, despair, violence, hysteria and frustration. Juxtaposed against this is the story of Sada.

The story of Sada, as all those who read the film reviews will know, is: maidservant runs off with employer's husband and eventually strangles him in the course of a sexual game. (Accidents will happen.) What happened then seems to me to belong solely to the realm of psychopathology; she sheared off his penis, wrote SADA AND KICHI-SAN FOR EVER in blood on his hapless trunk, wrapped his penis up in a handkerchief and was found, a few days later, wandering the streets of Tokyo with the bloody relic in her bosom. She told the police she cut it off because she didn't want him to sleep with another woman. She received a very light prison sentence because, I was told, most people thought she was nuts – a reasonable hypothesis Oshima does not explore. She ended her days, I believe, again as a maid in an inn. People would come for miles to have her pour saké for them.

It is a singularly bizarre variant on the classic theme of the love suicide; and the lightness of her sentence and the levity, albeit terrified levity, with which her crime is discussed, suggests the lack of seriousness with which women are treated in that country. Oshima certainly does not treat her with levity. He treats her with such lugubrious solemnity that the movie made me wish that men would just leave off making films about female sexuality until they stop feeling threatened by it, for good intentions can lead them into old traps.

Coming out of the Gate Cinema after Sada had finally strangled and castrated the poor hulk, after an infinitely prolonged session of foreplay, I overheard some idiot braying: '*That* was a liberated lady for you!' As if erotic anti-feminism wasn't one of the great staples of all romantic art and we hadn't just seen a particularly glittering celebration of it. For all I know, Oshima himself does indeed believe his heroine is striking a blow for all women, everywhere, when she garottes her lover, even though, by that time, he has turned the actress who plays her into a demented fiend with dishevelled hair and a crazy smile, robed in a kimono of the bloodiest, most ominous red.

Then he makes her stand over the corpse in an attitude strikingly reminiscent of Max Ernst's castratory painting, *The Robing of the Bride*, gloatingly stroking her exceptionally large knife. I know Kichi-san was asking for it; but that doesn't mean a girl has got to give it to him. Need female submission go so far?

Ai No Corrida is a pornographic film. I don't see why anybody should argue about whether it is or isn't, or should care. Films about people having sex are pornographic in the way that films about cowboys are western; it is a description, not a value judgement. (Now *Love Story* was obscene.) Most major film-makers (of whom Oshima is one) have made pornographic films during the 1970s and I don't think this is to do solely with market pressures. Sexuality is a hitherto taboo area of human experience which it is now possible to explore for the benefit of large audiences. It always raises, in the most provocative fashion, the nature of the relation of the individual to society. Which is one of the reasons why pornography as a genre attacts radicals. However, pornography presents a number of artistic problems – not least because it has even more stringent intellectual limitations than the western. It also necessarily involves a discussion of the nature of realism.

Since pornography, almost more than any other cinematic genre, must depend on its audience suspending disbelief, the audience must be persuaded through a suave and, as it were, invisible photographic technique, that they are watching a couple actually screwing. (Or whatever else they are getting up to.) But, at the same time, the audience must be persuaded by a variety of means – Oshima uses a heavy overlay of period Japonaiserie detail – from asking themselves whether the couple they are watching *are* actually screwing. Because, if you start wondering whether the actors personating, say, Sada and Kichi are indeed getting it on in the studio, then the illusion of reality is broken at once. And once this illusion is gone, then the whole thing flies out of the artistic control of the director.

Upon the beautiful image of the privacy of the lovers, the busy, populous, brightly lit image of the film-studio superimposes itself. We are no longer eavesdropping on the activity of desire; we are watching, instead, an elaborate mimetic paraphrase of desire, the appearance of realism which is, *per se*, unreal. And even if they *are* doing it, we are not watching *them* do it. We are watching the people they are pretending to be do it; that is part of the bargain we made with the nature of reality when we entered the cinema. But now everything you see is false; it all means something other than the spectacle before us, but the genre itself denies you access to that meaning!

So the film-maker perforce plays a game with the audience's perception of his creation which the essential, and probably crippling, discipline of pornography – that it must look as real as he can make it – prevents him from acknowledging. Alienation is the essence of pornography. In *Casanova*, Fellini coped with the presentation of alienated sexuality with characteristic brio; Donald Sutherland never took his trousers off, all his diverse adventures, were conducted in a stylised mime, at high speed. The effect was harsh, satiric and anti-erotic – as if to say, repressive desublimation will get you nowhere fast. Yet *Casanova* is not a puritanical film, while *Ai No Corrida*, with its abundance of fictive copulations, *is* deeply puritanical. No movie with the central message that the price of gratified desire is madness and death could fail to be puritanical. That love should end in the death of the object of the other's desire is a refinement of a notion of sexual love as transgression, which is not unique to Judaeo-Christian culture. If the film is intended as a critique of the social basis of this notion, then I simply don't think pornographic realism can cope with this kind of input.

Near the beginning of the film, there is a sequence where a group of children poke open a robe of a sleeping tramp with Japanese flags; they reveal his senescent tool. This they then pelt with snowballs. Oshima's other films have made very free use of expressionist devices; and this extraordinary image of nationalism and impotence dominated the film, and made me wonder: what does he mean by all this screwing, what does he *mean*? The emblematic tramp cannot get it up at the sight of Sada's carelessly revealed nudity; perhaps *Ai No Corrida* is a film about a less specific kind of inadequacy than that which Kichi, and who can blame him, finally exhibits. Liberalism, perhaps? Or, what? About female sexuality it is not, although it exploits male fear.

It is, finally, bitterly ironic that Oshima, who has made some profoundly serious films about modern Japan, should achieve his breakthrough to critical acclaim in the West with a film that enshrines certain Western stereotypes of Japanese culture in the glossy context of a period piece. Oshima is himself, perhaps, aware of this irony.

New Society, 1978

Much, Much Stranger than Fiction

Review of Diana Dors, *Behind Closed Dors*; Kenneth Anger, *Hollywood Babylon*; A.E. Hotchner, *Doris Day: Her Own Story* and *Sophia – Living and Loving: Her Own Story*; Hildegarde Knef, *The Gift Horse*; Joan Collins, *Past Imperfect*.

Autobiography is closer to fiction than biography. This is true both in method – the processes of memory are very like those of the imagination and the one sometimes gets inextricably mixed up with the other – and also in intention. 'Life of' is, or ought to be, history: that is, 'the life and times of'. But 'my life' ought to be (though rarely is) a clarification of personal experience, in which it is less important (though only tactful) to get the dates right. You read so-and-so's life of somebody to find out what actually happened to him or her. But so-and-so's 'my life' tells you what so-and-so thought about it all.

This obviously presupposes the autobiographer to possess a reflective bent but, as Diana Dors (in *Behind Closed Dors*) says: 'The urge to "tell all" is probably within most of us,' and the success of Miss Dors's own set of 'gossipy memoirs' proves that movie actresses, at least, don't need a reflective bent in order to satisfy the curiosity of the general public. Movie actresses often live in a margin of fictionality that runs parallel to real life – the twilight world of what Norman Mailer called 'factoids': items invented by the publicity department.

Movie actresses' 'my life' experience is, to a very large extent, not what you would properly call *personal* experience at all. It belongs in the public domain. The nature of their daily work, when they are lucky enough to get it, consists of impersonating other people, and sometimes incarnating other people's fantasies. This necessary element of fantasy removes the movie actress memoir from the realm of autobiography altogether, and makes of it a fairy tale, sometimes a fable for our time. Kenneth Anger says of Judy Garland in *Hollywood Babylon:* 'She was *She,* who had stepped into the Flame once too often' – victim of the intense exploitation of the star system, and maybe of the emotional disturbance that makes somebody want to be a star in the first place.

Hollywood Babylon is a poison banquet of foul scandal and gossip, spanning Hollywood from the Gish sisters to Sharon Tate. It uses exclusively 'unauthorised' material. The 'unauthorised' show-business memoir always has a greater air of authenticity about it than the authorised one. The showbiz autobiography itself is patently a public relations job; in most cases, to tell all would presumably mean you never worked again.

Here, the 'as-told-to' steps in to clarify the issue: 'in her own words, as told to'. When Doris Day tells A. E. Hotchner, her as-told-to, that she wants to do an autobiography because: 'I'm tired of being thought of as Miss Goody Two-Shoes', you immediately smell a rat. She and her as-told-to will be concerned with reshaping her slightly outmoded image.

And Hotchner, a real old pro, indeed officiates at the birth of a revamped Doris Day, kind of a Ms Goody Two-Shoes, with up-to-date ideas about pre-marital intercourse, and a thing about earning her own living. A plucky little woman, with enough inherent innocence of heart to make her passion for dogs touching and her enthusiasm for Christian Science inevitable. And the undertext of *Doris Day: Her Own Story* is indeed gripping; all the bewilderment of Middle America faced with the stark facts of life. Her third husband, Marty Melcher, up to some very tricky business with taxes before he passed on, leaving Miss D in the lurch; her son, Terry Melcher, smirched by the beastly Manson business.

The line that Doris and her as-told-to fall back on is consistent with this bewilderment. Stardom, box-office ratings, etcetera, etcetera, were thrust upon her. For herself, she would rather have been successfully married with lots of kids and lived happily anonymous in Cincinnati.

Most PR hypes are crass, and the Poor Little Rich Girl hype is the crass-est of the lot. Doris and her as-told-to are sailing near the wind, here, since Hotchner has indeed created, out of taped transcripts of interviews, a per-sonality of some complexity and internal tensions. Nevertheless, perhaps due to his sterling work on the Day file, we next find Hotchner tackling a rather more ambitious job – nothing less than the secular canonisation of one of the leading sex-symbols for her time, incorporating the richest hype of all, the Cinderella hype.

Sophia – Living and Loving: Her Own Story, by A. E. Hotchner (see –he's credited with a full by-line, again; all for transcribing and editing tapes) features a stunning cover picture of Sophia ('ripeness is all') Loren as she is today. On the back flap is a faded snap of Sophia as a gaunt, wide-eyed child attired for her first communion, the kind of heart-wrenching photo-graph you find in Italian graveyards. But the whole thrust of Hotchner's first-person rendering of Sophia's life is that the glorious condition of her latter years is the logical culmination of her early vicissitudes and iron-clad virtue. A portentous quote from Chaplin – 'Out of chaos comes the birth of a star' – introduces the book and sets the tone.

Nowhere is there any discussion of what a star actually is. Such a dis-cussion might involve a historical analysis of the economics of the film industry, and a certain amount of metaphysical speculation about the nature of vicarious experience and projective fantasies. (Hildegarde Knef, in her memoirs, discusses the changing role of the movie director in this context.) Sophia-as-told-to does venture her own opinions: 'It seems to me that adoration of a hero figure is universally as basic as hunger.' Which contains certain implicit, unpleasant assumptions. But Sophia-as-told-to leaves you with the impression that stardom is an exemplary condition which certain people, especially women, arrive at through being very beautiful and very good, and after striving to overcome immense odds such as poverty and illegitimacy.

Sophia – Living and Loving starts off with a parable: 'There was once a little girl with very thin legs, huge eyes and a worried mouth.' Guess who. This little girl: 'had been born in a knot of bitter roots, in the flower of which she eventually discovered the world'. Profiting by this discovery, she eventually: 'embraced the whole universe'. Hotchner dedicates this book to her, 'and to all the little girls with big eyes and spindly legs who are born in a knot of bitter roots'. This hushed reverence is characteristic of Hotchner in full gear. He ends his collaboration with Doris Day by quoting a friend of hers: 'I think God did a little dance round her [D.D.] when she was born.' The stars are, in some sense, chosen people.

This reverential language tones down the PR hype aspects of Sophia's Cinderellaesque trajectory, which needs some work on it, anyway, since the marriage to the prince occurred *in medias res*. Sophia's universal embrace – the love of the star encompassing us all – now forms the happy end. The flesh-and-blood dimensions, which Sophia and her amanuensis wish to give to the voluptuous Neapolitan of the screen, are neither the spiky ones of *real* life nor the melting ones of erotic fantasy.

Sophia-as-told-to is warm, glowing, serene, serious, sensible, kind, resolutely monogamous and a hero mother, to boot. Hotchner quotes Sophia's secretary: 'I still marvel at the way she sacrificed herself to have that child. Nine months in bed, no activity at all, not even talking on the telephone, and not one word of complaint.' Such dedication to mother-hood that, four years later, Sophia went through it all again.

The sanctity of motherhood! Perfect protective camouflage for a super-star – especially one who started out squabbling with Gina Lollobrigida about who had the biggest tits.

It is instructive to compare Sophia-as-told-to's account of Naples at the end of the second world war with Hildegarde Knef's description of that war in Berlin. Sophia-as-told-to, starving and lousy in Naples, is at her blandest, the miseries are recounted quickly. Here in this terrible crucible was, presumably, forged the steely spirit that took her into the high life; but she doesn't want to let on all that much about it, perhaps because it contains an element of the controversial.

Admittedly, Knef was rather older – old enough, as a UFA starlet, to have had a supper invitation from Goebbels, which was brusquely fielded by a true friend. Nevertheless, the first part of her autobiography, *The Gift Horse*, is improbably enough, a *tour de force*. It uses all the techniques of fiction, para-doxically, to create the impression of complete veracity. It is a document about a generation that you could file alongside Günther Grass's *Dog Years*. Her subsequent, bumpy career in show business is less fascinating – though her quizzical disaffection tells you far more about the film industry, and the making of a star, than any as-told-to. *The Gift Horse* isn't really a show-busi-ness autobiography at all. Knef says things like: 'Success and failure are both greatly overrated, but failure gives you a whole lot more to talk about,' that no as-told-to would dare. Curiously, her most recent screen appearance was in Billy Wilder's *Fedora*, which is about stardom as self-destruction.

These memories and pseudo-memoirs all enshrine cultural myths. Day is 'true grit', in the American grain. Loren, combines physical lavishness with the taboo against screwing your mother, in a typically Italian fashion. Knef is the paradigm of those nervously intelligent, high-strung European actresses who, like certain wines, do not travel well. The interesting thing about Diana Dors and Joan Collins – both of whom have recently thought their memoirs worth publication – is that neither of them can boast the critically and commercially respectable filmographies of any of the above. Indeed, Dors's bizarre cameo role, as a football fetishist, in Skolimovski's *Deep End,* is her unique claim to any kind of cinematic class. But both really do believe themselves to be movie stars, relating the most trivial events of their careers with absolute self-assurance.

Dors is British as Blackpool rock; well-nigh – one would think – incomprehensible outside her native shores. She is a direct linear descen-dant of the Wyf of Bath, and her two publications, *For Adults Only* and *Behind Closed Dors*, have a raucous good humour that, give her her due, no as-told-to would dare to emulate. A typical Dors quip: 'Why was Richard Burton's father the greatest carpenter in Wales?' 'Because with just one screw he made the biggest shithouse in the country.' Mae West herself would have thought this one a mite vulgar, but conspicuous vul-garity is Dors's style, the flip side of the English lady, the *truth* about Mrs Miniver. Her reflective bent takes her as far as: 'To be born with the name of Fluck, particularly if one is a girl, can be nothing less than disastrous.'

If Dors is the very personification of the buxom backside of the other Britain, the one we cannot export because nobody believes it exists, then Joan Collins is the pits. Just the pits. Like Dors, she evidently eschews as-told-tos. On the cover of *Past Imperfect*, it says: 'In her own words', and who could doubt it. No competent ghost would have let through a cul-tural reference such as: 'I had just read F. Scott Fitzgerald's *The Girl in the Green Hat*.' Day, Loren, Knef, Dors, Collins, are all now well into middle age, but Collins is the only one who is still in the business as a sex symbol, pure and simple. I can only conclude that she penned her sniggering memoirs in order to give her drecky movies, *The Stud, The Bitch*, an extra touch of notoriety. See the naughty girl in characteristic action.

'My cocoon of baby pillows and sheets was rumpled from last night's lovemaking, and my mouth was dry from too much wine and too many cigarettes.'

Miss Collins's style is, aptly enough, copywriter's kitsch:

'Dollink, I know a wonderful man who is MAD about you,' Zsa Zsa Gabor bit crisply into a shrimp and surveyed me shrewdly.' (The man in question is Raphael Trujillo. Oh, my God.)

And so on. Here is the little girl from RADA who went to Hollywood, made a number of movies which contributed to the decline of the motion picture industry, might have starred in *Cleopatra* had Elizabeth Taylor died, and screwed a number of exceedingly dull men. A perennial naughty girl, a celluloid courtesan: the perfect product of a dream factory that is now almost defunct, and can (ironically) only stimulate interest in its fantasies with the aid of the printed word.

Joan Collins's blend of the meretricious, the salacious and the self-exploitative is a peculiarly depressing one. It is difficult not to see – in her iron-clad eye for the main chance, her glorification of her well-preserved charms, her conscious re-warming of her life as cheap fiction – the perfect projective fantasy of Margaret Thatcher's Britain. *Past Imperfect*'s parallel reality is a bit too near the nerve.

New Society, 1979

Bertolucci: La Luna

In a *Sight and Sound* interview with Richard Roud Bertolucci says he first had the idea for his film *La Luna* during a session with his psychoanalyst. 'I suddenly realised that I had been talking about my father for seven or eight years – and now I wanted to talk about my mother.' It seems to have taken them an unconscionable time to get around to discussing the person Freud calls a child's 'first seducer', the authentic, original source of love and hunger, but Bertolucci certainly now attacks the subject with brio. He says that, in *La Luna*, 'I wanted to say the obvious – that every man is in love with his mother.' Which, put like that, is something like dedicating a movie to the proposition that rain is wet. Nevertheless, *La Luna* is concerned to reveal this psychoanalytic truth via the artistic method of the lushest kind of forties and fifties Hollywood melodrama.

And much of the satisfaction of the movie comes from the spectacle of watching stock themes and characters of the Dream Factory – illicit sex, drug addiction, glamorous career women, troubled adolescents, poor but honest schoolteachers – graphically presented in terms of *The Interpretation of Dreams*, even if Bertolucci, throughout, seems rapturously uncritical of both kinds of dream – indeed, of dreams in general. The Dream Factory effect is enhanced by an 'international' production with all the stops out – American leads, American dialogue, sumptuous photography, sumptuous design, set mostly in a Rome bathed in sumptuous corn-syrup sunlight like adolescent afterglow.

Few of the characters are not variants of Hollywood stereotypes. The heroine, played by Jill Clayburgh, even has the traditional girlfriend/confidante. But Jill Clayburgh, seizing by the throat the opportunity of working with a great European director, gives a bravura performance: she is like the life force in person, and this subtly alters the movie's entire distribution of emphasis, because it isn't supposed to be about her as a mother at all, but about a son's relation to his mother.

Clayburgh plays Caterina, née Catherine, an American opera singer returning more or less triumphantly to sing in Rome. (She had previously studied in Italy.) After her husband-manager suddenly dies in New York, she sweeps along with her to the Eternal City her spoiled, neglected, bored, troubled, adolescent son, Joe (Matthew Barry). To Caterina's guilty horror, she discovers Joe has become addicted to heroin. They are sexually drawn towards one another, but, after Joe has lain between her thighs for a few tense seconds in a seedy hotel room, she tremulously reveals the existence of *another* father. Her late husband was only Joe's legal father. Joe has a real father, a biological father. The Great Taboo, just as it is about to be broken, raises itself again.

Joe immediately quests off in search of his biological father, and all ends happily with Joe coming off smack in the sunshine of his new-found father's smile. So, in spite of the come-on promotional slogan, 'Catherine and her son share a desire that will shock you!' the film is not so much about incest as about incest successfully averted. And, since sleeping with your mother is but half the Oedipal package deal, it is also about parricide successfully circumvented. The father whom Joe saw die a few moments after he'd suggested to his mother that they ditch him – 'there's nothing dad can do that I can't' – was a false, a decoy father. Joe never killed him, not even in thought.

All the taboos are, in the end, respected. Father is, as it were, resurrected and restored to his rightful position at the pinnacle of a boy's world. Joe has his Oedipal cake and eats it: no wonder he is able to abandon the forbidden food of heroin. In the final sequence, where the long-parted lovers

meet at the instigation of their child, as in a late Shakespeare comedy, a
young girl arrives to snuggle up to Joe, to indicate he is now mature
enough to acquire sexual playmates of his own age. Even the trivial convention against cross-generation sex is scrupulously respected.

So what we have here is really an old-fashioned 'problem' movie, in
which a 'controversial' theme gets all its teeth drawn by the simple process
of evading the real issues. (The real issue being, I would say, the repressive
nature of patriarchy, but I've been asking myself what Jocasta felt about
that unpleasant business at Thebes for a long time now.) Anyway, this,
surely, accounts for all *La Luna*'s curiously cosy charm, and, together with
Bertolucci's easy and voluptuous skill as a film-maker, makes it a
thoroughly enjoyable wallow that titillates but never remotely disconcerts,
let alone disturbs. It is instructive to compare it with those films of Douglas
Sirk – *All that Heaven Allows, Imitation of Life, A Time to Love and a Time to
Die* etc. – that are, apparently, soapy weepies but contain within, because
of their rigid adherence to genre conventions, descriptions of the way
human beings are cut up to fit the procrustean bed of social norms.

Well, Caterina and Joe cut themselves up, too, but Bertolucci, following the letter and not the spirit of Sirk, and lugubriously authorised by
Freud, seems to think this is perfectly all right. It is a very odd film for the
maker of *The Conformist* to have made, but, on the evidence of *La Luna*,
Bertolucci appears content to reserve politics for his specifically political
movies, as though politics had nothing to do with human relationships,
and gives the film a 'happy end' that leaves Joe with all the rebellion of his
desire crushed.

The film begins wth a specifically Freudian prologue. A blonde, freck-
led young woman dribbles honey on the mouth of a sulking boy child,
licks spilled honey off his skin. (Bertolucci is blessed by Clayburgh's ability
to exhibit polymorphous sexuality in relation to virtually everything.) It is
a beautiful day. A shadowy, vaguely menacing figure strums a piano inside
the house on the sunny terrace of which mother and baby play. The
amniotic sea glitters. A young man is filleting a fish. The sensuous young
mother teases the child with an unfilleted fish. A mirror is propped against
the wall in a little homage to Jacques Lacan. The blonde young woman,
to the irritation of the invisible piano-player, now puts a record of a sexy
dance on the player and pulls the fish-gutter to his feet. The baby doesn't
like this at all and grizzles. When the pair conclude their vigorous 'twist'
with a kiss, the baby howls and totters off to the arms of the shadowy person, his ankles tangling in the unwinding wool from a ball with which he
has been playing.

This self-contained episode, which yet reverberates throughout all the
ensuing action, is so replete with Freudian symbolism – knitting wool/

navel string, sexy dance/primal scene, and oh, that phallic herring! – that one expects a transformation scene as dramatically explicit as the one in Buñuel and Dali's *L'Age d'Or*, in which the archbishops suddenly turn into skeletons. (The movie is so jam-packed with screaming symbols that, later, when a chance acquaintance tells Caterina how he went fishing with Castro and he caught a big fish but Castro caught a little fish, it sounds like an unnecessary slight on the virility of the President of Cuba.)

What *does* come next is a brief scene – according to Bertolucci, a child-hood memory of his own – in which Jill Clayburgh's wonderfully vivid and alive face is elided with the sterile features of the romantic but uncomfortable moon. Now she is riding a bicycle along a country road, cooing to the baby tucked into the basket in front of her, and the mother of mysteries, white, inviolable, luminous, mysterious, rises behind her. The surrealists, Freudians themselves, celebrated the bicycle as the perfect image of self-sufficient sexuality, but self-sufficiency, sexual or otherwise, isn't going to be Caterina's quality at all. The bike is a red herring: the moon is the thing – Caterina embodies the mysterious female principle.

It is an extraordinary and very beautiful image, a direct visualisation of the actual process of mystification – the real woman transposed into metaphor before your very eyes. (And, so crass is Bertolucci's use of symbolism, it is a wonder he never thinks to have Caterina sing the Queen of Night, especially since she was also a demanding parent and appears in – nudge – *The Magic Flute*.)

But the vision of Caterina as the mothering moon is interesting because it indicates the only way in which Bertolucci is prepared to subvert the genre of the 'woman's picture' within which he is working, and which Jill Clayburgh remains magnificently working towards, whatever happens, even when he takes the film's significance away from Caterina and gives it to Joe. Bertolucci converts the 'woman's picture' material into the background for a boy's movie, a movie of special interest to boys of all ages.

The moon is a dead planet, with no light of its own. Caterina is seen externally, always from the outside. Even when she is singing on the stage, we watch her, not for her own sake, but because Joe is watching her. Truly like the moon, she is visible only because we see her in the light reflected by Joe's perceptions of her. Since he is a spoiled brat, Caterina emerges strangely, as a bewitching, unpredictable giantess, and, for all her abundant liveliness, she is quite inscrutable because Joe, since he is a child, doesn't have the faintest idea what makes adults tick and, with the crystalline egocentricity of childhood, would answer Freud's question, 'What does a woman want?' with the triumphantly assured cry: 'Me! Joe! Me!' However, there is more to it than that. Bertolucci himself may well regard this absence of a sense of self in the character of Caterina as part of the existential characterisation of the New Dramaturgy, of which he claims *La Luna* to be an example.

But surely this absence of gravity, in the sense of weight, this depthless yet mysterious quality of Caterina, is no more than the romantic notion of Woman as Other which is characteristic of Bertolucci's treatment of women in all his movies. The wantonly destructive Maria Schneider in *Last Tango in Paris* functions only as Brando's externalised id; Dominique Sanda, in both *1900* and *The Conformist*, is a self-conscious sphinx. Both these share with Caterina'Clayburgh a magnificent moral irresponsibility, as though this is in the very nature of women. Gérard Dépardieu's red wife in *1900* is cut from a different cloth, but Bertolucci kills her off very quickly – in childbirth, significantly enough.

Only when women are over forty is he able to allow them to have any decent solidity. Alida Valli in *The Spider's Stratagem* may be a mystery to other people but never to herself: made of steel, she is the unmoved mover of the entire plot. It is no surprise to discover that the shadowy pianist in the primal scene, to whom baby Joe runs for sanctuary when his parents ignore him, Joe's granny, turns out to be Alida Valli all the time. And if *she* eventually acquires custody of the lad, after his Oedipal quest is over, then heaven help him, because she means war. Caterina, therefore, is doomed to a feckless and mercurial personality because her director can portray a woman of her age on the screen in very few other ways.

But the point of the movie is not that Joe is in trouble with himself because he sees his mother as the romantic other: seeing a woman as the romantic other is presumably what Bertolucci means by being 'in love', anyway. Nevertheless, both of the principals lose a good deal of their dignity by virtue of the film's refusal to admit any significant life for Caterina except in relation to her son, who, at the conclusion of the extended overture that prefigures all the main themes, metamorphoses into a petulant, pudgy, fractious, self-centred fourteen-year-old – not an attractive child, the kind whom, as they say, only a mother could love. Which, in such a remorselessly Oedipal movie, is only right and proper.

Yet. Oedipally speaking, the movie is rather confused. Joe's quest for a father has its own metaphysical strangeness. The whole theory of Oedipal conflict is based on the cultural fact of patriarchy rather than on the biological accident of paternity, and the person Joe has, for fourteen years, seen as a rival, the man of whom he boasts to his mother that he can do anything dad can, is dead. The schoolmaster he eventually discovers, surrounded by other people's children (a bathetic touch), is, in real, emotional terms, a perfect stranger, even if one act of impregnation, years ago, has assisted in Joe's arrival on earth. The schoolteacher, like the bicycle, is a red herring but, unlike the bicycle, Bertolucci doesn't intend him to be.

The dramatic nub of *La Luna* is really the moment when the sexual desire of the woman and the boy becomes overt. This is not the scene in which she masturbates him – Clayburgh performs this function with tight-lipped, clinical precision: there is no pleasure in it for her. Rather, it is a later scene, when she suddenly kisses him 'as one kisses a lover', as Bertolucci says in the *Sight and Sound* interview. He confesses himself confused by this scene. 'I don't quite understand it myself. I guess it's the New Dramaturgy.' Why is it the New Dramaturgy? Because it's inconsistent, and 'one must avoid consistency if one is to portray the sudden contradictions which we find in life.' But this lover-like kiss isn't inconsistent at all. It is the moment when both of them appreciate that a taboo may be broken; the moment of transgression is at hand. God is dead and anything can happen. Patriarchy is about to take it on the nose.

Although, in the bedroom scene a little later, intercourse is apparently interrupted only by Joe's more urgent desire for a fix, the feverish maternal embrace is soon explained and censored. Caterina is softening the boy up for the revelation that fourteen years of love, care, paid dental bills and shared baseball games do not make a father: only sperm does that. This is the authentic irrationality of patriarchy, the triumph of nature over nurture, the consecration of seminal fluid as the supreme unction of human bonding. Curiously enough, the news that father is alive makes mother untouchable, again, as though Big Daddy were watching. But I wonder what would have happened if Caterina had said: 'I'm not your real mother.'

Of course, they've only got into this embarrassing intimacy because Caterina is not a 'real' mother, and Joe's addiction to heroin is an unweaned dependence on a metal nipple transmitting a chemical substitute for the nourishing milk she has denied him through her selfish insistence on continuing her career. At this point, it becomes obvious that Bertolucci, unlike Fassbinder, who has also worked out an aesthetic based on a radical reinterpretation of Hollywood melodrama, has been unable to transcend the kitsch excesses of the genre and give it real life. Perhaps it is because Bertolucci seems to be entirely without irony. At one point, Caterina goes to see Joe's Arab dealer, Mustapha. Mustapha, dripping with patronising concern for his hapless client, is clearly the Third World's revent on that overprivileged youth. Yet Bertolucci presents him almost as a little guru, in a white robe, comforting Caterina and giving her good advice. This isn't the inconsistency of real life: it is sentimentality of a peculiarly self-deluding and unpleasant kind.

In a movie constantly teetering on the verge of self-parody, there is one delirious moment when it looks as though the New Dramaturgy might nudge Bertolucci profitably into just that higher kind of Sirkian melodrama. Joe goes on a ramble through Rome, is picked up by a young man who takes him to a bar and dances with him. (Although Mustapha tells Caterina that Joe finances his habit by stealing from her, she is not as rich as all that, and Joe is more likely to be earning Mustapha's pay-off from honest prostitution, though it seems likely that whoever holds the purse-strings of the Yankee dollars behind *La Luna* would have upheld, with absolute sternness, the taboo against sleeping with your own sex.) It seems as though Joe's pick-up may indeed prove to be the mysterious fish-gutter of the primal scene and all will end in hysteria of an epic and exemplary kind. No such luck.

London Review of Books, 1980

Hal Ashby: Being There

Hal Ashby's movie, *Being There*, presents itself as a parable of how-to-succeed-without-really-trying in the land of high capitalism. But it isn't really about America, although its apolitical cynicism accords very well with the mood of a year which witnesses a presidential election in which neither principal contender could ever, in any circumstances, no matter who directed, have been personated on celluloid by Henry Fonda.

Nor is it about television. Its hero, if 'hero' be not too emphatic a word for Chance the gardener, is created and circumscribed by the experience of television. But television remains no more than the film's central metaphor, a metaphor for a state of dynamic non-being. And non-being is really the theme of *Being There*: the dialectics of non-being, you might say, done in terms of such comic-book crudity that you end up feeling that non-being is the only way to be.

Being There is scripted by the Polish emigré writer, Jerzy Kosinski, from his own slender, enigmatic novel of the same name; and more than a touch of the middle European fable, the Kafka that dare not speak its name, blurs the all-American edge of things. Kosinski, an interesting, even brilliant novelist with a professional speciality in the social sciences, has lived in the United States since 1957. He called this novel, as a work in progress, either *The Blank Page* or *Dasein*. Dasein is a 'philosophical term, difficult to translate, which could mean the state in which one "is" and "is not" at the same time' (to quote Kosinski from a *Paris Review* interview). His screenplay follows the novel very closely. One major and significant change is a shift of location, from New York City to Washington. The character of

Chance the gardener remains exactly the same; he is a perfect null. Peter Sellers plays him.

It's apt and fitting that *Being There* should conclude Seller's career as shape-shifter extraordinary, that the Man of a Thousand Identities should leave as his screen monument a role in which he has no identity at all except that with which other people supply him. He functions as a *tabula rasa*. His pale, bland, oblong face bears an unnerving resemblance to a TV screen laid on its side. An occasional flicker of sub-clinical awareness ripples across it like static. In Jerzy Kosinski's novel Chance was young and handsome: Sellers is neither, but exudes a kind of negative charisma.

If Chance the gardener had been played *à la* Candide, by, say Kris Kristofferson, the logic of his beauty would have made the fable considerably less acrid. It would have become a dumb blonde apotheosis and dumb blondes (like Marilyn Monroe) always variants of Holy Fools. The movie sub-edits residual trace elements of the Holy Fool from the character of Chance. Sellers plays him as a perfect idiot and most of the laughs in *Being There* are at his expense. If you do not find the spectacle of the feeble-minded in itself amusing, you will not enjoy *Being There* much.

The novel tells us all about Chance in its second paragraph: this is perfectly recapitulated in visual terms in the movie, when we see him in, and at one with, the garden of the house owned by somebody called the Old Man, who is perhaps his father. Chance, brain-damaged son of a brain-damaged mother, is unknowing and intentionless as the plants he tends. A plant 'cannot help growing, and its growth has no meaning, since a plant cannot reason or dream'. Chance, the plant, is watered by television. He wakes, eats and sleeps to television. He exists in an amniotic fluid composed of warm sounds, colours and random images that he changes with god-like arbitrariness by flicking the buttons on his remote control switch.

Chance's sense of television as the world and the world as television is rendered on the big screen by a sequence in which he attempts to deflect the attention of a street gang by pressing the remote control switch he has brought with him after his expulsion from the garden.

For the Old Man dies and Chance must leave the garden. He steps out into the unknown world to the accompaniment on the soundtrack of a jazz version of the Strauss tone poem, *Thus Spake Zarathustra*. This not only tells us that God is dead but also summons up from the vasty deeps of space the floating human foetus and its twin, the world, the transcendental final image of Kubrick's *2001*. (Any movie-buff knows that *Zarathustra* is the *2001* music.) Chance, therefore, is foetus as superman.

But, by the way, wasn't Adam a gardener, like Chance, and wasn't Christ the second Adam? At this point, I felt like Mr Jones – that something was happening and I didn't know what it was but I knew damn well I didn't approve of it.

In the streets, in his piteous simplicity – a simplicity, however the audience is never allowed to pity – Chance asks a busy shopper to give him some lunch; he's hungry. Guffaws rocked the auditorium at her affronted stare, a laughter which validates welfare cuts; the idea on offer here is that it is inexpressibly comic in itself that the hungry should expect to be fed. It is instructive to find we live in times when the hunger of the innocent is a cause for mirth. But here Chance is no more than following Christ's own precepts, or that of any mendicant order of any faith whatsoever that allocates to humanity some kind of heart. However.

Chance then suffers a mild traffic accident and Eve (get that – *Eve*) Rand takes him home in her car. Eve Rand is played by Shirley MacLaine, looking stunning as a sexist stereotype. Eve Rand's home turns out to be the Xanadu-like mansion of her dying billionaire husband, Ben.

Chance gives his name and occupation – Chance the gardener; she mishears this as the impeccably WASP 'Chauncey Gardiner', and that, plus the classy wardrobe Chance has culled from the effects of the Old Man, sets the blank page on its career as doodle pad for the projective fantasies of others. Serious phenomenolgoists begin here.

The Rands applaud his stupidity as profundity. When he chatters on about gardening, everybody, from the president himself to the media pundits, takes his talk of the turn of the seasons as a profound analogy with the state of the nation.

Chance, for whom television is the world, takes to TV exposure like a duck to water. He is, presumably, the lowest common denominator with whom the masses can identify. Overnight, by simply *being there*, Chance is precipitated to nationwide fame. Rand, the kingmaker financier, dies. The pall-bearers at his funeral discuss the highest political future for Chauncey Gardiner, media star, backed by big business, chum of presidents, politically OK because null.

The film abandons Chance/Chauncey as he is walking on the water. Literally. He is picking his way across a barrier in a lake on the Rand grounds, scarcely wetting his feet as he advances across the little waves. Difficult to resist the notion that, in an oblique way, the movie was partly up to investigate that hoariest of chestnuts, who would Christ be were he alive today? And indeed, Christ would probably shine like a star on the media but, loath as I am to summon up a good word for the Son of Man, the gospels demonstrate he was intellectually no slouch and the Diggers and Levellers were not the first to point out that, on the basis of his own theories, had he found himself in political office, he would have been very radical indeed.

Be that as it may, this final receding image of Chance – baggy trousers, cane-like rolled umbrella, weird insouciance – has a touching, Chaplinesque quality; and the arbitrariness of real life has dowered it with an additional poignancy. This backview is the last we shall see of Peter Sellers. What a shame this strangely gifted and rather sinister mimic should exit as a hollow man, headpiece stuffed with straw, alas, even if Sellers' talents were never particularly suited to the cinema, whose great stars depend on unchanging essence rather than the flux of appearances. That this *is* the last of Sellers also sets the final necrophiliac seal of box office success on *Being There*. Perhaps one message of *Being There* is that every cloud has a silver lining.

The transportation of the action from New York in the novel to Washington in the movie means that the dome of the Capitol can hang over the proceedings ominous as a mushroom cloud. The persistence of Washington in the visual imagery is also a reminder of Frank Capra's populist comedies of the 1930s, *Mr Deeds Goes to Town, Mr Smith Goes to Washington*, that affirmed, if not the triumph of good over evil, at least the inexorable victory of niceness over nastiness, that down-homey decency and common sense of the ordinary little man (John Doe as in *Meet John Doe*) must, by the power of sheer decency, send the connivers of big business into the outer darkness. Capra wanted to show, as Chance might say, that the roots were sound.

Being There could almost be read as parody Capra. A brain-damaged zombie, John Doe for the American 1980s, given the spurious reflexive spasms of life due to total immersion in television, rises effortlessly and without intention to a probable presidential candidacy because the represetatives of big business are, not bigger idiots, but different kinds of idiots than he.

But this sour little fable is a one-joke movie which, in style and content, would best have suited a ten-minute animated cartoon. It has been stretched out to two hours primarily by the device of having Sellers speak his lines very, very slowly. And it has achieved a very considerable degree of critical acclaim. It has already won prizes and will undoubtedly win more.

I think it stinks, morally and artistically. It is yet another example of the current *trahison de clercs* that has produced the renaissance of the intellectual right, if the concept of an 'intellectual right' be not a contradiction in terms. It's too morally flaccid to be decently reactionary, though; it is reactionary only by virtue of the inertia it celebrates, a movie too exhausted to extract meaning from the images it half-heartedly articulates. If, indeed, it is Capra for our times, then God help us all. Yet it is really just a bland, timeless, placeless fairy tale – itself a blank page, on which it seems some people find it possible to project all sorts of significance. It fits the mood of the times. God is dead and the devil take the hindmost.

By far the most interesting thing about *Being There* is its supercilious, non-anayltic, besotted attitude to television itself. In some respects, *Being There* is a protracted anti-commercial for television mounted by the medium it threatens most. It implicitly suggest, by just being there, that it is a far better thing to sit in a cinema auditorium watching this protracted piece of magnificent yawnorama than to sit in the privacy of one's own home and allow the random variability of piped-in imagery to play on the screen of one's own mind.

Well, is it? This is a real question, to which I don't know the answer, at all, although that *Paris Review* interview with Kosinski tells you exactly what *he* thinks about television: 'the ultimate hope of religion was that it would release us from trauma. Television actually does so'. It does so by turning the viewer into a disinterested bystander at every human event, like Chance. The viewer is man in an exacerbated state of continuous alienation, even from sex. He will never know how to act. Perhaps this sub-theme of television as religion accounts for all those biblical overtones in the film. Who knows?

And the trouble with *Being There* is, after seeing it, having summoned up the question, who could care about the answer? Because, in this particular year, the most horrid irony of all is that Chance would indeed be a fine thing. I'd much rather have *his* finger on the button than any other finger on offer at the present time, providing no madman told him it was only a remote control switch, of course. You never know where you are with a madman but you can always trust a fool to persist in his folly.

But by making this particular fool a brain-damaged living vegetable, Ashby and Kosinski pre-empt the notion that the fool, were he to persist in his folly, would become wise. (Compare and contrast Werner Herzog's treatment of a similarly inadequately socialised person in *The Enigma of Kaspar Hauser*; but Herzog didn't allow himself the easy way out of using brain damage.) By cutting the Holy Fool down to size, *Being There* truly turns him into a suitable candidate for a closed institution, of which the White House is probably indeed a fitting image.

New Society, 1980

The Draughtsman's Contract

Over the credits of Peter Greenaway's *The Draughtsman's Contract*, and very elegantly chaste and discreet credits they are, there's a voice, singing – the ringing, thrilling, brilliant, somehow artificial-sounding voice of a counter-tenor, or male soprano.

And that's a very fitting prelude to a film that is just as brilliant and thrilling, just as much the product of high artifice and baroque convention. The singer and the song also 'date' the period in which the film is set – the late seventeenth century, to be precise – the film is very precise about this – the year 1694, just as the British bourgeoisie consolidates itself. But though in some ways the movie parodies the 'period romp', nothing could be further from a period romp than it.

The Draughtsman's Contract is the best British film for years, and it's good in what seems at first a very un-British way – it's highly self-conscious; it makes few gestures towards naturalism; and, above all, it possesses a visual glamour of the most seductive kind . . . a luscious sensuality mostly to do with light, with the way light falls . . . with candlelight on flesh; with sunlight on brick; most ravishing of all, the light that Turner painted, the light that irradiates the mists of mornings of high summer . . . the whole film is, in a way, a tribute to the uncertain glories of English light, light of an Atlantic island, various, changeable, subtle . . . the light of pure romanticism with which Peter Greenaway bathes a movie that is profoundly sardonic, bitterly funny and utterly without sentimentality.

The story-line: a young artist, the draughtsman of the title, makes a contract with a mature beauty, a certain Mrs Herbert, to draw a series of views of her husband's country house while her husband himself is away. Her intention, apparently, is to effect a reconciliation with her cold, indifferent, neglectful husband – on the other hand, the terms of the contract look suspiciously as though she's hiring herself a lover.

The young man sets to with a will, cock-sure in the possession of his talent – the thing he has officially for sale; and also of his – sexiness, his sexual allure . . . he has a rather touching faith in himself as the universal object of female desire; and, perhaps, of his class ascendancy. In the year 1694, bourgeoisie like the Herberts may be rich enough to commission pictures of their homes, but tradesmen – artisans like Mr Neville are on the up and up, too, ready and waiting to service them . . . to despise them, too. Mr Neville is making an almost piratical sortie among his betters, for fun and profit until his patroness's hustand is murdered. And things turn serious.

If *The Draughtsman's Contract* is un-British in its self-consciousness – you can't believe in its characters for one moment, nor are you supposed to; you never forget you are watching, not a slice of life but an elaborately constructed artificial reality – nevertheless, its plot is a combination of two characteristic British genres, the country house murder mystery and the comedy of manners. Agatha Christie articulated in terms of William Congreve.

It isn't a who-dunnit so much as a who-has-done-or-is-about-to-do-

what-to-whom-and-why; or even a now-you-see-it, now-you-don't –
because the drawings Mr Neville makes contain certain visual clues as to
what is really going on, even if he himself doesn't quite know.

The Draughtsman's Contract is a conundrum, or a rebus – a set of riddles
about sex, snobbery and death, executed with the sprightly heartlessness
characteristic of both the murder mystery and the restoration comedy . . .
until, that is, the very last moments, when the lovely light has died away;
night comes; in Pope's lines from the end of *The Dunciad* – 'a universal
darkness covers all'.

I'm not castigating the movie for 'sprightly heartlessness', by the way;
far from it. It is because of this formalist 'lack of heart', one of the thousand and one ways of achieving an alienation effect, that Greenaway has
been able to extract such brilliant ensemble acting from his cast.

Because the actors are always called upon to *act* – to perform, not to
embody feeling. This means that, at one bound, Greenaway has leapt over
the great stumbling block to good British cinema – that is, the entire
tradition of British theatrical acting.

Trained for the stage, that is, display, that is, trained always to act in long
shot 'for the back of the gallery', trained to pretend to be imaginary people
and to keep their own personalities out of the way, British actors usually
mess up movies by persistently *acting* – they never stop, they act all the
time, always doing busy things with their hands, twiddling their parasols,
fidgeting with props, they seem to think that if they keep still, they're not
earning their keep.

There's a little scene towards the end of the movie where Janet Suzman
reaches out and pats a teapot – God knows why she does this, why the
director told her to or let her do it, because this is typical *actor's business* –
meaningless clutter imitating life.

But, mostly, Greenaway is using stage-trained British actors in the only
way they *can* usefully be used in movies – in a context of high, artificial
theatricality. And he gives them long, complicated, well-constructed sentences to speak, too . . . stylised as 'actorspeak' itself.

This isn't to say the movie isn't well acted – that's the point! It is! It is!
if least strenuously by Anne Louise Lambert, as Janet Suzman's daughter,
Lambert, an actress gifted with the most sinister repose. (She does know
how to keep most menacingly still.) But Janet Suzman and Anthony
Higgins, as lady, Mrs Herbert, and draughtsman, Mr Neville, give truly
'glittering' performances – they create characters as if those characters were
stunning artefacts, with the happiest results, since that is precisely what
these characters are.

In fact, they don't look human, in their baroque elaboration of their
summer whites . . . Mr Neville states his difference by his black clothes,

his black wig, and, alone of them all, sometimes he may be seen in his own, cropped hair.

Those wigs. They make the men look like sheep, sheep Mr Neville thinks he's come to fleece, perhaps. Wigs; white, powdered faces; rouged lips. Like characters in *commedia del arte* . . . elaborate, exotic, unnatural.

And the women, too, with their tall, stiff headdresses like crests of birds, the still-lifes of rigid curls on their foreheads, curls as glossy and artificial-looking as if carved from wood by Grinling Gibbons . . . the complicated clothes in which they barricade themselves, from which they must be cut free: but don't let that clip deceive you. The sensuality of this extremely sensuous film is confined to an appreciation of things, not human flesh: to fruit . . . fruit, fruition, fecundity and the lack of fecundity, artificially induced fecundity . . . fruit and fruition are an elaborate, on-going metaphor within the film, and if the metaphor is extended to Mrs Herbert herself – if she is a neglected fruit-tree: there is, as you can see, no sensuality at all in the treatment of their sexual relation.

If our first suspicion is, that Mrs Herbert has hired Mr Neville for her own pleasure, it is soon evident that her motives are more complex. What pleasure is there in it for her . . . while Mr Neville himself, the hired hand, takes only a brisk satisfaction out of humiliating the lady. His desire, or her desire, does not enter the picture at all. Until the very end, when it may be Mr Neville's delusion of her desire. The lady's daughter takes over the contract after a while, inserts a few clauses that *seem* to concern her own libidinal gratification. Cock-sure Mr Neville never smells a rat! He perceives *her* sexual humiliation of him as another conquest of his own.

And then, murder. After that, the white/black colour scheme is reversed; Mrs Herbert and her entourage all in mourning, Mr Neville now in white – first hint of his näivety, his innocence, that he's no black sheep after all, but, perhaps, a sacrificial lamb . . .

Oddly enough, although *The Draughtsman's Contract* wouldn't be conceivable in any medium but film, it doesn't really owe much to the movies. Although it reminds me a little of Borowczyk's *Blanche,* perhaps because of that bravura singing over the credits, also because *Blanche,* too, presented the past as *mise-en-scène* . . . important for its decorative function, a glamorous commodity. And *The Draughtsman's Contract* also reminds me of Stanley Kubrik's underrated *Barry Lyndon,* a designer's fiesta of the eighteenth century that equated production values with property value in the most striking way. The opulent surfaces of Kubrik's movie, the sheer prodigality of it, lavished on the story of a young man who squanders a 'great estate'. *The Draughtsman's Contract* isn't nearly as unnervingly insolent though it has the same cold intelligence in the way it puts production values squarely at the service of an investigation of the nature of property.

Barry Lyndon acquired his 'great estate' through marriage. So, it turns out, did Mr Herbert. The sexual politics of *The Draughtsman's Contract* do *not*, in fact, centre round the women's use of Mr Neville as sexual hireling – they centre round the ownership of the estate itself.

Marriage not only makes these women the property of these men but dowers the men with property.

We are fairly and squarely in the terrain of patriarchy. Property passes through the women to the men. Mrs Herbert's son-in-law, the repellent Mr Tallman, surveys his wife's home with as much proprietorial satisfaction as if it were his own.

Only very gradually does the power of the women reveal itself. Mother and daughter – known only by their husband's names, Mrs Herbert, Mrs Tallman – are deep in complicity together; their complicity is profound and beautiful. They plot against the men, and, in the end, in a rather appalling way, they triumph not by subverting patriarchy itself – but by rendering the idea of paternity farcical. And I won't spoil the final riddle of the plot by telling you how they do that.

Sumptuous, glossy, witty, literate, sensuous and coldly sexy . . . an elaborate tourist brochure for the Kentish countryside . . . a tribute to the English country house . . . a hymn to English light . . . an extended commercial for wig-makers . . . teasingly cerebral as a Borges short story and immediately pleasurable as a bowl of flowers . . . *The Draughtsman's Contract* has all the makings of an art-house hit.

That is, a movie for people . . . who don't like movies. No. That's not fair. It is a movie that may be best enjoyed, perhaps, by people who don't have movies in their bloodstream – who wouldn't dream of trekking out to the Classic Hendon, to catch, oh, *Gunfight at the OK Corral* for the seventh time. It is a film richly enjoyable on other terms than those of pure movie and this, increasingly, is the quality of the art-house hit – a film with closer relations to other media, and in *The Draughtsman's Contract*, those relations are rather with fine art, than to the medium of film itself. As such, it runs perilously near, at times, to foundering on its own, impeccable good taste . . . because good taste has its own vulgarity, and, terrific as *The Draughtsman's Contract* is, I could feel, treacherously, that it would do very, very well as a coffee-table book.

Because it makes very few concessions to its own status as a movie. Ridley Scott's *Blade Runner*, for example, gains most of its impact from a vast range of cinematic references – from Lang's *Metropolis* to Godard's *Alphaville*. As such, it's a typical contemporary 'commercial' movie – as full of quotations as *Hamlet* and geared to a generation weaned on saturation exposure to old movies. (You can catch five or six on TV now, without going out of the house, after all.) *The Draughtsman's Contract* is not like that. Not at all. It isn't concerned with its own historical relevance to the movies, I think – not a film *about* film, but, perhaps, about the *act of seeing*.

And that is why the final minutes are so profoundly distressing, why the fate of Mr Neville – which you must find out for yourselves – is so appalling.

It's a film made to be looked at, as paintings are. About the act of seeing – and the difference between *seeing* and *looking*, and how, in the gap between looking and seeing, truth might lie.

One or two things jar. First, the score. As soon as the credits are over, that counter-tenor signs off. Michael Nyman has composed music which is an elaborate 'reconstruction' of themes from Purcell, a reconstruction in the modern manner, that is, a ransacking of the past. I can understand why Greenaway wanted to get away from the cliché of the 'classical music sound track to the art movie' – remember how *Elvira Madigan* murdered Mozart. But *this* score gets thoroughly out of hand; from time to time, it even starts to sound like another kind of cliché – those pop versions of the classics, a kind of electronic Swingle Singers. So loud and assertive, too, that it seems to be pushing the images to one side, as if it's saying: 'I can do better than that on my own.' It already sounds like an LP of itself, *Theme from the Draughtsman's Contract*, that could be tucked into Xmas stockings all over Posy Simmonds land, too much – altogether *too* irrelevantly tasteful.

And another thing. There is an extraordinarily crass running joke about a living statue, a piece of British whimsy of the kind that makes me squirm . . . as though Greenaway is hedging his bets . . . He's made a spectacularly arresting film, of the most serious kind, yet he's prepared to undercut its seriousness, which is both aesthetic and moral, with a limp joke about a *mannequin pis*. Why is this? What final lack of conviction in the essential power of the image?

Visions, Channel 4, 1982

The Belle as Businessperson

Look, if you can't see what's so irresistible about Clark 'Jug Ears' Gable of the Jack o'Lantern grin, then much of the appeal of *Gone With the Wind* goes out the window. Furthermore, if Vivien Leigh's anorexic, overdressed Scarlett O'Hara seems to you one of the least credible of Hollywood *femmes fatales*, most of whose petulant squeaks are, to boot, audible only to bats . . .

And, finally, if you can't seen anything romantic AT ALL about the more
than feudal darkness of the Old South, then, oh, then, you are left alone
ith the naked sexual ideology of the most famous movie ever made in all
its factitious simplicity. Macho violence fersus female guile, bull v. bitch.

The first time I saw this meretricious epic, it was the 1950s, on one of
the many occasions when they dusted off the reels and sent it on the road
again to warp the minds of a new generation. Though I was but a kid in
short pants, then, with zilch consciousness, truly I thought it stank. But –
I was of that generation whose sexual fantasies were moulded by Elvis
Presley and James Dean.

Presley, white trash with black style, in his chubby, epicene and gyrat-
ing person himself the barbarian at the gates of Tara – talk about irresistible, how could even Scarlett have resisted had Elvis pleaded with her
to let him be her teddy bear? As for Dean – impossible to imagine James
Dean carrying a girl upstairs. I used to fantasise about doing that to *him*.
Fifty-six was, perhaps the best year in which to view *Gone With the Wind*.

But the big question. Why, oh, why did the BBC shoose to empty out
Gone With the Wind, that hoary sackful of compulsive trash at this point in
time? More – why did the Corporation decide to play Santa with this
thing at the fag-end of Christmas, when, softened up by grub and booze,
the notion might be deemed to be uniquely vulnerable? Impossible not to
smell a rat. Part of the Women's Lib backlash?

I still think it stinks, this movie famous for being famous: that reduces
the American Civil War to the status of spectacle (the Hollywood attitude
to war, which reaches its apogee in *Apocalypse Now*); that advertises the
masochistic pleasures of tight lacing – did you notice how often Mammy
is depicted brutally compressing Scarlett into her corset? What kind of an
image is that?

But, goodness me, how enjoyable it is! I curled up in my armchair, giggling helplessly, weakly muttering: 'Break his kneecaps', about every five
minutes, sometimes more often.

Whose kneecaps? Well, Ashley Wilkes's, obviously! What a whingeing
creep. *Not* those of Big Sam, patently the Best Man on the entire planta-
tion even if touched with Uncle Tom, such an obvious father figure that
I can't see why Scarlett, father-fixated as she is, doesn't marry *him*, thereby
giving the plot a whole new dimension.

But it is, of course, Rhett Butler's kneecaps that seem ripest for the
treatment. That Rhett Butler and his travelling salesman's lines: 'You need
to be kissed often, by somebody who knows how to do it.' This is the
authentic language of a sexually incompetent man whistling in the dark,
but let me not continue with that train of thought or else I'll start feeling
sorry for him. And who could feel sorry for a man who says, as he closes

in for the clinch: 'This is what you were meant for'?

Since Scarlett is characterised as a Maggie Thatcher *manquée,* I would have thought she was meant for high office rather than low innuendo. And, give *GWTW* its due, implicit in the script is just how ill at ease Scarlett is with the role in which the plot has cast her. Given any other option than that of the Southern belle, even that of a poor white farmer, she grasps it with both hands. Her sexual manipulations seem to spring from sheer boredom rather than actual malice, from the frustrated ambition of a baulked entrepreneur of the kind who has given capitalism a bad name. A bitch, not from sexual frustration (that old chestnut!) but from existential frustration.

After all, as soon as she gets her hands on that lumber mill, she starts coming on like the Godmother and Rhett can't think of a way to stop her.

Yet all this is going on in the gaps of the overt ideology of the movie. Which is very simple – no more than *The Taming of the Shrew* in hooped skirts. But in a film so extravagantly long, the viewer has ample time to ponder the socially determined nature of the shrew, which is often that of a woman forced to live for love when she really isn't interested in love at all, and why should she be, dammit.

Not that Rhett Butler does manage to tame *this* shrew, in the end. He may give out with genuinely unforgivable things such as: 'I've always thought a good lashing with a buggy whip would benefit you immensely.' But he never does batter her. Since he is the sort of macho weakling who is off like a long dog at the whiff of a genuine emotional demand, the obvious strategy to be rid of him is to say you truly love him.

So Scarlett wins out; off goes Rhett, thank goodness, and tomorrow is another day. Now Scarlett can get on with amassing a great estate and bankrupting small businessmen, for which activity breaking hearts must always have been an inadequate substitute.

There is, of course, the one really disgusting scene, that of the famous marital rape, which, in the late 1930s was deemed the very stuff of girlish dream and is now grounds for divorce. As a teenager, I'm bound to admit I didn't find this scene as repellent as I do now. Since it occurs three-quarters of the way through the second half, it is high time for Scarlett's come-uppance and, God help us, the whole scene is set up so that the viewer *wants* Rhett Butler to rape his wife!

Not that there is any suggestion it i*s* rape. Irresistible Rhett, his ears rampant as if ears were secondary sexual characteristics, is but asserting his rights over the body of the woman who has rejected him out of selfish, narcissistic reasons such as a disinclination for motherhood. 'This is one night you're not turning me out.' He scoops her up in his arms.

Cut to the morning after. Scarlett stretches luxuriously in bed, smiling, singing a happy little song to herself. See? That's just what the bitch needed all the time.

And if you believe that, you will believe anything.

But. Perhaps. Perhaps she had broken his kneecaps, at that! Surely that is the only thing that could make her smile, at this juncture! And that must be the real reason why he has to go off to Europe, to visit a good kneecap specialist. Of course, they can't say that in the script, but I am sure that is what happened, really.

Observer, 1982

Jean-Luc Godard

Jean-Luc Godard is the perennial adolescent of film – all the arrogance, the romanticism, the monomaniac intensity, the readiness to risk. To carry on thus into middle age is rare and if, like Godard, you've pulled it off, you're bound to get up the noses of the ones who think ripeness is all and anguish, like acne, is the product of disturbed hormones.

To know Channel Four proposes to expose the enigmatic genius of Godard to a fresh generation of disaffected adolescents fills me with nervous, delighted glee.

Twenty years ago, what a revelation, those early movies! Everything from *A Bout de Souffle* (1960) to *Weekend* (1967) stated emphatically: sex, politics and the movies are the only things that matter. No more than French intellectuals had said for years, in fact. But set forth in images of such energy even stolid Brits became afflicted with that blessed acne of the soul, recognised ourselves, at last, as part of the great international conspiracy of the disaffected.

Not, as we'd been told, the children of F. R. Leavis and the Welfare State but, in Godard's famous definition, children 'of Marx and Coca-Cola'. And more. Children of Hitchcock, Dostoevsky, Brecht – and of pulp fiction, phenomenology and the class struggle. Heady stuff, that changes you.

We were his meat, my generation of British adolescents that ripened, some would say like a boil, towards the end of the 1950s. We were the apotheosis of the 1944 Education Act, the grammar school kids who took further education as a right. We sat down at the table of privilege and – complained about the food.

In our haughty innocence, we didn't even know what such precursors as Kingsley Amis had picked up so quickly – that anti-intellectualism is the traditional characteristic of the British intelligentsia. When Godard quoted Hegel, Lautréamont, Fanon, we didn't groan. We pricked up our ears. And we took to film like ducks to water.

Godard's movies are themselves an education in cinema and how to see it. In the marvellous *Vivre sa vie*, there's a sequence where Anna Karina, made up to look like Louise Brooks, watches Dreier's *Passion of Joan of Arc*. We learned to call this kind of thing a 'homage'. Complex homage, connecting the erotic magic of Brooks to the martyrised virgin of Dreier's imagery.

Godard shows how to read movies as just such systems of connotations. To see them three-dimensionally, never to take narrative as an end-in-itself, to comprehend *Vivre sa vie* as both the story of a prostitute who sells her body but retains her integrity – and also a film about prostitution as a description of the condition of all women in our society. Dynamite. It still looks like dynamite. I promise.

Godard's sixties' movies uniquely crystallise the vertigo of that decade. The vertigo that had nothing to do with the ephemeral pop mythology of the Beatles or mini-skirts, but with Vietnam, with the Prague spring, culminating in the events of May in Paris, '68, when, however briefly, it seemed imagination might truly sieze power. Vertigo that came from the intoxicating, terrifying notion that the old order was indeed coming to an end, vertigo of beings about to be born.

But his last prophetic film, about the end of everything, pre-dates '68 – *Weekend* came out in 1967, concludes apocalyptically 'fin du cinema, fin du monde'. And, indeed, it seemed the rest was silence because, although he kept on making movies, it got harder and harder to *see* them. He went back to the nuts and bolts of dialectics with a vengeance. He abandoned narrative, took up agitprop. And, during the 1970s, the cinema itself betrayed the film-maker.

The communal rituals in the dark became a thing of the past. Cinema became privatised. Movies have turned into things you watched on TV in the privacy of your own home. The little box to which we scornfully left our parents glued all those years ago gobbled up the dream factory and the reality factory, too.

For the past decade, Godard has grappled with this predicament – that the most public of art forms has been transformed by technological change into the most intimate. It may be that, in his most recent movie, *Passion*, to be previewed in the 'Visions' Godard documentary, it will turn out he's resolved that dilemma and will dominate the 1980s as he did the 1960s. For clearly he remains, in the irritating way, young at heart.

1983

Robert Coover: A Night at the Movies

The American cinema was born, toddled, talked, provided the furniture for all the living-rooms, and the bedrooms, too, of the imagination of the entire world, gave way to television and declined from most potent of mass media into a minority art form within the space of a human lifetime. In the days when Hollywood bestraddled the world like a colossus, its vast, brief, insubstantial empire helped to Americanise us all.

A critique of the Hollywood movie is a critique of the imagination of the twentieth century in the West. Could this be what Robert Coover, most undeceived and quintessentially American of writers, is up to in this new collection of stories, characterised as they are by his particular quality of heroic irony? Certainly they are located almost entirely within the territory of the American film except for a side-trip into a British one, 'Milford Junction 1939: a Brief Encounter', which gets on to the bill for *A Night at the Movies* under the description of travelogue.

Strangers used to gather together at the cinema and sit together in the dark, like Ancient Greeks participating in the mysteries, dreaming the same dream in unison. But Coover is no respecter of mysteries. The book kicks off in the cinema, with a story called 'The Phantom of the Movie Palace'. But nowadays the cinema is a rat-haunted, urine-scented wreck, inhabited only by a lonely projectionist screening reels at random for his solitary pleasure.

'The Phantom of the Movie Palace' describes the method of much of what is to follow, as the projectionist puts together his flickering collages:

> He overlays frenzy with freeze frames, the flight of rockets with the staking of the vampire's heart, Death's face with thrusting buttocks, cheesecake with chaingangs, and all just to prove to himself over and over again that nothing and everything is true. Slapstick *is* romance, heroism a dance number. Kisses kill.

At last the projectionist finds himself flattened into two dimensions, up there on the screen, 'surrendering himself finally . . . to that great stream of image activity that characterizes the mortal condition'.

Coover exacts a similar surrender from the reader. There is some exceptionally strenuous image activity ahead in these stories that precisely reactivate the magnificent gesticulations of giant forms, the bewildering transformations, the orgiastic violence that hurts nobody because it is not real – all the devices of dream, or film, or fiction. Coover is also diabolically, obscenely, incomparably funny.

The collection includes, besides the travelogue already mentioned, a weekly serial, some shorts, a cartoon, a musical interlude, and not one but three main features – a western, a comedy, a romance. Every aspect of the mortal condition, besides every type of Hollywood genre, is comprehensively covered. Some of the movies invoked are imaginary; some, like the musical, *Top Hat*, reinvent the familiar in hallucinatory terms: 'he had some pretty fancy moves, but all that nimble-footedness looked to me like something he mighta learned tippytoeing through the cowshit.'

'Shoot Out at Gentry's Junction' starts off deceptively straightforwardly: 'The Mex would arrive in Gentry's Junction at 12:10. Or had arrived. Couldn't be sure . . . Sheriff Henry Harmon grunted irritably and eased his long pointed boots to the floor.'

So far, so good: already the stereotypes are briskly in play and, as so often in westerns, the set-up is strictly Freudian. If Hank Harmon, clearly the Henry Fonda role, 'a tough honest man with clear speech and powerful hands', stands for the Superego, then the Mex is, as ever, the Id incarnate. 'Here he is in the schoolhouse demonstrating for the little children the exemplary marvels of his private member.'

The presence of the Mexican bandit, his grotesque Hispanic accent, that amazing private member, the appalling stench of his fart – 'The goddam Mex had let one that smelled like a tomb' – his presence transforms the genre. With the Mex at the centre, all becomes a bloody carnival of sex and death.

It soon becomes obvious the terrible Mexican must triumph at the shoot-out. 'Adios to Gentry's Junction! . . . The storekeeper, the banker, the preacher, they swing with soft felicity from scaffolds and the whisky he is running like blood.'

The two other main features exhibit no less manic invention. 'Charlie in the House of Rue – yes; it *is* that Charlie – takes slapstick via its own remorseless logic of paranoia and anxiety to a place of the deepest anguish and disquiet, as darkness, 'like the onset of blindness', irises in on the clown. 'What kind of place is this? Who took the light away? And why is everybody laughing?'

If Coover turns a western into a savage fiesta and a Chaplin two-reeler into an analysis of the compulsion to repeat, he is cruellest of all to the love story that is, of all film romances, most precious to buffs, for he turns *Casablanca* into a blue movie in which Rick and Ilsa get it on again in no uncertain manner: 'he's not enjoyed multiple orgasms like this since he hauled his broken-down black-listed ass out of Paris a year and a half ago. . .'

This is desecration on the grand scale, a full frontal attack on – or, rather, a full frontal revision of – one of the sacred texts of American cinema. But Rick and Ilsa also founder amongst gathering shadows and uncertainty. The other characters wait downstairs in the bar for the lovers to get up and dress and the action to continue but is that possible, now? Hasn't everything been changed? The story, nostalgically titled 'You Must Remember This', ends the book; the ending is an unanswered, unanswerable plea: 'And then . . . Ilsa . . .? And *then* . . .?

It is a wild night, this marathon night's viewing, in the semi-derelict picture palace of twentieth-century illusion, from which gangsters can whisk you away in an unmarked car during the 'Intermission', send you spinning through a dozen different hazards – 'sharks, seraglios, dud parachutes, etc., and drop you back in your seat in time for the shorts.

But, wait. Something has happened while you have been away. Now the audience is 'all sitting stiffly in their seats with weird flattened-out faces, their dilated eyes locked onto the screen like they're hypnotized or dead or something'. The most virtuoso single exercise in the book, the strangest, the most exemplary in its demonstration of the transforming resources of narrative, 'After Lazarus,' concludes with a coffin being lowered towards the camera. 'Sudden blackness.'

At this moment, impossible not to recall, as if they were prophecy, the final words of *Weekend,* Jean-Luc Godard's great film of the sixties, 'Fin du cinema. Fin du monde'.

Guardian, 1987

Hollywood

Review of David Bordwell, Janet Staiger and Kristin Thompson, *The Classical Hollywood Cinema*, Paul F. Boller Jr and Ronald L. Davis, *Hollywood Anecdotes* and Danny Pearcy (ed.), *Close-Ups*.

In its heyday, the period 1917–60 dealt with in *The Classical Hollywood Cinema*, Hollywood was a gold-rush boom town, a place of pilgrimage, when the young and the beautiful, the cynical and the depraved, the talented, the lucky, and the doomed thronged to seek their fortunes. That was how it was supposed to be, at any rate, and, oddly enough, that was really the way the capital city of illusion was, as if Hollywood itself were its own greatest production.

Easy to forget, nowadays, how unprecedented the movie industry was in its mobilisation of vast amounts of capital, both financial and human, in the production of pleasure. Easy to forget the religious fervour that possessed the audiences, those communities of strangers crowded together in the dark. (How appropriate that, according to *Hollywood Anecdotes*, one of the abandoned Art Deco picture palaces in New York has been consecrated as a Pentecostal tabernacle.)

Hollywood was, still is, always will be, synonymous with the movies. It was the place where the United States perpetrated itself as a universal dream and put the dream into mass production. 'We take Hollywood seriously, treating it as a distinct mode of movie practice with its own cinematic style and industrial conditions of existence,' state the authors of *The Classical Hollywood Cinema*, and proceed, comprehensively to do so.

But there was an extra dimension of scandal and glamour that was also an essential part of the product. John Ford said that you couldn't geographically define Hollywood. Almost as soon as the studios went up, the town was recreated via the twentieth-century arts of publicity as the home of an ever-increasing pantheon of deities; major, minor, and all sizes in between. Star worship wasn't a perversion but a genuine manifestation of the religious instinct. (Some of that sense of the sacred rubbed off the movies on to the US itself, too, which is why we all venerate the Stars and Stripes.)

Janet Leigh thought the MGM lot in the 1950s was like fairyland. Other actresses did not. 'Darling,' drawled Tallulah Bankhead to Irving Thalberg, 'how does one get laid in this dreadful place?'

But did she really say it, or did somebody put the words in her mouth? 'Hollywood thrives on apocryphal aphorisms,' say the authors of *Hollywood Anecdotes*. At least one of their stories – the one about the cameraman who apol,ogises for not getting as good shots as he did ten years before – has a variable heroine, either Greer Garson or Marlene Dietrich or Norma Shearer. The authors categorically deny that another story, told by Elizabeth Taylor about herself, ever happened at all. A favourite story of Hitchcock's has no basis in fact, either.

This is genuinely folkloric material. 'Telling a story is the basic formal concern,' according to *The Classical Hollywood Cinema*. That is what the Hollywood cinema is there for. Telling stories about the people engaged in telling stories is a basic informal concern, and no matter if these are twice-told tales – they gain richness and significance with repetition.

Much of the contents of *Hollywood Anecdotes* will be familiar to buffs, and loved because it is familiar. There is the MGM lion ('Ars Gratia Artis') who in old age, had to be fitted with dentures, and also the lions (25 lions at 25 dollars a head) who pissed on the assembled Christian martyrs in Cecil B. de Mille's *The Sign of the Cross*. Though, alas, the toothless lion of whom Victor Mature (*Androcles and the Lion*) said, 'I don't want to be gummed to death', is missing.

Sam Goldwyn's famous deformations of English are lavishly quoted: 'You've got to take the bull by the teeth,' etc. Boller and Davis are fond of funny accents; they wouldn't dream of omitting Michael 'Bring on the empty horses' Curtiz.

They cite genuine curiosities, like the brothel. Mae's, staffed by film-star lookalikes ('Claudette Colbert' spoke excellent French). Ben Hecht's celebrated dictum gets another airing: 'Starlet is a name for any woman under thirty not actively employed in a brothel.' Otherwise, Boller and Davis are decently reticent about the abundant sexual folklore of Hollywood, which the prurient are advised to seek in Kenneth Anger's two volumes of *Hollywood Babylon*.

All in all, the tone of *Hollywood Anecdotes* is oddly similar to those little Sunday school compilations of the sayings of saints and worthies. Any incident, no matter how trivial, is worth recounting if it concerns a star or near-star. Christopher Plummer, it is said, hated *The Sound of Music* so much he nicknamed it *The Sound of Mucus*. Abbott and Costello once threw a suitcase of condoms at their director in the middle of a scene. Well, well, goodness gracious.

Close-Ups – designed to look like a mock-up of a thirties' movie annual – is the very stuff of legendary history, a collection of star ephemera spanning seventy-odd years complete with iconic representations. Odd little snippety articles go with the photographers, some of them historic documents such as Alvah Bessie's obituary of Marilyn Monroe and Budd Schulberg's weird threnody for Judy Garland, other bits of makeweight scribble even if the by-line makes you blink – Sergio Leone on Henry Fonda, for example.

Danny Peary, the editor, describes *Close-Ups* as a scrapbook. Leafing through it is an unnerving experience; like flicking through the channels late at night on television, catching snatch after snatch of old movies diminished by their transmission through the indifferent air. When we talk about Hollywood nowadays, we talk about nostalgia, but Brecht described his own experience in Golden Age Hollywood: 'Every morning to earn my bread,/I go to the market where lies are bought/Hopefully/I take up my place among the sellers.'

The hell of it was, they made wonderful movies, then, when nothing in Hollywood was real except hard work, mass production, the conveyor belt, the tyrants, and madmen running the studios.

The Classical Hollywood Cinema quotes François Truffaut: 'We said that the American cinema pleases us and its film-makers are slaves. What if they were freed? And from the moment that they were freed, they made shitty films.'

Guardian, 1988

Barry Paris: Louise Brooks

I once showed G. W. Pabst's 1929 film version of Wedekind's *Lulu* plays, Louise Brooks's starring vehicle, *Pandora's Box*, to a graduate class at the University of Iowa. I was apprehensive. These were children of the television age, unfamiliar with the codes of silent movies, especially of German silents – the exaggerated gesture, the mask-like make-up, the distorted shadows – but I badly wanted to show them this great film about the unholy alliance between desire and money as part of a course about twentieth-century narrative I'd titled, quoting from Thomas Wolfe, 'Life is strange and the world is bad'. Nothing else but *Pandora's Box* would do.

Happily, they did not fidget or shuffle but sat like mice. Finally Jack the Ripper stabbed Lulu just as, or just because, she turns towards him the full force of her radiant sexuality; like the sun, he cannot bear to look at her for long. The film was over. There was a silence. Then a young man said: 'That was the most beautiful woman I've ever seen in the movies.'

And they all said, yes. The most beautiful. The best performance. Who is she? What else did she do? This biography provides a comprehensive answer to that question. Note how no attempt has been made to gussy up the title; Louise Brooks is a name that carries with it all the resonance of a quotation. The name that instantly evokes her personal logo, that haircut, those eyebrows. There are sumptuous photographs on front and back flaps – oh! the patented Brooks version of the Giaconda smile, the one that, as Barry Paris says, isn't so much a 'come hither' look as a look that says, to each and every gender, 'I'll come to you.' (If, that is she likes the look of you, a big if, in fact.)

That straightforward look of hers is what makes these sixty-year-old photographs of Louise Brooks so provocative, so disturbing, so unchanged by time. Like Manet's Olympia, she is directly challenging the person who is looking at her; she is piercing right through the camera with her questing gaze to give your look back, with interest. 'This provocative eyeful', as *Picturegoer* magazine called her in the brief springtime of her youthful fame, is not presenting herself as an object of contemplation so much as throwing down a gauntlet. She is 'the girl in the black helmet', she'd have you know. She is the one they call 'the exotic black orchid'. She has a Cartier watch and a copy of *A La Recherche du temps perdu* tucked into her purse. Essentially, her attitude is one of: 'Now show me what *you* can do.'

It is still an unusual attitude for a woman to adopt. Many men, even if aroused by it, would think it was a bad attitude; so would those women who were neither aroused, nor felt complicitous with her.

'Women of exceptional beauty are doomed to unhappiness,' says Theodor Adorno. Beautiful is as beautiful does; Brooks's features in repose can look doll-like, chocolate boxy. The spirit that animated them was the exceptional thing. Roddy McDowell, who knew her in old age, said, 'when she was young she must have been like a whirling dervish. She must have been like a shot of oxygen right into the brain.'

And, on the evidence of this book and of her own book of essays, *Lulu in Hollywood*, I don't think she was unhappy, exactly. She was certainly, as she says, 'inept' at marriage, trying it briefly twice; it never took. She quarrelled with her best-loved brother shortly before he died, as if to insure herself against grieving for him. She was a vain, imperious bitch with a tongue like a knife, yet she was loved far more than she deserved, or acknowledged, and, even during her bleakest periods of despair, she always seems to have been buoyed up by a mysterious, self-sustaining glee. Drunk or sober (more often the former than the latter), flush or destitute, star, salesgirl, call-girl, or, final incarnation, *grande dame* and *monstre sacrée*, she never lost a talent for living memorably. Born a self-dramatiser, she always enjoyed the spectacle of herself.

It was an unusually picaresque life, for a woman, one of varied sexual encounters, booze, violent reversals of fortune, a good deal of laughter, and fairly continuous intellectual activity — Lotte Eisner, the critic, first spotted Brooks on the set of *Pandora's Box*, immersed in a volume of Schopenhauer's *Essays and Aphorisms*. She thought it was a publicity stunt, but changed her mind after they became friends.

Neither guilt nor remorse were items in Brooks's repertoire. It was a life like a man's, complicated by her beauty, and by the unimpeachable fact she was *not* a man. Far from it.

It was a life centred around, given meaning by, an extraordinary accident — that this young American adventuress and budding glamour star, on the advice of her handsome but sinister millionaire lover, accepted, without reading the script beforehand, the role of the Life Force incarnate, Wedekind's earth spirit, the Dionysiacally unrepressed Lulu, who must die because she is free. She went off to Berlin to shoot the film because she and her lover felt like an ocean cruise.

The role of Lulu itself is one of the key representations of female sexuality in twentieth-century literature. Brooks, under Pabst's direction in the movie, perhaps did nothing more than what came naturally. As Dorothy Mackail, a colleague from early Hollywood days, remarked: 'All they had to do with Brooksie was turn the camera on.' Mackail did not realise that therein lay the essence of a great screen performer. Pabst did.

But Brooks's chaotic life had an enormous artistic logic to it, as if Mr

Pabst himself defined its parameters that day in Berlin, when Brooks was twenty-two, hungover from partying till all hours with rich American friends; finally Pabst, exasperated, said to her: 'Your life is exactly like Lulu's and you will end the same way.'

Another Pabst movie, *Diary of a Lost Girl*, also 1929, shows that *Pandora's Box* isn't a fluke, that Brooks could do it twice. It isn't as good a film as *Pandora's Box* but Brooks is, if anything, even more luminous, more like a transparency through which joy and pain, pleasure and heartbreak are transmitted directly to the audience. The 'lost girl', seduced and abandoned, finds herself in a brothel.

At one point, Brooks is raffled off as a prize. Brooks, laughing, preening her extraordinary neck like a swan, looks as if it is the most exciting adventure in the world, that random chance will bring her partner for that night. Her particular quality is, she makes being polymorphously perverse look like the only way to be.

In her thirties, after she hit the skids, was doing a bit of this, a bit of that in New York, she and her great friend Tallulah Bankhead used to go out on the town together, bar-hopping, up to God knows what. Behaviour of Henry Miller buddies. But, however scabrous the circumstances, Brooks never lost a thoroughly un-Millerian elegance and self-irony and when she finally took up her pen and wrote, in her sixties and seventies, she wrote, not about life in the lower depths, but about her work in the movies, and if she wrote very little, she wrote very well, with an acute critical intelligence, and much showing off. (She was a culture vulture, an intellectual snob, an autodidact – good for her!)

Although her life spiralled downwards, like Lulu's, no victim, she. She died, unregenerate, in her own bed, at the ripe age of seventy-eight. But she was also the lost girl; in 1976, she wrote to an admirer, 'Remember when the prodigal son returned the father said, "He was lost and is found." It was the father who *found* the lost son. Somehow I have missed being found.' But this kind of existential rhetoric may only be the gin talking. Barry Paris makes it plain that somebody, somewhere, always did arrive in the nick of time to bail Brooks out. Always magnificently ungrateful, she would then scornfully retreat to the tried and tested company of 'my beloved Proust', her Ortega y Gasset, her Goethe.

We are dealing with a complex phenomenon, here.

She was born deep in the American grain, in Kansas, in 1906, of pioneer stock – her father, aged three, had been brought out West in a covered wagon. Her first dancing teacher had a name straight out of Mark Twain, Mrs Argue Buckspitt. In *Lulu in Hollywood*, she describes an unconventionally idyllic childhood, full of books, music and freedom. It sounds too good to be true; yet proves to be true in every detail, even to the music her beautiful, unhappy mother played all day on the piano. Bach, Debussy, Ravel. . .

All true. Except that Brooks edited it. Her parents preferred the company of books and music to that of their children, whose freedom was the product of indifference. Louise, the elder daughter, the image of her beautiful mother, was 'more or less a professional dancer by the age of ten', performing at fairs, junkets, jamborees all over south-eastern Kansas, whether to fulfil her mother's thwarted ambitions or, more simply, to coax from her, however fleetingly, attention and praise is now beyond surmise. Probably a bit of both.

At fifteen Brooks left home, an act most bourgeois parents would consider premature even in these permissive times; Brooks père was a highly respected lawyer. Nevertheless, with parental blessing, off she went to join a modern dance troupe, the Denishawn company. Barry Paris is succinct about Denishawn: 'In effect, Denishawn founded American modern dance.' It was also as chaste an establishment as a convent.

One of Denishawn's then stars was Martha Graham. Later, Brooks would say she learnt to act by watching Martha Graham dance, and to dance by watching Charlie Chaplin act. This explains her technique.

Brooks wrote in her journal, reminding herself how hard she must work 'as I someday intend to rise high in the ranks'. There is something very touching, something uncharacteristically earnest, about that phrase. She worked extremely hard, but it did her no good. Yet dance was Brooks's first and probably abiding love; at seventy, hair scraped austerely back from her vividly mobile face, the lovely old bones sticking out everywhere, she looks not in the least like an antique movie star but exactly like a retired dancer, as if, as a final indulgence to herself, she has decided to allow herself to look like the thing she'd wished she'd always been.

She never became a match for Martha Graham because she was thrown out of Denishawn after two years, not for dancing badly but for hell-raising. Sex, mostly. The sexual double standard was to haunt her for the rest of her life. No young man would have been censured in this way for sexual experimentation. At the same age, the impenetrably respectable Kafka regularly spent one evening a week at a brothel and was not dismissed from his insurance company. Nor turned out of home.

Her revenge on Denishawn and all it stood for in the way of High Art and Plain Living was swift and spectacular; soon, in beads and feathers, she starred in Ziegfield's *Follies,* and engaged in a brief but highly visible affair with Chaplin, then at the dizzy height of his fame. *The Gold Rush* was freshly out. Crowds followed them in the streets of New York.

The dedicated dancer, moved by some 'inner vision' that Martha Graham, for one, saw in her, was now well on the way to becoming a *grande horizontale*. Men bought her furs. She let them take her out to tea. The management accused her of 'using the theatre simply as a showcase – a place to publish her wares'. She was capricious, promiscuous, petulant; she could have said, in the words of another great 1920s beauty, Lee Miller, the muse of the surrealists, 'I was terribly, terribly pretty. I looked like an angel but I was a fiend inside.'

Almost absentmindedly, because it was the thing for showgirls to do, she started to make movies. Then came Hollywood.

I'd always assumed her Hollywood movies were negligible, her career there a non-starter, but Barry Paris makes out a convincing case, based on the amount of fan mail she received, the sheer *attention* she got, her rise from supporting player to fledgling star, that she was set fair to be one of the major stars of the 1930s. Sound would have posed no problem; she went to make a very successful stab at radio, dramas and soaps, in New York in the l940s, before she trashed *that* career, in a fit of pique.

But that terrible accident intervened. She fell in love, broke up her new marriage, broke up her contract, went off to Berlin and made a huge flop of a movie. Because, in its time, *Pandora's Box* proved dead on arrival at the box office in both Germany and the USA. The last great silent, it was rendered obsolete before the première by the arrival of sound. She stayed on in Europe to make a couple more movies that scarcely saw the light of day and when she finally got back to California, she found her own career was floating belly up, expired in her absence, beyond recall.

Perhaps it had to do with her capricious libido; although accustomed to follow the promptings of her own desires wherever they might lead, they tended to stop dead at the casting couch. For a year or two, she coasted, doing bit parts in lousy films, until at last she was offered a chance at re-habilitation - the lead in *Public Enemy*, opposite James Cagney. When in doubt, Miss Brooks always burned her boats. She turned it down. It went to Jean Harlow.

And that, barring a few minor roles in 'B' features, was that. Eventually she went home to Wichita; home is where you go when nobody else will have you. But they wouldn't have her there, either. Her blue period began.

Until, like a miracle, *Pandora's Box* emerged in the 1950s after years of neglect as one of the greatest of all silent movies, and the young woman who always believed she could not act, and was not beautiful, either was too 'black and furry', who approached the movies as though they were modern dance, became, retrospectively, a great star, and one of the icono-graphic faces of the cinema, because of a role she had forgotten, in a film she had never seen all the way through.

She could have got the Myrna Loy role in *The Thin Man* series, opines

Barry Paris. And, God . . . think of missing out on *Public Enemy*! What a great star Hollywood lost!

So what. Think of this as a possible analogy. After *Niagara*, Marilyn Monroe got a phone call. Let us bend time a little, and say it was from Tarkovsky, who had read in a smuggled copy of *Photoplay* how she'd always wanted to play Grushenka in *The Brothers Karamazov*. It just so happens, if she can get a release, that Mosfilm are preparing a production he has scripted. Puzzled, flattered, Monroe accepts. No problem about her English. She'll be dubbed.

After six months in Moscow, with no Russian, she's no longer sure if she's shooting *The Brothers Karamazov* or *Carry On, Comrade*. Tarkovsky pours mud over her and barks at her to keep her clothes on every time she tries to take something off. However late she is on the set, she is always the first one there. She lets her hair grow out. And being Grushenka all that time breaks something inside her. She stops shaving her armpits. She stops worrying about her weight. She returns home to find she has gone out of fashion overnight; no place in Hollywood for overweight brunettes with too much body hair. Because I am fond of Marilyn Monroe, I will find her congenial work in a children's home, perhaps. How the children love her! Count your blessings, Marilyn; you missed out on Arthur Miller.

Meanwhile, back in the USSR, the Tarkovsky movie is shelved for painting a negative picture of life in the Urals. The years pass. Glasnost. Tarkovsky's *The Karamazov Brothers* opens at the Venice Festival. His greatest picture. Who is the stunning girl with the blonde halo? Can it be possible she is still alive? So the lovely, fat old lady, resurrected, becomes a staple of film festivals. She is in a position of absolute security. Fame has come too late to bewilder or corrupt; it can only console. She is something better than a star; she is an eternal flame in the holy church of cinema.

I'm sure that Louise Brooks could have been, had she wished, had she even so much as lifted her little finger, as big and as durable a star as her contemporary, Joan Crawford. But she was presented, without either her knowledge or consent, a choice between Art and Fame, as straightforwardly as it might have been offered in a Renaissance allegory, and, without even being aware of it, she plumped, as it were, for the eternity promised by the poet. I do believe that, in her heart, she knew just what it was she wanted. She wanted 'to rise high in the ranks'. It was the reverse of a Faustian bargain. She bartered her future in exchange for her soul.

London Review of Books, 1990

In Pantoland

'I'm bored with television,' announced Widow Twankey from her easy chair in the Empyrian, switching off 'The Late Show' and adjusting his/her falsies inside her outrageous red bustier. 'I will descend again to Pantoland!'

In Pantoland, everything is grand. Well, let's not exaggerate – grandish. Not like what it used to be but, then, what isn't. Even so, all still brightly coloured – garish, in fact, all your primaries, red, yellow, blue. And all excessive, so that your castle has more turrets than a regular castle, your forest is considerably more impenetrable than the average forest and, not infrequently, your cow has more than its natural share of teats and udders.

We're talking multiple projections here, spikes, sprouts, boobs, bums. It's a bristling world, in Pantoland, either phallic or else demonically, aggressively female and there's something archaic behind it all, archaic in the worst sense. Something positively filthy.

But all also two-dimensional, so that Maid Marian's house, in Pantoland's fictive Nottingham, is flat as a pancake. The front door may well open when she goes in but it makes a hollow sound behind her when she slams it shut and the entire façade gets the shivers. Robin serenades her from below; she opens her window to riposte and what you see behind her, of her bedroom is only a painted bedhead on a painted wall.

Of course, the real problem here is that it is Baron Hardup of Hardup hall, father of Cinderella, stepfather of the Ugly Sisters who, these barren days, all too often occupies the post of minister of finance in Pantoland. Occasionally, even now, the free-spenders such as Prince Badroulbador take things into their own hands and then you get some wonderful effects, such as a three-masted galleon in full sail breasting through tumultuous storms with thunder booming and lightning breaking about the spars as the gallant ship takes Dick Whittington and his cat either away from or else back to London amidst a nostalgic series of *tableaux vivants* of British naval heroes such as Raleigh, Drake, Captain Cook and Nelson, discovering things or keeping the Channel safe for English shipping, while Dick gives out a full-throated contralto rendition of 'If I Had a Hammer', with a chorus of rats in masks and tights, courtesy of the Italia Conti school.

Illusion and transformation, kitchen into palace with the aid of gauze etc. etc. etc. You know the kind of thing. It all costs money. And, sometimes, as if it were the greatest illusion of all, there might be an incursion of the real. Real horses, perhaps, trotting, neighing and whinnying, large as life. Yet 'large as life' isn't the right phrase, at all, at all. 'Large as life' they might be, in the context of the auditorium, but when the proscenium arch gapes as wide as the mouth of the ogre in *Jack and the Beanstalk,* those forty white horses pulling the glass coach of the princess look as little and inconsequential as white mice. They are real, all right, but insignificant, and only raise a laugh or round of applause if one of them inadvertently drops dung.

And sometimes there'll be a dog, often one of those sandy-coloured, short-haired terriers. On the programme, it will say: 'Chuckles, played by himself', just above where it says: 'Cigarettes by Abdullah'. (Whatever happened to Abdullah?) Chuckles does everything they taught him at dog-school – fetches, carries, jumps through a flaming hoop – but now and then he forgets his script, forgets he lives in Pantoland, remembers he is a real dog precipitated into a wondrous world of draughts and pungency and rustlings. He will run down to the footlights, he will look out over the daisy field of upturned, expectant faces and, after a moment's puzzlement, give a little questioning bark.

It was not like this when Toto dropped down into Oz; it is more like it was when Toto landed back, also, in Kansas. Chuckles does not like it. Chuckles feels let down.

Then Robin Hood or Prince Charming or whoever it is has the titular – and 'tits' is the operative word, with this one – ownership of Chuckles in Pantoland, scoops him up against her bosom and he has been saved. He has returned to Pantoland. In Pantoland, he can live for ever.

In Pantoland, which is the carnival of the unacknowledged and the fiesta of the repressed, everything is excessive and gender is variable.

THE DAME: double-sexed and self-sufficient, the Dame, the sacred transvestite of Pantoland, manifests him/herself in a number of guises. For example, he/she might introduce him/herself thus:

'My name is Widow Twankey.' Then sternly adjure the audience: 'Smile when you say that!'

Because Twankey rhymes with – pardon me vicar; and,

> Once upon a distant time,
> They talked in Pantoland in rhyme

but now they talk in *double entendre,* which is a language all its own and is accented, not with the acute or grave, but with the eyebrows. *Double entendre.* That is, everyday discourse which has been dipped in the infinite riches of a dirty mind.

She/he stars as Mother Goose. In *Cinderella,* you get two for the price of one with the Ugly Sisters. If they throw in Cinders's stepmother, that's a bonanza, that's three. Then there is Jack's Mum in *Jack and the Beanstalk* where the presence of cow and stem in close proximity rams home the 'phallic mother' aspect of the dame. The Queen of Hearts (who stole some tarts). Granny in *Red Riding Hood,* where the wolf – 'Ooooer!' – gobbles her up. He/she pops up everywhere in Pantoland, tittering and squealing, 'Look out, girls! There's a man!!!' whenever the Principal Boy (q.v.) appears.

Big wigs and round spots of rouge on either cheek and eyelashes longer than those of Daisy the Cow; crinolines that dip and sway and support a mass of crispy petticoats out of which comes running Chuckles the dog dragging behind him a string of sausages plucked, evidently, from the Dame's fundament.

'Better out than in.'

He/she bestrides the stage. His/her enormous footsteps resonate with the antique past. She brings with him the sacred terror inherent in those of his/her avatars such as Lisa Maron, the androgynous god-goddess of the Abomey pantheon; the great god Shango, thunder deity of the Yorubas, who can be either male or female: the sacrifical priest who, in the Congo, dressed like a woman and was called: 'Grandma'.

The Dame bends over, whips up her crinolines; she has three pairs of knee-length bloomers, which she wears according to mood.

One pair of bloomers is made out of the Union Jack, for the sake of patriotism.

The second pair of bloomers is quartered red and black, in memory of Utopia.

The third and vastest pair of bloomers is scarlet, with a target on the seat, centred on the arsehole, and this pair is wholly dedicated to obscenity.

Roars. Screams. Hoots.

She turns and curtsies. And what do you know, she/he has shoved a truncheon down her trousers, hasn't she.

In Burgundy, in the Middle Ages, they held a Feast of Fools that lasted all through the dead days, that vacant lapse of time during which, according to the hairy-legged mythology of the Norsemen, the sky wolf ate up the sun. By the time the sky wolf puked it up again, a person or persons unknown had fucked the New Year back into being during the days when all the boys wore sprigs of mistletoe in their hats. Filthy work, but *somebody* had to do it.

By the fourteenth century, the far-from-hairy-legged Burgundians had forgotten all about the sky wolf, of course; but had they also forgotten the orgiastic non-time of the Solstice, which, once upon a time, was also the time of the Saturnalia, the topsy-turvy time, 'the Liberties of December', when master swapped places with slave and anything could happen?

The mid-winter carnival in Old Burgundy, known as the Feast of Fools, was reigned over in style by a man dressed as a woman whom they used to call Mère Folle. Crazy Mother.

Crazy Mother turns round and curtsies. She pulls the truncheon out of her bloomers. All shriek in terrified delight and turn away their eyes. But when the punters dare to look again, they encounter only his/her seraphic smile and, lo and behold! the truncheon has turned into a magic wand.

When Widow Twankey/The Queen of Hearts/Mother Goose taps Daisy the Cow with her wand, Daisy the Cow gives out with a chorus of 'Down at the Old Bull and Bush'.

THE BEASTS: the Goose in *Mother Goose* is, or so they say, the Hamlet of animal roles, introspective and moody as only a costive bird straining over its egg might be. There is a full gamut of emotion in the Goose role – loyalty and devotion to her mother, joy and delight at her own maternity; heartbreak at the loss of egg, fear and trembling at the wide variety of gruesome possibilities which might occur if, in the infinite intercouplings of possible texts which occur all the time in the promiscuity of Pantoland, one story will effortlessly segue into another story, so that *Mother Goose* twins up with *Jack and the Beanstalk*, involving an egg-hungry ogre; or with *Robin Hood*, incorporating a goose-hungry Sheriff of Nottingham.

Note that the Goose, like the Dame, is a female role usually, though not always, played by a man. But the Goose does not represent the exaggerated and parodic femininity of Widow Twankey. The Goose's femininity is real. She is all woman. Witness the centrality of the egg in her life. So the Goose deserves an interpreter with the sophisticated technique and empathy for gender of the *onnagata,* the female impersonators of the Japanese Kabuki theatre, who can make you weep at the sadness inherent in the sleeves of a kimono as they quiver with suppressed emotion at a woman's lot. Because of this, and because she is the prime focus of all attention, the Goose in *Mother Goose* is the premier animal role, even more so than . . .

DICK WHITTINGTON'S CAT: Dick Whittington's cat is the Scaramouche of Pantoland, limber, agile, and going on two legs more often than on four to stress his status as intermediary between the world of the animals and our world. If he possesses some of the chthonic ambiguity of all dark messengers between different modes of being, nevertheless he is never less than a perfect valet to his master and hops and skips at Dick's bidding.

His is therefore less of a starring role than the Goose, even if his rat-catching activities are central to the action, and it is as difficult to imagine Dick without his cat as Morecambe without Wise.

Note that this cast is male almost to a fault, unquestionably a tom-cat, and personated by a man; some things are sacrosanct, even in Pantoland. A tom-cat is maleness personified, whereas . . .

DAISY THE COW is so female it takes two whole men to represent her, one on his own couldn't hack it. The back legs of the pantomime quadruped are traditionally a thankless task but the front end gets the chance to indulge in all manner of antics, flirting, flattering, fluttering those endless eyelashes and, sometimes, if the co-ordination between the two ends is good enough, Daisy does a tap-dance, which makes her massive udder with its many dangling teats dip and sway in the most salacious manner, bringing back home the notion of a basic crudely reproductive female sexuality of which those of us who don't lactate often do not like to be reminded. (They have lactation, generation all the time in mind in Pantoland.)

This rude femaleness requires two men to mimic it, as I've said; therefore you could call Daisy a Dame, squared.

These three are the principal animal leads in Pantoland, although Mother Hubbard, a free-floating Dame who might turn up in any text, always comes accompanied by her dog but more often than not, Chuckles gets in on the act, here, and real animals don't count.

Pantomime horses can crop up anywhere and mimic rats are not confined to Dick Whittington but inhabit Cinderella's kitchen, even drive her coach; there are mice, and lizards, too. Birds. You need robins to cover up the Babes in the Wood. Emus, you get sometimes. Ducks. You name it.

When Pantoland was young, and I mean really young, before it got stage-struck, in the time of the sky wolf, when fertility festivals filled up those vacant, dark, solstitial days, we used to see no difference between ourselves and the animals. Bruno the Bear and Felix the Cat walked and talked amongst us. We lived with, we loved, we married the animals (*Beauty and the Beast*). The Goose, the Cat and Daisy the Cow have come to us out of the paradise that little children remember, when we thought we could talk to the animals, to remind us how once we knew that the animals were just as human as we were, and that made us more human, too.

THE PRINCIPAL BOY: What an armful! She is the grandest thing in Pantoland. Look at those arms! Look at those thighs! Like tree trunks, but like sexy tree trunks. Her hats are huge and plumed and feathers; her gleaming, exiguous little knicks are made of satin and trimmed with sequins. As Prince Charming, she is a spectacle of pure glamour although, as Jack, her costume might start off a touch more peasant and, as Dick, she needs to look like a London apprentice for a while before she gets to try on that Lord Mayor schmutter. For Robin Hood, she'll wear green; as Aladdin, the East is signified by her turban.

You can tell she is supposed to be a man not by her shape, which is a conventional hour-glass, but by her body language. She marches with as martial a stride as it is possible to achieve in stiletto heels and throws out her arms in wide, generous, all-encompassing, patriarchal gestures, as if she owned the earth. Her maleness has an antique charm, even, nowadays, a touch of wistful Edwardiana about it; no Principal Boy worth her salt would want to personate a New Man, after all. She's gone to the bother of turning herself into a Principal Boy to get away from the washing-up, in the first place.

Despite her spilling physical luxuriance, which ensures that, unlike the more ambivalent Dame, the Principal Boy is always referred to as a 'she', her voice is a deep, dark brown and, when raised in song, could raise the dead. Who, who ever heard her, could ever forget a Principal Boy of the Old School lead the chorus in a rousing military parade and rendition of, say: 'Where are the boys of the Old Brigade?'

Come to that, where *are* the Principal Boys of the Old Brigade. In these anorexic times, there is less and less thigh to slap. Girls, nowadays, are big-bosomed, all right, due to implants, but not deep-chested any more. Principal Boys used to share a hollow-voiced, bass-baritone bonhomie with department store Father Christmases but: 'Ho! Ho! Ho!' is heard no more in the land. In these lean times, your average Principal Boy looks more like a Peter Pan and pre-pubescence isn't what you're aiming for at a fertility festival, although the presence of actual children, in great numbers, laughing at that which they should not know about, is indispensable as having established the success of preceding fertility festivals.

The Principal Boy is a male/female cross, like the Dame, but she is never played for laughs. No. She is played for thrills, for adventure, for romance. So, after innumerable adventures, she ends up with the Principal Girl in a number where their voices soar and swoon together as in the excrutiatingly erotic climactic aria of Monteverdi's *L'Incoronnazione di Poppaea*, performed as it is in the present day always by two ladies, one playing Nero, one Poppaea, due to male castrati being thin on the ground in spite of the population explosion. And, as Principal Boy and Principal Girl duet, their four breasts in two décolletages jostle one another for pre-eminence in the eyes of all observers. This is a thrill indeed but will not make babies unless they then dash out and borrow the turkey-baster from the Christmas dinner kitchen. There is a kind of censorship inherent in pantomime.

But the question of gender remains vague because you have to hang on to the idea that the Principal Boy is all boy and all girl at the same time, just as the Dame is Mother Eve and Old Adam in one parcel; they are both doors that open both ways, they are the Janus faces of the season, they look backwards and forwards, they bury the past, they procreate the future, and, by rights, these two should belong together for they are and are not ambivalent and the Principal Girl (q. does not v. in this work of reference) is nothing more than a pretty prop, even when eponymous as in *Cinderella* and *Snow White*.

Widow Twankey came out of retirement and, gorged on anthropology, dropped down on stage in Pantoland. 'I have come back to earth and I feel randy.'

She/he didn't have to say a word. The décor picked up on her unutterance and all the pasteboard everywhere shuddered. The Dame and the Principal Boy come together by chance in the Chinese laundry. Aladdin has brought in his washing. They exchange some banter about smalls and drawers, eyeing one another up. They know that this time, for the first time since censorship began, the script will change.

'I feel randy,' said Widow Twankey. What is a fertility festival without a ritual copulation.

But it isn't as simple as that. For now, oh! now the hobby-horse is quite forgot. The Phallic Mother and the Big-Breasted Boy must take second place in the contemporary cast list to some cricketer who does not even know enough to make an obscene gesture with his bat, since in the late twentieth century, the planet is over-populated and four breasts in harmony is what we need more of, rather than babies, so Widow Twankey ought to go and have it off with Mother Hubbard and stop bothering Aladdin, really she/he ought.

Do people still believe in Pantoland?

If you believe in Pantoland, put your palms together and give a big hand to . . . If you *really* believe in Pantoland, put your – pardon me, vicar.

A fertility festival without a ritual copulation is . . . nothing but a pantomime. Widow Twankey has come back to earth to restore the pantomime to its original condition. But, before scarlet drawers and satin knicks could hit the floor, a hook dropped out of the flies and struck Widow Twankey between the shoulders.

The hook lodged securely in her red satin bustier; shouting and screaming, with a great display of a scrawny shin, she was hauled back up where she had come from, in spite of her raucous protests, and deposited back amongst the dead stars, leaving the Principal Boy at a loss for what to do except to imitate George Formby and sing: 'Oh, Mr Wu, I'm telling you . . .' As Umberto Eco said, 'An everlasting carnival does not work.' You can't keep it up, you know; nobody ever could.

The essence of the carnival, the festival, the Feast of Fools, is transience. It is here today and gone tomorrow, a release of tension not a reconstitution of order, a refreshment . . . after which everything can go on again exactly as if nothing had happened.

Things don't change because a girl puts on trousers or a chap slips on a frock, you know. Masters were masters again, the day after Saturnalia ended; after the holiday from gender, it was back to the old grind . . .

Besides, all that was years ago, of course. That was before television.

Guardian, 1991

The Granada, Tooting

My father had a permanent free pass to the Granada chain of cinemas, due to something to do with his work – he was a journalist – and the big Granada at Tooting was our nearest Granada, so sometimes, on Friday nights – he worked at nights but he had alternate weekends off – he would bring me here, to the pictures.

There's something glorious, for a small girl about going out with her father anyway, and with Dad it was the big-screen experience. This was the austere world of the Welfare State, remember – and I owe everything I am, my education, my sense of self, to the Welfare State and the Attlee government. But to step through the door of this dream cathedral of voluptuous thirties wish-fulfilment architecture was to set up a tension within me that was never resolved, the tension between inside and outside, between the unappeasable appetite for the unexpected, the gorgeous, the gim-crack, the fantastic, the free play of the imagination . . . and harmony, order. Abstraction. Classicism.

This cinema, with its mix of the real and false – real marble huggermugger with plaster, so you have to tap everything to see if it sounds hollow or solid – this apotheosis of the fake. There was a functioning cyclorama, in my day, clouds, stars, a sun, a moon, drifting across a painted sky. I held my breath in the gallery of mirrors – anything might materialise in those velvety depths, monsters, beauties, my own grown self. I would have been seven or eight.

This was the first great public building that ever impinged on me – and even though it was then jam-packed with queues, the marble steps polished by uniformed ushers, all the same, from outside it was just a concrete bunker. So there was always the element of surprise. It was, like the unconscious itself – like cinema itself – public and private at the same time.

I fell in love with rococo here, unaware it *was* rococo, or kitsch, or camp – I drank in the mix of styles with a pure eye. It seemed purely wonderful.

I fell in love with cinema although I scarcely remember the movies I watched with my father, only the space in which we sat to watch them, where we sat with all those wonderful people waiting in the dark.

Omnibus, BBC1, 1992

The Box

Theatre of the Absurd

I suppose that, of any art form, the television commercial has most in common with the limerick. It shares the same qualities of brevity, allusiveness and inherent absurdity. Just as the matter of the limerick is arbitrarily determined by the geographical derivation of its unique hero (the young lady from Riga, the young man from Devizes), so that of the commercial is dictated by the product he or she espouses. Exigencies of rhyme scheme alone ordain the tiger-rides of these Latvian adventuresses, the testicular irregularities of those adolescent Devonians, just as that warbling Italian copper haplessly creates his traffic jam due to the rigour with which his celebration of ice-cream transcends logic or reason.

This is what is marvellous about the commercials, marvellous in the surrealist sense. There's a kind of lateral imagination at work that makes it no wonder so many poets work in advertising. This quality of allusiveness is what roots the television commercial so firmly in the absurd. Maybe that is what makes it the dominant art form of our time – the unacknowledged, despised, low culture art form spontaneously generated in the twilight kitsch of the Krazy World of Kapitalism.

Nightly, the commercial channels spill out a cornucopia of images that would make a surrealist weep for joy. That caged and roaring Fiat, for example, with its direct, below-the-belt appeal to the id, the beast in you. And the child and dog at play with an immense roll of toilet paper. I can't get over that one. Admittedly, both small children and dogs are magnificent, uncontrollable shitters. That must be the, as it were, under-correspondence, the thing you can't help but think of when you see the commercial. So that the refulgent voice-over is *really* saying a polite version of: 'So and so's bog paper cleans up more shit, better.' Yet this seems to me a perfectly acceptable slogan, if linguistically arguable (better than what?), and not absurd at all. That, I suppose is why it can't be used.

Brevity necessitated by technical limitations need not be an artistic straitjacket; witness the succinct classics of early jazz and rock and roll, honed to a fine edge of formal perfection by the need to fit everything into three minutes' playing time. And, artistically, the most satisfying commercials are those that make a virtue of their extreme brevity, that either describe the product in terms of pure allusion (these are often lyric in technique, with sung or chanted texts and lots of fancy camerawork), or else compress information into almost an epigrammatic form, like the mininarrative about the lady who faints when she sees how cheap a certain brand of tea is.

The television commercial may be roughly divided into three principal genres; the lyric anthem, often sung and danced; the mini-narrative; and the straightforward exhortation. There is a lot of cross-fertilisation between these forms, needless to say; it's a living form, for God's sake, not defunct like the movies. These little kinetic and aural limericks, piped directly into your home, are, however, very rarely about the dissemination of information. Indeed, the exhortatory genre, which *is* specifically about the virtues of a brand, often suggests desperation, as if, throughout the campaign, all concerned with it have been gripped by a deep fear the product will be a non-starter and are trying to convince themselves it is all worthwhile, not us. (There's an ad for some kind of orange drink on the box at the moment that has this frenzied lack of conviction written all over it.)

Indeed, the television commercials are now so predominantly absurdist that I have the impression advertising agencies have perhaps at last acknowledged that people buy things in a random, *ad hoc* and wilful way and if you've made the consumer chuckle, at least she might remember you kindly in the supermarket. Unless dissemination of information was never the real point and persuasion was only theoretically what television advertising was ever all about.

And few commercials, now, even try to persuade. As performance rather than form, the analogy is with vaudeville. The commercial breaks are gaps in the fictive reality of the television evening through which a magic otherworld of lights, bustle and glamour is glimpsed – the magic otherworld of art. The commercial breaks perform the function, three or four times an hour, of interpolating a welcome breath of the magic of music-hall – a laugh; a song; a sketch; a pretty girl; cute chorusing kids; performing animals – where all round is turgid and parodic actuality.

The television evening is already in itself discontinuous, on any channel, with advertising or not; it is segmented into half-hour or hour-long or ninety-minute chunks of disparate material. And, on the commercial channels, there is an even greater discontinuity within the very programme breaks that break up your already discontinuous viewing. The commercial breaks contain a number of finite episodes, complete in themselves and absolutely unrelated to one another, though often related to other, similarly styled ads for the same product.

Kids who watch much commercial television ought to develop into whizzes at the dialectic; you have to keep so much in your mind at once because a series of artificially short attention spans has been created. But this in itself means that the experience of watching the commercial channels is a more informal one, curiously more 'homely' than watching BBC.

This is because the commercial breaks are constant reminders that the medium itself is artificial, isn't, in fact, 'real', even if the gesticulating heads, unlike the giants of the movie screen, are life-size. There is a kind of built-in alienation effect. Everything you see is false, as Tristan Tzara gnomically opined. And the young lady in the St Bruno tobacco ads who currently concludes her spiel by stating categorically: 'And if you believe that, you'll believe anything,' is saying no more than the truth. The long-term effect of habitually watching commercial television is probably an erosion of trust in the television medium itself.

Since joy is the message of all commercials, it is as well they breed scepticism. Every story has a happy ending, gratification is guaranteed by the conventions of the commercial form, which contributes no end to the pervasive unreality of it all. Indeed, it is the chronic bliss of everybody in the commercials that creates their final divorce from effective life as we know it. Grumpy mum, frowning dad, are soon all smiles again after the ingestion of some pill or potion; minimal concessions are made to mild frustration (as they are, occasionally, to lust), but none at all to despair or consummation. In fact, if the form is reminiscent of the limerick and the presentation of the music-hall, the overall mood – in its absolute and unruffled decorum – is that of the uplift fables in the Sunday school picture books of my childhood.

No copulation, no full frontals, no bad language, no gays, no exploitative human relations, no schizophrenia, so that none of it touches the heart. So that a television commercial cannot be serious, though it may be immoral; it cannot be serious because anger, passion and desire are banished, together with reason, from this art form, which is what cripples it, reduces it to decoration.

This is what makes the commercials for the regular army currently warping the small screen so disturbing; in a context of universal joy and harmony, propaganda for institutionalised killing must willy-nilly pertain to a world of universal joy and harmony. They are offensive because, under the carapace of pleasurable viewing, they *are* serious, they patently do have the intention to persuade and are factitiously inserted into a frivolous context in a far more sinuous way than those soft-sell ads about drunken driving ever were, although they had a perfect right to persuade.

That particular campaign rammed its well-meaning head right up against the gross limitations of the commercial.

There seems to be no way in which to utilise this most immediately attractive form of advertising for the purpose of moral restraint, just because it cannot contain real feeling. It proved, simply, impossible to put a tragic mini-narrative about the consequences of human folly into the commercial form. It was as futile an exercise as when the comic doffs his false nose, rolls pious eyes, sings 'Ave Maria'.

The regular army commercials are not of the same order as the moral restraint propaganda, of course, although part of their infernal cunning is that they use some of the same heavy naturalism, all the resources of a social-realist mini-narrative with an overlay of comedy that would seem more queasy if it were not for the lengthy British tradition of services farce. It was extraordinary to find a regular army commercial slotted cheek by jowl to a movie, *The Virgin Soldiers*, in which soldiers actually killed people and were killed during one of the murkier periods of British post-imperial history. For one thing, the movie was saying loud and long that the army is horrible and dehumanising and is often in the wrong place at the wrong time, and the commercial was using exactly the same kind of comic naturalism to assure viewers the army is loads of fun. The agency who've perpetrated this gross evasion of moral responsibility have even gone so far as to employ a token black model for some commercials, as if to further disarm liberals.

The most purely offensive one I've seen so far ends on a freeze-frame, a device often used in commercials for 'fixing' a pseudo real-life situation in your mind, real as a snapshot. The freeze-frame somehow makes everything that went before it look unfaked. This one is of a gentle, slight, shy, immature boy collecting a luscious dinner from a serving hatch at his training camp. He is not a figure to strike terror into the Queen's enemies (yes, the commercial really does talk about 'the Queen's enemies') though, by God, he strikes terror into me.

The voice-over intones paternally: 'The professionals – if you've got it in you, we'll bring it out.' Bring out what? Blood-lust, sado-masochism, authoritarianism, blind submission? Be warned – the army experience turned my grandfather from a ploughboy into a Bolshevik, though such had not been the intention of his officers. But if it makes a man of you, you can't say nastier than that. These commercials freeze my blood. The comic doffs his red nose and sings a recruiting song: it's a lovely war.

Then, wham! from the ridiculous to the sublime, as our master of ceremonies would say. The sweet, dissonant hymnals of the Malt Street Kids; the antiphonal Mr Bradford and Mr Bingley, plus chorus; and child and dog play for ever with bog paper in a glade. Then the curtains swish to on this absurdist vaudeville and, if regular television is often more artistically boring, then real life seems richer, fuller, somehow, more rewarding, by contrast, which *is* one of the things art can do.

New Society, 1978

Acting It Up on the Small Screen

The main difficulty about television drama is that it has to compete with old movies. When I watch British television drama, especially the sort of prestige production for which they use well-known 'classic' actors, that is, actors trained for the theatre, I remember why I stopped going to the theatre (it was some time in the late 1950s) and started going to the movies, instead.

'Live' theatre – though it might be better to call it 'undead' theatre – used to embarrass me so much I could hardly bear it, that dreadful spectacle of painted loons in the middle distance making fools of themselves. But these loons have truly come into their own, now. They have inherited the small screen and are inescapable, they spread themselves across all three channels mopping and mowing and rolling their eyes and scattering cutglass vowels everywhere.

Television has extraordinary limitations as a medium for the presentation of imaginative drama of any kind. It has an inbuilt ability to cut people down to size, to reduce them to gesticulating heads or, in long shot, to friezes of capering dwarfs. The *Rock Follies* series and Dennis Potter's *Pennies from Heaven* utilised this diminished reality effect in various sprightly ways and British actors, given good scripts, can do quite nicely under these conditions. Two-dimensional characters present them with no problems, unless the script is by Noël Coward. (Oh, that dreadful *Design for Living*.)

This is because most of them can't stylise for toffee. Two dimensions, yes; four dimensions, no. They think stylisation means over-acting. But the problem remains; the image on the television screen is very small. Television drama is more like the movies than it is like the theatre, obviously, but it is like the movies through the wrong end of a telescope. Watching *real* movies on television is very much an all-round reduced experience, though the opportunity to catch up on something like the current Douglas Sirk season is the main reason for owning a set.

In the cinema, we accept the convention that the images on the screen

are much larger than life without even thinking about it. This means that
we accept, also without thinking about it, a far higher degree of expres-
sionism than television could ever tolerate on its own terms.

Double Indemnity turned up – what a treat – as the midnight movie a
few weeks ago. Take the famous close-up of Barbara Stanwyck's high
heels, with the teasing anklet, as she walks down the staircase in order
to lure Fred MacMurray to his doom. What this shot means, of course,
is that MacMurray's whole attention is focused, not on the woman but
on the erotic potential he, she and we know she is exploiting. On television, this whole point is lost. The image of Stanwyck's lower limbs is
simply no longer large enough to sustain a metaphor. In television
drama itself, there is not sufficient artistic space to contain this kind of
device, and when directors try to perpetrate it it looks phony and
contrived.

A close-up on television is about the size of one's own face in a mirror.
Two is a crowd; scenes involving three or more people involve abrupt
changes of the focus of attention. In three-quarter shot, the actors are
already receding rapidly backwards, turning into wee folk before your
very eyes. This question of scale, that only faces are life-size and everything else is far smaller, means that television narrative is somehow always
composed at a distance, in the third person.

Movies aren't. There is always someone to identify with, even if it's
only the director. And scheduling that cruelly juxtaposes vintage
Hollywood classics, great movies, quaint movies, boring movies, freaky
movies against inept American telefilms and worthy but dull British high-
class custom-made drama suggests only that television drama has not yet
found its Lilliputian D.W. Griffith.

Nevertheless, one test of the viability of television drama *as* television is
whether or not it would look better on a big screen. If it would, then it's
lousy television. I would have thought this stood to reason, due to the limitations of the form creating the aesthetic of the form. But sometimes one
suspects television drama is made for preview theatres rather than transmission. It is interesting to see television falling into some of the old
Hollywood traps, though.

For example, it is a well-known fact that good novels make bad movies.
Obviously, what makes a novel good are just those qualities that make it
difficult to translate it out of fiction into anything else. (Conversely, who'd
want to read the book of the film of *Citizen Kane*?) Why, then, should it
be accepted as a self-evident fact that great novels make great television?
God knows. But the BBC keeps on churning out its 'classics' series, working remorselessly through Tolstoy, Hardy, Robert Graves (*Robert Graves?*)
amid a chorus of sycophantic yawns.

These series certainly give the painted loons a chance to show their paces. British actors adore period costume and facial hair; that's what they went to RADA for. The just-ended *Crime and Punishment* on BBC 2 really brings out the worst in them, even more than Chekhov does. They love to get their tongues round those lilting patronymics, they seem grotesquely liberated by personating groovy Slavs, it's an excuse to act your head off. Everybody knows how histrionic Russians are. Yet what looks, if not good, then at least lifelike in a parodic kind of way on a stage, looks like the theatrical equivalent of S. J. Perelman's pastiches of Dostoevsky when it is virtually delivered into your lap, which is what television does.

At the end of *Queen Christina*, Garbo was presented with the problem of a lengthy close-up as she sailed away from Sweden, having given up her throne to run off with a gentleman who had unfortunately just been eviscerated. Should she look glum? brave? Rouben Mamoulian told her to keep her face a perfect blank, so that the audience could read into her features whatever they felt should be the appropriate response. It works, too. Triumph of reticence; her face has the weary immobility of the obsessed. In this benighted *Crime and Punishment*, John Hurt feels it necessary to contort every single facial muscle, until the very hairs within his nostrils seem to rhumba, in a balked effort to convey spiritual turmoil. This is no way to sift out the human truth from a script based on a writer whose strong suit was just that very thing. Mind you, I don't want to put John Hurt down. He is a highly competent character actor in the classic British theatrical style; but that style, as Norman Mailer suggested in another context, is designed to evade truth and celebrate simulation.

In an interview (in the *Radio Times*) Hurt is quoted as saying: 'If an actor can make you listen and watch and believe him, he's achieving quite something.' This fetchingly modest statement contains within it the very definition of that sort of 'naturalistic' acting that drove me out of the theatre, blushing for them, all those years ago.

He's talking about the fictive reality of naturalism, which necessitates the creation of an illusion as an end in itself. (No wonder British actors make such a pig's breakfast out of Brecht.) But 'naturalism' as a mode which deals with the recreation of reality as a credible illusion is quite a different thing from the mode of realism itself, which is a representation of what things actually *are* like and must, therefore, bear an intimate relation to truth or else, well, it isn't any good. (And, of course, it doesn't have to *look* real.)

Hurt's remark reminds me of something gnomically ambiguous that Erving Goffman says about the fictive reality of commercial photography: 'It is through such practices that those who make a living reproducing appearances of life can continue further to stamp the real things out.'

Television, as a medium for drama, is, as I said, more like the movies than it is like the theatre. In fact, it is more like the movies than the movies are themselves, since so much of it is done in close-up. Most British actors are trained to project emotion rather than embody it. Nobody needs to project in close-up, unless he or she is selling something. British actors are very good at television commercials.

In fact, by far the most *realistic* acting in *Crime and Punishment* was Frank Middlemass as Marmeladov, but Marmeladov is a piece of cake for any British actor because Marmeladov is a posturing fake. The peculiarly external quality of the British school of acting, as if it were done in the third person, suits the personation of posturing fakes very well. It also suits the personation of other actors and of people who live with a high degree of self-consciousness; the upcoming *Brideshead Revisited* serial ought to turn out rather nauseatingly well because of this. It was also probably, in another way, why ITV's gangster series, *Out* worked.

John Hurt was terrific, truly, as Quentin Crisp, though *Crime and Punishment* hit the high peak of embarrassment, for me, when he threw himself at Sonya's feet with such an abrupt lurch that one half-expected the poor girl to snap: 'What you obviously have in mind will be five roubles extra.' But it certainly wasn't John Hurt's fault he couldn't bring off Raskolnikov's spontaneous act of homage from the murderer to the pious harlot. Probably only somebody as vulgarly Dostoevskian as Douglas Sirk would have known how to orchestrate Hurt's theatricality with the demented theatricality of the image.

I doubt if it would occur to a BBC2 classic serial television director to watch Sirk to pick up tips, though I hope I'm wrong. But the only thing at all like this exchange between Raskolnikov and Sonya that I've seen on television recently was when Susan Kohner threw herself on her mother's coffin in Sirk's *Imitation of Life*. Funnily enough, in the terms of British classic theatre, Susan Kohner probably can't act at all.

The BBC 'classic' serials are really no more than upmarket versions of the Classic Comics on which I was raised and which did indeed lead me in time to a curiosity about great literature that I eventually satisfied. It is probably unfair to discuss them as if they were drama, really. After all as somebody pompously opined about Crime and Punishment, if it makes one person who had never heard of Dostoevsky pick up the book and start to read, it will have served its purpose . . . and also have the rather self-defeating result of, presumably, making him switch the telly off.

But if the BBC really does feel a compulsion to tackle projects like *Crime and Punishment*, it seems shabbily unimaginative of them not to treat the insane melodrama about guilt and redemption, which is, after all,

Goffman's 'real thing', as richly unnatural as life, in the mode of realism. Maybe they could have thrown it open to the school of television social realism – Garnett-Loach-Allen *et al.*, let the cast make up their lines as they went along, shot it in Bradford which really does look like a Russian city, instead of what a Russian city is supposed to look like. Television pseudo-documentary social realism, after all this time, remains the only genre of television drama in this country that has the marks of a coherent style in which form and content fuse so that the actors appear to believe in what they are doing rather than trying to put one over on you.

New Society, 1979

The Box Does Furnish a Room

The more I watch television, the more I wonder what it's *for*. OK, so it's just afforded the entire nation vicarious participation in the summer solstice grass court ritual: players in white like Morris dancers, the final triumphs of the Summer King and Summer Queen. These spectator events – tennis, football, royal weddings, horse racing, general elections – are the occasions when the set really does plug you into the throbbing heart of things: one of the crowd but with a far better view, and no chance of heat stroke, a drenching or being hit over the head with a broken bottle.

These fiestas, most enjoyed by those who stay away, contain some of the essential oddness of television as a medium, the sense of uninvolved participation, of being there and doing nothing. It was the archetypal British fiesta, the coronation, that seemed to turn the country truly on to television all those years ago. The coronation spread its electronic tentacles all over the British Isles; it needed to be witnessed and the means to do so were newly available, in the comfort of one's own home. Privatisation of experience, of course.

But even so there is the optional bonus, on all such occasions, that if you actually manage to drag yourself to the last night of the Proms or whatever, and make sufficient exhibition of yourself, you too may be picked up by the camera and appear unscheduled on television. The extroverts who grin and gesticulate in between the television interviewer and his prey are really the ones who are using television as a medium of communication, not the hapless broadcasters, who are only doing what their roles demand.

These kinds of transmission, which are records of real life, are also the only times when the unscheduled can be seen to happen. This is the attraction of televised actuality events. Real life can burst through its simulacrum, the whole charade falls apart, life is there and *not* like it is on television. As when Jim Callaghan called Pat Arrowsmith up from the audience to 'speak out about Northern Ireland' after his election results were read out, and then ostentatiously left the stage with his entourage. A bit too much like Pontius Pilate washing his hands, Jim.

Television as a medium is not 'for' showing the disjunction between different kinds of reality, but it cannot help do so because of the disjunction between the kinds of life shown on the screen and the one which the viewer knows to be real. And since one cannot fool all of the people all of the time, television may be implicitly radical all the time, in spite of itself.

But however much television engages in what Hans Magnus Enzensberger calls 'consciousness shaping' that doesn't answer the question why people watch it in the first place. This is a wholly different question.

In thirty years or thereabouts, television has come to operate as a technological margin around most people's waking lives, something neither welcome nor unwelcome, nor even especially thought about except by specialists. Just there. 'See what's on the box.'

Its presence is something that continually bewilders me. I grew up without it. I'm not *used* to it as kids today are. I resent having to pay attention to it. For which Enzensberger raps me smartly across the knuckles: 'Potentially the new media do away with all educational privileges and thereby with the cultural monopoly of the bourgeois intelligentsia. This is one of the reasons for the intelligensia's resentment of the new industry.' It's no good saying that I'd like *everybody* to have enjoyed that broadcast of Alban Berg's *Lulu*, I suppose.

My father says that television is a 'great comfort'. Well, he did without it for sixty-five years, never missed it; we were the last house in the street to have a set. But if he hadn't got it now, he'd be so bored he'd have to come and live with me. Before I got my own television set, last year, a little child came visiting. At first she didn't believe I hadn't got television, thought I was hiding it, to tease her. At last, convinced, she said: 'But what do you do in the evenings?' If they both came to live with me, they would share the traditional complicity of those who do not yet work and those who've stopped working, but I bet they wouldn't stop watching television: they'd watch it together. It has replaced the story book.

And who am I to sneer? A television-less childhood I might have had, but it was *Saturday Night Theatre, Monday Night at Eight, ITMA, Take It From Here*. Less pure junk than you get, these days, but a lot more corn. And it is almost impossible, nowadays, to imagine the funereal hush of houses before the Industrial Revolution entered the cultural field, the dreadful isolation of those whose families predeceased them, the morbid reclusiveness of the respectable poor who didn't even have the nerve to get pissed on a Saturday night.

There are, apparently, more homes in the US without indoor lavatories than there are without television sets. This need not necessarily represent a set of priorities gone awry. It's usually easier and cheaper to install electricity than it is to install a proper sewerage system. Since the contemporary interpenetration of broadcasting and daily life can only be compared with that of yesteryear's religions, well, nobody would think it odd to find an outdoor lavatory and an indoor Sacred Heart in Ireland. In Japan, you'll find a cesspit, which they call a 'godshelf', and a colour television set in most rural homes and many in the cities too. There's more profit in electronics. I'm not saying that television *is* a religion, mind, only, that it functions rather like a religion – as consolation, entertainment and a method of relating to the real world by proxy. Perhaps these in themselves are sufficient reasons why people want television so much.

Only a fraction of the British intelligentsia manage without it, now, and most of *them* sneak off to friends when there's something they really want to watch, like *Fawlty Towers* or *Days of Hope*.

Nowhere is safe from it, nowhere. There was a picture in the paper the other day of a shop window in Peking, stuffed full of television sets for which, apparently, Chinese workers in the post-Gang-of-Four liberalisation are clamouring – though who knows if they're clamouring for them in inner Mongolia or Tibet.

God knows what they transmit on the things. They look like items of pure conspicuous consumption and, ain't it always the same, the minute people get a bob or two in their pockets, the demand for 'luxury goods'. Washing machines, refrigerators, television sets . . .

Which is an interesting set of luxury goods. Because nobody who has ever washed a pair of double sheets by hand would ever describe a washing machine as a luxury. Refrigeration, especially in a hot climate, does not mean ice cubes clinking in a gin and tonic; it means gastro-intestinal disorders reduced to a bare minimum, fresh milk, and meat without maggots in it. Both these so-called luxury goods significantly simplify the domestic labour of women and leave them more time to enter the work force, improve their minds and generally comport themselves in a way God – or man – did not intend.

If, therefore, a washing machine or a refrigerator turns out to be not really a luxury good at all, then it seems to me quite possible that from the point of view of pure function, a television set is not a mere item of conspicuous consumption, either. In its function of electronic companion and nanny – a function we systematically undervalue – television makes family life possible in a high-rise flat on a wet day. Never mind what's on it. Look instead at what it does.

I know a household that pays the television rental before it pays the rent, and they're not idiots, they certainly don't sit in front of the box in a glazed trance. Nevertheless, their life is conducted against a continuous stream of electronic babble because one or more members of the household are likely to be seriously watching any given programme at any given time. The set, obviously is sited in the (only) living room. A kind of fictive privacy may be obtained among the domestic group by focusing on the television screen. This privacy is respected – 'He's watching his programme.'

It's a piss-poor household with several teenage children, very badly housed and they all need a little privacy from time to time. Their method of creating it is to retreat into the television, not into the action on the screen so much as into the act of viewing. I don't know how what they see on the screen affects them, and, yes, it would be a far better thing if they were reading Tolstoy or raising their consciousnesses, not having them shaped. Nevertheless, this is how they use television, and the rental is money well spent as far as that family is concerned, keeping them a viable unit in circumstances where they might very well be hitting one another with chair-legs. I don't know if this is repressive or not.

John McGrath (*Sight and Sound*, spring 1977) quotes a gnarled old scriptwriter telling him, in his early days at the BBC: 'What is television? I'll tell you: television is a piece of furniture.' And this seems rather a good way to begin thinking about the social fact of television. Cut all the crap about the popular arts – which, except for certain kinds of drama and, possibly, wrestling, are certainly not represented on or by television – and cut all the stuff about mass media and communications theory, the exponents of which still seem to be reeling, stunned, before the magnitude of the task they have set themselves, which is no less than the interpretation of the world.

We could start, instead, with a box in a room, which transmits pictures when you press a switch. Now why should anyone want to look at that, when the world is so full of a number of things? Don't think it's going to catch on.

New Society, 1979

Monkey Business

Perhaps the BBC felt that the Christmas season wasn't a suitable time for the transmission of overt Buddhist propaganda. Anyway, the other

Friday, settling down in front of the set for what has lately become the happiest time of the week, imagine my indignation to be confronted by the Beatles, like skeletons from a cupboard. I can't imagine what the purpose of the Yuletide exposure of the atrocious movies perpetrated at the height of their meretricious fame by the erstwhile mop-top four was supposed to serve, unless it was to make the surviving Sex Pistols feel good. But a lady at the BBC assured me that *Monkey* will be back this week.

Monkey is an ongoing, metaphysical series about animal spirits, demons, ethics, sex-swapping Boddhisattvas. It is something like the kind of thing Ken Campbell might do if he were given access to three-quarters of an hour of early evening television every week, a great deal of money, and the proviso that children were watching.

Monkey is by far the oddest thing on television at the moment, and also the most engaging. It is structured like a strip cartoon, with real actors, wild special effects and a horrible rock music score. It is a Japanese version of a sixteenth-century Chinese fairytale cum allegory about the pilgrimage undertaken by the monk, Tripitaka, to India from China to bring back the Buddhist scriptures. Perhaps the only equivalent of this in the west would be the Grail Quest, although, according to Arthur Waley, Tripitaka was a real person ('better known to history as Hsuan Tsang') which is more than can be said for Parsifal. And the Grail didn't exist, either.

Whether the real Tripitaka rode a white horse that was transformed from a dragon and was accompanied on his mission by a monkey, a pig and a lugubrious, indeterminate beast which the script, following Arthur Waley's translation of Wu Cheng'-ên's novel, calls a 'water monster', is another matter. Tripitaka himself is personated by a stunningly beautiful actress in a bald wig, which adds a further dimension of conspicuous un-reality to a scenario in which time and space are presented as modes of thought. The whole thing is dubbed, so that everybody sounds like speak-your-weight machines, a surreally harmonious effect.

Not that the pig and the water monster are *real* animals, although Monkey began life as a monkey, even if a rather special kind of monkey – stone, in fact. Piggsy and Sandy (as, again following Waley, this oddly sinister person is called) were originally high-ranking officials in a heaven run with the bureaucratic efficiency of British Leyland. Both were suspended from celestial duties – one for rampant sexism, the other for clumsiness. But they've been offered reinstatement after an aeon or two on condition they make the pilgrim's progress with Tripitaka. Sandy wears a necklace of human skulls, a nasty touch, and an inverted dish on his head. I worried about this dish a good deal, wondering if it had some esoteric Buddhist significance, until I remembered there is a Japanese mythical beast called a *Kappa* who has a head like an inverted dish. I think there is no more to it than that. Nevertheless, it remains disconcerting.

Not that it's the only thing the occidental will find disconcerting. Oceans materialise and dematerialise: things constantly change into other things – Monkey himself frequently turns into a fly, amongst other things: and he is equipped with an invincible magic staff that can shrink down to almost nothing and grow very, very big indeed at will, a piece of apparatus my five-year-old godson finds particularly satisfying as any Freudian can understand.

Indeed, all of *Monkey* has the authentic quality of dream, often gently boring, never less than terribly confusing, bursting with latent content, mysterious and full of marvels. If a sinuous fluidity of being is common to most of the characters, then Tripitaka, the pure in heart, always stays reassuringly the same. In fact, Tripitaka is so pure in heart he is a pain in the neck. Nag, nag, nag, all the time; and the Buddhas have slipped him a beastly little long-distance nerve tightener so that he can give Monkey a nasty headache when Monkey is about to act in a particularly unenlightened way. (I suspect this is a fable about the origin of conscience.)

Tripitaka's companions, prone as they are to gluttony, fighting, sulking and running after women (who always turn out to be immaterial demons), are constantly grumbling about Tripitaka's moral totalitarianism, especially since they are always having to rescue him from the tight spots he has got himself into by assisting old ladies (who often turn out to be demons, too) or forgiving some murderous brigand too expeditiously. Yet even when hanging by the heels over a slow fire, Tripitaka cannot be seduced into a single murderous thought. He is ethically impeccable.

But Tripitaka isn't the real hero. Monkey is – 'the funkiest monkey that ever bopped', as the regrettable lyrics of the theme song have it. And Monkey is wonderful, even more wonderful than Piggsy, in spite of Piggsy's lovely, pink silky ears and coyly insinuating smile. These ambiguous beings are only subtly animalised: Monkey's eyebrows meet and he grins a lot. He walks like a monkey. He jumps like a monkey. That's all.

Monkey, as shown in the pre-credit sequence, burst out of a stone egg one fine day: 'the nature of Monkey was . . . irrepressible'. According to Arthur Waley, in the introduction to his translation of the novel, *Monkey*, Monkey's allegorical significance is 'the restless instability of genius'. The series plays Monkey rather more for broad comedy, and the transportation device that Waley translates as his 'cloud trapeze' turns into a busy little fluorescent pink cloud that comes when he whistles for it and speedily whizzes him anywhere.

Monkey acquires immortality by gorging himself on the forbidden peaches in the garden of the immortal deities, but, unlike the consequences of a not dissimilar fruit theft in our own cultural heritage, he does not, thus, let sin and guilt into the world. Instead, the immortals are somewhat perplexed as to what to do about this transgression. They tentatively award him the title, Great Sage, Equal of Heaven. Then he pisses on the Buddha's hand.

The Buddha, for inscrutable reasons of his or her own – and I use the form, 'his or her', advisedly in this context – is manifesting, well, itself as a woman for the duration of the series, perhaps to point up some of the ways in which the ideology of this ethical system differs from that of God the Father Inc. (The Japanese don't miss much.) Monkey, high on the peaches of immortality, boasts he can whizz on his cloud to the ends of the universe Buddha, in a full lotus on top of the Himalayas, assures him he can go where he likes but never, never will he leave the palm of the Buddha's hand.

Whee! Off goes Monkey, until he comes to three enormous pillars. Clearly the pillars at the end of the universe. (Note it's a steady state model.) Monkey scrawls his name on the central pillar, to show he's been there, and slips round it to take a pee. He jets proudly back to the Buddha but she laughs and raises her hand.

At the base of her third finger, there is Monkey's name, and, on the other side, a spreading damp patch.

And it was genuinely, breathtakingly magical, an image of such grace and beauty and imaginative gaiety that you very rarely see on television at all, least of all in the etiolated pap they provide for children.

Anyway, Monkey was dismissed from the great civil service in the sky (for such is the sixteenth-century Chinese kingdom of heaven) for chronic insubordination, slammed under a rock for a millennia or two and let out to acquire enlightenment on the way to India with Tripitaka. At the time of writing, he has shown no sign whatsoever of acquiring any such thing.

The last episode before the Christmas break concluded with the gnomic reminder: 'The world is a product of mind'. Chew on *that* with your cold turkey, kids. Although real Buddhists may find all this as wincingly embarrassing as a self-confessed atheist like myself finds *The Life of Brian*, and the intricacies of Buddhist theology remain as hermetic to me as hitherto, I still think *Monkey* is a spendid corrective to the stuff they teach them in RE in school.

Of course, Wu Cheng'-ên's *Monkey* is a fairytale and not a holy book, even if Arthur Waley does it no more than justice when he calls it 'unique in its combination of beauty with absurdity, of profundity with nonsense', which is more than you can say of most holy books.

New Society, 1980

The Wonderful World of Cops

There's a story, as follows: coppers in, say, Glasgow, fret because children, given as an essay subject, 'Our police,' submit reams and screeds of abuse. A particularly hurtful essay comprises one word: 'bastards'. Determined to improve relations, the coppers organise a big party with clowns, balloons and ice cubes in the orange squash. The essay subject is set again. This time, happily, all the kids unite to praise the police. Except for one, who just adds a qualifying adjective: 'cunning bastards'.

I feel that way about *Hill Street Blues* (ITV), the most widely acclaimed of recent US cop-operas. Even the radical *City Limits*, for once evidently blind to the contradictions inherent in liberalism, thinks it is marvellous, and there's no doubt it has heralded a whole new style of presentation of the work of the police in media entertainment.

One tends to think of those who work from the Hill Street Precinct as 'the gang', as in 'the gang's all here'. Under the kind but firm guidance of Frank Furillo, they deal with the detritus of human misery and crime in the insalubrious neighbourhood known as 'the Hill', making mistakes, sometimes – but always ready to see the funny side, to josh with quaint, Runyonesque figures such as the midget hispanic gang-leader, Jésus, on his way to pick up his mother from the dentist before a rumble.

The series is taking a breather for a while but one hopes it will soon be back, opening up as it does whole new, hitherto unimagined areas of repressive tolerance, a concept that itself seems to have gone to ground only, as the French say, to recoil in order to jump better.

Hill Street Blues's wacky influence may be traced in another of this past summer's imports, *Cagney and Lacey* (BBC), with its eponymous women cops, low-profile case-work, often involving children, and mood of gritty sentimental realism. But *Cagney and Lacey* goes considerably further than *Hill Street Blues* in creating fictions about US law enforcement in which it is possible to suspend disbelief.

The point about *Cagney and Lacey* is not that they are wise, wonderful police-women but that they are tough, wearily competent, occasionally tender women who work as police officers. The recently concluded six-part series has been remarkable in several ways, not least because the class origins of the two women – both 'lower class', as the Americans put it – are depicted with a firmness and a precision very rare indeed in American mass media entertainment, which tends to the depiction of a blandly homogenised middle class.

Cagney is the daughter of a uniformed cop. There is a suggestion her own career as a 'tec fulfils some of her Irish father's thwarted ambition. Lacey is happily married to an unemployed construction worker, who functions, cheerfully, as house-husband. They share the rearing of their two kids in an apartment on the crummy side of the not-so-great. If Lacey's home-life is overt propaganda, I'd be the last one to knock it. But much of *Cagney and Lacey* is propaganda, not for the police but for women as free, equal citizens.

There is the impression the entire production team worked very hard on the series to make it special, and it does break altogether new ground. Simply and unpretentiously, it describes ordinary women, tousled, behind on their paperwork, smoking too much, working together as friends and partners.

It may have done this too well, since CBS apparently proposes to replace the marvellous woman who plays Cagney in the next series, on the grounds she is too dyke-like. Somebody must have spotted that the series wasn't *really* about cops at all and, puzzling their heads over it, concluded that therefore it must be about *that*.

Of course, by showing law enforcement as just the job these admirable women do, the series does beg the question of the peculiar nature of police work. Cagney and Lacey are really depicted as kinds of investigative social worker who just happen to pack guns.

The insertion of *real* problems, either social or personal, into the context of television mass entertainment serials always presents some problems. *Hill Street Blues* has always attempted to overcome these by offering a surface naturalism upon which real problems may be dealt with appropriately superficially. With its cast of raffish, street-wise, plain-clothes cops, it has exactly the air of what William Empson once called 'urban pastoral', with this difference: the law-enforcers have taken over wholesale the deviant charm which, in those far-off days when popular art was less mediated than it is now, used to pertain to the outlaw. It is not unlike an inverted *Beggars' Opera*, with Furillo as a benign MacHeath.

There is a tension between the pseudo-improvisational technique, the overlapping dialogue and plotting and so on, and an implicit stylisation. The Hill Street precinct is set in a generalised inner city that the British viewer vaguely takes to be New York . . . or somewhere like that, and the American viewer, presumably, takes as Everytown. The Hill is, in fact, a paradigmatic social problem, inhabited by a criminal underclass of poor blacks, hispanics and one or two stranded whites.

The depiction of the Hill as a vast generalisation equating poor America with criminal America is the main thing that gives *Hill Street Blues* its liberal credentials – that, and the series' tacit admission cops can make mistakes and look silly. But a few ritual genuflections to the idea, hoary in

Mayhew's day, that poverty breeds crime just isn't good enough, especially when the series' treatment of blacks is so dicey – black actors,
doomed yet again to be side-kicks, cold-blooded street killers, whores or
– new stereotype – crisp, efficient social workers, which is just the whore
image turned inside out.

And things have come to a pretty pass when the notion that a US law
enforcement officer might sometimes shoot his own foot while it is resisting arrest is hailed as a breakthrough for a refreshing new attitude to cops.

However, I hope the series returns to the small screen, soon, because
the last one concluded on a note of irony and paradox: Captain Furillo's
girlfriend, the improbably glossy attorney, Joyce Davenport, galvanised
into action by the wanton murder of a colleague, has bent the law to
acquire, like Nancy Reagan, a hand-gun with which to defend herself.
And, in the realm of *real* gunshot fatalities, the person whom Joyce
Davenport is most likely to shoot is not a mugger or street assassin but, of
course, Frank Furillo.

The reason why Joyce has bought her little gun takes us straight to the
compromised heart of the series, to a theme that recurs again and again in
all the cop shows. It is: that justice is no longer good enough. Nowadays,
it lets the wrong people off and, as far as one can tell, this means all those
of the accused who have not been found guilty. Therefore, the thing to
do is to shoot the punks first, before they shoot you.

This motif is introduced by formulae like: of course we have proof but
it just won't stick in a court of law. Planting of evidence may be heralded
by such a line as: we need something to really nail him with. Physical
intimidation of suspects, prisoners and even witnesses has become so much
a part of the arrest and investigative procedure of cop-operas that we don't
blink when we see suspects flung across car bonnets and searched with
grunts and gestures more appropriate to anal rape.

The cop-operas hold firm on one ethical principle: cops don't, except
in certain exceptional cases, shoot to maim or kill unless they are shot at
first. But being shot at automatically empowers a cop with the right to kill;
and these shootings, more and more, are presented as the ultimate form of
law enforcement – which, indeed, they are.

However, to be shot while resisting arrest cannot in any way be construed as 'cruel and unusual punishment' because it pre-dates, just as it
precludes, the trial, which would ascertain – beyond a reasonable doubt –
whether punishment was necessary or appropriate. The recent TV screening of the film *Twelve Angry Men* (1957), enshrined a morality as of before
the flood. There was Henry Fonda, pleading that justice involved no
question of guilt or innocence but only the existence of that 'reasonable
doubt' and, furthermore, striving to ensure that real justice and not class

justice was administered to the ghetto punk accused of parricide. *Twelve Angry Men* concludes with just the sort of acquittal the Hill Street Gang would regard, not as justice in action but as gross perversion of justice. Those were the days of a militant, crusading liberalism that could be mobilised at the idea of the death penalty.

Today, it is the cops themselves who mete out the death penalty, which appears to be the standard if unwritten punishment for threatening a policeman. Only Lacey, in recent cop-operas, refused to be consoled by the knowledge that the person she killed had tried to kill her first. Since she is a woman and a mother and therefore the embodiment, not the custodian, of morality, she is permitted grief and remorse denied her male colleagues, in the course of the endless stream of simulated public executions in which it is axiomatic that the victim is guilty or else he would not be dead. *Hill Street Blues* concurs at every point with this morality of the medieval witch trial. Cunning bastards, indeed.

New Society, 1982

Making Art

Berthold Hinz: Art in the Third Reich

This is a remarkable, deeply affecting and also rather disquieting book. Disquieting not simply because the iconography of fascism freezes the blood because we know what it means, but also because some of the pictures reproduced here are what quite a lot of people might rather like – if they were shown the pictures of pretty girls and rolling landscapes cold.

The art of the Third Reich was certainly produced for, and, one suspects, by people who didn't know much about art but knew what they liked; and Hinz's pictorial material reflects the uncanny kind of art made in a country where there were no artists, for the artists were all either dead or exiled. And this results in an art in complicity with ideology in an absolutely unmediated way – a political pseudo-aesthetics, as he says. But the banality is that of the international language of third-rate representational painting, which is part of the irony of it all.

The National Socialists, however, also knew what they didn't like. They didn't need to define it because as Hinz says: 'All the National Socialists needed was to look at the various studies on modern art and to note who was mentioned and considered important.' Armed with this information, the resultant purge of twentieth-century artists was staggeringly impressive in its scope – not just Jews, Slavs, Bolsheviks, homosexuals, abstractionists, surrealists, cubists, dadas, but a special *enfer* reserved for realists like George Grosz and Kathe Kollwicz. What is striking about the way the National Socialists cleared the ground for 'a new and genuine German art' was how they repudiated every painter with any class at all in any German collection.

The entire faculty of the Bauhaus, that powerhouse of modernism, was sacked. The famous exhibition of Degenerate Art in Munich in 1937 (attended by over two million people) was, of course, one of the finest and most comprehensive exhibitions of the art of this century ever held. (Most of the exhibits were burned, except for the impressionists Goering picked out for himself and a handful, including a Van Gogh, that turned up on the international market.) This exhibition coincided with the first Great

German Art exhibition of the ideologically immaculate painting that Hinz convincingly demonstrates were simply those still being churned out by provincial ateliers that stuck to the conventions of the nineteenth-century salon. A year later, opening the second Great German Art exhibition, the Führer stated his case: 'I thought it essential . . . to give the decent, honest artist of average talent a chance.' What such artist would not be grateful and toe the line?

If the conscious break with international modernism was part of a general aesthetic project of 'revolutionary discontinuity,' as Hinz suggests, then this 'revolutionary discontinuity' was a parodic inversion of that with which Malevich and Tatlin celebrated the Russian revolution in art that expresses an authentic liberation of the human spirit. For the National Socialists, it was not a 'revolutionary discontinuity' with the past, but with the present. Time would stand still; or even, for 1,000 years, run backwards. This, Hinz argues, was the true intention of this bizarre aesthetic, an absolute denial of time.

Third Reich art is a closing in, a shutting down, a deliberate cauterisation of the imagination. Stylistically, it might involve an engineered return to Dutch and Flemish 'genre' painting, but genre recreated in an un-historic vacuum, where women, animals, even landscapes, soldiers – especially soldiers – scenes of family life, are not sufficient in themselves but are pressed into the service of symbolising 'the sacred mysteries of the natural order'. On these canvases, labour, such as farming or stone-breaking, is consciously archaised, old implements are used. Women are solely objects; the nudes, slick as if their flesh was moulded margerine, are genuinely obscene in their static lifelessness.

There is a haunting ambiguity about the title of a painting of a troop of cavalry: 'They Carry Death With Them'. These paintings, differentiated by subject matter but unnervingly similar in academic competence of exe-cution, were intended for sale at low prices and for reproduction in the form of cheap prints. Painting was only of interest as a political instrument, and was effective as glorification of the Reich only through wide dis-semination.

Hinz believes that the function of the art of the Third Reich was the denial and elimination of every conceivable reflection of reality and history in art in order to validate an illegitimate political system further. 'The painting of German fascism no longer reflected reality but presented it in such a way that it paralysed consciousness.' Art as cultural anaesthesia.

It is the banality of these canvases, the prettiness of the healthy farm girls, the solidity of the old men, that might numb the mind as to their factitiousness, until you turn the page and see the swastikas.

Hinz's exemplary text concludes with an exposition on architecture, the arms industry and war itself. His subtle, complex book is a most important account of the sensibility of National Socialism, and also of its deathly cynicism.

New Society, 1980

Treasures of Ancient Nigeria

The 'Treasures of Ancient Nigeria', on display at the Royal Academy until 23 January, are imbued with a perfectly genuine mystery which is not that of mystical strangeness but to do with the hard fact that we know, as yet, very little about most of the people who produced them. Not only have the cultures that created these beautiful objects vanished, but most of those cultures provide the European historical imagination with little or none of its favourite nourishment – that is, chronicles, documents, laundry lists and so on. There are no written records of the kingdoms of West Africa before the sixteenth century.

Therefore what manner of people shaped and fired those terracotta heads of the so-called Nok culture, dating from around the time of Socrates, is unknown to us. What they had for dinner, what they used for money, how they felt about their parents . . . all lost, as if swept away by the rivers which archaeologists believe once swept away these statues from the riverside villages where, probably, they were made. The floods rent many of the statues limb from limb; we are left, mostly, with suggestive fragments.

Fragments that are not, however, suggestive in the same way as the 'vast and trunkless legs of stone' stumbled upon by Shelley's traveller in an antique land. They do not seem to signify either ancient *folie de grandeur* or the overweening vanity of artists or models. The bronzes of the coastal Benin empire, of some two millennia later, certainly do address the spectator as if to say: 'Look on my works, ye mighty, and beware!' And indeed, they are genuinely intimidating, especially those warriors armed to the teeth; awesome, in fact, though not in size. And we know quite enough about the Benin empire, to which the British put a stop in 1897, to appreciate its artefacts were not awesome to no purpose.

However, though there *is* a trunkless Nok leg on display at the Royal Academy, it does not look as if it once upheld an Ozymandias, an effigy that was supposed to scare you rigid. With its blunt-toed foot and crust of anklets, it looks like – a well-dressed leg.

Everything Nok is just about lifesize, except some tiny terracottas a few inches long, the size of fossils. Evidently these people were not giants, nor did they aggrandise themselves as such. We know from their faces, stylised as their features are, that they were as African as the 'Africa man original' of the song of the Nigerian jazz musician, Fela Anikulapo Kuti: 'I no be gentleman at all, I be Africa man original.' Fela Anikulapo Kuti's music is the product of the hectic and volatile modern city of Lagos, which is where the exhibits at the RA come from, although they live in museums, there, and he does not (his biography, *Fela Fela*, has recently been published).

We know, from the evidence of this earliest sculpture of black Africa, that the people who made them took great trouble with their hair, arranging it in coils and little chignons and possibly decorating it with feathers, which they might have stuck in little holes left in the hairdos, unless these holes were intended for some other purpose. They also enjoyed jewellery. Their dandyism argues a concern with the public presentation of self, a sign of a society with sufficient leisure in which people thought a lot of themselves. Excavations show they farmed, and smelted iron, too.

The sculptured heads have big, surprised-looking, triangular eyes and mouths with an apprehensive pout to them. There is the head of an elephant and he has three-cornered eyes, too. They enjoyed modelling animals, evidently, but whether the enjoyment of the thing was the reason for doing it, or whether there was some ritual or religious purpose behind it, we do not know.

This school or tradition of sculpture is named after the village where the first piece was found, by a clerk in a tin mine who took his terracotta head home to use as a scarecrow in his yam field. ('Let the past serve the present,' as Mao Tse-tung said.) The forms tend to geometric abstractions based on spheres, cones and cylinders; nothing, so far, has been dug up that might show how the artists of the Nok school came to see this way, or if this way of seeing influenced anything that was to come.

Because of this tendency to see natural forms in terms of unnatural geometric structures, the Nok heads look modern in almost an outmoded way – they look, of course, cubist. They do not surprise, as the vividly lifelike portrait heads of Ife sculpture surprise, because, for historic reasons, we associate African art with twentieth-century art and the cast-metal and terracotta heads of Ife look more like the sculpture of the European fifteenth century, the work of Donatello or somebody like that, with whom these artists were roughly contemporary.

In fact, some of the Ife heads, and especially some of the rather later heads from Owo – a Yoruba city-state lying roughly halfway between Ife and Benin, as it might be between Florence and Rome except the distances are larger – are almost too much. Almost kitsch in their sweet prettiness. (I'm thinking particularly of No. 60 in the catalogue, head of a pretty minx in a turban.) For this prettiness, we must presumably blame the prettiness of the model rather than the art of the craftsman, because it would appear to be almost a speaking likeness,

Most of the work in the exhibition has been excavated very recently, within the last forty years, and its serene classicism is new to Europe. Some of the bronzes of Benin, however, have been here before, after they were sold off to defray the costs of the British Punitive Exhibition of 1897 which consigned the 400 or 500 years of the Benin empire to one of the minor sideshows of European history. The Benin bronzes are more familiar – ten of them used to be in the British Museum, before they returned to Nigeria – and must have helped to shape our ideas of what West African art ought to look like. Suffice to say that it looks primarily like itself.

The most extraordinary, if not the loveliest, objects in the exhibition aren't really sculpture, however one defines it; they are pieces of metal-work – dishes and jewellery and potstands and fly-whisk handles – of the most paranoid complexity of design. The highly decorated surfaces of these bronzes look as if covered with several kinds of lace, lace in which flies and other small insects, and snails, and spiders, and birds, and frogs, have somehow got themselves trapped. There is a pendant in the shape of a ram's head with flies on its nose. One imagines, possibly quite incorrectly, a kind of playfulness. The makers were functioning around the ninth century AD in south-eastern Nigeria and seem to have enjoyed using exceedingly complicated methods of manufacture, perhaps for the sheer hell of it, perhaps because they were in love with technology.

As to their baroque, nay, rococo style, the catalogue says: 'We know nothing of where it came from and almost nothing of what it led to.' It can't have led to European art nouveau, of which it is reminiscent, because no art nouveau craftsperson could have clapped eyes on it. The first pieces were found in 1938, by a farmer who liked the look of them and kept them for luck.

EX AFRICA SEMPER ALIQUID NOVI, as the imperialist Africanophile and writer of sadistic, racist adventure stories used as a motto for his novel of 1887, *Allen Quatermain*. Rider Haggard was addicted to the idea of a Lost White Kingdom somewhere in the heart of what he often called 'the dark continent'. Somewhere with a pleasant climate, naturally, and peopled by descendants of Persians or Phoenicians, perhaps.

It was as though he couldn't get his mind round the idea that there might exist an entire continent which harboured no peoples at all to whom he could relate on the matter of pigmentation. For him, Africa was a vast, picturesque, beautiful elsewhere, full of savage beasts and magnificent savages whom his heroes respected just to the extent they put up a good fight before being killed. Haggard's Africa is a terrain somewhat like an unexplored galaxy in modern science-fiction, a marvellous elsewhere in which, at journey's end, a beautiful blonde princess waits to welcome you. It is startling, and shaming, to read in the catalogue that many early twentieth-century European art historians simply could not believe that Africans had thought of the bronzes of Ife and Benin all by themselves.

Sponsored by Mobil, they look well in the well-carpeted silence of the London gallery, pregnant with a meaning to which the original key has been mislaid, but provided with a new meaning by the context of this exhibition, at which they have arrived in order to be *looked at*.

In glass cases, under spotlights, these beautiful objects of clay, stone and bronze are presented purely as triumphs of the artistic imagination and the craftsman's skill. (And also, of course, of the skills and dedication of the archaeologist.) But the exhibition also has a didactic purpose. It is intended to correct certain European assumptions about Europocentricity, assumptions that are immoral when held by Europeans themselves and tragic if held by those who are not.

And yet, looking in the glass cases at the exquisitely presented portrait heads, the bronze plaques, the jewellery, one cannot help but think of Brancusi, and Donatello, and Rodin, and Fabergé — of European artists and craftsmen who made and sold signed commodities in a market-place dominated by fashion. The exhibition implicitly invites us to look at the anonymous craftsmen of cultures with quite different value systems to those of Europe since the fifteenth century as if their work was the same sort of thing. As if, that is, the concept of the art object were a human universal; as if the metaphysic of 'art for art's sake' was something that held good for the work of all modellers in clay, bronze, stone or ivory, in all places and at all times.

There are some lovely soapstone figures from a place called Esie in the Nigerian exhibition. Their date is undetermined; before 1850, says the catalogue. About 800 of these figures were found by the present inhabitants of Esie when they migrated there 200 years ago. The people of Esie like these statues very much, and tell a story about how they are the remains of petrified visitors from a distant land.

Every year during the reign of the last fifteen kings of Esie, there has been a festival for the images. The Esie Museum, officially opened in 1970, where they are now housed, contains an altar where this worship continues. This is another kind of metaphysics than the secularised religion of art-object worship. This is how the people who have inherited the Elsie figures feel about them, in the context of their lived history, and whether I think they are 'art' or not is not the point.

But as art, pure and simple, it is a magnificent exhibition and everybody should go.

New Society, 1982

Artists of the Tudor Court

At the entrance to the latest Victoria and Albert Museum super-spectacular, 'Artists of the Tudor Court', a couple of television screens relay an endlessly repeated commercial for the exhibition. The commentary is intoned by Radio Three's Patricia Hughes, whose voice is synonymous with culture; music by Giles Farnaby and William Byrd squeaks and tinkles. You know at once this is going to be a class show.

On the monitors, a succession of Tudor and early Jacobean miniatures appears, first blown up big and then shrunk down to very, very small, presumably to emulate the experience of looking at them through a microscope – the catalogue makes great play of the fact the things have been studied 'in laboratory conditions'. This is evidently an ethically superior activity to looking at them as if they were pictures.

When the wee goodies expand to fill the TV screens, the portrait heads look like photographs of bit-players in the BBC Shakespeare series, such as might appear in the *Radio Times*. They are 'lifelike' to a degree unusual in art, something that argues a basic artlessness in both the painters and the appreciators.

There is also, hanging among the audio-visuals, a big portrait, to welcome you – a proper, life-size portrait, in oils, not in the luminous watercolours of the miniatures, though it was painted by George Gower, who also painted miniatures. It is of a woman. Perhaps she is Lady Walsingham. She is very elaborately dressed; her clothes are loaded down with gold embroidery and jewels. She represents a walking fortune. One of her jewels is a minature portrait of, presumably, her husband, set in a jewelled locket hanging from a ribbon at her waist. She holds out the opened locket, displaying its contents somewhat impassively, keeping her eye on the spectator as firmly as if she suspects he might be thinking of stealing it.

She has a nasty, mean, assessing face, thin lips, a bony nose, pale eyes – a face repeated again and again among the Elizabethan faces assembled here, the female face most celebrated by the Elizabethans so that those who possessed versions of it enjoyed their unique heyday as beauties then. This face became fashionable because Elizabeth I looked like that.

The two faces in this portrait, the big one and the little one, are both at odds with the presumed Lady Walsingham's body. Unlike those faces, her body is obviously not made of flesh, but of fabrics and jewellery. It is impossible even to guess at the shape of the skeleton under the clothes; indeed, it looks as if there is nothing at all under the hugely elaborate armour of her dress, which is stiff enough to stand by itself. And her hands have a Grand Guignol look, as if cut off somebody else, possibly a corpse, and tacked on to the lace cuffs of her sleeves.

This portrait is dated at 1572. In later life-size portraits, especially those painted by such masters of the minuscule verismo as Nicholas Hilliard, the disjunction between the painted faces and the bodies – no, these are not bodies! they are merely clothes – is even more striking. That is because the clothes themselves grow ever more preposterous as Elizabeth's reign proceeds, until the women acquire invented bodies like T-squares, architecturally distorted by the long, straight, narrow corset that appears to extend below the pubis, and wide, stiff, stuffed petticoats that look disproportionately short.

The image of Elizabeth I manifests itself everywhere in the exhibition. One of the oddest representations, life-size, from the studio of Nicholas Hilliard (query? it says in the catalogue), shows her stiff as an ironing board and stuck with pearls like lice, water-monsters embroidered on her skirt.

The men fare just as strangely, equipped with vast, steatopygous buttocks by their padded bloomers. The unisex ruffs and spiky lace collars seem to guard all their necks in a lethal and decorative barbed wire. None of these, of course, are everyday clothes; yet that unaccommodating stiffness, the almost mineral glitter and gleam of these garments weighted down with metallic threads and precious clothes, these are the clothes in which those people wished to be remembered.

The most stunningly dressed figure of all the dandies and peacocks in the exhibition is Richard Sackville, Third Earl of Dorset, painted full-length by William Larkin in 1613, well after Elizabeth's time. But his costume takes the Elizabethan mode to its extreme. He is all black velvet and white satin and lace and his vast, swollen breeches bulge down almost to his knees. What calves! Calves of a champion cyclist, fittingly displayed by white silk stockings, with gold, silver and black silk clocks embroidered on them. And all his clothes are as lavishly embroidered with gold as if he has been scribbled all over in gold ink in a strange script. Rosettes of gold-edged black lace decorate his embroidered shoes. The rosettes are the size of prize-winning dahlias. He sports black garters. Above all this, the face of a mafioso, rendered with what appears to be absolute fidelity.

There is some schizophrenic discord between the faces and the rest of the

full-size portraits which is not simply the result of the unfamiliarity of most
of the painters with the conventions of rendering perspective. These models look as if they had posed in those fairground booths, where you stick
your head through a hole above a body already painted on a wooden board.

Evidently it was the custom for the subjects of these painters to send
their clothes round, separately, so they could be hung up in the studio and
reproduced with absolute fidelity to the degree of conspicuous consumption they represented, an arduous task best undertaken without the easily
bored subject inside them. This custom may account for some, at least, of
the uncanny *unlived-in-ness* of the apparel from which the heads pop out
like apparitions from another order of being, or kind of art.

Although the subjects of the miniatures are no less jewelled and gorgeous, the little pictures usually represent only faces, or faces and torsos, so
they give less sense of a period in which people's private sense of self
stopped short at the neck, to be replaced from there downwards by a public announcement of one's finances. The miniatures, in fact, look far more
like what we know art ought to look like, or people ought to look like.
Indeed, what Elizabethans ought to look like.

The catalogue states categorically that the miniature is 'this country's
unique contribution to the art of the Renaissance'. If this be so, no doubt
it helps to explain why the rest of Renaissance Europe thought the English
were so vulgar and *arriviste*, such coarse voluptuaries, so – when you got
down to it – *uncultured*.

Roy Strong, whose beloved brainchild the entire exhibition is, also
compares the miniatures to Victorian photographs. Though some of them
– especially those of Isaac Oliver – certainly look like photographs, the
analogy is all wrong. Victorian photographers tried to encompass the
whole world; the world Oliver, Hilliard and the rest depict is as tiny as the
dimensions of the playing cards on which they mounted their gold and
silver-crusted watercolours. (Why did they use playing cards? Was there
some emblematic point being made about the game of life, about destiny
dealing the cards? Apart from stating that the painters usually obliterated
the ill-omened spades on the backs of the cards, the catalogue is silent on
this point.)

It is a partial world, exclusively that of the immensely powerful – kings,
queens, princes, aristos. Henry VIII, looking like a fat thug; his wives; his
daughters; Mary Queen of Scots, a reassuringly plain face; lords and ladies
in droves. (One lord with the inexpressibly Wodehouse name, Peregrine
Bertie, Lord Willoughby D'Eresby.)

The Elizabethans publicised themselves so well that many of the names
are familiar. It's good to put a face to the name of Henry Wriothesley,
Third Earl of Southampton, Shakespeare's patron and, teasing possibility,

perhaps the Mr W. H. of the sonnets. Like several other of the young men, Henry Wriothesley looks like delicious trouble, with the brooding sensuality of his regard and the curls tumbling over his shoulder in careful disorder and an air of too fast to live, too young to die. A 'dysshe', as no doubt the boys in that well-known gay hangout, the Mermaid Tavern, frequently opined.

The entire exhibition, by the way, is not free from a relish in that 'quaynteness' which we ascribe with hindsight to the bloodiest, most grown-up and most verbally sophisticated of our forebears, a 'quayntness' we perceive even in the relaxed unorthodoxies of their spelling. We think of them as 'quaynte' to protect ourselves from a reality of a society that was as splendid and horrible as that of the Benin empire just before it fell.

The miniaturists reflect none of the violence, or indeed, of the intellectual turbulence of the age. If the miniaturists resemble photographers, it is rather the society photographers who go to posh dances and weddings there to take snaps for the *Tatler* rather than those who risk their asses in Vietnam or El Salvador or haunt Toxteth looking for riots.

Yet, sumptuous as they are, the miniatures are intended to give only a peculiarly personal and private gratification. If some were worn, now and then, in the form of jewellery, most were kept concealed in lidded cases since the colours faded quickly with exposure to light. A Lilliputian tendency towards increasing diminishment furthers the impression of looking, not into a mirror, but through a keyhole. One peers at these faces like a voyeur.

There is a set of Hilliard miniatures of Elizabeth I that descend from small, to tiny, to teeny-tiny – the teeny-tiniest of a size to fit on the head of a pin. It is accompanied by a companion head, the Earl of Leicester. The catalogue hints suggestively: 'The presentation of the Earl as consort manqué' indicates that these miniatures were once part of an object of extreme intimacy.'

Elizabeth, apparently, kept her miniatures in the innermost sanctum of the royal bedroom, each one carefully wrapped up with a label bearing the name of the sitter. She showed them occasionally to specially favoured guests, as if they were dirty pictures.

'This country's unique contribution to the art of the Renaissance.' The self-absorbed and obsessive products of an offshore island removed from the mainstream of European culture by its Protestantism as much as its geographical isolation. An art in which the rich and powerful observed themselves in their best clothes in the form of paintings which themselves could, at a pinch, be worn like the jewels they so much resemble – but pictures that, in spite of that, were rarely seen, stored away from the light in little ivory boxes, much as a sensible rich woman of today keeps her necklaces in a safe. An art of narcissism and privacy, produced by an age of massive, brutal vulgarities, which the exhibition 'Artists of the Tudor Court' is dedicated to presenting to us as some kind of rare, exquisite peak of civilisation, seasoned whimsically with the 'quaynte'.

New Society, 1983

Pontus Hulten: The Arcimboldo Effect

Familiarity does not dull the peculiar shock, almost horror, given by the paintings of Guiseppe Arcimboldo, especially those 'composed heads' of which the features, with the logic of dream or child, are built up from material objects – flowers, vegetables, birds, beasts, books.

Other paintings of his – the saucepan filled with vegetables that turns into the face of the gardener when you up-end it; the dish of roast meats that reverses to become the cook – are jokes that haven't lost their point over the years. But the whole point of the 'composed heads' is their enigmatic self-sufficiency, objects that inhabit only a ceremonial space, as if the canvas was a theatre. And yet, there is no play, no performance – only the actors.

These grotesque portraits have the troubling, festive inhumanity of carnival heads, and represent just as simple concepts. Spring has roses for cheeks – literally; the nose of Summer is composed of a small vegetable marrow; Autumn has a mushroom for an ear and Winter is made up mostly of roots and fungi. The imagination at work here is a curiously literal one.

If there is a theatricality to the composed heads, then indeed one of Arcimboldo's jobs at the court of the Emperor Maximilian was to invent carnival costumes and design pageants. (Some of the designs are reproduced in *The Arcimboldo Effect*.) Arcimboldo went to Vienna from Milan in 1562, to become court painter to Maximilian and subsequently to his son, that connoisseur of the bizarre, Rudolf II.

Rudolf commissioned Arcimboldo to paint him as Vertumnus, god of gardens: the result is a man wholly subsumed to the condition of a harvest festival. Rudolf loved it and made him a Palatine count.

The sensibility of this period is both familiar and strange to us. 'Emblems, devices, anagrams, riddles, puzzles were accounted sublime achievements of art,' commented Mario Praz in his book about the baroque, *The Flaming Heart*. It was as if Renaissance painting had exhausted the idea of the beautiful, something more cerebral became the vogue.

The twinned categories of the grotesque and the marvellous opened up to aesthetics and Rudolf filled an entire treasure house with art works and curious objects. Like Cocteau four centuries later, he wanted to be astonished. Arcimboldo was one of the people he employed to astonish him. At one time, Arcimboldo was in charge of buying curios for him. Rudolf patronised alchemists and collected mandrake roots.

Arcimboldo's name is almost entirely absent from art history between the end of the sixteenth and the beginning of the twentieth centuries. The surrealists, whose entire aesthetic was based on an appreciation of the marvellous, rescued him from the historical cul-de-sac of the quaint.

The Arcimboldo Effect is the catalogue of Arcimboldo's recent one-man show at the Palazzo Grassi, in Venice. A gorgeously illustrated, hefty collection of essays by diverse hands, it relates Arcimboldo convincingly to the surrealists – no surprise there – and less convincingly to the cubists. It is a characteristic of Mannerism that it is more interesting to talk about than it is to look at and I have a feeling that the book is rather better value than the exhibition, even at the price. No amount of explanation removes the strangeness from the pictures.

Guardian, 1987

Three Women Artists

Review of Laurie Leslie, *Portrait of an Artist*; Nicholas Callaway (ed.), *Georgia O'Keeffe*; Cecily Langdale, *Gwen John*; Baroness Kizette de Lempicka, as told to Charles Phillips, *Passion By Design*.

Ida O'Keeffe, who also painted, used to annoy her illustrious sister by claiming that she, Ida, would have won just as much fame and fortune as Georgia if only she, too, had found herself an Alfred Steiglitz as husband, dealer, arbiter of taste, publicist of genius and, last but not least, photographer, to give protection and promotion.

Laurie Leslie thinks Ida deceived herself and, to prove it, describes snapshots Steiglitz took of the sisters. Georgia, so slender, so stern, black-clad like a nun. Ida, beaming in floral prints, already the plump hausfrau type. 'Georgia seemed to be willing herself to become extraordinary, while Ida remained ordinary . . .'

The premises underpinning this statement are shaky and illustrate the main weakness of Laurie Leslie's biography of O'Keeffe, which is that she doesn't know much about art, nor, it would seem, how its practitioners wear their faces.

The early portraits of Gwen John, some by her brother, Augustus, some by herself, make her look like a mouse squaring up to an assault. Less, you might say, than ordinary. While the photographs of a teenage de Lempicka, in contrast, show somebody already quite extraordinary enough without even trying. A teenage shocker who would blossom into an improbably luscious adventuress whose relation with the brush is entirely more problematic than that of the other two but seems to have been as driven as either, though God knows to what end.

These three women, a mid-western farmer's daughter, an English provincial lady, a Polish siren, all embarked on careers as painters at roughly the same time, the end of the nineteenth century and the beginning of the twentieth, the time when it became possible for a woman painter to think of 'fame' in the same way that it had been possible for a man since the Renaissance.

Whether you see this pursuit of 'fame' as a challenge, as part of the great confidence-trick of bourgeois art, or as an open invitation to megalomania, it certainly made megalomania an attractive possibility for women painters, one of which O'Keeffe and de Lempicka certainly took advantage in their different ways, and of which Gwen John, perhaps having seen the effect on Augustus, did not.

It also presented a problem; how is fame created? Because it is made in quite a different way than art. Can a woman make fame as well as art?

That Steiglitz was a photographer, and a good one, proved important for O'Keeffe. His studies of her, exhibited in 1921 in the early days of her professional career, made of her both artist and art object at the same time. 'Many (of the photographs) were semi-nudes and although those of her most private parts were withheld, people whispered about their existence,' notes Laurie Leslie in an ambiguous aside.

The gossip was sufficient to superimpose the image of her naked body between the eyes of the viewer and those canvases depicting ferocious flowers which she was soon offering the public, so that both the idea of the woman painter and the paintings themselves were thoroughly eroticised. As Leslie observes, 'Her gigantic flowers . . . were painted frontally and revealingly, much the way Steiglitz photographed her.

Famously austere and dignified, O'Keeffe nevertheless made her mark first as a perpetrator of erotic outrage and achieved fame speedily. Fame seems to have been a part of her strategy for survival as an artist; fame created a privileged space in which to work. Besides, she liked it.

Gwen John also posed in the nude, most notably for Rodin, when she worked as an artist's model in Paris some years before O'Keeffe stripped down in New York, but she provoked no furore, although she herself painted naked women often and also painted herself wearing nothing but the simple mortal envelope of her not uncomplicated soul. To the pure all things are pure: Gwen John's ambitions were not secular.

Cecily Langdale's monograph describes a reclusive, transcendental spinster who might have come from the pages of a novel by Patrick White. Her paintings, quiet depictions of rooms, the street outside, women reading or sewing, are disconcertingly resonant of an inner life so intense that it finally devoured her completely, for she seems, in the last decade of her life, to have given up painting in favour of the more intellectually and spiritually demanding task of thinking about painting.

As for de Lempicka, the 'Grande Dame of Art Deco' as Charles Phillips calls her in his engagingly soap operatic version of her daughter's memories, what was a refugee down on her luck in Paris after the Russian Revolution to do? Why, pick up her brush and paint!

She perfected a line in super-kitsch society portraits and sub-cubist nude ladies hugging one another that hit the spot in Europe between the wars and brought her wealth, a title, and the green Bugatti at whose wheel she painted herself with Vaselined eyelids, subject of her own object, frozen in the ghastly limbo of pure glamour. An adventuress using to the hilt a strange, cold, semi-pornographic, rather horrible facility with paint to get places, fast. Art, in fact, as a green Bugatti, fame as the accelerator.

O'Keeffe and de Lempicka both died in their beds at ripe old ages, with scads of dollars tucked away. Think of Rothko, Pollock, Arshile Gorky before you say how tough it is to be a woman painter. Gwen John's death at sixty-three, essentially of self neglect, is as miserable as that of any great painter of any sex in the twentieth century, yet she may have received it ecstatically.

O'Keeffe's floral orifices look wonderful in a coffee table book. Some of them do indeed look like sexual organs, because that is precisely what they are – the sexual organs of plants. I learned that in O-level biology. In the end, O'Keeffe got rather tired of flowers and snapped: 'I hate flowers – I paint them because they're cheaper than models and they don't move.'

Guardian, 1987

Frida Kahlo432

Frida Kahlo loved to paint her face. She painted it constantly, from the first moment she began seriously to paint when she was sixteen up till the time

of her death some thirty years later. Again and again, her face, with the
beautiful bones, the hairy upper lip, and batwing eyebrows that meet in
the middle. She liked to be photographed, too, but she could not do that
for herself so other people did it for her, although portrait photographs of
Frida Kahlo resemble the face in her own pictures so closely that her eyes
seem to have had the power to subvert the camera, making it see her as
she saw herself, as she makes us see what she sees when she paints.

Women painters are sometimes forced to specialise in self-portraiture
because they can't afford models. Gwen John, for example. That wasn't
the case with Frida Kahlo. I think it was the process of looking at herself
that engaged her. Because the face in the self-portraits is not that of a
woman looking at the person looking at the picture; she is not addressing
us. It is the face of a woman looking at *herself,* subjecting herself to the most
intense scrutiny, almost to an interrogation.

But we will never know what this urgent self-interrogation concerns.
Frida Kahlo uses narcissism, exhibitionism, as a form of disguise.

This is the face of a woman looking into a mirror. We cannot see the
mirror but we must always remember that it was there. These paintings
are a form of self-monitoring. She watches herself watching herself. When
she does that, she is at work.

The painted face is that of a woman working at transforming her whole
experience in the world into a series of marvellously explicit images. She
is in the process of remaking herself in another medium than life and is
becoming resplendent. The flesh made sign.

The wounded flesh.

Her raw material was herself, just as the raw material of the New York
performance artist, Cindy Sherman, who also specialises in self-
portraiture, is herself. (In many ways, Frida Kahlo was ahead of her time;
hers is a remarkably total kind of artistic vision, including such things as
shoes and bed-linen.)

But, with Frida Kahlo, the raw material remained – raw. The wounds
never healed over.

Her husband, Diego Rivera, said: 'Frida is the only example in the
history of art of an artist who tore open her chest and heart to reveal the
biological truth of her feelings.' How painful he makes it sound. It *was*
painful. The expression on that painted face, unchanging over the years, is
one of enigmatic stoicism and she displays her wounds like a martyr. The
woman who would dig an ornamental comb through her hair deep into
her scalp with what a friend called 'coquettish masochism' was a connoisseur of physical suffering.

Speaking of hair, what she does with it in the pictures is extraordinary.
If wild, flowing hair is associated with sensuality and abandon, then note

how the hair of Frida Kahlo, the most sensual of painters, hangs in disorder down her back only when she depicts herself in great pain, or as a child.

Sometimes her hair is scraped back so tight the sight of it hurts; or it is unnaturally twisted into knots; plaited with flowers and ribbons and top-knots and feathers in any one of fifty different ways; arranged in fetishistic, architectural compositions of braids. She puts her poor hair through such torture it is a relief, in the picture of 1940, after her divorce from Rivera, to see it all cut off at last and lying on the ground, as if she'd finally got rid of an unpleasant, demanding pet.

But there is a phrase from one of the popular songs she liked to sing at the top of the picture:

> look,
> if I loved you, it was for your hair
> now you are hairless
> I love you no more.

And she wears, not the folkloric Mexican finery with which we associate her but a man's suit. When she was a girl, before her accident, before she married Rivera, she used to pose for photographs *en travestie*. Even for family photographs. Quite the little dandy. But in *this* picture, the jacket and trousers are much too big, billowing, voluminous. Has she put on her enormous ex-husband's clothes, in order to comfort herself? Or do men's clothes no longer fit her, as they once did? One thing is plain: whoever no longer loves her like this, she certainly does not love herself. They were remarried later that year. She grew her hair and braided it again.

Although Frida Kahlo, born in 1907, liked to give 1910, the year of the Mexican Revolution, as the date of her birth, you could say she was not really born until the disastrous accident that broke her. Her work as a painter came out of that accident; she painted in order to pass the time during the lengthy period of recovery nobody had really expected. (Before the accident, interestingly, the woman who was to become the lifelong patient of doctors had intended to study medicine and become a doctor herself.)

The accident and its physical consequences not only made her start to paint; they gave her something to paint about. Her pain. In fact, the accident itself, horribly, turned her into a bloody and involuntary art object. After a streetcar ploughed into the bus on which Frida Kahlo was travelling through Mexico City, a metal bar pierced her back; somehow all her clothes came off in the crash and the bag of gold powder carried by a fellow passenger spilled over her. It is an image from a nightmare, more horribly glamorous than any she imagined, or recreated.

There's a deer with Frida Kahlo's face, its habitual changeless intensity of gaze; the deer's side is pierced with arrows. She is not often so subtle. She depicts her body enclosed in one of the plaster-of-Paris corsets prescribed for her crumbling spine, her torso stuck with tacks; she paints the fresh incision of the surgeon's knife; her own blood, and other people's, too; her miscarriage; her restless dual nature, part European, part Mexican; her broken heart.

She made of her broken, humiliated, warring self a series of masterpieces of mutilation and she did so in real life, too, submitting herself to more than thirty surgical operations between 1925 and 1954, culminating in the amputation of a foot.

And that loss seems to be what killed her. What made her not want to live any more, finally. As if they could cut her, carve her, burrow away within as much as they pleased, just so long as they did not take anything away.

Most of her operations did not alleviate the many and various conditions that ailed her; possibly some of them, at least, were needless, even harmful. If she was an invalid all her life, she did not act like an invalid unless forcibly bedridden; had she treated her physical fragility with more respect and less awe, she might have lived longer, and painted more still lives of fruit and flowers, more portraits of monkeys and children. More cruel truths. As it was, she became addicted to pain-killers and to alcohol. In addition, she may have suffered from syphilis. In the circumstances, her narcissism becomes triumphant, a carnival. (Never forget the black humour in her paintings.)

Married to Rivera almost all her adult life with only the brief respite of a year's divorce, she was tormented by jealousy and paid back his infidelities in kind, although her husband's own jealousy prevented her from the pleasure of regaling her conquests to him, as he did to her.

Monstrously ambiguous couple – Frida with her moustache, Diego with his fat man's breasts. The sexiest couple in Mexico, who did not fuck. (According to Rivera, one of the conditions Frida made for their remarriage was, no more sex.) Mr and Mrs Jack Spratt, he so fat, she so skinny. Their division of labour was absolute: he did the large-scale public works, the great political murals. She did the colour postcards of heightened states of mind, the politics of the heart.

Rivera, I suppose, was her muse. At least two self-portraits, one of 1943, one of 1949, show he of the bullfrog features ensconced upon her forehead, in the place where I imagine that Cain was marked. Obsession. Devotion. Inspiration. Muses aren't supposed to make you happy, after all. Then, again, men are warned against marrying their muses. Women sometimes have no option.

She became a great painter because of, not in spite of, all this.

Women painters are often forced to make exhibitions of themselves in order to mount exhibitions. Fame, notoriety, scandal, eccentric dress and behaviour – Rosa Bonheur, Meret Oppenheim, Leonor Fini, Georgia O'Keeffe, Frida Kahlo. Fame is not an end in itself but a strategy. Being famous means she can stake out her own territory, can even determine, wholly or in part, the way her paintings will be looked at. Frida Kahlo's transition from the status of maker of tiny, charming paintings on tin in the naïve style to publicly acknowledged major artist was assisted, not hindered, by her growing fame as the beautiful wife of the Mexican muralist. Indeed, she became famous as a symbol of Mexicanness.

After her marriage, after she gave up trousers, she always wore the most elaborate Mexican traditional dress and quantities of jewellery, pre-Columbian antiques, beads bought from the market, anything, everything. She spent hours arranging herself for the day. She turned herself into a folkloric artefact at a time when the Mexican bourgeoisie, from which she came, did not indulge in fancy dress and even high Bohemia, to which she now belonged, only kept it for parties.

If she started to wear her long petticoats to hide her crippled leg, then the enchantment of disguise, of the perpetual festival of fancy dress, soon overcame her. In New York, children followed her in the street: 'Where's the circus?' When she dressed up for some big event, she took the plain gold caps off her incisors and replaced them with caps set with rose diamonds. Even the dazzle of her smile was artificial, and her living exposition of the vitality of the peasant culture of Mexico which turned her appearance into a piece of political theatre could easily find itself trapped in the world of commodity high fashion. In Paris in 1939, Schiaparelli liked her dress so much that she designed a *robe Madame Rivera* and Frida Kahlo's hand, with its crust of marketstall rings, graced the cover of *Vogue*.

Like Walt Whitman, if she contradicted herself, it was because she contained multitudes.

After her death in 1954, Diego Rivera turned the blue painted house in Coyoacan, a suburb of Mexico City, where she had been born, where they lived, into the Museo Frida Kahlo. He didn't have to change a thing; she had already made of their home a shrine dedicated to their entwined, if complicated, lives. Herself a work of art, she produced art works inside another one. Rivera left the unfinished portrait of Stalin on the easel in her studio, with her wheelchair next to it. The little earthenware mugs spelling out DIEGO Y FRIDA on pegs in the kitchen. Her most precious fetishes in her bedroom, for this thwarted mother kept a pickled foetus in a jar by her bed, surrounded herself with dolls.

In the magic and artful universe of this house, a beautiful and wholly invented life of flowers, fruit, parrots, monkeys and other people's children went on while Rivera paused from mural painting to conduct visiting Hollywood film stars on guided tours of the work of the Revolution in Mexico. (Both husband and wife were more than the sum of their contradictions.) She, sometimes in her orthopaedic corset, sometimes in her wheelchair, sometimes in bed and painting with the aid of a mirror, sometimes miraculously whole, plaited and unplaited her hair; sang rude songs and violent ballads; laughed and was enchanting. Yes. I believe that. I believe that she was enchanting.

When she was well enough, she painted the strangeness of the world made visible. Her face. Her friends. A bowl of fruit. Flowers. The victim of a *crime passionel*. The sun. A dead child. The curse of love, the disasters to which the female body is heir. 'VIVA LA VIDA', she scrawled on her last painting, when she was about to die.

Preface, Images of Frida Kahlo, 1989

STORIES AND TELLERS

Tell Me a Story

Jorge Luis Borges: An Introduction to English Literature

Resnais's early documentary, *Tout le memoire du monde*, about the Bibliothèque Nationale, has a long dream-like sequence of tracking shots down endless, winding corridors, past shelves stacked to the ceiling with books, rooms filled up with books almost past the tops of the doors. It's a cumulative effect, like a trip round the labyrinthine information-retrieval system of the brain – the model of all libraries, or of which all libraries are the memory. (See: already, a Borgesian inflection.) Labyrinths, libraries, a lonely, claustrophobic inwardness – Resnais might have been filming the interior of Borges's head.

Nevertheless, Borges's *Introduction to English Literature,* far from being such a hallucinatory trip round the stockroom, is an idiosyncratically bland little book. The tone is resolutely commonplace; the observation varies between received opinion tersely expressed – of D. H. Lawrence: 'Tuberculosis, which finally killed him, exacerbated his sensitivity and justifies his extreme positions'; and the more familiarly Borgesian oblique: William Morris is 'an indefatigable, energetic and probably happy man'. It is the modest unexpectedness of the last adjective, modified by that particular adverb, that gives the expected tingle of strangeness.

It would be interesting to know how Borges and his collaborator, Maria Esther Vazquez, divided up the work. Did Borges concentrate mainly on his favourites: the Anglo-Saxons, Stevenson, Chesterton, and perhaps, the little chapter on the seventeenth century? How odd to find him writing about D. H. Lawrence, the prophet of the flesh; there is precious little fucking in the Borges oeuvre, and the dark gods are different.

There are huge gaps, perhaps because – as we know from his autobiographical essay, published in the collection called *The Aleph* – he does not like novels, except the picaresque. (One could argue, from his observations on Joyce, that he has never grasped the principles of the construction of the novel.) No Jane Austen, then; no Brontës; no George Eliot – and no Hardy, either, so these omissions are not due to Latin *machismo*. All the predecessors of Dickens are consigned to limbo, with the exception of Walter Scott, curtly named as the father of the historical novel and then dismissed. Borges posits the influence of *Don Quixote* on Pickwick; he perks up a bit at that.

Similarly, his interest in Milton seems to quicken when dubbing him a heresiarch and he is at home with dreamers. We learn that Kublai Khan, as well as Coleridge, saw the plan of Xanadu in a dream. De Quincey actually sounds like a Borges character. 'His image lives in the memory of men like a character in fiction, rather than a reality.' His prose is described with a wonderful rhetoric: 'delicate and intricate paragraphs open like cathedrals of music'. Quite Mallarmé. Lewis Carroll, predictably, dreams on the edge of nightmare.

Writers of special interest to Argentinians – W. H. Hudson and Robert Bontine-Cunningham (who?) – take up perhaps too much of the limited space. But the latter writer has a peculiarly Borgesian claim to attention, that of allusive survival in footnote, appendix, or commentary; Shaw described him 'vividly' in the preface to *Captain Brassbound's Conversion*.

This little book is of limited use as an introduction to English literature, if only because of the curious omission of the eighteenth- and nineteenth-century novel. It may persuade one or two Borges fans to study a little Anglo-Saxon, or Middle English, which will be very good for them. But let us examine it as a guide to the Borges version of our literary heritage.

It appears to have been composed in the cosiest of panelled libraries at some eternal teatime. Not, here, the lonely involutions of the interior of the Bibliothèque Nationale; another kind of library altogether. A resonant quotation from Novalis, 'every Englishman is an island', justifies perhaps this air of the cosiness which has always expressed the English resistance to the notion of existential solitude. Disquiet, unease, have been banished from these more or less complacent pages. Though references to mazes, kaleidoscopes and the nightmare recur from time to time, they do not destroy the impression that all the books mentioned here have been bound in leather and tooled in gold. The bibliography cites solid critics from the age of Elgar, such as George Saintsbury, Andrew Lang and G. K. Chesterton.

It is tempting to read the little book as a hoax, just as one has combed it for hoaxes, knowing beforehand the Master's tricksy ways. Are he and his collaborator trying to foist off on a generation of Latin American students a pseudo-tradition of English literature, which will elevate G. K. Chesterton to equal status with Milton and persuade hundreds of innocent young minds dutifully to repeat that Joyce should have tried to write poetry, and not tried his hand so disastrously at fiction?

Indeed, Vita Sackville-West gets almost as much space as Joyce; and up crops Charles Morgan though he, like James 'Ossian' Macpherson, was always more highly thought of on the continent than at home – a rare, possibly unique, example of native English literary taste and discernment. But this may be Miss Vazquez's choice. I can't somehow imagine Borges ploughing through *The Fountain*.

An aesthetic emerges. Literature itself is a kind of dreaming. Charm, he quotes Robert Louis Stevenson with apparent approval, is the supreme criterion of literature, a contentious point; charm is the most treacherous of qualities and the perfect disguise for a heart of stone. Charm is not the signal quality of Borges's own finest stories, which radiate an icy, serene disquiet, sometimes a mysterious and desolating anguish. Very rarely has the rationale of bourgeois despair been advertised with such cool luminosity, mystification made so persuasive or so attractively rational-seeming.

Nevertheless, his little autobiographical essay reads like a conscious attempt to disarm. Perhaps he frightens himself so much, sometimes, with his metaphysical riddles, that he has to be very, very charming indeed to convince himself he is still human and that he will kindle and burn when a flame is applied.

His Eng Lit textbook contains very little of Borges the riddler, trapped in his own labyrinth – that is, Borges the artist – but a great deal of Professor Borges, who is not alienated at all, thank you, but much beloved by a wide circle of friends and universally acclaimed, as well. Should one *never* trust the teller, only the tale? Certainly, the laconic tales of Borges's blindness show a major and uncharming obsession with knives and violent death, as though these things are the inevitable concomitant of life outside the library.

For we have come out of the labyrinth of books into the dark of common day. Goodbye to the baroque echoes of the cadences of Sir Thomas Browne (to whom, he says, Milton is 'not superior'; which is one of those irritating judgments that are both true and not true, like saying a rose is not inferior to a lion). Hello to Kiplingesque terse vernacular plain tales from the pampa.

Borges, a lovably, booksy, bespectacled little boy (who, however, from *The Meeting*, may have longed to see a man killed), was deeply impressed by rare glimpses of gaucho life. The most cerebral people are most vulnerable to the glamour of a vitality perceived as a quality of appearance, rather than a way of life which cannot be known for itself. Sartre didn't canonise Genet for nothing. Borges's stories of gauchos and gangsters in the Argentine at the turn of the century are not exercises in realism at all, but put a formal realism to work that is the same kind of literary invention as *The Dictionary of Imaginary Beings,* though it invokes memory rather than dream.

The language of these heroes is the knife; sometimes the knives speak of their own accord, as though in a specific language of death. He wrote one very weak tale, *Guayaquil,* which reads like a re-running of an earlier story and betrays an indecorous element of camp, which Borges does not do well when he does it consciously. But there is one stunner, *The Gospel According to Mark.* Patrick White (who is omitted from Borges's *Introduction*), a writer infinitely superior to Charles Morgan, or G. K. Chesterton, used a devastating version of the same theme in *Riders in the Chariot,* a comparison which illuminates some of the necessary limitations of a miniaturist who is content, as S. J. Perelman said of himself, to stitch away at his little embroidery hoop. Nevertheless, in four pages, very fine and haunting, Borges redefines the gospel as a book that kills.

Perhaps Borges's work may be expressed through two dominant images. The marvellous tales using devices from traditional logic and a highly-decorated neo-platonism, are those of the labyrinth. The solitary in the labyrinth is a chilling image of alienation from being. Add to this familiar Borges image, a new, most gothic implement, a knife that kills of its own accord.

Now the necessity for charm becomes imperative.

New Society, 1974

The Hidden Child

'We were sitting on a dilapidated seventeenth-century tomb in the late afternoon of an autumn day, at the old burying ground in Arkham, and speculating about the unnameable.'

So, with characteristic brio, in a characteristic setting, H. P. Lovecraft begins a characteristic tale of terror. The Lovecraftian – 'tale of terror' is primarily an aesthetic convention; so it defines evil on aesthetic terms – that is, as a visible ghastliness. The thing that jumps up out of the pit when darkness falls turns out to be a construction of gelatine and ectoplasm. It gores the narrator and his friend with its retractable horns in order to demonstrate motiveless, supernatural malignity, and also teach the friend – hitherto a crass materialist – a concrete lesson in phantomology.

Lovecraft tacitly assumes that the 'unnameable' is the temporary embodiment of a free-form, cosmic evil like a blasting dew. This is a convention of the genre in which he works. Evil *is* . . . It is not what men *do*. Evil is an abstraction, something like mathematics. It may be studied in arcane law. It can concretise and become objective, like a theorem; then an unfortunate can accidentally stumble on it. (Aaaaaaagh!) It can become embodied in a place: houses, landscapes can acquire evil as a quality. Sometimes it is an inheritance, a hereditary blight that may not be evaded: the Doomed family motif, with its residual Calvinism, at the hypothesis of a necromantic or vampiric chromosome.

Some of the consolatory quality of the tale of supernatural terror lies in this; that it removes evil from the realm of human practice and gives it the status of a visitation from another realm of being. It is an affliction. It is a possession.

So the 'tale of terror', like pornography, with which it has much in common, represents a carefree holiday from ethics. That is the source of its enduring charm. The tale of terror, the horror movie, the horror comic, are genres which show positively vampiric longevity: Lovecraft himself (1890–1937) is far better known today than he was during his lifetime, when he eked out a meagre existence writing for *Weird Tales*. 'Step into a nightmare world of hellish horror,' says the legend on the cover of the paperback edition of *Dagon and Other Macabre Tales*. What should I want to do that for? Why, to luxuriate in a world where I may be just as beastly as I wish entirely without moral responsibility. And people go on queuing up for *The Exorcist* in spite of the authentic smell of sulphur emanating, not from little Regan (who is only doing what most kids want to do a lot of the time), but from the box office.

The tale of terror lacks even the element of human and judicial retribution which provides the dynamic of the detective story, where the confession or exposure of the criminal reinstitutes the pact with society the crime had broken. But this moral function of the detective story may be waning. The success of the movie, *Murder on the Orient Express,* may be due to the ethical sleight of hand by which a group of people take the law into their own hands and, without benefit of trial, rid the world of a wrongdoer, get off scot-free, and are applauded by the detective or priest figure.

Lovecraft wrote tales of terror which impose an expressionist landscape of dread and menace upon the mundane geography of New England. Some of these tales (like 'The Picture in the House', 'At the Mountains of Madness', perhaps, and one or two others) conform to the surrealistic aesthetic of convulsive beauty. He can invoke the marvellous, usually when he is not trying too hard to do so. He invented a bizarre cosmogony full of ambivalent deities with names that look like typing errors. Hastur, the Unspeakable, Chthulhu, who lies in the watery depths. Nyarlothotep, the Messenger. Shub-Niggurath, the black goat of the woods with a thousand young. Lovecraft had a great vogue during the acid honeymoon of the last decade. I recall a rock band named after him. Loud music, especially that of flutes and drums, had a ghastly effect on his delicate nerves. It was an ironic tribute.

He was from faded, genteel, poverty-stricken New England stock, and scarcely (if ever) worked. Mother-dominated, he expressed the standard nostalgia for his 'wistful boyhood', but was curiously free enough from artistic hypocrisy, when it came to the crunch, to depict the 'great, good place', the prelapsarian Eden of the womb, as a nightmare forest of poison oaks.

Inevitably, he was drawn to fascism. 'I knows he's a clown but God, I *like* the boy!' he wrote to a friend in 1930. 'The boy' was Hitler. But this infatuation, and the pash on Mussolini, mercifully did not last. His dealings with the American pulp press may have been his first encounter, in all his sheltered life, with human wickedness. It belatedly made something of a pinko of him, a New Dealer, a Roosevelt fan. And he painfully weaned himself away from the racism in youth so cherished.

The typical Lovecraft protagonist is something in his own image – a booksy, reclusive, middle-aged bachelor with antiquarian predilections. Lovecraft, a high-school dropout, revenged himself by creating Miskatonic University at Arkham, Massachusetts, and awarding himself occasional professorships at it. He adored erudition, like the Argentinian Borges, to whom he has an odd stylistic resemblance. But he took the easy way out and invented all his own references. So his work provides all the appearance of pedantry but none at all of the substance. He devised whole libraries of books to validate his mythologies. They have the most wonderful titles. The Pnakotic Manuscripts. The Seven Cryptical Books of Hsan. The 'delirious' *Image du monde* of Gauthier de Metz. The suppressed *Unaussprechlichen Kulten* of von Junzt.

One could write a very Lovecrafty tale about the arrival at his door late, very late, one night of a (preferably) demented student clutching in his hand an actual copy of the dreaded *Necronomicom* of the mad Arab, Abdul Alhazred, bound in human skin, stolen from the *enfer* of the Bibliothèque Nationale and brought triumphantly to the Maestro of the Twisted Nerve, who has so often mentioned it.

Shocked horror of the master, who never thought the vile thing existed. Has he *thought* the abomination into existence? Or did it always exist, has he always been unconsciously quoting it? Opening the pages with trembling fingers, he discovers cryptic marginalia on the time-seared pages, penned what centuries ago in what fearful city yet, unmistakably, *in his own handwriting*.

Dementia of the master. It always ends in dementia. Even to handle, touch these sacrilegious covers is to invite unquiet sleeps; unexpected visits from ten-foot, rugose cones, a powerful attraction to graveyards. But not damnation. Lovecraft's universe is resolutely secular.

It is also remarkably sexless. The only nubile woman I can think of off-hand in the Lovecraft oeuvre is an ambivalent figure called Rosa Dexter, who falls into the clutches of three androids who have all, for some reason, disguised themselves as Edgar Allan Poe. An octopodal thing does horrid things to her, which are so very far from the Lovecraft's usual form that I suspect he wrote the story to fit an already commissioned illustration. Fond as he was of tentacles, he never – being a fine, old-fashioned, New England gentleman – allowed them to sully the flesh of a white woman.

There are several eldritch beldames. A 'clod-like Polish woman' loses a baby to the witches; a 'slatternly, almost bearded Spanish woman' runs a lodging house. (Lovecraft is tough on lesser breeds and mongrel races.) And that is just about all. Even the pantheon of Chthulhu rather conspicuously lacks a mother goddess. It is as masculine a preserve as a London club.

Nor is there any homo-erotic content, either latent or manifest. Erotic libido is either absolutely repressed or – more likely – has not yet made its appearance. Its lack is amply compensated for by a strong sado-masochistic element. Carnage, ghouls, cannibalism. Ravages of 'demon claws and teeth'; corpses 'mangled, chewed and clawed'. The necrophagic passion is very strong in Lovecraft. It is genuinely disturbing because so unmediated by art. He loses control of himself entirely when confronted by a charnel house. Cannibalism and human sacrifice recur so often as the ultimate horror – are greeted with such squeaks of delicious dread – that the dread is clearly a screen for relief.

Is it any wonder, when evil finally manifests itself, that it does so as an obscene and huge ejaculation? 'Out of the fungus ridden-earth steamed up a vaporous corpse-light, yellow and diseased, which bubbled and lapped to a gigantic height in vague outlines, half human and half monstrous' ('The Shuttered House'). The doctor who posthumously refrigerated himself leaves behind him, when the machinery breaks down, pools of 'something unutterable', a ghastly pus. 'A burst of multitudinous and leprous life – a loathsome, night-spawned flood of organic corruption . . . seething, stewing, surging, bubbling like serpent's slime' ('The Lurking Fear'). On examination, this stream proves composed of uncountable thousands of dwarfed, monkey things, oddly reminiscent of the teeming homunculi early researchers observed when they put their semen under the microscope. This pus-like matter turns out to be the last of an old Dutch colonial family. Evolution has wound them backwards; they have reverted to their own seminal fluid in three generations.

Lovecraft did indeed find his way back to his 'wistful boyhood' and described all he found there with remarkable vividness and accuracy. The beastly world of childhood, with its polymorphously perverse imaginings; its wild, inconsolable fears; its terror of darkness, of loneliness, its hatred of strangers. Its love of long, strange words and facility for inventing private languages. Its ability to construct elaborate mythologies out of the cracks in the crazy paving or the patterns on the wallpaper. Fear of cold. Weakness. Clawing, screaming temper tantrums. Self-abuse, old wives' tales. A lonely childhood. Childhood is the world before the knowledge of good and evil. A Hobbesian and terrible place. Such is the genesis of Lovecraft's aesthetics of the horrid. Maybe the source of all aesthetics of the horrid.

New Society, 1975

The Art of Horrorzines

There's no denying, Vampirella's got a lot more class in French. Yankee horror always has. *Suivez-moi. Je vous attendais. Vous serez ma proie.*

That's something like it! Almost, if not quite, the voluptuous imperatives of the Baudelairean vampiress. In translation, she awakes far more resonances, does Vampirella, the chunky-thighed, horrorzine superheroine in her scarlet single garment ingeniously cut to conceal her nipples whilst sumptuously exposing her navel, with her long black hair, her bat-shaped earrings and her fangs – ineffable Vampirella, the most beautiful vampire '*Demoniaque!* . . . *Irréel* . . . *Fantastique!* . . . *Envoutante!*' Yet she has a certain innocence; no damned undead she, but an extra-terrestrial from the planet Draculon, where blood's the natural diet and that means her tastes are not dictated by perversity but by physiology. So, according to the rather complicated ethics of the horrorzines, she is on the side of good versus evil, on the whole.

Her figure, with those plump hips, is down-homey American. In England, she was marketed as a glossy comic in the style of the sword-and-sorcery comics that picked up the last of the psychedelic trade two or three years ago. But in France she becomes the eponymous heroine of a plump and erudite magazine retailing at a whacking eight francs; a magazine replete with exhaustive articles on Italian westerns and authentic surrealist film-makers. The modification of this strip during its international distribution is a demonstration of cultural differences. The Americans like vulgarity. The English like fantasy. The French like a veneer of intellectualism. Baudelaire's version of Poe helps to distort, to etherealise, to surrealise the original image of the chubby Vampirella in all its native sexploitativeness and sensationalism.

So *Vampirella* and the other publications of Club Creepy (from whom may be obtained a six-foot poster of the girl herself, for twenty-five francs) are something other than horrorzines pure and simple. *Creepy* ('*le premier et le meilleur magazine illustré d'épouvante*') reprints American horror classics. There's a special number devoted to King Kong and it advertises reprints of *Tales from the Crypt* and other comics of the 1940s that gave horror comics such a bad name.

The French *Vampirella* magazine is full of the kind of heavy camp, an erudition only imperfectly aware of its own frivolity. This is the antithesis of that aspect of the British intellectual tradition typified by F. R. Leavis and those unable to see anything extraordinary in the juxtaposition of an umbrella and a sewing machine on a dissecting table.

The iconography of the American horrorzine originals is not filtered through such a tradition: 'Beyond Hell . . . Beyond Fear . . . Beyond the Terror that lurks in Man's Mind . . . DRACULA LIVES! He lives to stalk innocents. He thrives on the blood of mortals. He lives . . . and he wants YOU!'

With truly Draculian vivacity, the shadow of the Fatal Count falls across a whole stable of Marvel comics. Remember Marvel? The company who, in the 1960s, brought you Batman, Spiderman, Captain Marvel, Captain America, the Incredible Hulk and many other superheroes – some of whom had themselves been resuscitated from the comic book heyday of the 1940s. At the time, Marvel Comics Group looked like the heralds of McLuhan's post-literate man. Latterly they branched out into a range of Kung-Fu comics and a series derived from *Planet of the Apes* movies, reflecting a curious symbiosis between comic strip and film. And then they went into horrorzines, spurred perhaps by the success of *The Exorcist;* but don't seem to have prospered. Not quite horrid enough, maybe; Marvel always had a wholesome image.

The editorial (headlined 'Support your local monster') in vol.1, no.1, of *The Legion of Monsters,* dated this September, suggests that Marvel comics rather overstretched themselves in pursuit of the macabre market. It announces the demise of *The Haunt of Horror, Monsters Unleashed, Tales of the Zombie, Dracula Lives and Vampire Tales.* 'It's my personal feeling that the market which wasn't great enough to carry *five* monster-oriented titles *will* support *one* such publication,' says the editor.

The Legion of Monsters relies heavily on source material. There's a comic strip adaption of Bram Stoker's original *Dracula,* and a strip featuring yet further adventures of Frankenstein's monster, now come a long way in space and time from Mary Shelley. There's also one really nasty story, about a retarded microcephalic with surgeon's hands, that ought to guarantee bad dreams for any sensitive child.

All the same, considering the fuss there was about horror comics in the 1940s, it's surprising how unnoticed the revived genre passes on the newsstands now. My newsagent, a bit of a buff, says he sells most of them to students. He himself likes the sword-and-sorcery ones, like *Savage Sword of Conan* and *Kull and the Barbarians.* He says they're shipped over from America as ballast. He says he can't get enough of them to meet the demand.

The subculture of the comic buff has about it an air of parody academe, with its bibliographies, collectors' items, annual conferences, encyclopaedic knowledge of artists, writers, styles. This rococo obsessional erudition is reflected in the readers' letters, which often concern themselves with technical minutiae: 'The muddying of greys with blacks continued in this issue,' complains one reader and suggests: 'Use a lighter concentration of grey wash (dilute it in some manner), so that the individual blacks (letters) stand out against the grey background.' A typical Marvel-maniac critique.

However, those in the 'Archaic horror mailbag' in *Psycho* (my newsagent calls this 'one of the sick ones') have a rather different, more hysterical style. ' "I, Slime", is the story that drove me *insane,'* writes one satisfied customer, allegedly from a locked ward, in an issue that features, surely rather late in the day, a review of Murnau's *Nosferatu* by 'emotionally disturbed film buff Ed Fedory'.

Psycho shares some advertising with the Marvel comics. I wish all of them would stop advertising a book about freaks called *Very Special People.* With a come-on which goes some way beyond kitsch: 'As a youngster, Francesco Lentini was so shocked at what he saw in an institution for the severely handicapped that he never complained about his third leg again.' Among the ads for build-your-own-monster kits and potato guns and body-building courses, this ad strikes a very unhealthy note.

But in spite of the shared ads, *Psycho* appears to emanate from a different stable, where its mates include *Nightmare* and *Scream* (' "I Was a Vampire for Hire" was the second coolest story in the macabre history of *Scream,'* writes a reader.) And also a couple of horses of an altogether more sinister colour, to my mind – *Hell-Rider,* 'the original bike-riding superhero magazine,' and *Crime-Machine,* the 'most violent street horror magazine'. These publications offer cheap, well cheapish, library boxes – 'Get your macabre library organised off the floor where the rats have been chewing your magazines to shreds.' Rats and bats form perennial decorative motifs.

The woman's angle in the horrorzines seems influenced by the woman's movement in rather a complex way. *Devilina* a New York production, offers stories of 'female-filled fantasy'. Devilina herself, the sister of Satan, is physically a version of the superbly equipped Wonderwoman, who never quite got off the ground back in the 1940s as a rival to Superman; in her standard superheroine's two-piece bathing costume and boots, she has a period air. Theologically, her origins are obscure. She is in revolt against her satanic brother and exorcises his ministers: 'In the name of the Light of the World!' But Satan himself is no more than the horned, fanged nostalgia of a secular age; it's a very campy strip, together, though Devilina is one tough cookie and definitely on the side of Good, even if she looks like a Munch on the cover, with bulging thighs and wee horns peeping through lots of red hair.

Lilith, daughter of Dracula, featured in *Vampire Tales* and retained for *Legion of Monsters,* is rather a different conception. 'Within the lissom frame of Angel O'Hara there dwelled a raven-tressed *she demon,*' a Jekyll and Hyde variant. Angel O'Hara has a sophisticated pick-up technique and is sexually liberated; as her Lilith alter-ego, she sinks her teeth exclusively in the necks of wrongdoers, muggers, rapists, sex murderers. Once again Angel, a merciful amnesia blots out her vengeances. It is as if the notion of woman-as-aggressor can't be quite tolerated yet, and so must be presented in this schizophrenic fashion.

Here, the vampiress personifies righteous indignation, a one-woman lynch mob. The theme of evil-in-defence-of-good appears often; in one story, the People's Defence Association of Harlem enlisted a vampire in its struggle against inner-city decay. 'And *drug traffic* is down . . . The crime rate is down . . . The streets are safe.' And the price? Cheap – a soul for Satan is all.

But the vampire as tragic protagonist consumed with self-loathing and repugnance for his role is a favourite theme: Drac with scruples and post-prandial guilt, an existential kind of vampire. Michael Morbius the 'living vampire', has a scientific explanation for his condition. 'I was dying from a rare blood disease . . . experimented with the extract from a bat and electro-shock but it didn't work . . . turned me into a monster requiring *blood to survive.'* This strip has something of the authentic, crazed, obsessive quality that characterises those nineteenth-century French decadents with whose prose style the captions are heavily tinged.

'The sky a vast grey canvas of troubled cloud . . . a canvas clawed by jagged talons of lightning . . . a canvas ripped and shredded by elemental fury.' The rain spills forth, turns the earth to mud; and Morbius perhaps, identifies with that 'which cannot be cleansed'. The self-loathing is so exuberant it might almost express a degree of self-contempt on the part of the artists who have to churn out this stuff; but the Morbius strip has a lot of malign energy, and utilises a number of gothic hardy annuals. For example, he works on his test tubes and a cure – Dracula crossed with the mad scientist. Yet he, too, puts his dementia at the service of vengeance upon evildoers; he wipes out a band of murderers and then, overcome with self-hate, makes a pact with God teasingly reminiscent of a similar one in Buñuel's *Milky Way*. 'The only faith I'll believe in is that which *strikes me dead where I stand!*' And lightning strikes the shattered corpse at his feet, ironically bypassing Morbius. The rain continues to fall. Nothing is cleansed. And over the page falls the long shadows of the *poètes maudits*, longer by far than that of Dracula, even.

Here's a writer who knows that he's doing! Very heavy camp indeed. Who's got the French translation rights?

New Society, 1975

The Better to Eat You With

It doesn't need the horrid example of the painter Richard Dadd, the aptly named parricide, to suggest there is something peculiar about a grown man who devotes his life to an obsessional exploration of fairyland. The realm of faery has always attracted nutters, regressives and the unbalanced, as though a potential audience of children granted absolute licence. Children lack the tools of critical analysis; they can only defend themselves against disturbing input by a display of boredom which their masters, the adults, don't take seriously. Tellers of fairytales must have felt they could perpetrate the most excessive fantasies without fear of censure, provided everything took place in that domain of psychoanalytic privilege, fairyland.

Look at Hans Andersen – what a tortured dement! Those Arthur Rackham illustrations to Anderson are all wrong; Münch would have been far more suitable. Remember the little red shoes, with the feet still inside them, dancing off all by themselves into the forest, after the dreadful executioner with the axe had relieved poor Karen of them. Even worse in some ways, the feet the little mermaid bought for herself in order to walk on dry land; the price she paid for them was the perpetual sensation of walking on knives. And, in spite of all, she did not win the love of the prince. (A touch of Calvinism, there; Protestantism is a hard taskmaster.)

Please God, make it stop, I used to say, when they read Hans Andersen's
stories to me at bedtime. Is there no end to human suffering?

But they kept on assaulting my sensibilities with Andersen's fairytales
with a grand air of self-satisfaction. Weren't these dreadful stories
Children's Classics? Weren't they only doing their cultural duty by forcing them on me? Isn't the function of a good fairytale to instil fear, trembling and the sickness unto death into the existential virgin, anyway? And
why *should* children have a good time? The sooner you learn your own
impotence in the face of universal despair, the better.

Most children's classics of the fantasy and imagination – that is, the fairytale – are books for bewildered adults sailing under false colours, using the
free conventions of the fairytale to project a private world of terror and
dread. Sometimes, I admit, of luminous ambiguities, too. I got a lot of very
positive input from the splendid little robber girl in *The Snow Queen*. She
rode upon reindeer (I think it was), a small image of emancipation.

For Hans Andersen had genius; that is the hell of it. Good art is always
infinitely more pernicious in its influence than bad art, which can be dis-
regarded. A sensitive child might come to less emotional harm if he sticks
to soft-core porn, rather than Andersen. That extraordinary series of
French comic books called *Contes Féerotiques,* for example, in which the
seven dwarfs sport erections larger than themselves, and one is left in no
doubt as to exactly what kind of Beast it was that Beauty married.

Further, the free conventions of fairytale, fantasy and imagination are
the perfect excuse for super-kitsch. Oscar Wilde's over-upholstered fairytales must often have been the middle-class child's first lamentable introduction to Fine Writing – paving the way for a later passion for
Christopher Fry, and fatally confusing several generations as to the nature
of poetry.

Poetry and the fairytale. Yes. In Britain, it's considered a fine thing for
poets to turn out the odd imaginative piece of fantasy for sensitive kids and
grown-ups who want to take an intellectual holiday. This is a reflection
on the status of the poet in our society. Unacknowledged legislators of
mankind, indeed!

The notion of the fairytale as a vehicle for moral instruction is not a
fashionable one. I sweated out the heatwave browsing through Perrault's
Contes du temps passé on the pretext of improving my French. What an
unexpected treat to find that in this great Ur-collection – whence sprang
the Sleeping Beauty, Puss in Boots, Little Red Riding Hood, Cinderella,
Tom Thumb, all the heroes of pantomime – all these nursery tales are purposely dressed up as fables of the politics of experience. The seventeenth
century regarded children, quite rightly, as apprentice adults. Charles
Perrault, academician, folklorist, pedant, but clearly neither nutter nor

regressive, takes a healthily abrasive attitude to his material. Cut the crap about richly nurturing the imagination. *This* world is all that is to the point.

Here all the stories are – sprightly and fresh, and so very worldly. It is the succinct brutality of the folktale modified by the first stirrings of the Age of Reason. The wolf consumes Red Riding Hood; what else do you expect if you talk to strange men, comments Perrault briskly. Let's not bother our heads with the mysteries of sado-masochistic attraction; we must learn to cope with the world before we can interpret it. The primitive terror a young girl feels when she sees Bluebeard is soon soothed when he takes her out and shows her a good time, parties, trips to the country and so on. But marriage itself is no party. Better learn that right away.

The ghastliness of the rest of the Bluebeard story is clearly almost too much for Perrault: the dismembered wives lying in their own blood in the secret chamber, the bloodstained key that won't wash clean . . . an extravagance no modern writer could dismiss so lightly. The weeping woman, and Bluebeard with his cutlass raised ready to chop her head off: it's all too much. It's easy to see all this took place long ago, consoles Perrault in his moral tag at the end of the story. Modern husbands wouldn't dare to be so terrible. He blithely dismisses all the Freudian elements in the tale that galvanise the twentieth century. The troubling and intransigent images are incorporated into a well-mannered scheme of good sense. Perhaps the very presence of a rich imaginative life is an indication that the circumstances of real life are unsatisfactory.

Archaic patterns of ritual initiation; forbidden thresholds; invitatory incantations to pubertal rites such as 'Lift up the latch and walk in'; virgin martyrs and sacrificial victims (for why else should the folkloric original of Little Red Riding Hood dress up in such a bloody colour?): all the elements that our more barbarous times rejoice in for their own sakes as part of the rarest show of the unconscious, are subsumed by Perrault into a project for worldly instruction. It is a very precise kind of world in which money and self-advancement are the roads to happiness. Bluebeard's widow uses her inheritance to buy good husbands for herself and her sister Anne. Marital content may only be acquired in the marketplace, after a good deal of consumer research. She's learned that much.

The story of *The Sleeping Beauty* is a perfect parable of sexual trauma and awakening. But Perrault resolutely eschews making any such connections; and quite right, too. Never a hint that a girl's first encounter with a phallic object might shock her into a death-like trance. She's the victim of a power struggle among the heavy female fairy mafia. We're dealing with the real world, not the phantasia of the unconscious. Children get quite enough of that in the privacy of their own homes.

Of course, Perrault's great hero — hero of an age and a class — is Puss in Boots, or the Cat as Con Man. I'd forgotten what a masterpiece of cynicism this story is. 'Keep quiet and leave everything to me,' the cat requests the miller's son, and forthwith embarks on a career of guilt, blackmail and low cunning that advances his master to the highest station in the land, with a lot of gravy left over for Cat as well. Perrault adds a moral as a sop to the emergent bourgeoisie — hard work and ingenuity will take you further than inherited capital.

The Cat has certainly plenty of ingenuity, but his idea of a hard day's work is one spent collecting protection money; and the only task the miller's son himself performs is to pretend to drown. It's almost the frame work for a Stendhalian parable. Were the Cat not a small, furry animal but a Figaroesque valet — a servant so much the master already that he doesn't need the outward apparatus of the role because then he'd become powerless — then *Puss in Boots* would be in no way suitable for children.

Even Perrault's specifically magical beings, the Lilac Fairy and Cinderella's godmother, and the guests at the Sleeping Beauty's wedding, have rather less the air of supernatural beings derived from pagan legend about them than of women of independent means who've done quite well for themselves, one way and another, and are prepared to help along a little sister who finds herself in difficulties. It's little Mae West comforting the young girl who's been seduced and abandoned in *She Done Him Wrong:* she gives her nice clothes and good advice. 'When a girl goes wrong, a man goes right after her.'

'We all need a fairy godmother of some kind or another,' says Perrault sagely. Hard work and ingenuity, virtue and beauty are all very well. But somebody's got to run the racket.

And what a craftsman Perrault was! *Little Red Riding Hood* is a classic of narrative form. The plot arises from the interaction of the wolf and his hunger, and the child and her ingenuity. The suspense springs from our own knowledge of the predatoriness of wolves and our perception of Red Riding Hood's ignorance of it. No child reared on these austere and consummately constructed narrative forms is going to be easily fobbed off with slipshod stream-of-consciousness techniques, or overheated poetic diction.

If there is something odd about a grown man who devotes most of his time on the *qui vive* for the horns of elfland faintly blowing, I don't think it's too good for children, either. Rather let them learn enlightened self-interest from Puss; resourcefulness from Tom Thumb; the advantages of patronage from Cinderella, and of long engagements from the Sleeping Beauty. The first bourgeois mythologies were the best bourgeois mythologies, look at *Robinson Crusoe,* than which no fictional text has ever been more specific on the nature of primitive capital accumulation and early colonialism. 'I told him his name was to be Friday, which was the day I caught him; I taught him to say, master, and let him know that was to be my name.'

Ban Tolkien, Ban Andersen. Too much imaginative richness makes Jack a dull boy; and no good at killing giants.

New Society, 1976

An I for Truth

Narrative in the first person implies a specific relation of intimacy and trust between writer and reader. It is the narrative mode of a good deal of down-market woman's magazine fiction. It is supposed to make you say: 'Yes: that's how it is,' and feel better.

True Story (ten complete real-life stories of love and marriage), *True Romances* (ten complete real-life love stories), *True* magazine (dramatic real-life stories), *Hers: True Life Stories* (thrilling confessions) all offer first-person narratives exclusively concerned with affairs of the heart.

And not only do you hear their voices, you can see their faces. Posed photographs illustrate all these magazines. The models are only the tiniest bit more glamorous than real life. They invite, presumably, absolute audience identification.

The whole format of what used to be called 'confession magazines' hasn't changed much: only a little slicker than I remember when my mother wouldn't let me read them. Some of the really lurid ones, with come-ons on the front like: 'I asked him in for coffee – a rapist!' and 'Married – to my own brother', are harder to find; indeed, seem to have disappeared from most newsstands and were, I think, American imports, anyway. Like the richest and primmest of the whole genre of pseudo-documentary magazines, the 'orrible murder mags.

The 'orrible murder mags are still around, with their grainy photographs of bloodstained pillows and ads for lucky charms, their irresistible come-ons, grown ever more sprightly with the passing years. A Hooker and a Hammer put Moses in the Slammers. Who Butchered the Beautiful Omaha Virgin? But the 'orrible murders, all taken from police files, are third-person narratives, and the photographs are of the actual accused. They are fact told as if it were fiction, rather than fiction presented as fact (which is what I should think the woman's magazines are, since no stories give any sources). The 'orrible murders belong to a healthy, well, vigorous tradition of folk Grand Guignol. The broadside ballad of gallowside confessions (like Maria Marten and the Red Barn) preceded them. They all say the same thing: justice triumphs.

No such gamey avatars prefigure the pseudo-documentary, first-person women-oriented magazines, and their message is more diffuse. They are directly related to the moral tale and derive from Sunday School literature, as Richard Hoggart observed about *Red Star* and *People's Friend* twenty years ago, in *The Uses of Literacy*. These two papers, still on limp newsprint, still decorated with simple line drawings, haven't changed format at all, and may still be purchased. Their content remains as in some prelapsarian time-warp, as if the Pill had never been, full of such cosy warmth it makes you feel like you've been buried alive in home-made scones.

The pseudo-documentaries are invisible friends who adopt a sympathetically hortatory tone, interspersing the good advice implicit in their adventures with fashion and beauty tips, and cookery of a kind that sometimes approaches the porno-cuisine of Millie in Altman's film, *Three Women,* where you chuck in a tin of soup and a grape and hey presto! Chicken *véronique.*

The magazines, also, like good friends, give you things: a free packet of Silvikrin 'Nature's Riches' strawberry shine conditioner, a sachet of Endocil clear moisturising lotion, a handy kitchen spatula. This, and the omnipresent 'I' of the real-life romances suggests that the producers anticipate that the consumers will be both lonely and grateful.

The ideology behind the romances and the confessions stinks. Really it does. Admittedly, it stinks in quite an interesting way. It isn't as rancid as that of the more sophisticated woman's magazine – which absolutely evades some of the problems (frigidity, prison, alcoholism, divorce) that these down-market productions deal with, even if only intermittently. And a happy ending is not, in these narratives, always synonymous with wedding bells. Sometimes it is synonymous with divorce.

What stinks is the assumption – common to all the 'I's in my random sampling of pseudo-documentaries catalogued above – that maturity consists of making the best of what you have. Even if what you have is pretty crummy.

'I've come to realise that life can never be one long romance,' says a girl who came to her senses after an adulterous fling, and has returned to her husband. Time and again, adultery is resolved by 'coming to one's senses', even if occasionally ('Patsy taught me a lot') a narrator – in this instance, male; nothing queer about *my* friends – acknowledges it has enriched a marriage. Sometimes, occasionally, a drab-voiced friend suggests a marriage might just erode, or adultery might be a symptom that Something More is Wrong. But in the main, marriage remains an unassailable institution, as does the family. This is the populist celebration of the status quo, all right. It is not surprising to find, here, a strong anti-women's movement motif that occasionally becomes quite explicit in a kind of knowing condescension.

'Your sister's far too wrapped up in her equality for women thing,' David tells his wife, who tells us. His sister-in-law, he goes on, is just as bad as the people who don't believe in woman's rights: a transparent piece of repressive tolerance. When this woman gives his son a necklace for Christmas and his daughter a toolkit, their mother and father are immensely gratified to see the children voluntarily exchange these gifts with one another. This is positive proof – they crow – that the boy and girl are free of sex-role stereotyping. They're each individuals, aren't they? Haven't they made a free choice?

Another girl, a secretary, is disgusted to find she is to work for a female boss. There is no conciliation between them. The girl hates her new boss until the end of the story. The female boss is quite incidental to the plot. She seems to have been introduced only for the sake of a bit of knocking copy.

Knocking copy, also, the cartoon in which a man (seated at table) says to a woman (standing, akimbo, a women's movement symbol round her neck): 'Have you ever considered getting involved in cooking?' (Has *he?* Get off your ass and cook your own supper, you lazy good-for-nothing. But I do not think the cartoon is intended to mock male chauvinism.)

A rather subtler story has a woman giving up a part-time job because her children show signs of deprivation. Propaganda for clearing women off the labour market at a time of high unemployment, I suppose. We leave this woman baking a cake for her beaming kids. Family togetherness is *more* important than the extra few bob she earned as a waitress. The children's delinquency is directly linked to her deflection from the maternal role, and there is no question that she worked for any other reason than additional income. Nor that such additional income might be essential to the family budget. The pseudo-documentaries approach the real conditions of life but evade them with solutions in the realm of fantasy.

The invisible friends constantly reassure the reader (who may have private doubts about it) that happiness is more important than money. They would, presumably, block any demands for a return to free collective bargaining on the part of their husbands' unions on these grounds alone. 'I'll bet I'm richer than all those "successful" people on Newlands Estate,' says Louise. 'I've got something infinitely more precious than their two-car homes and colour televisions – I've got love.' It would be socially divisive,

I guess, to suggest that the people on Newlands Estate might have love too.

This particular story has as its come-on: 'The man in my life wanted us to be lovers before I became his wife.' It is a pleasure, these days, to find that Judy regards this as an outrageous suggestion. Louise, her sister, suggests, not a visit to the family planning clinic, but a speedy marriage. Perhaps she does not know the way to the family planning clinic herself since she will be unable to act as matron of honour because her fourth child is about to be born: 'the price of love', she quips. There is no suggestion that it might be purchased more cheaply, or might prove too high.

They get married so young, these girls! Seventeen, eighteen, nineteen; and the babies come, to complete their happiness, except one girl miscarries and takes to the bottle, another miscarries and becomes frigid. These catastrophes are dealt with by the love and understanding of all concerned.

Sometimes things go wrong. A wife informs on her warehouse-breaker husband, and anxiously waits for him at the prison gate. Will he still love her? She sees 'a new maturity' on his face as he comes out. Prison has obviously made a man of him. The marriage, enriched, will continue.

Yet the straightforward populist celebrations of marital love and family life are interspersed with downbeat narratives by people, often in their late thirties or older, coming to terms with divorce, not necessarily by finding new partners. A certain drab veracity is the tone of these 'I's. Yet marriage remains the principle obsession, even here. It is as if marriage functions as the sexuality of women. It occupies the imagination of these magazines to the same obsessive extent that sexuality itself does in the tit mags. Perhaps, like the tit mags, these magazines do not truly reflect the central preoccupations of the readers.

Still, most women do get married and define themselves in relation to marriage, and will, no doubt, continue to get married. They marry men, of course. But you would never think that marriage was just as central to the lives of men from the evidence of the magazines that cater for a male readership. Which is a curious imbalance.

There are a number of illicit pregnancies in these forty or fifty first-person narratives that I've read. Two end in adoption, the others in miscarriage or stillbirth. The letters on the problem page ask about abortion and contraception. The pseudo-documentaries can't find room for these things in real life. The 'I's are a homogenous, upper-working, lower-middle, socially cohesive mass. There are no blacks, no trade union members, no dossers, freaks, unemployed manual workers, or socially discordant elements.

The small towns in which the 'I's live might be anywhere. They have the false universality of any other mythic places and the value system has the same false universality, too. And what is really pornographic is the titillatory exploitation of the human heart, which is a lot worse than the titillatory exploitation of human flesh.

The only consolation is, I'm sure the people who read them don't believe one word of them.

New Society, 1977

Latin Rhythms

Review of Gabriel García Márquez, *Innocent Erendira and Other Stories,*
and Jorge Luis Borges, *The Book of Sand.*

Monstrous critical overkill has hived Gabriel García Márquez off into an exotic limbo. Extravagant silliness greeted the arrival in English of his sinuous and accomplished novel, *One Hundred Years of Solitude.* The *Spectator* gushed: 'The most obvious comparison is with Homer's *Odyssey.*' Follow *that.*

Most of Márquez's non-hispanic readers can have but the haziest idea of the exact whereabouts of his native Colombia, its history or ethnic composition. It is therefore, easy to treat Márquez's books as though they were located, not in a heightened reality, but in a timeless, placeless dream world where the reader can relax and let the dream take charge.

In a sense, the dream *does* take charge in Márquez but, like most recent Latin American writers, he evidently imbibed surrealism with his mother's milk (see the early stories reprinted in *Innocent Erendira* which is translated by Gregory Rabassa). The dreams he recounts are not holidays from reality but encounters with it.

The novella here, the full title of which is: 'The incredible and sad tale of innocent Erendira and her heartless grandmother', is a specific parable of economic exploitation. The landscape is a desert. The mute, indifferent presence of the aboriginal Indians is also part of the landscape, through which the principal actors, of varied ethnic stock, cart a bric-à-brac of beds, coffins and pianos as if they were displaced persons. This powerful sense of alienation – it wasn't called *One Hundred Years of SOLITUDE* for nothing – and Márquez's method of closing the distance between the human figures and the inimical landscape by means of folkloric devices relate this novella to the earlier novel very closely.

The cruel bones of the story are: Erendira accidentally burns down her grandmother's house; she must work as a prostitute for her grandmother until she repays her for the cost of the house; due to the continuing expenses of the trade – laundry and so on – the grandmother never will be repaid and so must be murdered by Erendira's lover before Erendira can run away from them all.

Monstrous critical overkill of an even more upmarket kind has transformed the Argentinian *petit maître*, Borges, into one of the Great Writers of our Time and his most recent collection, *The Book of Sand,* (stories translated by Norman Thomas di Giovanni, and poems by Alastair Reid), shows signs that he is content humbly to acquiesce in this opinion.

There is a chillingly posthumous air about, for example, 'The Double', in which Old Borges meets the young man he once was by a trick of time. Neither likes nor understands the other much and the story is oddly paralleled by a poem, 'The Double' in which Borges addresses himself in the third person: 'Down to the last detail I abhor him. I am gratified to remark that he can hardly see. I am in a circular cell and the infinite wall is closing in.' The pervasive despair beneath the lapidary surface of Borges's work is breaking through at last in the form of acute self-dislike.

Unlike Márquez, Borges believes the dream is in itself a reality, not the product of or the illumination of social reality. 'Our obvious duty . . . is to accept the dream just as we accept the world'('The Double'). The title story, 'The Book of Sand', is a characteristically Borgesian tribute to the concrete dream, or world-as-fiction, about an inexhaustible, numinous volume, 'an obscene thing that affronted and tainted reality itself'. But which is which? As Alice said to the kitten. As Borges grows older and wearier, he finds that opposites turn out to have been precise equivalents all long.

He scrupulously documents yet another fake heresy, in 'The Sect of the Thirty'. The sect regards Christ and Judas, the only *intentional* actors in the Christian drama, as the same. Elsewhere, a narrator says: 'I was loved by a woman I shall never forget; I left her or she left me – it amounts to the same thing.' But, except at the level of the glibbest paradox, it doesn't, it doesn't, it doesn't! And Borges, exhaustedly, now seems to acknowledge himself trapped in his own solipsistic labyrinth, like one of his own creations, but still insisting that this is the only way to be. No wonder he is such a hit in Old World senior common rooms.

However, even Borges has been powerfully affected by that sense of estrangement which the peculiar colonial and post-colonial history of Latin America has produced. One of his finest stories, and one most full of real dread, 'Tlon, Uqbar, Orbis Tertius' (in *Fictions)* is about the imposition of a fictive culture that displaces reality. I understand this is what a lot of Latin Americans believe has, in fact, happened to them. It is curious that Borges, of all people, thus invokes, in a dead language, the very phrase, the

Third World. But Márquez writes about the contradictions of a most ancient and yet newborn society in a living language. If we are content to regard Márquez as a picturesque spell-binder, the literary equivalent of Don Juan the Yaquil sorcerer, then we are being very silly.

New Society, 1979

Yashar Kemal: The Lords of Akchasaz

Turkish is clearly a language that deploys the resources of rhetoric with greater vivacity than contemporary English does. Therefore Yashar Kemal's most recently translated novel comes through the language barrier disconcertingly like a sword-and-sorcery romance. Not only the style, with its magic touch of fustian ('I am Gazele, the gazelle-eyed, take my eyes, they are yours') but the content suggests a picturesque never-never world. It starts off with a mysterious horseman wrapped in a black felt cloak, his boots full of blood, arriving at Dervish Bey's mansion in the great Chukurova plain. Rain 'never-ending, lurid, yellow', streams down. Dervish Bey keeps an ivory handled revolver stuck in his silk sash; he lives at a high pitch of existential cruelty, autocratic dignity, deathly vanity. And so on. Gosh.

The thing is, it's perfectly possible, perhaps probable, that Turks themselves, and people who know that beautiful and under-developed country better than I, may very well not see anything particularly picturesque about all this. The idea that the Middle East *was* picturesque was propagated by nineteenth-century European travellers in the first place, so that we would not have to take it seriously. But the first real sign, for the common reader, that this novel is taking place, not in a mythic Turkic dream-time but around, say, last Thursday, is when the mother of Dervish Bey's mortal enemy urges him 'Kill him, my Mustafa! . . . Kill him and bring me back his heart . . . His heart and a jugful of blood.'

While, outside, one of the family henchmen gets the tractor ready. 'It was a bright blue one and it stood there in the middle of the yard like a huge freshly-blown flower. Like a fabulous blue insect . . .' And, in a way, the tractor, one of which can do the work of a thousand men, is the real hero of the story, symptom of the profound social changes that are transforming these feudal lords with their archaic rivalries and the hateful beauty of their lives into anachronisms, murderous dandies of the void. And, gradually, the vast plain, and the novel itself, fills up with dispossessed sharecroppers, with peasant entrepreneurs who invest in Mercedes Benzes, with policemen trained in the latest American methods of torture.

Kemal is, of course, using the same method as Latin American magic realism, a fusion of folkloric elements and social history in epic dimensions, at a very high imaginative level. And, even if you don't know any modern Turkish history at all, this first part of *The Lords of Akchasaz* is a very good read, indeed. And if you do, I suspect it takes on a massive allegorical grandeur. With its huge cast list, its splendid descriptive beauties, its ghastly violence, its occasional lurches into the purest kitsch, its exquisite sense of place and feeling for vastness, its capacity for making a grand gesture, it is the antithesis of the bourgeois novel as we know it. Indeed, like Fuentes's *Terra Nostra,* it makes you wonder if the novel is, in fact, a bourgeois form, after all.

The title page calls this book: *The Lords of Akchasaz: Part One, Murder in the Ironsmith's Market,* but, alas, hints nowhere at an imminent part two. Yet this volume leaves the principals of the blood feud alive, even if in a state of profound alienation, with a gnomic old man reprising the threnody that has echoed through the novel like a leitmotiv: 'They have mounted those beautiful horses, all the good people, and ridden away.'

I can think of few recent novels that reveal to us, by contrast, how small our world is, how narrow our imaginative range, how queasily terrified we are at confronting our own historic experience.

New Society, 1979

William Burroughs: Ah Pook Is Here

Ah Pook is Here is an apocalypse. Ah Pook is the Mayan death deity. John Stanley Hart, a young American student of immorality, searches the jungle for the lost Mayan codices that contain Ah Pook's secrets of fear and death. But, when he finds them, he reads them 'as one who reads Moby Dick to find out about whaling and to hell with Ahab'. For Hart is addicted to a personal immorality predicated on the mortality of others, 'gooks, niggers, human dogs, stinking *humans*'.

The arcane secrets of fear and death are utilised to make a world safe for John Stanley Hart to live (for ever) in. 'Is this terrible knowledge now computerised and vested in the hands of far-sighted Americans in the State Department and the CIA?' Burroughs is often so outrageously upfront about his moral indignation it is possible, I think wrongly, to dismiss it as a cheap effect.

But a fugue of deathless mutant boys precipitates a bizarrely ecstatic finale that looks like it's been choreographed by Hieronymous Bosch. 'A boy whipped with a transparent fish sprouts wings . . . Flying fox boy soars above a burning tree.' Wild boys lyrically ejaculate robins and blue birds. Nobody, it turns out, can Hire Death as a company cop. Or not for long.

This is by no means an adequate summary of the only hitherto unpublished text in this little garden of Burroughs. *Ah Pook Is Here* is infinitely more thematically complex, more uncomfortable and replete with far more deadpan black humour than I have begun to suggest. But you can't easily fillet the meaning out of Burroughs's work because he is against succinct verbal exposition which he sees as a sinister form of thought control. What he likes to do is hit you with an image and let the image act for itself.

No wonder, then, all these pieces reflect his interest in scripts composed of signs and hieroglyphs. *Ah Pook Is Here* was originally intended as a picture-book based on the Mayan codices. The second piece, 'The Book of Breathing', actually turns into pictures. In the third piece, 'The Electronic Revolution', Burroughs talks approvingly about Chinese, 'a script derived from hieroglyphs . . . [and therefore] more closely related to the objects and areas described'.

Elsewhere, he defines words as 'moving pictures'. The dialectic between the concrete and the discrete in Burroughs, between the solidity of the image and the arbitrariness of sequence, is what makes his own prose *move*, makes it kinetic, gives it, in spite of its obsession with death, mind-death, soul-death, death-in-life, its superabundant life.

Guardian, 1979

William Burroughs: The Western Lands

Since William S. Burroughs relocated from New York City to Lawrence, Kansas, the town blasted by IBMs in the antinuke TV spectacular, 'The Day After', he has evidently prefected a final loathing for the instruments of mass death and – 'no job too dirty for a fucking scientist' – their perpetrators.

Pointless to head for the hills, these days: 'What hills? Geiger counters click to countdown. Decaying lead spells out the last syllable of recorded time. Orgone balked at the post. Christ bled. Time ran out. Radiation has won at a half-life.'

The densely impacted mass of cultural references here – Macbeth, the western, Reich, Dr Faustus, pulp science fiction – isn't an isolated example of *The Western Lands'* intense awareness of literature and of itself as literature, suggesting that perhaps one of the things going on, here, is an elegiac farewell to all that. The peremptory demand on which the novel ends, 'Hurry up, please. It's time', is a straight quote from 'The Wasteland', reminiscent also of Cyril Connolly's remark about closing time in the gardens of the West.

Unless Burroughs is practising some complicated double irony (and I wouldn't put it past him), the West of Connolly's usage has nothing to do with the Old West of Burroughs's obsession, site of his last novel, *The Place of Dead Roads,* which was second in the trilogy of which *Cities of the Red Night* was first and this the last. The 'Western Lands' of Burroughs's title are, mythologically speaking, where the dead live. That is, the place beyond death.

Essentially we are talking about immortality, the immortality promised by the poet to Mr W.H. , which is no longer compatible with the weapons that cause 'Total Death. Soul Death'. 'Well, that's what art is all about, isn't it? All creative thought, actually. A bid for immortality.' Who is talking about immortality? William Seward Hall, for one, old man and blocked writer, who decides to 'write his way out of death' just as old novelists, like Scott, wrote themselves out of debt.

But, both in and out of this transparent disguise, Burroughs is talking about immortality, too. *The Western Lands* is structured according to an internal logic derived from an idiosyncratic reading of Egyptian myth; immortality, in its most concrete form, greatly concerned Egyptians.

In spite of a series of discontinuous story lines featuring a variety of heroes, the book often resembles a nineteenth-century commonplace book. The most urgent personal reflections are juxtaposed with jokes, satires, quotations, essays in fake anthropology, parody, pastiche, and passages of Burroughs's unique infective delirium – piss, shit, offal, disembowellings. This is slapstick reinterpreted by Sade.

Cats of all kinds weave in and out of the text; Burroughs has clearly taken to them in a big way in his old age and seems torn between a fear they will betray him into sentimentality and a resigned acceptance that a man can't be ironic *all* the time.

The method is eclectic and discrete and it is important, and essential, because Burroughs is doing something peculiar with the reader's time. He's stopping it. Or, rather, stop-starting it. Taking it out of the reader's hands, anyway, which is where we tend to assume it ought to be.

He'll give you a paragraph, a page, even three or four pages at a time, of narrative like a railway down which the reader, as if having boarded a train, travels from somewhere to somewhere else according to an already existing timetable. Then – the track vanishes. The train vanishes. And you find you don't have any clothes on, either. While all that's left of the engine driver is a disappearing grin.

This constant derailment of the reader happens again and again, shattering the sense of cause and effect, whilst all the time one is reassured in the most affectingly disingenuous manner: 'How can any danger come from an old man cuddling his cats?'

You cannot hurry Burroughs, or skim, or read him for the story. He likes to take his time and to disrupt *your* time in such a way that you cannot be carried along by his narrative. Each time it tips you out, you have to stand and think about it; you yourself are being rendered as discontinuous as the text.

In fact, Burroughs's project is to make time stand still for a while, one which is more frequently that of religion than of literature and there are ways in which Burroughs's work indeed resembles that of another William, the Blake of the self-crafted mythology of the Prophetic Books, although it must be said that Burroughs is much funnier.

He is also the only living American writer of whom one can say with confidence he will be read with the same shock of terror and pleasure in a hundred years' time, or read at all, in fact, should there be anybody left to read.

Guardian, 1988

The German Legends of the Brothers Grimm

Unlike the Grimms' collection of fairytales, without which no home is complete, their collection of German legends has never been translated into English before. What is the difference between a fairytale and a legend? The Grimms themselves scrupulously differentiate in their own Foreword to the first German edition of 1816. A fairytale, they say, can 'find its home anywhere', it belongs to the timeless, international zone of poetry; but the legend – ah! the legend, securely attached to a specific place, often a specific date, is the folk spirit recreating its own history. Is distilled essence of folk spirit. Is, in short, essentially, gloriously and unpollutedly *German.* 'Nothing is as edifying or as likely to bring more joy than the products of the Fatherland.' H'm.

Ironically, Donald Ward's scholarly notes on individual legends suggest that many of the German legends aren't so very German, after all – wild hunts, mermen, headless horsemen, dwarfs and giants distribute themselves throughout Europe and, indeed, the world with a grand disregard for frontiers.

Volume One is composed of odd, fragmentary bits and pieces of pseudo-history and folk belief taken, mostly, directly from the mouths of the German folk themselves. It is a feast of snacks. The very inconsequentiality is enchanting. 'There is a bridge outside of Haxthusen-Hofe near Paderborn. Beneath it lives a poor soul who sneezes from time to time.' Who? Why? You can almost see the Grimms' informant shrug. Who knows? Just take my word for it.

Early nineteenth-century Germany was rife with such spooks; many of them seem to have fallen out of a household tale, folk motifs in search of a narrative. What of the ghostly girl, carrying a bunch of keys, often seen washing herself in a certain spring? And another girl, with long, golden hair, who frequents the mountainside on which she was burned to death – what *can* they be up to?

The answer, usually, is nothing. Neither numinous nor ominous, they possess only the existential validity of being there, part of the imaginative furniture of the place, ubiquitous and homely as the village idiot.

Sometimes the legends are uncanny just because they are so enigmatic:

Once a man was riding through a forest late in the evening when he saw two children sitting next to each other. He admonished them to go home and not to tarry any longer. But the two began laughing loudly. The man rode on and after a while he encountered the same two children who began laughing again.

The pointlessness of it is the whole point; it is a free-form apparition, awaiting a random injection of significance, or the formal shaping of the storyteller's craft.

I wonder if the method of the collectors differed when they were out after *real* pseudo-history, serious German essence rather than frivolous invented narrative? How much did they themselves want their informants actually to believe in the things the informants were relating? The almost lunatic precision of dating and locating material – 'in 1398 . . . near Eisenach, in Thuringia . . .'; 'In 1519, just before the plague killed many people in the city of Hof . . .' – gives a specious appearance of authenticity to many a tall tale, though, indeed, some of these references come from old books to back up the memories of old people. All the same, these legends occupy a curious grey area between fact and fiction.

There are anecdotes, old wives' tales, tales of saints and miracles, marvellous lies designed to test the gullibility of the listener – most of them designed to be neither believed nor disbelieved, designed to court no more positive response than 'Well, fancy that!' It is a loose-jointed, easy-going way of decorating the real world with imaginative detail. As Lévi-Strauss says about such benign and cheering superstitions, they make the world 'more tasty'. It was a tasty old world that the Grimms found, all right.

Mermen are just the same as we are except for their green teeth. The edges of the petticoats of water-pixies are always sopping wet. The devil, a constant visitor, lends his name to inauspicious tracts of land like the Devil's Dance Floor, and the Devil's Pillow, a boulder on which the very mark of his ear may still be seen. Dwarfs borrow pots and pans for their weddings. Fairies borrow human midwives for their lyings-in.

Some narratives start out like true fairytales, only to collapse in grand anti-climax, pricked balloons from which the magic suddenly leaks out. A young man releases a dwarf from a spell but no good fortune accrues; he can't get rid of the dwarf, an unwelcome lodger, thereafter. A girl sees another dwarf pouring water in front of a house; shortly afterwards, the house is saved from fire. Some time later, the dwarf is out with his watering can again; and what happens this time? A big fat nothing happens this time.

Often the very magical matter of the fairytale comes down to earth with a bump in these matter-of-fact renditions of wonderful occurrences. The anti-hero makes his appearance. A poor girl who, like the Fairy Melusine, is a snake from the waist down, must be kissed three times by a chaste youth to regain her natural shape. But the lad from our village dared kiss her only twice! 'Each time, in great anticipation for the unhoped-for-miracle, the maiden made such dreadful gestures that he feared she was going to tear him to pieces. He, therefore, did not dare kiss her for the third time, and instead departed in haste.' Departed, in fact, to forthwith lose his virtue to an 'impure woman' and, with it, all his fairytale eligibility for the task of rescue.

Some of the legends are, in fact, shaggy-dog stories. The boy in Freiburg in 1545, for instance, who was cursed to remain standing up. Eventually his feet wore grooves in the floor. Because he was standing near the stove he got in everybody's way so they picked him up and stowed him away in corners. At last they all got bored with him and covered him up with a cloth.

Amongst many other such delights may be found the true stories of the Pied Piper of Hamelin and of Bishop Hatt and the Rats. There is a delicious little giant girl who scoops up plough, horses, ploughmen, and all in her apron and takes them home to play with: 'Oh, Father, it's such a marvellous toy!'

Volume Two is a very different kettle of fish, a collection of heroic legends very few of which come from the living traditions of real people. The Grimms say these stories could be called Legends of Teutonic Tribes and Royal Families and, here, they are as much concerned with myth-making as with folklore. They embrace the historic with disturbing enthusiasm: '. . . it is . . . a noble attribute of people . . . any people . . . when both the dawn and the dusk of their day in history consists of legends'. The relation between the rise of folklore studies and that of modern nationalism is an interesting one; there are things here that uncomfortably tease the mind.

To quote King Dagobert who, while he lay on his deathbed, said to his dogs: 'No company is so good, that one cannot take leave of it.'

Guardian, 1981

The Sweet Sell of Romance

Review of Judith Krantz, *Princess Daisy*.

Glamour has returned to the White House, according to the magazine headlines, and *Princess Daisy* has at last joined its stable-mate, *Scruples,* in the US paperback outlets, twinned in self-advertisement: '*Princess Daisy,* a novel by the author of *Scruples*'; ' *Scruples,* a novel by the author of *Princess Daisy.*' Judith Krantz is the author in question. Glamour has also returned to the bestseller lists. And how.

Though you couldn't quite say that Judith Krantz is to these troubled times what Scott Fitzgerald was to the Jazz Age, her two novels so far – she's reportedly working on a third – certainly offer some insights into the mood of the United States in these regrettable, even implausible days of disquiet, when the century trembles on the cusp of *fin de siècle*, and there is even an unstable undercurrent of *fin du monde* about it all. The manner in which her books have been sold to the public is certainly indicative of a new role for the novel.

According to an exhaustive blow-by-blow account of this entire marketing process, in a recent *New Yorker* article, a certain Morton L. Janklow, after first reading the manuscript of *Scruples* a year or two ago, told Judith Krantz: 'If you want to see that book covering the faces of every woman on the beach in America next summer, let me be your agent.' This statement lets the cat out of the bag. You are not reading a book if it is covering your face. Any fool can see that. Selling the book is more important than having people read it.

Presented with this notion of fiction as pure commodity, Mrs Krantz enthusiastically concurred. And is it any wonder! Because both *Scruples* and *Princess Daisy* are romances of high consumerism.

In *Scruples*, the incredibly rich Billie Ikehorn Irsini, after a period as a compulsive shopper, finds true fulfilment by opening a shop herself (the 'Scruples' of the title), and selling luxury items of personal adornment. In this novel, some tacky nostalgic stuff about the movie industry is thrown in towards the end as a glamour makeweight, but in *Princess Daisy*, consumption is allowed its own complete integrity. Princess Daisy, the eponymous heroine, achieves a more radical apotheosis. She herself becomes a brand name. Indeed, she is transformed into a perfume when a matching fragrance and line of cosmetics are named after her.

The final effect of both novels is of being sealed inside a luxury shopping mall whilst being softly pelted with scented sex technique manuals. It is a uniquely late twentieth-century experience and not without a certain preposterous charm, as of a champagne picnic on the crust of an active volcano.

I don't think that Mrs Krantz's novels offer a richly informative guide to the fantasy lives of Middle American woman. Rather, they are indications of what a lot of people think a lot of other people's fantasy lives *ought* to be like. They are prescriptive rather than descriptive. But I think this is unconscious. No doubt Judith Krantz believes she has merely tapped one or two veins of wish-fulfilment fantasy that have existed since time immemorial. The one about being a rich widow. The one about being a beautiful princess.

A *beautiful princess?* Yes! That one! In this day and age? Never, it seems, more potent. In republican America? You bet.

Krantz knows better than to repeat successful formulae. There are fascinating differences between the two novels. *Scruples* (1978) is a West Coast novel. The meat of the action takes place in and around Los Angeles. Billie's shop is on Rodeo Drive, where luxury boutiques create 'the most staggering display of luxury in the western world', *Princess Daisy* (1980) is basically a Manhattan novel. (Presumably the work in progress will be a sagebrush rebel novel, centred on Houston or Dallas, where the action is now said to be.)

Billie is an Amazon-tall, sexually voracious brunette whose wealth is her problem. Daisy is a fragile, sexually reticent blonde, a White Russian heiress who loses her family fortune because her father invests it in Rolls-Royce, which the British government then heartlessly nationalise. She becomes poor, that is *her* problem. She works hard, and practises elegant economies like dressing in old Schiaparelli suits bought at a jumble sales.

Though Daisy's period of poverty (in New York's new bohemia, SoHo) has elements of Marie-Antoinette playing milkmaid, her full-time job still gives her more quiddity as a character than Billie. In spite of her ludicrous pedigree, Daisy is more believable within the terms of the fictional convention. It is always difficult to empathise fully with somebody whose relation to the world is blunted at the edges by an excess of the green stuff.

Krantz makes a valiant attempt to promote Billie as a 'poor little rich widow', imprisoned in the magic castle of her wealth. But there's a lack of conviction about it because, in her heart, Krantz obviously believes (as I do myself) that if the rich are not seen to be happy, then there is no validity to the concept of personal wealth. It goes without saying that, in the Krantz world, money means gratification. More, it is a primary requisite of existence. After all, it takes a million dollars to make Daisy solvent – which is rather more than it would take, for example, me.

The difference in the treatment of sex between the two novels is the most startling single contrast. *Scruples* contains anatomically precise descriptions of the parts of the greater part of the male principals. Those of the hero of the sub-plot, 'Spider' Elliot, are constantly visible, in a state of excitation, beneath his jeans. Billie's own well-developed clitoris 'pouts' through her labia major in a manner which, in the real world, usually belongs only to the female orang-utang. Men and women fall to it in soft porn sequences at cannily spaced intervals. There is an interlude of men-only sex. Oral sex is high on the menu and Billie('got something to show you . . . you'll like it') is herself a *vade mecum* to sexual expertise.

But sex in *Princess Daisy* is soft focus rather than soft porn. It rises to infrequent peaks of the explicit only on special occasions – Daisy's father's boyhood initiation by an older woman; Daisy's rape at fifteen by her half-brother, a difficult boy; a lesbian episode which does *not* involve Daisy . . . big erotic set-pieces like that.

Krantz may have perceived that, even in the two short years between the books, the sexual hard sell is already *déjà vu*. The women's lib backlash supervened. Daisy's best friend, the 'ribald' automobile heiress, profligate as she is, must now descend to playing hard to get to stir the interest of the man for whom she really cares. Femininity is back in fashion.

If Billie is always fumbling in men's trousers, Daisy's sex life, somewhat inhibited by that rape, is done with a rose-tinted delicacy. Men part her thighs and whisper, 'May I?' proving that she is a real lady.

Krantz herself acknowledges that Billie, with her 'huntress's stride' and 'almost virile beauty', is an out-of-date model, when the cosmetics executive in *Princess Daisy* says: 'I think the time has come to return to a romantic sell in fragrance, a classy, feminine sell.' That romantic sell in fragrance is the one to which Princess Daisy lends (or, rather, sells, for a million bucks) her name. And the book is a 'romantic sell', too.

The novel's title suggests a fancy conflation of Henry James's *The Princess Casamassima* and *Daisy Miller*. It hints at sophisticated, cosmopolitan goings-on, and the novel spends time in London, Venice and other romantic European places, besides SoHo. To a certain extent, pure snobbery – an awed gasp at the divinity that still hedges White Russian royals, at least for Krantz – supplies the charge in *Princess Daisy* which sex has supplied in *Scruples*. Such good, old-fashioned snobbery is making a big come-back these days.

Scruples, however, has the more startling vision. It offers a total eroticisation of the idea of the shop, the shop as magic brothel. In Billie's boutique, not only do you pick 'clothes that are right for you, but you had to be hot for them, dizzy with a desire that can't be forced, any more than a faked orgasm can be enjoyed'.

Buying a dress is, or ought to be like a good fuck (*sic*). Customers are described as 'gratification junkies'. They spend freely, recalling the Victorian use of the verb, 'to spend', as a euphemism for ejaculation. Cash has an intimate relation to libido. Never, you might say, has it been so hard.

A shop like 'Scruples', we are told, will succeed in any city 'full of very rich, very bored, very elegant women'. All it needs is a large leisure class. It is an emporium that expresses the values of imperialism in a late Roman sense. Profit has no relation at all to productive labour. The shop could only have been conceived in a period of sharp inflation, where there has been a loss of faith in money as a medium of exchange. The wealth that the customers of 'Scruples' expend within it is real, but meaningless. Like fairy gold.

And Billie deeply needs her shop to be a financial smash, just because she herself doesn't need the money. Similarly, it is central to the mystique of Krantz as author that she herself is not short of a bob or two. She is, apparently, a well-to-do woman, married to a Hollywood film producer, and a graduate of classy Wellesley.

No rags-to-riches story, hers. The story of Judith Krantz, like that of her heroines, has as its motto the fiscal policy of the Reagan administration: 'Unto every one that hath shall be given'. The *real* poor exist in an unimaginable limbo.

That Krantz is rich and worldly-wise to start with is what gives authenticity to her account of the high life. Even if Kenneth Clark himself told you how lunch at the Connaught Hotel was 'one of the premier experiences of Western civilisation, the Uffizi gallery of dining', you might well think he was having you on. The serene self-confidence with which Krantz imparts this information puts it beyond question.

Throughout both novels, Krantz is always comfortingly *there*, not in person, but as an utterly authoritative authorial voice, imparting what purports to be solid information about the world, often in almost aphoristic cadences. From *Scruples*: 'Going into research is the only way a doctor can positively insure himself against making a decent living'; 'The [Cannes film festival] audience is the most purely vicious since Christians were thrown to the lions.' From *Princess Daisy*: 'There is no team so committed to their joint and individual successes as the homosexual husband happily married to a lesbian wife.' And so on, and on.

Her novels offer, at a modest price, what purports to be an insider's comprehensive knowledge of the inside workings of the tiny, glamorous world of the gossip columns and media fame. They are handbooks of a certain kind of social mobility, masquerading as good reads. The information about what to eat, how to dress, where to buy (she is hot on real restaurants, real brand names, and real shops as well as imaginary ones) is guilelessly presented in terms of fantasy.

This is fiction as service industry to an emergent class of media aristocrats; or, at least, would-be media aristocrats. Her initial success came with just such a class: with the people who bought the paperback rights, and the television rights, and God knows what other rights, and ensured that both novels would be bestsellers long before the books ever got to the wire racks in the paperback outlets, and thence to the person in the shopping market.

Towards the end of *Princess Daisy*, Judith Krantz starts playing a dangerous game, under the circumstances. Virgil to the reader's Dante in the inferno of the advertising industry, she invites us to inspect at close hand the very confidence trick which lures the cash out of the pocket in the first place. 'When cosmetics and perfumes start selling for anything *near* the price they cost to produce,' ruminates an executive, 'it'd be like fucking Russia.'

Here, in her desire to identify the reader/consumer with the men at the control boards of power, she forgets that the reader *is* consumer. She comes perilously close to labelling her or him as a credulous gull, and so disclosing, in all its luminous purity, the value system underlying her novels.

This is the value system of capitalism in its great rock-candy-mountain phase, where only money makes more money. Which is precisely where it's at in the United States now.

New Society, 1981

Robert Darnton: The Great Cat Massacre

Had Jacques Vincent not served up for dinner to his printing shop apprentices the gristly leftovers already turned down by his cats, those cats might have lived longer. As it was, the apprentices finally staged a mass trial and a public execution of not only their master's cats – paying special attention to his wife's beloved tabby – but of every other cat they could lay their hands on. In fact, of all the cats whose yowling made the apprentices' nights at the rue Saint Severin hideous, while they huddled in their cold and filthy garret scurrilously debating whether or not the vicar was screwing the missus.

We are in Paris, about a third of the way through the eighteenth century; coming events are casting their shadows before them, and the missus, returning horrified to the scene of the slaughter, will read the subtext of the incident at one glance: 'These wicked men can't kill the masters so they have killed my pussy.'

But as for the apprentices, the cat killers themselves, well, they can't get a word out for laughing. They are, according to one of their number, 'besides themselves with joy'. Each of them might have said, in Daley Thompson's words of only the other day: 'I haven't laughed so much since my granny caught her tit in the mangle.'

This metaphor would be quite bizarre enough to catch Robert Darnton's attention were his special area twentieth-century Britain rather than eighteenth-century France. What would he make of it?

This uproarious laughter of the apprentices is the kind of thing that excites Robert Darnton's curiosity. He pricks up his ears when he hears the laughter echoing out of the pages of the autobiography that one of them, Nicolas Contat, put together later on in the course of a life of no particular consequence.

Robert Darnton is concerned with the history of the way we think. It has taken a big change in the way we think of history to transform Nicolas Contat's account of artisan life under the Old Regime into something we are going to take seriously. Up until 100 years or so ago, most ordinary Europeans could not leave records of their lives and times because they were illiterate, and nobody literate bothered to do it for them: Nicolas Contat was able to take advantage of the literacy demanded of him by his craft of printer. Otherwise there is folklore, there are proverbs, songs, stories – the longest essay in this entertaining book of essays is to do with folktales – and there are memories, and there is silence. The everyday lives and habits of the vast majority of those who have lived in this world before us are as mysterious to us as the bottom of the sea.

Out of this abyss, in this instance, come the screams of dying cats and the heartless and immoderate laughter of younger men.

Just what is so funny about killing cats, ponders Darnton. And why did the apprentice printers laugh quite so much. He puzzles away at the problem. He worries it, like a puppy with a slipper. Because, if he can work out just what it was that made the lads go into such paroxysms, then he will obtain the key to 'an alien system of meaning'.

This is Darnton's method. He wanders through the archives as if on a kind of botanising walk, on the qui-vive for the obscure, the incomprehensible, the odd. 'By picking at the document where it is most opaque, we may be able to unravel an alien system of meaning. The thread might even lead into a strange and wonderful world view.'

He sees the past as the domain of absolute otherness, a definitive elsewhere of difference from a present which he sometimes forgets himself so much as to regard as a monolith of *non*-otherness, a here-and-now that covers the globe. For example, he says that Contat's description of the cat massacre 'strikes the modern reader as unfunny, if not downright repulsive'. It struck this modern reader as rather less unfunny than the notion of a poor old lady with her tit caught in a mangle, and I am a cat-lover myself.

The habits of mind and the interpersonal relations of craft apprentices are very important to the story; these have been considerably modified by changing material conditions, but remain striking in their archaism. Darnton makes much of the point that his eighteenth-century France, the France of the Enlightenment, is enlightened only in fits and starts and tiny pockets of the urban intelligentsia; that the past, in all its otherness, infiltrated the present at every moment, making a mockery of the notion of the modern. If we do think of the past as being very much like the present, that is because most human beings have always thought in that kind of continuum. Making the break, acknowledging that human nature is *not* continuous, is a very great and dramatic change in our grasp of reality.

These are immensely pleasurable essays to read, and perhaps Darnton's easy-going, almost ingratiating charm of manner is partially intended to disarm the reader into taking for granted a new way of looking at the world. He warns us that we must expect culture shock history; that we must never think of the past as just like the here-and-now in fancy dress. But in escaping with Darnton the danger of a false sense of familiarity with the past, his reader runs the risk of becoming a tourist of otherness. On every page, one is tempted to say: 'How quaint! How odd!' Darnton's explorations of unfamiliar views of eighteenth-century France are on the verge of becoming a display of the picturesque, which is the tried and true method of marginalising otherness.

Darnton remarks, disarming as usual: 'Straying from the beaten path may not be much of a methodology . . .' Disarmingly, and also disingenuously; he has a good deal more rigour about him than he will easily let on, even if that rigour sometimes stops short of his prose style and he is capable of letting slip lines like: 'there is an indefinable *je ne sais quoi* about cats' when opening discussion about the kind of cultural resonances the eighteenth-century French cat carried round with her.

Ten closely packed pages later, it turns out that the '*je ne sais quoi*' about cats is not indefinable at all; Darnton has just defined it, in all its folkloric and symbolic richness. In the first essay in the book, 'Peasants Tell Tales: the Meaning of Mother Goose', he has already dissected the significance of the tom of the same period, blotting the rigour of this copybook by ascribing to Puss in Boots of the well-known tale the status of embodiment of the essence of French pragmatism and guile. I think this is pushing it a bit; not by quarrying too much significance out of a fairy story, but by too free and unexamined a use of national stereotypes.

But Darnton is irresistibly engaging in the company of Mother Goose, and the savage brutality of the world described in the fairytale, where incest, sodomy, rape, bestiality, cannibalism are commonplaces. He puts the psychoanalytic interpreters of fairytales firmly in their place: 'Far from veiling their message with symbols, the storytellers of eighteenth-century France portrayed a world of raw and naked brutality.' A Hobbesian world, in which parents leave their children in the forest to spare themselves the sight of them starving to death in front of their eyes; in which guile and trickery are the only way out of the slow death-in-life of the 'immobile history' of the village; in which the best happy ending you can think of is a good dinner. This is the true otherness of the past, described by the illiterate storytellers; they depict the matrix of poverty, want and degradation which formed their real and their symbolic world.

Amongst other richly enjoyable essays is the one about the file on the intelligentsia kept by a Parisian police inspector during the 1740s, which turns out to be a collection of thumbnail sketches, potted biographies and jotted-down literary criticism. We learn, for example, that Diderot is 'a very clever boy but extremely dangerous'. And there is also a remarkable essay on the response of his readership to the work of Jean-Jacques Rousseau: in particular, the letters of a Jean Ranson, a merchant from La Rochelle, who organised his life according to the precepts of Rousseau – no greater honour can a fan pay – and, happily, organised it not unsuccessfully. More successfully than Rousseau himself in fact.

New Society, 1984

Irish Folk Tales, Arab Folktales

Review of Henry Glassie (ed.), *Irish Folk Tales* and Inea Bushnaq (ed.),
Arab Folk Tales.

Thomas Gray surely did not mean to be patronising when he referred to the 'mute, inglorious Milton' who might have been slumbering in the country churchyard. But if he indeed meant 'mute' metaphorically rather than physically, then it is difficult to imagine even an illiterate Milton refraining from discourse. Surely a ploughboy Milton would have made a lot of noise; and even if only other members of the rural proletariat heard him, that does not mean he would have been silent.

Few poets have been so intellectually well armed as the real Milton, yet the antique glamour of the blind singer still clings to him, so that one thinks of him in the same breath as Homer, who according to tradition, was also blind, and created epics too, and yet was almost certainly not illiterate but simply preliterate – that is, could not have been literate even had he wished to be so. Language exists before its own written form. The voice is the first instrument of literature; narrative precedes text.

These first two plump handsome volumes in the projected Penguin Folklore Library transform oral narrative into texts, so that the tales will survive the voices of their narrators. Inea Bushnaq notes: 'It is a wistful moment when interest in recording an oral tradition wakens.' It means that the culture of the illiterate, that is, the poor, is no longer being taken for granted. Sometimes it means that it has started to die. As the voices fall silent, one by one, so we lose irreplaceable parts of our past.

Robert Darnton, the historian says (in his essay 'Peasants Tell Tales: the meaning of Mother Goose') that folktales 'provide a rare opportunity to make contact with the illiterate masses who have disappeared into the past without leaving a trace'. This is rather an apocalyptic way of putting it. We may not know much about the lives of those 'illiterate masses' but most of us are directly descended from them, and we retain, if we have lost everything else from the oral tradition, a complicated folklore of family.

Besides, a flourishing illiterate culture has always wonderfully nourished the productions of the literati. Henry Glassie remainds us in his introduction to *Irish Folk Tales* that James Joyce named *Finnegans Wake* after a Dublin street song, even borrowed the plot.

But Ireland is a special case, In the last years of the nineteenth century, Yeats and Synge and Lady Gregory went out on purpose to listen to country storytellers, to strive consciously to reach out to those who had slipped through the huge holes in the net of history down which the common people vanish – to reconstruct from the mouths of the poor the basis for an authentically Irish literature, a project that bore abundant fruit. (It is interesting to read, in Inea Bushnaq's book, that there is 'a lively folklore department in the university at Bir Zeit', on the debated West Bank, and an increasing interest is the collection and preservation of Palestinian culture.)

The stories assembled by Henry Glassie include some from those collections made by Yeats and his friends nearly a century ago, some from other nineteenth-century collections, others recorded far more recently by the editor himself and by other collectors currently working in Ireland, a nation which no longer contains a significant proportion of illiterates, but is, folklorically, far from a worked-out seam.

An American academic who has made the English language folklore of Ireland his special study, he is scrupulous about notes and sources; his bibliography is enormous and comprehensive; his *Irish Folk Tales* is both scholarly reference book and a pleasure to browse in – but the spare fluidity of the language of his informants has not rubbed off on him, alas.

He is grievously afflicted with fine writing ('Pure darkness welcomes the winds that skim off the ocean', etc.), and embarrassingly lyrical about his informants. 'They call him eccentric . . . they call him a saint,' he says of one. What does his informant call Henry Glassie?

But here are stories about Finn MacCumhail and the Fenians, as Jeremiah Curtain noted them down in Donegal in 1887; stories about St Finbar, and St Brigit, and St Kevin who made apples grow on a willow tree; stories about true folk heroes – Robert Burns, Daniel O'Connell. Yes, indeed; here is an Irish Cinderella (in which the three sisters are called, Fair, Brown, and Trembling). And a giant who opines of a visitor: 'I think you large of one mouthful and small of two mouthfuls.'

There are also some moving examples of legendary history. For example, how Cromwell possessed a black Bible that was so big 'it would take a horse to draw it'. When his servant opened up this Bible on the sly, lots of little men came out of it and ran around until the servant cried: 'Off ye go in the name of the Divell!'

The circumstances of life in these stories are universally harsh and the happy endings few and far between. A good breakfast is a pot full of boiled turnips. Drink is a curse. A man named George Armstrong went to Australia but all he came back with was thruppence and when he got home again he weighed so little his mother put him in a basket and kept him by the fire.

Inea Bushnaq's tales from Libya, Iraq, Morocco, Algeria, Syria – from all over the Arab world – reflect a different kind of life, one full of delicious smells and sights and sounds, fresh coffee, baking bread, rosewater and incense, flowers, embroidery, cloth of gold, apricots, figs. The Iraqi

Cinderella wears golden clogs and a pearl comb in her hair. The people might be poor but the imagination is lavish.

The Arab countries have in common a language and a religion, Islam, and a still predominantly peasant culture in which storytelling as pastime and entertainment has survived in good order rather longer than it has in the advanced industrialised countries, although, as Inea Bushnaq says, television may well deal the *coup de grâce* with amazing speed.

Her method is quite different from Henry Glassie's: she has compiled an anthology from a variety of text materials, splicing some together and has selected stories 'most likely to interest the English reader'. It would be nice to know what criteria she used in picking them out.

She provides a vast amount of cultural background in a series of introductions to different sections of the collection, with their mouth-watering titles – Djinn, Ghouls and Afreets, Tales Told in Houses Made of Hair (that is, the goat-hair tents of the Bedouin), Beasts that Roam the Earth, and Birds that Fly with Wings. But this is not a scholarly collection so much as a triumphant shining, glorious labour of love.

Perhaps Inea Bushnaq is more cavalier with her sources than a professional folklorist because she has heard many of the stories herself when she was a child and truly feels that they belong to her for just that moment of the telling, when the storyteller makes the story his or her own, the fleeting gift of the storyteller.

The stories invent a world of marvels – flying carpets, girls from whose mouths fall lilies and jasmine each time they speak, a boy whose ears are so sharp he can hear the dew fall. The cry goes out: 'A calamity and a scandal! The king's new queen has given birth to a puppy dog and a water jug!' A green bird spells out the stark terror of family life: 'My father's wife, she took my life. My father ate me for his dinner.' And once upon a time, there was a woman called Rice Pudding . . . .

Guardian, 1987

Bruce Chatwin: The Songlines

It is now common knowledge that the people who lived in Australia before the island continent was given that name never got around to inventing the wheel because they were too absorbed in metaphysics.

This could be seen as a positive argument against metaphysics, for the contemplation of the transcendental did not equip the first Australians sufficiently against the sudden arrival of technologically adept and ethically unscrupulous invaders. But Bruce Chatwin's expository novel *The Songlines*, is both a defence of Aboriginal metaphysics as a way of life and a piece of metaphysical speculation in its own right.

Human beings, Bruce Chatwin posits, are born to wander; indeed, the source of all evil is to settle down. Appropriately, the form of his novel is that of a journey. Its hero, an Englishman named Bruce, travels into the magical aridity Australians call the Centre, in order, for compelling reasons of his own, to find out what a 'songline' is. His guide is a wise young man of Cossack extraction called Arkady.

Arkady is employed to map out the sacred sites of the Aboriginals so that a proposed new railway line will not destroy a single one of them. This, as he points out, is difficult, because, 'if you look at it *their* way . . . the whole of bloody Australia is a sacred site'.

A sacred site, which the totemic ancestors – the grand, original wallaby, and budgerigar, and lizard and so on – once, literally, sang into existence, stone by stone, thorn by thorn; they sang into being that vast, dry, almost supernaturally beautiful country. A country which is continually being sung into existence again and again during the ritual journeyings, the walkabouts, of the tribespeople. (I hope I've got this right. It is all very complicated.)

'In theory, at least, the whole of Australia could be read as a musical score,' says Bruce Chatwin. A musical score of stunning complexity and numinous significance, of which the learning is the most imperative business in the whole world. He quotes Heidegger, from *What Are Poets For?*: 'The song still remains which names the land over which it sings.'

The singing goes on and if there is no proof that it maintains the world in its precarious existence, neither is there proof that it does not.

The searcher after songlines meets and talks with strange, learned, displaced men and women, among them a policeman whose passions are weight-lifting and Spinoza; a furious old bush-crazed Communist who gives an account of the atom bomb tests at Maralinga in the mode of black farce; a naked philosopher of the bush who gives his occupation: Footwalking all the time all over the world.'

Footwalking is Bruce Chatwin's passion, too, and, in the course of nearly 300 pages, he investigates the significance not only of the songlines, that mythic and incorporeal map of Australia, but also of his own travels, especially those among the nomadic peoples of Africa, pulling everything together to form a grand theory of footwalking, and much more.

And all this springs from an obsession with what the Eskimos call 'the Great Unrest', a conviction that human beings, just as birds do, feel an irrepressible urge, from time to time, to migrate, to slough off attachments, to get on the move and stay there.

More specifically, Chatwin conjectures that 'Natural Selection has designed us – from the structure of our brain-cells to the structure of our big toe – for a career of seasonal journeys *on foot* through a blistering land of thorn-scrub or desert.'

The narrative of Bruce's journey is interspersed with digressions such as a visit to a solitary priest who has carved above the door of his hut the apt legend: 'Foxes have holes, birds of the air have nests But the Son of Man had no place to lay his head.' This priest says of a friendly marsupial: 'My brother the wallaby.' Who could resist the notion of an Antipodean St Francis.

There is an equally endearing account of another visit, to the Nemadi, wanderers of the Saharan Empty Quarter known as 'Outcasts of the Wilderness', where an ancient, deaf and dumb old lady gives Bruce a smile that lasts a full three minutes, a smile, he tells us, 'like a message from the Golden Age'. A smile that teaches him to reject out of hand all arguments for the nastiness of human nature. (As a tramp he meets outside the London Library finds out, Bruce is a very soft touch indeed; he seems to have lost all trace of cynicism on just those very roads where most travellers acquire it.)

The Australian journey eventually founders in a flash flood in a remote Pintupi settlement, where Bruce finds time to unpack his notebooks of a lifetime's journeying. The remainder of the book is largely composed of sections taken from these notebooks., a patchwork of quotations – Pascal, Gautama Buddha, the Bible and I don't know what else, memories, and increasingly, speculation. Here, the fictional Bruce and the real Bruce Chatwin seem to come together.

The patchwork is assembled with a good deal of art. Rimbaud's heart-felt cry from Ethiopia: 'What am I doing here?' is juxtaposed against an account of a vile town in Brazil: 'The stucco façade is painted a pale mint green with the words CHARM HOTEL in bold, black letters. A leaking gutter pipe has washed away the letter C, so that it now reads . . .'

Bruce Chatwin discusses the nature of the murder of Abel, the wandering herdsman, by Cain, the gardener; was Cain jealous of the free spirit? He proposes the superior ethics of the hunter-gatherers; he has an aristocratic disdain for what you could call roots and quotes a Bedouin proverb: 'Raids are our agriculture.'

He recalls an interview with Konrad Lorenz, who wrote *On Aggression* and this leads into a series of speculations on instinctual behaviour, the origins of human society, the possible origins of our fear of the dark, the nature of fear in babies, the instincts of mothers and children.

When he cites John Bowlby's work in this connection, however, I felt a tremor of unease, for Bowlby's work has very largely been discredited, if not by other child psychologists then certainly by women at the sharp end of babies. And the speculation shows signs of turning into very sophisticated science fiction – science fiction in the purest sense; speculative fiction about science.

So, at last, we arrive in the Transvaal, gazing with Bruce Chatwin at the fossilised bones of the earliest members of humanity, perhaps the very earliest, for it is out of Africa that many people now believe came memory and language, the qualities that make us human. Magnificently, rather crazily, Bruce Chatwin offers us his own version of the Fall of Man. But it is not a Fall at all; he hypothesises that, at the very beginning of the human race, we did not succumb to the Prince of Darkness but instead, vanquished him.

We arrive at this awesome piece of theological revisionism thus; in those days there roamed a beast – Bruce Chatwin thinks it may have been some kind of giant leopard – who preyed specifically upon primates. On the conquest of this fatal creature depended the fate of Man on earth.

When we invented the weapon, we overcame the forces of destruction the terrible Beast whose memory, to this day, scares little babies and haunts our own imaginations with needless fears. 'Compared to this victory, the rest of our achievements may be seen as so many frills'. Even if the Beast bowed out of history and left us with the weapon in our hands.

When Bruce finally returns to his own narrative, it is to conclude with Arkady's wedding, but the true romance of this always enchanting, sometimes infuriating book is not that of Arkady and Marian but the one between an Englishman and the wilderness. The journey of the one within the other leads to the only happy ending the traveller can honestly aspire to, a happy death.

In the bush, Bruce and his companions visit three old men at a ritual site; they have sung their way back where they belong. Three old men who knew where they were going, 'smiling at death in the shade of a ghost-gum'.

Guardian 1987

Through a Text Backwards: The Resurrection of the House of Usher

There is a certain kind of pictorial joke, a picture that presents the same image in two different ways. If you look at the portrait one way up, it looks like this; and if you turn it upside down, lo and behold! the elements of the representation turn themselves into a quite different representation. If it was a sad face, turn it upside down and it becomes a happy face. And vice versa.

The elements in Poe's voluptuous tales of terror – 'The Fall of the House of Usher', 'Ligeia', 'Berenice' – are over-determined, so that it is very difficult to find out what is going on. That is, to find out what is *really* going on, what is going on under the surface. Because at first it looks as if *everything* is on the surface; there is a grand theatricality about Poe, the true child of strolling players.

His theatricality ensures we know all the time that the scenery is cardboard, the blade of the axe is silver paint on papier maché, the men and women in the stories unreal, two-dimensional stock characters, yet still we shiver. The imagery is simply that of the most conventional tale of terror and easily translates into the medium of the conventional horror movie. His landscapes are those of the commonplace picturesque. We feel we know it so well just because it is so familiar; we feel we have been here before.

'I have been here before.' In *The Interpretation of Dreams*, Freud says this feeling of familiarity means that we are remembering the bodies of our mother. If so, Poe's mother's body is a haunted house, one haunted by allusion. Allusions to the blasted heath in *King Lear* perhaps. To the castle where Macbeth killed the king, in the play from whence flapped that 'raven over the infected house', perhaps. And mightn't the body of an actress contain within it just such abandoned, weathered stage sets?

But, within the terms of the conventions of the tale of terror, Poe's compulsive sexual pathology is presented as straightforwardly as if everybody loved corpses best. The latent content of these stories greets us first, as in that extraordinary story, 'Berenice', where the husband becomes obsessed with his wife's teeth and finally pulls them all out, each one. This strategy for defeating the vagina *endentata* is presented with such unselfconscious relish it is tempting to tease out a subconscious meaning, as those jokes about Freudian dream symbolism: a man dreams about his wilting penis, it means he has a great longing for a new necktie.

There is a slippery quality about Poe's tales of sexual terror. They are and they are not what they claim to be.

I decided to adopt the method of the painters of the double portraits I described a moment ago. I decided that I would invert 'The Fall of the House of Usher' – play it backwards, in the same way as one can play a movie backwards, and see what face is showed to me, then, and what story that face told about the Ushers and their author.

Consider the following story: 'The Resurrection of the House of Usher'. A storm rages.

We see before us a sullen tarn. Above, in the stormy sky, a blood red moon. We may suppose that the tarn reflects the moonlight and therefore looks as though it is filled not with water but with blood.

Out of this pool, the House that is synonymous with the Usher family reconstructs itself. Stone by fungus-eroded stone, the ancient mansion rises from the crimson tarn, refreshed by its bath of blood just as the Countess Elizabeth Bàthory, the Hungarian vampire, was by the baths of blood she used to take long ago, in Transylvania, in a benighted mansion not unlike this one.

The zig-zag fissure that runs from the base of the building to its roof now seals itself up so that we can no longer see the baleful head of the moon peering through the gap.

The wild tempest continues to rage.

The narrator – let us call him Edgar Allan Poe. For Poe consistently invites the reader to make this identification of the narrator with him. No matter how unreal the circumstances of the tale, how improbable Poe's presence there in the first person singular, the witness, the on-the-spot reporter, always lends them plausibility. It is the trick of an old news-paperman. Edgar Allan Poe arrives. He is the child of a pair of strolling players, David Poe and Elizabeth Arnold; picture his arrival as something like that of the Player King in *Hamlet*. Perhaps he has just arrived at the House of Usher, to perform a one-man show, perhaps. At the special request of Roderick Usher. A one-man show consisting, say, of a selec-tion of Hamlet's soliloquies for he wears a suit of Hamlet's colours, i.e. sable.

Fleeing the fury of the storm, the newcomer makes across the causeway with all speed towards the ambivalent hospitality the frightful walls of the ancient house may offer.

We are – or, at least, Poe was born and spent all his life in – a country where there are no castles, that is, the USA. At least, there are no indige-nous castles. There may be one or two that have, like London Bridge, been shipped from their original sites by millionaires nostalgic for the pic-turesque, sent across the Atlantic in boxes of numbered bricks and put together again in Texas, California, Tennessee . . . but these imported castles are few and far between and, besides, were shipped over well after Poe's day.

Unless he caught a glimpse of one during his brief period of schooling in England in his childhood (although there are no castles in Stoke Newington, now a suburb of London, then a village outside London) it is possible that Poe had never seen a real castle.

Not that he ever specifies a castle when he describes the great, crumbling mansions of his imagination, where his neurasthenic men and women play out their grim charades of love and death. Yet their interior design's that of castles, though not the castles of European fact but the castles of European fancy. The tapestries, billowing in chill draughts, the armorial trophies, the ancient furniture – we have seen all this before, too.

These great, doomed mansions and their melancholy, antique interiors may always be found in landscapes of the most extraordinary ferocity. The château in 'The Oval Portrait', a pile of 'commingled gloom and grandeur', lies in the wildest possible kind of countryside. Its isolation is absolute.

The abbey purchased by the hero of 'Ligeia' occupies a site in 'one of the wildest and least frequented portions of fair England' (one of the very few times that Poe gives some geographical location to these dream palaces). He describes the 'gloomy and dreary grandeur of the building, the most savage aspect of the domain'.

'The Masque of the Red Death' takes place in a 'castellated abbey'.

'There are no towers in the land more time-honoured' than those of the 'gloomy, grey, hereditary halls' of the husband of the unfortunate Berenice in the story of the same name.

The principal feature of the House of Usher seems to Poe to be 'that of an excessive antiquity'. Most of his mansions are indistinguishable from one another in terms of gloom and antiquity, but *this* house has a conspicuous deformity, 'a tangled web of fungus' that 'covers its exterior'. It must look as if it had been born in a caul.

There are no indigenous castles in the USA but the title of the Gothic melodrama in which Poe's mother first appeared on any stage was *The Mysteries of the Castle*. Elizabeth Arnold had just arrived in America with her own mother; it was April 1796, and Elizabeth Arnold was nine years old.

Horace Walpole's *The Castle of Otranto* had been published as long ago as 1765, setting in train a great vogue for tales of unease. Mrs Radcliffe's *The Mysteries of Udolpho* was published in 1794. The architecture of anxiety was a literary convention long before Poe was born.

Most notably, the castellated abbey and gaunt mansions of Poe, isolated, abandoned in the middle of the howling wilderness, resemble the most forbidden of all the forbidden places of de Sade: the castle in *The Hundred Days at Sodom* where ritual tableaux of the most extravagant sexual cruelty are acted out daily by a small group of aristocrats using imprisoned victims whose only hope of escape lies in death. (Poe's scheme of things differs in this particular from de Sade's; for Poe, death need not necessarily put an end to suffering'.)

The mansions, abbeys and castles where Justine is tortured and her sister, Juliette, wreaks her infamies are built of the same imaginative fabric as the castles of Poe. This room of Juliette's might just as well come from one of Poe's stories: 'A dim, a lugubrious lamp hung in the middle of the room whose vaults were likewise covered with dismal appurtenances . . .' but de Sade gives the game away, here; he goes on blithely: 'various instruments of torture were scattered here and there'. Poe retains enough self-control to keep the instruments of torture out of the bedchamber, at least where women are concerned — most of the time, at least. I don't know if Poe actually read de Sade; the dissemination of banned books is a difficult area to research. I do not even know if de Sade was translated into English at this period. Anyway, Poe would have denied reading de Sade.

To return to our inversions.

Edgar Allan Poe, the hero and narrator of 'The Fall of the House of Usher', the Ishmael of this *Moby Dick*, rushes headlong into the freshly reconstituted house. (Obviously, if we are running the story backwards, so is Poe himself running backwards, but I don't propose to retain that much fidelity to the conceit.)

He speeds up the worm-eaten stair and makes his way to an upstairs bedroom. There he stops, aghast. A man and a woman are clasped together on the floor, still as death, locked in what seems to be either the fatal embrace of a love suicide or else a post-coital slumber so profound it is as good as death.

A couple bear a marked physical resemblance to one another:

A cadaverousness of complexion; lips somewhat thin and very pallid; but of a surpassingly beautiful curve; a nose of delicate Hebrew model, but with a breadth of nostril unusual and similar formations; a finely-moulded chin, speaking, in its want of prominence, of a want of moral energy; hair of a more than web-like softness and tenuity; these features, with an inordinate expansion above the regions of the temple, made up altogether a countenance not easily to be forgotten.

They look like one another because they are twins, each the fatal double of the other, It is also a face that somewhat resembles Poe's own in the celebrated photograph, with his bulging brow, pale, delicate, intellectual features and curing, disdainful lips. (See how he writes himself into the script, as witness or voyeur, or second cousin twice removed of the protagonists.)

And perhaps this face also reminds him of the face of his own mother, if, indeed, he remembers it, because she died when she was twenty-four years old and he was two and perhaps retained no concrete memory, only a vague memory, an idea, an impression of the face of the woman he loved and lost, his lost dear one.

Certainly the two corpses on the floor look very much like Ligeia, the heroine of the authentic resurrection story, with her Hebraic nose and large, dark eyes; and the editors of the Harvard Editions of *The Collected Works of Edgar Allan Poe* claim, on I don't know what authority, that Ligeia looks like Elizabeth Arnold. (Who, therefore, must have given much of her face to her son, his only inheritance.)

Gazing in wonder at these felled lovers – or are they lovers? – our hero, whom we have decided to call Edgar Allan Poe, sees that there is blood on the woman's white robes, those robes that look so much like a shroud, and 'the evidence of bitter struggle upon every portion of her emaciated body'.

Perhaps she has just been raped and finally managed to wreak vengeance on her rapist.

Or perhaps her appearance is more like that of a woman who has just given birth. But in that case, what about the young man? Unless – it is he who has just been born?

They lie still, victims of some nameless and presumably erotic catastropohe, on the floor of the gloomy bedchamber, whilst the storm continues to rage outside and the narrator, with his face the mirror image of theirs, each of which is the mirror image of each other, gazes on, in horror, until the woman at last – oh, horror upon horror! – comes to life again.

Or was she only stunned? Or has she genuinely turned to life? Or is it something unspeakably else?

Be that as it may, now she rises up, as if the presence of Poe has set the action in motion – as indeed it has. Without him, nothing would be happening. He is more essential to the plot than either of the Ushers or their dilapidated habitation.

She rises up, her face a mask of horror. Screaming, she departs, backing out of the ebony doors of the apartment, leaving behind her on the air the vivid spook of her voice. The doors close behind her with a crash.

Her partner, her lover, her brother, her twin, scrambles unharmed to his feet, to discover that the newly arrived Poe is scarcely coherent from fear at what he has witnessed. Roderick Usher, believing the visitor to have been deranged by what he has just witnessed, exclaims: 'Madam!'

and then hastens to reassure: 'I tell you that now she stands without the door!'

And indeed she is gone.

A series of diminishing bangs and crashes indicate that the Lady Madeline is returning to from whence she came, leaving her brother and companion blessedly alone.

She is returning to her coffin.

For I do think the Lady Madeline is more undead than prematurely buried, and it was Poe's fate to have found her at her ungodly feast athwart the body of his friend, her brother, Roderick Usher. (Poe is suspiciously straightforward about his enthusiasm for dead and dying women.) 'The death of a beautiful woman is, unquestionably, the most poetical topic in the world,' he opined in 'The Philosophy of Composition', which should therefore, by rights, be retitled: 'The Philosophy of Decomposition'. It is a categorical statement. He will admit of no argument.

He was the child of a beautiful actress who died, of consumption, in his early infancy. If he remembered her at all, it would be the memory of a slow death. He watched his young wife die of the same disease; it took her somewhat longer, five years. His fascination for female morbidity is, however, a little over-determined; think how often the beautiful women in his stories turn out not to have been dead at all. Berenice wasn't really dead. Ligeia, by the sheer force of her will or of her husband's desire, returns to life through the possession of another woman's body. If Lady Madeline dies once, to rise again, might she not rise again and again and again from no matter how many deaths?

It is reasonable to suppose that Poe did not want his mother to die, or his beloved Virginia to die. It is reasonable to suppose that, somewhere, at some subterranean level of the unconscious, he did not really believe they were dead but only play-acting, isn't it?

The coffin of Lady Madeline rests, not in a graveyard, but in a vault in the cellarage of the House of Usher, a vault that at one time – renewed shades of de Sade – had been used as a torture chamber. Poe tells us so: 'the vault had been used in remote feudal times for worst purposes of a *donjon keep*'. The vault is sheathed in copper; apparently it was also used, at one time, to store gunpowder.

Lady Madeline's coffin is shut in by an iron door but now the men know she can get out whenever she wants to, in spite of all their precautions, so they may as well bring her coffin out of the vault, now, and let her be part of the household again.

They cannot resist opening the coffin and peeking at her face, which is their own face, and note that it has the freshness and liveliness characteristic of the undead, with 'the mockery of a faint blush upon the bosom and the face, and that suspiciously lingering smile upon the lip which is so terrible in death'.

But now they know that appearances are deceptive, that she is *not* dead. Or, more precisely, that she *is* dead, but that, for some reason, death, like an unsatisfactory injection, has not *taken*.

(If we start the story with her attack on Roderick Usher, and *then* she trots off back into her coffin, obviously we posit that her death – or an event similar to a death – has taken place before the story beings. The fiction cannot be tinkered with in such a way as to stop her dying, alas, but, seen retrospectively, her 'death' is a highly ambiguous state, even more ambiguous than it is if seen in the original sequence.)

The two young men lift up the coffin between them and bear it from the vault. And –

– and the text is silent. Presumably they take it to her bedroom. Poe doesn't say. Playing the story backwards as we are doing, all we see now is that now the coffin disappears, here one minute, gone the next.

Poe never tells us where the coffin has come from, anyway. The Ushers probably had a stock of empty coffins laid in, anyway, in case of sudden emergency. They probably felt about coffins like other people feel about spare beds. All Poe says about the coffin is incorporated in a verb: 'The body having been encoffined, we two alone (i.e. Roderick and the narrator) bore it to its rest.'

(Or, rather, to its presumed rest.)

If we invert this sequence of events, the two young men now bear the coffin *away* from its rest, into a silence broken only by the wild strains of Roderick's guitar. Perhaps she has been taken to the music room.

Like Pater's Mona Lisa, the Lady Madeline has been dead many times and learned the secrets of the grave. She lies on her bed in her somnolent, half-sleeping state, neither fully dead nor fully alive, the life of a sentient plant, waiting, waiting, waiting until the men downstairs call up for her to come and frighten them.

That is her lot. That is her fate. The reader's last glimpse of her is of a domestic spectre, not the angel of the health of Victorian domesticity but a house-ghost, the terrible beloved.

> the Lady Madeline . . . passed slowly through a remote portion of the apartment and, without having noticed my presence, disappeared. I regarded her with an utter astonishment mingled with dread – and yet I found it impossible to account for such feelings.

We know better to account for them, now. We cannot believe that those we love could leave us; we cannot believe that, in our hearts, we might have been glad that they were gone. That was how vampires were born, our of grief, relief and guilt.

'FEAR!' cries Roderick and, ecstatic with dread, collapses in a heap on the sofa. Poe judges he has worn out his welcome and quits at last the House of Usher. On his way down the stairs, he meets the family doctor hurrying up them, presumably on an urgent call to attend to Roderick. He casts a weird look at Poe; perhaps he thinks Poe's visit is to blame for this crisis, perhaps he blames the storyteller for the story.

Has Poe, who presents himself all the while as a blameless observer of a family tragedy, had more of an active role in this scenario for *folie à deux* than he pretends? Was it a *folie à trois?*

Shaking off his heels the dust of the House of Usher, Poe rides away, into the savage landscape; the Player King is off to another engagement. On with the show.

The house he leaves behind him continues to look at itself in the still waters of the tarn, gazing at its fungus-encrusted face, contemplating the 'remodelled and inverted images of the grey sedge, and the ghastly tree-stems, and the vacant and eye-like windows'. The House of Usher contemplates its double in the serenity after the story.

It is a haunted house and only the boldest enter it; only the boldest leave.

End of the story: 'The Resurrection of the House of Usher'.

Turn the story upside down and the face of Madeline Usher – which is also the face of her brother, and perhaps, of the narrator, Poe, who presence has set all this in motion – upside down, the face of Madeline Usher turns into that of a vampire.

The paraphernalia of the occult is conspicuously absent from Poe's tales of terror – no witches, no black magic, no werewolves, nothing so tangible as a ghost. It is pyschological terror he manipulates and though the décor of the tales is murky and theatrical beyond belief, the emotions of sexual guilt, of longing, of paranoia, are raw and real. The tension between the one and the other produces the genius of the tales.

All the same, it turns out that the latent content of 'The Fall of the House of Usher' contains – a vampire, a supernatural being of the kind that Poe usually rigorously rationalised as physical illness, as the promptings of a guilty conscience, or even, as in 'The Masque of the Red Death', as an allegorical figure.

The vampire. Especially, the female vampire, the *femme fatale,* epitomising the fear of and longing for sexuality, symbolising sex and femininity as compulsion and disease. She is the woman who takes by force the blood and life and potency of a man. A metaphor. A part of the décor, in fact – no lonely castle in these abandoned parts is complete without one.

The vampire is a tacky theatrical device, too, just like the collapsing house itself.

So the rawness of feeling turns out to be artifice, too. The sense of doom, the sense of impending psycho-sexual catastrophe that seems to permeate the tale is a device. We are left with the story as a self-defensive strategy, a mask; it tells us nothing about the writer, only about itself. The story is the story in a story. Its most significant images are the House of Usher looking at itself in the water, and the Usher twins gazing at one another's mirror image faces – images of gratified narcissism, entirely sufficient to themselves.

Metaphores, 1988

Milorad Pavic: Dictionary of the Khazars

According to Apuleius, Pleasure is the daughter of Cupid and Psyche – of Love and the Soul, that is, a sufficiently elevated pedigree, one would have thought. Yet the British still put up a strong resistance to the idea that pleasurability might be a valid criterion in the response to literature, just as we remain dubious about the value of the 'decorative' in the visual arts. When Graham Greene made 'entertainment' a separate category from the hard stuff in his production, he rammed home the point: the difference was a moral one, a difference between reading to pass the time pleasurably – that is, trivially – and reading *to some purpose*.

The 'great tradition' does not brook even the possibility of libidinal gratification between the pages as an end in itself, and F. R. Leavis's 'eat up your broccoli' approach to fiction emphasises this junkfood/wholefood dichotomy. If reading a novel – for the eighteenth-century reader, the most frivolous of diversions – did not, by the middle of the twentieth century, make you a better person in some way, then you might as well flush the offending volume down the toilet, which was by far the best place for the undigested excreta of dubious nourishment.

The Yugoslav writer Milorad Pavic's *Dictionary of the Khazars* is an exercise in a certain kind of erudite frivolity that does not do you good *as such*, but offers the cerebral pleasure of the recognition of patterning afforded by formalism, a profusion of language games, some rude mirth. In culinary terms, the book is neither tofuburger nor Big Mac, but a Chinese banquet, a multiplicity of short narratives and prose fragments at which we are invited, not to take our fill, but to snack as freely or as meagrely as we please on a wide variety of small portions of sharply flavoured delicacies, mixing and matching many different taste sensations. In other words, it is not like a novel by Penelope Lively. It will not set you up; nor will it tell you how to live. That is not what it is for.

The mother-type of these feast-like compilations is *The Arabian Nights Entertainment* – note the word 'entertainment'. That shambolic anthology of literary fairytales lined by an exiguous narrative was originally, and still is, related to the folktale of peasant communities and its particular improvisatory yet regulated systems of narrative. The whole of *Dictionary of the Khazars* is a kind of legendary history, and some of the individual entries have considerable affinities to the folktale ('The Tale of Petkutin and Kalina' in the section called 'The Red Book', for example): but, I suspect, not so much the influence of an oral tradition – though that's still possible in Yugoslavia – as the influence of an aesthetic owing a good deal to Vladimir Propp's *Morphology of the Folk-Tale,* first published in Russia in 1928.

Propp's thesis is that the traditional fairytale is not composed, but built up out of discrete narrative blocks that can be pulled down again and reassembled in different ways to make any number of other stories, or can be used for any number of other stories in combination with other narrative blocks. That is partly why there is no place for, nor possibility of, inwardness in the traditional tale, nor of characterisation in any three-dimensional way. If the European novel of the nineteenth and twentieth centuries is closely related to gossip, to narrative arising out of conflicted character, then the folktale survives, in our advanced, industrialised, society, in the anecdote. Gossip would say: 'You know the daughter of that bloke at the "Dog and Duck"? Well . . .' An anecdote might begin: 'There was this publican's daughter, see. . .' In our culture, the folktale survives in the saloon bar.

A traditional storyteller does not make things up afresh, except now and then, if the need arises. Instead, he or she selects, according to mood, whim and cultural background, the narrative segments that feel right at the time from a store acquired from a career of listening, and reassembles them in attractive, and sometimes new, ways. And that's how formalism was born. (Italo Calvino, the most exquisite of contemporary formalists, is also, it should be remembered, editor of the classic collection of Italian fairytales.)

Pavic advises the reader to behave exactly like a traditional storyteller and construct his or her own story out of the ample material he has made available. The main difference is, Pavic has made all this material up by himself. 'No chronology is observed here, nor is one necessary. Hence, each reader will put together the book for himself, as in a game of dominoes or cards.' The book is an exercise, not in creative writing, but in creative reading. The reader can, says Pavic, rearrange the book 'in an infinite number of ways, like a Rubic Cube'.

Pavic positively invites you to join in, as if opening his imagination to the public. 'It is an open book,' he says in the preliminary notes, 'and when it is shut it can be added to: just as it has its own former and present lexicographer, so it can acquire new writers, compilers, continuers'.

In a US review, Robert Coover suggested that computer hackers might make *Dictionary of the Khazars* their own as a prototype hypertext, unpaginated, non-sequential, that can be entered anywhere by anybody. This looks forward to a Utopian, high-tech version of the oral tradition where machines do all the work whilst men and women unite in joyous and creative human pastimes. It is a prospect to make William Morris's mind reel, publishers quail.

But who are, or were, the Khazars? 'An autonomous and powerful tribe, a warlike and nomadic people who appeared from the East at an unknown date, driven by a scorching silence, and who from the seventh to the tenth century, settled in the land between two seas, the Caspian and the Black.' As a nation, the Khazars no longer exist, and ceased to do so during the tenth century after 'their conversion from their original faith, unknown to us today, to one (again, it is not known which) of three known religions of the past and present – Judaism, Islam or Christianity.'

The *Dictionary* purports to be, with some additions, the reprint of an edition of a book published by the Pole, Joannes Daubmannus, in 1691, which was 'divided into three dictionaries: a separate glossary of Moslem sources on the Khazar question, an alphabetised list of materials drawn from Hebrew writings and tales, and a third dictionary compiled on the basis of Christian accounts of the Khazar question'. So the same characters and events are usually seen three times, each from the perspective of a different history and set of cultural traditions, and may be followed through the three books *cross-wise*, if you wish. The 'ancient' texts are organised according to the antiquarian interests of the seventeenth century. As in *The Arabian Nights,* an exiguous narrative set in the present day is interwoven throughout the three volumes of the dictionary and provides some sort of climax.

The most obvious immediate inspiration for this 'plot' is surely a certain Volume XLVI of the *Anglo-American Cyclopaedia* (New York, 1917), itself a 'literal but delinquent reprint of the *Encyclopaedia Britannica* of 1902,' in which Bioy Cesares and Jorge Luis Borges discovered the first recorded reference to the land of Uqbar. But instead of, like Borges, writing a story about a fake reference book that invades the real world, Pivac has set to and compiled the book itself, a book that contains a whole lost world, with its heroes, its rituals, its deaths, its mysteries, and especially its theological disputations, providing a plausible-enough-sounding apparatus of scholarly references that involve a series of implicit jokes about theories of authenticity just as the skewed versions of characters such as Princess Ateh, recurring three times, involve implicit jokes about cultural relativity.

Unless, of course, these aren't jokes at all. Yugoslavia is a federation of states with extraordinarily diverse cultural histories that came together as a nation almost by accident in 1918, with a sizeable Moslem population, to boot. This idea of a tripartite version of an imaginary history ought to appeal to the British since the United Kingdom is also a union of principalities with extraordinarily diverse cultural histories, and a significant Moslem minority, too.

There is a blatant quality of fakery about the *Dictionary*. One imagines Pavic gleefully setting to with a Black and Decker drill, inserting artificial worm-holes into his synthetic oak beams. This fakery, this purposely antiqued and distressed surface, is what makes Pavic's book look so postmodern as to be almost parodically fashionable, the perfect type of those Euro-bestsellers such as Patrick Suskind's *Perfume* and Umberto Eco's *Name of the Rose* that seem, to some British critics, to spring from an EEC conspiracy to thwart exports of genuine, wholesome, straightforward British fiction the same way French farmers block the entry of English lamb. However, Yugoslavia is not a member of the Common Market and the British have developed a nervous tendency to label anything 'postmodern' that doesn't have a beginning, a middle, and an end in that order.

In Yugoslavia, according to Martin Seymour-Smith, 'except for a few years after Tito came to power in 1945, Modernism has flourished almost, if not quite, as it wished (*Guide to World Literature*, edition of 1985). *Dictionary of the Khazars* fulfils, almost too richly, all Wallace Stevens's prescriptions in 'Notes towards a Supreme Fiction':

> it must be abstract
> it must change
> it must give pleasure.

Most of the time, Pavic speaks in the language of romantic modernism – that is, surrealism. Al Bakri, the Spaniard, dies 'dreaming of salty female breasts in a gravy of saliva and toothache'. The Princess Ateh composes a prayer: 'On our ship, my father, the crew swarms like ants: I cleaned it this morning with my hair and they crawl up the clean mast and strip the green sails like sweet vine leaves into their anthills.' A man, a certain Dr Ismail Suk, waking, blinks, 'with eyes hairy as testicles'.

Dr Suk is the hero of a section called 'The Story of the Egg and the

Violin Bow' that boasts all the inscrutability of surrealist narrative plus a quality of what one can only call the 'mercantile fantastic' reminiscent of the short stories of Bruno Schulz, with their bizarre and ominous shops and shopkeepers. 'The shop was empty except for a hen nestled in a cap in the corner. She cocked one eye at Dr Suk and saw everything edible in him.' The Polish woman who will murder Dr Suk is called Dr Dorothea Schulz.

In fact, there is a strong sense of pastiche everywhere, most engagingly in the collection of Islamic sources on the Khazar question, although the poem in question purports to have been written by the Khazar Princess Ateh. It is a piece of spoof Kafka. A woman travelling to a distant school to take a test is subjected to bureaucratic misinformation and then told: 'you can't reach the school today. And that means not ever. Because the school will no longer exist as of tomorrow. You have missed your life's destination . . .'

But this is a revisionist version of Kafka. Once her destination is withheld from her, the traveller searches for the significance of her journey in the journey itself – and finds it in one luminous memory, of a table with food and wine. 'On the table by the food a candle with a drop of flame on the top; next to it the Holy Book and the month of Jamaz-ul-Aker flowing through it.' A happy ending!

There is the casual acceptance of the marvellous common to both surrealism and the folktale: 'Ibn Ashkany was himself a very deft player. There exists a written record of his fingering for a song, so we know that he used more than ten fingers to play his instruments.' (In fact, Satan used this name for a time, and we learn how he played the lute with both his fingers and the tip of his tail.) A band of Greek merchants are 'so hirsute that the hair on their chests had a part like the hair on their heads'.

But the sense of the marvellous is most often created simply by the manipulation of language: 'Avram Brankovich cuts a striking figure. He has a broad chest the size of a cage for large birds or a small beast.' One way and another, the task of Pavic's translator, Christina Pricevic-Zoric, must have been awesome, for among the Khazars we are living in a world of words *as such*. The vanished world of the Khazars is constructed solely out of words. A dictionary itself is a book in which words provide the plot. The Khazars are nothing if not people of the Book, dithering as they did between the three great faiths, the sacred texts of Christianity, Islam, and Judaism. One of the copies of the 1691 edition of the *Dictionary*, we are told, was printed with a poisoned ink: 'The reader would die on the ninth page at the words *Verbum caro factum est*. ("The Word became Flesh".)' Almost certainly, something metaphysical is going on.

The Khazars indefatigably enter that most metaphysical of states, dreaming. 'A woman was sitting by her fire, her kettle of broth babbling like bursting boils. Children were standing in line with their plates and dogs, waiting. She ladled out the broth to the children and animals and immediately Masudi knew that she was portioning out dreams from the kettle.'

The Dream Hunters are a set of Khazar priests, 'They could read other people's dreams, live and make themselves at home in them . . .' That is the Christian version. The Moslem Dictionary is more forthcoming: 'If all human dreams could be assembled together, they would form a huge man, a human being the size of a continent. This would not be just any man, it would be Adam Ruhani, the heavenly Adam, man's angel ancestor, of whom the imams speak.'

The book of Hebrew sources is most explicit:

The Khazars saw letters in people's dreams, and in them they looked for primordial man, for Adam Cadmon, who was both man and woman and born before eternity. They believed that to every person belongs one letter of the alphabet, that each of these letters constitutes part of Adam Cadmon's body on earth, and that these letters converge in people's dreams and come to life in Adam's body.

(I am not sure that Pavic thinks of Freud when he thinks of dreams.)

So we can construct our primal ancestor out of the elements of our dreams, out of the elements of the *Dictionary,* just as Propp thought that if one found sufficient narrative elements and combined them in the right order, one would be able to retell the very first story of all – 'it would be possible to construct the archetype of the fairytale not only schematically . . . but concretely as well'.

Please do not run away with the idea that this is a difficult book, although it is flamboyantly and intentionally confusing. I first came across the *Dictionary of the Khazars* in the following manner. Last summer, on the beach of a rather down-market Italian resort, I was staying, for reasons I won't bore you with, at the best hotel. Under a beach umbrella there was a wonderfully extrovert French businessman and his wife, who originally hailed from Yorkshire ('I was passing through Paris thirty-five years ago and I'm still passing through'). He was recovering from a bypass operation; under the sun-tan oil his chest was ravelled. They first attracted my attention in the hotel restaurant because they ordered everything flambé. She, in a white jump-suit printed with huge orange flowers, danced on the beach with my little boy. Meanwhile her husband was reading *Dictionary of the Khazars.* It had just been published in France, it was his holiday book. He kept reading bits aloud to her: 'Kyr Avram is sometimes wont to say, "A woman without a behind is like a village without a church!"' 'I'm all right, then, she said. He was laughing so much I feared for his scars.

At dinner, they read bits to the waiter as he flambéd their steaks.

I thought that if this wonderful man and woman were enjoying the book so much, then so would I. In fact, perhaps the best way of tackling it *is* to read bits aloud, to treat it like a game. In his *New York Times* review, Coover suggested that, if marketed as a board game, it might soon outsell 'Dungeons and Dragons', which is probably true. It is a book to play with, to open up and take things out of, a box of delights and a box of tricks. It is a novel without any sense of closure, the product of a vast generosity of the imagination – user-friendly, you could say, and an invitation to invent for yourself.

The book, by the way, comes in two editions, a male one and a female one, differing by seventeen lines, perhaps because the scribe, Father Theoctist Nikolsky, avers that 'masculine and feminine stories cannot have the same ending.' Why not? But the gender difference between the editions is not crucial, in spite of the warning on the jacket, although the very concept is the only point in the book where Pavic's invention nearly founders under an access of sheer cuteness.

London Review of Books, 1989

Milorad Pavic: Landscape Painted with Tea

Central to the argument of this frisky but intellectually gripping work of fiction is the idea of two oppositional human types – the idiorrhythmics, who are solitaries, each moving to his own rhythm of life, unique, separate; and the cenobites, the *solidaries,* who join in brotherhood and live in common. And a person must be either the one or the other. Never both.

This is a classic either/or situation. Obviously, you can't be both existentially alone and warmly part of a fraternity at the same time. 'A man with a heart full of silence and a man with a heart full of quiet cannot be alike,' opines the narrator of *Landscape Painted with Tea* in one of the frequent aphorisms that adorn the text. The book twists and turns about this contradiction and various resolutions to it.

Although *Landscape Painted with Tea* is narrated in the third person from a traditionally omniscient and god-like point of view, the novel is constructed to let its reader in on the action at every opportunity, by a variety of means. If the text is a constant, then the ways of reading it are not. Pavic's reader is invited, via the formal device of a crossword puzzle and its clues, to read the book 'not in order of succession and across (as the river flows) but *down,* as the rain falls'.

This produces an effect of intentional randomness not unlike that of some of Calvino's writing – like that of the marvellous *Castle of Crossed Destinies,* for example, which based its constellations of stories on the various ways in which the cards in the Tarot pack fell. But Pavic isn't interested in a new way of writing. He is interested in a new way of *reading,* because 'any new way of reading that goes against the matrix of time, which pulls us towards death, is a futile but honest effort to resist this inexorability of one's fate'.

The traditional novel, like the traditional anecdote, begins and goes on until it ends. Like life. Pavic wants more than that. He wants to disrupt time, to challenge death.

And why not, dammit. It's filthy work but somebody's got to do it. Kingsley Amis isn't going to try.

Pavic sets out to seduce the reader into the text. There is even a blank page at the end of the book where the reader can write out the dénouement he or she has worked out by themselves. Pavic veers crazily between a particularly Balkan brand of cute surrealism ('I hear the birds' voices knitting endless socks and gloves with a thousand fingers') and the kind of high seriousness that can concern itself with the nature of narrative, with what it is and what it does. Sometimes, in his concern to massage the reader pleasurably into a rapt contemplation of what constitutes the act of reading, he can come a cropper. Most of the time, though he contrives to discuss this question and also give pleasure, no mean feat.

You can't be an idiorrhythmic and a cenobite at the same time, but you *can* change over from one to another. Think of Yoan Siropoulos; he was born and died a Greek but, in between 'entered a different time, where different waters flowed', in which he became Yovan Siropulov, the Bulgarian. His story is a miniature version of the bizarre epic of the lives of the book's major figure, the Yugoslav architect, Atanas Svilar, who converts himself into the Russian mathematician, Atanas Fyodorovish Razin, and, after numerous adventures, emigrates to the USA.

There seems to be a complicated political sub-text going on beneath the rich palimpsest of stories and counter-stories that provide the material for Pavic's crossword clues. The architect, Svilar/Razin draws, again and again, the plans of the grand summer villa of Josip Broz Tito, 'general secretary of the Yugoslav Communist Party and president of the republic', finally building himself a replica of this palace in the USA. Since irony is Pavic's medium, it is hard for the non-Yugoslav reader to tell precisely

what is going on, here. The central dichotomy between the idiorrhythmics and the cenobites has, of course, its own political resonance.

You need to take *Landscape Painted with Tea* slowly. You need to chew
it for a long time, like certain kinds of peasant bread. It will reward you
with constant shocks of pleasure. There is its pervasive lyricism: 'the
moonlight . . . was the kind you enter from the dark, like a room . . .' The
aphorisms are frequent, always witty, sometimes with witty little teeth:
'Nobody can be masculine every day, not even God.' There are incidental stories whose characters have the radiant two-dimensionality of fairytale, like the man who wears two wrist-watches and tells his lover: 'This
silver watch measures your time and this gold one mine. I wear them
together, so that I can always know what time you have.

It is the architect Razin who paints the landscapes in various kinds of
tea, fruit teas, tisanes, Darjeeling (the champagne of teas), green tea, every
shade and variation of colour executed in tea. But very early on in the
book, a traveller recounts how he became a painter by accident after his
wife 'wrote her signature in the snow, steering his penis like a fountain
pen, and for a while the signature steamed like tea, and then became perfectly legible'. (Soon she was drawing pictures using the same method.)
Landscapes Painted with Pee? Would this be a joke in Serbo-Croat?

Independent on Sunday, 1991

Writers and Readers

Lorenzo the Closet-Queen

A piece of comment I once read about that monstrous book, *The Story of O.,* suggested that only a woman could have written it because of some curious metaphor about, I think, curlers, somewhere in the book. The commentator, a French intellectual, probably a member of the Académie Française and God knows what else besides, said this sartorial detail could only have been documented 'by a woman', because it was uniquely revelatory of a woman's eye.

Such, then, was the opinion of this Frenchman, whose name I forget; but it seemed to me that *The Story of O.* bore all the stigmata of male consciousness, not least in that details about clothes are just the sort of thing a man would put into a book if he wanted the book to read as though it had been written by a woman. Cleland uses much the same device in *Fanny Hill.* All the same, many woman writers do themselves pretend to be female impersonators; look at Jean Rhys and Edna O'Brien, whose scars glorify the sex that wounded them. But the nature of female impersonation in art is a complex business and the man who sets out to do it must be careful not to let his own transvestite slip show, especially if he does not like women much.

The greatest drag artistes, of whom the most magnificent examples are the *onnagata,* the male actors who play the female roles in the kabuki theatre of Japan, betray their authentic gender only by too great a perfection of performance, so that a real woman looks butch beside them. Which brings me to the strange case of D. H. Lawrence, and the truism that those who preach phallic superiority usually have an enormous dildo tucked away somewhere in their psychic impedimenta.

I should like to make a brief, sartorial critique of *Women in Love,* Lawrence's most exuberantly clothed novel, a novel which, furthermore, is supposed to be an exegesis on my sex, trusting, not the teller but the tale, to show to what extent D. H. Lawrence personated women through simple externalities of dress; by doing so, managed to pull off one of the greatest con tricks in the history of modern fiction; and revealed a more than womanly, indeed, pathologically fetishistic, obsession with female apparel. *Woman in Love* is as full of clothes as Brown's, and clothes of the same kind. D. H. Lawrence catalogues his heroine's wardrobes with the loving care of a ladies' maid. It is not a simple case of needing to convince the reader the book has been written by a woman; that is far from his intention. It is a device by which D. H. Lawrence attempts to convince the reader that he D.H.L., has a hot line to a woman's heart by the extraordinary sympathy he has for her deepest needs, that is, nice stockings, pretty dresses and submission.

Yet Lawrence clearly enjoys being a girl. If we do not trust the teller but the tale, then the tale positively revels in lace and feathers, bags, beads, blouses and hats. It is always touching to see a man quite as seduced by the cultural apparatus of femininity as Lawrence was, the whole gamut, from feathers to self-abnegation. Even if, as Kate Millett suggests, he only wanted to be a woman so that he could achieve the supreme if schizophrenic pleasure of fucking himself, since nobody else was good enough for him. (The fantasy-achievement of this ambition is probably what lends *Lady Chatterley's Lover* such an air of repletion.)

Lawrence is seduced and bemused by the narcissistic apparatus of femininity. It dazzles him. He is like a child with a dressing-up box. Gudrun, witch and whore, is introduced in a fanfare of finery: 'She wore a dress of dark-green, silky stuff, with ruches of blue and green linen lace in the necks and sleeves.' The Brangwen girls habitually come on to the page dragging *Vogue* captions behind them, until you start looking for the price tag. (How could they have afforded to dress like that on teachers' salaries in those days?) It is the detail of the 'linen lace' that gives Lawrence away, of course. He is a true *aficionado* of furbelows. What the hell is linen lace? I'm sure I don't know. It is a delicious feminine secret between Gudrun and her dressmaker.

Gudrun completes her ensemble with emerald-green stockings. Gudrun's stockings run through the book like a *leitmotiv*. Very gaudy stockings. She will keep on drawing attention to the pedestals which support her, her legs, though these legs are rarely mentioned by name. Her stockings become almost a symbol of her contrariness. When she arrives at the Crich mansion wearing thick, yellow woollen ones, Gerald Crich is a little taken aback. 'Her stockings always disconcerted him,' notes Lawrence, to underline just what a bourgeois cow Gerald is, that he can't take a pair of Bohemian stockings with equanimity.

But Lawrence himself is so deeply disturbed by the notion of Gudrun's legs he cannot bear to see them uncovered; they must be conspicuously concealed. That will negate their discomforting, unmodified legginess. Stockings as censorship.

Stockings, stockings, stockings everywhere. Hermione Roddice sports coral-coloured ones, Ursula canary ones, Defiant, brilliant, emphatic stockings. But never the suggestion the fabric masks, upholsters, disguises living, subversive flesh. Lawrence is a stocking man, not a leg man. Stockings have supplanted legs; clothes have supplanted flesh. Fetishism.

The apotheosis of the stockings comes right at the end of the novel, where they acquire at last an acknowledged, positive, sexual significance. 'Gudrun came to Ursula's bedroom with three pairs of the coloured stockings for which she was notorious and she threw them on the bed. But these were thick, silk stockings, vermilion, cornflower blue and grey, bought in Paris.' With sure, feminine intuition, Ursula knows 'Gudrun must be feeling *very* loving, to give away such treasures'.

The excited girls call the stockings 'jewels', or 'lambs', as if the inert silky things were lovers, or children. Indeed, the stockings appear to precipitate a condition of extreme erotic arousal in Gudrun; she touches them with 'trembling, excited hands'. The orgasmic nature of the stocking exchange is underlined by a very curious piece of dialogue.

' "One gets the greatest joy of all out of really lovely stockings," said Ursula.

' "One does" replies Gudrun. "The greatest joy of all." '

What *is* Lawrence playing at? Or, rather, what does he think he's playing at? This sort of camp ecstasy more properly belongs in Firbank, who understood about dandyism in women, dandyism and irony, the most extreme defences of the victim. But Firbank, as plucky a little bantamweight as ever bounced off the ropes, had *real* moral strength.

I think what Lawrence is doing is attempting to put down the women he has created in his own image for their excessive reaction to the stockings to which he himself has a very excessive reaction indeed, the deepdown queenly, monstrous old hypocrite that he is.

Of course, at this point in the novel, Lawrence must be feeling very full of Woman since Birkin has just ingested Ursula, swallowed her whole in the manner of a boa constrictor. So he can really deceive himself with his own drag queen act, and it doesn't seem to him in the least incongruous that his heroines, who were initially scrupulously established as very heavy ladies indeed, are now jabbering away to one another like the worst kind of schoolgirl.

The girls have just met again in Switzerland, after Ursula's marriage and Gudrun's dirty weekend in Paris with the atrocious Gerald. They scuttle off immediately to Gudrun's bedroom to talk 'clothes and experiences', in that order. Curled up with a box of Swiss Chox, I dare say. My God, what an insult. Lawrence's prose gets progressively sloppier and sloppier towards

the end of the book, but weariness and laziness are no excuse for this kind
of patronising dismissal.

But cunning old Lawrence can have his cake and eat it, too. Earlier on,
in Derbyshire the miners' children call names after Gudrun. 'What price
the stockings!' they cry. This is realism, of course. The penalty of sartorial
eccentricity is always mockery. Some kinds of clothes are a self-inflicted
martyrdom. But D. H. Lawrence can put all those lovely garments he
himself desires so much on the girls he has invented and yet cunningly
evade the moral responsibility of having to go out in them himself and face
the rude music of the mob.

And he luxuriously allows himself the licence to mock the girls for
parading about in the grotesque finery he has forced them to don. He judi-
ciously allots Gudrun a sartorial crucifixion by the miners. Never, they
allow, have they seen night-soil in such a lovely bag but, with Pauline
resolution, they never lose sight of the fact that night-soil, nevertheless,
she remains. She has committed the solecism of wearing 'bright rose
stockings' for a walk in the village.

'What price, eh? She'll do, won't she?' See the emphasis on the cash
nexus. Her dandyism, her sartorial defiance, is only an invitation to humiliation. The miners look, not for the price-tag on the stockings as did the
relatively innocent children, but they are brute enough to perceive the
flesh beneath the stockings and speculate about the price-tag on *that*.

The old miner thinks she'd be worth a week's wages. Indeed, he would
put them down straight away. But the younger 'shook his head with fatal
misgiving'.

' "No," he said, "It's not worth that to me." '

Lawrence hates the miners with the lacerated, guilty passion of the true
class-traitor. All the same, he is delighted to use the frank speech proper to
the degraded status he gives them to put Gudrun, sashaying out in her
Lunnon clothes with her high-falutin ways, firmly in her place. 'Not
worth a week's wages', eh? So much for your subtle little carvings of
water-wagtails, girlie. Get down on your back for free.

All the same, Lawrence has given Gudrun a particularly shocking kind
of beauty, for God knows what masochistic reasons of his own. And it is
a perpetual affront to him. Not 'Beauty's self is she when all her clothes
are gone', by any means; never that. There is no sense of the tactile immediacy of undressing in Lawrence's relation with his unruly heroine.
Rather, it is like strip-tease in reverse; the more clothes he piles on her,
the more desirable she becomes, because the less real.

At the Swiss hotel, in her evening dress of green silk and gold tissue (and
where *does* she get the cash to pay for all this glamour? Not on the streets,
he's made *that* plain), ' she was really brilliantly beautiful and everybody

noticed her'. Which is an astonishingly mean and bald description of the effect of an erotically disturbing woman on a party. He has already had a stab at describing the effect of an erotically disturbing man on a party. (Gudrun's description of Gerald at the studio party in Paris.) But he can't get much about the cock-of-the-midden scenario. Perhaps he wants to say that Gudrun exerts the dominance of desire; but he is too mean to admit a woman can do that, and too hypocritical to let his heroes do it seriously. Birkin is described somewhere as extraordinarily desirable, but his dominance is not an erotic one; he is really what the Brangwen girls call him in one of their more lucid moments, an intellectual bully.

Hermione Roddice, inevitably, gets the full weight of the sartorial stick. She disappears under layer upon layer of cloth. Cloth of gold, fur, antique brocade, enormous flat hats of pale yellow velvet 'on which were streaks of ostrich feathers, natural and grey'. What an asset Lawrence would have been to those fashion writers who report the Paris collections where photographers are not allowed, so they have to remember everything.

Hermione's clothes are visible alienation. They verge on fancy dress, which is dress as pure decoration, unmodified by function or environment. 'Hermione came down to dinner strange and sepulchral, her eyes heavy and full of sepulchral darkness, strength. She had put on a dress of stiff, old, greenish brocade, that fitted tight and made her look tall and rather terrible, ghastly.' Lawrence is plainly terrified of her and full of an awed respect. Her exoticism, for Lawrence primarily an exoticism of class, is expressed in a self-conscious strangeness of apparel. Her dress defines the area of abstract power she inhabits.

Hermione is a portrait from life, and Ottoline Morrell did indeed get herself up like that, but she arouses Lawrence to such a heightened awareness of lace and trimming he might almost have spent lots of furtive, happy hours at Garsington, rummaging through her wardrobe.

The house-party at Breadalby sees them all going for a swim together. Gerald looks 'white but natural in his nakedness', with a scarlet silk kerchief about his loins. The ladies decorously expose their flesh, for once, but not much; Hermione approaches the water in a 'great mantle of purple silk', ornate, disguised, shrouded in baroque finery. Indeed, her appearance has the gilded formality of an icon. This is probably because she is an aristocrat and therefore holy.

If Lawrence is making some pseudo-philosophical point about these heavily over-dressed women, that they themselves retreat behind their clothes, he never makes it overtly, which is off, for him. But it is almost as if he is inverting the Baudelairean paradox, 'woman is natural, therefore abominable', and saying: 'Woman, when unnatural, is abominable', and making a platitude out of Baudelaire's thrust at the notion of 'natural man'.

For most of the women he dislikes in *Women in Love* end up as apparatuses constructed out of fabric, stalking clothes' horses which suggest only the appearance of women. Lawrence approaches these women via their apparel. Their clothes are the only thing he can hold on to. Like a drag-queen, but without the tragic heroism that enables a transvestite to test the magic himself, he believes women's clothes are themselves magical objects which define and confine women.

And his heroines cannot get out of the sartorial trap Lawrence has laid for them, though there is a connection between the amount of clothes he piles on them and their own erotic quality. Erotically disturbing women get bundled up more. Ursula starts off just as ostentatiously clothed as Gudrun, but descriptions of her apparel tail off after Birkin castrates her. But Gudrun, the Pussum (poor Carrington, again, getting hers), Hermione – always, always subsumed to their appearance, since that defuses their sexuality, their challenge. Unless, for Lawrence, their appearance alone constitutes their sexuality.

Yes, Hermione. She plainly functions as the most erotically disturbing of all the women in the novel, not because Lawrence apprehends her in a sensual mode – far be it – but because she is spiced with what, for him is the only potent aphrodisiac, that of class.

Clothes acquire such an elaborate significance as the armour of woman-hood it is striking that, when Ursula and Hermione meet for their *tête à tête* (chapter 22, 'Woman to Woman'), when they are tussling for posses-sion of Birkin, there is no mention at all of what either of them have on. They are stripped for battle, you understand.

Most of the time in *Women in Love,* Lawrence is like a little boy dress-ing up in his mother's clothes and thinking, that way, he has become his mother. The con trick, the brilliant, the wonderful con trick, the real mir-acle, is that his version of drag has been widely accepted as the real thing, even by young women who ought to know better. In fact, Lawrence probes as deeply into a woman's heart as the bottom of a hat-box.

He is too female by half. His surreptitious, loved and envied slip is always dipping a good two inches below his intellectual hemline. The stocking covers a hairy, muscular leg.

Next to this *onnagata*, Colette looks like Cassius Clay.

New Society, 1975

The Life of Katherine Mansfield
Review of Anthony Alpers, *The Life of Katherine Mansfield*.

There is the heroic myth of colonialism, the setting out across the sea to domesticate the unknown. It has its no less heroic reverse; the colonial's return, 'coming home', as they say, an unfledged arrival at a known yet unknown motherland that prefers to acknowledge no other reality than itself. Katherine Mansfield liked to present herself as a prodigal daughter in letters from England to her father in New Zealand, where he had prospered, becoming, unforgivably in terms of motherland snobbism, *nouveau riche*. But her own relation as unforgiven prodigal daughter to Britain, a culture of which she was subtly never a part, is something Anthony Alpers does not explore in this otherwise exhaustive, especially gynaecologically exhaustive, biography, which he intends to replace one first published in 1953, when many of Mansfield's contemporaries, including her husband, John Middleton Murry, were still alive and some capable of addressing writs.

Though Katherine Mansfield was one of the greatest of expatriate writers, she may never have fully realised that, in London, she *was* an expatriate, though her biographer, perhaps unconsciously, often stresses the point by referring to her as 'the Colonial' from time to time. Born in Wellington, she 'came home' first to school, in 1903, at fourteen; sailed back across the world to endure the rigours of a Wellington débutante ('violet teas' where sandwiches with violets in them were served); came home, again, at nearly twenty, to sow her wild oats. Tremendous youthful follies leading to cohabitation with and eventual marriage to Murry and a hectic shared life of little magazines and *literati*. Garsington and the Bloomsburys, a battery of hypocrisy and snobbery, she colonially innocent and unprepared. Death of tuberculosis at thirty-four. She left behind short stories, letters and, most traditional of all women's literary forms, a journal. All her written remains are capable of being construed as a fabulous – and I use the word advisedly – autobiography of the soul; one of the great traps for the woman writer is the desire to be loved for oneself as well as admired for one's work, to be a Beautiful Person as well as a Great Artist, and Katherine Mansfield was only saved from narcissistic self-regard by the tough bitchery under her parade of sensitive vulnerability. She also seems to have been ravaged by sexual guilt, which probably helped.

Inevitably, the best of her short stories, including 'Prelude', 'At the Bay', 'The Garden Party', are set in New Zealand, in everyday domesticity, and have a shimmering tenderness, as of memories of a happy land far away to which return would have been death. But she died, anyway, in

famously bizarre circumstances at Gurdjieff's fancy-dress commune outside Paris.

Mansfield's life, with its inherently tragic quality, a youth spent slowly
dying, a sexual freedom for which she paid such a price in mental and
physical pain, considerable artistic achievement and the early close
clouded by the occult, is bound to make her something of a heroine for
our times, not least because the period in which she lived here, 1903-23
now looks as though it was England's last artistically vital one. Indeed,
everyone who was anyone put her down – Wyndham Lewis, Bertrand
Russell, Gaudier-Brzeska – the list is endless. Virginia Woolf was 'shocked
by her commonness'. One wonders, at the end of Alpers's loving, even
besotted biography, why someone so gifted, so charming, should have
been so universally detested. It is good to get a hint of the reason in a crisp
note to a girlfriend of her husband's: 'I am afraid you must stop writing
these little love letters to my husband while he and I live together. It is one
of the things which is not done in our world.' She must have been formidable.

If magnificent Gudrun in *Women in Love,* the *castratrix triumphans,* is
partly about her, then the cutesy-poo way she snuggled up to Murry and
indeed, the world, must have seemed to Lawrence a shocking betrayal of
her true nature. Which does not excuse the unforgivably cruel letters
Lawrence wrote to her in her last illness. But Alpers somewhat underplays
the full complexity of the *ménage-à-quatre* of Lawrence and Murrys in
Cornwall in 1916. It is surely not enough to say that Lawrence took against
Mansfield because he was in love with Murry; wasn't Murry already sniff-
ing after Frieda? And 'Tig' and 'Wig' , the Murrys called one another.
They used to sit together writing poems about their happiness. Enough to
turn a stronger stomach than Lawrence's, especially if you smell the power
in her.

Alpers, to some degree, attempts to whitewash Murry, but the outlines
of a truly nauseating creep still show through and Mansfield's relation to
him seems less true love than a painfully sustained romantic illusion. Since
she called her lifelong champion, Ida Baker, her 'wife' and treated her with
a truly marital contemptuous affection, perhaps Mansfield had more sense
of emotional self-preservation than meets the eye.

And, after all, Alpers doesn't give much impression of his heroine's true
nature. Not because he doesn't try, almost too hard, sifting and resifting
contradictory evidence about a deeply ambiguous personality. But, then
she *was* mysterious and, in the manner of the colonialised, rather than the
Colonial, she used her charm to deflect attention from a core of mystery
she wished to keep to herself; perhaps the mystery was her very creativity.
It is right she should retain it.

The biography, impeccable in every other respect, suffers from a prurient intimacy of tone. For example, once Alpers has worked out the code Mansfield used in her journals to indicate her periods, she is allowed no outburst of temper or fit of depression without a reference to pre- or post-menstrual tension. He is so protective of 'Katherine', as he always calls her, that he appears to be conducting a posthumous affair with her. Presumably this is the fate of any attractive, mysterious and sexually experimental woman at the hands of a gallant male biographer.

Guardian, 1978

The Alchemy of the Word

Surrealism celebrated wonder, the capacity for seeing the world as if for the first time which, in its purest state, is the prerogative of children and madmen, but more than that, it celebrated wonder itself as an essential means of perception. Yet not a naïve wonder. The surrealist did not live in naïve times. A premonition of the imminent end of the world is always a shot in the arm for the arts; if the world has, in fact, just ended, what then? The 1914-18 war was, in many respects, for France and Germany, indeed the end of the world. The Zurich Dadas celebrated the end of the world, and of art with it. However, the Russian Revolution of 1917 suggested the end of one world might mark the commencement of another world, one in which human beings themselves might take possession not only of their own lives but also of their own means of expressing the reality of that life, i.e. art. It is possible for the true optimist to view the end of the world with sang-froid. What is so great about all this crap? Might there be something better? Surrealism's undercurrent of joy, of delight, springs from its faith in humankind's ability to recreate itself; the conviction that struggle *can* bring something better.

Any discussion of surrealism must, first of all, acknowledge that it was never a school of art, or of literature, as such. The surrealist painters and poets were not in the least interested in formal art or literature, and if they started to show signs of becoming so, André Breton, the supreme arbitrator, kicked them out of the group. It was the irreducible psychological element that makes a wonder out of the commonplace, the imagination itself that obsessed them. As for art, anyone can make it; so they made art, out of word and image, though their techniques were haphazard and idiosyncratic, and it must be said that some of them were better at it than others, though an unfair proportion of them all had that ability to light the blue touchpaper of the imagination and that retire, which a more élitist culture than the one at whose service the surrealists placed their work, or play, would have called genius.

Surrealism was not an artistic movement but a theory of knowledge that developed a political ideology of its own accord. Its art came out of the practice of a number of men and women who formulated and committed themselves to this theory of knowledge, some for a few years, some for their whole lives. They were practitioners and theoreticians at the same time. A poet, André Breton wrote the Surrealist Manifesto; a film-maker and a punk painter, Luis Buñuel and Salvador Dali, made the two most comprehensive surrealist visual statements, *Un Chien Andalou* and *L'Age d'Or,* though Dali later recanted on the whole thing. Buñuel never recanted, kept turning them out, the greatest poet of the cinema and of love, who used the camera like a machine-gun, the dialectic like a *coup de grâce.*

However, surrealist theory is derived from a synthesis of Freud and Hegel that only those without a specialist knowledge of either psycho-analysis or philosophy might have dared to undertake. Over the surrealists, or, rather, around them lie the long shadows of Plato, amongst whom they moved as if they were made of flesh. The immediate literary avatars are easier to assimilate: Baudelaire, Lautreamont, Rimbaud, Alfred Jarry. The surrealists soon incorporated Marx, yet, with digestions like so many boa constrictors, were greedy for occult phenomena and utilised a poetic methodology based on analogy and inspiration, the free play of the unconscious, tangling with the French Communist Party – losing Louis Aragon and Paul Eluard to it. Most of the painters found themselves prize exhibits in the Hitlerian gallery of decadent art. The poetry, especially that of Eluard, with its themes of freedom and love, was used as propaganda in the French Resistance.

Like most philosophical systems put together by artists – like neo-Platonism itself – surrealism was intellectually shaky, but artistically speaking, the shakier the intellectual structure, the better art it produces. (Christianity has produced some perfectly respectable painting, even poetry.) The British could never take its philosophic pretensions seriously; none of the surrealists knew any maths, and besides, they kept dragging sex and politics into everything, including the relations between men and women and the individual and the state, where every good Briton knows sex and politics have no right to be. Nevertheless, surrealist art is, in the deepest sense, philosophical – that is, art created in the terms of certain premisses about reality; and also an art that is itself a series of adventures in, or propositions and expositions of, this surrealist philosophy.

It was also a way of life; of living on the edge of the senses; of perpetual outrage and scandal, the destruction of the churches, of the prisons, of the armies, of the brothels. Such power they ascribed to words and images. A poem is a wound; a poem is a weapon:

> It has been said that it is not our right but our duty to start with words and their relations in order to study the world scientifically. It should be added that this duty is that of living itself, not in the fashion of those who bear death within them, and who are already blind walls, or vacuums, but by uniting with the universe, with the universe in movement, in process.
>
> Poetry will become flesh and blood only when it is reciprocal. This reciprocity is entirely a function of the equality of happiness among mankind. And equality of happiness will bear happiness to a height of which we can as yet have only a faint notion.
>
> (Paul Eluard)

Surrealism posits poetry as a possible mode, possibly the primary mode, of being. Surrealism was the latest, perhaps the final, explosion of romantic humanism in Western Europe. It demanded the liberation of the human spirit as both the ends and the means of art.

> Surrealism = *permanent revelation*
> Surrealism − *permanent revolution*

So it didn't work out. Those surrealists who are not dead are very old and some are very rich, which wasn't on the original agenda. Since poetry has to pay its dues at the custom-house of translation, it rarely travels, and, besides, the nature of outrage is not the same at all places and at all times. The Dadas are more fashionable at the moment, since we live in nihilistic times. Surrealist romanticism is at the opposite pole from classical modernism, but then, the surrealists would never have given Pound or Eliot house room on strictly moral grounds. A Mussolini fan? A high Tory? They'd have moved, noisily but with dignity, to another café. You don't *have* to collaborate, you know. *La lutte continue*. It continues because it has to. This world is all we have.

It is this world, there is no other but a world transformed by imagination and desire. You could say it is the dream made flesh.

Freud's *The Interpretation of Dreams* was a key book. When we dream, we are all poets. Everywhere, the surrealists left their visiting cards: 'Parents! Tell your children your dreams.' The Bureau of Surrealist Enquiries was opened at 15 rue de Grenelle, Paris, in October 1924. 'The Bureau of Surrealist Enquiries is engaged in collecting, by every appropriate means, communications relevant to the diverse forms which the unconscious activity of the mind is likely to take.' The general public were invited to visit the Bureau to confide their rarest dreams, to debate morality, to allow the staff to judge the quality of those striking coincidences that revealed the arbitrary, irrational, magical correspondences of life.

Antonin Artaud fired off letters to the chancellors of the European universities: 'Gentlemen: In the narrow tank which you call "Thought", the rays of the spirit rot like old straw.' To the Pope: 'In the name of Family and Fatherland, you urge the sale of souls, the unrestricted grinding of bodies.' And to the Dalai Lama: 'Teach us, Lama, material levitation of the body and how we can be held no longer by the earth.' Note the touch of oriental mysticism creeping into the last missive. A bit more of that kind of thing and André Breton, the Pope of surrealism, its theoretician, propagandist, and mage, expelled him from the group. Like many libertarians, Breton had, in action, a marked authoritarian streak. Artaud vanished from this world into that of madness.

In 1922 Max Ernst had already painted a group portrait: 'At the Rendezvous of Friends'. The friends were the poets René Crevel, Louis Aragon, Philippe Soupoult, Paul Eluard, Robert Desnos, André Breton, and Benjamin Peret; Dostoevsky had also arrived. Jean Arp, like Ernst a former Dada, was a poet as well as a sculptor; Giorgio de Chirico and Ernst himself are primarily painters, even if Ernst is the most literary of all painters and de Chirico wrote an enigmatic novel, *Hebdomeros*, that begins in the middle of one sentence and ends in the middle of another. The surrealist freemasonry encompassed all kinds of art because it saw all kinds of art as manifestations of the same phenomena.

The term 'surrealism' was coined by Guillaume Apollinaire in the preface to his play, *Les Mamelles de Tiresias,* to describe the human ability to create the unnatural. Man's first surreal act, he opined, was the creation of the wheel. The wheel imitates the physical function of motion but creates a form entirely independent of forms known to exist in nature. It was a product entirely of the imagination.

At the première of *Les Mamelles de Tiresias,* at the Conservatoire Maubel, on 24 June 1917, the young André Breton observed an acquaintance in the audience; this young man had come to the theatre with a revolver in his hand, and excited by the scandal of the performance, was threatening to fire into the audience. This Jacques Vache, a Baudelairean dandy, exercised a far greater influence over surrealism than his exiguous life would suggest; ten years later, Breton would write in the *Second Manifesto of Surrealism:* 'the simplest surrealist act consists of going out into the street revolver in hand and firing at random into the crowd as often as possible.' Fifty years later, Buñuel filmed just such a random assassin in *The*

Phantom of Liberty. A judge condemns the man to death and he walks into the street, free. Girls cluster round him for his autograph.

Put together your own set of connections between these events.

Vache wrote to Breton: 'Art is nonsense.'

In 1917, at the home of the ubiquitous Apollinaire, poet, art critic, modernist, Breton found issues of a magazine from Zurich, *Dada*. Which confirmed his intuition that, if art was nonsense – then nonsense might be art.

When Tzara arrived in Paris two years later, he, Breton, and friends organised a series of provocation-performances similar to those he had staged in Zurich; announcing a poem, Tzara would read from a newspaper, accompanied by bells and rattles. Breton would chew matches. Others screamed, caterwauled, or counted the number of pearls in the necklaces of ladies in the audience. But Breton could not keep up the pace for long. Nihilism can never be an end in itself.

Surrealism was born out of the row between André Breton and Tristan Tzara. It was the creative negation of destruction.

The young poets, the friends, who assembled around Breton concerned themselves with a direct relation to the unconscious: then ensued the period of automatic writing, of trance, of the recitals of dreams. Robert Desnos was so good at tranced pronouncements they thought he was faking it. A photograph of him, tranced, published in Breton's novel, *Najda*, in 1928, oddly prefigures the face of a man near death. It was by this photograph that a Czech student, working in the German concentration camp where Desnos lay dying of typhus, recognised him at the end of the Second World War.

What did these young people do with themselves when they were not engaged in the revolutionary act of sleep? For a start, they played games.

They played: the question game, in which you make a reply without knowing the question.

For example: Raymond Queneau: 'Who is Benjamin Peret?'

Marcel Noll: 'A zoo in revolt, a jungle, a liberty.'

They played: *l'un dans l'autre*, a thing described in terms of an analogy.

For example: George Goldfayn describes an armchair as if it were a hedgehog. 'I am a very small garden armchair whose springs pierce the leather cover under which I draw back my feet whenever someone comes near.

(This kind of exquisite whimsy is the only thing the British have ever found tolerable about the whole damn crew.)

They drew analogical portraits; they collaborated on portraits; they invented animals, the flora and fauna of dream; they compiled manifestos, put together magazines, quarrelled, demonstrated, shocked the bourgeoisie. There is a beautiful photograph I have seen of Benjamin Peret snapped in the act of insulting a priest.

The surrealists also fell in love. Love, passionate, heterosexual love, together with freedom, from which it is inextricable, was their greatest source of inspiration; their women live vividly on the page at second hand. Gala, who left Eluard for Dali. Elsa Triolet (for whom, and Communism, Aragon left surrealism). Youki Desnos. The three wives of Breton – he transferred his passion *en bloc* to each in turn. The surrealists were not good with women. That is why, although I thought they were wonderful, I had to give them up in the end. They were, with a few patronised exceptions, all men and they told me that I was the source of all mystery, beauty, and otherness, because I was a woman – and I knew that was not true. I knew I wanted my fair share of the imagination, too. Not an excessive amount, mind; I wasn't greedy. Just an equal share in the right to vision.

When I realised that surrealist art did not recognise I had my own rights to liberty and love and vision as an autonomous being, not as a projected image, I got bored with it and wandered away.

But the old juices can still run, as in the mouths of Pavlov's dogs, when I hear the old, incendiary slogans, when I hear that most important of all surrealist principles: 'The marvellous alone is beautiful' (*First Manifesto of Surrealism*, 1924).

Surrealist beauty is convulsive. That is, you *feel* it, you don't see it – it exists as an excitation of the nerves. The experience of the beautiful is, like the experience of desire, an abandonment to vertigo, yet the beautiful does not exist *as such*. What do exist are images or objects that are enigmatic, marvellous, erotic – or juxtapositions of objects, or people, or ideas, that arbitrarily extend our notion of the connections it is possible to make. In this way, the beautiful is put at the service of liberty.

An aesthetic of the eye at the tips of the fingers; of the preternaturally heightened senses of the dreamer. They liked William Blake; and they liked Lewis Carroll; and they liked Bishop Berkeley. Leonora Carrington was British and wrote, still writes, prim, strange, surrealist fictions but the movement never travelled across the Channel, not even in the 1930s, just as women never took it over. Breton died in 1966, securely ensconced as one of France's greatest modern writers.

So does the struggle continue?

Why not. Give me one good reason. Even if the struggle has changed its terms.

Harpers & Queen, 1978

F. Scott Fitzgerald: The Great Gatsby

The Great Gatsby is a romance, perhaps the most perfect romance, of high capitalism, which may be one of the reasons why the novel has proved so easy to merchandise. Because Fitzgerald is so upfront and unembarrassed – 'Her voice is full of money' – about this love story which is poignant solely because each word, each gesture, each caress of the two principals is determined by economic factors, it is easy to forget that he is but rehearing a universal truth and doing so with a peculiar and remorseless lucidity.

And it is one of the great middlebrow classics – a soft-edge production, in no way intellectually demanding: you lie back and have it done to you. It is a ravishing novel: but it does not ravish you to no purpose.

Indeed, in spite of its small scale, though it is the smallness of scale that helps give Gatsby its odd illusion of perfection, it is the most Balzacian of all American novels and certainly the only authentic American account of a sentimental education that I know of. Not that it is Gatsby who is thus educated: it is the narrator, Nick Carraway, who is the hero of the novel, and who acquires almost too much weary knowledge of the heart at Gatsby's expense. Gatsby himself is no hero. He is the dupe of the dream. Reality would spoil things. He believes it is possible to re-create the past.

So Gatsby is about *not* making it, about the intractability of social class, about the yawning gulf between wealth and money and that between love and marriage. It is also, very much so, about adultery, unusual for a Great American novel; but, then, Fitzgerald was raised a Roman Catholic. This is adultery in the grand manner: when Gatsby startles the staid midwesterner, Nick, by dismissing the relations between the woman whom he believes to be in love with him and her husband as 'just personal', Gatsby is, from the depths of his passionate naïvety, singing the very song Tristan sang before King Mark and the Queen of Cornwall.

This grand, rhetorical adultery is counterpointed by the sordid, realistic adultery between Daisy's husband and the wife of the man who looks after his car. The final twist of the plot restores marital propriety.

Daisy/Isolde triumphantly repossesses her deplorable but necessary husband after disposing of this mistress. Indeed, with one hit and run accident for which she evades the blame, Daisy contrives not only to rid herself of Tom Buchanan's woman but also unconsciously to set in motion the events that also rid her of Gatsby, the old lover turned up like the refrain of an old song – a lover with whom she rapidly becomes disillusioned. For, if Daisy has represented the Love of a Good Woman for Gatsby for all those years, then she, too must have polished the shining armour of his memory during her unsatisfactory marriage and found the reality did not match the dream either.

Right from the start, Fitzgerald makes no bones about Daisy's lack of moral fibre. There's a terrific bit at the beginning, when Nick goes to meet Daisy and her husband, Tom, at their sumptuous house (they're filthy rich, obviously). After a sticky dinner interrupted by a phone call from Tom's mistress, Daisy goes to great lengths to present herself to Nick as the wronged woman. 'I've had a very bad time, Nick, and I'm pretty cynical about things.' As she waves him goodbye, Nick, ever the rational man, thinks: 'It seemed to me that the thing for Daisy to do was to rush out of the house, child in arms – but apparently there were no such intentions in her head.' And that, apart from the amazing charm that leaps up off the page at you, is all you need to know about Daisy. If she will not leave her husband for the sake of her own self-respect, then she will scarcely be regenerated by the renewed offer of Gatsby's pure heart, even – especially – if it comes wrapped up in a great deal of funny money.

It's curious that this surgically anatomised can of worms should be popularly supposed to be a sort of bootleg 'Dolce Vita'. Certainly the consistency of tone – an unruffled elegiac irony – holds an exceedingly melodramatic plot in a firm, cool grip. And it is this consistency of tone that gives the novel its illusion of perfection which is an illusion because, technically, *The Great Gatsby* is put together with a knife and fork. Formal qualities were never Fitzgerald's strong suit and he wasn't too handy with negotiating the limited viewpoint of a first-person narrative, either.

But, since Fitzgerald was working in the context of a sudden accession of grace, the quickness of his hand deceives the eye. He decided to dower Nick Carraway with his own, bitter-sweet, Cole Porterish, sensual eye and appreciation of social nuance, but let him, otherwise, be something of a dull old stick. And Nick's carefully delineated decency of a 'squeamish provincial' both carries the clumsiness of the construction – one somehow doesn't expect him to be an accomplished raconteur – and also gives credibility to the complicated *crime passionel* (with the wrong victim!) that is the finale. Nick seems such a trustworthy person. Has he not 'disapproved of Gatsby from beginning to end'? Therefore it is possible to take Gatsby at Nick's estimation of him, to lament, with him, for Gatsby's terrible, implacable, pig-headed, corrupt innocence.

Stylistically, too, although one always remembers *The Great Gatsby* as seamlessly elegant, it is full of close squeaks. Fitzgerald takes the kind of risks with pretentiousness that only somebody very young and over-confident and hell bent on becoming a star would take. The miracle is, they mostly work. Reading *Gatsby* is like watching the daring young man on the flying trapeze: your heart is in your mouth. 'No amount of fire or

freshness can challenge what a man can store up in his ghostly heart.'
Oops. No wonder Fitzgerald thought Michael Arlen would be his successor as the most popular fiction writer of the day.

When Gatsby remembers his and Daisy's first kiss. Fitzgerald very nearly
takes a nasty tumble: 'He knew that when he kissed this girl, and forever
wed his unutterable visions to her perishable breath, his mind would never
romp again like the mind of God.' And worse to come! 'So he waited, listening for a moment longer to the tuning-fork that had been struck upon
a star.' Then, miraculously, he rights himself: how true all this is to
Gatsby's 'appalling sentimentality', how characteristic of the Jay Gatz who
'invented just the sort of Jay Gatsby that a seventeen-year-old boy would
be likely to invent and to this conception . . . was faithful to the end'.
What Gatsby is doing is making a pass at the first Nice Girl he has ever
met. What Gatsby truly believes himself to be doing is making the same
kind of Faustian bargain with fate and social mobility that Jude the
Obscure made.

And Gatsby could have done it only in 1917, in the social confusion of
the war that made him a lieutenant and gave him access to a Nice Girl in
the first place, sent him to Oxford, put his life in the way of his ambitions,
Only the postwar boom and Prohibition could have given him the chance
to make all that funny money. Of course, Gatsby is mixed up in even
murkier things than bootlegging, or so Fitzgerald hints. But he is content
to be as enticingly reticent about the real sources of Gatsby's wealth as
Emily Brontë was about Heathcliff's.

But Gatsby is such a creature of history, who gains his very universality
from his secure location in a specific place and time, that it is only right
and proper that those great set pieces, Fitzgerald's descriptions of his parties, should now seem the perfect embodiment of the Roaring Twenties,
with popular music of the period accompanying the most important
scenes. The piano – 'One thing's sure and nothing's surer, The rich get
richer and the poor get children – accompanies the first, untroubled
reunion of the parted lovers; a dance band pounds away heartlessly in the
Plaza ballroom as Tom brutally breaks Gatsby's cover in the suite above.
Indeed, the novel is composed almost theatrically, in a series of very consciously set and stage-managed scenes, that mirror, even parody, one
another: dinner with Tom and Daisy, with its conscious 'civilisation', its
undercurrent of nastiness, followed by a drunken evening with Tom and
Myrtle; if Daisy's dinner table is disrupted by an unwelcome phone call,
Myrtle's evening ends when Tom breaks her nose for daring to mention
his wife's name.

And, as the novel draws towards the ineffable dying fall with which it
ends, one realises that those parties, where the crowds only emphasise

Gatsby's isolation, prefigure that lonely funeral, to which, from all those revellers, only the bespectacled man who so admired Gatsby's leather-bound library goes. And this anonymous mourner, so appreciative of Gatsby's style as an idealistic parvenu, speaks the only fitting epitaph for one who was burdened with 'such an extraordinary gift of hope', who reached, tremulously, wondering towards the orgiastic future : ' The poor son-of-a-bitch,' he said.

Observer Magazine, 1980

Grace Paley: The Little Disturbances of Man and Enormous Changes at the Last Minute

What can put you off Grace Paley's stories is their charm. 'An Interest in Life' in the collection called *The Little Disturbances of Man* begins: 'My husband gave me a broom one Christmas. This wasn't right. No one can tell me it was meant kindly.' It is so scrupulously disarming an intro that it is bound to put people who like Joan Didion very much on their guard. And it is alarmingly easy to fall into the language of the Martini ad when writing about Grace Paley – wry, dry, tender, ironic, etc.

The snag is her work *has* all these qualities: it is an added irony that, since the *fin* has come a little early this *siècle* and anomie is all the rage, wry, dry tenderness is a suspect commodity. Not that Paley appears to give one jot for psychosocial hem-lengths. She is, as we used to say, 'for life', and clearly cannot imagine why anybody should be against it. Not that the wonderful world of Grace Paley is all sunshine: the heroine of 'An Interest in Life' is kept from despair only by a Micawberesque sustaining illusion that the broom-giver, now defected, will return. (It's obvious that, if he does, she'll really be in trouble.)

But the charm is a problem, though, both infuriatingly irresistible and, since couched in the *faux-naif* style, verging dangerously on the point of cloy. The title story of the collection called *Enormous Changes at the Last Minute* almost goes over the top. A middle-aged social worker, Alexandra, is surprised into bed with a feckless hippy. 'That's my bag. I'm a mother-fucker,' he crows complacently. He impregnates her. Her aged father is justifiably enraged. 'After that, Alexandra hoped every day for her father's death, so that she could have a child without ruining his life at the very end of it when ruin is absolutely retroactive.'

But Paley contrives to transcend this Shirley MacLainesque scenario completely. Alexandra reorganises her apartment as a refuge for pregnant teenagers, setting an interesting precedent in social work. Her father falls, bangs his head, clears his brain, begins again 'with fewer scruples'. The hippy composes a celebratory anthem about parent-child relationships that is a hit from coast to coast and is 'responsible for a statistical increase in visitors to old-age homes by the apprehensive middle-aged and the astonished young'.

That single adjective, 'astonished', is sufficient to illuminate retrospectively this everyday story of marginal folk. We see that it is not a quaint tale of last-minute motherhood so much as an account of that reconciliation with old age and kinship which is, in itself, a reconciliation with time. Extracted from the text, the characters are patently emblematic: an old man, his daughter, a young man, a chorus of girls, a boy child. There is even an off-stage cameo guest appearance by Alexandra's ex-husband, the Communist Granofsky. ('Probably boring the Cubans to death this very minute,' opines her father.)

As in the *News of the World,* the whole of human life is here, and, indeed, many of Paley's plots would not disgrace that journal. Other stories feature a man shot by a jealous cop, his neighbour's husband; a White runaway raped, beaten, dead, in a Black neighbourhood – Paley extends tenderness and respect even to the rapists. There are shot-gun marriages and catatonic boys. But do not think that, Ophelia-like, Paley can turn hell itself to favour and to prettiness. In *Enormous Changes at the Last Minute,* two stories – 'Gloomy Tune' and 'Samuel' – are done as straight as case-histories. 'Gloomy Tune' is an analysis of social deprivation. The problem children 'never stole. They had a teeny knife. They pushed people on slides and knocked them all over the playground. They wouldn't murder anyone, I think.' They are doomed. 'Samuel' is probably one of the great works of fiction in our century, although it is but four pages long. He is a bold child killed at dangerous play on the subway. His mother is young and soon pregnant again. 'Then for a few months she was hopeful. The child born to her was a boy. They brought him to be seen and nursed. She smiled. But immediately she saw that this baby wasn't Samuel.'

I love to think how Joan Didion would hate Grace Paley. If a continent divides Paley's seedy, violent multi-ethnic New York from Didion's neurasthenic version of LA as a city of the plain, their sensibilities are those of different planets. But, then, the poor always have an unfair moral edge on the rich, and most Paley characters are on Welfare.

Those who manage to keep their heads above water tend to come from good socialist stock. Even in retirement with the Children of Judea, one old man plots to organise the help. Ex-husbands constantly send committed postcards from developing countries. Ex-husbands are far more frequent on these pages than husbands, though, as in 'The Used-Boy Raisers' and 'The Pale Pink Roast', often turning up again like the refrain of an old song – mysterious, irrelevant, yet never quite consigned to oblivion.

Paley does not efface herself from the text. A homogeneous, immediately recognisable personality pervades everything she writes. Nevertheless, she is a ventriloquist *par excellence,* and speaks the American that has been moulded by Russian, Polish, and Yiddish as eloquently as she can personate the speech of Harlem. She can change sex, too: as a first person, she credibly becomes a man, young or old. Shape-shifting is no problem – thin, fat. 'I was popular in certain circles, says Aunt Rose. I wasn't no thinner then, only more stationary in the flesh'. This is 'Goodbye and Good Luck', in *The Little Disturbances of Man,* the only one of all these stories that has a strong flavour of another writer. In this case, Isaac Bashevis Singer, with whom Paley shares a tradition and an idiom.

All the same, all the narrative roles Paley undertakes are those of the same kind of marginal people, with essentially the same exhausted, oblique tolerance as those child-besieged women, usually called Faith (she has a sister, Hope), who seem most directly to express the real personality of the writer. One of them describes her own marginality: 'I was forced by inclement management into a yellow-dog contract with Bohemia, such as it survives.' And perhaps the continuous creation of this fictive personality, whom we are always conscious of as the moving force behind the narratives, is the real achievement of these two marvellous collections. As if, somehow, this omnipresent meta-narrator is, finally, more important than the events described. I think this meta-personality, is in fact, something like conscience.

The charm turns out to be a stalking-horse, a method of persuasion, the self-conscious defensive/protective mechanism characteristic of all exploited groups, a composite of Jewish charm, Black charm, Irish charm, Hispanic charm, female charm. It is part of the apparatus of the tragic sense of life.

Technically, Grace Paley's work makes the novel as a form seem virtually redundant. Each one of her stories has more abundant inner life then most other people's novels; they are as overcrowded as the apartments they all live in, and an enormous amount can happen in five or six pages. Her prose presents a series of miracles of poetic compression. There are some analogies for her verbal method – e.e. cummings, perhaps, also a smiler with a knife, but she rarely plumbs his depths of cuteness. She has the laconic street eloquence of some of the Beats. This is not *English* English; scarcely a Wasp graces these pages. Yet the cumulative effect of these stories is that of the morality of the woman of flexible steel behind them; most of all, because of her essential gravity, she reminds me, strangely enough, of George Eliot. But, within its deliberately circumscribed compass, Grace Paley's work echoes with the promise of that sense, not of optimism, but of *inexhaustibility,* which is the unique quality of the greatest American art.

London Review of Books, 1980

Colette

Review of Michèle Sarde, *Colette: A Biography.*

Colette is one of the few, possibly the only, well-known woman writer of modern times who is universally referred to simply by her surname, *tout court.* Woolf hasn't made it, even after all these years; Rhys without the Jean is incognito, Nin without the Anaïs looks like a typo. Colette, Madame Colette, remains, in this as much else, unique.

However, Colette did not acquire this distinction because she terrorised respect language out of her peers, alas; by a happy accident, her family name also doubles as a girlish handle and a very ducky one, too. One could posit 'Bonny' or 'Rosie' as some kind of English equivalent. It was by a probably perfectly unconscious sleight of hand that Colette appropriated for herself the form of address of both masculine respect and masculine intimacy of her period, a fact that, in a small way, reflects the whole message of her career. This is: if you can't win, change the rules of the game.

Her career was a profoundly strange one and necessarily full of contradictions, of which her uncompromising zeal for self-exploitation is one. Madame Colette, though never quite Madame Colette de l'Académie Française – one game she couldn't crack – was accorded a state funeral by the French government; this was the woman whose second husband's aristocratic family dismissed her as a cunning little strip-tease artist over-eager for the title of Baroness. As Madame Colette, she first appeared on pin-up pictures of 'Our pretty actresses: Madame Colette of the Olympia'. And, in these pictures, taken in her late thirties, she is very beautiful and sexy indeed; she looks out at you with all the invitation of the stripper, '*you* can call me Colette', a familiar show-biz trick, the relationship of artificial intimacy the showgirl creates between her named self and the anonymous punter, with its intention to disarm.

This artificial creation of a sense of intimacy with Colette herself is one of the qualities that gives her writing its seductiveness; Colette certainly wasn't on the halls all those years for nothing, although the extent to which a wilful exhibitionism kept her on the boards against the advice of the majority of her critics well into her fifties may be connected with a certain capacity to embarrass that often frays the edges of her writing.

Because 'you can call me Colette' isn't a statement of the same order as: 'Call me Ishmael.' The social limitations to experience in a woman's life still preclude the kind of unselfconscious picaresque adventuring that formed the artistic apprenticeships of Melville, Lowry, Conrad, while other socio-economic factors mean that those women who see most of the beastly backside of the world, that is, prostitutes, are least in a position to utilise this invaluable experience as art. Somewhere, Norman Mailer says there won't be a *really* great woman writer, one, you understand, *con cojones* and everything, until the first call-girl tells her story. Though it's reasonable to assume that, when she does, Mailer won't like it at all, at all, the unpleasant truth in this put-down is that most women don't have exposure to the kind of breadth of experience that, when digested, produces great fiction. (OK, so what about the Brontës? Well, as vicar's daughters in a rural slum parish, peripatetic international governesses and terminal consumptives, they *did* have such a variety of experience. So.) But the life of Colette was as picaresque as a woman's may be without putting herself in a state of hazard.

Her first novel, *Claudine at School*, and its sequels, appeared with the name of her husband on the title page. This man, the peculiar Willy, one of the best-publicised Bohemians of the Belle Époque, ensured that the little Burgundian village girl, Colette's favourite disguise, encountered not only numerous whores of both sexes at an impressionable age but also *everybody,* Proust, Debussy, Ravel, you name them. When Willy left her, his wife found herself in the unusual position of having written a number of bestsellers whilst being unable to take any financial or artistic credit for them. To earn a living in the years before the First World War, she felt she had no alternative but to go on the halls. Since she could neither sing nor dance she performed as a sex-object and subject of scandal, and not a particularly up-market sex object, either. Since Willy had enjoyed sexually humiliating her, no doubt there was a special pleasure in exploiting her sexuality whilst herself secure and unavailable; after Willy, she took refuge in the bosom of the lesbian Establishment of the period. Our pretty actress had an aristocratic protector, the Marquise de Mornay; nothing unusual, not even the sex of the Marquise, about this in those permissive times.

Then came a Cinderellaesque marriage to (Baron) Henry de Jouvenal, editor of *Le Matin,* later a politician of considerable distinction. One thing about Colette interests me; when did she stop lying about her age? The voluptuous dancer was pushing forty when she married de Jouvenal, 'But the registry office has to know your age!' she complained to a friend. There comes a time when a woman freely publicises her age so people can say: 'How young you look!' It seems to have come later than most to Colette, but when it did, she gloried in it, as in all else.

In tandem with this characteristically if rather Hollywood Edwardian career, not one but two writers are growing within Colette. One writes *La Vagabonde* in 1910, a novel which is still one of the most truthful expositions of the dilemma of a free woman in a male-dominated society. Perhaps because Colette, having the triumphant myopia of a vain woman, refused to acknowledge her society as male-dominated, she sees no dilemma; there is no real choice. One *is* free. In the same year, the other writer, the one more nearly related to our pretty actress, began work as a journalist for *Le Matin,* which is how she met its editor. Renée Néré, music-hall artiste, prefers to go it alone in *La Vagabonde,* but Colette, Colette married and married well. Her marriage also sealed her fate as a journalist, which in turn sealed her fate as a novelist, because the professions are mutually exclusive, even if simultaneously conducted.

Colette became literary editor of *Le Matin* in 1919 and thereafter was to work almost continuously in newspapers and magazines in one way and another, whilst continuing to write fiction and, from time to time, to act. In 1924, after her divorce from de Jouvenal, she started signing her work, for the first time, neither Colette Willy nor Colette de Jouvenal but simply 'Colette'. Her third marriage, some ten years later, would never make her dwindle into Colette Goudeket, even if Colette was not her own but her father's name. You can't subvert patriarchy *that* easily, after all, even if your father's name might be roughly analogous to 'Darling', and he so weak and feckless you have only acquired the very haziest grasp of the power of patriarchy. However, now 'Colette' she was, for all seasons.

As a writer, of both journalism and of some of her fiction, Colette exploits this intimacy of the stripper with her reader quite remorselessly. She trades on the assumption that you are going to care about Maman because this is the unique Colette's unique Maman. The details of her Burgundian childhood, endlessly recapitulated and, one suspects, endlessly elaborated over the years, are purveyed with a child-like sense of self importance, such a naïve expectation that the smallest details of the Colette family diet and customs are worth recounting that it seems churlish to ask: 'What is the point of all this?'

She puts herself into much of her actual fiction. Not so much that all her fiction tends to draw on childhood, on the music-hall or the sad truths distilled from unhappy marriages as that whole short novels – *Chance Acquaintances, Break of Day* – and many short stories are recounted in the first person of a Colette very precisely realised as subject and object at the same time. In the collection Penguin publish under the title, *The Rainy Moon,* most of the stories feature Colette herself, if not as a major character then never as passive narrator. She always gives herself a part, as though she could not bear to leave herself out, must always be on stage.

She stopped writing fiction altogether after *Gigi,* in 1942, a Belle Époque fable of the apparent triumph of innocence that would been nauseating were it not so cynical. Her later work, until her death in 1954, is mostly a series of extended autobiographical reveries, among them *The Blue Lantern, The Evening Star.* These, and the volumes of autobiographical journalism that preceded them, *My Mother's House* (given this curious biblical title in English – in French, *La Maison de Claudine) Sido, My Apprenticeships, Music-Hall Sidelights,* etc. are a peculiar kind of literary strip-tease in themselves, a self-exploitation that greedily utilises every scrap of past experience in an almost unmediated form.

Yet there is no sense of the confessional about this endless flow of memory. Colette never tells you about herself. Instead, she describes herself. Few writers have described their own physicality so often; 'savage' child, with the long, blonde plaits; bride with the 'splash of red carnations on the bodice of her white wedding gown', in dinner jacket and monacle; pregnant, looking like 'a rat dragging a stolen egg'. And so on.

But she gives the impression of telling all, in a literary form unclassifiable except as a version of what television has accustomed us to call 'fictionalised documentary'. Robert Phelps was able to construct a perfectly coherent autobiography from Colette's scattered reminiscences, and present *The Earthly Paradise* as if it were, not an imaginative parallel to her real life, but the real thing. All Colette's biographers rely heavily on the sources she herself provides, even Michèle Sarde's recent, exhaustive, lengthy life, as if Colette could be trusted not to keep her fingers crossed when she was talking about herself, even when remembering events across a great gulf of years. Also, as if her sincerity was in itself important. Such is the sense of intimacy Colette creates; you feel you know her, because she has said '*you* can call me Colette', although she says this to everybody who pays.

And yet these memories, this experience, are organised with such conscious art, such lack of spontaneity! She must have acquired from Balzac her taste for presenting those she loved best and admired most, including herself, as actors in *tableaux vivants,* as beings complete in themselves, as if unmodified by the eyes of an observer who is herself part of the tableau; she describes finished objects in a perfect perspective, almost *trompe l'œil,* stuck fast in the lucid amber of her prose. Her portrait of her friend, the poet, Renée Vivian, in *The Pure and the Impure,* has the finite quality of nineteenth-century fiction. 'I remember Renée's gay laughter, her liveliness, the faint halo of light trembling in her golden hair all combined to sadden me, as does the happiness of blind children who laugh and play without the help of light.' All that Colette has left out of this portrait is the possibility of some kind of inner life beyond Colette's imagining which belongs to Renée Vivian alone. This holds true for all the dazzling galaxy of heterogeneous humanity in Colette's fictionalised documentaries. The apparent objectivity of her prose is a device to seal these people in her own narrative subjectivity.

The portraits, of Renée Vivian, of actresses like La Belle Otéro and Polaire, even of Willy and, later of her own daughter, are exemplary because of their precision and troubling because of their detachment. Even in the accounts of her beloved mother, Colette's actual prose implicitly invites the reader to admire both the quality of the observation and the skill with which a different time and place are recreated; then, with a shock, you realise you have been seduced into applauding, not so much a remarkable woman, as the quality of Colette's love for her. Colette's actual prose is itself narcissistic.

So her apparently total lack of reticence tells us, in the end, nothing about her real relationships and her self-absorption becomes a come-on, a device like a mask behind which an absolute privacy might be maintained. Her obsessive love of make-up, of the stage, of disguises, suggest a desire, if not to conceal, then to mystify. The daughter of Captain Jules-Joseph Colette of the Zouaves could die happy in the notion she had never been on first-name terms with anyone outside her immediate family, not even, least of all, with any of her three husbands.

Since she appears to have been a profoundly disingenuous person, there seems no reason to think she did *not* die happy in this respect. The best lie is the truth, after all. Colette was indeed her name. Her childhood *was* a Burgundian idyll, even if one sister later killed herself, while a brother burned all of Colette's two thousand letters to her mother, as if to ensure that some things, at least, would remain sacrosanct from the daughter's guzzling, inordinate rapacity for material; Because the demands of journalism made Colette desperate for material; once a journalist has established the power-base of a cult of personality, he or she is positively encouraged to trot out their own opinions and anecdotes over and over again.

Colette's novels are of a different order of reality than her autobiographical pieces, because her novels are fiction and hence the truth; the rest is journalism and so may bear only the most peripheral relation to truth, even if a journalist tells you every single thing that actually happened.

In Colette's first novel, *Claudine at School,* she kills off Claudine's mother before the action begins. Claudine, her first *alter ego*. This is a far more interesting fact than all the obsessive gush about her own real mother, that spills out later in *La Maison de Claudine, Sido* and *Break of Day*. In this last novel, in fact a transparently fictionalised documentary using real Provençale locations and some real persons, Colette virtually apotheosises her dead mother, but leaves out altogether her third husband, Maurice Goudeket, who was happily ensconced by her side as she scribbled: 'I have paid for my folly, shut away the heady young wine that intoxicated me, and folded up my big, floating heart.'

The extent to which Colette came to believe her own mythology of herself is, of course, another question. Goudeket himself entered into the spirit of the thing wholeheartedly. His memoir of her last twenty years with him, *Close to Colette,* celebrates her peasant wisdom, her child-like enthusiasm. To him we owe the anecdote of her encounter with the cat in New York. 'At last someone who speaks French!' Michèle Sarde repeats this unblushingly, as if it told us something about the wit and wisdom of Colette. Michèle Sarde has swallowed the mythology whole; but the anecdote *does* tell us a good deal about Colette. It shows how wisely she picked her last companion, her Boswell, her PRO faithfully beyond the grave.

Goudeket rhapsodises: 'There were so many arts which she had not lost. With her the art of living came before the art of writing. She knew a receipt for everything, whether it was for furniture polish, vinegar, orange-wine or quince-water, for cooking truffles or preserving linen and materials.' French , he says – she was French to her fingertips, and provincial to boot, even after sixty years' total immersion in the heady whirlpool of Parisian artistic life. French and provincial as Elizabeth David's *French Country Cooking*, and just as much intended for publication.

I must say, now, that this ineradicable quality of the fraud, the fake, of the unrepentant self-publicist, is one of the things about Colette I respect most; indeed, revere. Michèle Sarde's biography, however besotted, however uncritical, however willing to draw illegimate parallels between art and life, nevertheless demonstrates how it was the passionate integrity of Colette's narcissism that rendered her indestructible.

It's possible to see her entire career as a writer, instigated as it was by Willy, who robbed her of the first fruits of her labours, as an act of vengeance on him. A certain kind of woman, a vain woman, that is to say, a woman with self-respect, is spurred on by spite. Had the Rev. Brontë supported and encouraged his daughters' ambitions, what would the poor things have done then? I don't think Leonard Woolf did his wife a favour by mothering her. After Colette met kind, sweet, intelligent, loving Goudeket, she wrote very little major fiction.

In Simone de Beauvoir's memoirs, there's a description of a dinner party de Beauvoir attended with Sartre, at which Colette, already the frizzed and painted sacred cow of French letters, babbling away to *les gars,* as was her wont, about dogs, cats, knitting, *le bon vin, les bons fromages* and so on, offered de Beauvoir only the meagre attention of an occasional, piercing stare. De Beauvoir thought Colette disliked women. Possibly Colette, never a one to be *bouleversée* by a great mind, and, perhaps, privately relishing boring a great mind into the ground with nuggets of earthly Burgundian wisdom, was no more than contemplating the question every thinking woman in the Western world must have posed herself one time or other: why is a nice girl like Simone wasting her time sucking up to a boring old fart like J.-P.? Her memoirs will be mostly about him; he will scarcely speak of her. Colette would have *known* so, intuitively.

Of course, Colette could no more have written *The Second Sex* than de Beauvoir could have danced naked on a public stage, which precisely defines the limitations of both these great ladies and it is this very self-exploitative, stripper quality that earths most of Colette's later writing. However, it is hard to imagine Colette, had she attended the Sorbonne, getting any kind of buzz out of coming second to Sartre in her final examinations, or, indeed, out of coming second to anybody. She had to be number one, even if she had to reinvent a whole genre of literature, and herself included, to do so.

Even after all these years, de Beauvoir still appears to be proud that only Sartre achieved higher marks in those first exams than she. What would have happened, one wonders, if she had come top? What would it have done to Sartre? Merely to think of it makes the mind reel. Only love can make you proud to be an also-ran. Would love have made J.-P. proud like that?

But Colette simply did not believe that women *were* the second sex. One of Goudeket's anecdotes from the declining years is very revealing. He carried her in her wheelchair into a holiday hotel; the lobby filled with applauding, cheering fans; she was a national institution in France, after all. Colette seemed touched: 'They've remembered me from last year.' This isn't modesty, though Goudeket pretends to think so; it's irony, I hope, because, if it isn't irony, then what is it? What monstrous vanity would think it was perfectly natural for a little old lady to receive a tumultuous welcome from her hotel staff? Of course she didn't believe she was really famous, towards the end. She knew she wasn't famous enough to gratify her unappeasable ego. Magnificently she did not know her place.

But to believe women are not the second sex is to deny a whole area of social reality, however inspiriting the toughness and resilience of Colette and most of her heroines may be, especially after the revival of the wet and spineless woman-as-hero which graced the 1970s. (The zomboid creatures in Joan Didion's novels, for example; the resurrected dippy dames of Jean Rhys, so many of whom might have had pathetic walk-on parts in Colette's own stories of Paris in the 1920s.) Colette celebrated the status quo of femininity, not only its physical glamour but its capacity to subvert and withstand the boredom of patriarchy. This makes her an ambivalent ally to the women's movement. She is like certain shop-stewards who devote so much time to getting up management's nose that they lose sight of the great goals of socialism.

Her fiction, as opposed to her journalism, is dedicated to the proposition of the battle of the sexes – 'love, the bread and butter of my pen', she observes in a revealing phrase. But, in Colette's battles, the results are fixed, men can never win, unless, as in the short story, 'The Képi', the woman is foolish enough to believe a declaration of love is tantamount to a cessation of hostilities.

In the brief, fragile, ironic novels that are Colette's claim to artistic seriousness, *Ripening Seed, The Vagabond, Chéri* and *The last of Chéri,* the men are decorative but useless. The delicious adolescent Phil, in *Ripening Seed,* lolls at ease on the beach while little Vinca arranges their picnic, her role is to serve, but this role makes him a parasite. The beautiful (and economically self-sufficient, as so many of Colette's heroines) lady who seduces him, whom he calls his 'master', is not really Vinca's rival at all, but her fellow conspirator in the ugly plot to 'make a man' of Phil with all that implies of futility and arrogance and complacency.

Renée Néré, the vagabond, tenderly consigns her rich suitor to the condition of a fragrant, unfulfilled memory since that is the only way she can continue to think kindly of him; she knows quite well the truth of the fairytale is, kiss Prince Charming and he instantly turns into a frog. Léa simply grows out of Chéri, which is tough on Chéri.

The two Chéri novellas probably form Colette's masterpieces, although they are now so 'period' in atmosphere that the luxurious Edwardian décor blurs their hard core of emotional truth. As they recede into history, the décor will disappear; we will be left with something not unlike *Les Liaisons Dangereuses.* They are her masterpieces because they transcend the notion of the battle between the sexes by concentrating on an exceptionally rigorous analysis of the rules of war. Léa's financial independence is, of course, taken for granted; otherwise, in Colette's terms, there would be no possibility of a real relationship.

Julie de Carneilhan, published in 1941, a brief novel about upper-class alimony, is interesting in this respect because it deals specifically with a woman as an economically contingent being. I suspect this is what Colette meant when she said it was as close a reckoning with the elements of her second marriage as she ever allowed herself, since de Jouvenal was theoretically in control of their joint finances for the duration of their relationship. Without financial resources of her own, Julie is duped and stripped of self-respect by her husband, finally taking refuge with her brother and father, an obvious fantasy ending to which the shadow of approaching war promises an appropriately patriarchal resolution. Curiously enough, another war, the First World War, provides the watershed between the two Chéri novellas; released from the maternal embrace of Léa, anyone but Colette would have thought the trenches would make a *real* man of Chéri. But she knew it wasn't as simple as that.

The Chéri novels are about the power politics of love, and Léa and Chéri could be almost any permutation of ages or sexes. It is not in the least like *Der Rosenkavalier,* although we first meet Léa in her graceful late forties, some twenty-five years older than her boy lover. But they could both as well be men; or both women. Psychologically, Chéri could just as well be Chérie and Léa, Léo, except that we are socially acclimatised to the sexual vanity of middle-aged men; a handsome, successful, rich, fifty-year-old Léo might well feel that Chéri, at twenty-five, after an affair of six years, was getting a touch long in the tooth for his tastes. But even the age difference is not the point of the stories; the point is, that Léa holds the reins. The only person who could film these novels with a sufficiently cold and dialectical eye is Fassbinder and he is the contemporary artist whom Colette most resembles. Not that she was a political person at all, in the Fassbinder sense, but she watched with a beady eye and drew the correct conclusions.

Given the thrust towards an idealised past of the major part of Colette's work, it is disconcerting to find that the moral of the Chéri novellas is: memory kills. When Chéri goes to see his ageing mistress, after the war and an absence of seven years, he finds, not the faded, touching ghost of love and beauty – no Miss Haversham, she – but a fat, jolly, altogether unrecognisable old lady quite unprepared to forgive him for once having flinched from her wrinkles. No tender scene of a visit to Juliet's tomb ensues, but a brisk invitation to grow up and forget which Chéri is temperamentally incapable of accepting. A bullet in the brain is the only way out for Chéri. Léa was forced to reconstruct herself as a human being in order to survive the pain of Chéri's first rejection of her; the reconstructed Léa inevitably destroys Chéri by her very existence.

Colette's 'personal' voice is altogether absent from this parable. All the leading characters are either whores or the children of whores. They are all rich. If Colette set in motion the entire Colette industry in order to create for herself the artistic freedom and privacy to construct this chilling account of libido and false consciousness, then it was all abundantly worthwhile.

Penguin continue to reissue translations of most of Colette by a variety of hands, some of them, especially Antonia White's (the *Claudine* books) conspicuously handier than others. These slim volumes are currently dressed up in melting pinks, tones of pink, mauve and almond green not unlike the colour of Léa's knickers' drawer. The exquisitely period photographs on the covers often turn out to depict Colette's own foxy mask, done up in a variety of disguises – a sailor suit for *Gigi*; full drag for *The Pure and the Impure*. The Women's Press put a charcoal drawing of the geriatric Colette, foxier than ever, on their edition of *Break of Day*. The cult of the personality of Colette, to which Michèle Sarde's biography, *Colette*, is a votive tribute, continues apace although it detracts attention from the artist in her, turns her more and more into a figure of historic significance, the woman who *did,* who occupied a key position in a transitional period of social history, from 1873 to 1954, and noted down most of what happened to her.

Apart from the *Chéri* novels and one or two others, her achievement as a whole *was* extraordinary though not in a literary sense; she forged a career out of the kind of self-obsession which is supposed, in a woman, to lead only to tears before bed-time, in a man to lead to the peaks. Good for her. I've got a god-daughter named after her. Or rather, such are the contradictions inherent in all this, named after Captain Jules-Joseph Colette, one-legged tax gatherer and bankrupt.

London Review of Books, 1980

Carol Ascher: Simone de Beauvoir

I recall an ad, years ago, in the early 1960s, in the *New Statesman* lonely hearts column, that went: 'De Beauvoirish woman seeks Sartre-type man.' For some reason, perhaps because of the couple's inherent genius for self-publicity, the premier existential pair have always been doomed to be vulgarised. Carol Ascher vulgarises them both separately and together in her book and I propose to vulgarise them in this review.

That *cri de coeur* in the *New Statesman* seemed to sum up the emotional aspirations of certain members of the female intelligentsia who came to maturity just before the women's movement got off the ground. Like de Beauvoir herself, we thought we were so clever we deserved to get the *really* clever men; never mind that Sartre-type men rarely, if ever, seemed to advertise for de Beauvoirish women, preferring instead to appeal quixotically for nineteen-year-old blondes (It turns out poor Simone suffered a lot due to this.)

Simone and Jean-Paul were already established as the Darby and Joan of intellectual camaraderie and companionate marriage, in those days, living proof that the Cleverest Man in the World needed by his side, if not always in bed, a woman almost so clever as he. We knew she was almost as clever as he was because, at that time, de Beauvoir still thought it worthwhile to tell the world via the autobiographical details on her back-flaps that she had come second to Sartre in their university finals. And, goodness me, wasn't coming second to Jean-Paul Sartre – *Jean-Paul Sartre!* – something to be proud of? De Beauvoir mentions somewhere how she wanted to live with an 'intellectual superior'; clearly only a deep thinker like Sartre could be intellectually superior to this cookie.

One of the most interesting projects of the life of Simone de Beauvoir has been her mythologisation of Sartre. Her volumes of memoirs are devoted to this project, one that Carol Ascher ignores. The publication of de Beauvoir's *The Second Sex*, still the subtlest and most complex analysis of the condition of women to be published since the war, only seemed to confirm the egalitarian rationality of their relationship. Fancy, one thought, him letting her write *The Second Sex* . . .

Carol Ascher isolates de Beauvoir's fifty-year relationship with Sartre for some rather odd criticism, *tutoying* de Beauvoir the while in an offensive and embarrassing manner: 'your decision to remain with Sartre, to make him the centre of your life, really, seems to have entailed a heavy sacrifice of eroticism and emotions in favour of your mind, which you knew he would always be able to nurture'. (Note the scrambled grammar.)

That de Beauvoir might have found a 'path to the self' by freaking out, as Ascher suggests, is a hypothesis that makes the mind reel; but, self-confessed feminist as Ascher is, all the same she still takes for granted, without even thinking about it, that Sartre *did* nurture de Beauvoir's mind. Yet what, one wonders, would have been the intellectual history of twentieth-century Europe had de Beauvoir somehow managed to scrape together that handful of extra marks and pip Sartre at the post? What might de Beauvoir not have done had it been objectively proved to her that *she* was cleverer than Sartre?

The career of Simone de Beauvoir is indeed rich in internal contradictions, not the least of which is that the author of *The Second Sex* did not commit herself to feminism until late middle age, until just the other year, in fact. Nor did this commitment appear to affect her relationship with Sartre, which seems peculiar. Many of these contradictions spring from the nature of Parisian intellectual life, and, indeed, from French history *in toto*, but Ascher shows little interest in cultural relativity.

Ascher's method is to approach de Beauvoir and her complex, incestuous, hermetic and cerebral world through Ascher's own experience, which is that of a nice, clean, liberal American girl. This means she can, with a straight face, deliver statements like: 'When I was a teenager, existentialism was making midwestern newspapers with such headings as: IF GOD IS DEAD, EVERYTHING IS POSSIBLE!' Even with a four or five line gloss about choice, responsibility, contingency and black turtleneck sweaters, I do not think this is a sufficient introduction to existential theory as manifested in the work of Simone de Beauvoir, and I can't see what mid-1950s midwestern newspaper headlines have got to do with anything whatsoever.

But since Ascher tells us she doesn't believe in objectivity and adds proudly that she 'cannot pretend her attitude is neutral', presumably she intends to forge a new style in which to write a new kind of book in which to interpret a new kind of woman. She describes her study of de Beauvoir as 'part biography, part literary criticism, part political and personal commentary'. You can tell right from the introduction that she isn't going to get bogged down in boring old masculine-type academic discourse. 'When I would tell people I was working on a book about Simone de Beauvoir, I usually received one or two reactions. 'Oh, wow, she wrote *The Second Sex*, I'm afraid I never quite got through it.' Or, 'She's Jean-Paul Sartre's friend, isn't she?'

To assure the reader at the start that de Beauvoir is unreadable clears the air and lets us know where we stand. Presumably, Ascher intends de Beauvoir to remain unread, since *Simone de Beauvoir: A Life of Freedom* turns out to be a crib on de Beauvoir for Women's Studies courses, to spare students the inconvenience and eyestrain of actually having to grapple with the texts.

It would be infinitely kinder to pass over this book in silence were it not for the richly fatuous self-regard that gleams off every page. Ascher succeeds in patronising Simone de Beauvoir almost continuously. She has succeeded in writing a book that resembles in almost every way an Anthony Burgess parody of a Women's Studies academic textbook. How has she managed to pull this off? Perhaps the phrase, somewhere, a 'supportive community of women writers', has something to do with it. Apparently this was what poor Simone lacked. That is why *The Second Sex* is so overwritten and crammed with meaningless detail.

However, patronising though Ascher is towards her austere madonna, my goodness me, but she adores her! And her own narcissism peaks in a curious anecdote in the afterword, where Ascher tells us how she finally managed to get it together to write to de Beauvoir: 'I expressed my confusion at having worked on her writings over a long period without her knowing me.' In reply, she receives the standard polite note, in which de Beauvoir is rash enough to say she is sure Archer's book will be a 'good' one.

This goes to Ascher's head in a deliciously dizzying way. 'I imagined turning every sentence of the book into a perfect gift to her'. . . 'the letter from Simone de Beauvoir made me fantasise about going off into the sunset with her'.

But she hasn't even *met* Simone! And, after all, de Beauvoir would hardly have written her she was sure the book was going to be a great, steaming heap of crap, would she? We Europeans don't normally abuse those to whom we have not been introduced, except in the course of book reviews.

The book is composed of chapters of almost equal lengths devoted to discussions of de Beauvoir's memoirs; her early fiction; the *roman à cléf, The Mandarins;* her later fiction; a chapter called: 'Death: a life-long obsession' (Ascher thinks de Beauvoir's fear of death is evidence of a lack of moral fibre); and another entitled 'Freedom and wholeness', which is about how women must return to the specificity of their own bodies. The introduction, an open letter to Simone de Beauvoir printed in the middle of the book, and the afterword are fan magazine ramblings.

Books Ascher dislikes she leaves out, which is one way of dealing with them. ('Spending equal amounts of analysis on works whose value appears doubtful seems to be a false kind of objectivity.') There is no bibliography. Ascher seems to be singularly ill-read in French twentieth-century texts besides translations of the more accessible works of her heroine, even though she confides in the afterword: 'One of the greatest gifts Simone de Beauvoir has given me, both before and during the writing of this book, is her conviction that it is all right to be an intellectual.'

I simply don't know what to make of this statement. It is, literally, stunning in the circumstances.

New Society, 1982

D. H. Lawrence, Scholarship Boy

Sooner or later, anyone who writes fiction in England has to come to terms with D. H. Lawrence, though this tussle is not necessary if you are writing fiction in the English language, Lawrence is central to the English novel, but by no means central to the novel in English – as far as that great mainstream is concerned, Lawrence is something of a cul-de-sac. But in England, he must still be dealt with and, even twenty years ago, he was a primary influence. Almost *the* primary influence.

Sons and Lovers remained, as it had been since it was first published in 1912, the paradigmatic first novel. Although it wasn't Lawrence's own first novel, it was nevertheless very much the first novel we all wanted to write. Those themes – that naked confrontation with the self, most passionate of all encounters for a bourgeois individualist; with the family; with sex; with the challenge of the world; the novel that justifies your own existence, the justification, above all, for that murder of the parent, which is to say, the murder of the self as child, which is the beginning of adult life.

I say, 'we'. Yet what resonance is lost if 'daughters' is substituted for 'sons' in that title, and how rich the internal contradiction, that the father himself should be largely absent from one of the classic novels of patriarchy. And that, in such an overtly Oedipal fiction, it is the *mother* whom the son murders. But Lawrence's eminence in the feminist Chamber of Horrors has contributed little to his slow but steady demise as a living influence on contemporary fiction – would to God sisterhood were as powerful as that!

But sermons writ in fire are no longer *à la mode* in this cool, ironic post-modernist world, though if you are influenced by Latin Americans, you can write sermons in *real* fire, if you want. Television has largely inherited the territory of the 'social' novel and, where social realism is concerned, has done something with it that would have made Lawrence take pot shots at the set.

So now coming to terms with Lawrence is an event that may be postponed almost indefinitely, though the uncomfortable fact remains that he is, simply, the greatest English novelist of this century.

This is not to celebrate Lawrence but to define and, indeed, limit him. There are few other major English novelists this century; and some of them, like Firbank, would have regarded both 'great' and 'English' as mild insults. Lawrence, however, was burdened by that dreadful sense of self-importance that an English child of the empire, such as he was, must have suckled with his mother's milk. This may account for his hectoring tone, a characteristic mode of imperialist discourse. He is English; he is not even British, he takes no account of the tripartite nature of the UK, and the England he so loved and so much hated has changed, since his death, beyond any of his imaginings. It is not so much changing fashions in fiction that have made much of Lawrence seem redundant, but the social changes that bring about these changes in artistic expression.

So the massive Cambridge edition of the complete works of Lawrence, and the matching massive Cambridge edition of the letters of Lawrence (seven volumes of text and one of index), of which the second volume has just been published, have something of the look of building blocks of a mausoleum in which Lawrence will be at last enshrined among the Great Unread. From this tomb no phoenix will be volatile enough to escape, for who can read anything with a quickening of the pulse while pausing to consult footnotes? And Lawrence's intention *is* to quicken the pulse; to change your life, in fact, although our lives have been totally changed since his death without his intervention.

The centenary of Lawrence's birth coming up in 1985, may well turn out to be a rum do. How Lawrence would have hated the late twentieth century! The oral contraceptives; *Gay News*, deconstructivism. Although he would have been furious if confronted by semiotics, that most serious of intellectual games – one consistent aspect of his Englishness was his anti-intellectualism – it is a small irony that Lawrence made one abiding con-tribution to the vocabulary of coarse signs. Whenever a gamekeeper lurches into a sketch in a TV comedy show, everybody knows what that means – for gamekeeper, read S-M-U-T. For this insight, I am indebted to Ian McEwan, who adds that he knows what D. H. Lawrence would have thought of him.

Exactly. Insect. Blackbeetle. Me too; I'm *proud* to be a blackbeetle. A female blackbeetle, adding her little bit to the demystification of DHL before it is too late, before he is forgotten, and it is less easy for me to do so than you might think because at university they taught me he was God.

I used to wonder why they did that. Now I think I know. Lawrence's three best novels, *Sons and Lovers, The Rainbow* and *Women in Love,* form, together, the most moving and profound account of the creation of the twentieth-century British intelligentsia – British, not exclusively English, of course, because the intelligentsia, itself a new phenomenon in Britain, recruited from all the grammar schools in Wales and Scotland, as well as England. It absorbed colonials and refugees from Europe besides.

Those three novels describe the birth of the upper working, lower middle, upwardly-socially-mobile-via-education class as a force to be reckoned with. In 1897 Lawrence, aged twelve, won one of the recently instituted county council scholarships, and a place at Nottingham High School; that, far more than him eloping with a German lady, is the key event in his life. There is nothing bathetic about this. We are talking about a new kind of person gaining hold of a means of power. (Not that I'm sure Lawrence himself thought knowledge was, in itself, power, but only a *means* to power.)

Trusting some sort of intuition that was not blood dark but, perhaps, based simply on the experience of teaching school with female colleagues, Lawrence chose the Brangwen girls as the focus of the *real* drama of the novels. Their position is more problematic, hence more dramatic; and in

choosing heroines for these two novels, Lawrence, probably quite accidentally, did indeed stumble upon absolutely *new* kinds of people, people
who could never have existed before.

Notice how we leave Gudrun, at the end of *Women in Love,* more or
less as we leave Paul Morel at the end of *Sons and Lovers*, disappearing into
an unguessable future. Never mind that we're supposed to believe Gudrun
is a damned soul. Don't trust the teller, trust the tale. She has whirled off,
from the close family life of her childhood, into the eye of the maelstrom
of the rootless urban intelligentsia, which accounts for that strange, exponential feeling of the end of the novel, as if everything were whirling apart.
As indeed it was.

What a typical blackbeetlish thing to do, to reduce Lawrence to his
socio-economic relevance! But the glory and the confusion of the
grammar-school kid were utterly new; and I read and reread those novels
again and again, looking for clues, not to how I should live my life, but
how it came to pass that my life has been lived in this way, since I am a
second-generation grammar school kid.

And this interpretation of the novels explains the extraordinary dominance of Lawrence over two or three generations of grammar-school kids,
who were actively (or passively, like my mother) involved in the same
drama. Those novels express the vitality and the bewilderment of an emergent class, for whom there were no guidelines laid down, who were
engaged in a new way of living. People for whom Lawrence was the
Messiah and F. R. Leavis his John the Baptist. And *Lucky Jim* the epitaph.

This vigour has more or less exhausted itself, now, without invalidating
the historic importance of that central drama, of which the upwardly
socially mobile romance (miner's son weds aristo) is no more than the
conventional fairytale ending, *Cinderella* in reverse.

The first two volumes of Lawrence's letters in the Cambridge edition
form an extraordinary subtext to what is going on in the great novels;
they take Lawrence from 1901 up to 1916, to the completion of *Women
in Love*. In fact, the letters make up a gigantic epistolary novel in themselves, a much more nineteenth-century one than any of his fictions,
because it is the story of a cad on the make who bit off more than he
could chew. Correction: a cad of *genius* on the make – and it is the
volatile, unquantifiable quality of genius that makes his letters painful to
read, even tragic, since his own genius was partly the undigestible bit:
for Lawrence, it was not sufficient to be a great novelist. That did not
satisfy him at all.

How the scholarship system worked was like this: it offered you a place
at a great feast, the feast of privilege and though they told you you were
lucky to get it, you knew you'd earned it because you'd worked so hard.

So there was conflict from the word go: they expected gratitude, you expected praise. All the same, you knew in your heart that all you had to do, now, was pull up your chair and use the right knife and fork and, as night followed day, you would be eventually admitted to the company of the blessed – that is, the people with the power.

Art it is that gets you out of the run and in at the front door with the nobs. As soon as *Sons and Lovers* was published, and unequivocally hailed as a great novel, Lawrence had the nobs eating out of his hand – Lady Cynthia Asquith, the prime minister's daughter-in-law! Sir Walter Raleigh; Rupert Brooke; H.G. Wells; nobs of all kinds, nobs in spades.

However, once one has obtained the nobs' interest, how is one to maintain it? Since the nobs make fame. Fame is infectious; you catch it by mixing with famous people. But you need to keep them continuously interested until you yourself are the infectiously famous one. Lawrence was not the first Englishman of working-class origins to convert himself into a prophet of the apocalypse in order to attract attention to himself. Blake did so, too, but the kind of attention Blake sought was more eternal than temporal. But Lawrence seems to have, almost overnight, turned himself into a guru. Not even the career of R. D. Laing in our own day parallels the amazing speed with which Lawrence became vatic and numinous.

'He is amazing: he sees through and through one. He is infallible. He is like Ezekiel or some other Old Testament prophet, prophesying. Of course, the blood of his nonconformist preaching ancestors is strong in him, but he sees everything and is always right.'

No impressionable adolescent summed Lawrence up thus in 1915, but Bertrand Russell. If, later that year, Russell backpedalled a little ('The trouble with him is a tendency to mad exaggeration'), he could still contemplate suicide, however briefly, when Lawrence accused him of 'perverted mental blood-lust', imprecise as this diagnosis of mental disturbance might be.

The role of the prophet, of the one crying in the wilderness to whom the truth hath been revealed, possesses, even more than the profession of journalism, that 'harlot's privilege' of power without responsibility. There seems every reason to believe that Lawrence, sensing within him the surging power of that emergent class whose final apotheosis was to be the election of the 1945 Labour government (but how Lawrence would have hated *that!*) – Lawrence, sensing he was somehow in an ascendant, tried to jump the gun. Not to alter the power structure, but to take it over. From the top.

If Lawrence came more and more to resemble the pictured image of the Son of Man, whether out of his own hubris or as part of a huge confidence trick in which he also managed to deceive himself, Lawrence did not adopt his original's methods of recruitment. If the Christ were content with humble toilers for disciples, that wasn't good enough for our Bert. He wanted dukes' half-sisters and belted earls wiping his feet with their hair; grand apotheosis of the snob, to humiliate the objects of his own awe by making them venerate him.

In his brisk youth, before he met Frieda and became a prophet, he was indeed a confidence man; the letters prove it. And, in Volume One of the Cambridge edition, there is a strangely moving account of Lawrence in 1910, by a beautiful poetess called Rachel Annand Taylor, with whom Lawrence attempted one of his inimitable cajoling courtships, unsuccessfully: 'He was a terrific snob, was definitely a cad, yet in this early period he was touching, he was so artlessly trying to find his way . . .'

And suddenly Lawrence becomes comprehensible. For the first time I feel I fully understand him . . . He is as the perfect type of those literary provincials in Balzac, fresh in Paris, naïvely unscrupulous, a disarming scoundrel who must, at that stage, have felt that everything was a terrific adventure and, characteristic of those who feel they have been undervalued (which is how the scholarship person often ends up feeling) – he must have thought that anybody who trusted him deserved what they got. And they did, at that.

I suspect it was the cad who was the artist and, when he ceased to be a cad – perhaps because Frieda took him at face value in all things – he started to believe in his own publicity. Which is the death of the soul.

New Society, 1982

Envoi: Bloomsday

'Now I will make my own legend and stick to it.'
Letter from James Joyce to Lady Gregory, 1904

Cities have sexes: London is a man, Paris a woman, and New York a well-adjusted transsexual, but – what is Dublin? Has it made up its mind? Yet if the Thames, as is well known, is Old Father, then Dublin's river is as famous a woman, is Anna Liffey, with her broad curves gracious as those of a *fin de siècle* bum. On 16 June, the name of the bridge at Chapelizod was officially changed to the Anna Livia Bridge, thus putting the unequivocal sex of Mother Liffey squarely on the map at last, even if in tribute to Dublin's most protean if least-grateful son, who irreverently changed 'Liffey' to 'Livia' after a Triestine housewife.

'. . . riverrun past Eve and Adam's from swerve of shore to bend of bay . . .' Invitation to the swell and ebb of sleeping and waking, to the world inside the book, which is the world, which is the river, which is the book. And so on. But *Finnegans Wake* is postgraduate stuff, still; as it turns out, *Ulysses* is for *everybody*.

Dubliners wished one another: 'A Happy Bloomsday'. Florists cashed in on a pardonable pun: 'Buy a bloom for Bloomsday,' and many, Anthony Burgess for one, sported Blazes Boylan bottonholes. Some said it should have been a national holiday. The entire inner city was *en fête* and, no, it did not rain. Thus Dublin ingeniously secularised and took back unto itself the first authentic post-modernist literary festival, a day devoted to the celebration of the fictional texts of James Joyce, in which the author took a back seat to his inventions.

For though 1982 is his centenary year, Joyce was not born nor did he die on 16 June, but chose to moor *Ulysses* to this point in time and place because, on that day, in 1904, Nora Barnacle consented to walk out with him. You could say that, on that day, Joyce's real life began for his greatest novels make of the role of Husband the peak and summit of masculine aspiration. Joyce was one of nature's husbands, incomplete until he found his wife, and none the less so because he did not marry her for a decade or two after; a husband, still, in his unconsummated dreams of cuckoldry.

On Bloomsday, though, it was not Bloom's imaginary and antlered head that graced the postage stamps, but the Brancusi drawing of Joyce's own, the gaunt, bespectacled, subtly odd, familiar face of the legend. But I prefer that infinitely moving photograph of young Joyce, every inch a Jim, taken when he was twenty-two in that very blessed 1904 itself, hands in his pockets, almost a *Boy's Own Paper*ly heroic stance. Such an undeniably handsome face you see why Nora fell, and his eyes not yet dimmed nor hidden away behind glasses. 'Asked what he was thinking when C. P. Curran photographed him, Joyce replied: "I was wondering would he lend me five shillings."'[*]

Note Joyce's syntax, here. His English, as he well knew, had been moulded by another tongue, by one not even his mother tongue since her monoglot English, too, had been moulded by the language long lost within it. (The name of Dublin, Baile Atha Cliath, in Irish so dignified and remotely foreign, turns, when Anglicised, into the almost comically accessible Ballyattaclee: the English knew how to make the languages of the ethnic minorities of the British Isles ridiculous.)

This questing young man is already determined on earth-shattering fame: 'Now I will make my legend and stick to it.' He stares at us with

[*] Richard Ellman, *James Joyce* (New York: Oxford University Press, 1959).

almost a Jack London look of purpose. He is, I think, already pondering a magisterial project: that of buggering the English language, the ultimate revenge of the colonialised.

'Aren't there words enough for you in English?' the Bliznakoff sister asked Joyce. 'Yes,' he replied. 'But they aren't the right ones.'

However many there were, there would never be the right ones, since Joyce spoke a language that had been translated into English and must always have suffered a teasing feeling that most of the meaning had been lost in the process. Somewhere, perhaps in the European languages, lurked that unimaginably rich original.

What is more, we carry our history on our tongues and the history of the British empire came to exercise a curious kind of brake upon our expression in the English language, as it became less and less the instrument of feeling and more and more that of propaganda. Something even odder has happened since Joyce's day, in these last years, when English, in the great world, has become synonymous with the language spoken in America, which, though it uses the same words, is an entirely other communications system. Indeed, American threatens to leave us entirely stranded, now, on a linguistic beach of history with English turning into a quaint dialect, another Old World survival, like Castilian Spanish, stiff, outmoded, unapposite.

And what shall we do then? Why, we shall be thrust back on Joyce, who never took English seriously and so he could continue, as we will do.

However, the worldwide provenance of English, its ubiquitous if fading *functionability,* the reason why there *were* enough words in it, even if they had to be kicked around a bit and shown their place, is inseparable from the history of the British empire, when English needed to be in a lot of different places at the same time. Happy for Shakespeare he did not speak Serbo-Croat and his Queen embarked on a policy of expansion. If you speak a language nobody understands, you can babble away as much as you like and nobody will hear you. Even had he wished to use it, the grand but archaic language of Ireland would not have suited a man who wished to straddle the world.

In *Ulysses*, only an Englishman is fluent in Irish. 'I'm ashamed I don't speak the language myself,' mutters a crone addressed in her native speech.

On the other hand, the Celtic revivalists were theoretically correct. The only way to get us off their backs was to ensure we could not understand what they were saying. But unfortunately, we *needed* to hear them and, by the turn of the century, Ireland was already committed to that tongue of the wicked stepmother – fortunately for us. And this is the tongue that Joyce systematically deformed, excavated, imploded, you might say; he made sufficient space within that appropriated language to accommodate the next phase of history.

He sheared away the phoney rhetoric that had been accreting over the centuries. In *Ulysses,* he transformed English into something intimate, domestic, demotic, a language fit not for heroes but for husbands, then did it over again, stripped it of its linguistic elements, in fact, and put it together in a polyglot babble that, perhaps, begins to approximate something like a symphonic Euro-language, in which English is no more than a dominant theme. He disestablished English.

Although American academia was especially prominent among the massed scholarship arriving in Dublin for Bloomsday Week and the VIII International James Joyce Symposium in order to get their heads down over a susurrating mass of learned papers, this question of the disestablishment of English is, of course, not an American problem. The American language had something exponential built into it from the start, although the chances are that American will harden its arteries somewhat if the United States dons the mantle of world leadership with too much enthusiasm. All the same, there is nothing culturally troubling about Joyce for Americans. There is for me. Troubling and consoling.

I do believe that, had Joyce opted for a career as a singer, as Nora wished, I, for one, as a writer in post-imperialist Britain, would not even have had the possibility of a language, for Joyce it was who showed how one could tell the story of whatever it is that is going to happen next. Not that he would have cared. Whatever it was he thought he was up to, it certainly wasn't making it easier for the British to explain their past and their future to themselves. He wasn't doing it for *our* sakes, he made *that* clear.

Nevertheless, he carved out a once-and-future language, restoring both the simplicity it had lost and imparting a complexity. The language of the heart and the imagination and the daily round and the dream had been systematically deformed by a couple of centuries of use as the rhetorical top-dressing of crude power. Joyce Irished, he Europeanised, he decolonialised English: he tailored it to fit this century, he drove a giant wedge between English Literature and literature in the English language and, in doing so, he made me (forgive this personal note) free. Free not to do as he did, but free to treat the Word not as if it were holy but in the knowledge that it is always profane. He is in himself the antithesis of the Great Tradition. You could also say, he detached fiction from one particular ideological base, and his work has still not yet begun to bear its true fruit. The centenarian still seems avant-garde.

'The value of the book is its new style,' he said of *Ulysses* to a friend in Paris.

And another thing. Poet of the upper-working and lower-middle classes as he was – that is, of the artistically most despised and rejected, poet

of those exiled from poetry – he never succumbed to the delusion that
people who do not say complicated things do not have complicated
thoughts. Hence, the stream-of-consciousness technique, to bring that
inner life into the open. It's simple, Just as, when you hear Joyce read
aloud in the rhythms of Irish, it, too, all falls into place.

That is what Radio Telefis Eirann did, for Bloomsday. RTE broadcast
Ulysses, read aloud, from early morning on 16 June till the next day. All
over the city, transistors fed it to the air. RTE proposed to sell cassettes of
this mammoth and inspired occasion for the sum of £1,000 each, which
would have gladdened Joyce's heart of a balked entrepreneur. (He set up
the first cinema in Dublin, the Volta, in 1909, with Triestine money. It
failed. RTE's project, with a market of American universities, will probably succeed.)

'History is a trap from which I am trying to escape,' said Stephen
Daedalus. The Bloomsday of 1982 takes place in the capital city of the
Republic of Ireland. It is a country which Bloom Joyce, the wandering
Irishman, would find amazing. A state reception was held for him in
Dublin Castle, and this reception turned out to be the very kind of riotous
party Joyce adored. American Express offered the city the Bloomsday
present of Joyce's head in bronze; the President himself, Dr Patrick
Hillery, unveiled it. (Nobody thought to gratify Joyce's gleeful and malicious ghost by slipping say, an item of ladies' underwear under the veil
and, indeed, it would have marred the dignity of the occasion.) Bloomsday
was celebrated with such stylish and imaginative joyousness it seemed a
pity the old boy missed it.

But the old city is pulling itself down. Freed at last from that 'hemiple-
gia of the will' which Joyce diagnosed as his country's most significant
malady in a letter to his brother in 1903, Dublin, all bustle, thrust, traffic-
jams, and businessmen concluding suave deals, is no longer the city I
remember from even twenty years ago, which, then, pickled in the sour
brine of poverty, was sufficiently like the city of the book to make you
blink.

Nobody knows what tomorrow will bring.

The squares, the terraces, the grand parades, going, going, deserted,
weed-grown, the city of the Raj, waiting for the demolition men, gone.
The city seethes with gossip, rumour, and speculation about the activities
of property speculators. Up go the mirror-clad slabs of office-blocks;
Ireland has at last followed Joyce into Europe.

Everything has changed. If 16 June was Bloomsday, 26 June was Gay
Pride Day. In the personal column of the magazine, *In Dublin,* the 'Legion
of Mary' finds itself at hazard of alphabetical listing, nudging against
'Lesbian Line'. Decorating each street corner, exquisitely spiked and stud-

ded Irish punks have, overnight, discovered Style. The city, the country, whose inhabitants once seemed to leap with one bound from babyhood to middle age now seethes with the youngest population in Europe who have a look in their eyes that suggests they will not be easily satisfied. One doubts both the old sow's appetite for *this* farrow and her ability to digest it.

But nobody lives at 7 Eccles Street any more. The house where the imaginary Blooms never lived is not a tumbledown shell. Its door graces the Bailey Bar, in Duke Street. Before this abandoned house, however, at three in the afternoon of Bloomsday, a facsimile of Molly Bloom disposed herself upon a makeshift bed while Blazes Boylan made his way towards her and her husband pottered pooterishly round the town. Because this is what Dublin did for Bloomsday: it peopled the streets of the city with the beings of the book: the Word made Flesh, in fact.

For one hour, just one hour, up they all popped, in costume, large as life, and even William Humble, Earl of Dudley, and Lady Dudley, accompanied by Lieutenant-Colonel Hesseltine riding out from the viceregal lodge in a cavalcade of carriages and antique horseless carriages. And exquisite children in pinafores and sunbonnets and ladies in tight bloomers on tricycles and blind men and one-legged sailors and look it up in your Bodley Head edition, the 'Wandering Rocks' episode in *Ulysses* (pages 280, 328), this slice of teeming 1904 Dublin life rendered as street theatre, like a marvellous hallucination. Nothing could have been more perfect, as the city adopted Bloomsday and revisited its own vanishing past with a tourist's eager curiosity and the devotion of a trustee.

These are, perhaps, the last few years when Joyce's fictional blueprints of Dublin will correspond at all to the real outlines of the city. Dublin appears, the final tribute, to be 'fixing' the city of the book as perfect fiction by tidying away the real thing so that Joyce's Dublin can gloriously survive as its own monument, the book which is the city, the metaphysical city of the word, while whatever it is that happens next gets on with it.

Jorge Luis Borges at the Bloomsday banquet, proposing the toast to Joyce and Ireland ('since for me they are inseparable'), opined that, one day, 'as with all great books', *Ulysses* and *Finnegans Wake* would become books for children. One day, one fine day, one universal Bloomsday, when, perhaps, the metaphysics depart from the book and it becomes life, again.

New Society, 1982

Alison's Giggle

In the Miller's Tale of *The Canterbury Tales* by Geoffrey Chaucer, a young woman, who has just played a sexual practical joke on a young man whom she does not want, emits a satisfied giggle. We know Alison giggles rather than bursts out laughing, because Chaucer tells us that she does so: 'Tehee quod she.' She giggles; and returns to bed with a more attractive partner. Her husband, meanwhile, has strung himself up in a tub under the rafters, awaiting the arrival of the Flood, which his wife and her lover have convinced him is imminent so that he will vacate his bed and leave it to them. (Alison's husband believes the tub will make an excellent improvised boat and proposes to launch it at the first sign of the inundation by cutting the ropes which attach it to the roof.)

Alison's giggle is not a sound which is heard very often in literature, although, in life, it can be heard every time a young girl successfully humiliates a would-be admirer. (My mother taught me to say this to young men in dance halls who wanted to buy me gin and orange even though they had spots: 'Does your mother know you're out?' Off they would squelch, abashed, on their two-inch thick crêpe soles. And we girls would giggle.) Perhaps given the traditional male narrator in literature, the sound is so rarely heard just because it expresses the innocent glee with which women humiliate men in the only way available to them, through a frontal attack on male pride. To reproduce this giggle, a man must identify with a woman rather than with another man and perceive some aspects of male desire as foolish. Indeed, in a sense, perceive the idea of the supremacy of male desire as foolish.

Admittedly, Chaucer, through the mouth of the Miller whom he has invented to tell this tale, is careful to present Alison's failed suitor, Absolon, the parish clerk, as a ninny; that makes it easier for them both to take Alison's point of view. All the same, Absolon, looked at objectively, is no more of a ninny than Don José in *Carmen,* who also attempts to thrust his attentions on a woman who is no longer interested. But Prosper Merimée saw nothing foolish about *his* hero. And even if he *is* a ninny, Absolon is so roundly humiliated – Alison tricks him into kissing her backside, rather than her mouth – most men would think she'd gone too far. But, in the tale, Absolon's vengeance goes badly wrong and misses Alison altogether; and, more significantly, Alison is not censured by her creator for asserting a woman's right to humiliate in however light-hearted and girlish a fashion.

Alison's giggle sets up a series of echoes disturbing our preconceptions whilst echoing our experience. If male narrators, in general, cannot bear to hear it, the female narrator, increasingly frequent over the last two hundred years, especially in those forms of the novel that purport to give an exact transcription of everyday life and so ought to tally better with our experience than medieval poetry does, have also tended to omit both the giggle and the kind of sexual circumstance that best provokes it.

Hard to imagine Jane Austen's Elizabeth Bennett playing a sexual practical joke on the curate in *Pride and Prejudice* who so richly deserved it, and not only because Jane Austen's genteel scenario, centuries away from that of the 'fabliau' of the Middle Ages, does not allow to take place the kind of events in the course of which Mr Collins might, literally, kiss Elizabeth's arse. (Indeed, linguistically, Elizabeth is not in possession of an arse.) And, apart from these limitations, Jane Austen arrives in history at that curious time when women, as a fiction-reading as well as a fiction-writing class, were supposed to affect ignorance of just exactly what it was Alison was up to in bed with her Nicholas when she was interrupted by the unwelcome serenade of the parish clerk.

Whether a *female* narrator of Chaucer's period would have felt the Chaucerian freedom of diction and situation is moot. The female narrators whom Chaucer invents himself are perfectly decorous in diction, although the Wyf of Bath's tale is not particularly decorous in content and her soliloquies on life, love and the management of husbands have badly upset centuries of male commentators. The Wyf of Bath is, however, a fictional invention, and her self-determined sexual appetites ('I folwed ay myn inclinacioun,' she says) and her robust speech belong to the sexual stereotype of the middle-aged woman, who may speak as she pleases since the sexual threat she poses has been removed by the menopause. She is the same kind of fictional person as the nurse in Shakespeare's *Romeo and Juliet;* and as Mae West. Situation complicated, here, by the fact that Mae West was both a fictional invention, a woman who re-invented herself in terms of the movies she wrote and starred in, and also a perfectly real woman who, it would seem, often behaved and spoke like the fictional Mae West. Stereotypes only become stereotypes, after all, because they correspond to certain kinds of real behaviour. It is possible to surmise, therefore, that there were sufficient middle-aged women rich enough and tough enough to behave not unlike the Wyf of Bath in England in the fourteenth century, which is, in many ways, a daunting thought.

Such a woman, with a perfectly good trade of her own (the Wyf of Bath was a famous weaver of cloth) and a very active sexual and emotional life, would scarcely have had the time to write poetry, nor, one imagines, would she have seen the point of the activity. And she may not have known how to read and write too well (although she could certainly count). Marie de France, the twelfth-century poetess (called 'De France' because she was a Frenchwoman who lived in England) composed infinitely elegant poetic tales of impeccably courtly love, befitting a person with a nice mind and, presumably, a private income. However, since women certainly contributed to the anonymous body of traditional lyric which survives in manuscript from the medieval period, and survives in other forms in folk songs collected in the nineteenth century, and which is often very rude indeed, it is possible that *illiterate* women may have had a freedom of creative expression and the opportunity to do so, denied to those of higher rank and accomplishment.

Whether women could, if the possibility had been widely available, have written in a 'Chaucerian' manner in Chaucer's time is an unanswerable question; but we know that medieval women, of whatever class, were not supposed to be shocked by Chaucer because *The Canterbury Tales* was intended for a mixed-sex audience. There are two women on the pilgrimage itself, one the Wyf of Bath and the other a nun, who listen and comment upon a collection of stories many of which, by Jane Austen's time, were not considered suitable for women at all, at all. When the Miller sums up his tale in the phrase, 'Thus swyved was the carpenterys wife' ('That's how the carpenter's wife got herself fucked'), it may be assumed that not only the male pilgrims and the Wyf of Bath but also the nun knew what 'to swyve' meant and did not think it reprehensible or unusual activity between consenting adults.

The representations of women in English literature by male narrators (and we can assume a dominant male narrator until the mid-eighteenth century) are, however much determined by contemporary notions of the position of women, based on the assumption that men and women share an equal knowledge of the basic facts of sexual experience up until, curiously enough, that very time in the eighteenth century when women in significant numbers take up their pens and write. The poet, the writer of fiction and the dramatist always write in the context of the assumed knowledge of the listener, the reader, the spectator; when, for whatever reasons, there comes about a time when rather more than half the audience for any given literary production is presumed to be in ignorance of the basic facts of the continuation of the human race. Then a whole group of literary productions becomes 'unsuitable for women', especially those in which women *are* shown as knowledgeable and active sexual beings. (Witness the wrath the nineteenth century inflicted on Restoration comedy and the way the female dramatist, Mrs Aphra Behn, became unmentionable, due to her 'indecent' wit.)

It is not a naïve question, that of whether Jane Austen, a provincial maiden lady, was herself precisely aware of the actual mechanics of sexual intercourse. It is reasonable to assume, from the degree of sexual tension between her female and male characters, that, even if she were unfamiliar with the practice, she was conversant with the theory, to some degree. The twanging eroticism of Austen's novels may even owe some of its power to the taboo upon pre-marital or extra-marital sexual intercourse and upon discussion of these things in any but the broadest terms. Yet the conventions of her time and class, conventions of both fiction and of actual behaviour, force her to deny to her heroines the practical use of the sexual allure with which she so abundantly equips them – assuming, that is, she did indeed know just what such use would mean.

The sexuality of Austen's heroines exists as a potential; as a potential, it is fully utilised as lure and bait. But her narratives ceased abruptly with the marriages of the heroines, although this is the point at which, for the British bourgeoisie of the late eighteenth century, a woman's life actually begins. That is, her *real* life, as mistress of a house and as a being-in-the-world; all this is symbolised by marriage as the beginning of a woman's sexual life.

Austen shares this cut-off point in her heroine's stories both with the nameless authors of fairytales and with most writers of fiction primarily intended for a female market in her own day and in ours. Her heroines remain electric virgins, charged with a power of which they know the value – indeed, perhaps they over-value it – just as long as it remains within their own control. But, as regards that power in the context of a marriage, when the woman herself is no longer in complete control of it – for Austen, and, perhaps, for many women, this remains unquantifiable, and not only if they remain unmarried. Austen ends her heroines' stories at the moment when the virgin is about to die as a virgin, and be born again as – and, you see, there is no word for it. No word for a 'respectable' woman as a heterosexual being except 'wife', that is, by definition, a contingent being.

If both words, 'virgin' and 'wife', define a woman by her sexual status, 'virgin' describes a condition-in-itself, while the word 'wife' implies the existence of a husband, just as the word 'prostitute' implies the existence of a client.

Even so, the conventionalised 'happy ending' of the wedding in fiction by and for women may signify not so much the woman's resignation of her status as autonomous individual, a status that might be at best problematic in a society with little available space for anybody's autonomy, but the woman's acquisition of a licence to legitimately explore her own sexuality in relation to a man, as well as acquiring part shares in her husband's public status and wealth, and inheriting all the folklore of sex and reproduction that is passed from generation to generation of married women. For a woman, to marry, in fiction, is to grow up; all the same, there is something rather honourable about the simple reluctance of fiction by and for women to accommodate itself to that kind of maturity. The narratives stop short at the altar, as if they cannot bear to go on. As if to travel hopefully, the chase, the courtship, the acceptance or rejection of suitors, were better than to arrive at this ambivalent destination. All such fictional narratives of women that end in marriage could just as well end with a death, because marriage means the death of the virgin, that is, the termination of her narrative as an individual, however hedged about with prohibitions that individualism might be.

Alison, the carpenter's wife, is brusquely defined by her sexual status in a perfectly straightforward way. Since she is a wife, we know she is not a virgin and also that her sexuality belongs to somebody else. Further, she carries her husband's social status around with her like a badge. Artisan class. (The Wyf of Bath, by the way, is simply a woman from the city of that name; she's had too many husbands to be easily defined by the status of one of them and has, besides, a perfectly good status of her own.) Alison's story does not end with marriage; she is married before her story begins and the plot quickens when she becomes the focus of male extra-marital desire. Alison is a contingent being in every way. We are not even given a hint of her former history as a virgin; whether or not she, like the Wyf of Bath, had 'other company in youth' is a mystery. But marriage has not robbed her of the ability to keep her hands on the reins of her own life; she can grab back control of her sexuality and compensate herself thereby for some, at least, of the more unpleasant consequences of marriage to a silly old man.

George Eliot's *Middlemarch,* unlike the novels of Jane Austen, begins with the marriage of its heroine, a marriage the success of which is indicated by the scene in which we find Dorothea Casaubon, on her honeymoon, weeping in a cemetery. The tears of Dorothea come from a different world, a different kind of experience and an utterly different narrator than the giggle of Alison. Eliot is a woman. Chaucer is a man. The two fictional women demonstrate the change in fiction in the intervening five hundred years: Dorothea, clever, sensitive, middle-class, aspiring towards she knows not what, is an inhabitant of the fully three-dimensional Victorian novel with its project of transmitting the whole of human life irradiated by a vision of a transcendent morality. If that, too, was Chaucer's project in *The Canterbury Tales,* he went about it in a different way, and his Alison is an inhabitant of the shadowless, two-dimensional world of medieval fabliau, the eighteen-year-old wife of an artisan whose class had disappeared from bourgeois fiction by George Eliot's day, except as picturesque extras mumbling proverbs and old saws in dialect. Alison is coltish and wild, slim as a weasel, with a 'likerous ye' (a lecherous eye). She is described as an object of desire, not from the inside. She is compared to a young pear tree, a colt, a calf, a flower; all in all, the typical young girl of male imagination. Yet, when she giggles, that 'Tehee! quod she' comes rippling across the centuries, giving that entirely spurious sense which only the greatest art gives us, that the past, in all its unimaginable difference from our lives, can nevertheless shiver, fall apart and reveal human beings who, for all they believe the sun went round the earth, lived on the same terms with themselves that we do and made the same kind of compromises with circumstances.

Dorothea's dilemma, marriage to a man she finds sexually odious and from which there is no way out except his death, is presented by George Eliot as a paradigmatic moral dilemma which has nothing to do with Dorothea's sexuality, nor with desire nor with pleasure – least of all, with pleasure. It is just possible to imagine Jane Austen, had she been born, not a vicar's daughter in the Home Counties but into that world of the amoral Regency aristocracy which scared her so much (see her treatment of the Crawfords in *Mansfield Park*) thoroughly endorsing Alison's strategy for the perpetuation of pleasure after marriage – that is, infidelity and the use of her sex as a weapon. Jane Austen's heroines have a glittering confidence in their own allure, even if it is always allure and never the lineaments of gratified desire. Fifty years later, Eliot, a writer of infinitely greater intellectual resources than Austen, effectively begged the entire question of the sexual nature of the heroine of her finest novel by presenting it in such an oblique way that Dorothea seems almost asexual and is constantly assimilated to unsexed female images of saints.

Yet Dorothea weeps on her honeymoon; and it is her husband Casaubon's attempt to regulate her actual sexual behaviour – according to his will, her inheritance depends on her *not* marrying the young, toothsome Will Ladislaw – that finally causes her to rebel. Casaubon, in his senile jealousy, noticed something that F. R. Leavis, in his commentary on the novel, did not, something Eliot veiled in sentimentality but did not entirely obscure – that Dorothea, even if she does look like a cinquecento madonna, is subject to the ancient sexual law of 'like unto like' upon which the Miller's tale is based. Dorothea wants to sleep with Ladislaw because he is young and handsome and so is she. In their social context, to 'sleep with' means to marry. So marry they must and, in order tactfully to indicate that there are no tears on *this* honeymoon, Dorothea's story ends, not with the marriage, but with the birth of her child.

What is odd about all this discretion is that George Eliot herself led a sexual and emotional life that would have been considered unusually rich and full even by liberal late-twentieth-century standards, and was perfectly well aware that marriage, in reality, is neither an end nor a beginning but only a legislative change, and also that one does not need to marry men in order to sleep with them. Within the bounds of the conventions of her time, Eliot succeeds in writing about sexual relationships as they are, not as they should be, to a quite remarkable degree; her grasp of emotional logic is as straightforward as Chaucer's was. All the same, those tears of Dorothea in the Italian cemetery are a kind of code, a code which, at that period, only married women, i.e. non virgins, were supposed to understand, although those tears tell us more, perhaps, than we might wish to know about Casaubon as a husband, and fill in many of the gaps in the idealised characterisation of Dorothea herself. Those tears, in fact, prepare the reader for her eventual remarriage; they tell us that Dorothea is a sexual being and her protracted intellectual disillusionment with her husband has started off from an equally unforgiveable sexual disappointment.

I suspect George Eliot would have been glad to have been able to describe the nature of that disappointment in more detail, if not in the self-same language used by Chaucer's Miller. However, it was not permissible for her to do more than hint; and, unsatisfactory and destructive as her marriage is, once Dorothea is married she is condemned to weep over her frustration without her inventor being able to tell us, in so many words, that this is what ails her. Both Dorothea and her inventor must present this aspect of the failure of the marriage between Dorothea and Casaubon as if it were of peripheral significance to Dorothea.

However, such is Eliot's respect for, and partial idealisation of the beautiful and saintly woman she has invented that, as well as convention and acceptability, a resistance to acknowledging Dorothea's sexuality in a more explicit way on Eliot's own part prevents *this* plot quickening at the notion of extra-marital intercourse. Small-town gossip would have singled out the friendship between Dorothea and the handsome Dr Lydgate as almost certain to blossom into the right, true end of two unsatisfactory marriages. Eliot hints at this as a might-have-been; a union that would have redeemed Lydgate from the besetting sin of his own vulgarity, if – even without the complicating factor of their two spouses – Dorothea had shown the least sign of being attracted to a 'manly' Englishman of Lydgate's type. Since Dorothea gladly throws up her inheritance in order to marry an effete, curly-headed Slav, it would seem that Lydgate was the last kind of man she'd find attractive. By the end of the novel, marriage has taught Dorothea one important lesson – now she knows just what and whom she wants, and takes it the moment it is offered her. She wants, in fact, the kind of pretty, malleable man strong women very often want. (It is odd how many people find this aspect of the novel unsatisfactory, or unlikely.)

But all this is dealt with in such a discreet way that Eliot seems almost to be censoring herself. Eliot is certainly capable of presenting women who *are* deeply aware of their sexual being; in the same novel, Lydgate's wife, Rosamund, is perfectly aware, and is presented by Eliot as a poisonous, manipulative bitch.

The sexual relations between the Lydgates are left, of course, unstressed, although they produce children in due order so we know the marriage has been consummated. If there is a suggestion Rosamund is frigid, this is depicted as no more than an aspect of her selfishness; Lydgate can't possibly have anything to do with it.

Eliot castigates Lydgate for his foolishness in thoughtlessly marrying a pretty girl in the same way as he might have acquired an attractive piece of bric-à-brac, but the piece of bric-à-brac in question is condemned for no more than – being a piece of bric-à-brac. (Which is just how Rosamund tends to think of herself; as a precious ornament for a home, a fine possession for a man. This is a bad way for a woman to be in, but Eliot spares her no pity.) George Eliot neither likes nor approves of Rosamund and treats her touching provincial aspirations to material comfort, to social position, to respect, with contempt. But the relish with which she describes Rosamund's long-term corrosion of Lydgate's self-satisfaction has something self-contradictory about it. Reprehensible as Rosamund might be, her campaign of attrition against her husband may be read as the prototype of the revenge of any disappointed wife. She does to Lydgate what Dorothea, were Dorothea not such a saintly human being, might have felt perfectly justified in doing to Casaubon. (And, of course, we know with hindsight that Lydgate's medical research into the origins of typhoid will, on the evidence the novel gives us of its nature, lead him up just the same blind alley as Casaubon's theological research has led *him* – not that Eliot could have known that, of course.)

But Eliot – and this is a recurring phenomenon with the female narrator – simply can't bear to put her beloved Dorothea in a bad light. Dorothea is not allowed to exhibit the least resentment. She must be the type of the 'Patient Griselda', who suffers in silence the tyranny of an appalling husband, gaining treasure in heaven thereby. 'Patient Griselda' is the idealisation of one type of medieval wife as Alison is the crystallisation of a more down-to-earth variety. Rosamund Lydgate, with far more of the Alison in her make-up than the Griselda, is offered to us as a 'bad woman', in contrast to Dorothea's 'good woman'. Rosamund is judged in the text by her narrator for her embittered attitude to her husband and found wanting; Dorothea is celebrated for concealing her bitterness. Yet both suffer the same affliction, which was Alison's affliction, too; all are married to men whom they do not, to use a shorthand phrase, love.

The nineteenth-century bourgeois novel is in the business of making judgements. The medieval fabliau was not. Chaucer, and the Miller, suspend judgement on everyone. Yet it's noticeable that Absolon, Nicholas and even the carpenter – all the men in the story, in fact, suffer some kind of hurt, either of the feelings or the body. Absolon is tricked into kissing Alison's backside; intent on revenge, he returns with a red hot iron bar and asks for another kiss. However, Alison's lover, Nicholas, decides it would be fun if *he* were to stick his backside out of the window, this time, and so it is Nicholas, not Alison, who is branded on the buttock. When Nicholas cries out for water to cool his smart, the carpenter believes the Flood must have at last arrived, cuts the rope keeping his tub hanging in the rafters, and falls to the floor, breaking an arm. Only Alison, the adulterous wife and heartless humiliator of men, ends the story in as fresh, lively and 'likerous' a way as she began it.

Unjudged, perhaps, because not deemed responsible for her own actions, being so young, so coltish, so female? When the Miller concludes: 'Thus swyved was this carpenterys wife' the use of the passive mood is striking. But at least Alison managed to get herself fucked by the man of her choice, to her own satisfaction and with no loss of either her own self-respect or the respect of her male creator, which is more than a girl like her will be able to do again, in fiction, for almost more than half a millennium.

Very well. Alison is a character in an extended joke, not in a three-decker novel, even if that extended joke forms part of a long novel in the form of a poem that describes Chaucer's world and preoccupations as fully as *Middlemarch* does George Eliot's. But when she giggles, after Absolon has kissed her bum in error, she turns into a person who is literally uncontainable within the limitations of the kind of novel Eliot wrote and even, perhaps, uncontainable within Eliot's ability to imagine.

Alison will have one or two naughty sisters in other medieval fabliaus, a handful of rather more vicious great-great-grand-daughters in Restoration comedy, but nobody in literature quite like her, with her light heart and her guiltlessness, until Colette summoned up her own girlhood in order to invent Claudine, nearly six hundred years later. And even Colette would have been unable to express, with such limpid simplicity, what it is that Nicholas does to Alison, could not have written down the Burgundian dialect equivalent of 'to swyve' and assumed all her readers would know what she meant without a gloss, would have been able to count on her readers not needing to have the activity spelled out blow by blow or euphemistically mystified.

In fact, Chaucer *does* expand a little on the swyving. He tacitly assumes his audience is perfectly familiar with the organs involved and so on, an assumption it might be gross to make even today, so he has no need to describe thrusting pistons or yielding walls or anything like that. He sums up the encounter thus:

> And thus lith Alison and Nicholas
> In bisynesse of myrthe and of solas.

Laughter and consolation. Nothing Lawrentian or metaphysical about *this* coupling; simply, it is as much as any sane person can hope for from sex and more, perhaps, than Alison deserves.

Then the serenader interrupts them. Alison humiliates him and giggles. If Colette could have entertained the possibility of that giggle, the female narrators who followed her in the latter part of the twentieth century would find it difficult to let their heroines get away with it. Anna in *The Golden Notebook;* the lugubrious heroine of Marilyn French's *The Women's Room;* the moonstruck demi-vierges of Jean Rhys – to none of them, is adultery less than an existential challenge, while sexuality, either male or female, is no laughing matter and good women do not behave badly to men but gain treasure in heaven by letting men behave badly to them.

These heroines must be blameless, or else they cannot be heroines. They are recycled Patient Griseldas, tyrannised, not by one man as Griselda was, but by the entire sex, and now idealised by women themselves, rather than by men. The very question of sexual pleasure is hedged around with ambiguities and the desire to please is often mistaken for the desire for pleasure. When these heroines go to bed with their men, 'myrthe and solas' are the last things on their minds, which is just as well, since these things are rarely on offer.

There is a moving passage by Theodor Adorno, in *Minima Moralia:*

> Society constantly casts woman's self-abandon back into the sacrificial situation from which it freed her. No man, cajoling some poor girl to go with him, can mistake, unless he be wholly insensitive, the faint moment of rightness in her resistance, the only prerogative left by patriarchal society to woman, who, once persuaded, after the brief triumph of refusal, must immediately pay the bill.

Well, yes. Frigidity in the Victorian married woman, the headaches, the neurasthenia, the fabled vague ill-health that drove her husband into the arms of whores, may be seen as no more than a strategy of self-preservation, in the light of the maternal mortality statistics. (In the light of the ravages childbirth often inflicted upon women before the introduction of antisepsis and modern surgery, the lingering malaise of the married woman may, of course, have been genuine, protracted ill-health.) The nature of sexual repression in a society where heterosexual activity usually results in pregnancy and pregnancy may result in death is quite different from that of sexual repression in a society where birth control is freely available and childbirth is not feared, although, as Adorno implies, the ghosts of the old pain may not be so easily exorcised as all that.

Alison, unrepressed, giggles in the medieval fabliau, creation – however sympathetic – of a male narrator (and Chaucer is as sympathetic a male narrator as one will find in English literature, himself.) She and Chaucer live in a pre-bourgeois world, where women, as women, have somewhat more autonomy as workers and as beings-in-the-world than they will have by the time the novel, the bourgeois form of literature *par excellence,* is established. When this form becomes established, it becomes largely dominated by women themselves, as both readers and writers of fiction, and there seems to arise a conspiracy to deny women access through fiction to certain aspects of real life which are deemed unsuitable for them largely because they are concerned with sexual practice. There is some logic at work, here, a logic of repression related to the price of experience which is to do not with submission to the notion of the supremacy of male desire but an evasion of that presumed supremacy.

It should be noted that Alison seems untroubled by the idea of fertility. Perhaps, like the Wyf of Bath, she is fully aware of the 'remedies of love' (by which Chaucer presumably means abortificants); or, more likely, Chaucer temporarily forgot that sex often leads to babies. This is the characteristic sign of the male narrator everywhere in fiction. Either their mothers never told them, or the connection slipped their minds.

At the end of Colette's novel, *Ripening Seed,* the boy looks up at the window in which the girl whom he has just deflowered greets the morning with a song.

> From the window came a faint, happy little tune that passed over his head. Nor did the thought strike him that in a few weeks' time the child who was singing might well be standing in tears, doomed and frantic, at the same window.

The thought strikes Colette, of course; but it rarely strikes the male narrator. Phil continues meditating on how little the encounter has meant to his Vinca:

> A little pain, a little pleasure . . . That's all I shall have given her, that and nothing else . . . nothing.

So the novel ends, on a note of the bitterest irony; it is obvious from this that Colette intends the reader to understand that Vinca *has* conceived, and the seaside idyll of the teenage lovers is going to end very badly indeed. The connection between sex and reproduction does not slip a woman's mind so easily.

It is almost a cliché of orally transmitted poetry, that is, folk song, that one unprotected act of intercourse will lead inevitably to pregnancy; the pleasure principle remains undivorced from the reproductive function. Since performance of traditional song is fairly evenly divided between women and men, and the anonymous material is kept alive and often considerably altered in performance, it is fair to assume that women not only shape the songs they sing but invented some of them, long ago, in the first place.

> When I wore my apron low
> He followed me through frost and snow.
> Now I wear it to my chin
> He passes by and says nothing.

Although always found in the song called 'Died for Love', this is a 'floating' verse, that may be used at appropriate moments in all manner of different versions of different songs. Sex; pregnancy; desertion. That is a woman's life.

> I wish my baby little were born
> And smiling on its nurse's knee,
> And I myself were dead and gone
> For a maid again I'll never be.

Such songs were, no doubt, intended to help proscribe extramarital sexual activity on the part of young village girls. Whether they had any effect on illegitimacy rates is now unguessable.

However, the study of the representations of women in unofficial culture, in orally transmitted songs and stories, even in bar-room anecdotes, may prove a fruitful method of entry into the lived reality of the past. So may research into those forms of fiction that pre-date the bourgeois novel, in which the giggle of Alison, however disingenuous, suggests the possibility that, at some time in the past, a male narrator has been able to laugh at the pretensions of his own sex and therefore it is possible this may happen, again, in the future.

Eileen Philips (ed)., *The Left and the Erotic* (Lawrence & Wishart, 1983).

Trials of a Booker Judge

Both *Private Eye* and *City Limits,* from their different corners, find the novels shortlisted for this year's Booker McConnell prize 'unsurprising' and 'uninspiring', respectively. This seems a bit unfair. At least two of the shortlist items, John Fuller's metaphysical *jeu d'esprit* about dissection and putrefaction, *Flying to Nowhere,* and that epic of anal penetration and heresy in the first century AD, *The Illusionist,* by Anita Mason, are as unlikely contenders for Britain's premier literary prize, going on that prize's past form, as may be.

Past form, of course; but not its present form. Indeed, this year's Booker shortlist might suggest the eccentric had become the norm in British publishing. It comprises, also, an epic, didactic fairytale, *Shame,* by Salman Rushdie, who won in 1981 and is eligible to enter again, and to win again, if necessary, because whoever drafted the rules in the first place did not have sufficient faith in Britain's literary capacity to entertain the notion that somebody might write two – or, dammit, more than two – good novels in the course of their lifetime. Or perhaps nobody remembered that giants such as Joseph Conrad, D. H. Lawrence and John Galsworthy – all potential prizewinners, especially the last-named – ever existed.

There is also an exercise in imaginary linguistics, *Rates of Exchange,* by Malcolm Bradbury; J. M. Coetzee's South African political allegory, *The Life and Times of Malcolm K;* and an epic, didactic novel about adolescent sexuality, the life cycle of the eel, and British social history, *Waterland,* by Graham Swift. Unsurprising, uninspiring it might be but the *Sunday Times* called it 'highbrow', as if with faint surprise.

But of course, the odd has *not* become the norm. It is simply that, over the last three or four years, the odd has become visible, even if those which were odd before the tip of the iceberg emerged are still, Booker-wise, in limbo. Two of the very oddest fiction writers eligible by nationality for the prize, Wilson Harris and J. G. Ballard, remain in the proud position of Most Eminent Figures never to have made it on to a Booker shortlist.

However, out of the hundred or so submissions this year – dear God! A *hundred!* – a significant number were not in the least odd in any way, because people neither levitated in them nor had *verismo* abortions on kitchen tables in them. (If magic realism is coming up, then social realism appears to have vanished virtually without trace.) There remained a sterling residue of novels of personal experience divorced from public context, the fiction of a middle class apparently reassessing experimental territory in which it feels newly secure.

The housing estate downwind may pong a bit, kids at university some-times pick up the Wrong Type, a bogeyman or woman may lurch up from the lower orders now and then to give us all a nasty shock but, in this fic-tion, nobody ever needs to worry about the price of butter. These neo middle class novels bear no relation whatsoever to the 'adultery in NW3' novel. Writers of fiction would appear, on this showing, to have been mostly priced out of Hampstead, leaving it to Arabs and media personali-ties who often have better things to do with their time. In fact, there is no particular location for these scenarios. Events take place indifferently in the Home Counties and London suburbia. If the latter, the area is often newly gentrified, an interesting sociological touch.

The only way of characterising this kind of novel is to call it a typical *library book*. You read it to pass the time but you wouldn't dream of buy-ing it; and what passes my understanding is how a halfway competent pub-lisher's editor can say to him or herself about such a book: 'This is indeed worthy of winning ten tax-free grand in hand, plus publicity and prestige galore; *everybody* should read it and the world must have it whether it wants it or not!' And pack-a-bag it off, rejoicing in the richness of distilled experience the Booker judges will be about to relish. Because surely, if the prize is to mean anything, that is how anyone who submits a novel should feel.

Now what I've given you here, is a vast, parodic generalisation. There was a lot more going on among the submissions than that, even novels about the civil war in Northern Ireland (one out of more than 100), about Zimbabwe's independence (one out of more than 100) and at least two dealt either directly or obliquely with the nuclear menace. There were novels about old folks and working-class childhoods and much more.

However, among a widely disparate spread of themes, the 'library book' novel – and some of them are very skilfully written indeed, almost worth keeping – asserted itself as a definite genre. It can usually, though not always, be identified by the presence of a charlady among the minor char-acters. Not a continental au-pair; she's disappeared from middle-class mythology. But an authentic throwback, your proper old-fashioned char-lady.

All kinds of charladies. The traditional, comic charlady, no less amusing for nowadays taking her holidays in Spain. Charladies present but invisible, like the servants in Jane Austen, keeping the narrative going by ensuring the characters don't have to stop emoting every few minutes to wash up. Memorably, a mystic charlady given to visions of the Blessed Virgin Mary – the charlady as holy fool. These charladies are sometimes dignified with the title, housekeeper, but they carry on behaving like chars from the good old days; and there was a notable absence of any novel done from the charlady's point of view, though it would seem an excellent method by which to approach in a fresh light the bitter-sweet tragi-comedy of middle-class life.

There is a fictional subtext underwriting the much-vaunted renaissance of British fiction and it is to do with as-you-were. The collective profile of the entrants remains predominantly WASP, in spite of Salman Rushdie.

As a Booker judge, I'd confidently expected all manner of good things to happen between the day the season opened, in June and shortlist selection day, in September. Fat lunches from publishers, perhaps; bottles of bubbly delivered in plain wrappers; flattery and sycophancy on all sides. Not on your life. This *is* Britain. The only unsolicited gift that arrived took the form of a package containing yet *more* books from a publisher who must remain nameless, lest that name become mud – books *in addition* to the ones this publisher had already submitted, sent, not for the competition, obviously, but to me, personally, as a freelance lover of literature. This package coincided with the peak period towards the end of August, when fiction was arriving at the house by the crateful. I leafed through the offerings it contained to check if there were any tenners slipped among the pages, but no such luck.

Then tales began to filter through to me of hysterical scenes in publishers' offices as writers begged and pleaded on their knees to be submitted for the Booker. A certain literary agent is said to have inserted a clause in a certain writer's contract to the effect that publication of the said writer's novel be contingent on Booker submission of that work.

I'm sure the hysteria surrounding the Goncourt is just as bad, if not worse. But the Goncourt has been around for a long time and, besides, hysteria characterises the daily life of the French intellectual at the best of times. Further, the French, or at least Parisians are, as is well known, a booksy lot. The British, not.

Or – are the British turning into a booksy lot, under the influence of a literary prize promoted as if it were a sporting event?

Of course, the name 'Booker McConnell' helps. The 'Booker', for short. With the built-in word, 'book', as a mnemonic as to what the prize is for and a suggestion, too, that one should visit Ladbroke's and place one's bet now. Nevertheless, the evidence, piling up over the years since 1969, when the first prize was awarded (no bullseye, that; an unmemorable novel by P. H. Newby), suggests the existence in Britain of a market for fiction that only needs to be told what to buy in order to activate itself.

That sounds cynical. It isn't meant to be. The existence of this market implies the existence of an appetite. And so many novels are published, these days, its hard to find your way among the maze of even those reviewed. It is also quite difficult actually to *buy* hardback fiction and the

Booker business ensures that the shortlist at least achieves a very wide distribution.

After that false start, the then Booker judges struck gold in 1972 and 1973 with two of the best novels published here since the end of the war – John Berger's G and J. G. Farrell's *The Siege of Krishnapur*. Both were guaranteed to cause a degree of bewilderment, for different reasons. The attitudes of both these writers to the prize evidently caused offence. It seemed the prize was on its way.

But after that, for a long period, the judges seemed to take collective fright and award the prize for the Most Inoffensive Novel of the Year and no excitement accrued therefrom. The prize money went up from £5,000 to £10,000 – though this scarcely keeps pace with inflation; £5,000 in 1969 was worth a lot more than £10,000 is today. It is only since 1980, when William Golding won it, that the prize began to acquire a general audience and the Booker shortlist of five or six novels started to turn into an annual checklist for busy people of what is going on in the world o' books.

There remains the problem of what the Booker McConnell prize is actually given *for*. Is it for the Book of the Year, plus a handful of highly commendeds, like an Oscar? Or ought it to be the reward for a lifetime's contribution to culture – in which case, what then is the status of the shortlistees, poor things. If the judges increasingly opt for the former, they could easily oscillate to the latter view this year, next year. . . Iris Murdoch presumably won it for a body of work, since it can't have been for *The Sea, The Sea;* Doris Lessing ought to. So should Anthony Burgess. (No surprises? No surprises. But that isn't the point of this sort of prize!)

The judges could do that, could change the entire nature of the prize and the direction in which it is taking the readers of Britain, because the judges change every year themselves. This year, Fay Weldon, chairperson; Peter Porter, Terence Kilmartin, Libby Purves, me. A certain bias towards booksiness, here – two novelists, a poet, a literary editor (and translator of Proust), a highly literate journalist.

Next year, it might be – who can tell?

But who the actual team of judges comprises isn't really the point. What matters, what affects the whole nature of the prize and the kind of writing it helps to promote, is the fact this team isn't stable.

If the team of judges, any team, were given a fair run of, say three years, it would be possible for them to define the scope of the Booker prize, to continue to open up the crack it has willy-nilly inserted in the traditional philistinism of the British and help to start some kind of discussion as to what a novel is supposed to do in the general scheme of things. (Apart from making money, of course.)

The Booker is fun, already, a kind of football pools for publishers and writers. The hype and the hysteria and the vulgarity are all part of the process that has actually made the general public aware of it; so one can't knock them. But the prize could, and should, do rather more than it does now to help, not readers, but publishers, discriminate among their own wares.

New Society, 1983

J. G. Ballard: Empire of the Sun

J. G. Ballard says he's an optimist, which, given his penchant for apocalypses, initially seems unlikely but is nevertheless reassuring. He convinces me Reagan won't start World War III because he's too gaga to locate the whereabouts of the red button. Since, back in the sixties, Ballard was the only sane person in the entire Western world who predicted the ex-movie actor would one day rise to the dizzying heights of the presidency, maybe Ballard-the-prophet will hit target on this one too. Cross fingers.

It was in a story titled 'Why I want to Fuck Ronald Reagan', written, Ballard thinks, in 1966, that he foretold Reagan would run for the White House and that 'the profound anality of the presidential contender may be expected to dominate the US in the coming years'.

Not that he presented it as a prophecy exactly, or that 'Why I want to Fuck Ronald Reagan' is a short story on the terms of V. S. Pritchett or William Trevor. It is a piece of fiction, a set of ferocious images, a fragment of Swiftian satire, and it subsequently formed part of a book called *The Atrocity Exhibition,* published in 1970, which is one of the important works of British fiction produced in those exploding years.

I read 'Why I want to Fuck Ronald Reagan' to a class of English Literature majors at a liberal East Coast college in one of the four states in the Union that stayed with Jimmy Carter that November day in 1980 when a British Science-fiction writer's mad notion came true. They laughed until they cried, except those who vice versa'd , and then they demanded: 'Who is this man? He is one of your great writers! Why haven't we heard of him before?'

Perhaps it was just because they *were* Eng. Lit. majors that they hadn't heard of him before. He was certainly big stuff in the semiotics department already. Besides, Ballard doesn't like to think of himself as a 'literary man'. He bridles and huffs at the very thought. He is an imagery and ideas man, surreal, troubling – 'sensitive and enigmatic', *The Times Literary Supplement* once characterised his work, making him sound like Denton Welch, for God's sake. He is *not* a fine-writing man:

> I see myself primarily as an imaginative writer, and the imaginative writer isn't primarily concerned with his own medium. The fact that I express myself in a prose narrative is in a sense incidental – if I'd had a different facility, it could have been painting. It's the images I produce, and the ideas enshrined in the images that are the key things – their translation into words is the least important part of the enterprise.

In spite of that, Ballard is one of those rare beings who talk in grammatically correct sentences. His fiction has been characterised by restless and brilliant formal innovation, highly stylised, extreme and shocking violence, pitch-back humour . . .all the post-modernist characteristics. But you are still less likely to find Ballard on the shelf next to Barth and Barthelme and Coover than you are to find him filed along with Bug-Eyed Monster. After the publication of his new novel, *Empire of the Sun,* however, he will be among the bestsellers.

But up until now, Ballard has lived – very happily; he's not one of those sf writers who grumble about being ghettoised – in the privileged seclusion of genre. That is, as a science-fiction writer, he's been able on occasion to be as adventurous with narrative as he may be; to refer to Hans Bellmer or Max Ernst or Alfred Jarry as often as he feels the need without anybody putting him down for pretension. In fact, to carry on with all the freedoms of the 'experimental' writer who has an intelligent and sympathetically critical audience ever eager to find out what he has been up to, this time.

The price of all this? Even if he is greatly admired by Kathy Acker, has been a massive influence on performance art, and an inspiration to musicians and painters, Ballard is rarely, if ever, mentioned in the same breath, or even the same paragraph, as such peers as Anthony Powell or Iris Murdoch. Fans such as Kingsley Amis and Anthony Burgess praise Ballard to the skies but they themselves are classified differently, as, God help us, 'serious writers' in comparison.

This is a price Ballard has been happy, nay, positively ecstatic to pay. He has fans at the very top of the market, and fans in the pulps. The mainstream parts around him, leaving his feet comfortably dry. It has been thus ever since the delirious days of Michael Moorcock's magazine, *New Worlds,* twenty years ago, when science fiction started to excavate a whole new era – inner space, i.e. the unconscious – and joined hands with surrealism.

Ballard was attracted to science fiction in the early days because, when he arrived in Britain from China, where he was born, after the war was over and as a stranger with a strange, cold eye, he found that the reality of British society seriously overstretched the traditional resources of British naturalistic fiction:

I wanted a revolutionary fiction; I wanted the recognition of the whole domain of the unconscious, something British naturalistic fiction never attempted. I wanted a fiction of the imagination which would tell us the truth about ourselves. I wanted the future, not the past – I wanted the future of the next five minutes.

One of the results of this desire was that Ballard became the great chronicler of the new, technological Britain. A man prone to thrust himself into the grip of obsessions – 'I *am* my obsessions!' – he grew increasingly obsessed by the aspects of our landscape those of us who grew up with the culturally programmed notion of Britain as a 'green and pleasant land' conspire to ignore. Motorways. High rises.

There eventually ensued novels of pure technological nightmare – *Crash!*, *High Rise*, *The Concrete Island*. These were the vinyl and broken glass, sex 'n' violence novels, describing a landscape of desolation and disquiet similar to that of the novels of William Burroughs; the fame they brought was of a kind distinctly parallel to the norm of the world o' books. Burgess and Kingsley Amis could go on admiring him in comfort, free from the suspicion he might creep up behind them and pinch their laurels, even if the younger Amis, as big a fan as his father, showed signs of picking up a trick or two from his hero.

Ballard's thirty-odd-year career as a cult classic is, however, about to come to an end. He has, in his mid-fifties, produced what they call a 'breakthrough' novel. No doubt the 'literary men' (and women) will now treat Ballard as the sf writer who came in from the cold. Who finally put away childish things, man-powered fight, landscapes of flesh, the erotic geometry of the car crash, things like that, and wrote the Big Novel they always knew he'd got in him.

Yet *Empire of the Sun*, which is indeed a Big Novel, is manifestly the product of the same unique sensibility as his last major novel, *The Unlimited Dream Company* (1979), and has a great deal in common with it. They share the theme of death and resurrection, the earlier one in a radiant, visionary mode, the later one as delirious obsession. But *Empire of the Sun* is a recreation of the recent past, not a myth of the near future, and the well-loved Ballardian leitmotifs, confinement, escape, flight, have the gritty three-dimensionality of real experience. The novel is even about a kind of apocalypse, the destruction of the British community in Shanghai by the Japanese.

All the same, the chapters have titles that recall those of earlier Ballard short stories: 'The Drained Swimming Pool', 'The Open-Air Cinema', 'The Fallen Airmen'. It is a shock to find so much of the recurrent, hypnotic imagery of J. G. Ballard moored to the soil of an authentic city, at an authentic date in real time – Shanghai, as the European residents of that city of salesmen are engulfed ineluctably in war. It was the place of Ballard's childhood.

Empire of the Sun is, very notably, a novel about the fragility of the human body, and the dreadful spillability of that body's essential juices, shit, piss, blood, pus. It is also about the resilience of children; and about the difficulty experienced by the British in adjusting to changing circumstances. More specifically, it is about one child's war, and hence an investigation of twentieth-century warfare, in which non-combatants such as children and also the old, the weak, the sick increasingly fare worst. It is about one child's war in a prison camp, and how he came to feel at home there.

There has, notes Ballard, been surprisingly little fiction about the war in the Far East, perhaps because the British lost it. No, he hasn't read J. G. Farrell's *The Singapore Grip,* which is an account of the fall of Singapore. 'Was Farrell there?' Ballard asked sharply. He obviously doesn't trust book-based research in this area. A note at the front of *Empire of the Sun* says the novel 'draws on my experiences in Shanghai, China, during the Second World War and in Lunghua C.A.C (Civilian Assembly Centre) where I was interned from 1942-45'. The strange, cold eye which Ballard turned on Britain when he first came here was evidently trained to look on, unflinching, in Lunghua.

He says:

I always intended to write a novel about China and the war, but I put it off because I always had more urgent things to do, in fiction. Then, two or three years ago, I realised if I didn't write the China book soon, I would never do so. Memory would fade, apart from anything else. It took a very long time, 20 years or so, to forget the events that took place in Shanghai and it took a very long time to remember them, again. . . I don't just mean to bring them to mind, but to flesh them out, to remythologise them.

Jim 'my young hero', misses his Scripture exam because the Japanese attack Shanghai; at first that missed exam seems the most important thing.

Although he mislays his parents early on, it is a long time before he finally surrenders his school cap and blazer. This well-brought-up boy goes to the Cathedral School. His father's house in Amherst Avenue has a swimming pool (soon to be drained) and nine servants. Jim has the sense of security only privilege can bring.

He is too young to be surprised when he finds the servants gone and the house deserted. He is on his own; it is an adventure. Trying to surrender to the Japanese is more of a problem. They don't really want any more prisoners, but the camp, for all its privations, offers more safety than the dangerous chaos of the city, where a thief will cut off your arm for the sake of a watch, kill you for your shoes, where there is no food left, where the water is full of cholera. Where privilege has evaporated.

Once in the camp, Jim adjusts quickly. Too young to feel nostalgia, he focuses his memory forward. Soon he will be reunited with his parents! One day. Soon. Until then, he lives the present. He scavenges. He runs errands. He keeps himself busy. He sneaks and wheedles extra sweet potatoes. If his ingratiating smile drives the Japanese guards into paroxysms of fury and all the other children are afraid of him, he is free from self-pity, sustained by the very business of living, and his dreams are nourished by contraband copies of *Readers Digest* scrounged from American prisoners.

Jimmy Ballard lived in Lunghua Camp; he lived in the very hut that his young hero inhabits. The entire context of the novel is true, but Jim's adventures are invention. The book is by no means autobiographical. Ballard was with his parents and his sister in the camp and he knows that children, particularly when they are with their parents, can witness appalling events and feel no fear.

It was a peculiar life for the business community in Shanghai, before the war, after the war, even during the war – until the crunch came and internment began.

'Like my young hero,' Ballard says,

one witnessed, on a daily basis, the most appalling events – starvation, disease, brutality – but through the window of a chauffeur-driven car. So that one was very, very close to the terrible brutalities inflicted on the Chinese by the Japanese, who surrounded Shanghai, and by the Chinese themselves on one another, but one could do nothing about it. And one wasn't directly involved. And, in a way, writing the book may be an attempt to go back and put emotion in.

Only at the end of the novel, reunited with his parents, about to leave China forever, does Jim, now sixteen, a child no longer, see that Shanghai is now and always was a 'terrible city'; and these, the last words of the

novel, restore to the adjective 'terrible' all its original force. The last image
of the novel is the haunting one of the paper flowers that decorate the
coffins the Chinese, too poor to afford burial, launch into the sea, the
drowned flowers that come back to the city, along with the corpses.

Empire of the Sun is a rich, complex, heartrending novel, in characteristically Ballardian prose – a prose with a curiously metallic quality, cold as
steel, that makes the imagery shine out, as he wants it to, with the hallucinatory clarity of that of naïve painters. The image of those paper flowers
decorating the corpses, not of the Chinese dead, but of British sailors dying
in the Yangtze River; the mask of flies on the face of the dead airman; the
silvery shapes of the American bombers Jim sees from the corner of his eye
when he is sick with fever, that are the emissaries of death.

It is easy to think of *Empire of the Sun* as the logical culmination of a
career, the book towards which Ballard has been working all his life. Since
he is far too young to retire, to think that would be an error. The novel
has the look of a significant change of direction for Ballard, yet its appearance of naturalism is only superficial – it is, once again, a triumph of the
imagination. The imaginative recreation of that 'terrible city' and the resurrection of its teeming population of dead are to do with the notions of
transformation that have always informed his work.

It is hard to imagine – top that! – what he will do next. But, then, it
always has been. Meanwhile, here is the fruit of that obsessiveness Ballard
so much admires, the obsessive single-mindedness of, as he puts it, 'long-
incarcerated mental patients who remain totally faithful to their few obsessions throughout their long lives, the sort of dedication shown by Japanese
soldiers hiding out in the jungle for 30-odd-years. . .' The obsessive pursuit of his own imagery to its origins has brought us this riveting and sombre and, yes, funny (humour blacker than black, this time) and humane
novel, that is the kind of novel we used to think we no longer had the
energy to write, that Ballard was writing all the time.

Time Out, 1984

The End: Reading South Africa

Review of André Brink and J. M. Coetzee (ed.) *A Land Apart: A South
African Reader* and Norma Kitson, *Where Sixpence Lives.*

The situation in South Africa is such that, by the time this review appears
in print, the two books with which it deals may already belong to the past,

both in their different ways witnesses to the haunted tensions, torture and bloodshed of the period of minority rule. The anthology of fiction, *A Land Apart*, was, say its editors, André Brink and J. M. Coetzee, 'compiled amid the tumult of the uprisings of 1985', although the writers they choose to represent had not then had the time to reflect upon that tumult in their work, and almost certainly have not had sufficient time since. Outside South Africa, *A Land Apart* will be read against the background of silence created by that country's recently imposed censorship of its internal news. Inside South Africa, who will read it? The editors note that, at the outset, they agreed that 'we would proceed as if the apparatus of censorship did not exist'. This is an anthology for export only.

André Brink took primary responsibility for selecting the work translated from Afrikaans; J. M. Coetzee for that in English. They do not represent their own work. Both are novelists of international reputation, and the bias of the collection is towards writers little known in Britain, especially younger ones. All the Afrikaans-language writers and the great majority of the English-language writers live and work in South Africa at present. This is one of the points of the collection, that it is utterly contemporary.

Perhaps most black South Africans do not feel that their country is now entering upon its final tragedy: they may, rather, believe that their tragedy is finally coming to an end, even if it is doing so amidst great suffering. But the writing in *A Land Apart* is largely by white writers and, especially that translated from Afrikaans, is almost entirely pervaded by a deep sense of dread. The preface speaks of this mood in Afrikaans fiction as 'an intimation of apocalypse, which implies not just the death of the individual or the end of his hopes, but the destruction of the entire known world or way of life'. All the same, it warns: 'If the outline of a map of contemporary South African writing does seem to emerge, the map should be used cautiously'. This is a necessary warning: if the guilt, the self-loathing, the sheer demoralisation of much of this fiction were the predominant mood of the real South Africa, not just of its fictional representation in the pages of *A Land Apart*, Nelson Mandela would be prime minister before the year was out.

In the Afrikaans section, the narrator of Elsie Joubert's story, 'Back Yard', says: 'I live on the periphery of an existence which I don't understand.' She meditates upon the fact that even if she learned her black maid's real – that is, African – name, she would be unable to pronounce it. In the servant's room, outside in the yard, the tumultuous lives of the poor are carried on. However good the narrator's heart – and she *does* have a good heart – their lives are unutterably alien to her. The deserted wife in Lotte Viljoen's '*Lament for Koos*' longs for human contact with her black servant, but 'my domestic help is unreachable'. Estrangement would seem to be the essence of middle-class Afrikaans life; poverty, misery, superstition, violence and an iron sexual puritanism are present as the lot of the rural poor. E. Kotzé (Day of Blood'), Hennie Aucamp ('For Four Voices') and Pirow Becker ('Under a Shepherd's Tree') offer glimpses of poor whites with lives almost as circumscribed and open to hazard as those of the Tennessee sharecroppers described in the 1930s by James Agee in *Let Us Now Praise Famous Men*. Other stories reveal small-town life as a hot-bed of hypocrisy. Sexual relations are poisoned and poisonous everywhere from the farmstead to the gleaming suburb. And, bitterest of ironies, young men must die in defence of all this. Several stories deal with the war against South Africa's neighbours. The young paratrooper in Etienne Van Heerden's 'My Cuban' broods: 'Oh how we float, the flower of the Republic's youth. Green our uniforms, red the flush on our cheeks, fresh the wind, Africa an open hand beneath us. . .'

The Afrikaans section, eighteen writers, is confined to prose fiction. The times have produced such an abundance of writers that the editors say this number could easily have been doubled, and doubled again had poetry and drama been included. Afrikaans as a literary language is barely a century old; its linguistic catchment area is not extensive. The need to record and interpret experience must be felt very urgently, although most of the fiction – Etienne Van Heerden and, less successfully, Fransi Phillips are exceptions – is written in a straightforwardly naturalistic style that offers scant opportunity for prophecy, denunciation or rhetoric of any kind.

The English section, which has seventeen writers – Nadine Gordimer is represented twice – stretches itself to include poetry and autobiography. Because of the presence of black and Coloured writers, there is less psychological violence here and more of the ordinary, physical kind. Joel Matlou's harrowing account of a spell of work in a platinum mine, 'Man Against Himself', suggests there are worse things in life than an inability to pronounce one's maid's name. The excerpt from the tape-recorded diary of Mario Tholo includes a description of the local mortuary in 1976: 'What happens is that they put all the unidentified bodies in one place and you have to search through them like a pile of old clothes to find yours.' Most imaginative fiction would pale in significance beside this kind of direct and unmediated recounting of experience and the stories in *A Land Apart* are no exception.

Or perhaps it is fiction itself that is the problem: perhaps the fiction of bourgeois realism, the fiction that was invented to order to let the middle class inspect itself in its mirror, in inappropriate to the representation of the historic crisis of white South Africa, even if the need to try to represent that crisis is pressing in the extreme, even if the work of Nadine Gordimer suggests the moral stature which the uncompromised writer may achieve in such circumstances.

There is a rare kind of hopefulness about Jeremy Cronin's splendidly and unashamedly sentimental prison poem, 'Walking on Air', about a white, working-class Communist, that comes from the South Africa of heroic struggle rarely hinted at elsewhere in the book. He says to his wife:

> – Dulcie, I will never betray my comrades.
> And with a frog in her throat she replied
> – I'm behind you. One hundred per cent.

The John Matthews of the poem ends up with a sentence of fifteen years. Norma Kitson's husband, David Kitson, was sentenced to twenty years for work connected with the early days of the ANC. Like Dulcie, she was a hundred per cent behind him and remained so. Her spirit is unquenchable, even if she is something like the little boy in 'The Emperor's New Clothes', and something like Cassandra – she keeps on shouting out loud that the Emperor is stark naked but nobody will believe her. She recalls:

> There was very little support among the white people for the liberation struggle in the Fifties. I thought that the minute I informed them about the things I knew, about the injustices and the laws, they would be sure to join in. But they looked at me blankly. They didn't want to know.

When Norma Kitson, or Cranko, as she was then, was a little girl, she lived in a big house in Durban. The small son of her mother's maid Sarah was allowed to come and stay for a few weeks every year; the Crankos used to call him 'Sixpence'. The rest of the year, Sixpence lived miles away in Zululand with his brothers and sisters. Whenever Sarah lost her temper with the Cranko kids, Norma wondered whether it was because she resented looking after them instead of looking after her own children. Sixpence's real name was Zolile, which Mrs Kitson knows very well how to pronounce. Her own daughter has been given a Zulu name, Amandla.

The first chapters of *Where Sixpence Lives* are the raw material for a certain kind of colonial novel: the grand house with its huge staff, the spoiled, capricious, beautiful mother, the liberal father with his bedtime stories about the French Revolution and his repressed homosexuality, the scapegrace brother – all pulled this way and that way by the turbulent undercurrents of a failing marriage. All the glamorous misery of a novel of sensibility.

The family, especially on her mother's side, was flush with new money.

Perhaps it was the awareness of the money that helped to tune Mrs Kitson's eye so finely to questions of cash and class. Edith, their old black housekeeper, had been passed on by Auntie Ettie, who had 'graduated to getting a Coloured woman, who cost more'. The children's status was confirmed by a stern Anglo nurse. Affection came from the blacks. When Mrs Kitson's mother arbitrarily abandoned her marriage, separating her children from one another and scattering the constellation of servants to the four winds, Philemon the chauffeur doubled up with ironic laughter: 'You white people make so much destruction you even do it to yourselves!'

That is where, if it were a novel, *Where Sixpence Lives*, would end, although the story of a life spent in opposition to white privilege is the real story and is only just beginning. But, though her book is emphatically not a novel, Mrs Kitson hasn't been able to resist the use of page after page of reconstructed dialogue and a fiction-like presentation of events. As when, during the Kitson's London courtship: 'One Saturday night at the Finsbury Park Odeon, when I was six months pregnant, David handed me an orange ice-lolly and said: 'How about getting married?' Yet her jauntiness and guts are so engaging that these tricks seem the natural buttonholing devices of an incorrigible raconteuse rather than a deliberate reinvention of the past.

Another tactic is less engaging: she frequently employs a device familiar from the didactic fiction of my youth, in which ideological problems are introduced in the form of debates in the homely setting of a family meal or in answer to the innocent query of a bystander. This sometimes gives her memoir the flavour of a tract, when its matter-of-fact and unsentimental account of torture and violence ought to make its own points.

Shortly after her husband was imprisoned in South Africa in 1964, Mrs Kitson and her young children returned to Britain, where her son had been born, continuing to devote herself to the struggle from abroad. This led to her founding the City of London Anti-Apartheid Group, who conducted the notorious non-stop picket in front of South Africa House in London for eighty-six days and nights in 1982. One of the (successful) aims of the picket was to embarrass the South African authorities into moving David Kitson from Death Row, where he was spending the last months of his confinement. The picket is out there again, as I write; this time it says it won't budge until Nelson Mandela is free.

It is during this period of exile that the tale goes murky, as Mrs Kitson recounts, in a tone of startled innocence, her experience of the internecine factionalism of the exiled South African Left. But at the end of the book, her husband free again, Mrs Kitson's hope for Africa's future remains radiant, her faith in the inexorability of natural justice absolute. The Kitsons are looking forward to being able to go home soon. It is still possible that they may not have to walk through a sea of blood in order to do so.

London Review of Books, 1986

Christina Stead

To open a book, any book, by Christina Stead and read a few pages is to be at once aware that one is in the presence of greatness. Yet this revelation is apt to precipitate a sense of confusion, of strangeness, of anxiety, not only because Stead has a rare capacity to flay the reader's sensibilities, but also because we have grown accustomed to the idea that we live in pygmy times. To discover that a writer of so sure and unmistakable a stature is still amongst us, and, more, produced some of her most remarkable work as recently as the 1960s and 1970s, is a chastening thing especially since those two relatively recent novels – *Cotters' England* (1966) and *Miss Herbert (the Suburban Wife)* (1976) – contain extremely important analyses of postwar Britain, address the subject of sexual politics at a profound level, and have been largely ignored in comparison with far lesser novels such as Doris Lessing's *The Golden Notebook.* To read Stead, now, is to be reminded of how little, recently, we have come to expect from fiction. Stead is of that category of fiction writer who us restores to the entire world, in its infinite complexity and inexorable bitterness, and never asks if the reader wishes to be so furiously enlightened and instructed, but takes it for granted that this is the function of fiction. She is a kind of witness and a kind of judge, merciless, cruel, and unforgiving.

Stead has just reached the age of eighty and, according to Australian newspapers, is still writing. Born in Australia, she has lived in Britain, Europe and the US and has written novels set in cities in various countries as if she were native to them all. This phenomenon of ubiquity helps to explain her relative obscurity: she appears to acknowledge no homeland and has therefore been acknowledged by none until her return to her native country after almost a half-century of absence. Lawrence, in exile, remained British to the core; Joyce took Dublin in his back pocket wherever he went. Stead becomes absorbed into the rhythms of life wherever she finds herself. Furthermore, although she has always written from a profound consciousness of what it is to be a woman, she writes, as they say, 'like a man': that is, she betrays none of the collusive charm which is supposedly a mark of the feminine genius. As a result, because she writes *as* a woman, not *like* a woman, Randall Jarrell could say of *The Man Who Loved Children* (1940): 'a male reader worries: "Ought I to be a man?"'

Jarrell thought that *The Man Who Loved Children* was by far Stead's best novel and believed its commercial and critical failure blighted her subsequent development. (Why did he say that? Was it revenge for having his machismo deflated?) However, at least three of her other novels – I'd say *For Love Alone* (1945), *A Little Tea, A Little Chat* (1948) and *Cotters' England* (1966) – equal that novel, and in some ways surpass it, while *Letty Fox: Her Luck* (1946) is, unusually for Stead, a fully achieved comic novel of a most original kind.

However, it wasn't surprising that *The Man Who Loved Children* should acquire the romantic reputation of a unique masterpiece, especially when it was the only novel of hers in print. The single-minded intensity of its evocation of domestic terror gives it a greater artistic cohesion than Stead's subsequent work, which tends towards the random picaresque. And Stead permits herself a genuinely tragic resolution. The ravaged harridan, Henny, the focus of the novel, dies in a grand, fated gesture, an act of self-immolation that, so outrageous has been her previous suffering, is almost a conventional catharsis. One feels that all Henny's previous life has been a preparation for her sudden, violent departure from it and, although the novels appals, it also, artistically, satisfies, in a way familiar in art. Later, Stead would not let her readers off the hook of life so easily. She won't allow us the dubious consolations of pity and terror again.

Since Stead went home, she has become more and more known as an Australian writer. This geographical placement is, of course, only right and proper and geographically correct, and contains within it the enticing notion of a specific kind of post-colonial sensibility which might serve as a context for her illusionless power. But only one of her novels has a wholly Australian setting, and that the earliest, *Seven Poor Men of Sydney* (1934). Even here, she has already established her characteristic milieu as that of the rootless urban intelligensia, a milieu as international as it is peculiar to our century. Teresa Hawkins in *For Love Alone* is the only major Australian character in Stead's later fiction, and Teresa is the most striking of these birds of passage, who sometimes become mercenaries of an ideology, sometimes end up as flotsam and jetsam.

Stead is also one of the great articulators of family life. There is no contradiction here. Stead's families – the Pollitts in *The Man Who Loved Children*, the Foxes in *Letty Fox: Her Luck*, the Hawkinses in *For Love Alone*, the Cotters of *Cotters' England* – are social units that have outlived the original functions of protection and mutual aid and grown to be seedbeds of pathology. These are families in a terminal state of malfunction, families you must flee from in order to preserve your sanity, families it is criminal folly to perpetuate – and, on the whole, Stead's women eschew motherhood like the plague. (Stead's loathing of the rank futility of home and hearth is equalled, in literature, only by that expressed by the Marquis de Sade.) These are degenerated, cannibal families, in which the very sacrament of the family, the communal meal when all are gathered together, is a Barmecide feast at which some family member, wife or child, is on the emotional menu. One characteristic and gruesomely memorable family dinner, with its exaggerated hysteria and elements of high, diabolic farce, is that in *Cotters' England*, at which raw chicken and dementia are served. Once away from the nest, Stead's birds of passage tend to eat in the neutral environments of restaurants – as do the runaway lovers in *The Beauties and Furies*.

These rancid, cancerous homes may provide a useful apprenticeship in the nature of tyranny (several times in *The Man Who Loved Children* Stead stresses that children have 'no rights' within the family): that is all. The only escape is a plunge into an exponential whirl of furnished rooms, cheap hotels, constant travelling, chance liaisons, the blessed indifference of strangers. Stead's families, in fact, produce those rootless, sceptical displaced persons she also describes, who have no country but a state of mind, and yet who might, due to their very displacement and disaffection, be able to make new beginnings.

In *For Love Alone,* we actually see Teresa Hawkins performing this trajectory, from the mutilating claustrophobia of her father's house – 'home' in Stead is almost always the patriarchal cage – into that homelessness which is the prerequisite of freedom. In *The Beauties and Furies* this process founders. Elvira leaves her husband in London for a lover in Paris, but Elvira is a dreamily narcissistic, emotionally contingent being, who scarcely knows what freedom is and who will, inevitably, return home. (There is a remarkable consistency in Stead. Elvira, the romantic, self-obsessed Englishwoman, of this, one of her earliest novels, has much in common with the Eleanor Herbert of her latest.) But Stead does not direct us to condemn Elvira – nor to pity her. Stead's greatest moral quality as a novelist is her lack of pity. As Blake said,

> Pity would be no more,
> If we did not make somebody poor,

and, for Stead, pity is otiose, a self-indulgent luxury that obscures the real nature of our relations with our kind. To disclose that real nature has always been her business. Essentially, she is engaged in the exposition of certain perceptions as to the nature of human society. She does this through the interplay of individuals both with one another and with the institutions that we created but which now seem to dominate us. Marriage; the family; money.

. She has, obviously, from the very beginning – her first publication was a collection of short stories modelled on the *Decameron* - been a writer of almost megalomaniac ambition. The literary project of Louie, the unnatural daughter of *The Man Who Loved Children*, was to compose for an adored teacher 'the Aiden cycle . . . a poem of every conceivable form and also every conceivable metre in the English language', all in Miss Aiden's praise. This seems the sort of project that would attract Stead herself. Hers may even be the kind of ambition that is nourished by neglect, of which she has received sufficient. (Had people believed Cassandra, she would have known something had gone badly wrong.) To read some of Stead's more possessed and driven novels – *Cotters' England* and *A Little Tea, A Little Chat,* in particular – is to be reminded of what Blake said about his Bible of Hell: 'which the world shall have whether they will or no'. If, as seems the case, we are now ready to accept Stead as one of the great writers of our time, this does not mean the times are going well.

It is possible to be a great novelist – that is, to render a veracious account of your times – and a bad writer – that is, an incompetent practitioner of applied linguistics. Like Theodore Dreiser. Conversely, good writers – for example, Borges – often prefer to construct alternative metaphysical universes based on the Word. If you read only the novels Stead wrote after *The Man Who Loved Children,* it would seem that she belonged to the Dreiser tendency. She patently does not subscribe to any metaphysics of the Word. The work of her maturity is a constant, agitated reflection upon our experience in *this* world. For her, language is not an end-in-itself in the current, post-modernist or 'mannerist' mode, but a mere tool, and a tool she increasingly uses to hew her material more and more roughly. Nor does she see the act of storytelling as a self-reflexive act. Therefore, as a composer of narrative, she can be amazingly slipshod. She will allow careless lapses in continuity. People can change names, parentage, age, occupation from page to page, as though she corrected nothing. They can also slip through holes in the narrative and disappear. Miss Aiden is honoured, arrives for a typically vile family supper with the Pollitts, and is then written out of the script like a soap-opera character with a contract elsewhere. All this would be unforgivable if, in Stead, narrative mattered, much. It does not. Her narrative is almost *tachiste:* she composes it like a blind man throwing paint against a wall. Her narratives shape themselves, as our lives seem to do.

Interestingly enough, she started her career as a very mannered writer indeed. *The Salzburg Tales* of 1934 is a collection of glittering, grotesque short fictions, parables and allegories not dissimilar to the *Seven Gothic*

Tales that Isak Dinesen published in the same year. *The Salzburg Tales* are contrived with a lush, jewelled exquisiteness of technique that recurs in *The Beauties and Furies,* which first appeared in 1936. At one point in that novel, Coromandel, the antique-dealer's daughter, recites just such a little Gothic tale, 'The Story of Hamadryad'. Oliver's adventures in the Club of the Somnambulists at the end of the novel and the dreams of several of the characters have a similar overblown, highly decorated, romantic extravagance. It is rather unusual for Stead's characters to dream with quite such abandon – 'She saw a rod with two headless snakes emerging from a dusky ivory egg. . .'- and it is tempting to hypothesise some influence from the surrealists, especially since this novel takes place in a Paris that is decidedly Paul Eluard's *capitale de la douleur.* And, at this stage, Stead is assimilating influences from every conceivable source. She is a self-consciously brilliant young writer. *The Beauties and Furies* is evidence of a love-affair with language which produces felicities such as: 'Not a blade of grass moved and not a bird flew down the perspective of the great water, but, under thickety trees, officers and children skated with coloured cloaks and gloves over a pond. Beyond, dazzling and enchanted, lay the leafless forest.' Very finely crafted, too, though this love-affair can induce logorrhoea, and the same novel contains much purple: 'Imprisoned by her marauding hair, she lay, and turned dark, silent eyes upon me.' And so, on. Fine writing must have come easily to her; roughness, ungainliness, ferocity were qualities for which she had to strive.

In *House of All Nations* (1938), which comes after *The Beauties and Furies,* the puppy-fat is already beginning to fall away from the bare bones of Stead's mature style, and of her mature purpose, for this is a novel straightforwardly about the root of all evil: that is, banking. However, the complications of its plotting recall the Jacobean drama at its most involuted, so that it is quite difficult to tell exactly what is going on. In fact, the elaborately fugal plotting of *House of All Nations* is beginning to dissolve of its own accord, just because too much is going on, into the arbitrary flux of event that characterises Stead's later novels. And she is beginning to write, not like a craftsman, but like an honest worker.

At the time of *The Man Who Loved Children,* she relinquished all the capacity of the language of her narrative to bewitch and seduce. But Sam Pollitt, the father almighty or Nobodaddy of that novel, uses a babbling, improvised, pseudo-language, a sort of Pollitt creole, full of cant words – 'cawf' for coffee, 'munch-time', 'orfus' – with which to bemuse, delight, and snare his brood. This is the soft, slippery, charming language of seduction itself. Louie invents an utterly opaque but grammatically impeccable language of her own and confronts him with a one-act play in it, acted by her siblings. 'Mat, rom garrots im.' (In translation: 'Mother, father is strangling me.') Sam is very angry. Louie's ugly language is vengeance. Stead does not go as far as Louie. Her later style is merely craggy, unaccommodating, a simple, functional, often unbeautiful means to an end, which can still astonish by its directness: 'With old Mrs Cotter after the funeral, time had been, time was and time might be again, but it was all one time: she knew no difference between the living and the dead.' So, without pathos or elaboration, she depicts senility in *Cotters' England*.

Since she is technically an expressionist writer, in whose books madmen scream in deserted landscapes, a blue light turns a woman into the image of a vampire and a lesbian party takes on the insanely heightened melodrama of a drawing by George Grosz, the *effect* is the thing, not the language that achieves it. But there is more to it than that. The way she finally writes is almost as if she were showing you by demonstration that style itself is a lie in action, that language is an elaborate confidence trick designed to lull us into acceptance of the intolerable, just as Sam Pollitt uses it on his family, that words are systems of deceit. And that truth is not a quality inherent in any kind of discourse, but a way of looking at things: that truth is not an aspect of reality but a test of reality. So, more and more, Stead concentrates on dialogue, on language in use as camouflage or subterfuge – dialogue, or rather serial monologue, for Stead's characters rarely listen to one another sufficiently to enable them to conduct dialogues together, although they frequently enjoy rows of a polyphonic nature, in which it is not possible for anybody to hear anybody else. If the storytellers in *The Salzburg Tales* reveal their personalities through the gnomic and discrete fables they tell, Stead's later characters thunder out great arias and recitatives of self-deceit, self-justification, attempted manipulation, and it is up to the reader to compare what they say with what they do and draw his or her conclusions as to what is really going on. The monologue is Stead's forte, dramatic monologues comparable to those of Robert Browning.

In *Letty Fox: Her Luck* (1946) she extends this form of the dramatic monologue to the length of an entire novel. It is an elaborate imitation autobiography almost in the manner of Defoe, a completely successful impersonation of an American woman, in which we are invited to extract bare facts from Letty's account of her own life – the life of a 'generous fool' who has no luck with men because of the careless magnificence with which she throws herself away on them – and construct from the bare facts the *real* life of Letty Fox. Letty, it turns out, is joylessly promiscuous, hysterically demanding, a self-righteous bitch, and a heartless betrayer. But Letty does not know any of these things about herself and when, as from time to time happens, her friends tax her with them, she hotly denies them. The disjuncture between what she is and what she thinks she is, is wonderfully comic. It is, curiously, not comic at Letty's expense. Letty finally does no harm to anyone but herself, and Stead graciously allots her the best one-liner in her entire *oeuvre:* 'Radicalism is the opium of the middle-classes.' Letty is as full of bad faith as Nellie Cotter but is saved by her unpretentiousness and by what Stead calls somewhere the 'inherent outlawry' in women. Letty is not named after the predatory and raffish fox for nothing and if her only ambition is to marry, which defines her limited aspirations, it takes two to tie the knot. Letty longs for children and is only truly happy when pregnant, but any social worker would recommend a termination when, at the novel's end, we leave her pregnant, in a cheap hotel, with a penniless playboy husband – all she has finally managed to ensnare. The final joke is that this greedy vixen of an amateur prostitute will, as a wife, be the perfect poacher turned gamekeeper: all her life she has been a matriarch manquée – hence her ill-success as a free woman – and now the matriarch has found herself and can begin. The amoral predator will become the solid citizen. Why rob banks when you can run them, to paraphrase one of the maxims in Brecht's *Threepenny Opera,* and Letty is too dishonest to live for long outside the law.

Others in Stead's gallery of monsters of existential bad faith – Sam Pollitt, Nellie Cotter, Robert Grant in *a Little Tea, A Little Chat* – are not treated so genially. They are killers. They precipitate suicide and madness in those who come close to them. Letty uses bad faith to bolster her faltering self-respect: these pernicious beings base their entire self-respect on bad faith. The mouths of these grotesque, nodding carnival heads are moving all the time as they rage, bluster, cajole, manipulate, provoke, enlightening us as to what bad faith does.

Stead's fictional method obviously presupposes a confidence in the importance of fiction as the exposition of the real structures on which our lives are based. It follows that she has gained a reputation as a writer of naturalism, so much so that, in her Introduction to the Virago edition of *The Beauties and Furies,* Hilary Bailey seems disconcerted that 'this great writer of naturalism' should have produced a novel so resistant to a naturalist reading. (Any novel in which a prostitute advertises her wares by reciting the poetry of Baudelaire is scarcely in the tradition of George Gissing.) Stead is certainly not a writer of naturalism nor of social realism, and if her novels are read as novels about our lives, rather than about the circumstances that shape our lives, they are bound to disappoint, because the naturalist or high bourgeois mode works within the convention that there exists such a thing as 'private life'. In these private lives, actions are informed by certain innate inner freedoms and, however stringent the pressures upon the individual, there is always a little margin of autonomy which could be called 'the self'. For Stead, however, 'private life' is itself a socially determined fiction, the 'self' is a mere foetus of autonomy which may or may not prove viable, and 'inner freedom', far from being an innate quality, is a precariously held intellectual position that may be achieved only at the cost of enormous struggle, often against the very grain of what we take to be human feeling.

Teresa Hawkins achieves selfhood only through a fanatical, half-crazed ordeal of self-imposed poverty and an act of willed alienation which takes her across half the world, from Australia to England. But this ordeal does not prepare Teresa for any reconciliation with the world: it only toughens her up for what is going to happen next. Louie, in *The Man Who Loved Children,* plots her parents' murder and succeeds in abetting her stepmother's death to a point beyond complicity. Then she runs away, leaving a houseful of small children to the tender mercies of Sam Pollitt. That is what Louie must do, in order to enter the fragile state of freedom-in-potential which is all Stead will offer in the way of hope. (She sometimes reminds me of what Kafka said to Max Brod: 'There *is* hope – but not for us.') But many, in fact most, of Stead's characters remain trapped in the circumstances which have produced them. These include Sam Pollitt, Letty Fox, Nellie Cooke and her brother, Robert Grant and his blonde, fatal mistress – and the eponymous 'Miss Herbert, the Suburban Wife'. (*Miss Herbert* is one of the oddest novels and, after much thought, I take it to be a reversion to certain allegorical elements present in her earliest writing and always latent in it: to be nothing more nor less than a representation of the home life of Britannia from the 1920s until almost the present day.) The lovers in *The Beauties and Furies* are incapable of responding to the challenge of their romantic attachment: they drift, vacillate, betray one another and all in a kind of lapse of consciousness – like the sleepwalkers their friend Marpurgo says they all are. 'I prefer to be a somnambulist. I walk on the edge of precipices safely. Awake, I tremble.' Earlier, Elvira has said: 'I am a dead soul; life is too heavy for me to lift.' Happily for them, they never wake; happily for her, she never gets sufficient grip on life to give it a good shove.

The hard edges and sharp spikes of Stead's work are rarely, if ever, softened by the notion that things might be, generally, other than they are. It is tempting to conclude that she does not think much of the human race, but it is rather that she is appalled by the human condition. It is illuminating that Teresa, in *For Love Alone,* says to herself, near the end of the novel: 'I only have to do what is supposed to be wrong and I have a happiness that is barely credible.' Teresa has freely chosen to be unfaithful to her beloved lover, to follow her own desire. To become free, she has exercised her will; to remain free, she follows her desires. Stead rarely states her subversive intent as explicitly as this, nor often suggests that the mind-forged manacles of the human condition are to be so easily confounded. But when Teresa meditates, 'It was easy to see how upsetting it would be if women began to love freely', she is raising the question of female desire, of women's sexuality as action and as choice, of the assertion of sexuality as a right, and this question, to which she returns again and again in various ways, is at the core of Stead's work. The latter part of *For Love Alone*, the section in London where Teresa learns to love freedom, is rendered as a mass of dense argument within Teresa herself, unlike the discussion of women and marriage that occupies most of the earlier, Australian section of the book, where it is dramatised through the experiences of women in Teresa's circle. As a result, the triumph of desire simply does not strike the reader as vividly as the early grisly *tableaux vivants* of repression, such as Malfi's wedding. Perhaps Stead found this subject of the triumph of desire almost too important to be rendered as pure fiction; it is the exultant end of Teresa's ordeal.

For Love Alone is an account of a woman's fight for the right to love in freedom, which the anarchist Emma Goldman claimed as 'the most vital right'. (All Teresa's meditations on free union recall Goldman.) This is a fight we see one woman, Teresa herself, win: Teresa, who has the name of a saint, and also – Hawkins – kinship with a bird of prey noted for its clear vision. Stead then published *Letty Fox: Her Luck*, a crazy comedy about a girl who fights, and fights dirty, to get a ring on her finger. It is as if Stead were saying: 'There is Teresa, yes: but there is also Letty.' ('Letty Marmalade', as she signs herself, 'Always-in-a-Jam'.) It is as if the successive novels were parts of one long argument.

Stead's work always has this movement, always contains a movement forward and then a withdrawal to a different position. *A Little Tea, A Little Chat*, her New York novel of 1948, presents us with another kind of woman: the thoroughly venal Barbara Kent, who is depicted almost exclusively from the outside. She is a mystery, with a complicated but largely concealed past, and she does not say much. She is like a secret agent from the outlawry of women, on a mission to destroy – but that is not her conscious intention. She and the shark-like war-profiteer, Robert Grant, form a union of true minds. They are both entrepreneurs, although Barbara Kent's only capital is her erotic allure. However, she is able to, as they say, screw him. Grant, for himself, screws everything that moves. The novel makes a seamless equation between sexual exploitation and economic exploitation. It thoroughly trashes all the social and economic relations of the USA. It etches in acid an impressive picture of New York as the city of the damned. It is also, as is all Stead, rich in humour of the blackest kind. It occurs to me that Stead has a good deal in common with Luis Buñuel, if it is possible to imagine a Buñuel within a lapsed Protestant tradition. A Calvinist Buñuel, whose belief in grace has survived belief in God.

However, this definitive account of a New York fit to be destroyed by fire from heaven is followed, in 1952, by *The People with the Dogs,* a description of a charming clan of New York intelligentsia who are modestly and unself-consciously virtuous and, although bonded by blood, are each other's best friends. Why is Stead playing happy families, all of a sudden? What, one wonders, is she trying to prove? Perhaps, that amongst the infinite contradictions of the USA, where anything is possible, even Utopia might be possible. In the USA, Utopias have certainly been attempted. The generously loving Oneida Massine, not matriarch – that would be too much – but principal aunt of this extended family, is named after one of the Utopian experimental communities of nineteenth-century America. And, like perfect communards, the Massines exist in harmony and tolerance with one another in a New York which has transformed itself from the City of Dreadful Night into the shabby, seedy, comfortable kind of place where birds of passage, Stead's habitual displaced *dramatis personae,* can all roost happily together – a city of strangers, which is to say a city with infinite possibilities. Tiring of the city, the Massines can enjoy pastoral retreats in an idyllic country house left them by a wise father who has had the decency to die long before the action begins. Stead seems to be saying that, given a small private income, beautiful people can lead beautiful lives, although the very circumstances which nourish their human kindness are those which succour the morally deformed profiteers and whores of *A Little Tea, A Little Chat.*

But there is something odd about *The People with the Dogs,* as if the dynamo of her energy, ill-supplied with the fuel of distaste, were flagging. She permits the Massines to be charming and even writes about them in a charming way, as if she herself has been moved by the beautiful promise of the Statue of Liberty, which always touches the heart no matter how often it is betrayed. There is nothing fraudulent about this novel, although, perhaps revealingly, it is exceedingly carelessly written. It would be interesting to know whether an unpublished novel, *I'm Dying Laughing,* set during the period of the HUAC investigations, was written before or after *The People with the Dogs.* According to a recent Australian newspaper article, this novel remained unpublished because of subsequent tragedies in the lives of the people involved. Certainly *The People with the Dogs* may be softening up the reader for a blow which, in the end, was never delivered.

An internal logic of dialectical sequels connects all Stead's work in a single massive argument on the themes of sexual relations, economic relations, and politics. There has been scarcely any large-scale critical appraisal in the UK, to my knowledge, though at the moment more of her fiction

is in print, here, than at any single time before. If I were to choose an
introductory motto for the collected works of Christina Stead, it would
be, again, from Blake, from *The Marriage of Heaven and Hell*. It would be:
'Without contraries is no progression. Attraction and repulsion, Reason
and Energy, Love and Hate, are necessary to Human existence.' One
might take this as a point to begin the exploration of this most undervalued
of our contemporaries.

London Review of Books, 1982

Christina Stead completed the original manuscript of *I'm Dying Laughing*
in 1966 and was urged to revise it, to clarify its background of politics in
the US in the 1940s. For the next ten years, she worried away at the novel
until at last she bequeathed a mass of confused material to her literary
trustee, R. G. Geering, with instructions to publish it after her death.

The Stead connoisseur will note that Mr Geering's editorial hand is evident in an internal consistency far from characteristic of the novelist in her
later years. *I'm Dying Laughing* is a mess, but a tidy mess. Characters do not
change their names and appearances from page to page; events do not
occur in an entirely arbitrary manner. All the same, it has that chaotic sense
of flux that makes reading Stead somehow unlike reading fiction, that
makes reading her seem like plunging into the mess of life itself, learning
things, crashing against the desperate strategies of survival.

Thematically, it belongs with the group of political novels she completed
much earlier, in the 1940s – *Letty Fox: Her Luck, A Little Tea, A Little Chat,
The People with the Dogs,* novels about the life and times of the American
Left. *I'm Dying Laughing* concludes this sequence; it is a kind of obituary.

I'm Dying Laughing begins at a time that now seems scarcely credible,
those far-off days when the Left was in fashion in the US. In those days,
careerists joined the party and the party itself was a career. In 1935, Emily
Wilkes and Stephen Howard meet, fall in love, and marry, to the strains
of the Internationale.

They are superficially an odd couple. She, a big, gaudy, loquacious mid-
Westerner with huge appetites and mighty laughter. He is the scion of an
upper-crust East Coast family. He has abandoned his patrimony for the
party. The Howards' greatest bond is the struggle. They love passionately,
with a quality of *amour fou* that already suggests a tragic outcome.

Emily is a writer, and Stead makes us believe this comic, greedy, self-
deceiving, self-dramatising woman might possess some kind of genius,
although her husband spends a good deal of time attempting to convince
her she has only the profitable fluency of a hack. This does not make the
portrait of their marriage any less gripping; it is one of the happiest if most

tempestuous marriages in literature, and destructive precisely to the degree of their mutual passion.

Stephen, however, is more an all-purpose Marxist intellectual. Emily ritually defers to Stephen's superiority in dialectics but it is she who rakes in the money. The Roosevelt years are ripe for her home-spun tales of small-town life.

By the end of the war, they are in Hollywood, hobnobbing with a Communist élite of script-writers and living high on the hog's back. They are already very partial to a place on the hog's back.

In his Preface, R. G. Geering observes that *I'm Dying Laughing* is 'not a political novel in the manner of Koestler's *Darkness at Noon* or Orwell's *Nineteen Eighty-Four*'. Quite so. It is certainly not a novel about the bankruptcy of an ideology. Stead takes the validity of the ideology for granted. The world of her fiction is analysed as consistently from the left as Evelyn Waugh's world is described from the right. She gives her own characteristically bleak and sardonic account of the novel's protagonists: 'At the same time they wanted to be on the side of the angels, good Communists, good people, and also to be very rich. Well, of course . . . they came to a bad end.'

But the side of the angels has its drawbacks. The first full-scale set-piece in the novel is a trial – an informal one, conducted after a good dinner in a spirit of the most sanctimonious self-righteousness, by a cabal of Hollywood Communists. The Howards, it seems, have been judged deviationist. Especially roaring, ranting Emily, who is 'making deviationist speeches every time she opens her mouth. It's a very serious thing.'

Their crimes are individualism. Bohemianism. They won't accept party discipline. They are unreconstructed Marxist-Leninists and the 'good party Communists' don't see why such disordered creatures should be permitted to take care of Stephen's daughter by his first wife. Indeed, they are prepared to go to court to help contest his custody of the girl.

It is an extraordinary scene, a 'trial without jury, entirely in the spirit of the mid-century and their society'. The Howards are subjected to what is virtually a moral crucifixion – 'It was thought necessary by us all to get you here and be frank and clear,' they are told.

At this point, the Hollywood Communists have a great deal of power and do not even realise when they are abusing it. With hindsight, one knows all those gathered in the room will shortly face real trials of their own; it is one of Stead's singular achievements to make us understand fully some of the powerful bitternesses that came to flower in the days of HUAC.

But the Howards remain proudly unreconstructed. 'Still on the train that started from the Finland Station,' as Stephen says, he is determined to stay on it until the end. They compile a litany of the sins of the Soviet Union, the 1923 party purge, the expulsion of Trotsky, the labour camps. 'And to think we're losing our shirts and our faces, standing up for such a nation, such betrayers of all that's dear to the romantic hearts of the parlour pinks,' says Emily. Then she damns herself: 'Heigh-ho! History doesn't bear scrutiny.'

The Howards flee, not the party but their country. Like the representatives of the Lost Generation immediately preceding them, they go to Paris. They set up a vast entourage of children, nannies, maids, cooks, governesses, and proceed to live the life of Riley although, in the aftermath of the Second World War, the necessities of life are scarce and luxuries virtually unobtainable. But the Howards live happily, lavishly, off the Black Market, financed by Emily's earnings. Slowly, the contradictions of their situation destroy them.

They meet former collaborators and former resistants and people whose experience under Fascism has driven them to despair. The Howards are at sea. Increasingly corrupted by money and the privileges it can buy in a poor country, they guiltily discover they enjoy the company of the collaborators, their style, their fine food, rather better than the European comrades, with their dour air, their poverty, their patronage of typical little workers' bistros where the food wreaks havoc with Stephen's ulcer and on Emily's increasingly refined palate.

Emily gives herself over to gluttony, soon they are like Mr and Mrs Jack Spratt. Stephen querulous, dyspeptic, is increasingly given to shady practices with the money that has been settled on his daughter and the nephew whom they have adopted, for Emily's earning power is on the wane.

But still they spend, spend, spend, as news comes of the witch hunts at home. The leaders of the red élite that so berated them, those 'pious, stiffnecked people', as Emily calls them, are now in prison; they pleaded the First Amendment, they refused to name names. Communism has fallen out of fashion with a vengeance in the US.

The European comrades, the governesses, and shabby businessmen who turn out to be great heroes of the Resistance, are not interested in living well, to which the Howards by now are fatally addicted although Emily's writing, like Communism, has gone out of fashion and their debts are piling up. Has the time come at last to get off that 'slow train from Finland'?

Emily, half-mad with worry and balked ambition, gives in first, hoping that if she recants she will be forgiven and once more be rich and famous. Once she has done so, Stephen, heart and spirit broken, follows suit. Stead does not make a big issue of the scenes where the Howards name names, as if she cannot bear to linger on it.

Emily might have been able, out of her chronic Bohemianism, to patch herself together and go on, Stephen has nothing left to live for. That 'bad end' their author has prepared for them is nigh.

Guardian, 1987

Vladimir Nabokov: The Enchanter

The Enchanter is an erotic fable composed in a perfumed style that affords a queasy contrast to the straightforward brutality of the plot, describing as it does how a paedophile marries a dying woman in order to obtain sexual access to the latter's twelve-year-old daughter. The effect is that of raw liver exquisitely arranged in a pink frilly box.

But not a very large helping of raw liver. So the novella's scant seventy pages have been bulked out with two prefaces culled from Nabokov's assorted prose and some notes by the translator, his son Dmitri. Much of this impedimenta circles round the question of the relation of the hitherto unpublished *The Enchanter* to the great novel with which the elder Nabokov first sprang to international fame. Lolita.

The Enchanter was written in Russian in Paris late in 1939; and then, evidently, lost. The much longer, infinitely more complex *Lolita* was written in English some ten years later, in the US. In 1956, in the note on *Lolita* reprinted here, Nabokov declared 'the nymphet. . . was really much the same lass and the basic marry-her-mother idea also subsisted but otherwise the thing (i.e. Lolita) was new and had grown in secret the claws and wings of a novel'.

This suggests that Nabokov was prepared to accept that it was not only length but quiddity that *The Enchanter* lacked, even if, in 1959, in a letter used as a second preface, he refers to it as 'a beautiful piece of Russian prose'. All the same, no claws, No wings. It is startling but frail.

The Enchanter begins with a forty-year-old jeweller's meditations upon his own paedophiliac tendencies whilst he sits on a bench in a public park. His pondering is interrupted by the arrival of a schoolgirl on roller skates. And he is lost. (So is she, of course; but this is not *her* story, and her feelings and fate are not taken into consideration by either would-be seducer or her creator.)

There is a distinction between *amour fou* and sexual obsession. Humbert Humbert will be a fully self-aware pervert mad with love. The eponymous 'enchanter' is a constantly self-justifying but hitherto thwarted pervert who suddenly spots the possibility of gratification and thereafter pursues it through thick and thin.

Almost as soon as she has been resentfully married, the sick mother dies. The 'enchanter' gleefully carries his stepdaughter off by car to a distant hotel, in a brief, pale, trial run for Humbert Humbert's later wanderings. He seizes the opportunity of masturbating over her sleeping body. She wakes up, catches him at it and screams; he rushes out into the street, to be abruptly terminated by a passing vehicle, a curiously moralistic and awesomely rapid punishment.

Nabokov does not care to give a proper name to any of the characters in *The Enchanter*, except to allot the ubiquitous name, Marie, to the minimal presence of a maid in the absent-minded manner of one tipping a servant. The nymphet of *The Enchanter* may have Lolita's russet curls but she has none of her presence on the page. She is an assemblage of dimples, curls and schoolgirl underwear, uncharacterised beyond a reference to her 'slightly vacuous' eyes.

We learn in passing that she has a tendency to car sickness but otherwise are told more about her panties than we are about her personality. She is the hapless object of desire, the pure anonymous creation of soft-core pornography.

The jeweller is a little more three-dimensional; at least, he possesses a few more than merely physical attributes. For example, he is full of self-deceit; the miserable creature reassures himself that at least he made the last months of his wife's life happy. He is a hypocrite, too. He fondly imagines how he will be a good father to her child, as well as a considerate lover. These moral posturings endow him with a certain twitching life.

But there is also a hypocrisy within the narrative itself, in the succulent way in which the child's sexuality is presented. It is not so much that the reader is drawn helplessly into the paedophile's obsession; rather, that obsession is depicted in the conventional language of voluptuousness, 'suedelike fissures' (whatever that means), 'shapely thighs' and all.

The narrative is written in the third person and therefore cannot retain its objectivity when undressing the little girl, so that the paedophile's idea of the little girl's irresistibility is presented as a universal truth that is obviously apparent at the same time as it is castigated as 'unnatural'.

As a result, the paedophile's desire starts to seem as feasible as the next man's and the moral underpinning of the story falls away, leaving, surely unintentionally, only the infrastructure of pornography.

In Lolita, Nabokov solves the technical problem of the specious objectivity of the third person narrative by telling the story in the person of Humbert Humbert, and Humbert Humbert can constantly remind the reader of the unsanctified nature of his desires.

The nameless paedophile of *The Enchanter* meets his end in the soiled raincoat characteristic of the habitué of dirty bookshops; but of course, I am not assuming that it was indeed Nabokov's intention to write a dirty book, even if the masturbator's consummation is written in such a way that it looks as if he is having his titillatory cake and eating it. Indeed, I would not put it past Nabokov to be parodying a dirty book, though Paris in the winter of 1939 seems an odd place to play this game.

The text is adorned with a number of modernist arabesques. There is a 'black salad devouring a green rabbit' that would have seemed a little dated and expressionist in 1939 but now, thanks to changing fashions, comes up as fresh as paint. Nowhere is the expression less than elegant and the translation reads like an original. The wonder is, that *Lolita*, in its irony, complexity and verbal felicity, sprang in part from this scanty wee seedlet once it was transferred to the fertile, if alien soil of the United States.

Guardian, 1987

Peter Carey: Oscar and Lucinda

It is instructive to see how Peter Carey beings off a fusion of the epic and ironic modes in this marvellous novel, *Oscar and Lucinda*.

He constructs his narrative out of short or shortish, sentences, often of an off-beat ferocious elegance. (His is a style that calls attention to itself not insistently but unequivocally.) These sharp, highly coloured splinters are assembled into very many short, or shortish, chapters. Gradually, all builds into a novel of extraordinary size, in every sense of the word; yet the method of it is not unlike the way a person might set out to construct a model of the Taj Mahal out of matchsticks, and the general effect of *Oscar and Lucinda* does indeed have some of the unselfconscious strangeness of folk art.

It is just this strangeness that undercuts the tendency towards irony, and gives Oscar Hopkins his genuinely tragic dimension. Oscar and Lucinda are in predicaments which, in the twentieth century, to a twentieth-century sensibility, are absurd – but never, for one moment, seems so to themselves, nor to their creator. The circumstances of their lives, and the environments from which they spring, are recreated in hallucinatory detail.

The novel is set in England and Australia in the middle of the nineteenth century and wears its research so openly on its sleeve it is obviously intended to demonstrate just how very different a country the past was, and how, in that country, salvation and damnation were not only a constant topic of intellectual debate but a matter of profound emotional concern to the individual.

The novel is narrated by somebody we never learn much about, except he tells us that he looks like his great-grandfather, the Reverend Oscar Hopkins, and that it is because of a Christmas pudding that there is a story for him to tell, in the first place.

This information is delivered deadpan; there is nothing quaint about the story of the Christmas pudding, nor of the section of family history that devolves thereon for *Oscar and Lucinda* belongs to the category of novels that reach back into the past to explicate the present, although the connection between Oscar and the family who call him their great-grandfather is as shockingly arbitrary as the white presence in Australia itself.

Everything begins in the red mud of a Devon village. Oscar is the child of a fundamentalist Christian of the most austere kind whose system of belief and practice reflects obsessional characteristics that will come to fine flower in his son. It is the illicit Christmas pudding an incorrigible servant cooks for the little boy one Christmas Day that sparks Oscar's first crisis of belief, for his father, opposed to Christmas pudding on theological grounds, makes the child vomit his helping.

Yet it was fatherly love made him do it. But God smites him for his austerity, or so Oscar believes, and Oscar flees him for the less rigorous Anglicans – abandons his father and the obsessional tenets of his faith only to discover in himself an untold capacity for obsessional gambling.

Carey makes us believe, not only in Theophilus Hopkins's religious mania, but also in his goodness of heart and when Oscar abandons his father he is himself abandoned, from that moment driven only by the demands of his obsessions and his phobias, his genuine humility, his genuine disregard for self. At last, ordained, he sets out to Australia to convert the heathen, only to encounter on the boat a young woman as driven as himself, the half-emancipated heiress, Lucinda Leplastrier.

The novel deals with sin, guilt, obsession, compulsion, the nature of religious belief and the destructive innocence of God's elect but nothing rumples the bright precision of the writing and the observation behind it. This precision gives the writing its profoundly unsettling quality. For example:

A fox terrier was placed in the ring. The fox terrier was called Tiny. It wore a woman's bracelet for a collar. It took the rats one by one, picked them up like fruit from a bowl, broke them while the clock ticked and the men roared so loud you could not hear your companion speak to you.

To bet on the results of this small massacre is the most degrading thing the Rev. Oscar Hopkins can imagine. He will do so, of course, soon after, and on a Sunday, too, 'because it was a sabbath and there was no other betting to be had'.

If Oscar is a Myshkin-like sacred innocent and holy fool – and he is all that – then he shares the pet vice of Myshkin's creator, and the young woman with whom he falls in love is as unruly and passionate as those heroines of Dostoevsky who tremble on the verge of becoming New Women. If Oscar is an obsessional gambler, then Lucinda is a compulsive one. There is a difference: see the difference between Oscar's coolly systematic gambling on his first day at the races in Chapter 29 ('Epsom Downs'), and Lucinda's crazed chase through the dark and dangerous night-time city of Sydney in search of the glamour and intoxication of a game where she can lose all her money (Chapter 65, 'The Multitude of Thy Sorceries'.) But it is inevitable they fall in love, the wild, rich girl and the by now unfrocked clergyman with his red hair and gangling legs, his saintliness, his lack of guile.

Their love, and their fates, are sealed with a wager concerning a folly even more extravagant than a model of the Taj Mahal made of matchsticks – a church made out of glass. A glass church that can be packed flat and transported through the bush to be raised again where the wasps and butterflies and bees don't know the nature of glass, have never met it before, will bang themselves against the suddenly solid air; and Oscar can praise God in the wilderness.

The detail and precision with which Carey has constructed the novel makes this wager seem not only possible but plausible, for Lucinda, known as the Glass Lady, bought herself a glass-works with her inheritance and the peculiar strengths and fragilities of glass as a substance is one of the things the novel is about.

Octavio Paz says somewhere that the most mysterious thing is absolutely transparent, and the glass church, that beautiful, preposterous 'batboned' thing, 'its walls like ice emanating light, as fine and elegant as civilisation itself', floats at last down the Bellinger River after Oscar has brought it through the bush at the cost of tremendous human suffering, not only to those on the crazy expedition, but to the tribal people whom the expedition kills, and to whom the civilisation represented by the glass church is deadly.

Oscar is presented with a final conundrum which the novel never properly resolves: Was the vision of the glass church built to the glory of God in reality a snare of the Evil One all the time? (It must be said that a glass church, in a country as sun-struck as Australia, is something of a lethal folly even if, as Lucinda suggests, it is erected under a shady tree.) This conundrum isn't resolved because it is one Oscar asks himself but one the novel never asks. It is possible that the folly – the great heartbreaking folly – was no more than a folly all the time.

Oscar and Lucinda is a novel of extraordinary richness, complexity and strength – it is a peopled world, humming, buzzing, dancing with life and liveliness; it brings the past, in all its difference, bewilderingly into our present. It fills me with wild, savage envy, and no novelist could say fairer than that.

Guardian, 1988

Salman Rushdie: The Satanic Verses

Somebody switches on a tape recorder, a meretricious disco version of a psalm of David, 'How shall I sing the Lord's song in a strange land', booms and twitters into a semi-apocalyptic version of London. Ellowen Deeowen, as the childrens' rhyme has it. And even in its vicious decay, Salman Rushdie still accords the glamour of a child's dream to this 'great rotting, beautiful, snow-white, illuminated city, Mahagonny, Babylon, Alphaville'.

But the vexed question of the Lord's song and how to sing it in Mahagonny, Babylon, Alphaville, concerns most of the characters in Salman Rushdie's new novel, for they are mostly displaced persons of one kind or another. Expatriates, immigrants, refugees. Perhaps, finally, the answer lies in the 'satanic verses' of the title; might not the Lord's song be utterly transformed by time and distance, just as the two heroes of this long, complicated, exhilarating novel are transformed in the course of a journey.

Formally, *The Satanic Verses* is an epic into which holes have been punched to let in visions; an epic hung about with ragbag scraps of many different cultures. In Bombay, another city this novel celebrates, the beautiful Zeenat Vikal, doctor, activist and art critic, seeks

> an ethic of historically validated eclecticism, for was not the entire national culture based on the principle of borrowing whatever clothes seemed to fit, Aryan, Mughal, British, take-the-best-and-leave-the-rest?

Rushdie gleefully follows this prescription. *The Satanic Verses,* as if in tribute to Zeeny's Indian ethic, is eclectic as hell.

It kicks off *in medias res,* astonishingly: two brown men, clasped in a reluctant embrace, hurtle out of the clouds towards the English coast, singing at the tops of their voices in raucous discord. They have burst out of the exploded pod of a hijacked aircraft, to miraculously survive impact and be extraordinarily reborn.

Mind you, one of them, Gibreel Farishta, the movie star, has already scraped through a brush with death and is now prey not only to an obsessive, clearly doomed passion for the iceblond mountaineer, Allelia Cone, but also to hauntings from a former mistress who killed herself for love of him. In addition, he suffers from halitosis; and strange, terrible dreams in which he features as his own namesake, the archangel.

These dreams form a phantasmagoric narrative within the novel itself, with themes and characters that echo and reflect the rest of the action and inventions such as the city of Jahilia, 'built entirely of sand', that gives a nod to Calvino and a wink to Frank Herbert; and a girl who subsists on a diet of butterflies such as might have sprung from the pen of Gabriel García Márques, himself another archangel.

These dreams have a cineramic quality that befits the unconscious of a Bombay superstar even if their intellectual content seems pitched high for someone as gloriously, irrepressibly vulgar as Gibreel. Indeed, his vulgarity is so irredeemable, so comic, so full of vitality as to seem a kind of grace, and yet his author punishes him for it with madness and a brief incarnation as Azreel, the worst of all possible angels.

Seduced at an early age by the imperial promise of those magic syllables, Ellowen Deeowen, he went to great lengths to tailor himself to fit his adopted city, paring down his hilariously unwieldy name to Saladin Chamcha, only to find the slimline version makes him a laughing stock – chamcha means 'toady' – when he returned to his native Bombay.

Like Gibreel, he is an actor but an actor in England; his face 'is the wrong colour for their colour TV' so he has pursued with success a uniquely late twentieth-century career, that of delivering the voice-overs for television commercials. This week, he personates a ketchup bottle; next week, a packet of crisps. It is a bizarre way to sing the Lord's song and that return visit to Bombay has revealed his inner emptiness to him, whilst Gibreel, full of himself, is hastening to meet his love when he sits down beside Saladin on that fateful flight.

After they tumble through the air entwined, they find, when once again on terra firma, that one has grown horns and the other a halo.

At first the devil fares worse. Picked up as an illegal immigrant, Saladin joins in a mass escape from a detention centre – a scene of great power and strangeness. He finds his wife in bed with his best friend. And moment by moment he grows hairier, smellier, goatier. He takes refuge in the Shandaar Café, an establishment you might find in a Hanif Kureishi film script or on the next corner – home cooking, skinhead whites who spit in the meals of Sikhs, rooms full of rackrent tenants upstairs, outside the mean streets of a marvellously evoked eighties London.

These mean streets team with deracinated flowers who are tough as old boots. Mischal, for instance, the nubile daughter of the café, with her enthusiasm for the martial arts. And the clients of the Club Hot Wax, with its effigies of Mary Seacole and Ignatius Sancho, and other, sometimes anonymous black men and women who once lived by the waters of Babylon. In this wilderness of a city, haloed Gibreel pursues a career as a full-fledged archangel that end in blood and fire and disaster and a veritable massacre of supporting players before the two actors return, separately, to Bombay, there to finally engage with the complicated dialectic of good and evil that occasioned their transformations in the first place.

The novel, after its roller-coaster ride over a vast landscape of the imagination, ends calmly – for one of the portagonists, at least – in reconciliations and home-coming and a necessary grief.

As to the fate of the other, and which one of the twinned pair of opposites it is who achieves such wholeness in the teeth of the mess and horror of the world, you must read this populous, loquacious, sometimes hilarious extraordinary contemporary novel to find out.

Guardian, 1988

Love in a Cold Climate

Some Problems of Passion, Protestant Culture and Emily Brontë's *Wuthering Heights*.

One of the most successful plays of recent years in London's West End was a farce called: *No Sex, Please! We're British.* It ran to packed houses for something like a decade. The title conveniently sums up both the stereotypical European attitude to the passionate, erotic life of the British (that is, given the reluctance with which the British exhibit any evidence of erotic initiative at all, it is a wonder the race has contrived to perpetuate itself); and also the attitude of the British bourgeoisie towards itself – its own furious reticence about the life of the senses and the life of the emotions. Here is Tusker Smalley, in Paul Scott's novel, *Staying On,* writing to his wife, Lucy, whom he loves but whom he's treated badly:

'Can't talk about these things face to face, you know. Difficult to write them. . . Don't want to discuss it.'

This is the familiar imaginative territory of Celia Johnson and Trevor Howard and *Brief Encounter,* where a woman's heart breaks silently under her pastel-coloured twin-set and, in moments of extreme emotion, a man might clench his strong, white teeth around the stem of his briar pipe. Repression, not ecstasy, is the goal towards which British lovers strive and which they applaud themselves upon achieving. The language of passion is extruded with extraordinary difficulty through the stiff upper lip. George Bataille opines that 'the essence of mankind lies in sexuality'. That may be true on the continent, perhaps. In Britain, no.

However, the British popular press has always recorded, in lip-smacking and salacious detail, a sexual culture and a sexual folklore of bizarre vitality. This is a phallic, aggressive culture, leering, comic, serving up naked women as dish of the day. If, for the bourgeoisie, sex is unspeakable and hence remains unspoken about, the proletariat has no such problems – the white, male, heterosexual proletariat, that is.

For many years the *News of the World* boasted the largest circulation of all British newspapers. It was published on Sundays, when its public had the leisure to enjoy its tradition of uninhibited court reporting, especially of juicy divorces, atrocious rapes and sexual crimes. (The *News of the World* used to advertise itself with the slogan, 'All human life is here', a sad reflection on our species.) It has lately moved into the area of sexual gossip, centred on pop music or television celebrities and, when it gets the chance, the royal family. The rich diet it offers has been recently augmented by the arrival of the nude sexploitation daily newspapers, the *Sun* and the *Star*.

The enormously popular bi-weekly, the *Sport* is entirely devoted to the reporting of sexual news and scandal to the exclusion of virtually all else except a little sports coverage. The *Sport* also carries advertisements for telephone sex. 'Hanky Panky! White Panties, Red Cheeks.' They charge calls at thirty-pence-per-minute cheap rate, forty-four-pence-a-minute at all other times.

A recent lead story in the *Sport* was as follows:

Disc jockey Ernest Hughes sexually aroused his wife with a bizarre collection of fruit, vegetables and household items, a court heard yesterday. Candles, bananas, cucumbers . . .

('My vegetable love', as Andrew Marvell said, 'shall grow, Vaster than empires. . .')

The British bourgeoisie, however, prefers to represent itself as the embodiment of the superego, pure, clean, above reproach – even if the Conservative Party is periodically wracked by sex scandals, of which the Profumo case ('Cabinet minister shares mistress with Soviet spy') is the most famous and the Cecil Parkinson affair the most recent ('Cabinet minister reneges on promise to wed pregnant mistress.') On the other hand, perhaps it is only in Britain that these predictable goings-on would be scandals at all.

But, if the British bourgeoisie thinks of itself as superego, the working class is happy to identify itself with id, pure id, and nothing but id, and a positively gendered, masculine id, at that. Not only to identify itself with id, but also to approximate the most riotous manifestations of the id in its public behaviour – riotous, brutal, murderous, obscene, given to Dionysiac displays of public debauchery when it runs howling through the streets. At international football events, it destroys everything it can lay its hands on.

In fact, this orgiastic, working-class culture, culture of the Saturday night drunken spree, the fist-fight, the gang-band, retains a profound resemblance to Tusker Smalley's culture of repression, even if it is more energetic. Both are based on a denial of the power of language to communicate feeling. This orgiastic riotousness is the *inversion* of the bourgeois culture of repression and is based on the same set of existential premises, on a sense of self with rigidly defined boundaries, on a fear of the expression of emotion as, perhaps, eroding those boundaries.

Of course, actual practice does not conform to its representation either in the mock-Tudor palaces of the stockbroker classes or in the tower blocks of subsidised housing. The couple in the farce, *No Sex, Please! We're British,* did not, it turns out, object to sex as such; they had become the unwilling targets of a massive publicity campaign on the part of a mail-order sex-aids firm and were rapidly being submerged in 'a rising tide of filth', that is, were being deluged with mail containing many copies of publications like the *Sport*. The representation, not the actuality, irked them.

And another story in the *Sport* suggests the sad reality of sexual mores among the British working class, for whom, it would seem, energy might be eternal delight but foreplay is a waste of time. Listen, for once, to the voice of a British, working-class woman, asked, during the course of a court case, if her husband would normally kiss her during sexual intercourse, she replied: 'Not really.' Georges Bataille once diagnosed the problem, here: 'Utilitarian sexual activity is in conflict with eroticism,' he opined, albeit in another context.

In short, ours is an orgiastic, not an ecstatic, culture. The morning after orgy comes a hangover; 'never again', we cry. But the morning after ecstasy comes enlightenment, and the desire to do it again as soon as possible. Passion is the metaphysics of ecstasy but we are a pragmatic nation. We invented empiricism. But although I am a good pragmatist, too, and am perfectly happy to ascribe the state of ecstasy to an explosion of body chemistry, that does not change the nature of the *feeling*. You can explain why ecstasy happens but you cannot explain it away.

The language of sexuality in Britain admits of no chink through which ecstasy might shine.

The *Sport* has been instrumental in popularising the verb currently in common use in English to signify the sexual act, that is, 'to bonk'. The verbal adjective, 'bonking', is used with a freedom that surprises me, even though I am a child of the permissive 1960s. For example, the tennis player, Boris Becker, became nationally known as 'Bonking Boris' during the Wimbledon championship a few years ago, evidently solely on the grounds that he was accompanied by his girlfriend. (What would the papers have said, one wonders, if the girlfriend had been a boyfriend?) The explicit euphemism is tolerated everywhere; but the verb for which 'to bonk' is a transparent substitute still provokes a furore if it is used on television or in the newspapers.

'Bonking.' Onomatopoeic, almost. The sound of clinking bodies. Bodies that are not animated by soul. If British bourgeois culture posits a sexual relation like that which Milton attributed to the angels, a kind of non-physical 'mingling', these are animal passions, the product of a culture of sexuality that has a pagan simplicity and excess.

If there is an abyss, the diabolic abyss of transcendence without mysticism, between sacred and profane love, the abyss over which Pier Paolo Pasolini teetered on a tightrope, the abyss into which Jean Genet plunged with joy, then my native culture is rich indeed in simple profanity.

Profane love is often expressed in a language continuously subverted by innuendo, where tone of voice or body language are as important as the words themselves. The flicker of an eyebrow can convert a simple inquiry, 'How's the missus,' say, or 'Keeping perky?' into something over which blows might be exchanged. Marie Lloyd, the turn-of-the-century music hall artiste, used to reduce her audience to tears of mirth when she announced her arrival: 'Sorry I'm late . . . I was *blocked* in the Strand.'

When it is *not* expressed in innuendo, the language of profane love is not suitable for public consumption because it is not the language of love at all but the language of vulgar abuse.

When D. H. Lawrence single-handedly attempted to put the profane language of proletarian sexuality in English at the service of a higher vision of class mobility in *Lady Chatterley's Lover*, something went badly wrong. It proved impossible to cleanse the words of the delirious violence that a millennia of use as the basic weapons of non-physical brutality had given them. Whatever else Anglo-Saxon might have been in its time, it turned out that it was *not* the language of passion. Lawrence did not manage to resanctify a system of sexual signifiers that had been transformed over the centuries into the cruellest kind of verbal abuse. Instead, he repeated them as farce.

However, by restoring the ancient nouns and verbs to their dictionary meaning, Lawrence did succeed in doing something very odd. He reminded us that things, words, concepts, the pig, women, the organs of generation, blood, the verbal adjective, 'fucking', only become prohibited, taboo, unclean, 'filthy', if, once upon a time, they have been sacred. The profane language of proletarian sexuality in English is a kind of blasphemy – indeed, it has a far more profound effect as swearing than blasphemy does itself. 'Fuck', like 'shit', is a far stronger exclamation than 'damn', 'For fuck's sake!' is stronger usage by far than 'For God's sake'. The sacred is absent even when its very name is taken in vain.

In fact, we British do not have a very clear notion of the 'sacred' as a special sort of category at all. The rending, sadomasochistic savagery of the idea of 'passion' – passion as a litany of exemplary suffering, illumination, transcendence, as an access of desire, not necessarily gratified desire, in which 'opposites vanish, in which life and death, time and eternity, are mixed', – in Octavio Paz's phrase, well! . . . 'Don't want to discuss it,' as Tusker Smalley would say.

The very word, 'passion' in English has lost almost all trace of its Latin root; it no longer has any relation to suffering. We think it is about rough sex. I wrote a novel some years ago with the title, *The Passion of New Eve*. The 'passion' of the title refers not only to the erotic attraction between the two principal characters – a man who has been changed into a woman, Eve, and a man who has elected to become a woman in appearance, Tristressa – but also to the process of physical pain and degradation that Eve undergoes in her apprenticeship as a woman. This led to some confusion in Britain. In its first English paperback edition, the novel was issued with a cover depicting a woman in tight jodhpurs and transparent blouse, flourishing a riding crop. 'Hanky-Panky.'

There is no visual tradition in Britain to correspond to the Renaissance one of the representations of 'sacred and profane love' – the Reformation and the English Civil War effectively terminated the possibility of that kind of theological speculation in paint: the Protestant faith, like Islam, does not approve of painted idols. You cannot get away with the idea that a naked lady represents a higher form of spiritual truth. In Britain a naked lady is implicitly lewd. We are essentially a Northern peasant culture, of the earth, earthy.

It is therefore very difficult, in English, for profane love to collide with any version of the sacred kind in order to create that explosion of transcendence the surrealists called 'amour fou'. Indeed, there is no adequate translation of 'amour fou' in English. 'Mad love' isn't quite right; the translation already contains an implied value judgement. There is also very little space in the national sensibility in which that grand confusion of the senses might take place, 'I want you to be madly loved,' wrote André Breton to his infant daughter. We would not want that for *our* children. A. A. Milne wrote *Winnie-the-Pooh* for *his* infant son, with a very class-and-culture-specific vision of eternity at the end of what turned into a series of much-loved children's books, a boy and his teddy bear playing together endlessly in a sunlit wood, a prepubescence without end, unless, perhaps, boy and bear might finally 'mingle' like Miltonic angels.

Milton, having allowed himself to believe in the physical integrity of angels, since to believe in them solely as spiritual emanations went against the grain of his intellect, was then forced to construct their theoretical reproductive and digestive systems so that he could go on believing in them. He was a good empiricist, in his way. He could not allow angels to exist purely as sacred beings, sufficient to themselves according to some metaphysical law we do not understand.

Milton is the greatest of all Protestant poets and the culture of the English language is essentially a Protestant culture. The language itself as we know it today was standardised out of a welter of dialects in the sixteenth century by the widespread dissemination of a single book – the book whose exis- tence was itself predicated by the Reformation – the Bible in English, in which the Old Testament had equal importance with the New Testament. The theological imagination was kept in check by the presence of the text, which also restricted metaphysical speculation about the events described in the Bible to a marked degree. The doctrine of the Virgin Birth is cer- tainly not something that Tusker Smalley would care to discuss and is cer- tainly not something that the average reader of the *Sport,* with his 'hands-on' approach to human reproduction, would entertain for one moment. In the Protestant communion service, the bread stays bread, the wine stays wine – the drama of the Christian liturgy passes us by. The majestic tragedy of Good Friday passes us by – Easter has never been an important popular festival in Britain since the Reformation. But the festi- val of Christmas – in England a thoroughly orgiastic festival – grafted as it was originally on to celebrations of an impressively orgiastic and pagan nature, has always had more hold on the popular imagination. A number of intellectually influential Protestant sects – in particular, the Unitarians – posit a Holy Family that is not, in itself, divine. The Scots inherited Calvinism and Original Sin; the English constructed a form of Protestant humanism out of Lutheranism and then rarely gave it another thought.

And if the Old Testament urged us to contemplate the Fall of Man rather than the Passion of our Lord, nevertheless the vicissitudes of our later history as Great Britain have more or less wiped out a sense of sin from our consciousness. A sense of sin is a gross impediment to an empire-builder. Graham Greene deplores this lack of a sense of sin; of my immediate contemporaries, Ian McEwan enjoys it and Martin Amis, without quite knowing what it is he is missing, seems as though he would rather like to have a sense of sin all to himself. But it is gone for good, especially where sex is concerned, and with it, the glorious transgressive impulse the surrealists valued most of all about passion. I cannot imagine that André Breton would identify the 'Hanky Panky' girl with her white panties and red cheeks with a practitioner of one of the 'mysterious perversions' with which he believed 'amour fou' surrounded itself.

Yet we cannot blame our lack of passion and our conspicuous profanity on the Reformation alone. Geoffrey Chaucer predates the Reformation by some two hundred years and some of the stories in *The Canterbury Tales* wouldn't seem out of place in this week's the *Sport*. Some of the others he borrowed from Boccaccio, who was not a Protestant, either.

Furthermore, it was the twenty-five-year-old daughter of a Protestant clergyman living in the most unaccommodatingly rugged and dissenting part of England, the Yorkshire moors, who wrote *Wuthering Heights,* an impossible novel that ought not to exist, a novel that makes us believe the world can crack apart like an egg when its shell is blown apart by the irrepressible force of human desire.

Wuthering Heights is one of the greatest, if not the greatest, love story ever written but it is not in the least like *Anna Karenina,* because it is a ferocious celebration of exactly those imperious qualities of desire for which *Anna Karenina* is a lament. It is a love story that takes for granted, that takes a perverse pleasure, an insane joy, in fact, in the way desire rips through the fabric of society and demands the sacrifice of status, family, honour. And finally of life, probably.

Ivan Karamazov, in one of the three or four nineteenth-century novels that may be compared with *Wuthering Heights*, was thrust into existential terror at the thought that, if God were dead, then anything might be possible. In the story of this phosphorescent man and woman, Heathcliff and Catherine Earnshaw, Emily Brontë seems to be saying: God *is* dead. Anything *is* possible. If . . . you have the will. This violent and extraordinary romance is about a desire that is stronger by far than death, that does not acknowledge death as in any way an impediment to passion. If the price of the lovers' desire is damnation – and there is a strong suggestion that this is so, for, if God is dead, then surely the Devil has been left in charge – then Heathcliff and Catherine will delight in being damned.

It is a mistake to think that *Wuthering Heights* is about Heathcliff, about

the charisma of that fatal, demon lover. This is not so. There is no denying that Heathcliff has sold his soul, probably to the Devil, quite early in
the narrative, but Catherine it is who emulates Lucifer. She dreamed,
once, that she went to heaven, and:

> 'heaven did not seem to be my home; and I broke my heart with weep-
> ing to come back to earth; and the angels were so angry that they flung
> me out into the middle of the heath on the top of Wuthering Heights;
> where I woke sobbing for joy.'

Milton's Lucifer fell from 'dawn to dewy eve . . .' but even he did not
weep for joy when he found himself exiled from God for ever. Catherine's
is the authentic voice of the rebel angel and it is easy to forget, because of
her gender, that, if Heathcliff is a demon lover cast in the same mould of
diabolic grandeur as the romantic poets, revisionist reworkings of Satan,
then so is Catherine Earnshaw, too. Perhaps more so, a Lady Lucifer.

She, like Heathcliff, effortlessly devastates tranquillity, domesticity,
honest affect. When she falls ill with fever, Mrs Linton, mother of the
unfortunate man she eventually marries, takes her off with her to conva-
lesce. 'But the poor dame had reason to repent of her kindness; she and
her husband both took the fever and died within a few days of each other.'
Cathy is literally, a 'femme fatale'.

Heathcliff's problematic humanity is constantly discussed throughout
the novels: 'Is Mr Heathcliff a man? Is so, is he mad? And if not, is he a
devil?' 'Is he a ghoul, or a vampire?' And so on. Catherine herself is quite
explicit that, if something is wrong with him, then the same thing is wrong
with her. 'Whatever our souls are made of, his and mine are the same . . .'
She, too, is daemonic. Nelly Dean, the housekeeper, who knows her very
well, does not believe that heaven can hold her but neither Nelly nor anybody else think of Catherine as resembling a vampire or a ghoul herself,
even though we first meet her in the novel when she is manifesting herself as a phantom, and one should not think that Emily Brontë composed
the passage about Catherine's dream in ignorance of Milton. (We are the
first generation of readers of English literature who haven't read Milton
with the same closeness and concentration with which we read
Shakespeare.)

Nelly Dean, always the voice of normative repression, speaks disap-
provingly of Cathy's 'fits of passion', meaning, in that curious Victorian
usage, bad temper. (Passion is perceived as irritability.) By passion, Nelly
means Cathy's wilfulness. Her uncontrollability. Her deep *unfemininity*.
But Catherine Earnshaw's passion is – passion. She and Heathcliff are
cloaked in the mutual incandescence of 'amour fou'.

The author of this novel wrote it when she was almost as young as that other rebel angel, Arthur Rimbaud, when he wrote *Les Illuminations*. She belongs more fittingly with him than with those who died young because the gods loved them, like Keats. Emily Brontë died at the age of thirty, but not from some tragic accident or chance infection. She appears to have died as the result of an exercise of will, to have deliberately starved herself to death a few months after the death from consumption of her brother, Branwell. In the period shortly before she died, she destroyed all her personal papers, which probably included another novel. She covered her tracks almost completely before she concluded this last, most ambitious project, her own death.

It is one of the strangest and, in a way, least tragic deaths one can imagine, and all of a piece with the stray images of Emily Brontë it is possible to glean from her sisters' accounts. We know she kept a pet hawk, called Hero; that once, shopping with Charlotte and Anne, she bought a dress length of white fabric printed with a design of purple thunder bolts and lightning flashes. They were horrified, they preferred the subfusc, wanting to go unnoticed in the crowd, by Emily the recluse never went out in crowds and wanted to be attired in the tempest. Once she was bitten by a mad dog, took up a red-hot iron and cauterised the wound herself. *Wuthering Heights* is the work of a woman capable of all these things.

Heathcliff's death, also the result of self-starvation, may have suggested to her her own passionately wilful suicide — but his death is not an act of will, rather, the result of a giant *absence of mind*. He forgets to eat in his eagerness for union, or reunion, with the dead beloved. He forgets, you could say, to live . . . but then, Catherine is both dead, yet not dead, a restless phantom maintained in the limbo between heaven and hell by her passionate will. And Heathcliff does not so much die as abandon his body.

Let me quote those wonderful lines of Joseph Glanvill, that Poe used as a motto for *his* story of the passion that transcends death, *Ligeia*. Remember, Legeia and Catherine Earnshaw are both Protestant revenants, that is, not supernatural beings so much as beings with a passionate excess of will to live.

And the will therein lieth, which dieth not. Who knoweth the mysteries of the will, with its vigour? For God is but a great will pervading all things by nature of its intentness. Man doth not yield himself to the angels, nor unto death utterly, save only through the weakness of his feeble will.

But Emily Brontë *died* by willpower, unless death appeared to her as a form of escape from a world which denied the existence of the elemental passions in which her fiction delights like the albatross delights in the storm. Octavio Paz: 'Women are imprisoned in the image masculine society has imposed on them; therefore if they attempt a free choice it must be a kind of jail-break.'

Emily Brontë seems to have been singularly unconcerned with the image masculine society imposed on her. Nevertheless, the only free choice she appears to have entertained was that between life and death and perhaps her death was in itself a kind of jail-break.

Catherine Earnshaw *is* imprisoned in an image of femininity. The process is described in no uncertain terms. She is socialised as a woman by the Lockwood family. They take her off the moors, a savage child as fierce, violent and impetuous as her adopted brother, and transform her. When she comes back home again to 'Wuthering Heights', she is utterly changed. 'Instead of a wild, hatless little savage jumping into the house, and rushing to squeeze us all breathless, there alighted from a handsome black pony a very dignified person with brown ringlets falling from the cover of a feathered beaver, and a long cloth habit which she was obliged to hold up with both hands that she might sail in.'

Together with her new clothes and her new femininity, she has put on repression. ('Today put on repression and a woman's name.') She can't play with the dogs any more for fear of messing her new clothes. She can't hug Nelly Dean because Nelly is covered with flour from cake-making – now Catherine can't even associate herself with the unclean activities of lower-class images of femininity. She has become not only a woman but a bourgeois woman, an object of conspicuous display, something to be looked at, not touched. She can't forbear to rush towards Heathcliff when she sees him, to hug him – the Earnshaw children are physically exceedingly free and demonstrative. But she draws back when she sees he is dirty – covered with farm-boy muck. He is *filthy*. Cathy retreats with a prim shudder from what she suddenly perceives as a 'rising tide of filth'. (I do not apologise for the *double entendre,* here.)

She has already made her choice between the dirty and the clean. She will make the *sensible* choice, the asexual choice, the clean and passionless choice. She is going to marry into heaven – to marry the good angel, the clean, blond, rich, squirearchical Edgar Linton. She is going to ascend, on the ladder of social mobility, into the paradise of the lower reaches of the upper-classes.

All post-sixteenth-century English art contains a subtext concerning class and *Wuthering Heights* is no exception to this. All the same, such is the furious endorsement of transgression in the incandescent personages of Heathcliff and Cathy that it comes almost as a shock of anticlimax to realise that all they are transgressing is the barrier of social class. One feels that at least they ought to be brother and sister, to make the transgression really worthwhile.

'Why did you betray your own heart, Cathy?' asks Heathcliff in that extraordinary love scene that culminates in Cathy's death, a scene of great emotional and physical violence given an added dimension of horror by the fact that Catherine is seven months' pregnant. She 'betrayed her own heart' – she betrayed the pure imperative of 'amour fou' – because she did what was expected of her. She reneged on free choice. She failed to make the jail-break in life – although her death has also a suspiciously willed quality about it. (Her last words are: 'Heathcliff, I shall die.' More of a promise than a threat.)

But Cathy certainly makes her jail-break posthumously. She comes back for Heathcliff. She returns and she *takes* him, as if, now all that remains of her is passion. The novel is a triumphant celebration of that 'amour fou' of which there is no adequate translation in English.

Wuthering Heights – together with *Alice in Wonderland* – was a favourite book of the surrealists. Luis Buñuel prepared a script in the 1930s but was unable to make a film until he was living in Mexico in 1953. Then he found himself saddled by the producers with a cast who had been hired for a musical, including a rhumba dancer named Lilia Prado who played Isabella Linton. In spite of the surreal aspect of all this, the random juxtaposition of Mexican song and dance team with this blazing text did not produce one of those accidental miracles so beloved by André Breton. The film creaks; so does the chocolate-box conjunction of Laurence Olivier and Merle Oberon in the William Wyler Hollywood version. But Buñuel at least knew he was dealing with some kind of blasphemy; William Wyler was content to film a romance.

There is a profound impropriety in *Wuthering Heights* that seems to touch some even more sensitive subject than that of the female libido, although certainly the novel states categorically that Cathy's mortal being, though not her ravenous immaterial part, is destroyed by her betrayal of her own desire. The relation between Cathy and Heathcliff seems almost too intense to be normal, to be transgressive *in itself*.

It should be said that, in the novel, incest occurs in every respect except the actual. Heathcliff marries Cathy's sister-in-law; their son marries Catherine's daughter, also named Catherine; after his death, the second Catherine marries the son of her mother's brother, a boy whom Heathcliff has reared according to his own deplorable methods and for whom he feels the closest possible affinity. (He seems, says Heathcliff, 'a personification of my youth, not a human being'.) The intricate matings demanded by the plot, a series of permutations on the marital possibilities of two nuclear families, skirt around potentially incestuous relationships in every case and, though Catherine and Heathcliff are *not* biologically brother and sister, they grow up together as brother and sister – closer than most siblings, in fact.

But, then, again, *Wuthering Heights* is is in no sense about physical consummation. The question of whether Heathcliff and Catherine ever had sex is beside the point. Theirs is a pure passion, pure transgression, an eroticism so violent it does not need to name itself. Virginia Woolf said about the book: 'There is love, but it is not the love of men and women.' Well, not perhaps as the love of men and women manifested itself in the Bloomsbury group. The US critic, Camille Paglia, puts it more clinically: 'Heathcliff and Catherine seek sadomasochistic annihilation of their separate identities.'

At one point, Catherine tells Nelly Dean, who is her servant and confidante, that she would certainly have married Heathcliff – she could have envisaged no other partner but Heathcliff – had not her brother, Hindley, set out to humiliate and degrade Heathcliff, to return him to the condition of savagery in which he first came to them.

But it is impossible to imagine these beings of sulphur and lightning as Mr and Mrs Heathcliff. If they touched, we feel, they would explode. That final, terrible love scene is a battle. She pulls out a handful of his hair, he leaves blue bruises on her arms. Their final embrace is like the inexorable mingling of two drops of mercury. 'An instant they held asunder and then how they met I hardly saw, but Catherine made a spring, and he caught her, and they were locked in an embrace from which I thought my mistress would never be released alive,' says Nelly Dean.

She *is* released alive – just. Heathcliff gives her back to her husband in a coma which is the prelude to her death. Flesh is too fragile a receptacle for this amount of feeling. They suffer a fire which burns and is not consumed; they burn in a mutual flame; they transcend the unique individuality of the body; they distil from physicality a pure spirit . . . and so on.

They aspire to the language of mysticism in their relationship, although Emily Brontë does not allow herself to use the language of mysticism.

What could they possibly want from one another? They want what Octavio Paz wanted – 'an instant of that full life in which opposites vanish, in which life and death, time and eternity, are united.' It is the high romantic vision of passion. And, in the end, what Catherine Earnshaw and Heathcliff want is precisely what they get. In no other novel in English is passion permitted to triumph. Emily Brontë even permits passion to triumph over death.

The ending of the novel is ambiguous. Emily Brontë gives the last words to the fatuous, town-dwelling, stranger, Lockwood. He pays a visit to the three graves, Catherine, her husband, her lover. The graves seem quiet enough, to him. 'I lingered round them under that benign sky; watched the moths fluttering among the heath and harebells, listened to the soft wind breathing through the grass, and wondered how anyone could ever imagine unquiet slumbers for the sleepers in that quiet earth.'

But don't forget that Lockwood is a fool, and a fool without imagination. A shepherd boy has just told us he saw a couple on the moors: 'They's Heathcliff and a woman, yonder, under t'nab!' The ghosts have even been seen at the windows of unused rooms in Wuthering Heights itself, as if waiting until the house is empty enough for them to move downstairs. Even Nelly Dean doesn't like to be out late, on the moors, these days.

Catherine Earnshaw dreamed the angels threw her out of heaven and she sobbed with joy to find herself back on the moors again. Perhaps her dream came true. Listen to the sound of the tears of joy of the rebel angels; it is the authentic sound of passion and we do not hear it often in England.

A paper given at a Conference on the Language of Passion,
University of Pisa, Italy 1990.

Colin Greenland: Michael Moorcock: Death Is No Obstacle

The first thing you feel when you read Michael Moorcock's lengthy and illuminating responses to Colin Greenland's subtle, intelligent, informed probing, is: 'The crazy fool! He's giving everything away!' Moorcock recklessly imparts all the trade secrets – how he does it, how to do it. How to construct a sword and sorcery novel, as follows: divide your 60,000 words into four sections ('15,000 WORDS apiece'), then each section into six chapters. Allow a major event, something jaw-dropping, to happen every four pages. What about plot, though? How about running through the requisite number of variations on the theme of, say 'Only six days to save the world!' That should do nicely.

Now draw a map of the new world you've just invented, so that you know exactly where you are at any given time. Then make a detailed plan of action, so that you know what is happening. Now sit down.

Begin.

Easy, isn't it. Can't think why everybody doesn't do it.

If you're a fast typist, perhaps you can match the daily totals Moorcock clocked up when he was young and limber and, he claims, fifteen thousands words *a day* at the keyboard wasn't too much. Mercifully, he's slowed down a bit, since then, or soon the world might well fill up with the Moorcock fiction that, seemingly, curls off his typewriter in an endless stream.

So it's all down to industry, enthusiasm and good typing speeds, you see. At least, that's what Moorcock seems to be saying. He appears to be intent on removing all the mystery from the craft he so masterfully plies. He concentrates on the 'craft' aspect – structure. It's all a matter of structure.

Industry, application, technique. How do you acquire industry and application? By doing it. What about technique? You acquire that by reading. If you want to write a novel, you really ought to read one, first. Read several. Read history, geography, anthropology. Read ancient epics, myths, romances. Read cigarette cards, the back of cereal packages, yesterday's newspapers. He himself emerges as an omnivorously well-read man, but the inexhaustible curiosity that lies behind all that is something that can't be acquired, is something you are born with.

And the harder Moorcock works at cutting his own mystery down to size, the more extraordinary the exuberant fecundity of his achievement becomes. He throws off lightly one extra piece of advice to the aspiring fantasy writer: 'You need a list of images that are purely fantastic; deliberate paradoxes, say, "the City of Screaming Statues", things like that.' But this is the bit that people who *aren't* Michael Moorcock find a little tricky. This is when they start chewing the end of their pencils and staring vacantly into space. For most of us, inventing something like a 'city of screaming statues' is a day's work in itself, even if the speed at which Moorcock works suggests that his imagination can sometimes go on automatic – that is, he reaches a point where, in a sense, his imagination starts to write *him*. He takes the ability to conjure up picturesque paradoxes at the drop of a hat for granted.

And he also takes for granted a due sense of the *serious* nature of the entire project of story telling. 'If you believe, as I do, in simple good and tangible evil, and that evil starts with petty greed and tends to get the ascendancy, you've got to find ways of expressing that in fiction, while still giving everything its proper shadings and subtleties,' he says.

For Moorcock, fiction is primarily and essentially a moral entertainment. He believes, he says, that 'morality and structure are very closely linked'. His obsession with form, 'always the solution to an artistic problem', must not be confused with a reliance on formula, even if he can gleefully give you all the formulae for every kind of story there ever was, because he's tried and tested all of them.

These interviews with the master storyteller of our time provide an invaluable record of his working methods, and take the reader phase by phase through an extraordinary career; they show us the workmanlike way he sets to and builds a narrative as if it were a house. But, finally, it is Moorcock's own lived experience and sense of the real world, his ability to censure and to judge, not in the least to censure and to judge himself, that gives his fiction its outstanding qualities, even the ability to put down 15,000 words a day stuns me into awed silence. (Really 15,000 words a day, Mike? How long did you take out for meals? How often did you break to go to the bathroom?)

He doesn't give anything away, because it isn't possible for him to do so. There are no real trade secrets. Fiction is as individual as a fingerprint, even if all the history of story-telling is somehow involved in every story.

Moorcock calls himself a 'popular' writer, always scrupulously making that distinction between 'popular' writer and 'literary' writer that his own work consistently blurs. Moorcock likes to put himself firmly on the other shore, in another country to the Booker prize winners, invoking as positive proof of his differences to, say, Julian Barnes, those early days as a page filler for the Sexton Blake library in an atmosphere of sweated fiction not unlike that of the Grub Street hacks of Victorian London. But very few Booker prize winners are more saturated in literature than he. Among his best loves are Conrad, also an influence on J. G. Ballard; and, especially, George Meredith, one of the most 'literary' of all writers but now virtually unread by the literati. Moorcock consciously compares his own prodigal production with that of Dickens.

Dickens was a 'popular' writer in his day, of course, one of the most popular writers of all time, and Moorcock is making an important point here – that all the BBC classic serials, the Armchair Theatre classics, were hugely popular bestseller novels in their own day. But that day was the day before, first, the cinema, and subsequently television took over many of the entertainment functions of the novel. Families used to gather round Father of an evening, for their fix of Dickens – that week's instalment of *Little Dorrit* or *The Old Curiosity Shop* as serialised in *Household Words*. The television soap opera, the thirteen-part serial, the three-decker mini-series have directly taken over a good many of the functions of those serialised novels and are often enjoyed communally in the same way, although they often seem to have a rather more tenuous relation to life, and even to fantasy, than their predecessors. But even the most avid fans don't assemble for family readings of this week's freshly published instalment of Moorcock, although it occurs to me that the Elric stories would make a terrific on-going television series.

Therefore to be a 'popular' writer, these days, means giving the reader something that the reader can't get from television – an excitement, an impulse of play, a *seriousness*. If Moorcock is Dickensian in his mode of production – get those words out! get those books out! – he is also Dickensian in his delight in the grotesque, the eccentric, the unpremeditated. If his essential generosity of spirit refuses to be contained by the orthodox rules of space, time and narrative, he is also, in a complex but irreducible way, very English. Not, never! In the 'teddibly English', self-congratulatory way of, well, your average Booker short-list victim, but English in the great tradition of music hall and penny dreadful, seaside pierrot show and pantomime, of radical dissent and continuous questioning, the other side of imperialism, if you like.

If the great body of Moorcock's work represents, in its totality, a vast morality play of the battle between good and evil, then it is presided over by a Lord of Misrule, whose work is the nearest thing we have in modern English fiction to a never-ending carnival.

1991

Appendix

Introduction to Expletives Deleted

I am known in my circle as notoriously foul-mouthed. It's a familiar paradox – the soft-spoken, middle-aged English gentlewoman who swears like
a trooper when roused. I blame my father, who was neither English nor a
gentleman but Scottish and a journalist, who bequeathed me bad language
and a taste for the print, so that his daughter, for the last fifteen-odd years,
has been writing book reviews and then conscientiously blue-pencilling
out her first gut reactions – 'bloody awful', 'fucking dire' – in order to give
a more balanced and objective overview.

My father kept a shelf of Penguin classics in translation by his bed.
Homer, Thucydides, Apuleius. My mother preferred Boswell, Pepys – she
adored gossip, especially antique gossip, but she mistrusted fiction because
she believed fiction gave one an unrealistic view of the world. Once she
caught me reading a novel and chastised me: 'Never let me catch you
doing that again, remember what happened to Emma Bovary.' Both my
parents had left school at fifteen, they were among the last generation of
men and women whose minds were furnished out of curiosity about the
printed word.

In the medieval morality play of *Everyman*, Knowledge says: 'Everyman,
I will go with thee and be thy guide, In thy most need to go by thy side.'
The old Everyman editions used to print this on the inner covers, it was their
motto. (The revived Everyman editions happily use the same motto.) I
remember another slogan: 'A good book is the precious life blood of a great
master', or words to that effect. We sat at meals with our open books. My
mother liked to read cookery books between meals, especially during the
period of food rationing. We were the only family in my class at school who
didn't have a television set. They got one at last, when my father retired,
ostensibly so that he could watch the news; things went downhill, after that.

Although I grew up with books and have spent a good deal of my adult
life among them, make my living out of writing them and very much

---

*From the essay, 'Readers Respond to Rousseau', in Robert Darnton, *The Great Cat Massacre* (London:
Allen Lane, 1984).

enjoy writing about them, I can contemplate with equanimity the science-fiction future world that every day approaches more closely, in which information and narrative pleasure are transmitted electronically and books are a quaint, antiquarian, minority taste. Not in *my* time, anyway, I say to myself. And, anyway, a book is simply the container of an idea – like a bottle; what is inside the book is what matters. Even so, I admit to having a fetishistic attitude to books, to their touch, their smell. All the same, human beings told each other stories, instructed one another in the names of things, speculated about the meaning of it all (and came to few if any conclusions), discussed the habits of animals, composed recipes, before there was such a thing even as writing and will doubtless continue to do so because the *really* important thing is narrative.

All books, even cookery books and car-maintenance manuals, consist of narratives. Narrative is written in language but it is composed, if you follow me, in time. All writers are inventing a kind of imitation time when they invent the time in which a story unfolds, and they are playing a complicated game with *our* time, the reader's time, the time it takes to read a story. A good writer can make you believe time stands still.

Yet the end of all stories, even if the writer forbears to mention it, is death, which is where our time stops short. Sheherezade knew this, which is why she kept on spinning another story out of the bowels of the last one, never coming to a point where she could say: 'This is the end.' Because it *would* have been. We travel along the thread of narrative like high-wire artistes. That is our life.

But there is more to it than that. The Balinese embark on a marathon session of reading aloud after they have prepared a corpse for burial. They read stories from collections of popular tales without stopping, twenty-four hours a day, for days at a time, in order to keep out the demons:

> Demons possess souls during the vulnerable period immediately after a death, but stories keep them out. Like Chinese boxes or English hedges, the stories contain tales within tales, so that as you enter one you run into another, passing from plot to plot every time you turn a corner, until at last you reach the core of the narrative space, which corresponds to the place occupied by the corpse within the inner courtyard of the household. Demons cannot penetrate this space because they cannot turn corners. They beat their heads helplessly against the narrative maze that the readers have built, and so reading provides a kind of defence fortification . . . It creates a wall of words, which operates like the jamming of radio broadcast. It does not amuse, instruct, improve or help to while away the time: by the imbrication of narrative and the cacophony of sound, it protects souls.*

And that is quite enough about the importance of narrative and ought to explain why the largest section of this book is devoted to pieces of writing about storytelling in its purest form, that is, to invented stories, and the strategies writers have devised to cheat the inevitability of closure, to chase away the demons, to keep them away for good.

Don't think I don't like real novels, though, the kind of novel in which people drink tea and commit adultery – I *do* like novels! I do! In spite of my mother's warning. Although, if a comic charlady obtrudes upon the action of a real novel, I will fling the novel against the wall amidst a flood of obscenities because the presence of such a character as a comic charlady tells me more than I wish to know about the way her creator sees the world.

Because all fiction, all writing of any kind, in fact, exists on a number of different levels. 'Never trust the teller, trust the tale,' said D. H. Lawrence, and he was right, even if he did not want this to happen to *his* tales. If you read the tale carefully, the tale tells you more than the writer knows, often much more than they wanted to give away. The tale tells you, in all innocence, what its writer thinks is important, who she or he thinks is important and, above all, why. Call it the sub-text.

I don't really think that writers, even great writers, are prophets, or sages, or Messiah-like figures; writing is a lonely, sedentary occupation and a touch of megalomania can be comforting around five on a November afternoon when you haven't seen anybody all day. But one or two of the people I'm writing about, here, have aspirations in the Messianic direction and I'm all for pretension; besides, I'm *glad* that Iain Sinclair did his bit to bring about the resignation of Margaret Thatcher. But, rather than the gift of prophecy, it seems to me that the times *shine through* certain writers, so that we think they see more clearly than we do, whereas in reality they are making *us* see more clearly. Calling such writers seers, or prophets, is a form of shorthand. I suppose I'd include John Berger and William Burroughs in this category, probably J. G. Ballard, certainly Christina Stead.

Otherwise, I like to write about writers who give me pleasure. Pleasure has always had a bad press in Britain. I'm all for pleasure, too. I wish there was more of it around. I also like to argue. There is also a strong irascibility factor in some of these pieces. A day without an argument is like an egg without salt.

I've divided up this mass of evidence of fifteen years writing about books into sections according to various enthusiasms. Storytelling, yes. Food and the semiotics of food. My country, this messy, post-imperialist Britain, which is not the country of my childhood in Atlee's austere, dignified egalitarian forties, nor yet of my young womanhood in the ecstatic sixties but something much more raucous and sinister. And there is also Amerika. Note I have adopted Kafka's spelling for the title of this section.

Like most Europeans of my generation, I have North America in my bloodstream. It started with the food parcels we used to receive just after the war, with the sticky American candies all over nuts and the cans of peaches, each half-peach as round, firm, golden, and ersatz as (had I but known it then) a silicone breast. I remember, possibly a trick of memory but even so, copies of *Glamour* and *Mademoiselle* and *Seventeen* thrown in as makeweights that showed me a world, as pastel-coloured and two-dimensional as a *Loony Tunes* cartoon, where people with good teeth on permanent exhibition in wide smiles ate inexplicable food, hamburgers, hot-dogs, French fries, and there were teenagers, bobby-sox, saddle Oxfords.

It was the bright, simple world of the post-war Eisenhower Utopia and I didn't encounter it again until Pop Art, when I realised it had been a vicious fake all the time.

But it was the movies that administered America to me intravenously, as they did to the entire generation that remembers 1968 with such love. It seemed to me, when I first started going to the cinema intensively in the late fifties, that Hollywood had colonised the imagination of the entire world and was turning us all into Americans. I resented it, it fascinated me.

It still does – that giant, tragic drama of American history, the super-spectacle of the twentieth century, the nation that invented itself and con-tinually reinvents itself through its art. I've lived in the midwest, with its pastoral simplicity and the endless promise of the land, and in upstate New York, on the upper reaches of the most beautiful river in the world, the Hudson, and other places, too, though less passionately, and I think of the United States with awe and sadness, that the country has never, ever quite reneged on the beautiful promise inscribed on the Statue of Liberty . . . and yet has fucked so much up.

So there is an American section. And since my life has been most sig-nificantly shaped by my gender, there is a section titled 'La Petite Différence'. I spent a good many years being told what I ought to think, and how I ought to behave, and how I ought to write, even, because I was a woman and men thought they had the right to tell me how to feel, but then I stopped listening to them and tried to figure it out for myself but they didn't stop talking, oh, dear no. So I started answering back. How simple, not to say simplistic, this all sounds; and yet it is true.

I've ended the book with a little piece about James Joyce, in Dublin, because for any writer in the English language, the twentieth century starts on 16 June 1904, Bloomsday, and shows no sign of ending yet.

The pieces aren't arranged chronologically because I didn't start reviewing seriously until I was thirty-five years old and fully grown up; my tastes were pretty much formed, I knew what I liked although every now and then something new would astonish me and still does. But there is a consistency of taste, if not chronology. I haven't changed much, over the years. I use less adjectives, now, and have a kinder heart, perhaps.

My thanks to the literary editors who commissioned these reviews or, in some cases, acceded to my requests for commissions to review books they themselves might not have thought of: Karl Miller, Tony Gould, Blake Morrison, Waldemar Januscek, Tim Radford, above all Bill Webb. Thanks to Susannah Clapp. My dear friend, Carmen Callil, thought this collection was a good idea, and found me Mark Bell, my amanuensis, without whom this book could not have been assembled. My thanks, above all, to the staff of the Foulis Gallery, the Brompton Hospital, London, also without whom . . .

For more than three years, Salman Rushdie, Britain's most remarkable writer, has suffered the archaic and cruel penalty of a death sentence, passed on him for writing and publishing a book. All those who work in the same profession are affected by his dreadful predicament, whether they know it or not. Its reverberations upon the freedoms and responsibilities of writers are endless. Perhaps writing *is* a matter of life and death. All good fortune, Salman.

CHRONOLOGY OF JOURNALISM AND OCCASIONAL WRITINGS (1964–92)

Abbreviations

ED   *Expletives Deleted: Selected Writings* (Chatto & Windus, 1992)
LRB   *London Review of Books*
NS   *New Society*
NSa   *Nothing Sacred: Selected Writings* (Virago, 1982; rev. edn, 1992)
Nonesuch   *Nonesuch Magazine* (Bristol University Student Magazine)
NYTBR   *New York Times Book Review*
TES   *Times Educational Supplement*
TLS   *Times Literary Supplement*

For books reviewed, the place of publication is London, unless otherwise stated.

Introductions and writings which form chapters of books are listed at the start of the relevant year.

Writings included in the previous collections, *Nothing Sacred* and *Expletives Deleted*, are marked (*NSa, NSa 92* and *ED*). The title given is that of the original article, which was sometimes altered in the collections.

This list does not include interviews, radio and television broadcasts, or articles that exist only in draft form.

We would welcome information about any further articles that have escaped our net.

1964
"Now Is the Time for Singing"   *Nonesuch* Autumn, no. 122

1966
'Bob Dylan on Tour: or,   *London* August
Huck Finn reaches Puberty'   *Magazine*

'Crime and Punishment', review of Tony Parker, *The Unknown Citizen* (Harmondsworth: Penguin)	*Nonesuch*	Summer–Autumn, no. 127
'Proles' Palgrave', V. de Sola Pinto and A. E. Rodway (eds), *The Common Muse: Popular British Ballad Poetry from the 15th to the 20th Century* (Harmondsworth: Penguin)	*Nonesuch*	Spring, no. 126

1967

'Fred Jordan, Singer'	*NS*	23 February
'A Busker (Retired)'	*NS*	30 March
'Tin Sheets and Crimson Gore'	*NS*	1 June
Charles Hindley, *Curiosities of Street Literature* (Broadsheet King)		
'Venturing Backwards', review of Richard Henry Horne, Memoirs of a London Doll (André Deutsch), Joan G. Robinson, *When Marnie Was There* (Collins) and Sarah Stafford Smith *The Ink-Bottle Club* (Harrap)	*NS*	7 December
"Notes for a Theory of Sixties Style'	*NS*	14 December (*NSa*)

1968

'The Good Old Songs'	*NS*	21 March

1970

'Bradford: Industry as Artwork'	*NS*	22 January (*NSa*)
'Tokyo Pastoral'	*NS*	11 June (*NSa*)
'Stealing Is Bad Karma'	*Listener*	25 June
'People as Pictures'	*NS*	8 October (*NSa*)
'My Maugham Award'	*The Author*	Autumn

1971

'Living in London'	*London Magazine*	March

| 'Mishima's Toy Sword' | NS | 18 March |
| 'Once More into the Mangle' | NS | 29 April (NSa) |

1972

'Poor Butterfly'	NS	16 March (NSa)
'Death in Japan'	NS	20 April
'Pupils' Voices'	NS	15 June
'Fin de Siècle'	NS	17 August
'The Back of Beyond'	NS	12 October

1973

| 'Triple Flavour' | NS | 2 August |
| 'Donovan's Dog', interview with Terence Donovan, review of film, Yellow Dog | Nova | October |

1974

'Afterword' to Angela Carter Fireworks (Quartet)		
'Sore Throat', review of Linda Lovelace, Inside Linda Lovelace (Heinrich Hanau)	NS	18 July (NSa)
'A Fertility Festival'	NS	5 September (NSa)
'Ancient Regime', review of Robert Gathorne Hardy (ed.), Ottoline at Garsington (Faber & Faber)	NS	12 September
'Fat Is Ugly', review of Mara Selvini Palazzoli, Self-Starvation (LSP Books)	NS	28 November
'Labyrinth of Charm', review of Jorge Luis Borges, An Introduction to English Literature (Robson Books)	NS	26 December

1975

| 'The Naked Lawrence (Lorenzo the Closet-Queen)' | NS | 13 February (NSa) |

'Unfair Sex', review of Rosalind Miles, *The Fiction of Sex* (Vision Press)	*NS*	20 February
'Eden Regained', review of Robert Gibson, *The Land Without a Name: Alain-Fournier and His World* (Elek)	*NS*	27 February
'The Hidden Child', H. P. Lovecraft	*NS*	6 March
Review of Patricia Walby and Andrew Goodman, *A Book About Men* (Quartet)	*NS*	10 April
'The Wound in the Face'	*NS*	24 April (*NSa*)
'The Oss Has His Day'	*NS*	29 May
'A Well-Hung Hang-Up'	*NS*	3 July (*NSa*)
'Wagner and the Mistral'	*NS*	7 August
'Bathed in Englishness', Bath	*NS*	18 September (*NSa*)
'Wolfe at the Writer's Door'	*NS*	23 October
'Trouser Protest'	*NS*	20 November
'The Art of Horrorzines'	*NS*	25 December

1976

'The Mother Lode'	*The New Review*	
'Giants' Playtime'	*NS*	29 January
'The New Vegetarians'	*NS*	4 March
'Saucerer's Apprentice', Elizabeth David	*NS*	8 April
'What the Hell It's Home!'	*NS*	13 May
'Family in a Landscape'	*NS*	17 June
'Good To Be Poor', review of Jocasta Innes, *The Pauper's Homemaking Book* (Harmondsworth: Penguin)	*NS*	15 July
'The Better to Eat You With'	*NS*	22 July

'Blooming Baboons' (At the Zoo)	NS	2 September (NSa)
'Animals in the Nursery'	NS	30 September
'The Donnie Ferrets'	NS	11 November (NSa)
'Health on the Brain'	NS	9 December

1977
Foreword to *The Fairy Tales of Charles Perrault* (Gollancz)

'Food Fetishes', review of Barbara Tims (ed.), *Food in Vogue: Six Decades of Cooking and Entertaining* (Harrap)	NS	13 January (ED)
'No Angels', review of Stuart Holroyd, *Psi and the Consciousness Explosion* (Bodley Head)	NS	20 January
'That Arizona Home'	NS	27 January
Review of Murasaki Shikibu, *The Tale of Genji* (Secker & Warburg)	Guardian	17 February (ED)
'In the Bear Garden'	NS	24 February
'Viv and Let Live', review of television drama, *Spend, Spend, Spend* by Jack Rosenthal	NS	24 March (NSa)
'Power of Porn'	Observer	10 April
'Life into Art', review of Clifford Irving and Richard Suskind, *'Project Octavio': the Story of the Howard Hughes Hoax* (Allison & Busby)	NS	28 April
'Wet Dream City'	NS	19 May
'The Paris of the North'	NS	30 June
'D'You Mean South?'	NS	28 July
'Time to Tell the Time' (Mother Lode)	New Review	September
'Behind the Mask', review of Edwin O. Reischauer, *The Japanese* (Cambridge, Mass.: Harvard University Press)	NS	1 September

'A Petrified Harvest'	NS	1 September
'Cash and Marry', review of Charles Castle, Model Girl (Newton Abbot: David & Charles)	NS	6 October
'Bread on Still Waters'	NS	13 October
'An I for Truth'	NS	17 November
'A Feeling of Fun' (Fun Fairs)	NS	15 December (NSa)
'Fantasy World', review of Jane Walter (ed.), A Man's Book: Fashion in the Man's World in the Twenties and Thirties (Duckworth) and Ernestine Carter, The Changing World of Fashion (Weidenfeld & Nicolson)	NS	15 December
'Roast or Boiled', review of Jessica Kuper (ed.), The Anthropologists' Cookbook (Routledge & Kegan Paul)	NS	22–9 December
'Year of the Punk'	NS	22–9 December

1978

'Little Lamb, Get Lost'	NS	26 January
'Femmes Fatales'	NS	16 March (NSa)
'No Satisfaction', review of Judith Williamson, Decoding Advertisements: Ideology and Meaning in Advertising (Marion Boyars)	NS	23 March
'Room with a Loo', review of Marilyn French, The Women's Room (André Deutsch)	NS	20 April
Review of Anthony Alpers, The Life of Katherine Mansfield (Jonathan Cape)	Guardian	8 May (NSa)
'Dorothy's Devotion' (Wordsworth)	NS	11 May (NSa)
'Japanese Erotica'	NS	15 June (NSa)
'Dress Rehearsal', review of Ted Polhemus (ed.), Social Aspects of the Human Body (Harmondsworth: Penguin)	NS	22 June

'Derrière Pensée (The Bridled Sweeties)'	*NS*	28 July
'Theatre of the Absurd'	*NS*	31 August
'The Good Life', review of Ronald Dore, *Shinohata: a Portrait of a Japanese Village* (Allen Lane)	*NS*	28 September
'On with the Dance', review of Philippa Puller, *Gilded Butterfly: the Rise and Fall of the London Season* (Hamish Hamilton)	*NS*	5 October
Review of Günter Grass, *The Flounder* (Secker & Warburg)	*Guardian*	13 October
'Dressing Up and Down', review of Ted Polhemus and Lynn Procter, *Fashion and Anti-Fashion: an Anthropology of Clothing and Adornment* (Thames & Hudson)	*NS*	30 November
'The Alchemy of the Word'	*Harpers & Queen*	(ED)

1979
'The Language of Sisterhood', in *The State of Language* (Berkeley: Univ. of California Press)

'All Creatures Great and Small', review of David Attenborough, *Life on Earth*, BBC	*NS*	15 March
'Sex as Blasphemy', review of Georges (ED) Bataille, *Story of the Eye* (Marion Boyars)	*NS*	22 March
'Who's Kidding', children's television	*NS*	19 April
'V for Victory', review of Desmond Morris, Peter Collett, Peter Marsh and Marie O'Shaughnessy, *Gestures: Their Origins and Distribution* (Jonathan Cape)	*NS*	10 May
'Culture of Survival', review of John Berger, *Pig Earth* (Writers and Readers)	*NS*	24 May (ED)
'Acting It Up on the Small Screen'	*NS*	7 June (*NSa*)
'Towards Maturity', review of Alix Kates Shulman, *Burning Questions* (André Deutsch)	*NS*	21 June

'Latin Rhythms', review of Gabriel García Márquez, *Innocent Erendira and Other Stories* (Jonathan Cape) and Jorge Luis Borges, *The Book of Sand* (Allen Lane)	NS	28 June
'The Box Does Furnish a Room'	NS	19 July
'Dandies of the Void', review of Yashar Kemal, *The Lords of Akchasaz: Part One, Murder in the Ironsmith's Market* (Collins & Harvill Press)	NS	2 August
'Time to Tell the Time' (The Mother Lode)	New Review	September
Review of Sheila Rowbotham, Lynne Segal and Hilary Wainwright, *Beyond the Fragments: Feminism and the Making of Socialism* (St Paul's Road, London)	NS	4 October
Review of William Burroughs, *Ah Pook Is Here* (John Calder)	Guardian	10 October
Review of J. G. Ballard, *The Unlimited Dream Company* (Jonathan Cape)	Guardian	26 October
'Man Does/Woman Is', review of Patricia Stubbs, *Women and Fiction: Feminism and the Novel 1880–1920* (Brighton: Harvester Press)	NS	8 November
'Bored, Bothered and Bewildered'	TES	7 December
'Much, Much Stranger than Fiction': review of an article on Diana Dors, *Behind Closed Doors*; Kenneth Anger, *Hollywood Babylon*; A. E. Hotchner, *Doris Day: Her Own Story* and *Sophia – Living and Loving: Her Own Story*; Hildegarde Knef, *The Gift Horse*; Joan Collins, *Past Imperfect*	NS	20–7 December

1980

'Monkey Business'	NS	10 January
F. Scott Fitzgerald, *The Great Gatsby*	Observer Magazine	24 February
Angela Carter Responds to Bertolucci's	LRB	6 March

Movie, *La Luna*

'Yen in South Ken': review of exhibition, *Japan Style*, Victoria and Albert Museum	NS	20 March
Review of Grace Paley, *The Little Disturbances of Man* (Virago) and *Enormous Changes at the Last Minute* (Virago)	LRB	17 April (*ED*)
'Between the Sheets', review of Reay Tannahill, *Sex in History* (Reay Tannahill)	NS	12 June
'Titillation', review of Jay Tarese, *Thy Neighbour's Wife: Sex in the World Today* (Collins)	NS	26 June
'Cultural Anaesthesia', review of Berthold Hinz, *Art in the Third Reich* (Oxford: Blackwell)	NS	10 July
'The Apotheosis of John Doe', review of Hal Ashby's film, *Being There*	NS	21 August
Review of Michèle Sarde, *Colette: a Biography*	LRB	2 October (*NSa*)

1981

'Snow-Belt America'	NS	5 March
'The Sweet Sell of Romance', review of Judith Krantz, *Princess Daisy* (Sidgwick & Jackson)	NS	2 April (*NSa*)
'The Rise of the Preppies'	NS	14 May
'Being Oneself at School One'	NS	11 June
'Absurdities', review of Lisa Alther, *Original Sins* (Women's Press) and Lorna Tracy, *Amateur Passions* (Virago)	LRB	2–15 July
Review of Donald Ward (trans. and ed.), *The German Legends of the Brothers Grimm* (Millington Books)	Guardian	(*ED*)

1982

Introduction to Walter de la Mare, *Memoirs of a Midget* (Oxford: Oxford University Press)		(*ED*)

'About the Stories', afterword to *Sleeping Beauty and Other Favourite Fairy Tales* chosen and trans. Angela Carter (Gollancz)		
'The Flamboyant Career of an African Superstar', review of Carlos Moore, *Fela Fela: This Bitch of a Life* (Allison & Busby)	*NS*	23–30 December
'The Intellectuals' Darby and Joan', review of Carol Ascher, *Simone de Beauvoir: A Life of Freedom* (Brighton: Harvester Press)	*NS*	28 January
'Fools Are My Theme, Let Satire Be My Song'	*Vector*	*Easter no. 109*
'The Painful Pleasure of a 15-inch Waist', review of David Kunzle, *Fashion and Fetishisms: a Social History of the Corset, Tight-Lacing and Other Forms of Body-Sculpture in the West* (George Prior)	*NS*	22 April (*ED*)
'D. H. Lawrence, Scholarship Boy'	*NS*	3 June
'Carmen Callil – *Common Sense Sensitivity*'	*Vogue*	July
'A Happy Bloomsday', Envoi: Bloomsday	*NS*	8 July (*ED*)
'The Cult of the True Loaf', review of Elizabeth David, *English Bread and Yeast Cookery* (Harmondsworth: Penguin)	*NS*	12 August (*ED*)
Review of Christina Stead, *The Beauties and Furies* (Virago)	*LRB*	16 September (*ED*)
'The Wonderful World of Cops'	*NS*	23 September
'So There'll Always Be an England'	*NS*	7 October
'Munch and Anti-biotics'	*NS*	21 October
'Africa Man Original', review of exhibition, *Treasures of Ancient Nigeria*, Royal Academy	*NS*	25 November
The Draughtsman's Contract, script for *Visions*, Channel 4	Channel 4	10 November
'The Belle as Businessperson' (*Gone with the Wind*)	*Observer*	(*NSa*)

1983

'Notes from the Front Line', in Michelene
Wanda (ed.), *Gender and Writing* (Pandora
Press)

'Anger in Black Landscape', in Dorothy
Thompson (ed.), *Over Our Dead Bodies:
Women Against the Bomb* (Virago)

'Sugar Daddy', in Ursula Owen (ed.),
Fathers (Virago)

'Alison's Giggle', in Eileen Philips (ed.), *The Left and the Erotic* (Lawrence & Wishart)		(*NSa* 92)
'The Recession Style'	NS	13 January (*NSa* 92)
'Rights and Rites', review of Bob Bushaway, *By Rite: Custom, Ceremony and Community in England, 1700–1880* (Junction Books)	NS	3 February
'Black Museum of Female Afflictions', review of Edward Shorter, *A History of Women's Bodies* (Allen Lane)	NS	24 February
'Obsessed by the Devil', review of John Putman Demos, *Entertaining Satan: Witchcraft and Culture in Early New England* (Oxford: Oxford University Press)	NS	31 March
'Jean-Luc Godard', for *Visions*, Channel 4	Channel 4	11 May
'Masochism for the Masses: Election '83'	*New Statesman*	3 June
'Through the Tudor Keyhole', review of exhibition, *Artists of the Tudor Court*, Victoria and Albert Museum	NS	21 July
'Shoot the Wolf', review of Jack Zipes, *Fairy Tales and the Art of Subversion: the Classical Genre for Children and the Process of Civilisation* and *The Trials and Tribulations of Little Red Riding Hood: Versions of the Tale in Sociocultural Context* (Heinemann Educational)	NS	8 September

'The Priviatisation of grief and mourning', *NS* 22 September
review of Lou Taylor, *Mourning Dress:*
a Costume and Social History (Allen & Unwin)

'Trials of a Booker Judge' *NS* 20 October

'Notes from a Maternity Ward' *New* 16–23
Statesman December

1984
'An Omelette and a Glass of Wine and *LRB* 24 January
Other Dishes', review of Ann Barr and *(ED)*
Paul Levy, *The Official Foodie Handbook*
(Ebury Press); Elizabeth David, *An*
Omelette and a Glass of Wine (Hale) and
Alice Waters, *Chez Panisse Menu Cookbook*
(Chatto & Windus)

'Mother in Bondage', review of Ian *NS* 15 March
Buruma, *A Japanese Mirror: Heroes and*
Villains of Japanese Culture (Jonathan Cape)

'Le Chat, c'est lui', review of Robert *NS* 30 August
Darnton, *The Great Cat Massacre, and Other*
Episodes in French Cultural History (Allen Lane)

Review of J. G. Ballard, *Empire of the Sun* *Time Out* 27 September
(Gollancz) *(ED)*

'The Asphalt Jungle', review of Anne *TLS* 14 December
Campbell, *The Girls in the Gang: A Report*
from New York City (Oxford: Blackwell)

'Woman Made', review of Isabelle *NS* 20–7
Anscombe, *A Woman's Touch: Women in* December
Design from 1860 to the Present Day (Virago)

1985
Preface to *Come Unto These Yellow Sands*
(Newcastle upon Tyne: Bloodaxe Books)

'The Written Garment', review of Roland *NS* 28 March
Barthes, *The Fashion System* (Jonathan Cape)

'Totalitarian Man', review of C. L. R. James, *NS* 21 June
Mariners, Renegades and Castaways: the Story

*of Herman Melville and the World We
Live In* (Allison & Busby)

'Angela Carter on the Latest Thing', review   *LRB*   5 December
of Elizabeth Wilson, *Adorned in Dreams:
Fashion and Modernity* (Virago)

1986
Introduction to ed. Angela Carter, *Wayward
Girls and Wicked Women* (Virago)

'From Rags to Breeches', review of Sarah   *NS*   7 February
Levitt, *Victorians Unbuttoned* (Allen & Unwin)

Review of Rana Kabbani, *Europe's Myths of*   *Guardian*   3 April
Orient: Devise and Rule (Macmillan)

'The Odd Couple', review of Junichiro   *NS*   11 April
Tanizaki, *Naomi* (Secker & Warburg)

Review of Redcliffe Salaman, *The History*   *LRB*   22 May (*ED*)
and Social Influence of the Potato, ed. J. G.
Hawkes (Cambridge: Cambridge University
Press)

Review of Carlos Fuentes, *The Old Gringo*   *Guardian*   29 May
(André Deutsch)

'The End: Reading South Africa', review   *LRB*   18 September
of André Brink and J. M. Coetzee (ed.),
A Land Apart: A South African Reader (Faber
& Faber) and Norma Kitson, *Where Sixpence
Lives* (Chatto & Windus)

1987
'Nabokov's Nymphet Novella', review of   *Guardian*   9 January
Vladimir Nabokov, *The Enchanter* (Picador)

Review of Louise Erdrich, *The Beet Queen*   *Guardian*   27 February
(Hamish Hamilton)   (*ED*)

Review of Christina Stead, *I'm Dying*   *Guardian*   27 March (*ED*)
Laughing (Virago)

Review of John Berger, *Once in Europe*   *Washing-*   29 March
(New York: Pantheon Books)   *ton Post*

'Irish Folktales, Arab Folktales', review of   *Guardian*   1 May (*ED*)
Henry Glassie (ed.), *Irish Folk Tales*
(Harmondsworth: Penguin) and Inea
Bushnaq (trans. and ed.), *Arab Folktales*
(Harmondsworth: Penguin)

'A Dream of Revenge on Youth', a   *Independent*   21 May
re-reading of Angela Carter, *Love Carter*
(Chatto & Windus)

Review of Ian Jack, *Before the Oil Ran Out:*   *Guardian*   5 June (*ED*)
Britain 1977–86 (Secker & Warburg);
Beryl Bainbridge, *Forever England, North and*
South (Duckworth/BBC Books) and *Norma*
Dolby's Diary: An Account of the Great Miners'
Strike (Verso)

'A Literal Vision', review of Pontus Hulten   *Guardian*   19 June
and others, *The Arcimboldo Effect* (Thames
& Hudson)

'A Song of the Sacred', review of Bruce   *Guardian*   26 June
Chatwin, *The Songlines* (Jonathan Cape)

'Woolfing It', review of Patience Gray,   *LRB*   23 July (*ED*)
Honey from a Weed: Fasting and Feasting in
Tuscany, Catalonia, the Cyclades and Apulia
(Prospect Books)

Review of Robert Coover, *A Night at*   *Guardian*   7 August (*ED*)
the Movies, or, You Must Remember This
(Heinemann)

'Constructing an Australia: Letter from   *Guardian*   2 October
Down Under'

'Girls in Flower', review of Laurie Leslie,   *Guardian*   27 November
Portrait of an Artist: a Biography of Georgia
O'Keffe (Heinemann); Nicholas Callaway
(ed.), *Georgia O'Keffe: One Hundred Flowers*
(Phaidon); Cecily Langdale, *Gwen John*
(New Haven: Yale); Baroness Kizette de
Lempicka-Foxhall as told to Charles Phillips,
Passion By Design: The Art and Times of
Tamara de Lempicka (Phaidon)

1988
'Truly, It Felt Like Year One', in Sarah
Maitland (ed.), *Looking Back at the 1960s*
(Virago)

Introduction to Gilbert Hernandez, (*ED*)
Duck Feet (Titan Books)

'Through a Text Backwards: The *Metaphores* January
Resurrection of the House of Usher'

Review of Edmund White, *The Beautiful* *Guardian* 22 January
Room is Empty (Picador) (*ED*)

Review of William Burroughs, *The Western* *Guardian* 11 March (*ED*)
Lands (Picador)

'Oscar for Envy', review of Peter Carey, *Guardian* 1 April
Oscar and Lucinda (Faber & Faber)

'Doing It to Mama', review of Eric Rhode, *LRB* 19 May (*ED*)
On Birth and Madness (Duckworth)

Review of Michael Moorcock, *Mother* *Guardian* 24 June (*ED*)
London (Secker & Warburg)

'Hollywood', review of David Bordwell, *Guardian* 19 August
Janet Staiger and Kristin Thompson, *The* (*ED*)
Classical Hollywood Cinema: Film Styles to
1960 (Routledge); Paul F. Boller jr and
Ronald L. Davis, *Hollywood Anecdotes*
(Macmillan), and Danny Peary (ed.),
Close-Ups: The Movie Star Book (New York:
Fireside)

'Angels in Dirty Places', review of Salman *Guardian* 23 September
Rushdie, *The Satanic Verses* (Viking)

1989
Preface, Exhibition Catalogue, *Images of* (*NSa* 92)
Frida Kahlo (Redstone Press)

'I Could Have Fancied Her', review of *LRB* 16 February
Arthur Marwick, *Beauty in History: Society,*
Politics and Personal Appearance c. 1500 to the
Present (Thames & Hudson)

Review of Danilo Kis, *The Encyclopedia of the* NYTBR   23 April (*ED*)
Dead (New York: Farrar, Straus & Giroux)

Review of Milorad Pavic, *Dictionary of the*   *LRB*   1 June (*ED*)
Khazars (Hamish Hamilton)

Review of Paul Theroux, *My Secret History*   *Guardian* 23 June (*ED*)
(Hamish Hamilton)

1990
Introduction to *Virago Book of Fairy Tales*
ed. Angela Carter (Virago)

Introduction to Charlotte Brontë, *Jane Eyre*   (*ED*)
(Virago)

'Love in a Cold Climate: Some Problems of   (*NSa* 92)
Passion, Protestant Culture and Emily
Brontë's *Wuthering Heights*' (Pisa Lecture)

'Brooksie and Faust', review of Barry Paris,   *LRB*   9 March
Louise Brooks (Hamish Hamilton)   (*NSa* 92)

Review of Hanif Kureishi, *The Buddha of*   *Guardian* 29 March (*ED*)
Suburbia (Faber & Faber)

Review of Phyllis Rose, *Jazz Cleopatra:*   *Tatler*   March (*ED*)
Josephine Baker in her Time (Chatto & Windus)

1991
Introduction to Colin Greenland, *Michael*
Moorcock: Death is No Obstacle (Manchester:
Savoy)

Review of Iain Sinclair, *Downriver* (Paladin)   *LRB*   7 March (*ED*)

Review of Milorad Pavic, *Landscape Painted*   *Independent* 12 May
with Tea (Hamish Hamilton)   *on Sunday* (*ED*)

'In Pantoland'   *Christmas* 24 December
                                               Guardian

1992
'The Granada, Tooting', for *Omnibus*, BBC   BBC1   January

Index